NEXT OF KIN

NEXT OF KIN

An International Reader on Changing Families

Edited by

Lorne Tepperman, Ph.D
University of Toronto

Susannah J. Wilson, Ph.D
Managerial Design Corporation
Oakville, Ontario, Canada

with the assistance of
Sandra Badin

PRENTICE HALL
Englewood Cliffs, New Jersey 07632

Library of Congress Cataloging-in-Publication Data

Next of kin : an international reader on changing families / edited by
 Lorne Tepperman and Susannah J. Wilson : with the assistance of
 Sandra Badin.
      p.   cm.
   Includes bibliographical references and index.
   ISBN 0-13-617564-3
   1. Family—Cross-cultural studies.   2. Marriage—Cross-cultural
studies.   I. Tepperman, Lorne.   II. Wilson, S. J. (Susannah Jane)
HQ515.N49   1993
306.8—dc20   92–16896
                                                       CIP

Editorial production: Helen Brennan
Acquisitions editor: Nancy Roberts
Cover design: Michelle Paccione
Prepress buyer: Kelly Behr
Manufacturing buyer: Mary Ann Gloriande

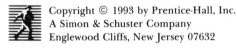
Copyright © 1993 by Prentice-Hall, Inc.
A Simon & Schuster Company
Englewood Cliffs, New Jersey 07632

Printed in the United States of America

10 9 8 7 6 5 4 3 2 1

ISBN 0-13-617564-3

Prentice-Hall International (UK) Limited, *London*
Prentice-Hall of Australia Pty. Limited, *Sydney*
Prentice-Hall Canada Inc., *Toronto*
Prentice-Hall Hispanoamericana, S.A., *Mexico*
Prentice-Hall of India Private Limited, *New Delhi*
Prentice-Hall of Japan, Inc., *Tokyo*
Prentice-Hall of Southeast Asia Pte. Ltd., *Singapore*
Editora Prentice-Hall do Brasil, Ltda., *Rio de Janeiro*

Contents

PART II
Marriage and Family Formation

PART III
Reproduction and Childbearing

PART IV
Parenting and Childcare

PART X
The Future of Family Life

Acknowledgments

Although academic writing is typically a solitary pursuit, creating a book of readings is definitely a team effort. This book had its beginnings in an earlier analysis of the Canadian family. Lorne Tepperman, working with Charles Jones and Sandra Badin, was convinced that students would find the wealth of material describing family life throughout the world both interesting and useful. Lorne talked to Sue about working together on a project to make this body of material accessible. From the outset the goal was to describe family processes throughout the world, without using North America or Western family life as benchmarks. We were delighted when Prentice Hall reacted favorably to our proposal.

From Sue's first meeting with Gordon Johnson and Nancy Roberts in Orange County, California, to the contract signing in Lorne's Toronto office, to our mailed exchanges of various stages of the manuscript with Helen Brennan and Fred Dahl in New Jersey, this project has proceeded smoothly. We know that dealing with the exigencies of book publishing (and the eccentricities of authors) is not always as easy as this Prentice Hall group has made it seem, and we appreciate their work.

Our greatest debt, of course, is owed to the authors who have agreed to have their work reproduced here. We thank them for their willingness to participate, and hope that they are pleased with the result. The final collection represents a modest effort on our part to bridge the geographic, linguistic, racial, and ethnic gaps that exist among social scientists.

In preparing the collection, Sandra Badin did a wonderful job helping us identify dozens of articles for possible inclusion. Once the final selection was made, Alan Wain edited the excerpts down to their present size. Clearly, it is a challenge to capture the essence of each article in a much shortened excerpt without losing either the flavor or the main arguments of the original. As he has done in other collaborations with Lorne, Alan once again did a sensitive and professional job, and we are grateful for this.

Finally, we want to publicly thank our spouses and children for their private support through this and so much more.

LT and SW

NEXT OF KIN

INTRODUCTION

Who Are Your Next of Kin? An Overview of Trends

At one time or another, you have probably filled out a school, job, or insurance application, and identified your "next of kin." These are people who would want to know if something bad happened to you—people you could expect to help you out of a jam. You may have named a parent, spouse, or sibling. In the past, next of kin were usually family members like these. Today, they are less likely to be; the connections between kin are looser, maybe less important than they were in the past.

In fact, we even have trouble defining our "kin" today. Around the world, people differ in how they define "the family," or their own family. They also disagree on what part "the family" ought to play in their personal lives, school lives, and work lives.

This lack of agreement suggests that the topic of "family" is a complex one. It is also emotionally charged and often biased by personal experience and values. Ideologies tend to creep into discussions of the family. Social, cultural, and political ideas shape ways of thinking where this topic is concerned. So discussing the family is no simple matter any more. Nor is it a simple scientific issue that can be solved by measurement and theory testing. Our thoughts about family life are tied up in a complex of ideas about society and living, whether we are scientists or not.

Is the Family Getting Better?

Many people still look for simple answers when they discuss these complex, emotional family issues. They focus on the changes in family life over the last five, ten, or twenty years and scratch their heads in dismay. "Terrible," say some of them. "Wonderful," say the others. They cannot get away from thinking about the moral meaning of these changes. Almost everyone seems to have a view on whether the family has gotten better or worse as a social institution.

But can we really answer this question as stated? Let's look at the difficulty involved. Taking the long view, we might ask, "Are families today better for the average person than they were in the past?" Well, on most counts, they are. Most people today believe it is better to have a low infant mortality rate than a high one, and a high life expectancy than a lower one. We also think it is better to make family decisions in an open manner and base family life on freedom, not constraint. On these grounds, family life today generally is better than it was, say, a century ago.

"But what about the emotional content of family life—hasn't that diminished?" ask the critics of family life today. "And what about the high divorce rates and frequency of domestic violence? Don't these all suggest family life is worse than it used to be?" Yet, recent scholarship suggests that glowing accounts of family life in the past are only partly true. So much for the "good old days."

Families are changing dramatically, all around the world; of that we can be certain. And, for the most part, the changes seem beneficial. But, as you will soon learn as you read this book, we are far from knowing all the facts about this change, and farther still from knowing all the causes of change we shall be discussing. In this field, even the simplest issues are surrounded by controversy.

For example, there is a debate as to whether the small, nuclear family with which we are all familiar first appeared before the Industrial Revolution or after it. By and large, we find extended (not nuclear) families in settled agricultural communities, and nuclear families in modern cities. Yet nuclear families were common in agricultural (preindustrial) England and some other societies of the past as well. Indeed the Western family has its origins in pre-Christian Europe. At best we can say that industrialization tends to encourage the spread of nuclear families and the decline of extended families. There are no "iron laws" in the study of family life.

Having said that, nuclear families do seem to fit in with various features of modern life—for example, geographic mobility. They become more common as societies "modernize": industrialize, urbanize, provide higher education to larger numbers, and lower their mortality and fertility rates. The spread of literacy, mass media, travel, and exposure to different ways of life also help to modernize a society and change family life (Inkeles and Smith, 1982). In all, "modernization" is a package of change that revolutionizes lives around the world: work lives and family lives included; and change is all around us.

The Inevitability of Change

The pace of social change was faster in the 20th century than ever before; and faster in the 19th century than any time before that. In general, each century, each decade, each year brings us more change to grapple with than we have experienced before. And so much dramatic change in our lives can frighten us. Some people try to imagine that change is avoidable. Imagining that they can return to "traditional family" offers some people relief from the constant uncertainty of rapid change.

Perhaps there has been even more change for women than men. Along with exposure to Western culture, city living and a living wage let people choose their own lives. And, with incomes of their own, women don't have to marry (or stay married to) anyone at all, and certainly not someone they despise. Old customs like arranged marriage, or staying together for the sake of the children, disappear into history like whalebone corsets and powdered wigs, when people have a chance to choose their own fate. Given a chance, people invariably choose freedom. People appear to want free choice more than they want certainty and tradition.

The growth of a cash economy invariably erodes parents' control over their children. So, for example, with the development of a cash economy in Iran, children gain independence from their parents. For the first time, they become able to choose their own mate and plan their own wedding, as they wish. There is nothing their parents can do to keep them from marrying the person they want, when they want.

In more developed countries, people exercise this freedom-to-choose with a vengeance. Here people are much less inclined to marry, or stay married, than they were only a few decades ago.

Cohabitation—living intimately with someone who is not a legal spouse—is an increasingly popular alternative to marriage. It gives people most of the benefits of marriage without the same expectation of permanent, binding obligation. Cohabitation is also coming to take the place of remarriage in many countries. By improving childcare, welfare, and work opportunities, Scandinavian societies for example, have given women—even single mothers—little reason to marry or remarry in the event of a divorce. Singlehood is a viable option, as is cohabitation.

However, the institution of marriage is not about to die from lack of interest. Marriage still has a symbolic importance, if less practical importance than in the past. People continue to see marriage as a decision to commit themselves sexually. In North America, people are more and more tolerant of sexual variety and premarital sex (subject, of course, to the anxiety about AIDS). But the majority are still strongly committed to the notion of exclusive intimacy within a spousal relationship. Survey data show that opposition to extramarital sex remains almost universal (Niemi, Mueller, and Smith, 1989: 194).

Changes in marriage and divorce—more generally, in the freedom to choose our intimate lives—have consequences for childbearing too. In urban industrial societies, we find smaller, even childless families because adults do not have the same need for children they once did. Many couples choose to have no children at all. Voluntarily childless couples attach little importance to childbearing. Nor do they expect to feel pride and achievement in raising a child. They get their feelings of pride and achievement from work, leisure, friendship, and so on. These couples, who postpone or reject parenthood outright, are usually well-off, career-oriented city dwellers.

Women, in particular, are opting for fewer children because they are busy pursuing education and working for pay—pursuits incompatible with childcare. Today, North American women are half as likely to bear two children or more as they were twenty years ago. In Europe, no state intervention has been needed to reduce high levels of preindustrial fertility. A "second demographic transition" is underway there, and people are spending ever less of their lives as parents (van de Kaa, 1987).

Historically, high fertility has been associated with a high marriage rate, low divorce rate, the domination of women by men and young people by old. For childbearing to decline, these family characteristics have to change. In the traditional family system, high fertility provides three main benefits to those who control the family: old-age support, child labor, and insurance against risk. Once they no longer provide income, labor, or insurance against risk, fewer children are needed.

The availability of contraceptives has an important impact on childbearing where people want to reduce their fertility; and that motivation is growing around the world. Sterilization and abortion also play important roles in reducing fertility. In some societies, state policy has also played an enormous role. For example, the Chinese people have been very responsive to state efforts to lower the birth rate (Chen, 1984). Compliance with state childbearing norms has been remarkable so far.

It's true that family planning programs may succeed less than expected if they pay too little attention to people's desire to insure themselves against risk by bearing children (especially, sons). However the state can jump this hurdle by giving people old-age security so they don't need sons to provide for them in their old age.

No Single Pattern of Family Life Prevails

There is no denying very powerful forces are at work modifying family life all around the world, and they tend to have the same outcomes: less marriage, more divorce, fewer children, more women working for pay, more sexual tolerance and cohabitation. But despite these main trends we have identified, there is no convergence of family forms around the world—no single modern family. We continue to find a wide variation in the forms of family life.

In Western societies, intimate relationships work similarly, whether they are legal marriages or common-law marriages, for example. In your own lifetime, you are likely to pass through a variety of intimate relationships. Each will provide you with some combination of sexual intimacy, emotional closeness, economic support, and personal identification—just as families have always done. Yet all, some, or none of these intimate relationships may be family relationships, in the traditional sense.

The forms of parent-child relations are changing too. These relations are no longer as unequal, or as predictable as they used to be, even in the rural areas of developing countries. To some degree, these changes demonstrate the pervasive influence of Western cultural notions about the life cycle—about childhood, the importance of formal education, and the need to prepare children for an urban, industrial lifestyle. To some degree, they are the simple result of wage labor giving children a chance to earn their own way, and go their own way.

In industrial and industrializing countries, more and more married women are working for pay, even if they have young children at home. In effect, they are rejecting traditional notions of domestic responsibility. This creates conflict between old and new ways; old beliefs and new behaviors. Employed women everywhere are overburdened trying to do both paid work and domestic work, without much help from other family members.

In postindustrial societies of North America and Western Europe female labor force participation is no longer tied to marital status, education, or number of children at home. Women of all types are likely to work for pay if there is a decent chance to do so. Yet, interestingly, women are continuing to build lives very different from men's, and very different from one another's. Women have more scope and responsibility for defining their own goals than ever before in the past. This produces ever more confusion and anxiety.

Change Brings Problems to Solve

Confusion and anxiety are two problems arising out of the rapid pace of change in the family. Divorce and its aftermath is a third. Divorce rates have increased as legal divorces have become easier to get. When divorce laws are liberal, divorce rates go up. But perhaps the most important changes here are no-fault laws first instituted in California in the 1960s. A key assumption of no-fault divorce law is that a woman can support herself, and her children, soon after divorce. Of course, this assumption is unwarranted in many cases. Still, as more women become self-supporting, divorce rates rise. Women who have the financial means to free themselves from an unhappy marital situation usually do so.

As divorce becomes a more common experience, more people experience the problems associated with divorce. For divorce works a hardship—indeed a threat to health—on both spouses and children. Many children end up in single-parent families and they are disadvantaged in comparison to children living in two-parent families. On average, they do not do as well at school, for example. In many cases this problem is due to impoverishment and the stress that poverty produces. Children also suffer from the pain and stress caused by loss of a parent. For all of these reasons, children who experience divorce or separation tend to suffer a deterioration in health. Rates of reported illness are higher for children in families that have experienced separation than for those who have not.

These are some of the common elements in a world-wide pattern of family changes. Now let's put them together in a more coherent explanation of the change that is taking place.

A Model of the Changing Family

ↄↄ

Change by Modernization

As we read the literature, we see a pattern of change in family life being repeated over and over, from one country to the next. This pattern seems to be related to what social scientists call "modernization," and it works in the following sequence:

(1) Industrialization changes how people earn a living. Industrialization changes lives by creating new jobs and offering new kinds of people a chance to enter them. The faster new jobs are created and men and women get a chance to fill them, the more opportunities adults in the society will have for personal change.

(2) People's lives individualize. A growth in jobs hence leads to what Jones, Marsden, and Tepperman (1990) have called "individualization": an increase in variety, fluidity, and idiosyncrasy in personal lives.

In family life, we find more variety, fluidity, and idiosyncrasy in all of the major demographic processes: in migration, union formation, union dissolution, child-bearing, familial decision making, women's personal and working lives. Invariably, when people have a greater opportunity to choose—for example a mate, a living arrangement, the number of children they will bear—they exercise this choice. Traditional constraints begin to fall with the exercise of new choices and the cultural definition of new norms.

(3) Choice produces uncertainty. With a growth in choice, people become less certain about the social norms—the rules of the game. This creates what Durkheim, a century ago, called a condition of anomie. For example, people may be confused about the propriety of same-sex couples, births to unmarried women, or male custodial parents. As uncertainty increases, people make new efforts to define what is socially acceptable. This struggle to create new norms is especially important for people, like women, who have been excluded from a wide range of choices until very recently.

(4) Uncertainty produces cultural creativity. With a growth in normative uncertainty come adaptations which may resolve the problems. They include:

(a) Formal Facilitation. This includes formal efforts by government and business to define marriage and its rights and obligations, support gender equality and affirmative action for women, improve daycare, and encourage childbearing or fertility control. At the extreme, the state attempts an ideological redefinition of the family (as in China).

(b) Informal Facilitation. This includes informal efforts to "negotiate" new social roles and norms. For example, within their own homes and offices, people work out rules for disciplining the children of their spouse's first marriage, interacting with their mother's latest lover, or getting to know a co-worker's same-sex spouse.

(c) Conservative Reaction. This includes popular mythologizing of existing arrangements (for example, exaggerating the contribution of fathers) and earlier family arrangements. At the extreme, it is a traditionalist reaction to recent changes in the family.

Some social conditions favor conservative reactions to change, while other conditions favor more creative solutions. In general, anything that slows down the rate of growth in opportunities, or speeds up the rate of entry of competitors, or slows the creation of new cultural "meanings" and "norms," or otherwise produces uncertainty (for example, a war or environmental disaster) will produce a backward-looking mythology of the family and resistance to change.

Likewise, anything that imports traditional ideas about the family (for example, through the immigration of rural people into a developed, urban society) will promote resistance to change.

(5) A new culture of intimate life emerges. All of these social and cultural changes, in turn, change the original cultural context within which industrialization occurred. They bring pressure for further structural change in the economic arena. For example, the growth in part-time work, "Mommy tracks," work sharing, and workplace childcare, all reflect a changing conception of the relationship of work to family life. Pressures on employers to pay health, retirement, or death benefits to nontraditional "spouses" tend in the same direction.

These changes further increase choice, uncertainty, and cultural change; so the cycle of change continues.

Change by Impoverishment

By and large, this cycle of change works similarly in different cultural milieux. Cultural conditions affect: (1) the time of introduction of economic growth; (2) the pace of economic growth; (3) the rate at which economic growth translates into more choice, and (4) the particular forms those increased choices take. However economic growth sets off a sequence of changes in intimate life, wherever it occurs; and this sequence is irreversible. There is no evidence a change in family life can be prevented, reversed, or mythologized out of existence.

Of course, modernization (industrialization, urbanization, education, and the like) is not the only source of change in family life. Tradition-smashing changes in family life come from other sources too, especially from poverty. It costs money to keep up traditions. Often poor people, not rich, educated ones, are the first to ignore old traditions because they cannot afford to honor them and lose little (in social standing) by ignoring them entirely.

Consider these examples we shall explore at greater length in the excerpts that follow:

- The age of marriage is rising in Bangladesh because people can no longer afford to get married at the traditional (younger) age (see Excerpt 8). Marriages used to be delayed by personal poverty in Europe too, before Europeans became prosperous (see Excerpt 55).
- Elopements increase in rural Thailand whenever there is a poor harvest because peasants don't want to wait until they can pay for a wedding (see Excerpt 10).
- The Chinese are mass producing IUDs because it is cheaper to do that than to manufacture birth control pills. Also their main motivation for lowering the country's birth rate seems to be the fear of economic disaster if population growth doesn't stop soon (see Excerpt 16).

These facts remind us that people can be pushed, as well as lured, into breaking with tradition. And because necessity can be the mother of invention, in the Third World the innovators often come from the least Westernized segments of the population. For example:

- The slum dwellers of Bangkok are the group most likely to forego the traditional marriage ceremony and brideswealth payment, presumably because these are too expensive (see Excerpt 10).
- The Persian Gulf women (rather than the better-educated, more widely traveled men) are more willing to abandon some of their traditional attitudes and values regarding family life (see Excerpt 9).

So one notes that traditions are dying for many reasons. The same types of intimate life—easy premarital sex, widespread cohabitation, women working for pay, no-fault dissolution of unions, and permissive childrearing—can be found among the wealthiest, most educated North Americans and Europeans and the poorest, least-educated city dwellers of the Third World. When prosperous people live this "modern" way, liberal observers label it a "progressive" form of family life. When poor people live this way, the same observers label it "social disorgani-zation," or a social problem.

This suggests a bias in social science against changes initiated by the poor, or in poor countries. Many like to think the West is at the "cutting edge" of history, leading the rest of the world to enlightenment. In the family literature, this is cap-tured in the image of Sweden (more generally Scandinavia or northwestern Europe) representing "the future of the family," even the future of social life as a whole. It also suggests a readiness to see middle-class "modern" people as acting on reason and enlightened values, while lower-class "traditional" people act on habit, in-stinct, and in response to immediate financial pressure.

The family decisions of people in rich, contemporary Western societies are rarely attributed to their finances. Many seem to assume that everybody in the West today has high wages, full wallets, and social security; and that therefore, their family decisions have a noneconomic basis in social values or personal goals. So the analysts use concepts like "post-materialism," "progressiveness," and the modern citizen's "quest for greater individual self-fulfilment" (see Excerpt 55) in order to explain behavior that, in other circumstances, is explained in terms of people's financial situation.

Many others put forward an opposite view. They argue that modern people are rational, not idealistic, about family life. Other writers also argue there are sound economic reasons why modern Western people delay marriage and child-bearing, cohabit instead of marrying or remarrying, and "choose" a demanding, two-income lifestyle. It is not all in the service of self-actualization; there are bills to pay, and a single breadwinner is no longer sufficient. Large families are too ex-pensive a luxury in a modern urban society.

So we must be careful, in reading the excerpts that follow and thinking about the issues they raise, to avoid applying a double standard to explanations of family behavior. (This would mean seeing actions in a positive light if done by the rich, and in a negative light if done by the poor.) The fact is, similar changes in the family are appearing both high up and low down the social structure, in countries all around the world. Economic pressures, value changes, and new opportunities are all playing a part.

Ethnocentrism and Sexism in Family Studies

To explain the same behavior differently if the actors are peasants or kings is not the only bias in the study of the family. Sexism, the tendency to see all behavior through a male lens, has been well documented in the social sciences. The experi-ence and voice of women have been underrepresented, ignored, or distorted in much social science research. Even in the study of the family—women's domain, if one exists—male experience was the norm. The examples are innumerable. Childbirth, motherwork, or housework were not studied until feminist researchers raised the questions. Family violence was hidden until uncovered by feminists. Women's accommodation to employment was taken for granted as was family ac-commodation to men's employment. Parenting until the 1980s meant mothering.

Another bias is ethnocentrism—the tendency to see the familiar as normal, the unfamiliar as abnormal. When we explain patterns of behavior in other cultures through a Western lens, we are being ethnocentric. Cassidy and Lee (1989) argue that even the objective study of polyandry has been hindered by ethnocentrism and sexism. (Polyandry is the marriage of one women to more than one man.) Researchers who made the erroneous and sexist assumption that men have strong sex drives and are more predisposed to sexual variety concluded that polyandry was "unnatural." The fact that polyandry is rare reinforced their interpretation.

Some Westerners saw the difficulty of establishing paternity in polyandrous marriages as problematic; but in societies that practice polyandry, kinship and not biology determines group membership. Another example of ethnocentrism is the assumption that sharing a wife will lead to sexual jealousy among men. (Indeed, jealousy among co-wives has not been a subject of particular curiosity among anthropologists.) Yet "In polyandrous societies, cooperative behaviors are highly valued; sexual exclusivity is not." (Cassidy and Lee, 1989: 4). So we must try to escape sexist and ethnocentric assumptions in studying the family. Once we do, at least four kinds of future family swim into view; and they are all nuclear families.

Four Types of Family

We can distinguish among nuclear families along two main dimensions: role separability and personal interchangeability.

"Role separability" means people can satisfactorily fulfill one central family role, for example spousehood, without having to satisfactorily fulfill any other, for example parenthood.

In some societies, such a separation is both culturally and legally difficult, if not impossible. The household unit is so tightly organized it compels the senior male—the *paterfamilias* in old terminology—to play both husband and father, the senior female to play both wife and mother. A "failure" in either role is generally considered a failure to perform adequately as an adult household member.

In North America today, no one assumes a woman's husband will be (or act like) her child's father. If he does, that is an added benefit to family cohesion. Conversely, children may consider they have more than one father. There is the biological one, who may not live with the child and may, or may not, act fatherly; and a mother's mate, who also may, or may not, act fatherly—and may indeed be a woman.

"Personal (and personnel) interchangeability" means family members can come and go without significantly influencing the way the family unit functions. Family members are important only as satisfactory role performers. They are not valued for the unique way in which they play their familial role.

Thus, the traditional family order values a husband for being a good provider; a wife, for keeping house well and producing sons; a mother, for being nurturant; and a father, for dispensing justice. Such idiosyncratic and role-irrelevant characteristics as beauty, wit, intelligence, or imaginativeness may be an added bonus, but are not part of the basic package. The institution of arranged marriage, found in

Bangladesh (see Excerpt 8), Libya (see Excerpt 40), China (see Excerpt 56), and many other parts of the world, assumes personal interchangeability.

On the other hand, our Western marriage pattern based on romantic love makes sense because it reverses the order of priorities. People select a mate for his or her unique characteristics—intelligence, wit, beauty, and so on—because he or she is Mr. or Ms. Right. The mate's ability to contribute income, cook dinner, produce and raise children—all practical or instrumental considerations—are secondary. If they are present, all the better!

As a result, people in Western societies have very different marriages over time, and one from another. Even more than our work lives, our family lives become individualized. Your second marriage may be very different from your first: everything depends on the mates you have chosen on each go around, and on their unique characteristics. And your marriage will be very different from mine, since mate selection largely shapes the character of each marriage.

Within the constraints of the mating market, for example, limits on whom you will meet, Western marriages will reflect the personalities of the participants. For good reason, people will be known by their spouses (and secondarily, by their children). This is one reason why, as Rosabeth Kanter points out (1977), executives' wives are very important to their husbands' careers: other people view them as symbols of their spouses' good judgment.

In cultures with arranged marriage, the opposite is true. We learn little about a person by knowing his or her spouse. People are expected to fit into their familial roles, whatever their personality types, secret hopes and fears, and so on. Marriages are similar, though personalities vary.

From a Western standpoint, families featuring personal interchangeability have many psychologically horrible aspects. Contact with new ideas about, and opportunities for, personal freedom makes family life a psychic war zone. Still, these families have a strong ability to survive under even the most adverse economic conditions. By contrast, marriages based on romantic mate selection may be less stable in times of hardship. Indeed, the romantic quest for uniqueness is only possible in prosperous times. So different kinds of societies are likely to get, and keep, different kinds of marriage patterns.

We can cross-classify families along these two dimensions. Doing so yields four possibilities: call them the (1) corporate, (2) collected, (3) concatenated, and (4) cyclical family, respectively.

The Corporate Family

The corporate family is characterized by inseparable family roles and personal interchangeability. Recall that, there, the husband serves as father to the younger generation in the household, and the wife serves as mother. In this kind of family, people can come and go without changing the essential structure and functioning of the family. This resistance to change is well-suited to high rates of mortality.

It is only in a society of corporate families that people can reasonably speak of "the family" as a clearly understood, stable social institution. In culture and by law, "the family" has a social importance, enjoys its own resources, and commands its members' loyalties. Families identify and protect their members, under a system Banfield (1962) has called "amoral familism."

In turn, the institution of "the family" is protected by religion as well as by the state. This kind of family is best suited to a theocratic, undifferentiated social structure. The state, the law, and religion are closely tied together and, typically, all lean the same way on "family matters."

In a society like this, the belief that individuals have rights and liberties has little support. But as individualism grows, the corporate family loses its hold. In modern societies, this kind of family has ever less support in law or public opinion, despite its idealization in the mass media and churches.

The Collected Family

The collected (or reconstituted) family is characterized by separable roles and inter-changeable performers. Like the corporate family, the collected family demands that family members conform to traditional, stereotyped notions of husband, wife, father, mother, and child. However, with the increased incidence of personnel change, people concede the impossibility of compelling mates to be both good spouses and good parents to the resident children. They settle for people being either good spouses or good parents.

In collected families, the component roles—not the family as a whole—are the locus of loyalty, meaning, and resources. Children are permitted to feel close to their mothers without having to love their mother's spouse or call him "daddy," for example. A woman can feel she is doing her duty as a "good mother" even if she mates with someone whom she has reason to believe will not turn out to be a "good father."

In societies with a significant number of such reconstituted families, govern-ments increasingly deliver social resources to spouses or to parents or to children, not to the paterfamilias. Legislators do not assume that a paterfamilias exists, nor do they think it is proper to invent one for the purpose of dispensing state funds to individuals. So, for example, Canadian family allowance checks are made payable to the custodial parent of a child, typically the mother. The notion of "family head" is dead.

Such legal rethinking has taken a lot of effort around the world. The change is opposed by people who live in, or idealize, corporate families. That is because this kind of change admits that corporate families are now a minority, and norma-tively, they are less important to modern life than they once were. Yet the change goes on.

The Concatenated Family

The concatenated family is characterized by separable roles and unique perform-ances. From the outside, the concatenated family is a chance event—individuals colliding in time and space to form a household. Indeed, the concatenated family is little more than a household at a particular moment in time, an emotional parking lot.

Here, meanings, loyalties, and resources are vested in individuals, not roles. Families exist only so long as their members share these meanings and resources. For a family to "survive," its members must constantly affirm and renegotiate the bases for this sharing.

In such a family, the meaning of "spouse" or "parent" is no longer certain. It varies from one person to another, and from one household to another. Sometimes definitions will mesh for long periods of time. Sometimes, a shortage of alternatives will keep the household/family from dissolving, despite a failure of definitions to mesh. We cannot assume that, in such families, there is a permanent commitment to "the family" in general, or even to current spousal and parental responsibilities.

Mothers are more likely than fathers to remain with their children in the event of a marital dissolution. For this reason, concatenated families (with children) tend, in practice, to be matrifocal. Men come and go; women and children are "the family."

The concatenated family is a lifestyle or consumer choice—a supermarket for intimate relations. Not surprisingly, this family type creates an enormous number of kinship connections: step siblings, half siblings, multiple grandparents, and so on. Along with this comes a lot of confusion about family responsibilities and property rights (for example, inheritance).

At bottom, all family dynamics are influenced by "the pleasure principle." As noted earlier, mating is motivated primarily by considerations of the spouse's unique characteristics; these may or may not continue to allure. Marital dissolution is very likely, because of the high premium put on varied experience.

Childbearing is also a form of self-expression—a psychic consumption of children for personal pleasure. For this reason, childbearing is increasingly rare in these families, since it is expensive, limits marital satisfaction, and makes household dissolution more difficult.

Some concatenated families are a response to dire poverty. Often poor people, especially males, will feel driven to flee their family responsibilities because they cannot earn a living and support the family. This economic failure robs them of dignity and value; they cannot live with this image of themselves—a failure in a society that only respects success. Without hope that the future will improve, they (or their partners) see little advantage in staying in the household. They imagine another place, another relationship, another family will work out better. In any event, they think they have nothing to lose in trying it.

A fourth type of family, the cyclical family, is nearly the opposite for it is a return engagement.

The Cyclical Family

Like the corporate family, the cyclical (or recycled) family features inseparable roles, with the husband and wife behaving in a traditional fashion. Unlike the corporate family, the cyclical family does not exhibit personal interchangeability.

Rather, the performances of its members are unique. Each is a "return engagement" entered into because of the unique relationship of family members.

This return engagement may be a second marriage of the same people. More often, it is a second parenthood, in which people are called upon to parent their now-adult children (sometimes called "boomerangs") a second time.

Many reasons can account for these children's returns. They include unemployment, insufficient income for accommodation, the need for additional education, baby-sitting help, or saving towards a house.

Such families are not without their problems. The parents may expect their children to be tidy, follow curfews, and be independent. The children may expect to be looked after, even to the point of receiving an allowance, and yet be independent of rules regarding the use of stereo systems, the family car, and so on. Given these differences in expectations, problems may arise out of feelings of guilt or a desire to maintain good relations with one another (usually, parents trying to maintain good relations with their children). Norms to guide behavior in these circumstances are not yet established; therefore much stress will be found in these families.

The Future of the Family

How are these families likely to spread and evolve in our lifetimes? This, of course, is a very hard question to answer, for many reasons. One reason is that families change in response to a variety of forces—new values, state policies, and economic change among others. Social scientists are notoriously bad at predicting the future course of any of these variables. So we can do no better than sketch how a few changes in these variables will affect family life in the future.

The collected family is likely to be the modal family of the foreseeable future, if only because it is intermediate between the more extreme corporate (traditional) and concatenated (nontraditional) versions of family life. Given the firm and growing hold of individualism on societies worldwide, we are unlikely to see a shift back toward the corporate family. And given the apparently tenacious desire for stable intimacy (not just sex) and parenthood (at least once), we are not likely to see the concatenated family become the dominant form of family life in the near future.

Much depends on the economy. If the economy worsens in the future, the cyclical family may become more common. Young adults will find it ever harder to establish themselves on their own and will take longer and longer to complete their education. An adverse economy tends to drive people together in tighter, more stable kinship groupings, as we see demonstrated in Israel (see Excerpt 59).

People tend to have more choice in their lives when the economy is booming. People with good jobs and good incomes will be more likely to flow in and out of relationships—in effect, creating concatenated families. They will be exercising their freedom to choose. Other people, without good jobs and incomes in an otherwise prosperous society, will also be more likely to flow in and out of relationships, creating concatenated families. They will feel they having nothing to lose by it and, in a prosperous society, will feel particularly unsatisfied if they remain in a traditional family.

We predict that in our lifetimes, around the world

(1) The corporate family will continue to be rare.
(2) The collected family will continue to be common.
(3) The cyclical family will become more common where economic conditions are poor; in other places, it will remain rare.
(4) The concatenated family will become more common where general economic conditions are good but there is a wide gap in income between the haves and have-nots.

More specifically, we can see the following kinds of changes occurring in family life, given the trends we have reported (and discuss throughout this book).

The Future of Kinship

It is by no means certain how many children parents are likely to have in the future. However most children will have at least two living parents, even if the people occupying these roles may change. What's more, parents will be "available" to their children for more years, due to increased longevity.

Thus, in the future, children will receive more person-years of parenting than in the past. This parenting becomes ever more significant by the increasing time it takes to get an education and escape dependency. Children need more and more parenting, particularly in periods of economic recession when unemployment is high and so are the costs of education, food, and separate living arrangements.

Parents in the future are going to have fewer children available to them, because they bore fewer children. However, due to increased longevity, they will have more person-years of availability from each child. Indeed, by age seventy, people may have as many living children as parents did a century ago, when they bore twice as many shorter-lived children.

Parents will also be physically and economically strong for a longer period of time. However, this has its downside too: they will live longer in economic dependency after retirement from the work force. In due course, they will need the "parenting" that their (few) children may or may not be willing to provide.

In the future, there will be fewer siblings to share the tasks of taking care of younger children and the elderly. Young children will be less likely to have older brothers and sisters. And because their own parents did not have many brothers and sisters, people will grow up with fewer uncles and aunts. In general, we can foresee a shortage of lateral extended kin at every age, including cousins, nephews, nieces, and so on. The vertical extended kin group will persist, through a longer survival of parents, grandparents, and even great-grandparents; however, the lateral extended kin network—for example, the social significance of uncles and cousins—may disappear from the stage of history.

Other social processes may compensate for these losses of kin support. They could include adoptive caring roles (where young people care for older people who are not their natural parents or kin by conventional definition), increased time and effort expended by the kin who are available, or kinship inventions (such as "step-grandchildhood" or "half-nephewhood") which would increase the number of kinship roles and obligations for young people over what people had in the past. We may also see older people caring for foster grandchildren.

The Future of Marriage

Like kinship, marriage is changing dramatically and its future is by no means certain. The trends we have examined tell us that some things have not changed very much in the last century (or longer). For this reason, we may be right to suppose they will not change much in the foreseeable future. First, the evidence shows that most people still marry at least once in their lives and almost everyone has at least one "spousal" relationship—whether in marriage or cohabitation.

Second, most people still have their first marriage (or cohabitation) in the second quarter of their lives. As lives get longer and childhood dependency is extended, the age of first spousehood is delayed, but the delay is strictly proportional. Thus, if future people live to 160 years of age and complete twice as much education in their youth as they do now, they may cohabit for the first time between the ages of 40 and 80, being too busy with education, travel, and sexual experimentation before that time to give any thought to marrying. (Questions: Will the experienced 72-year-old bride still wear a flowing white gown? Will friends of the 64-year-old bachelor still throw a stag party?)

Third, spousal dissolution rates are likely to remain high. There is no sign of a decline in legal divorce rates and, indeed, we find even higher rates of dissolution exist in Scandinavia than in North America. People increasingly prefer cohabitation to marriage. At the same time, cohabitation produces higher rates of dissolution than marriage does. So family "breakdown" is not likely to diminish. We are probably going to have to find a better term than "breakdown" to describe this transition—one that implies normality and growth, not failure and deviance.

Fourth, despite changing partners, people are likely to spend about the same proportion of their adult lives in spousal relationships as they have done in the past.

Those are the "constants" of married life. Other things will continue to change. Cohabitation has already become very popular, at the expense of such earlier practices as dating, marriage, and remarriage. This increase is likely to continue. As well, women are spending more years in the paid workforce; this too is likely to continue increasing. As a result, the number of two-income and two-career families will continue to increase.

As noted earlier, the result is greater individualization. People's lives, and especially women's lives, will become more and more different—more varied, fluid, and idiosyncratic—from one another. The individualization of lives will continue to increase both at work and at home. At home, women will have an increasing average number of spouses over a lifetime, and spouses will appear and disappear from the household in demographically unpredictable ways.

As a result, mothers and children will be the constant family unit—the nuclear family of the future. Caring, sharing fathers have yet to materialize in any numbers.

People will also spend more years as "singles" in the future. They will do this as bachelors and spinsters before the first marriage, or as divorcees and widows or widowers after the first marriage. It is likely we shall develop new words that adequately describe the many varieties of single status—whether short-lived or long-lived, intentional or unintentional, following a legal marriage or informal cohabitation, and so on. In general, people will spend a smaller proportion of their lives as widows or widowers than in the past.

The Future of Parenthood

In the future, parenthood will remain the same in at least one way: the proportion of adults experiencing parenthood at least once is not likely to decline by much. The total number of children born will continue to fall as fewer people produce large families. One- or two-child families will be much more common than they are today and families with three or more children will be relatively rare.

What will increase will be the proportion of life that people spend with no children around. This period will extend because people will marry slightly later than in the past. Mainly, it will extend because women will bear few children and will bear them within a short space of time. Other things being equal, this will mean fewer years until the youngest child leaves the family home. Partially offsetting this is the continued extension of child dependency and the return of formerly independent children who, for economic reasons, need renewed economic support.

All countries that now count as developed have seen a decline in fertility over the last one hundred years. In a broad perspective, the "baby boom" years of the 1950s and early 1960s can be seen as a temporary aberration before the restoration of the long-term downward trend in fertility with the introduction of oral contraception in the late 1960s.

It is difficult to predict how future couples in general, and women in particular, will use reproductive technology. We do not know whether it will ever be possible for a woman to choose the sex of her child and if so, what effect this might have on fertility. In general, sex preference is weak in North America although the births of sons seem to hold marriages together better than the births of daughters (Chen and Balakrishnan 1988).

Further, we do not know whether the childbearing period will ever be lengthened by as much as ten years. Finally, we do not know whether a male oral contraceptive pill will be invented and what effect this might have on decision making about fertility.

Continued efforts by well-educated people to limit their fertility will be partly offset by continued high fertility in certain subgroups such as native peoples, teenagers, and recent immigrants. Teenagers may ignore birth control out of indifference, having little stake in an educational and economic future that would make childbearing costly. Or birth control may offend their feelings by suggesting a lack of romantic spontaneity. Nationalistic or fundamentalist religious movements will try to encourage higher fertility rates. Recent immigrants may temporarily continue high fertility patterns that were normal in their countries of origin, until they assimilate socially and economically.

But despite these aberrations, the evidence argues that most women will bear only a few children, early in their lives. Some will bear them later, because of (1) increased professional education and careers for women and (2) remarriage and reentry into childbearing in second marriages. However these patterns may remain unusual. Research on individualization (Jones, Marsden, and Tepperman, 1990) argues women will not shape their family concerns around career concerns; rather, the reverse will continue. Reentry into childbearing after divorce will, for biological (and possibly social and economic) reasons, remain less common than childbearing in first unions.

Recall that our model of changes in the family is largely driven by economic change and cultural adaptation to that change. What would happen to family life if the dire economic conditions of the 1890s or the 1930s depressions returned? On our argument, this would clearly diminish choice and reduce individualization, however, this does not mean that people will simply go back to earlier forms of the family. Changes tend to accumulate through a discontinuous layering of new ideas and practices. The transition in women's lives that is taking place today is so fundamental, universal, and pervasive that one cannot conceive of a return to the exclusion of women from the work world and the world of public responsibility; nor, to a patriarchal corporate family.

In North America we have witnessed a remarkable transformation of women's work and intimate lives in the last twenty or thirty years. Family life in North America may be a decade or two behind family life in Sweden and a decade or two ahead of family life in Greece, Singapore, or Argentina. But everywhere, women's lives and family lives are individualizing.

Who, then, are our "next of kin"? Are they still mother and father, husband or wife? Or are they the people we will live with at some future point in our personal odyssey through life? Are they the next form of family life our society will experiment with? Or, the kinship system found in a nearby country?

Who will be our intimates and loved ones—our next of kin—fifty years from now? We will examine all of these questions in the readings that follow.

References

BANFIELD, E. (1962) *The Moral Basis of a Backward Society*. New York: Free Press.

CANABAL, M. E. (1990) "An economic approach to marital dissolution in Puerto Rico," *Journal of Marriage and the Family*, 52(2), May, 515–530.

CASSIDY, M. L., and G. LEE (1989) "The study of polyandry: A critique and synthesis," *Journal of Comparative Family Studies*, 20(1), Spring, 1–11.

CHEN, P. (1984) "China's other revolution: Findings from the one in 1,000 fertility survey," *International Family Planning Perspectives*, 10(2), June 48–57.

CHEN, J. and T. R. BALAKRISHNNAN (1990) "Do gender preferences affect fertility and family dissolution in Canada?'' Discussion Paper No. 90–7, Population Studies Centre, University of Western Ontario (London, Ontario).

INKELES, A. and D. H. SMITH (1982) Becoming modern. Cambridge: Harvard University Press.

JONES, C., L. MARSDEN and L. TEPPERMAN (1990) *Lives of their Own: The Individualization of Women's Lives.* Toronto: Oxford University Press.

KANTER, R. M. (1977) *Men and Women of the Corporation* New York: Basic Books.

NIEMI, R. G., J. MUELLER and T. W. SMITH (1989) Trends in Public Opinion: a compendium of survey data. New York: Greenwood Press.

PART I

How Families Change: An Overview

ↈↈ

This section provides an overview of changes in the family around the world. Excerpts presented here discuss the preindustrial family in England, and changes in family life in Albania, Latin America, the Persian Gulf, China, and Korea. The section begins with a discussion of changes in the definition of *family*.

What is a Family?

People used to have a pretty clear understanding of the meaning of "family." If someone told a friend, "I live at home with my family", or "I'm going home to see my family this weekend", he or she could be sure that friend would understand the message. Of course, the friend might not know precisely who the speaker meant: whether brothers and sisters, a mother and father, a grandmother or grandfather, aunt or uncle would be present "at home." Yet this never seemed to pose a problem. What's more, the listener as well as the speaker could reasonably suppose that the same people would be "at home" a month later, a year later, maybe even a decade later. The "family" was "at home" forever.

Well, that fiction is gone now, and so, in a great many cases, is the reality. I would not dare to guess who I would meet if you brought me home to meet your "family." Worse still, once I reached your home it could prove embarrassing and confusing to ask who is married to whom, who is the parent of whom, and so on. Family relations today are an unacceptable topic for speculation.

So talking about family life with friends is complicated. Just think of how this has affected the work of social scientists who study the family. Social scientists have found their job of theorizing complicated by the new difficulty in defining exactly what a "family" is. On the one hand, this problem has led to confused and confusing argument. On the other hand, it has fueled fears that "the family" is dead or in decline.

As you might imagine, theoretical arguments take different turns when the "family" is defined in different ways. Some new definitions of the family are so broad that almost any living arrangement is a "family." But families are qualitatively different from "the people we live with," or "the people in our household."

Families embody enduring, emotionally important relationships but some families are more emotionally binding than others. And, some emotionally binding families are quite unconventional in their organization. A great many kinds of families seem to work, by one criterion or another. Are emotionally binding "families" that have a nontraditional form, same-sex marriages for example, still families? Are they any less familylike than unhappy but legally married couples?

If you live with two friends over a long period of time—share income and secrets with them, make plans with them, let other people know that you intend to live together for as long as you can—haven't you formed a family, for all important purposes? Many theorists would say "yes."

Defining Families

That we find little consensus on the question of what families are, and how they ought to be defined, suggests that the "family" is a complex and emotionally charged topic. Debates on the family usually have an ideological undercurrent. Ideas about family life often reveal the deepest beliefs, hopes, and fears of the speaker.

They also reflect cultural, social, and political influences from a wide variety of sources (not least, the mass media and organized religion). Discussing the family is not a simple scientific process, not a problem of measurement and theory testing. The topic is also "political," in the broadest sense. It forces us to think through our notions of fairness and the good life. This fact will become clear in later sections of this book, when we discuss policy making about families.

For the time being, let's adopt the following definition: a family is a group of people who share, or shared, a stable living arrangement, intimacy, and dependency. If we accept this general definition, we can see that people will continue changing the ways they characterize the family. That is because living arrangements, and needs for intimacy and dependency within the household, will all continue to change as much as they have in the last century or so.

As defined by one of the pioneers in the field (Murdock, 1949: 1) the family is a social group characterized by common residence, economic cooperation, and reproduction. The term *nuclear family* describes a particular configuration of husband-father, wife-mother, and their children. Typically, nuclear families are two-generation families who live neolocally. In other words, they live apart from either set of in-laws. Extended families are related nuclear families sharing a household. Some are multigenerational; some are horizontally extended. Multigenerational families can exist only where life spans of grandparents and grandchildren overlap. Because of high mortality, such overlaps are rare in the nonindustrial world.

The Western family is one particular kind of nuclear family, characterized by monogamous marriage between consenting adults, neolocal residence, and bilateral kinship recognition. This pattern was first found in Western Europe, and differed from the extended households of Eastern and Southern Europe, Africa, and Asia. Western European immigrants maintained their family structure when they moved to North America, so the Western family also became the typical American family.

Unfortunately, social scientists writing about the family tend to use the concept of Western family without defining it properly (Walter, 1989). They underestimate the variation that exists, and has always existed, in family life within countries, across countries and over time. In fact, there is no single Western family, any more than there is a single world family. As we shall see, many variations are possible.

Another way to define the family is to focus on a family's most fundamental components. Instead of speaking of "family," we may want to speak of a "parent-child unit" and "spousal unit" as the basic relationships of family life (Trost, 1988). "Spousal units" are founded on closeness, even sexual exclusivity. "Parent-child units" are more complicated. They seem to require at least one of the following: coresidence, dependency, affection, or a blood tie. If a group consists of at least one parent-child unit and/or at least one spousal unit, Trost says it can be called a family. (*Ibid.* p. 307)

Traditional notions of the family have tended to focus on reproduction. This suggests that "normal" families contain children and are concerned with parenting. Yet many familylike relationships do not have this characteristic. People's lives are becoming varied and fluid—even idiosyncratic (Jones, Marsden, and Tepperman, 1990). We must be careful not to presume what kinds of people we are likely to find in a "family" setting. Today, children may be conspicuous by their absence.

People have traditionally evaluated families on whether they provide close, satisfying relationships, enhance a person's well-being, promote children's upbringing, and increase members' self-esteem and sense of security. A social institution that does all of these things well would be considered a "good family." But don't other institutions do the same things today? For example, consider the Israeli kibbutz. By some standards, the kibbutz is functionally equivalent to, or a substitute for, a family. Both perform the same objective functions and give people the same feeling of belonging to an organized, intimate group. In principle, the kibbutz should be able to function without families at all, because it functions as if it were a family, and because its members see each other as kin. (In practice however, communes do not replace families, at least not in the long run (see Excerpt 19).

The failure of actual families to be like ideal ones leads many of us to identify some families as "problem families" (Eichler, 1981). One result is that many of us feel guilty or ashamed of our families, since they are not living up to the (unattainable) ideal. Applying this monolithic model may also stigmatize people who live in alternative family forms. It may make spouses without children, or adults without spouses, or children without both parents present, feel as though they are odd. In fact, real families vary widely in both structure and function. Some families provide love but not economic support, and others do the opposite. One is not necessarily more healthy or normal than the other. The common denominator of families is variety.

How Has Industrialization Changed Family Life?

We began this section by noting that I cannot be certain who I would meet if you took me home to meet your "family." In one sense this is a new situation—families have changed very dramatically in the last thirty years. In another sense, it is a problem that is centuries old.

As Goldthorpe (1987: 10) points out, many features of the Western family—neolocal residence, bilateral kinship recognition and possibly monogamy—are pre-Christian in origin. But industrialization has had a great impact on family living. First, it separated public and private domains as men left the household to earn a living. Second, it stimulated a demographic transition, from high mortality and fertility to low mortality and fertility. The demographic transition in turn transformed the social meaning of children, childraising, and women's place in the family—all issues about which we shall have much more to say in later sections.

In the last hundred years, more and more societies have industrialized. As more young people seek wage work in urban centers, neolocal residence becomes more common. Because of the demographic transition, especially lower fertility, people have fewer kin available to them today than they did in the past. Many of us have fewer uncles and aunts, brothers and sisters, nephews and nieces, grandsons and granddaughters than our parents (let alone grandparents). And, largely because of urbanization, more people today live alone or outside conventional families than their parents or grandparents would have done. In general, domestic forms are becoming more varied.

This presents a rosy picture of family modernization, as though families and individuals were choosing to change. In fact, families have also been forced to change. William Goode (1984, pp. 57–8) has pointed out that families change when societies industrialize because industrialism "fails to give support to the family."

1. The industrial system fires, lays off, and demands geographical mobility of the individual, ignoring the family strains these actions may cause.
2. The economy increasingly uses women in the labor force, thus putting a still larger work burden on them; but few corporations have developed programs for helping women with child care, or making it easier for men to share in these tasks.
3. The industrial system has little place for the elderly. The neolocal, independent household, with its accompanying values in favor of separate lives for each couple, leaves older parents and kin feeling abandoned.

4. The family is relatively fragile because of separation and divorce, but the larger system offers little help in these crises for adults and their children.

So industrialization produces great opportunities, and great dangers, for family life. Some societies respond better than others to these dangers and opportunities. In some industrial countries, families receive much more support from the state than they do in others. By the laws and policies it makes, a state can influence the "costs" associated with marriage, divorce, childbearing, childraising, and so on. In this way, it can influence the patterns of family life in that society. That is why industrial societies do not have identical family forms; why there is far from complete convergence or uniformity of families in modern societies. For that matter, nuclear families are not the mere product of industrialization. As we see in an excerpt from Laslett in this section, nuclear families were common in England long before industrialization. English adults apparently never had a great desire to live with their uncles, aunts, and cousins; nor even with their parents or grown children. Like us, the preindustrial English preferred to set up their own households, containing only spouses and children.

So industrialism does not create nuclear families, nor (necessarily) destroy them. Throughout European history, many family forms have existed. Families of the past were full of movement, change, uncertainty, and variety. Just like today, families in the past changed with the economic, political, legal, and social conditions surrounding them. And today, many family forms exist. For example, an excerpt from Susan De Vos in this section shows that Latin American families are not quite like "Western" or "Eastern" families, nor are they all like one another.

Changing Families

All this makes defining the "family" very difficult. It also makes generalizing about changes in family life very risky. Still, a number of changes in intimate life seem to go along with modernization. These connections are especially evident in Eastern Europe, Asia, and Africa where the nuclear family has not had the same historic prominence it has in Western Europe. For example, with opportunities for paid employment, young people are more apt to form separate households upon marrying, though they may continue to live near their parents. Prospective brides and grooms become less willing to accept a mate their parents have selected for them. Where polygyny has existed before, it largely disappears. Endogamy may persist, but it does so in a modified form. So, for example, people may continue choosing mates from within their tribe (or ethnic group), but not from among their kinfolk.

Women increasingly seek more education, delay marriage, and delay (and restrict) childbearing. Men seek more educated wives; also, wives closer to them in age. In general, marriages become somewhat more egalitarian, in the sense that family power is shared between spouses more equally than in the past. That is not to say that all marriages become equal and fair; they don't. But most marriages used to be even less equal and fair. Despite the desire to imagine a "Golden Age" of family life to which we might someday return, families in the past had a great many shortcomings indeed—especially for women and children. In truth, there never was a Golden Age of the family against which we should compare modern families.

In some cases urbanization has a greater effect on family life than industrialization per se. That is largely because households (who lives with whom) are determined by the type of property ownership; and this varies between urban and rural areas. Typically, households are larger (that is, extended) and family life is more psychologically important to people in rural than in urban areas. In many parts of the world, people still spend an important part of their lives in the extended household, though they spend another important part of their lives in nuclear families.

Another factor that changes family life is political will and ideology. For example, China has attempted to mobilize its families in support of social development. Planned change of the family has gone hand in hand with economic and political change. In an excerpt by Kejing in this section, we can see both the hardship, and the progress. Many conditions of life in China remain difficult, yet there is no doubt that family life is improving, especially for women. Despite a lack of prosperity, state efforts to regulate marriage, fertility, and the rights of women are starting to pay off.

Cross-Cultural Variation

Around the world, both families and states provide social support for dependent social groups: children, old people, the infirm, and so on. However, demographic changes associated with modernization have reduced the availability of kin members. Declining mortality and fertility have led to a restructuring of the individual life course and family cycle. Increased longevity has been followed by diminished parenting, family size, sibships, and child dependency; by lengthened prechildbearing and "empty nest" periods for intact couples; but also by extended parental survival and dependency. In turn, this has reduced the potential quality and quantity of support dependent people can obtain (Keyfitz, 1988; Matras, 1989).

In some cases as families become less able to meet people's needs for support, state support has tried to fill the gap. But there are still major gaps in service in most societies, and wide variation from one society to another.

Against a backdrop of convergence in family forms, owing to modernization, we find great variation in families around the world. Family life changes in response to changing social conditions. Throughout this book we argue that many family forms are not only possible, but desirable, and indeed work well throughout the world. What we name the relationship—marriage versus cohabitation, nuclear family versus extended family—is less important than the way the relationship works.

Even in the smallest rural communities, parent-child relations are changing, even though traditional family forms persist (Caldwell, Reddy, and Caldwell, 1984). This change demonstrates the pervasive influence of Western cultural notions about the life cycle and, specifically, about childhood. It also shows the growing importance of education even in rural areas, and the socialization of new generations in preparation for an urban, industrial lifestyle.

An excerpt from Melikian and Al-Easa in this section describes changes in the Persian Gulf. In Qatar as elsewhere, a modern industrial economy means people earn wages that their families cannot control. Young people, especially, get more information from schooling and the media than any generation before them; and they learn to value a high material standard of living. All of these changes may conflict with traditional family norms and values. They certainly set up a conflict between parents and their children and, often, between religious and state institutions. Yet the outcome is not preordained; there is no certainty the modern Islamic family will be identical to the modern Christian, Hindu, or Jewish family.

There is No Simple Evolution of Family Life

Finding so great a variation in contemporary family forms, and so complex a relationship between family form and industrialization, once again forces us to reexamine our own past. There is no evidence of a single evolutionary path in family life—from simple to complex, extended to nuclear. There are no simple conclusions we can draw about family life and its relationship to major forces of social change like industrialization, urbanization, and even education.

Indeed, in two of the very most industrialized countries, Japan and Sweden, we find very different family forms. In Japan, we find traditional family and gender norms persisting; in Sweden, a high rate of cohabitation, divorce, and women working for pay.

The section ends with an excerpt by Kim arguing that, in Korea, modernization has led to a new kind of family life that stresses family interests over communal interests. Industrialism has led to a pursuit of individual (and familial) interests, "destroying the traditional cooperative mechanisms of human interaction in peasant society." We are faced with a seeming paradox: well-functioning families can contribute to a worsening of social life for all.

So the facts of family life, when we examine them, make it hard for us to draw simple conclusions about what a family is, what the main factors in family change are, and whether family life is getting better or worse. To those who want simple answers, this may seem like a disappointing conclusion. To others who want to understand the modern family, it tells us that we still have a lot of work to do.

References

CALDWELL, J. C., P. H. REDDY and P. CALDWELL (1984) "The determinants of family structure in rural south India," *Journal of Marriage and the Family,* 46(2), February, 215–229.

GOODE, W. J. (1984) "Individual investments in family relationships over the coming decades," *Tocqueville Review,* 6(1), Spring–Summer, 51–83.

JONES, C., L. MARSDEN and L. TEPPERMAN (1990) *Lives of their Own: The Individualization of Women's Lives.* Toronto: Oxford University Press.

KEYFITZ, N. (1986) "Canadian kinship patterns based on 1971 and 1981 data," *Canadian Studies in Population*, 13(2), 123–150.

LASLETT, P. (1971 [1965]) The world we have lost. London: Methuen (University Paperbacks).

MATRAS, J. (1989) "Demographic trends, life course, and family life cycle—the Canadian example: Part I. Changing longevity, parenting and kin-availability," *Canadian Studies in Population*, 16(1), 1–24.

TROST, J. (1988) "Conceptualizing the family," International Sociology, 3(3): 301–308.

WALTER, L. E., (1989) "Who are they? When is then? Comparison in histories of the western family," Journal of Comparative Family Studies, 20(2) Summer: 159–173.

Introduction

The World We Have Lost is the title of a classic book by Peter Laslett, from which we have selected the first excerpt of this book. This title evokes a host of sentiments and unconscious associations we should examine.

Imagine losing a world; what a loss! And what a world—the preindustrial world of sixteenth-century England. Instantly our minds fill with rustic images: the gentle sound of cattle, the sharp clang of a blacksmith's hammer; the smells of candle wax, cut grass, and baking bread. The slow, regular pulse of life—like blood flowing, like water and wind, and butterflies. What we imagine, in this world we have lost, is more often natural than of human making; and what humans have made is rough, personal, and, above all, small.

The world we have lost is small. People live in small communities where they all know one another. They rarely have reason to gather together; but when they do, their number is small—perhaps a few dozen or, at most, a few hundred souls. Their houses are small. Even their "great" public buildings are small: small doors and windows on all but the grandest churches remind us of that. Even the cities, by our standards, are small.

In this world, everyone has a place—a "station" or status. Everyone's station is connected with a line of work, as in our own society; but, far more than today, it is marked by family and kinship. Each person is part of a household and family, which supplies most human contact. Each household is commanded by its (male) head; the children, women, and servants of that age are largely faceless, unremembered today. Like domestic animals and lunatics, the women, children, and servants are legally nonpersons.

Is it better to be a nonperson in a quiet world of families, or a legal person in a noisy world of individuals? What have we lost, and what gained by this change, asks Laslett.

1

English Society Before and After
the Coming of Industry

Peter Laslett

In the year 1619 the bakers of London applied to the authorities for an increase in the price of bread. They sent in support of their claim a complete description of a bakery. . . . There were thirteen or fourteen people in such an undertaking: the baker and his wife, four paid employees who were called journeymen, two apprentices, two maidservants and the three or four children of the master baker himself. . . .

A London bakery was undoubtedly what we should call a commercial or even an industrial undertaking, turning out loaves by the thousand. Yet the business was carried on in the house of the baker himself. There was probably a *shop* as part of the house, *shop* as in *workshop* and not as meaning a retail establishment. . . . Most of the house was taken up with the living-quarters of the dozen people who worked there.

It is obvious that all these people ate in the house since the cost of their food helped to determine the production cost of the bread. Except for the journeymen they were all obliged to sleep in the house at night and live together as a family.

The only word used at that time to describe such a group . . . was 'family'. The man at the head of the group, the . . . employer, or the manager, was then known as the master or head of the family. He was father to some of its members and in place of father to the rest. There was no sharp distinction between his domestic and his economic functions. His wife was both his partner and his subordinate, a partner because she ran the family, took charge of the food and

managed the women-servants, a subordinate because she was woman and wife, mother and in place of mother to the rest.

The paid servants of both sexes had their specified and familiar position in the family, as much part of it as the children but not quite in the same position. At that time the family was not one society only but three societies fused together; the society of man and wife, of parents and children and of master and servant. But when they were young, and servants were, for the most part, young, unmarried people, they were very close to children in their status and their function. Here is the agreement made between the parents of a boy about to become an apprentice and his future master. The boy covenants to dwell with his master for seven years, to keep his secrets and to obey his commandments.

Taverns and alehouses he shall not haunt, dice, cards or any other unlawful games he shall not use, fornication with any woman he shall not commit, matrimony with any woman he shall not contract. He shall not absent himself by night or by day without his master's leave but be a true and faithful servant.

On his side, the master undertakes to teach his apprentice his *'art, science or occupation with moderate correction'.*

Finding and allowing unto his said servant meat, drink, apparel, washing, lodging and all other things during the said term of seven years, and to give unto his said apprentice at the end of the said term double apparel, to wit, one suit for holydays and one suit for worken days.

Apprentices, therefore, and many other servants, were workers who were also children, extra sons or extra daughters (for girls could be

Source: Laslett, Peter (1979) "English society before and after the coming of industry" Chapter 1 in *The World We Have Lost*, London: Methuen & Company. Reprinted with permission of Methuen & Co.

apprenticed too), clothed and educated as well as fed, obliged to obedience and forbidden to marry, often unpaid and dependent until after the age of twenty-one. If such servants were workers in the position of sons and daughters, the sons and daughters of the house were workers too. John Locke laid it down in 1697 that the children of the poor must work for some part of the day when they reached the age of three. The children of a London baker were not free to go to school for many years of their young lives, or even to play as they wished when they came back home. Soon they would find themselves doing what they could in *bolting*, that is sieving flour, or in helping the maidservant with her panniers of loaves on the way to the market stall, or in playing their small parts in preparing the never-ending succession of meals for the whole household.

. . . The patriarchal arrangements which we have begun to explore were not new in the England of Shakespeare and Elizabeth. They were as old as the Greeks, as old as European history, and not confined to Europe. And it may well be that they abused and enslaved people quite as remorselessly as the economic arrangements which had replaced them in the England of Blake and Victoria. When people could expect to live for so short a time, how must a man have felt when he realized that so much of his adult life must go in working for his keep and very little more in someone else's family?

But people very seldom recognize facts of this sort, and no one is content to expect to live as long as the majority in fact will live. Every servant in the old social world was probably quite confident that he or she would some day get married and be at the head of a new family, keeping others in subordination. . . .

It will be noticed that the roles we have allotted to all the members of the capacious family of the master-baker of London in the year 1619 are, emotionally, all highly symbolic and highly satisfying. We may feel that in a whole society organized like this, in spite of all the subordination, the exploitation and the obliteration of those who were young, or feminine, or in service, everyone belonged in a group, a family group. Everyone had his circle of affection: every relationship could be seen as a love-relationship.

Not so with us. Who could love the name of a limited company or of a government department as an apprentice could love his superbly satisfactory father-figure master, even if he were a bully and a beater, a usurer and a hypocrite? But if a family is a circle of affection, it can also be the scene of hatred. The worst tyrants among human beings, the murderers and the villains, are jealous husbands and resentful wives, possessive parents and deprived children. In the traditional, patriarchal society of Europe, where practically everyone lived out his whole life within the family, though not usually within one family, tension like this must have been incessant and unrelieved, incapable of release except in crisis. Men, women and children have to be very close together for a very long time to generate the emotional power which can give rise to a tragedy of Sophocles, or Shakespeare, or Racine. . . .

All this is true to history only if the little knot of people making bread in Stuart London was indeed the typical social unit of the old world in its size, composition and scale. There are reasons why a baker's household might have been a little out of the ordinary, for baking was a highly traditional occupation in a society increasingly subject to economic change. . . . A family of thirteen people, which was also a unit of production of thirteen, less the children still incapable of work, was quite large for English society at that time. Only the families of the really important, the nobility and the gentry, the aldermen and the successful merchants, were ordinarily as large as this. In fact, we can take the bakery to represent the upper limit in size and scale of the group in which ordinary people lived and worked. Among the great mass of society which cultivated the land, . . . the family group was smaller than a substantial London craftsman's entourage. . . .

. . . In the baking household sex and age were

mingled together. Fortunate children might go out to school, but adults did not usually go out to work. There was nothing to correspond to the thousands of young men on the assembly line, the hundreds of young women in the offices, the lonely lives of housekeeping wives, which we now know only too well. Those who survived to old age in the much less favourable conditions for survival which then were prevalent, were surprisingly often left to live and die alone, in their tiny cottages or sometimes in the almshouses which were being built so widely in the England of the Tudors and the Stuarts. Poor-law establishments, parochial in purpose and in size, had begun their melancholy chapter in the history of the English people. But institutional life was otherwise almost unknown. There were no hotels, hostels, or blocks of flats for single persons, very few hospitals and none of the kind we are familiar with, almost no young men and women living on their own. The family unit where so great a majority lived was what we should undoubtedly call a 'balanced' and 'healthy' group. . . .

To every farm there was a family, which spread itself over its portion of the village lands as the family of the master-craftsman filled out his manufactory. When a holding was small, and most were small as are the tiny holdings of European peasants today, a man tilled it with the help of his wife and his children. No single man, we must remember, would usually take charge of the land, any more than a single man would often be found at the head of a workshop in the city. The master of a family was expected to be a householder, whether he was a butcher, a baker, a candlestick maker or simply a husbandman, which was the universal name for one whose skill was in working the land. Marriage we must insist, and it is one of the rules which gave its character to the society of our ancestors, was the entry to full membership, in the enfolding countryside, as well as in the scattered urban centres.

. . . Some peasants did well: their crops were heavier and they had more land to till. To provide the extra labour needed then, the farming householder, like the successful craftsman, would extend his working family by taking on young men and women as servants to live with him and work the fields. This he would have to do, even if the land which he was farming was not his own but rented from the great family in the manor house. Sometimes, he would prefer to send out his own children as servants and bring in other children and young men to do the work. This is one of the few glimpses we can get into the quality of the emotional life of the family at this time, for it shows that parents may have been unwilling to submit children of their own to the discipline of work at home. It meant, too, that servants were not simply the perquisites of wealth and position. A quarter, or a third, of all the families in the country contained servants in Stuart times, and this meant that very humble people had them as well as the titled and the wealthy. Most of the servants, moreover, male or female, in the great house and in the small, were engaged in working the land.

. . . A boy, or a girl, born in a cottage, would leave home for service at any time after the age of ten. A servant-in-husbandry, as he might be called if he were a boy, would usually stay in the position of servant, though very rarely in the same household, until he or she got married. Marriage, when and if it came, would quite often take place with another servant. All this while, and it might be twelve, fifteen or even twenty years, the servant would be kept by the succession of employers in whose houses he dwelt. He was in no danger of poverty or hunger, even if the modest husbandman with whom he lived was worse housed than his landlord's horses, and worse clothed than his landlords servants. . . .

But poverty awaited the husbandman's servant when he got married, and went himself to live in just such a labourer's cottage as the one in which he had been born. Whoever had been his former master, the labourer, late servant in husbandry, would be liable to fall into want directly his wife began to have children and he lost the earnings of his companion. Once he found himself outside the farming household his living had to come from his wages, and he, with every member of his family, was subject for his labour to the local vagaries in the market. . . .

The removal of the economic functions from the patriarchal family at the point of industrialization created a mass society. It turned the people who worked into a mass of undifferentiated equals, working in a factory or scattered between the factories and mines, bereft for ever of the feeling that work was a family affair, done within the family. Marxist historical sociology presents this as the growth of class consciousness amongst the proletariat, and this is an important historical truth. But because it belongs with the large-scale class model for all social change it can also be misleading. . . . Moreover it has tended to divert attention from the structural function of the family in the pre-industrial world, and has impeded a proper, informed contrast between our world and the lost world we have to analyse. . . .

With the 'capitalism changed the world' way of thinking goes a division of history into the ancient, feudal and bourgeois eras or stages. But the facts of the contrast which has to be drawn between the world we have lost and the world we now inhabit tends to make all such divisions as these into subdivisions. The time has now come to divide our European past in a simpler way with industrialization as the point of critical change.

The word, alienation, is part of the cant of the mid-twentieth century and it began as an attempt to describe the separation of the worker from his world of work. We need not accept all that this expression has come to convey in order to recognize that it does point to something vital to us all in relation to our past. Time was when the whole of life went forward in the family, in a circle of loved, familiar faces, known and fondled objects, all to human size. That time has gone for ever. It makes us very different from our ancestors.

Introduction

In the last twenty or so years, many North Americans have despaired about the "crisis" or "breakdown" of the family. To judge from the next excerpt, just imagine what the old people of Albania must be thinking!

Albania was insulated from major social changes after the Second World War. A dogmatic Communist regime, under Enver Hoxha, prevented all outside influences on thinking—even those originating in other parts of the Eastern bloc. So there has been no liberalization of sex, marriage, or other social norms until very recently. Albania has remained a relatively traditional, pastoral, small-scale world—something like an Eastern version of the miniature world Laslett described in the last excerpt.

Now, all of a sudden, Albanian families are starting to face the same conflicts as other families around the world. Children, especially the educated ones, want more power to decide who they will marry; and they are meeting a wider variety of possible mates. What's more, they are putting a higher premium on love—typically a female concern—as a basis for harmony, than on fidelity—a traditional male concern. Generally, domestic power is shifting away from traditional male domination.

In years to come, will historians in Tirana write longingly about the "good old days," when family life was so very meaningful (especially to older men)?

2
Traditionalism and Modernity in Albania

Berth Danermark

Haluk Soydan

Gramos Pashko

Ylli Vejsiu

... In this article we examine how Albania's transition from traditionalism to modernity is reflected in three fields: decision-making in choosing a marriage partner, arena of choosing a marriage partner, factors of importance for harmony in the marital relationship.

ↄ

THE TRADITIONAL FAMILY

... A review of certain aspects of the traditional family in Albania is essential to understanding the survey material presented in this article. Due to the medieval laws of Albania (Canon of Lek) people lived in tribes or clans, each having its own tale of origin. The family was extended. Each tribe was headed by a male. The office passed from father to son, or ... to the next heir male. Tribes practised exogamy. Women's subordinance to men was absolute and definite. As unmarried, the woman was dominated by father, brother and mother, and as married she was in the hands of her father-in-law, husband and mother-in-law. ... Marriage was an economic institution where women were welcomed as labour power and child rearers. They did the heaviest work in the household. ...

Wedding was considered the most important happening in one's life. Arranged marriage was

the rule. Senior members of extended families acted as intermediaries. ...

Another aspect of the traditional family was ... that "honour and shame" (Peristiani, 1965) ... regulated interpersonal relations. "Honour" was connected to respect, prestige, reverence while "shame" had to do with disdain, contempt and disrespect. "Honour" in Albania was ... associated with men and symbolized male superiority and supremacy. "Shame" was seen as a female attribute. ...

The traditional family structure and its customs and values prevailed into the 1960s. ... There has been, during the socialist era, and especially since 1967, an active government policy, in terms of legislative reforms and social policy measures, to stimulate and promote women's emancipation and to counteract patriarchal customs and values in Albanian society.

MATERIAL AND METHODS

The empirical material stems from a survey conducted in 1984. The respondents were 1,303 people of both genders of productive age (about 20 to 55 years old). The survey was administered by the Faculty of Economics at the Enver Hoxha University of Tirana. The sample procedure was not random. ... Instead a number of workplaces were selected, stratified in order to cover all the regions, different branches of economic life, different educational level among the employees, etc. In each workplace a number of employees or workers were selected more or less

Source: Danermark, Berth, Haluk Soydan, Gramos Pashko and Ylli Vejsiu (1989) "Women, marriage and family—traditionalism vs. modernity in Albania," *International Journal of Sociology of the Family*, Vol. 19 (Autumn): 19–41. Reprinted with permission from *International Journal of Sociology of the Family*.

randomly. They were all interviewed by trained interviewers and guaranteed anonymity. . . .

INDEPENDENCE OF DECISION-MAKING IN CHOOSING A MARRIAGE PARTNER

. . . Independence is reached if the marrying young person is autonomous vis-a-vis his/her parents in deciding matters concerning the marriage. . . . As indicated earlier, decision-making in general was the privilege of elderly men in the traditional Albanian family. Young men and women were subservient in . . . decision-making concerning marriage arrangements. . . .

The proportion of marriages decided by the couple with the consent of parents has risen from 46.5% . . . before 1960 to 72.6% during the period from 1980 and on. The opposite and logical tendency is to be found in the proportion of marriages by parents with the consent of the couple, and it shows a drop from 41.9% during the period before 1960 to 19.8% during the period from 1980.

Decisions taken by the parents without the consent of the couple indicates extreme traditionalism and most probably a high degree of intergenerational conflicts. The figures indicate the proportion of marriages decided in this way has almost disappeared over the periods studied here. . . .

These figures . . . indicate . . . a strong transition . . . to modernity, and that the actors prefer harmony across generations and tend to refrain from strain-generating behaviour in decision-making.

Decision-Making by Level of Education

The proportion of marriages, decided by the couple (with the consent of their parents) . . . becomes larger as the educational level gets higher. 75.9% of the respondents with a university degree decided themselves with the consent of their parents, while only 16.2% of this group let their parents make the decision.

The figures show also that most decisions are made by the couple with the approval of parents, although this tendency is stronger among better educated persons.

. . . Marriages decided by the parents without the approval of the young persons, . . . are non-existent among the university graduates and almost non-existent among high school graduates. Decisions made by the couple without the consent of the parents, vary little with level of education. . . .

Decision-Making by Social Class and Gender

. . . In Albanian statistics two social classes are used: cooperativists (peasants), and workers. A third category, employees, is understood as a social stratum or group. "Cooperativists" are exclusively a peasant population who live in the countryside. . . . "Workers" are employed by the state, . . . mainly in the industrial, mining and forestry sectors. . . . "Workers" include peasants, of the state agricultural farms and enterprises.[1] "Employees" refers to white-collar employees of the political and administrative apparatus.

. . . Independence in decision-making is highest among employees and lowest among cooperativists. Among the employee class 76.0% of decisions were made by the couple with the consent of parents, while among the cooperativists only 45.3% of the decisions were made by the young people with the consent of parents. Among the workers the corresponding figure was 61.0%. . . . Decisions made by parents with the consent of the couple are consequently highest (41.3%) among the cooperativists and lowest (16.9%) among the employees. The proportion of decisions made by the parents without ap-

---

[1]The type of work done by this sub group has the same characteristics as the work performance by cooperativists. The Albanian statistics do not take into consideration the sociological state of affairs. We think that a reduction of the statistical categories used by the official statistics should, most probably, amplify the tendencies found in the present material.

TABLE 1. Independence of Decision-Making in Choosing Marriage Partner by Period of Marriage

Period of Marriage	Couple's Initiative without the Consent of Parents	With the Consent of Parents	Parents' Initiative with the Consent of Couple	Without the Consent of Couple	(n)
–1960	3.5	46.5	41.9	8.1	86
1961–1967	8.2	56.6	33.0	2.2	182
1968–1979	8.5	67.5	23.3	.7	718
1980–	7.2	72.6	19.8	.4	318

proval of the couple is almost non-existent among the employees. The highest figure in this context is to be found among the cooperativist men (4.7%). . . . There is very little difference between men and women among each group. . . .

ARENA OF CHOOSING MARRIAGE PARTNER

In our study, special interest is directed to . . . the arena used in order to meet and establish acquaintance with one's future marriage partner. . . . Did our respondents use arenas typical for traditional or for modern societies?

Arenas used in the questionnaire . . . are a) family and kinship systems, b) childhood, c) working place, and d) school, action-place for socialistic activities, military service. In our scheme, family and kinship systems, and childhood, correspond to traditional arenas while the other categories are modern arenas. . . .

The figures show, during the first two periods, . . . a major shift from traditional arenas to modern arenas. The role of the family and kinship is diminished from 60.5% during the period up to 1960 to 42.5% in the 1970's. . . . The relative importance of working place is changed from 11.6% to 26.9% between the early 1960's and the 1970's. . . . In the arena of educational settings; the change is from 4.6% to 19.3% during that period.

Figures . . . show little change however from the 1970's and on. For modern arenas the figures are around 26.9–26.7% and 19.4–20.8% respectively. For traditional arenas the figures are around 42.5–42.1% and 6.5–5.3% respectively. . . .

Workers/employees used modern arenas more often than the cooperativists did. . . .

It is striking that major changes in the behaviour of people entering marriage correspond to major changes in the economic structure of the country. Behavioural changes stagnated since the 1970's and this corresponds to a stabilization in the economic sphere. The period from the end of the 1960's has been an era of ideological offensive within various sectors of daily life. The situation of women, traditional family relationships, traditionalism and reactionary attitudes are focused on in the ideological offensive of the Party. But judging from the figures it seems the impact of economic and structural changes is far more important than the impact of ideological measures. . . .

The results verify our findings in the area of decision-making in choosing a marriage partner. Working class people and employees are more modernistic than the cooperativists.

FACTORS IMPORTANT FOR HARMONY IN A MARRIAGE

This indicator reflects whether there have occurred any significant changes in people's attitudes towards family life. The respondents were told to rank seven factors of importance for harmony in the marital relationship according to their appraisal of the factors' contribution. The factors were *love; fidelity; economy; equality* between the partners according to reciprocal responsibility for the family's tasks; sharing the same *interests*; *fertility*; and *intra-kinship harmony*. . . .

We give love high priority as an indicator of a modernistic view of marriage. It mirrors a change from marriage as an economically based institution to an emotionally embeded contract.

Similarly, a concern for equality and the mutuality of the partners' interests reflect an emancipatory and equalitarian change in attitudes. . . . The other factors reflect more traditional attitudes towards marriage. . . .

In sum, if there is a general shift from traditionalism towards modernity one can expect that the importance of love, equality, respect for the partner's interests has increased while the importance of good relations, fertility, economic condition and fidelity has decreased.

The Most Important Factor

Two factors are ranked as the most important by 82.1% of the respondents: love, ranked first by 43.4%, and fidelity, ranked first by 38.7%. Love is considered to be the most important by women and fidelity by men. . . .

The rest of the five factors play a minor role. . . .

The Relative Importance of the Factors

As the respondents were asked to rank all seven factors from 1 (the most important) to 7 (the least important) it is possible to calculate the average position for each indicator and thereby get a more comprehensive picture of attitudes. This . . . calculation suggests fidelity is the most important factor for both men and women, closely followed by love. This statement is not contradictory to what we said in the previous section. A reasonable explanation seems to be that those who ranked the low-scored factors as number one give higher importance to fidelity than to love. This means that among a large group (43.4%) love was important but for the rest of the respondents love was not so important. . . .

The disappearance of the differences between gender in their evaluation of fidelity implies the number of women who placed fidelity in second place is higher than the number of men who did so.

In general the order between the factors is the same irrespective of age. There are, however, two exceptions. Love and fidelity are considered equal among those under 30 years while for the others fidelity is more significant than love. . . .

The second deviation is that young people give greater emphasis to equality. They rank it number 3 while the other groups rank it number 4. This difference indicates a more modern way of thinking among the young. . . .

Modernistic indicators (love, equality, interests) are more highly valued among the younger respondents and one traditional indicator (good relations) has lost its importance. Fidelity, fertility and economic condition do not show any consistent pattern according to age. . . .

One's level of education is strongly correlated with one's attitudes. All modernistic indicators . . . increase with increased education. . . .

CONCLUSIONS

In . . . decision-making, there is a strong modernistic tendency and couples and parents tend to avoid strain-generating choices. They seem to prefer harmony across generations. The forerunners of the modernistic view are the educated. This difference is also reflected in the class structure; the cooperativists are more traditional than the working class while the employees are the most independent in this respect. . . . We only found a marginal difference between the genders.

When we turn to the arena of choosing a partner we note that Albania has experienced a rapid shift away from traditionalism to modernity in this field too. However, this process slowed down during the '70s and has . . . stabilized since then. The cooperativists are less modernistic in their choosing behaviour.

In attitudes towards factors that are important for harmony in the martial relationship there has also occurred a shift towards modernity. As in the first field of evaluation, the level of education seems to have a significant impact; more educated people held more modern attitudes.

The impact of the socialist construction of Albanian society is seen in two main areas: economic and material progress, and changes in attitudes and value systems. . . .

The entrance of women into the labour market and the high level of education and professionalization among the women strongly influence the social position of the women. Legislative reforms, social policy measures and the ideological propaganda promoted as well women's emancipation and raised their social status through revision and, abolition of patriarchal customs and values.

To be fair, the Albanian context should be compared with what we are observing in other developing countries. Where almost all the developing countries have been unsuccessful, the Albanian case stands as a unique example of rapid and explicit amelioration of the social position of women.

REFERENCES

LERNER, G. 1986 The Creation of Patriarchy. Oxford: Oxford University Press.

PERISTIANI, G. J. (ed) 1965 Honour and Shame. The Values of Mediterranean Society. London: Weidenfeld & Nicolson

ALBA, R. D. 1976 "Social assimilation among American Catholic national origin groups." *American Sociological Review* 41:1040–44.

ALBA, R. D. 1981 "The twilight of ethnicity among American Catholics of European ancestry." *The Annals* 454:86–97.

ALBA, R. D. 1986 "Patterns of interethnic marriage among American Catholics." *Social Forces* 65:202–223.

BARON, M. L. 1972 "Intergroup aspects of choosing a mate." Pp. 36–48 in Milton L. Barron (ed.), *The Blending American: Patterns of Intermarriage.* Chicago, Illinois: Quadrangle Books.

GOLDSCHEIDER, C. and A. S. ZUCKERMAN 1984 *The Transformation of the Jews.* Chicago, Illinois: University of Chicago Press.

GORDON, M. 1964 *Assimilation in American Life.* New York: Oxford University Press.

HUTTER, M. 1988 *The Changing Family: Comparative Perspectives.* Second edition, New York: Macmillan.

LYMAN, S. M. and W. A. DOUGLASS 1973 "Ethnicity: Strategies of collective and individual impression management." *Social Research* 40:344–65.

McGOLDRICK, M., J. K. PEARCE, and J. GIORDANO 1982 *Ethnicity and Family Therapy.* New York: Guilford.

MERTON, R. K. 1941/1972 "Intermarriage and the social structure: fact and theory." Pp. 12–35 in Milton L. Barron (ed.), *The Blending American: Patterns Of Intermarriage.* Chicago, Illinois: Quadrangle Books. Originally published in *Psychiatry* 4:361–74.

YANCEY, W. L., E. P. ERICKSEN, and R. N. JULIANI 1976 "Emergent ethnicity: A review and reformulation." *American Sociological Review* 41:391–402.

Introduction

What kinds of families would you get if you transplanted a northern culture into the southern hemisphere? If you used force to impose Catholicism and semifeudal politics on the native hunter-gatherer population? If you then imported black slaves to work on plantations made out of land seized from the local people. If, then, a century of revolution, civil war, military rule, labor protest, foreign intervention, debt and inflation stirred up people's personal lives. And all the while, ordinary people mixed together, moved around, married and made families.

What would you get? You would get Latin American families, described in the next excerpt from De Vos. The author points out that, in making their theories about family change, researchers have relied far too heavily on the evidence gained in Western Europe, England, and North America (perhaps because that is where most of the researchers have lived).

The result has been an oversimplification of reality: models that can only distinguish between Western and non-Western (or industrial and preindustrial) families, with no gradations in between. De Vos's Latin American data show us that such efforts are simply not good enough. They cannot make sense of the "typical" Latin American family, which is neither purely Western nor non-Western; and they cannot make sense of the diversity *among* Latin American families.

The problem with traditional family theorizing is not merely a result of generalizing. After all, we always risk (small) errors when we put things into categories. Rather, it is due to a failure to build family theories with the unique Latin American experience at the front of our minds.

3

Latin American Households in Comparative Perspective

Susan De Vos

. . . The purpose of this paper is to examine survey data on household composition in six countries that can lead to tentative suggestions about the similarities and distinctions between a Latin American household system and that of Northwestern Europe or elsewhere. To do so, I examine: (1) household complexity, (2) age at marriage and the separate residence of conjugal couples, (3) the propensity to have unrelated household members and (4) female headship. I use data from Mexico, Costa Rica, the Dominican Republic, Panama, Colombia and Peru gathered in the middle 1970s.

◑

BACKGROUND

. . . The Spaniards brought with them from traditional pre-industrial Southern Europe the notion that an older male should preside over a

Source: De Vos, Susan (1987) "Latin American households in comparative perspective," *Population Studies,* Vol. 41, No. 3, November, pp. 501–517

family that extended beyond his own nuclear unit to include married sons and other kin. The older male was supposed to head an economic unit of production and consumption, and he was supposed to have authority over the life and death of his wife, children and grandchildren. . . .

Related to the idea of the patriarchal family was a set of ideas about the ideal roles of men and women. The ideal man was supposed to be forceful, daring and virile whereas the ideal woman was supposed to be submissive and oriented towards her family. Whereas the virile man could engage in sexual 'exploits' outside marriage, a woman was expected to be chaste before and faithful within marriage. The 'macho' idea is consistent with the formation of casual sexual unions, whether or not a man could or would support a family.

A third factor underlying household organization in Latin America is the region's distinctive marital pattern. As in Western Europe, ages at first marriage are high for both men and women, about 22 years for women and 26 years for men.[1,2] (Consensual union is considered to be a type of marriage for this purpose.) Unlike in Western Europe, however, consensual union instead of civil or religious marriage is quite common.[3] Many consensual unions are stable, especially after children have been born; the spouses simply wanted to avoid paying the relatively high cost of a wedding. They may live with one set of parents until children are born, and establish their own household thereafter.[4,5]

Other consensual unions are not stable, however, and marital instability in Latin America is relatively high. For instance, an average of 77 and 68 per cent of women aged 35–44 and 45–54 respectively were currently married in the six Latin American countries, compared with between 85 and 90 per cent and 81–85 per cent in the Netherlands, Spain, Poland and Japan. A relatively high proportion of women in these age groups were divorced or separated. . . . It is not uncommon in the lower classes for households to be matrifocal, and children to be 'fathered in

a series of free unions in which men move in temporarily with the mother'.[6-8] . . .

A fourth factor influencing household organization in much of Latin America is the high rate of rural-urban migration.[9] One consequence is that wives and children may be left behind in rural areas as husbands seek work in urban areas. Another consequence is that young unmarried women may migrate to cities in search of employment. . . .

DATA

Data . . . for this study comes from six World Fertility Survey household samples gathered in the middle 1970s (1975 to 1977). . . .

Data for different countries were recoded into a relatively standard format. In this process, original information on relationship to household head was converted into a standard variable referring to the individual's generation in the household relative to the head (e.g. whether of the parental, head's or child's generation). . . .

Lodgers are not considered part of the same household if they do not take their meals with the people with whom they reside.

HOUSEHOLD COMPLEXITY

The Ratio of Adults per Household

. . . The adult per household (A/H) ratio is often used to compare household complexity around the world. This index only requires information on the number of households in a population and the number of adults. . . . I have

[1]Mohammed Kabir, 'The demographic characteristics of household populations', *WFS Comparative Studies*, No. 6, 1980.

[2]Jacob S. Siegel, 'El hogar y la familia en la formulacion de programas de vivenda'. *Estadistica*. June (1963). Reprinted in Thomas Burch *et al* (eds.), *La familia como unidad de estudio demografico* (San Jose, Costa Rica: Centro Latinoamericano de Demografia (CELADE), 1963).

[3]See also Susan De Vos, 'Using world fertility survey data to study household composition: Latin America', CDE Working paper 85–22, University of Wisconsin, Madison: Center for Demography and Ecology, 1985.

[4]Carmen Diana Deere, 'The differentiation of the peasantry and family structure: a Peruvian case study', *Journal of Family History*, **3** (1978), pp. 422–438.

[5]Carl Kendall, 'Female-headed households and domestic organization in San Isidro, Guatemala: a test of Hammel and Laslett's comparative typology', *Journal of Comparative Family Studies*, **9** (1978), pp. 129–141.

[6]Howard I. Blutstein, J. David Edwards, Kathryn T. Johnson, David S. Morrise and James D. Rudolph, *Colombia: A Country Study* (Washington, D.C.: U.S. Government Printing Office, 1983).

[7]Thomas E. Weil, Jan Knippers Black, Howard I. Blutstein, Kathryn T. Johnston and David S. McMorris, *Mexico: A Country Study* (Washington, D.C.: U.S. Government Printing Office, 1982).

[8]Winifred Weekes-Vagliani, 'Dominican Republic', pp. 291–327, in *Women in Development* (Paris: Organization for Economic Co-operation and Development Centre Studies, 1980).

[9]Carmen A. Miro and Joseph E. Potter, *Population Policy: Research Priorities in the Developing World* (London: Frances Pinter Publishers, 1980).

been using two ages for the beginning of adult status, 15 years and 25 years. . . .

The average household size and the crude A/H ratios in the six Latin American countries were larger than in the United States or Ireland. The mean household size was around 5.4 compared to 3.2 in the United States and 4.1 in Ireland. The crude A/H ratio was around 3.0 compared to 2.3 and 2.8. When standardized for age however, the A/H ratios of the six Latin American countries were intermediate between those of countries of low and high complexity. On one side were the Netherlands and the United States with (15+) A/H ratios of 2.5 and 2.6, on the other Japan and Ireland with relatively high A/H ratios of 3.1 and 3.4. Ratios in the six Latin American countries ranged from 2.7 to 3.0. . . . When the adult population is defined as consisting of individuals 25 years old and older, the differences are reduced but the same pattern emerges.

The Distribution of Households by Type

. . . In this study, simple family households consist of: (a) husband-wife households with or without children, and (b) single-parent households. Extended households are divided into (a) 'special' households containing relatives but without a conjugal couple,[10] (b) extended family households with one couple (e.g. a nuclear family with an unmarried elderly parent). The purpose of this latter sub-division is to discern the incidence of co-residence among non-married kin which might otherwise be overlooked if the primacy of the nuclear family or the conjugal unit were emphasized.[11]

Consistent with the proportion indicated by the A/H ratios, the proportion of complex households in the six countries of Latin America was intermediate between that found in histor-

ical samples for the West and Japan. Whereas the proportion of complex households did not exceed 21 per cent of the households in the pre-industrial North American or Western European samples and never dropped below 39 per cent in the two Japanese samples, the proportion in the six Latin American countries ranged between 25 and 36 per cent. This is roughly the range for the samples from Southern and Eastern Europe (Bertalia, Italy and Belgrade, Serbia).

. . . Compared to Southern and Eastern Europe or Japan, however, the proportion of multiple family households with two or more conjugal couples was relatively small in the Latin American samples. In addition, . . . household extension in Latin America appears to have involved more combinations of vertical and lateral extension. . . . In contrast to the other samples, lower proportions of the complex households in the six Latin American countries were extended only vertically, and larger proportions were extended both laterally and vertically, than appears to have been the case in the other samples. . . .

The reasons for the difference in household complexity between Latin America and elsewhere appears to be a combination of: (1) the relative independence of conjugal units together with the tendency for conjugal couples to extend their households by including unmarried relatives, and (2) the tendency for many households headed by women to be extended as well. . . .

MEN'S HEADSHIP AND THE SEPARATE RESIDENCE OF CONJUGAL COUPLES

Like Western households, households in Latin America rarely contain more than one conjugal couple. The most common exceptions to this rule occur when the couple are young and do not yet have any children, or when they are old. Even under these circumstances however, couples tend to live in their own household. The clearest indicator of this that can be compared

---

[10]These 'special' extended households are sometimes considered 'no family' households.

[11]See also De Vos, *loc. cit.*

households, and the tendency for many households headed by women to be extended.

A second distinction found between the household organization of pre-industrial North-western Europe and present-day Latin America is the low proportion of households headed by women in the former area compared to . . . the latter. Between 14 and 21 per cent of the households in the sample of six Latin American countries were headed by women. This appears to be one result of the relatively high marital instability in Latin America, compared to the West in the past, although households headed by women are becoming increasingly common today in countries like the United States.

A third distinction between household composition in Latin America and the pre-industrial West concerns young people who were not related to the household head. In the West, young unmarried adults of both sexes often became servants in others' households before they themselves married and formed a household of their own. In Latin America, in contrast, there appears to be a concentration of unrelated individuals only among young unmarried women in urban areas. Men, or people in rural areas do not commonly live in households with non-related persons.

The implication of these findings is that the nuclear-family household is not the best focus for theories of social reproduction in Latin America, because the extended family household is important there, whether or not it contains a husband/wife nucleus. The findings also imply there is a Latin American household form that needs to be distinguished from the rather simplistic dichotomy of households into a 'Western' or 'Eastern' form. . . .

Introduction

Traditional family loyalties and practices can have a strong staying power. Males, in particular, stand to gain from maintaining traditional family patterns. So it is not surprising to find, in this next article, that Arab women are more eager to make changes—to marry outsiders, marry at an older age, be allowed to disagree with their husbands, and have fewer children than their mothers' did—than Arab men are. Like the earlier Albanian article, this one makes us wonder "For whom was traditional family life 'the good old days'?"

In the Persian Gulf, change has come from the outside. In the small Moslem Arab country of Qatar, it has been due to sudden affluence—a result of oil revenues—and the inflow of Western ideas alongside Western capital. Like college students in other countries, the Qatari college students surveyed here want more choice in their own lives. This means that they also want more choice in whom they marry, when they marry, and how they will relate to their spouse.

In Qatar as elsewhere, a modern industrial economy has meant people earn wages that their families cannot control; they get more information from schooling and the media than any generation before them; and they learn to value a high material standard of living. All of these may conflict with traditional family norms and values, as we shall see later in this book. They certainly set up a conflict between parents and their children and, often, between mosque and state.

But, to repeat, the most interesting fact is the great receptivity of young Qatari women to the possibility of change.

4
Oil and Family Change in the Gulf

Levon H. Melikian
Juhaina S. Al-Easa

The objective of this study is to report the findings of a survey conducted between 1974 and 1978 among Qatari college men and women students. . . .

The State of Qatar is situated on the west coast of the Arabian Gulf. . . . The indigeneous population is of pure Arab stock. It consists mainly of nomadic tribesmen who became sedentarized and settled along the coast. . . . The annual rate in the increase of the indigeneous population is estimated at 8 per cent. This is attributed to an increase in the birth rate as well as to a liberal policy of naturalization whereby Arabs from the surrounding Gulf areas could take up Qatari citizenship. The increase in the number of expatriates, estimated to be 8.1 per cent, was mainly due to the increasing demands for experts, professionals, teachers, laborers and others needed for its development and industrialization programs. . . . Though Qatar was never isolated from other cultures the present contact with foreigners is higher than at any other period of its history. . . .

Since the early fifties Qatar has been enjoying a boom economy because of the spiraling increase in oil revenues. These revenues are utilized to provide a free education up to the university level, free medical services, free electricity and water, low cost housing as well as opportunities for work with a regular income. . . . The present industrialization program is aimed at the diversification of the economy. . . . All of these developments . . . influence the structure and function of the family.

Source: Melikian, L.H. and J.S. Al-Easa (1981), "Oil and social change in the Gulf," Journal of Arab Affairs, 1, 1, Oct. 79–98.

I

In Qatar, the tribe, clan and family (extended) represent the three levels of the kinship system. Kinship shapes almost all the individual and group patterns of behavior. The net of relationships extends to many generations and connects each tribe with its branches outside of Qatar. . . . The family remains the primary institution for economic and social control as well as for the protection of the rights of its members. It retains the traditional characteristics of being patriarchal, extended, patrilineal, patrilocal, endogamous and occasionally polygamous.

The large extended family was the dominant type. It consisted of grandfather, grandmother, their married sons with their wives and children, and their unmarried children all living under the same roof. Other relatives . . . may also have lived in the same household. . . .

Extended families living near each other generally belong to the same lineage, clan or tribe. Prior to the oil era, almost fifty per cent of the families living close to each other were related. This figure had dropped to 37 per cent by 1975[1] the tendency for proximal living of relatives is still reflected in the residential areas of the capital which are named after the clans or tribes which originally lived, or still reside, in them. . . . The residential pattern of the extended family has somewhat changed. Whereas previously all members lived under one roof, the grandfather and each of his married sons now live in separate dwellings within one compound. They still share a common kitchen and a common majlis or guest room. The classical extended family is, however, on the decline with the nuclear family slowly replacing it as the dominant type.

Role and status are traditionally determined by age and sex. Men are considered superior to women and older people command more respect than younger ones. . . . At the wider social level education and wealth have begun to assume a greater role in determining status. The husband is responsible for the economic affairs of the family, while the wife is expected to take care of all domestic affairs. . . . Among the more conservative sections of the population all shopping, . . . is made by the husband or an older son. Women are not supposed to go to the market place or leave their house unless accompanied by their husband or son. The role differentiation is reinforced by the segregation of the sexes at age ten. However, variations from this strict code are slowly becoming more common.

Relationships between husband and wife, parents and children, and between siblings themselves, are hierarchical . . . The young are expected to obey the old and females are expected to obey males. A study conducted by Melikian in Saudi Arabia, . . . found that among university students who had lived outside of Saudi Arabia for a minimum of one year or more, the mother shared the peak of the power hierarchy with the father and the eldest son.

These findings indicate that the concentration of power—power being defined as obeying others least—is in the hands of the father and the eldest son in the traditional families while among the exposed families—those who have resided abroad—the mother's position is equal to that of the father and to that of the eldest son. The position of the eldest son may have been enhanced by his level of education which far exceeds that of his father. Most fathers in this study did not have more than three years of schooling.[2]

The father not only controls the money, but decides who his sons and daughters are to marry, who they can mix with and when to change their place of residence. . . . The mother exercises authority over her daughters-in-law, her unmarried daughters and grandchildren.

But most students of the Arab family feel the wife wields more authority over husband and children than is commonly recognized. . . .

The Qatari family plays a major role in socialization. . . . Strong emphasis is placed on training a child to conform to the patterns laid down by his elders. Corporal punishment is employed as well as withdrawal of privilege. Fathers become active in bringing up their sons between the ages of 5 and 7. At that time the father starts taking his son along to the *majlis*, the guest room, in which the elders and men of the family and their male guests congregate in the evenings. . . . The father also takes his sons to the mosque to join other men in prayers. Here the child experiences a sense of a community which extends beyond the confines of the family. As the boy grows older he is encouraged to participate in communal activities but mainly with children from the same family and clan. As the boy grows up he may accompany his father to work. . . .

The mother sees to it that her daughter grows into an adult who can play the role prescribed by society. By age seven she is given simple household duties, which progressively become more difficult. She is told she will have to serve and respect not only her husband, but her in-laws and other kin living in the same house. . . .

Even though no definite studies have been made on the socialization of the Qatari child it can be said that the process instills conformity and docility. In addition religious injunctions teach that obedience to parents and grandparents comes second to obedience towards God and the Prophet. . . .

. . . Marriages tend to be arranged by the parents when the son is able to support a wife and expresses his desire for marriage. The girl does not initiate this procedure but is given a chance to reject her suitor. Early marriages, especially for girls are common. On average women marry men 5 to 10 years older than they are.

Preference is given first to marriages contracted within the extended family, next to a marriage within the lineage followed by marriage within the tribe. . . . Marrying from within the family insures the principle or condition of equal descent is fulfilled. Thus a man ought to marry one of equal descent status, but if no such suitable spouse is available he may marry a woman of lower descent. Such a marriage is allowed because the children will take the descent status of their father. A woman, however, is never allowed to marry a man of a lower descent though she may marry someone of a higher status. Descent takes precedence over wealth . . . A man chooses a wife from a series of possible spouses graded in order of preference ranging from his patrilineal parallel cousin, father's brother's daughter, to any other woman within the stratum. Preference for marriage from within the descent group is not, however, a religious injunction. . . . and even before the oil era paternal-cousin marriage was not prevalent.

. . . Qatari college students perceive marriage as inevitable. Most men are practical about it while the women idealize it. More men than women see it as restricting their freedom. More men than women appear concerned with its sexual and procreative aspects. Almost all expect to get married and remain monogamous.

The same group was asked the age at which they expected to get married. The men expect to get married at an average of 25.9 and the women at 23.4 years.

How endogamous are they in their preferences? . . . Sixty-four men and 34 women students were asked to indicate which one they preferred to marry: paternal cousin, a close relative, from the same clan, from Qatar, from the other Gulf States, from other Arab countries, or a non-Arab.

The results show . . . that 61 per cent of the men preferred to marry either a paternal cousin, or someone from the same lineage or clan while the remaining 39 per cent preferred to marry an outsider. By comparison only 24 per cent of the women preferred to marry a relative while the remaining 76 per cent opted for an exogamous marriage. . . .

Assuming the respondents marry the partner of their choice, what are the personal qualities they would like this person to have? To answer this, the same group of men and women were asked to rank three personal qualities in order of preference.

Some interesting differences appear. A larger proportion of women than men preferred companionship and a pleasant disposition in their spouses. Secondly, over twice as many men want their future wives to share in their beliefs and opinions. The same proportions of men and women rank intelligence and common sense first. Over half the women emphasized pleasant disposition and companionship in a husband.

The traditional attitudes of the men were further confirmed . . . When the subjects were asked to choose one of two alternative questions seen in Table 1. . . .

Both men and women wanted fewer children than they expected to have . . . Men also appear to want and expect more children than women. Both men and women also appear to expect and want more boys than girls with the trend being more marked in the case of the men. Qatari college students neither expect nor want as many children as their parents had. Seventy nine per cent of the men and 82 per cent of the women in this study indicated they favor limiting the number of children.

TABLE 1.

	Men (N = 99)		Women (N = 76)	
	F	%	F	%
1. (a) A man should feel closer to his wife.	44	63	33	87
(b) A man should feel closer to his family (father & mother)	26	37	5	13
2 (a) A wife should be allowed to make decisions on her own even though she disagrees with her husband.	15	21	27	71
(b) A good wife obeys her husband always.	58	79	11	29

The findings are summarized as follows:

1. More men than women see marriage as a practical and inevitable event that restricts their freedom. While women also see the inevitability of marriage, more of them idealize . . . it as a mutual bond, a companionship, which contributes to the security of the couple.
2. Men prefer to marry at the same age as their fathers did. The age of the women they prefer to marry is less than the age at which women prefer to get married.
3. Most of the men prefer to marry a relative, from within the tribe, who shares their opinions and ideas, while most of the women prefer to marry a non-relative, from outside the tribe, who has a "pleasant disposition" and who will be a "good companion."
4. Both men and women expect to have more children than they would like to have. Men want more children than women.
5. Most of the attitudes of the women . . . are less traditional than those held by the men. College women appear to press for a more egalitarian status with the men—at least within the family.

What does the future hold for the family in Qatar . . . Here are some projections:

1. The extended family will be replaced by the nuclear family.

2. Most young men would upon marriage live in separate households. The trend for proximal living will, however, continue.
3. Both young men and women will insist on getting to know each other before getting married.
4. Polygamous marriages will continue to decrease.
5. . . . The age differences between husband and wife will decrease, with women marrying at an older age than their mothers did.
6. There will be fewer paternal-cousin marriages and fewer marriages from within the same lineage. The shift will be towards marrying within one's tribe and country.
7. Couples will have fewer children than their parents did.
8. Women will strive for a more egalitarian partnership in the family.

NOTES

1. Juhaina S. Al-Easa, "Acculturation and the Changing Family Structure in Qatar," unpublished Masters Degree Thesis (Cairo: Cairo University, 1975).
2. Levon H. Melikian, "Modernization and the Perception of the Power Structure in the Saudi Arab Family," paper presented at the International Congress of applied psychology, Munich, 1978.

Introduction

The preceding excerpt showed how an economic boom is producing rapid changes in family life in Qatar. The effects are easiest to see among prosperous, educated young people. However, not all developing societies are as fortunate as this. Many economies improve much more slowly than Qatar's. As a result, ideas about family life also change more slowly.

A case in point is the Republic of China, that giant of a country with well over one billion people. In China, economic change has gone hand in hand with political change since the Revolution of 1949. As in many other developing countries, progress has been fitful. In some decades, as during Mao's "cultural revolution," people's lives may have actually worsened. In part, the Chinese economic problem is simply due to bad luck. There is no single export resource (like oil in the Persian Gulf) to drive the engines of change in China. The Chinese people have to win all their change inch by inch, modernizing age-old agricultural and industrial practices as they go.

In this excerpt, we see the hardship of this change in interviews with two generations of rural Chinese women. The interviews show that many conditions of life in China remain difficult, but there is no doubt that family life is improving—especially for women. Prosperity is yet to come, but state efforts to regulate marriage, fertility, and the rights of women are starting to pay off.

The Chinese example demonstrates that families can change in poor societies as well as rich ones, where the political will to make changes is strong (as it is in China).

5

The Experience of Chinese Rural Women Over Two Generations

Dai Kejing

How and to what extent China's rural women's status has been changing and what situations women of different ages are facing, are the major foci of this paper. It is based mainly on two surveys in which the author participated in May to June of 1986, and October 1987, in Kongsu village, Zhenghai County, Zhejiang Province and Yiaotang village, Tianchang County, Anhui Province, respectively. . . .

In order to describe how the status of rural women has been changing, I would like to divide them into two age groups: the young (aged between 18–36) and the old (over 56 years of age).

🔁

THE LUCKY AND BLESSED YOUNG (AGED 18–36)

Women of this age group were born after the 1949 Revolution and the establishment of the People's Republic of China. . . .

Generally speaking, women of this age group are much happier and far better off than their mothers and grandmothers. They live a far bet-

ter life, have more educational opportunities, greater job chances and, enjoy greater freedom to choose their own spouses. Since the establishment of New China, women have gained equal rights with men in education, work, and self-determination in marriage, which are guaranteed by law and the constitution (Marriage Law 1950; Constitution 1983).

. . . The percentage of free choices in marriage has been rising, while that of arranged marriages has been falling. In our interviews with 346 married women in Zhejiang Province, the proportion of arranged marriages by year of marriage declined from 83 per cent in 1946 to 38 per cent in 1953, 11 per cent in 1965, 9 per cent in 1976, 2 per cent in 1986. The free choice of marriage partners increased from zero in 1946 to 14 per cent in 1953, 16 per cent in 1965, 17 per cent in 1976, 22 per cent in 1986. Partner selection is now based on individual women's own ideas first, following which they seek their parents' opinion, or vice versa; and also on introduction through a third party, that is, through friends, relatives or neighbours of the parents or the young.

Peasant girls, usually when reaching school age, are sent to local primary schools and later to middle schools. Most girls or women of this

Source: Kejing, Dai (1991) "The experience and status of Chinese rural women from observation of three age groups," *International Sociology*, Vol. 6, No. 1, 5–23.

age group had from 3–4 years in primary school to two or three years in junior middle school. However, many dropped out of school for various reasons (for example, due to their parents' traditional idea that learning to read and write is of no use to girls; some parents could not afford their daughter's schooling, while other parents preferred to finance their son's schooling etc.). . . .

According to our 1986 survey in Kongsu village, Zhejiang Province, the village had four township enterprises producing: bricks and tiles, hemp bags, badminton equipment, and a small printing workshop. The badminton equipment unit and printing workshop employed 300 workers, 266 females and 34 males. Most of the female workers were aged 18–35. Of the two managers in the badminton equipment unit, one was a 33-year old female. The manager of the printing workshop was also a woman, aged 35. The social and family status of such females was undergoing a significant change. They earned their own salary and no longer needed to rely entirely on their husbands for food and pocket money. Rather their salaries had become an indispensable part of the shared family income. They went to work in the local enterprise units every day where they had a six- to eight-hour working day. Before and after work, they still managed to find time for housework, to grow vegetables and to raise a flock of poultry. Their mothers, mothers-in-law, husbands or sisters who worked on the farm, would look after their children while they were not at home. Although not all women of this age group were able to work in the enterprise units, those who did felt quite satisfied with their economic independence, ever increasing status in the family, and generally greater equality in their relationships with their husbands. it meant they had more say in the family.

I visited a 33-year-old female rural worker who was the deputy manager of the badminton unit in Kongsu village. . . . She said that when a woman finds a job in an enterprise unit it means a great improvement in her economic circumstances and family relations. As a consequence more women became managers of their household budgets. According to her experience in the village, females were better at saving money. They were less likely to spend money in an extravagant way. Thus the family was able to save to buy some consumer durables. She pointed to a colour TV set and said it had been the couple's joint decision to buy it. She said further: 'I buy what I need and think worth buying'.

It is very different now that women in the village can make decisions to buy something for their own use. In contrast, women of the older generation, were not allowed to buy things for themselves when they were young. They had to consult their husbands for the smallest purchase, although they worked hard for the family. Their work on the farm was no less than that of the young women in the enterprise units, yet they were penniless. According to Fei Xiaotong's study of the rural family in the thirties, married women could only take the lowest place at the table and sometimes were not even allowed to appear at the table (Fei Xiaotong 1939). They had to serve their husbands, in-laws and children first. They were only able to eat something after everybody had eaten . . .

The young female rural workers now are not very different in clothing and appearance from urban women workers. They also wear wristwatches, the only difference being that their watches are bigger in comparison with the small and stylish ones worn by urban women workers. They have their hair permed and some ride bicycles to their workplace. Some even wear golden rings. . . .

The situation in the township enterprises in Tianchang County, Anhui Province, was similar. Among the 187 women workers, 4.8 per cent were illiterate (three of whom were 45 years old, while six of them were aged 33–40). Of these 187 women workers, 126 were not married at that time. . . .

According to one relevant study, the rural female average age at marriage all over China rose from 17.9 in 1945 to 19.4 in 1970 and 21.9 in 1980 (Smith and Wei Jingsheng 1986). The rural women's horizons have broadened. They are no longer willing to be fettered by the traditional Chinese norm that 'women's virtue lies in their ignorance and inability'. When asked whether they expected to further their education, all answered 'yes'. Most did not want to discontinue their studies at an early stage to marry and stay at home to care for their husbands and children for the rest of their lives. Many had a great desire to work in the township enterprises, to earn a regular income and to save money for their future dowry. They wanted their ideal partners to be moral, healthy, capable, good-looking, to be educated to a higher level than their own and to earn a higher income. Though they were peasants of peasant origin, they wanted to marry workers in cities, towns and township enterprises. These findings are similar to those in the study of other Chinese villages (Fei Xiaotong 1983).

The young rural women's selection of a partner is also different from that of the older generation. Marriages in the past were predominantly arranged by parents in which case the couple did not get to know or see each other before marriage. Increasingly young rural women now insist on free love and self-determination in marriage. Young people often formed relationships before marriage with classmates or schoolmates, others met by working together in the same production team or township enterprises, while some knew each other because they grew up in the same village or were neighbours. . . .

It became quite common in rural areas for a pattern of two-way selection to emerge: either the parents select a partner for the young people first, and then ask the young people's opinion, or the young select first and ask for their parents' opinion. When the young people's and the parents' selections are acceptable to both, or if they can negotiate, things go smoothly; if not, there will be conflict.

In the underdeveloped parts of rural society nowadays young people are still facing greater interference from their parents than do their urban counterparts. Girls' parents in particular usually overemphasize the economic status of the future son-in-laws' families and personal prospects, or demand a bride price that is too high. This undermines young people's right for a freely chosen marriage partner.

It is a custom in China that most married couples are brought together by a third party. This can be regarded as the result of a long feudal culture and the transition from arranged marriages to marriages of absolutely free choice. In Kongsu village we found that married couples being brought together by a third party had steadily grown even during the 1970s and 1980s. The proportion of marriages introduced by a third party was: 17 per cent among those married between 1946–1949; 48 per cent between 1950–1953; 38 per cent between 1954–1957; 73 per cent between 1958–1965; 74 per cent between 1966–1976; 76 per cent between 1977–1986. . . .

After the 1949 Revolution and forty years of societal growth, young rural women's values concerning marriage are changing, and although not all of them dare to make their own decisions in love and marriage, there are more girls who do so.

THE SURVIVING OLD (AGED 56 AND OVER)

Women aged 56 and over were born around the 1920s and the early 1930s, while some of them were born even before the 1911 Revolution during which China was a feudal, semi-feudal and semi-colonial society. The early life of most women of this age group was sad and miserable.

Among the 493 households I visited in Kongsu village, Zhejiang Province, there were 111 women over the age of 56 . . . Of the 111, there were 60 women over the age of 63. Of the 111 women, 97 were illiterate, 7 were semi-literate; six had about four years of elementary schooling, and one had six years of elementary education.

Virtually without exception they were married off by their parents. It was taken-for-granted that the parents should 'find a mother-in-law's home' for their daughter when they came to marriage age. Many elderly women told me that they were married simply to give them a home to go to. The popular saying among them was, '*Jia Han, Jia Han, Chuan Yi, Chi Fan*', which means, 'Marry a man, marry a man, for clothing and bread'. The parents on the husband's side took in a daughter-in-law to continue the family line, to have an additional helping hand for the farm and household chores, to attend to their son and themselves. . . .

Generally speaking, the elderly were supported by their sons, although they had barely enough to eat and keep warm. This shows, on the one hand, that the Chinese traditional family ethic of filial piety is still alive and, on the other, that it is more or less gradually changing. . . . It was not uncommon in traditional society for a mother to sacrifice her health, at times even her life, for her children, especially her sons. Even now the old mother often restrains herself from asking much of her sons. She would rather suffer even if she was sick. She well knows the traditional principle that 'there is no filial piety at the bedside of chronically sick parents'. That means she would always be ready to forgive her undutiful sons.

When asked about their lives, they first of all expressed the opinion that life is better now than when they were young. They often recalled how they first arrived in the village as child brides. Some came to escape from a famine-stricken area. Some women over seventy and eighty were still able to recall their painful histories of giving birth. Giving birth to 4 or 5 children was few for them. Some had given birth 8 or 9 times or even more. After they had given birth to a child, they had to go back to working in the fields after barely a month. It was a common custom that women should have maternity leave or be well taken care of to recover physically for at least one month after giving birth to a baby. The family would, almost without exception, celebrate or congratulate on the month's safe and sound passage both for the mother and baby. Others painfully recounted how they themselves managed to dispose of their miscarriages or dead babies who had been alive only for a few hours or days.

One old woman told me her father had been too poor to bring her up. Her father sold her as an eleven-year-old to her husband's family as a child bride. She told me that she had been scared of her husband. The more afraid she became, the more he wanted to beat her with an iron bar. She was subsequently so frightened that she did not dare to stay at home. She ran away several times, but her father forced her to return. Later on, as she was growing up, her mother-in-law did not allow her to make love with her husband.

Another women aged 81 told me she had married before menstruating and reaching physical maturity, and hence suffered a great deal. At the time of the survey she lived with her youngest son, but cooked and ate separately from his family. Each of her three sons provided her with unhusked grain, while her eldest son was responsible for giving her 60 Yuan towards living expenses every year. . . .

Some old women who took turns to eat and live with their sons, hinted they had no alternative but to be content with second best. Apparently there was agreement between the siblings that the obligation should be shared equally.

In sum, the final years of this older generation of peasant women could be considered comparatively peaceful. But they were far from happy and comfortable. They were leading merely a frugal and miserable existence. Thus they sometimes envied the very much better and more independent lives of their daughters-in-law. They said that when they themselves were daughters-in-law, they had to toil and attend not only to their husbands but also their mothers- and fathers-in-law. They were absolutely at the mercy of the latter. The elderly women therefore often grumbled that 'nowadays things are reversed, mothers-in-law like us have become daughters-in-law—we are at their mercy'. This demonstrates dissatisfaction with their daughters-in-law, on the one hand, and the changing status of the young women, on the other. Daughters-in-law now have their own farm work, are involved in township enterprises and have their own income. They are no longer willing to be entirely dominated by their husbands and mothers-in-law. . . .

Introduction

Earlier excerpts have noted some of the mechanisms of family change, and their consequences: in Qatar, a rapid and wholesale revision of family thinking in the face of prosperity and Western ideas; in China, a struggle to remake the family in the light of poverty and concerns with equality, for example. In each case, we are left wondering whether the "new family," if it arrives, is better than the "old family."

In this excerpt, the author leaves no doubt on that issue: the new family is worse. Kim points out that the new family ethic is not completely bad, because it has contributed to Korea's phenomenal economic growth. However, the family now receives loyalty and resources that Koreans used to funnel into the community at large. The noneconomic (social, cultural, and political) consequences of this change are not all good!

As Banfield found in his study of Italian peasants, Kim finds "amoral familism" among the growing number of urban middle- and upper-class Koreans. By this, Kim means that industrialism has led to a pursuit of individual (and familial) interests, "destroying the traditional cooperative mechanisms of human interaction in peasant society."

This seeming paradox—that well-functioning families can contribute to a worsening of social life for all—is quite in keeping with the first excerpt in this section, and others since. In every society, there is bound to be some conflict between the family and the state, the family and society, or the family and the economy. Where the family-economy connection is strongest, as in Korea, the society may suffer. (Where the family-state connection is strongest, the economy may suffer.)

REFERENCES

FEI XIAOTONG, 1939. *Peasant Life in China*. London: Routledge.

FEI XIAOTONG, 1983. *Chinese Village Close-up*. Beijing: New World Press.

SMITH, P. C. and WEI JINGSHENG, 1986. *The Evolution of a Late Marriage Regime in China*. Honolulu: East-West Population Institute.

6
The Transformation of Familism in Modern Korean Society

Dongno Kim

I will investigate in this paper how a traditional social norm in South Korea (hereafter referred to as Korea), familism, has been transformed into a modern, amoral one during her transition from a peasant society to industrial society. . . . More, I intended to look into the influence of industrialisation on the traditional normative structure, and the change of social norms at the macro-level will be explained in terms of individual rationality at the micro-level.

🔁

TRANSFORMATION OF FAMILISM IN KOREAN SOCIETY

1. *Familism in traditional peasant society.* The essential element of traditional social norms in Korean society is familism, 'a form of social organization in which all values are determined by reference to the maintenance, continuity, and functions of family group' (Kulp 1966 : 188). Under this orientation, all purposes, actions, gains and ideals of individuals were referred to and evaluated by comparison with the fortune of family groups. The family was the most powerful social unit which had priority over any other social entities. In external relations, a man acted not as an independent social being but as a member of the family. Thus, familism was a central force in regulating one's daily activities, and, in cases of conflict, the familistic orientation took precedence over all others.

The influence of familism . . . also worked as

Source: Kim, Dongno (1990) "The transformation of familism in modern Korean society: From cooperation to competition," *International Sociology*, Volume 5, No. 4, December, 409–425. This is a revised version of the paper submitted in 1989 to the International Sociological Association's 'Worldwide Competition for Young Sociologists'.

a norm of interaction in the rural community. One study (Brandt 1972 : 25) on traditional Korean villages established two basic principles of village structure: the lineage ideology and the egalitarian community ethic. The lineage ideology was embodied in the consanguineous village, . . . which usually consisted of four or five generations of extended families (Lee 1982 : 121). . . . The consanguineous village was founded upon the sharing of ancestors and common ownership of land (Choi 1976 : 31). . . . Economic and cultural solidarity laid the foundation for the 'cooperation' of community members as a basic mechanism of interaction. . . .

To get maximum output from the limited areas, peasants could not but concentrate their labour power on such large projects as land reclamation and irrigation. These projects required a large amount of labour which could be obtained only by cooperation among neighbours. And to these cooperative projects the second principle of village structure, the egalitarian community ethic, applied. . . .

In Korea, the traditional peasant village had two mechanisms of political control: the formal domination of the central government and the informal authority of a headman of the consanguineous village. . . . To formal political leaders, informal leaders were useful because they directly regulated the cooperative mechanisms in villages to maximise agricultural outputs. They were also eager to prohibit any systematic rebellion from below with their powerful moral authority in order to keep their privileges and interests. This mechanism of political domination, accounts for the stability of peasant society. . . .

After being forced to pay a tribute to political elites, the peasants confronted their most urgent problem, to survive with insufficient material resources. Since the chances for political revolution were slim, a realistic option open to the peasants was to adjust to the given circumstances.

. . . The economic interests of peasants to produce economic surplus also made them prepared to cooperate. To maintain agricultural products at least at the subsistence level, cooperation among peasants was indispensable due to the nature of rice paddy farming which required the concentration of labour power for big projects, such as irrigation, seeding and harvest. And since the labour of other peasants could not be purchased with money but could be acquired only by exchanging their own labour power, cooperation among villagers who also shared blood lineage was inevitable. . . .

Individual interests were consistent with the interests of the social collectivity to which an individual belonged. That is, the social welfare or social insurance system was beneficial to their interests, because their agricultural harvest varied greatly from year to year. All peasants were potential victims of economic disasters and thus also beneficiaries of public goods. Thus, it was more lucrative and safer for them to invest some proportion of surplus, if any, in public goods in good years and then receive it back in bad years.

2. *The transformation of familism in industrial society.* . . . Modernisation theorists argue that industrialisation changes family structure from the extended to the nuclear or conjugal family, since the latter fits better the needs of industrialism (Goode 1963 : Ch. 1). This appears to explain the change of family patterns in Korea. The most typical family pattern in modern Korea has turned out to be nuclear, approximating about 70 per cent of all households (Choi 1982 : 20).

The change in family structure, however, means neither that the network of interactions among individuals has become confined narrowly to the nuclear family members, nor that an individual is liberated from the constraints of the traditional extended family. One study (Cho 1975) reveals that the network of interactions among modern Korean people is still oriented toward the traditional extended kinship ties, showing the persistence of traditional familism. The coexistence of the nuclear family structure and extended family kinship ties can be referred to as the emergence of the modified extended family. . . .

The network of the modified extended family has provided a favourable foundation for the emergence of modern familism. Modern familism takes a disjunctive view of family and social interests. The community is no longer regarded as an extension of one's blood relationship, and the social conditions which unified individual interests with collective interests in peasant society are radically altered. One's responsibilities for society are not emphasised, and one's obligation begins and ends with family groups. Loyalty is given to this modified extended family, not to . . . the village or the state. . . .

I can summarise more features of modern familism: the priority of family interests, the dominance of economic interests in kinship ties, and the exclusiveness of the kinship network. The priority of family interests means the precedence of family interests over any other social interests. . . . The second trait is that interactions among individuals in a modified extended family primarily originate from economic and instrumental objectives, contrary to emotional and expressive ones in traditional society. . . .

The third feature, the exclusiveness of modern familism, means that the perceived range of family membership is greatly reduced, from all villagers sharing blood relationships and brotherhood in traditional familism to the members of a modified extended family in modern society. . . . The limitation in membership is based on the attitude that in an insecure and unstable society one can only depend on the strongest family ties.

Modern familism, thus identified, is similar to the image of 'amoral familism' which Banfield (1958) describes. . . . Like amoral familists in Banfield's study, individuals in modern Korean society are eager to maximise material, short-term advantages for their family by mobilising all the resources available in the modified extended family networks, under the assumption that all others will do likewise. Nobody furthers public interests, except when they are related to their immediate private advantages. . . .

Why has this change occurred. . . ? And what social conditions destroyed the harmony between public goods and individual interests . . . ? To answer these questions, we need to investigate the . . . influence of extensive geographical and social mobility which accompanied industrialisation, on human consciousness and behaviour. . . .

Due to these two kinds of mobility, Korean society has witnessed the emergence of a new social stratum, the urban middle class. This new class was unprecedented in a traditional dichotomous class structure, which was largely composed of Confucian political elites and peasants. The middle class has consolidated its position by accumulating wealth through industrialisation, and thus emphasises the maximisation of individual economic interests at any cost. The emergence and expansion of this class satisfies a condition for the rise of a new social norm: that is, 'there should be a group of people who assert a different kind of norm and the old social network does not support the punishment for not conforming to it' (Goode 1960 : 254). . . .

The political leaders who pushed industrialisation programmes in Korea captured power by an illegitimate coup d'Etat headed by General Park in 1961. The illegitimacy of their power decisively determined the future direction of social development. The main purpose of their political action was to legitimate the military revolution. From this purpose the new government announced a revolution to modernise their country, to liberate the people from poverty, and establish a self-reliant economy (Park 1970 : 119–20). To accomplish these goals, there were two alternative means: balanced economic growth and unbalanced economic development. . . . The policy of balanced economic development requires an enormous quantity of capital and time to get substantial results to be appropriated for political propaganda. On the other hand, unbalanced economic development is designed to develop a disproportional economy by concentrating investments in a few strategic economic sectors. Thus, the results of economic growth are available more rapidly and conspicuously, though its long-term effects are detrimental to the balanced and indigenous development of the national economy.

The political leaders of Korea chose unbalanced economic growth. In addition to the general economic conditions of Korea which favoured the adoption of this policy (for example, underdevelopment of capital savings and technology and insufficient natural resources), the policy was taken up because it was more advantageous to the interests of political elites. The elites' primary concern was to gain support from the people to reduce the costs of political control required to suppress dissidents. . . .

Political leaders favoured this policy for another reason as well: it was more beneficial to their property rights. Unlike the model of balanced economic development, this model requires the participation of foreign capital and technology, especially when the heavy and petrochemical industries are of central importance, since they demand a large amount of capital and highly developed technology. Some dependency theorists (Dos Santos 1970; Cardoso 1972; Amin 1974) argue that the penetration of foreign capital into Third World countries distorts the economic structure and creates a monopoly of internal markets which are manipulated by comprador capitalists and state bureaucrats. In fact, a ruler frequently finds it in his interest to grant monopoly rights rather than property rights which would lead to more competitive conditions (North 1981 : 28). This happened in Korea.

This strategy of economic development was successful in terms of quantitative economic indices. . . . The GNP of Korea in 1975 was nine times larger than that of 1962. . . . Between 1962 and 1976, the value of exports increased from 55 million dollars to 77 billion dollars, and exports shifted from primary products to industrial goods (Lee 1981 : 177–85).

Economic development, however, generated a structural distortion in Korean society, as was evinced in economic inequalities among social classes. The distortion was expected even before developmental plans were executed, since the Korean government was unconcerned about the social redistribution of wealth and the development of a social welfare system. With the given programmes of industrialisation, a large number of industrial workers were 'planned' to suffer from low wages, since the cheap and disciplined labour forces were indispensable for Korea to keep ahead in international markets.

Ordinary people had to decide how they should behave. Here, two responses were predictable: to comply with the *status quo*, while pursuing their interests within the given conditions, or to protest and rebel against the established political power, while challenging the economic development plans. The former was dominant in the 1960s and 1970s, whereas the latter became more widespread in the 1980s. I shall consider only the former and will briefly explain why the people behaved in this way to bring forth and maintain modern familism.

. . . The intensification of industrialisation made more people tend toward acute conflict and competition among themselves. Why? An answer can be provided by examining the psychological mechanism operating among those who participated in industrialisation.

As stated earlier, the amount of economic and social resources with which individuals were endowed was almost identical at the initial point of industrialisation. Yet, the rewards they received in the middle of that process revealed an extremely skewed distribution. This . . . outcome was sufficient to generate 'relative frustration' between those who benefitted from industrialisation and those who did not. . . .

Notwithstanding this 'relative frustration', the people did not resign from the game of gaining economic wealth. The main reason is that

there remained the hope of being a winner in the game, since everyone had ample chances of upward mobility, provided they were equipped with higher education and the economic resources necessary for it. Thus, people were eager to mobilise all the available resources within the network of a modified extended family to take a favourable social position in promoting their family interests. . . . In the absence of an adequate rule controlling the game of economic gains, individuals began to perceive others as potential rivals who could take away material resources which would otherwise be theirs.

The development of competitive behaviour and amoral familism was furthered by the underdevelopment of the social welfare system . . . until the government began to establish a national welfare policy in 1976 (Jun 1980). . . . It is natural that where public law cannot guarantee adequate protection against breaches of non-kin contracts and where no cultural patterns of cooperation between non-kin exist to guide the required relationship, kinsmen may become parasitic upon one another (Wolf 1966 : 10). The final result is that an individual no longer invests in the public welfare or insurance system, but relies instead upon the personal family welfare system in the modified extended family.
. . .

CONCLUDING REMARKS

Traditional familism and its behaviour pattern, cooperation among community members, were established in peasant society, because they were efficient in realising the interests of both political leaders and peasants. In industrialisation, they have been transformed into a modern norm and a new behaviour pattern, because they no longer guarantee adequate returns for the pursuit of individual interests.

The 'direction' the transformation of familism took was not toward Western individualism . . . but toward a modern, distorted variant of itself. Here we find a dislocation between Western economic institutions and the continuation and distortion of the traditional normative structure (between economy and ideology), as is often observed in a transitional Third World society (Taylor 1979: 216–7). The dislocation was elicited from the industrialisation policy, which resulted in social inequalities between the haves and have-nots.

In closing, I need to add two qualifications concerning my arguments in this paper. First, a utilitarian analysis of the transformation of a social norm, in terms of individual interests and rationality never implies that social actions are solely interest-oriented. The strong ideological influence of Confucianism in traditional society encouraged cooperative behaviour among peasants. In the initial phase of industrialisation, the Korean government also utilised an ideology of nationalism to induce an enthusiastic participation of people in the process of industrialisation, even with insufficient returns. But in some cases, especially when individuals are strongly conscious of the consequences of their actions, these actions can be explained in terms of the motivation to pursue their own interests.

Secondly, I am not arguing that a modern amoral familism has been completely negative for Korean society, especially for its economic growth. . . . Korea could not have accomplished such an admirable outcome without the efforts of individuals to concentrate all resources in their family network. Thus, economic growth in Korea may be understood in a sense as an aggregated result of individual rationality oriented toward gaining maximum profits in industrialisation. But individual rationality, which encouraged rapid economic development, simultaneously seeded collective irrationality, thereby destroying the solidarity of traditional society based on communitywide cooperation. . . .

REFERENCES

AMIN, S. 1974. *Accumulation on a World Scale: A Critique of the Theory of Underdevelopment*. New York: Monthly Review Press.

BANFIELD, E. C. 1958. *The Moral Basis of Backward Society*. New York: The Free Press.

BOUDON, R. 1986. 'The Logic of Relative Frustration', in Elster, J. (ed.), *Rational Choice*. New York: New York University Press.

BRANDT, V. 1972. *Korean Village: Between Farm and Sea*. Cambridge: Harvard University Press.

CARDOSO, F. 1972. 'Dependency and Development in Latin America'. *New Left Review* 74.

CHO, H. 1975. 'The Kin Network of the Urban Middle Class Family in Korea'. *Korean Journal* 15.

CHOI, J.-S. 1976. 'Family System', in Chun, S.-Y. (ed.), *Korean Society*. Seoul: International Cultural Foundation.

CHOI, J.-S. 1982. *Hyundae Sahoe Gajok Yongu (A Study of the Family in Modern Society)*. Seoul: Il-ji Sa.

DOS SANTOS, T. 1970. 'The Structure of Dependency'. *The American Economic Review* LX.

GOODE, W. J. 1960. 'Norm Commitment and Conformity to Role-Status Obligations'. *American Journal of Sociology* 66.

GOODE, W. J. 1963. *World Revolution and Family Patterns*. New York: The Free Press.

JUN, N.-J. 1980. 'Establishment of the National Welfare Pension System in Korea'. Ph.D. Thesis, University of Chicago.

KULP, D. H. Jr. 1966. *Country Life in South China: The Sociology of Familism*. New York: Columbia University Press.

LEE, M. 1982. *Sociology and Social Change in Korea*. Seoul: Seoul National University Press.

LEE, Y.-H. 1981. 'Socio-Economic Transformation and Politcal Culture in Korea', in Lee, C.-S. (ed.), *Modernization in Korea and the Impact of the West*. Los Angeles: University of Southern California Press.

NORTH, D. C. 1981. *Structure and Change in Economic History*. New York: W. W. Norton.

PARK, C.-H. 1970. *Our Nation's Path: Ideology of Social Reconstruction*. Seoul: Hollym Corporation.

TAYLOR, J. G. 1979. *From Modernization to Modes of Production: A Critique of Sociologies of Development and Underdevelopment*. London: Macmillan.

WOLF, E. R. 1966. 'Kinship, Friendship, and Patron-Client Relations in Complex Societies', in Banton, M. (ed.), *The Social Anthropology of Complex Societies*. London: Tavistock.

Discussion Questions

1. Dongno Kim believes that modernization theories do a poor job of explaining changes in the Korean family. Why does he think so? Would Susan De Vos agree they do a poor job explaining Latin American families too? If so, would she say it is for the same reasons?

2. What are the important similarities and differences between the preindustrial families Laslett has described (in England) and those Melikian and Al-Easa describe (in Qatar)? Can we expect Qatari families to follow the same course of changes as English families did several centuries earlier?

3. Many people wax nostalgic about the past and picture the olden-day American family as snug, comfortable, loving, and protective. Is Dongno Kim guilty of doing this very thing when he describes Korean families of the past?

4. Dai Kejing focuses on the way changes in family life have affected women in China. By contrast, Peter Laslett has very little to say about women's experiences before or since the changes in English family life he studies. Why does Laslett seem to ignore women? Would he have found what Kejing did if he had looked?

5. Levon Melikian and Juhaina Al-Easa ask, "Will the family in Qatar continue to remain a source of security and support to the individual as it changes into the nuclear type?" How would Danermark and her colleagues answer that question, based on their analysis of changes in Albanian family life?

6. Susan De Vos suggests that the family history of Northwestern Europe should not be used as the basis for making simple distinctions between Western and Eastern families, or modern and preindustrial families. Do you agree? Would Dai Kejing agree?

Data Collection Exercises

1. De Vos bases her analysis of Latin American families on such things as average age at marriage, number of adults per household, proportion of households with one or more conjugal units, number of households with a female head, and presence of unrelated (and unmarried) young people in the household. Collect some census data on Qatar, or another Arab country, to measure at least three of these characteristics.

2. Despite an obvious fondness for "the world they have lost," neither Kim nor Laslett provides any hard data on the way people *felt* about family life in the past. Collect some convincing evidence of this kind about any society you wish—England, Korea, or the United States for example—and explain why it convinces you.

3. The Qatari research in this section focuses on people at the top of the social structure (urban, middle class college students), while the Chinese research focuses

on people at the bottom (poor rural women). Collect some American data comparing the rates of family change in each of these segments of American society.

4. The articles by Laslett and De Vos illustrate two alternative ways of studying family structures. One is a historical analysis of a single society, the other a cross-national comparison at a single point in time. Collect comparative data from at least three different countries to test any one of Laslett's conclusions. (Or, alternately, collect historical data from any Latin American country to test one of De Vos's conclusions.)

Writing Exercises

1. You are Susan De Vos. Write Peter Laslett a brief (250-word) letter telling him what you have found in Latin America, and how your findings bear on his English research. Now, you are Peter Laslett. Write Susan De Vos a brief (250-word) reply. Indicate which of her conclusions you are ready to accept, which you reject, and why.

2. "There is a real danger of amoral familism taking hold in Qatar." Defend or reject this view in a brief (500-word) essay.

3. Write a brief (500-word) drama in which Peter Laslett and Berth Danermark swap stories about "the good old days" of the family.

4. China and Korea have long historic and cultural connections with one another; and in both societies, the family is changing fundamentally. Are families in these two societies changing similarly? If not, why not? Write a brief (500-word) essay on the differences you would expect to find if you collected data from these two countries. Explain your reasoning.

Glossary

Amoral familism—A value system that puts one's own family's interests before everyone else's, including those of the community.

Cohabitation—A stable, sexually intimate living arrangement that is not legal marriage.

Convergence—A coming together, in this case, a coming together (or growing similarity) of different family systems around the world.

Demographic—Having to do with demography (the study of population) or population characteristics (such as births, deaths, and migrations).

Industrialism—A system of production which uses machinery and inanimate forms of energy (such as electric power) to mass-produce goods, often in large factories.

Institution(s)—Any set of social practices that are regular, repeated, and supported by the society's norms and values; major institutions include families, schools, and electoral systems.

Intimacy—A relationship marked by close acquaintance, frequent association and familiarity, often characterized by informality and privacy; may include sexual relations.

Modernization—A general process of social change which may include the development of (1) new political practices (for example, political parties and elective government); (2) new cultural practices (for example, secularization of the state, and development of nationalist sentiment); (3) new economic practices (for example, a greater division of labor, more specialization, and new technology); and (4) new social practices (for example, literacy, city living, and a decline of traditional authority).

Normative—Normative behavior is behavior that people in a society consider proper or correct; it follows rules or prescriptions that people consider legitimate, given their social values.

Urbanization—The process of growth of cities, and the movement of people from rural areas into cities.

Western—Historically, that part of the world that is located in Western (especially Northwestern) Europe, and those countries (such as the USA, Canada, and Australia) that began as colonies of these countries. In some circles, came to be used as a synonym for "modern" (see definition of "modernization")

Suggested Readings

EICHLER, MARGRIT. (1981) "Models of the family," *Canadian Journal of Sociology,* 6, 367–388. A fine examination of the problems people create when they try to apply "monolithic" models of the family in a complex, rapidly changing world. Not only do these images not apply to reality; they also display, and maintain, some ideas about gender and power that we would do well to get rid of.

GOODE, WILLIAM J. (1963) *World Revolution and Family Patterns.* New York: Free Press. This is one of the classic works on the way modernization changes families around the world. The arguments are put together with Goode's usual rigor and clarity, and draw on data from many different parts of the world, region by region.

INKELES, ALEX, and DAVID H. SMITH. (1982) *Becoming Modern: Individual Change in Six Developing Countries.* Cambridge: Harvard University Press. This book shows how the industrialization of jobs (also, city life and the spread of literacy and education) modernizes family relations, for example, equalizing the relations between husbands and wives, parents and children. The data are from Argentina, Chile, India, Pakistan, Nigeria, and Israel.

JONES, CHARLES, LORNA MARSDEN, and LORNE TEPPERMAN. (1990) *Lives of Their Own.* Toronto: Oxford University Press. This short book shows how women's lives have become more varied, fluid, and unlike one another in the last twenty years as a result of changes in family and work life. The data are mainly from Canada, with comparative materials from the United States, England, France, and other countries.

LASLETT, PETER. (1971) *The World We Have Lost.* London: Methuen and Company. Along with Goode's book, this is a modern classic on the family. It shows particularly well how a skilled researcher can reconstruct everyday life in the past from such diverse evidence as parish records of births and deaths, wheat prices, diaries, contemporary literature, and documentary evidence.

SCANZONI, JOHN. (1987) "Families in the 1980s: Time to Refocus Our Thinking," *Journal of Family Issues,* 8, 4, December, 394–421. This paper is chock-full of interesting ideas about the problem of defining "family" today. It forces us to rethink what families are supposed to be about—their functions, rather than their forms—and reminds us that forms may be less important than functions. Yet processes of family functioning (of intimacy and dependency, for example) are also changing.

PART II

Marriage and Family Formation

As far as social scientists have been able to determine, marriage is a universal institution. But marriages vary considerably from one society to another. They vary in structure, in residence patterns, and in the extent to which partners are freely chosen. The excerpts found in this section look at cross-cultural variations in the ways couples begin life together. Together they create an impression of variety, ingenuity, and adaptability. In the following paragraphs we will describe some of these cross-cultural differences.

Cross-Cultural Variation in Marriage Structure

Number of Spouses

The most obvious way to differentiate marriage structures is by number of spouses. Monogamous marriages are the most typical form of marriage now. Polygamous marriages (marriages of more than one man or more than one woman and a spouse of the opposite sex) are far less common. In most countries they are illegal. Monogamy has characterized Western marriage at least since very early Christian influence, and possibly before (Goldthorpe, 1987). However North America is not exclusively monogamous. Mormons practiced polygamy until 1890 when government pressure caused the practice to be officially discontinued. The Oneida community (see Excerpt 19) practiced what their leader, John Noyes, called complex marriage. "Under this system, monogamous relationships were forbidden and adult members of the community were encouraged to have sexual relations with a wide variety of partners."

It is impossible to determine the exact number of polygamous unions that exist in the United States or Canada today, because there is no way to count concurrent cohabiting relationships. One estimate suggests as many as 50,000 polygamous marriages in the Rocky Mountain States alone. (Kelly, 1991) A polygamous marriage profiled in a widely circulated American magazine for adolescents described a stable, long-term polygamous marriage of one man and nine women. Some of the women live communally, some live independently. All consider the other wives and the twenty progeny to be members of their family. (Kelly, 1991)

Most polygamous marriages are marriages of one man and two or more women. Anthropologists call this polygyny. Polyandrous marriages, which join one woman and more than one man are far less common, and polygynandry (multiple husbands and wives) rarer still. Although there are exceptions, polyandry tends to exist in very poor societies with marginal economies (Cassidy and Lee, 1989: 5). In these economies limited family size is an advantage. Polyandry is also linked to the practice of female infanticide.

It is impossible to estimate the extent to which polygamy is still practiced since many countries have legislated against group marriage. For example, the 1950 Marriage Act made polygamy unacceptable in China. Official Chinese statistics likely underrepresent the actual incidence. As recently as twenty years ago, polygamy was still widespread in much of Africa where it is now illegal. Nevertheless in 1977 almost 30% of married men in Zaire had more than one wife (Welch and Glick, 1981).

The first excerpt in this section asks why some societies endorse polygyny. Anthropologists have suggested two possible explanations: wives are either valued for the work they do, or for the offspring they produce.

Residence Patterns

The complexities of marital arrangements are reflected in the elaborate terminology developed to distinguish family forms and residence patterns. In much of Africa, India, and China, couples have typically taken up residence with the groom's parents. This is referred to as patrilocality. In Thailand, rural couples are more apt to live with the brides parents (matrilocally)—usually for a short time, not for life. Urban Thai newlyweds either live apart, or lucrilocally—with whichever parents can best afford it. (Chamratrithirong, Morgan and Rindfuss, 1988) Western marriages are described as being neolocal. Couples typically establish an independent household together. This doesn't necessarily mean that Westerners have smaller families. Smaller households, yes, but people in the West recognize a wide circle of relatives although they don't live together.

When couples live independently of their parents, they must (unless they are very rich) save enough money to establish their own household. So couples who live neolocally will necessarily marry at a later age than couples who live patrilocally or matrilocally. High rates of singlehood in the West (about 20%) are also tied to the tradition of neolocal residence. Not everyone can afford to live independently. Only about 5% of adults in non-Western countries stay single.

Late marriage has characterized Western family formation for several centuries. Men and women tend to marry earlier in Africa, Asia and China where extended family living is typical. In the post war years this age difference has narrowed as more and more young people in non-Western societies become economically independent.

The relationship between household structure and age of marriage is further complicated in countries where military or religious service is expected of young men before marriage. Such is the case in rural Thailand where young men have traditionally spent a period of time in Buddhist monasteries before marriage. (Chamratrithirong, Morgan, and Rindfuss, 1988)

In his classic study *World Revolution and Family Patterns,* William Goode (1963) predicted that one consequence of modernization would be a move away from extended-family living. Extended-family living arrangements developed in agricultural economies. Where land, or land rights, were passed from one generation to the next (from father to son) it was logical for sons to remain in their parents' home. It also made sense that marriages be arranged in order to consolidate wealth, and to minimize interpersonal conflict between in-laws.

Living Together, Living Apart

In Part One we talked about how Western families are characterized less by structures or functions than by the emotional ties that commit members to one another. Murdock's (1949: 1) classic definition of a family is ''a social group characterized by common residence, economic cooperation and reproduction.'' Clearly, an increased number of families don't fit Murdock's description. Couples don't necessarily remain married, don't necessarily have children, and don't necessarily live together even when happily married.

Couples may live separately because of immigration, imprisonment, or seasonal work. An increasing number of North American couples maintain separate households because of the career demands of both spouses. These are popularly called commuter marriages. Typically the commuting starts when one spouse accepts a job transfer and the other decides not to follow. Setting up two residences and commuting to spend time together is one solution to the dilemma of occupational and geographical mobility.

Several social trends predict more couples will commute in the future (Gerstel and Gross, 1982). More women have professional careers to which they are highly committed. These women may be just as successful as their husbands, and as well paid. Relationships in dual career marriages are more equitable and there is greater emphasis on individualism. Finally, individuals have more to risk refusing transfers in the tight job market we have experienced since the early 1980s.

A study of living arrangements of couples in central Thailand found a very high number who do not live in the same household (Chamratrithirong, Morgan, and Rindfuss, 1988). Indeed, 41% of the sample lived apart, including newlyweds and couples who had been married for some time. Remember that Thailand has a tradition of matrilocal residence. While it was not the preferred way to live, couples decided to live apart rather than postpone their marriage, or give up education or job. The most important reason for living apart was work. Some couples lived apart to avoid conflict with parents or in-laws, although the strong tradition of parental respect makes it difficult to measure this influence. The researchers also found indications that some wives were minor wives (mistresses or second wives) or had been prostitutes. Again these are not easy to quantify (Chamratrithirong, Morgan, and Rindfuss, 1988: 940).

Mate Selection

Arranged marriages occur where inheritance of family land, title, or name are very important and where family members live together in large households. In these instances marriages don't just join a couple, they join two kin groups. The choice of marriage partners is far too important to be left to the whims of youth! Spouses are chosen because the union is economically advantageous, or because of friendship or kinship obligations. Sometimes people marry someone they have never met. Anthropologists call these blind marriages.

In Excerpt 8 the author explains ways arranged marriages maintain social traditions. ''The arranged marriage performs the following functions: (1) it helps to maintain social stratification in general, (2) it affirms and strengthens parental power over the children, (3) it helps keep the family traditions and value systems intact, (4) it helps consolidate and extend family property, (5) it enhances the value of the kinship group, (6) it helps keep the tradition of endogamy if one desires, (7) it helps young people from getting into the uncertainty of searching [for a] mate.''

In India, marriage has traditionally been arranged between quite young children. In some cases the couple would not live together until the wife reached sexual maturity. In other cases young girls were initiated to sexual activity long before they reached puberty. While it is now illegal for children under the age of fifteen to marry, the practice continues.

In much of Eurasia, arranged marriages are the norm. Excerpts 8 and 9 look at two of these societies: Bangladesh and Iran. In both countries, as men are increasingly able to earn money, they are becoming more involved in the choice of their own marriage partners. But as Mir-Hosseini points out in Excerpt 9 this independence does not extend to women.

Declining opportunities in agriculture and increased industrialization mean that most young people look for work in urban centers now. Usually they must move away from the influence and support of their parents. Many young people will be the first members of their family to set up an independent household. Where a generation ago, married couples in Africa, Asia or China lived with a parent, an increasing number now live independently.

Dowry and Brideprice

In most societies gift giving is an important part of marriage ceremonies. In some cultures, brides bring a dowry to their marriage. The dowry typically includes personal items as well as household goods. Cross-culturally, dowry is relatively rare, occurring only in Mediterranean and East Asian societies. Brideprice or bridewealth (gifts to the bride's family from the groom's family) is more common.

In Iran (see Excerpt 9) brides bring a dowry to their marriage. In addition, families of the groom promise a payment to the bride (called a mahr). A portion of the mahr may be deferred to be paid to the bride in case of an unwarranted divorce. Wives who seek divorce forego the mahr.

Missionaries in Africa wanted to stop the practice of bridewealth because it seemed to them that brides were being treated as commodities. Anthropologists were more sensitive to the cultural role of bridewealth and its implications for marital stability. Bridewealth solidifies marriage, helps ensure that wives are well treated, and compensates the bride's family.

In Swaziland, Ferraro (1983) found it to be increasingly common for a groom rather than his father and kin group to pay the brideprice. Predictably, this change affects the ability of the groom to choose his own partner. It may also affect marital stability. When fewer relatives contribute to the brideprice, there are fewer people with a stake in maintaining the union.

Why are marriages in some societies accompanied by brideprice and others by dowry? Some argue that dowry offsets low economic contributions by wives. So dowry occurs where women are not active in agricultural production. A brideprice anticipates a substantial economic contribution by women. Another possible explanation is the competitive advantage held by husbands. Brides' families use dowry to compete for wealthy husbands.

Where elaborate gift giving is common bride and groom will typically come from similar class backgrounds. Endogamy refers to the tendency to marry people like ourselves. Although there have always been exceptions, marriages are generally endogamous with respect to race and ethnicity, social class, and age.

Endogamy

In some groups endogamy is a very strong value. Ahmed (Excerpt 8) explains the importance of endogamy in Bangladesh. Muslim men can marry non-Muslim women, but Muslim women cannot marry non-Muslims. And among Hindus, cross-caste marriage is rare.

As people become more geographically mobile, intergroup barriers break down. Indeed one of the distinguishing characteristics of "modern" societies is assumed to be a decreased reliance on ascribed characteristics such as race or ethnicity. Intergroup marriages join couples of different religious background (interfaith marriages), different race (interracial) or different ethnicity (interethnic).

International or cross-national marriages (Excerpt 12) are a particular type of intergroup marriage. Cross-national marriages may or may not also be interfaith, interethnic, or interracial. "An Indian who is an urban, Westernized Christian will have fewer cultural differences married to an American Christian than to an Indian who is an orthodox Hindu." (Cottrell, 1990: 152)

Since midcentury it has become increasingly commonplace for young people to live and work abroad. So, an increasing number of Western men and women have the opportunity to meet non-Westerners either in their own country or be-cause they are traveling. As Excerpt 12 points out, cross-national marriages are typi-cally between non-Western men and Western women. Usually both partners are from privileged backgrounds. In this they are very different from earlier cross-national marriages between Western servicemen and non-Western women (called war-bride marriages in Excerpt 12).

Is Marriage Declining?

Part One described a number of changes in Western family living. Marriage rates are declining, age of marriage is increasing, marital fertility is decreasing, cohabita-tion is increasing, and so is divorce. Nowhere are these changes as marked as in Sweden where marriage rates are lowest, and rates of cohabitation, divorce, and births to unmarried women are higher than anywhere else.

Marriage rates in Sweden began to decline in the 1960s when more people began to cohabit. Then, cohabiting preceded marriage. Couples typically married when they conceived or bore a child. Now cohabitation seems to be replacing marriage for a significant number of Swedes. Does the formalization of a relation-ship by marriage ceremony matter? Is cohabitation qualitatively different from mar-riage?

Some people in the West worry that increasing cohabitation and increased divorce signals a shift away from traditional family values. But, as we said in earlier sections, social historians are finding family life in the past was anything but the supportive atmosphere often imagined. Then, as now, family life could be problem-atic. Indeed illegitimacy, desertion, violence, and sexual abuse were not uncom-mon in "traditional" Western families.

Some societies give more weight to the act of becoming married in a legally recognized ceremony than others. Excerpts 10 and 11 focus on two societies where cohabitation is relatively common. Consensual unions and "visiting" relationships have long been an alternative to formal marriage in the Caribbean (see Excerpt 11). In Thailand, common law unions are approved by Thai Buddhism (see Excerpt 10). The determining factors in Thailand are whether couples can afford a wedding ceremony and whether they have parental approval. If the family is wealthy, and parents approve, the couple will marry. If not, they will either elope or live together.

In our society, the growing popularity of marriagelike relationships is begin-ning to challenge ideas about the rights and obligations of couples. Although fewer North Americans than Europeans cohabit, the number of couples living in common-law arrangements has increased in recent years. Here, common-law unions carry some of the obligations of formalized unions.

Gay-rights groups have become increasingly active in lobbying for legal recog-nition of same-sex marriages. Although gay couples can be married in some churches, these relationships are not legally recognized. Homosexual couples have difficulty establishing survivor rights, partner medical coverage, and so on.

Although more people are cohabiting now (or at least more people are open about their living arrangements) and divorce is increasing (see Part Seven), there is no reason to believe that marriage generally is on the decline. Most people (about 85% in North America) marry eventually.

Conclusion

For centuries, Western marriages have been monogamous, neolocal, and nuclear. Couples typically meet, "fall in love," court, marry, and establish a household together. The excerpts in this section show how aspects of marriage we may take for granted (choosing our own partners, establishing a home together) are not universal cultural expectations. Cross-cultural comparisons help us see how varied the possibilities are. We begin to frame our assumptions in a wider context.

References

CASSIDY, MARGARET L., and LEE, GARY R., (1986) "The study of polyandry: A critique and synthesis," *Journal of Comparative Family Studies,* Volume XX, No. 1, Spring, 1–11.

CHAMRATRITHIRONG, APHICHAT S., MORGAN, PHILIP S. and RINDFUSS, RONALD, (1988) "Living arrangements and family formation," *Social Forces,* 66, No. 4, June, 926–951.

COTTRELL, ANN BAKER, (1990) "Cross-national marriages: A review of the literature," *Journal of Comparative Family Studies,* Vol. XXI, No. 2, Summer, 151–169.

FERRARO, GARY P., (1983) "The persistence of bridewealth in Swaziland," *International Journal of Sociology of the Family,* 13, Spring, 1–16.

GERSTEL, N., and GROSS, H. E., (1982) "Commuter marriages: A review," in *Alternatives to Traditional Family Living.* New York: Haworth Press, 71–93.

KELLY, CHRISTINA, (1991) "This Cat has Nine Wives," *Sassy,* No. 41, August, 82–83, 98, 110.

MURDOCK, GEORGE P., (1949) *Social Structure* New York: Macmillan.

WELCH III, CHARLES E., and GLICK, PAUL, (1981) "The incidence of polygamy in contemporary Africa: A research note," *Journal of Marriage and the Family,* February, 191–193.

Introduction

Why do some societies endorse polygyny (marriage to more than one wife) and others not? What accounts for varied rates of polygyny among societies where it is practiced? What is the relationship between polygyny and wealth? polygyny and economic systems? The authors of the following article try to answer some of these questions. Their research is based on societies described in the Ethnographic Atlas.

Of this large sample of nonindustrial societies, only 15% do not practice polygyny. The rest are divided about equally into two groups. In about half of the remaining societies polygyny is practiced with some frequency. The authors use 20% of marriages as the dividing line. The rest practice polygyny infrequently.

It seems societies might be polygynous for two different economic reasons. Either they depend economically on women's productivity, or they depend on women's reproductivity. The first group are typically agricultural societies and women are valued as producers of food. The second group are fishing and hunting societies which depend on men for food. Women in these societies are valued as childbearers.

7

Economic Systems and Rates of Polygyny

Gary R. Lee
Les B. Whitbeck

INTRODUCTION

. . . Goody (1973) shows that women's contribution to subsistence are greater in East Africa, but rates of polygyny are higher in West Africa. He therefore concludes that variation in marital structure is not directly attributable to women's role in the productive economy: "The reasons behind polygyny are sexual and reproductive rather than economic and productive" (1973:189).

Analyses of rates of polygyny in industrializing societies (Clignet and Sween, 1971, 1974; Grossbard, 1976; Ware, 1979; Chojnacka, 1980) tend to support Goody's conclusion. These studies show that, in societies in which polygyny is allowed, it is most likely to be practiced by members of the wealthier strata. However, women in these strata do not have major roles in the production of wealth. . . . Polygyny may be a form of conspicuous consumption for the economically elite, symbolizing their ability to support nonproductive family members. . . .

Lee (1979) observed a small positive relationship between proportionate female contribution to subsistence (PFCS) and the practice of polygyny among societies in Murdock's (1967) Ethnographic Atlas. . . . The positive correlation was

found to hold among societies that depend primarily on gathering or agriculture for food. Among societies with economies based on fishing, hunting, or pastoralism however, the correlation was negative.

. . . Polygyny may contribute to a family's productivity as an economic unit in two different ways under different circumstances (see also Lee, 1982:81–88). Where women are highly involved in productive activities, families can produce food in direct proportion to the number of women they contain. Polygyny is thus a means of expanding a family's productive capacities directly, by increasing the familial labor force in gathering and agricultural economies. . . .

. . . In fishing, hunting, and herding societies (Lee, 1979:708) women are minimally involved in direct food production. Families may obtain economic advantage by maximising the number of male members.

Paradoxically, polygyny maximizes the number of male family members because these wives are potential mothers who may bear sons. While polygyny may marginally reduce the fertility of each wife in a polygynous union (compared to the fertility of monogamous wives), the mean number of children per family is directly related to the number of wives in polygynous societies (Smith and Kunz, 1976; Ukaegbu, 1977; Chojnacka, 1980). Thus, if males are the critical subsistence workers, families can increase their labor supplies by obtaining multiple wives to produce many children.

In fishing, hunting, and herding societies, the

Source: Lee, Gary R. and Les B. Whitbeck (1990) "Economic systems and rates of polygyny," Journal of Comparative Family Studies, Vol. XXI, No. 1, Spring, 13–23. This is a revised version of a paper presented at the annual meetings of the National Council on Family Relations, Atlanta, Georgia, November, 1987.

relationship between women's contribution to subsistence and the cultural endorsement of polygyny is negative (Lee, 1979: 710). In other words, the less women contribute to subsistence, the more likely the culture is to favor polygyny. Here, Lee (1979: 712) argues, wives are valued for their procreative capacities in direct proportion to the society's dependence on male labor.

Lee's (1979) data simply differentiated polygynous from monogamous societies regardless of whether polygyny is limited to a few of the nobility, or is common throughout the society. Our task in this paper is to expand this inquiry to include variation in rates of polygyny among polygynous societies. . . .

HYPOTHESES

We know from Lee (1979), that nonagricultural societies are more likely than agricultural ones to allow polygyny. Lee argues that gathering societies allow polygyny because they are heavily dependent on the labor of women, while families in hunting and fishing societies practice polygyny in order to produce large numbers of sons per family.

However, these exploitative economic systems are not labor-intensive. In a gathering economy, for example, per capita productivity does not increase as the size of the work group increases, because the amount of vegetation in any area is finite. . . . In fact, the larger the work group the more rapidly the vegetation is consumed, since each worker is a consumer and may be supporting non-productive dependents. Thus, even though polygyny is culturally valued because women are the primary producers of food, the proportion of families that would actually benefit from the presence of multiple wives is likely small. This implies that, in gathering economies, polygyny is culturally endorsed with great frequency but practiced much less frequently.

The same logic may apply in hunting and fishing economies. . . . More workers do not increase the supply of food in this environment. . . . Polygyny may be an effective economic strategy if the environment is lush, and may therefore be culturally endorsed, but is not likely to occur with great frequency in reality.

Rudimentary agricultural societies, on the other hand, are labor-intensive. Within limits imposed by the amount and productivity of available land, productivity per worker increases directly with the number of workers. Under these conditions, large work groups (large families) should be advantageous in a higher proportion of cases, and we expect polygyny to occur with considerable frequency in societies in which it is permitted. But as agricultural technology develops further, the productive system becomes less labor-intensive. In intensive agricultural economies, particularly those with irrigation technology, we expect polygyny to be practiced only occasionally.

. . . Therefore we predict that in agricultural economies PFCS and polygyny are positively related, but in exploitative economies PFCS is unrelated to the frequency of polygyny.

METHODS

Data were obtained from Murdock's (1967) Ethnographic Atlas, which contains precoded ethnographic information on 1,170 nonindustrial societies. This analysis includes only those cases where marital structure, primary subsistence base and proportionate female contribution to subsistence can be reliably estimated (see Lee, 1979); it excludes ten societies that practice polyandry. This leaves approximately 830 societies (actual sample size varies slightly according to the specific relationship being examined). . . .

. . . The data set permits differentiation of polygynous societies into catagories of "occasional" and "frequent," with frequent polygyny indicating ethnographers' estimate that twenty percent or more of all marriages in the society are polygynous. . . .

The Ethnographic Atlas also characterizes each society according to its primary subsistence base . . . gathering, hunting, fishing, animal husbandry (herding), incipient agriculture, extensive agriculture, and intensive agriculture (see Murdock, 1981, for definitions). Another variable allows the differentiation of intensive agriculture societies into those with and without irrigation. . . .

Finally, proportionate female contribution to subsistence (PFCS) is estimated by the sum of products of (a) the society's proportional reliance on each of five types of subsistence activities (gathering, hunting, fishing, herding, and agriculture); and (b) the proportion of each activity conducted by women. The higher the score, the greater women's role in the subsistence economy.

RESULTS

Table 1 shows the relationship between the primary subsistence base and both the occurrence of polygyny and mean proportionate female contribution to subsistence (PFCS). There are several interesting aspects to these distributions. . . . The lowest levels of frequent polygyny, and the highest levels of occasional polygyny, are found among gathering economies, even though

these societies evince the highest mean levels of female contribution to subsistence. . . .

Fishing and hunting societies have the lowest mean levels of PFCS, and are also least likely to be exclusively monogamous. Lee (1979) argued that, in these cases (along with herding societies), polygyny is practiced because it increases the supply of male labor via reproduction. Again, however, these societies are more likely to be characterized by occasional than frequent polygyny. The same is true of incipient agriculture societies, although PFCS is much higher in this case.

Frequent polygyny is most likely to occur in herding and extensive agriculture economies. In the latter, women contribute to subsistence by their agricultural labor, and the work is highly labor-intensive. . . . Women plant, tend, and harvest the crops. The more wives a family has, the more fields that family can tend, and the higher per capita production is likely to be. In herding societies PFCS is markedly lower, although there are many cases reported in the ethnographic literature where women do take considerable responsibility for tending animals. Here, a family with multiple wives produces many children, who are then able to tend flocks of animals that may be widely separated because of the amount of land they require or the need to move to different pastures in different seasons.

Intensive agriculture societies are most likely to be characterized by monogamy, and relatively

TABLE 1. Polygyny and Proportionate Female Contribution to Subsistence by Primary Subsistence Base

| | Subsistence Base | | | | | | | |
| | | | | | Agriculture | | | |
Polygyny	Gather	Fish	Hunt	Herd	Incipient	Extensive	Intensive	Total
None	12.2	9.1	3.8	13.0	16.7	12.5	28.2	15.0
Occasional	67.1	52.5	57.5	21.7	52.8	30.0	33.9	41.4
Frequent	20.7	38.4	38.8	65.2	30.6	57.5	37.9	43.7
Total	100.0	100.0	100.0	100.0	100.0	100.0	100.0	100.0
N	82	99	80	46	72	273	177	829

unlikely to have frequent polygyny. This subsistence type involves farming on permanent fields with some form of "fertilization by compost or animal manure, crop rotation, or other techniques so that fallowing is either unnecessary or is confined to relatively short periods" (Murdock, 1981:98). This usually, but not always, entails some mechanization. . . . The productive value of polygyny is decreased as agricultural technology develops.

This can be seen more clearly if we differentiate the 177 intensive agriculture societies into those with and without irrigation technology. Slightly over half (51%) of those societies without irrigation practice frequent polygyny, a proportion similar to that found in extensive agriculture. But frequent polygyny is found in less than one-fifth (19.2%) of the 73 societies with irrigation, suggesting the utility of polygyny decreases as agricultural technology advances. However, occasional polygyny increases in frequency from 23 percent to 49 percent with the advent of irrigation. . . .

Table 2 shows the relationship between proportionate female contribution to subsistence, divided into three categories, and the frequency of polygyny. . . .

. . . For agricultural societies PFCS and polygyny are positively related, with the strongest association occurring in intensive agriculture societies. As indicated above, in these societies polygyny is likely to be frequent where the labor of women is valuable, but where the agricultural enterprise is less labor-intensive polygyny occurs only occasionally, if at all. We suspect, but cannot demonstrate with these data, that polygyny

occurs primarily among the economically elite in the most advanced agricultural societies, as a symbol of their economic success. . . .

For the nonagricultural categories, however, the relationships are notably weaker . . . especially for herding societies. While herding is more often a male than a female activity, women contribute heavily to it in some societies. Large families, with multiple wives and many children, may be adaptive regardless of PFCS because families' economic enterprises require dispersal; larger herds require more land and multiple pastures. Different family members, or units consisting of wives and their children, may tend animals at different locations. The more wives and children, the more animals a family may tend. . . .

The smaller relationship for frequency than occurrence in exploitative economies is due to the fact that, when polygyny is practiced in these societies, it is much more likely to be occasional than frequent. While polygyny has the potential to be highly adaptive in these economies, natural resources are rarely sufficiently abundant to allow it to be practiced with great regularity. . . .

CONCLUSIONS

Although polygyny is allowed, in the vast majority of the nonindustrial societies represented in the Ethnographic Atlas, it occurs with frequency (more than 20% of all marriages) in less than half of these societies. . . .

Where women may perform central roles in the production of food, polygyny allows families

TABLE 2. Polygyny by Proportionate Female Contribution to Subsistence PFCS

Polygyny	.000–.299	.300–.299	.400+	Total
None	19.3	15.8	11.6	14.9
Occasional	43.7	45.8	37.7	41.4
Frequent	37.0	38.4	50.6	43.7
Total %	100.0	100.0	100.0	100.0
N	254	190	387	831

to contain more potentially productive female members. Where men are the principal actors in economic production, it increases the familial labor supply via reproduction. . . . Polygyny is more likely to appear where large and differentiated work groups are potentially adaptive, a situation which characterizes the vast majority of the world's nonindustrial societies.

The primary contribution of this study has been the identification of circumstances under which polygyny is culturally preferred but infrequently practiced. These circumstances involve situations . . . where an increase in the number of workers does not lead to increased per capita productivity. This occurs in exploitative and incipient agriculture economies. Pastoralism and extensive agriculture are labor-intensive and here we are most likely to find high rates of polygyny.

Further developments in agricultural technology, however, result in decreased frequencies of polygyny. In intensive agriculture societies there is a strong positive association between women's contribution to subsistence and the frequency of polygyny. However, PFCS is lower here than in extensive agriculture because the labor has become heavier and large numbers of workers are no longer required. Thus the advent of mechanization and irrigation mean agriculture becomes less labor-intensive (Boserup, 1970), and the economic benefits of multiple wives are decreased. Polygyny may be allowed in such cultures, but its function may be more symbolic than economic. Its historical association with greater wealth in labor-intensive agricultural systems means it may continue to convey status after its economic utility has dissipated. . . .

REFERENCES

BOSERUP, ESTER 1970. *Women's Role in Economic Development*. London: George Allen and Unwin.

CHOJNACKA, HELEN 1980. "Polygyny and the rate of Population growth." *Population Studies* 34:91–107.

CLIGNET, REMI, and JOYCE SWEEN 1971. "Traditional and modern life styles in Africa." *Journal of Comparative Family Studies* 2:188–214.

GOODY, JACK 1973. "Polygyny, economy, and the role of women." Pp. 175–190 in Jack Goody (ed.), *The Character of Kinship*, London: Cambridge, University Press.

GROSSBARD, A. 1976. "An economic analysis of polygyny: The case of the Maidguri." *Current Anthropology* 17:701–707.

LEE, GARY R. 1979. "Marital structure and economic systems." *Journal of Marriage and the Family* 41:701–707.

LEE, GARY R. 1982. *Family Structure and Interaction: A comparative Analysis* (revised second edition). Minneapolis: University of Minnesota Press.

MURDOCK, GEORGE P. 1967. "Ethnographic atlas: A summary." *Ethnology* 6:109–236.

MURDOCK, GEORGE P. 1981. *Atlas of World Cultures*. Pittsburgh: University of Pittsburgh Press.

SMITH, JAMES E., and PHILLIP R. KUNZ 1976. "Polygyny and fertility in nineteenth-century America." *Population Studies* 30:465–480.

UKAEGBU, ALFRED O. 1977. "Fertility of women in polygynous unions in rural eastern Nigeria." *Journal of Marriage and the Family* 39:397–404.

WARE, HELEN 1979. "Polygyny: Women's views in a transitional society, Nigeria 1975." *Journal of Marriage and the Family* 41:185–195.

Introduction

In many parts of India, China, and Africa, marriages are arranged by the families of the couple. Because marriages join two families, not just two people, the choice of suitable partners is a huge responsibility. Parents do the choosing for their children; young people have little say about who they marry. In some cases they will marry someone they have never met. However, the fact that marriages are arranged doesn't mean that love is not an important factor. Indeed marital love is highly valued. It's just that in arranged marriages couples expect love to develop after the marriage, not the other way around. (in a later excerpt on arranged marriages in China we will find out whether this expectation is justified.)

Child marriages, arranged by the parents of the couple have been common in Bangladesh. Traditionally girls were thought to be ready for marriage when they began to menstruate and boys when they became self-supporting. So strong was the tradition of early marriage that legislation identifying age fifteen as a minimum age for wives had little effect on marriage practices. But as this article explains, marriage patterns are beginning to change.

Bangladesh is a country plagued by population pressures, political unrest, and the exigencies of a tropical monsoon climate. It is one of the poorest countries in the world; 90% of Bengalis live in poverty. Ongoing economic woes in Bangladesh mean that people are simply too poor to marry as early as custom dictates. It is very difficult for a young man to earn enough to support a wife or children. Young women cannot work to make up the difference because the Muslim system of purdah restricts their social interaction.

As a result, the age of marriage is increasing in Bangladesh, and there are proportionately more young singles in the population than in the past.

8
Marriage and Its Transition in Bangladesh

Ashraf Uddin Ahmed

. . . In South Asian countries, irrespective of cultural conditions, a transition is visible in the pattern of family formation, the mating process, divorce and remarriage. . . . In the last few decades, Bangladesh has also experienced transition in these aspects. The deterioration of socioeconomic conditions has resulted in changes in the marriage pattern. For example, a dowry system is supplanting the older bride price system, and family background is no longer given its former importance in marriage negotiations. This paper attempts to evaluate these changing patterns, and their linkages with socio-economic factors in Bangladesh society.

Sources: Ahmed, Ashraf U. (1986) "Marriage and its transition in Bangladesh," International Journal of Sociology of the Family, 16, 1, Spring, 49–59. Reprinted with permission from International Journal of Sociology of the Family.

MARRIAGE

. . . Arranged marriage is dominant in most African and Asian countries. The proportion of marriages which are arranged nevertheless varies across nations. South Asian countries, except Sri Lanka, will probably be the highest in terms of the percentage of arranged marriages. . . .

The arranged marriage performs the following functions: (1) it helps to maintain social stratification in general, (2) it affirms and strengthens parental power over the children, (3) it helps keep the family traditions and value systems intact, (4) it helps consolidate and extend family property, (5) it enhances the value of the kinship group, (6) it helps keep the tradition of endogamy if one desires (Goode, 1963; Chekki, 1968), (7) it helps young people from getting into the uncertainty of searching for a mate.

(A) MUSLIM MARRIAGE

In Islam marriage is a civil contract as opposed to a sacrament (Korsen, 1979). The Qu'ran encourages marriage. For those who do not have enough money to set up a separate house or to provide the basic necessities, however, it encourages abstinance until their condition improves. Besides this economic restriction, Islam has put restrictions on the eligibility of marriage partners—such as uncle-niece, or aunt-nephew. Cross-cousin rather than parallel-cousin marriage is more common in Muslim societies, more so than any in other societies. For men to marry non-muslims is permissible, but for women it is not.

(B) HINDU MARRIAGE

From ancient times, marriage among Hindus has been considered as a ritual and a sacramental union. Marriage is an indispensable event of Hindu life, and the unmarried person is considered unholy. From the religious point of view, the unmarried person remains incomplete and is not eligible for participation in some social and religious activities. Except in a very few cases, the importance of marriage transcends not only the entire family but also the past ancestral line as well as future generations.

There are traditional norms describing the parental responsibilities in marrying off sons and daughters. The Hindu religion has given great importance to progeny whereby fathers and their ancestors are assured a peaceful and happy after life. The customs and the rites of Hindu religion demand male children from each married couple. Parents want to make sure their sons marry and continue to have male children. Pointing to the tradition and custom of the Hindu religion, Basham said, "a father who did not give his daughter in marriage before the first

menstruation incurred the guilt of procuring abortion (a very sin, worse than many kinds of murder) for every menstrual period in which she remained unmarried" (1963 : 167). These factors partly explain why marriage is universal and why child-marriage has been well accepted in the Indian sub-continent.

(C) CHILD-MARRIAGE

. . . The child-marriage system was started by the Hindus, and later adopted by the Muslims. . . . In the mid-nineteenth century, this practice became more common among Muslims and lower-caste Hindus. The proportions used to vary by regions. In some areas Muslims had a higher child-marriage rate, and in other areas, the Hindus did. After a long struggle, progressive Indian leaders with the help of the British government succeeded in 1929 in making a law on age at marriage, known as the Sarda Act. According to this act, the minimum age at marriage for girls was fifteen years. The law, however, has largely remained unenforced to this day.

Having a female child was considered by Hindus to be a sign of God's unhappiness with a girl's parents. If parents had a girl-baby, they were reluctant to mention it to friends and relatives. . . . Girls are always an economic burden to the parents until their marriage because they cannot contribute to the household income like sons. This has been strengthened by the partial acceptance of the Muslim *purdah* system, which does not allow them to work outside the household. Besides, the society places a high value on the chastity or virginity of the girls before marriage. Girls are also a psychological burden to the parents. If it is known that a girl is no longer a virgin, it will be difficult for her parents to find a husband for her. All these fears and responsibilities induce the parents to marry off their daughters as soon as possible no matter how old they are. The situation is gradually changing, however.

Economically, child-marriage is profitable to

the parents. The amount of dowry or bride price is usually significantly smaller when it is a child-marriage than a youth marriage. The overall cost of gifts is usually less. To minimize the ceremonial costs, parents sometimes try to arrange the marriage of two sons or daughters at a time, even if the younger one is not of marriageable age. . . .

Besides the economic factors, child betrothal, occurs in order to maintain social ties between families. In some cases, two couples who have been good friends commit to the marriage of their children even when their children are not yet born. For Hindus, this practice may occur among friends within the same caste or sub-caste. Among Muslims, it occurs among brothers and sisters, and this extends to friends. As most of the marriages are arranged, parents take it for granted that these marriages will eventually take place without objection from their children. . . .

MATE SELECTION AND SOCIAL MOBILITY

Most marriages in a traditional Muslim society are arranged by parents or guardians. Conventionally, parents of boys take the initiative. Sometimes they talk directly to the parents or propose through a *ghatak* (marriage broker) or through relatives and friends of either family. . . . When parents of both families find the would be in-laws are suitable, the marriage takes place. Where marriage is arranged, the interests of the families get priority over the interests of the couple. . . . Sometimes, the marriage partners do not get to see each other before the marriage. This is primarily a marriage between families and is termed as 'blind marriage' by Parish and Whyte (1978).

Classical Islamic law sets two conditions—consent of the parties involved and a contract specifying the bride price (mehr [mahr]) to be given by the husband to his wife in the presence of witnesses. The consent sometimes is not free from the influence of parents. . . .

Love marriage is thought to be disruptive to family ties, and is viewed as a children's transference of the loyalty from a family orientation to a single person, ignoring obligations to the family and kin group for personal goals. There is an old saying 'love is blind'. It overshadows the quality of spouses. It is a weak criterion for selection of a mate. People believe love after marriage is a heavenly or spiritual thing. God helps those who have sincere love for their spouses by giving them a peaceful life. . . .

If parents are looking for a mate for their son, they first inquire about non-economical factors—beauty, age, family status, modesty, religiousness and literacy—, and then economic factors—the amount of dowry and gift. Although dowry and gifts are important, there is no standard set for these. For daughters, parents inquire about the occupation, income, education and social status of the family of the would be son-in-law. The economic factors into which they inquire are the extent of land holding by his family if they are in rural areas, otherwise economic solvency or well-being of the family.

In Western societies, personal beauty of a girl is an important quality in the marriage market. A beautiful girl of low social class has a chance to marry a man at a much higher social class. She has a chance to trade her beauty at a higher price in the marriage market. Although this is true to some extent for every society, the chances of her upward mobility are much lower in a traditional society, where most of the marriages are arranged by guardians, so beauty does not get much importance in marriage negotiation. . . .

Among the factors considered as important determinants in mating, education appears to have a stronger influence in the marriage market. Education increases the chances for hypergamy. If a man with a good education reduces his expectation for dowry and increases his willingness to make bridal gifts, he might be able to marry into a higher social class than his own although this is forbidden in Islam. Education still has a strong influence in the marriage market, but it may not remain the same in the future if the employment situation in the non-agricultural sector does not improve. A business profession with some education is gradually overriding the value of an educated bridegroom.

Occupation, which has a strong relation with education, is another important factor for men. Employment in urban areas plus education has more demand in the marriage market. Of course, it depends on the type of occupation. Recently, men working in the Middle-East or in any foreign country have been preferred by the bride's parents. Parents think to marry off their daughters to economically solvent and socially well-placed mates. Economic solvency often gets the highest priority among the factors. On the other hand, when parents look for a mate for their sons, they place greater importance on the social status of the bride's family in addition to the economic factor. . . . Marriage is therefore emerging as one way social mobility might take place. . . . If the family status of a person is high, but achieved personal quality is low, the person has a chance either to marry in the same social class or one relatively lower than one's own. As a result, downward mobility takes place in one family and upward mobility in the other family. On the other hand, if the family status of a person is low but his achieved personal quality (or human capital) is high, the person has a chance to marry in a social class higher than one's own and thereby upward mobility takes place. Otherwise, most marriages occur within the same social class (homogamy).

Hindus practice endogamy. The first criterion is caste and sub caste identity. Within caste or sub caste, the factors of dowry and selection process are the same as discussed before. Cross-caste marriage does not occur unless it is love marriage. A negligible percentage of marriage can be found around the border line of subcastes. Love marriage seldom occurs among Hindus. . . . In Bangladesh, marriages between relatives appear to be declining. Three factors seem to have contributed to this fact. The first is the rise of dowry which resulted from the delay of men's marriages and a surplus of marriageable women. The second is the rise in men's spatial mobility resulting from increased literacy and non-agricultural occupations. The last factor is the diffusion of the Western belief that these marriages produce sickly children. . . .

IS THERE A MARRIAGE SQUEEZE IN BANGLADESH?

A few decades back, there was a scarcity of potential wives in the area. This shortage of marriageable women may be regarded as one cause of child-marriage. The impact of the demographic transition, high fertility and declining mortality, has resulted in an age-distribution with a broader base. Although the sex-ratio at birth has been about 105 males per 100 females for a long time, this does not imply the number of potential husbands is higher than the number of potential wives. This is because the age of eligibility for marriage is not the same for men and women. Parents of girls, particularly in rural areas, consider their daughters marriageable at menarche. On the other hand, men are not usually considered marriageable until they have stable source of income either from a job or from their parents' property. This contributes to the age difference between spouses. In urban areas, young men are deferring their marriages. Under present economic conditions, men are finding it difficult to marry because the amount of money they earn, cannot buy the basic necessities for even two people, aside from the problem of housing. As a result, men's demand for dowry is becoming a dominating factor in the marriage market, although the government has officially banned the dowry system. If the job market for educated women were better, the situation would be somewhat better; their potential earnings would be a substitute for dowry.

In rural areas, the situation does not differ

much. People who own cultivatable land and can earn their own living are more likely to get married earlier. The surplus of labor in rural areas has also affected the marriage pattern there. Besides these economic factors, the age distribution of a growing population demonstrates that the potential wives outnumber the potential husbands, since the population of the preceding age groups are often larger than the following age groups.

Another factor, labor migration to the Middle-East, has affected the marriage market. Most of these migrants appear to be single. This employment opportunity has delayed the marriages of some people. On the other hand, it has helped some people to afford to marry. In general, however, it has contributed to late marriage for most of the people involved.

Lastly, the liberation movement had some effect on the number of potential husbands, as the number of deaths of young men was much higher than other age groups.

These factors are working together for the creation of late marriage and for increasing the number of single people. This marriage squeeze has emerged in all the South Asian countries (Caldwell, Reddy and Caldwell, 1983), and in other parts of Asia.

among them is gradually declining due to their inability to produce a surplus. Human capital thus is becoming a dominant exchange commodity in marriage. The rationality of this consideration lies in the condition of the job market, which is to say on the demand for human capital.

The urbanites are gradually being highly exposed to Western culture. These people like to imitate the imported culture. Consequently, urban culture is not highly traditional. Also, the severity of economic pressures is making people less able to perform according to the demands of the traditional culture. Although this country is one of the least developed countries, nevertheless the society is experiencing a change in the pattern of family formation, family type and marriage decision. The characteristics of these changes are somewhat in the direction of the characteristics of the Western World, as limited by a poor economy.

Both demographic and socio-economic conditions have contributed to the marriage squeeze. The situation might improve if employment opportunities for women and the overall literacy rate increase. The concept of marriage as universal in the society may not remain as strong as it used to be. From the marriage squeeze, a positive effect, a reduction in population growth, is emerging.

DISCUSSION

. . . Social development has made changes in the society and culture of Bangladesh. The concept of marriage might have not changed much, but the process of family formation and mating process has. . . .

In mate selection, the persons involved in marriage are having more to say. Economic considerations are coming to have increasing importance, as are the achieved qualities of the marriage partners. In absence of other capital, human capital is becoming the strongest determinant in the selection since ninety percent of the population live below the poverty level in this country. As a result, transfers of assets

REFERENCES

BASHAM, A. L. 1963. The Wonder that was India. New York: Howthorn Books, Inc.

CALDWELL, J. C., P. H. REDDY and PAT CALDWELL 1983. "The Causes of Marriage Change in South India." Population Studies, 37:343–361.

CHEKKI, D. A. 1968. "Mate Selection, Age at Marriage and Propinguity Among the Lingayats of India." Journal of Marriage and the Family, 30:707–711.

GOODE, WILLIAM J. 1963. World Revolution and Family Patterns. London: The Free Press.

PARISH, WILLIAM L. and MORTIN L. WHYTE 1978. Village and Family in Contemporary China, Chicago: The University of Chicago Press.

Introduction

In Iran, as in Bangladesh, there is a strong tradition of arranged marriage. Because marriages in these societies tie two kinship groups together, parents and other kin have a vested interest in the relationship, and support the marriage through an elaborate exchange of money and gifts. This article describes the ceremonial exchanges that lead to marriage in Kalardasht, in Northern Iran.

In the Kalardasht district all of the expense of the marriage is borne by the groom's family. The groom or his family gives a cash payment to the bride's father who uses the money to pay for his daughter's dowry, and other expenses of the elaborate wedding celebrations. The fact that the dowry is openly displayed before the wedding ensures that he doesn't skimp.

Recently some of the traditional ceremonial aspects of the wedding have begun to change in the least isolated villages of the region. As the economy becomes increasingly dependent on wage labor and young men have increased opportunities to earn money, they become less dependent on their parents and other kin to pay for the marriage. This gives them more say in choosing a bride. The same cannot be said of young women. Because women in this part of the world are highly unlikely to earn their own money, they remain bound by custom.

On the other hand, there has been a huge increase in the value of *mahr* in recent years, and that benefits women. In fact, a woman is quoted in this article as saying that the low mahr in the old days reflected the fact that "women had no value" then.

9

Some Aspects of Changing Marriage in Rural Iran

Ziba Mir-Hosseini

In this paper I shall examine the impact of the availability of wage labour on some aspects of marriage, in Kalardasht, a rural area in northern Iran. I shall demonstrate how and to what extent the traditional ceremonies and the system of transactions at marriage have been modified under the influence of a cash economy, primarily as a result of the ability of young men to provide for their marriage and thus free themselves from their fathers' households. . . .

Source: Mir-Hosseini, Z. (1989) "Some aspects of changing marriage in rural Iran: The case of Kalardasht, a district in Northern provinces," *Journal of Comparative Studies,* 20, 2, Summer, 216–229.

The Kalardasht . . . district became a tourist attraction in the early 1970s. Now it serves as a summer resort for those wishing to avoid the heat in Tehran and the nearby coastal towns. Hence opportunities to work on non-agricultural activities became increasingly available. In recent years, wage labour has become an important source of income for some households. Although all the villages in the region have been affected by tourism and the subsequent availability of work opportunities, those with a better system of communications have been affected to a greater degree. Thus, the differential isolation and the resulting differential degrees of change provide scope for comparative analysis. The material drawn for this paper is based on fieldwork in four villages in the region, one of which, due to its scenic location and good means of communication, has experienced significant change as a result of expansion of tourism in the region; and the other three, due to their relative isolation, have retained their traditional way of life to a great extent. . . .

☉

TRADITIONAL MARRIAGE TRANSACTIONS

Three points should be made about traditional wedding ceremonies in this part of Iran. First, a large part of prestations is related to festivities whose scale indicates the wealth and prestige of the groom's household as well as that of the bride's. Second, marriage involves not only two individuals and their respective households, but also a wide range of other relatives. The groom's kin not only provide food staples but also present money which covers a large part of the expenses that the groom's father has incurred since the beginning of his son's betrothal. In the process of arranging his son's marriage, a man becomes indebted to other kinsmen and is, in his turn, obliged to reciprocate at the time of the marriage of their sons. . . . Third, sons are dependent on their fathers for arranging and financing their marriage: without his father's approval, a son cannot arrange his marriage as he will not receive any assistance from his kinsmen. . . .

To illustrate these points let us examine the marriage transactions in detail. Apart from the ceremonial offerings of food and gifts to the bride's natal household after the betrothal, the exchange of wealth can be subsumed under three categories: *shirbaha* (milk price), *jahiz* (dowry), and *mahr* (deferred dower).

Shirbaha consists of: (1) a cash payment from the groom or his father to the father or guardian of the bride; (2) food staples, wood for cooking, and other items provided for the wedding party which is held in the house of the bride.

Jahiz consists of household items such as kitchen utensils, carpets, bedding, and items of female clothing which the bride brings to the groom's household. Mothers usually start collecting *jahiz* for their daughters when they are still children, and some items are made by the girl herself. *Jahiz* is regarded as the exclusive property of the bride, although some items are for general household use. In the case of divorce or the death of the husband, the *jahiz* is returned with the bride to her natal household.

Jahiz is observed throughout the country, while *shirbaha* is mainly confined to rural Iran and to the urban poor. The two practices are integrated in that in Kalardasht the cash portion of *shirbaha* is expected to be spent on buying a *jahiz* for the bride. A father ought to provide his daughter with a dowry at least equal to, if not greater than, the value of the cash portion of *shirbaha* he receives. The public examination of the bride's dowry on the wedding day and one week later at a feast given by the bride's mother, makes skimping easily detectable.

The amount of *shirbaha*, which in turn influences the value of *jahiz* and the scale of wedding festivities, varies according to the social status of the two families concerned, as well as the nature of the marital union. It is lower for widows and divorcees, and the scale of festivities is also much curtailed. *Shirbaha* is also lower for marriages between close kin, as these are usually celebrated on a smaller scale. . . . The cash portion of the *shirbaha* has been rising in recent years.

While *shirbaha* and *jahiz* are sanctioned by custom, *mahr* is a component of every Muslim marriage and is sanctioned by Islamic law. It consists of money, property or valuables which the husband pays or pledges to pay to the bride upon marriage. According to Islamic law, even when a definite *mahr* is not stipulated in the marriage contract, the bride is still entitled to a *Mahr al mithal*, that is, a bridal gift befitting her family position and her qualities. Muslim societies differ greatly with respect to *mahr*; in some it consists of two parts: immediate and deferred. The immediate portion is given to the father of the bride or the bride herself prior to or upon marriage. The deferred portion is usually paid in case of an unwarranted divorce.[1] In Kalardasht, the *mahr*—as in most parts of the country—does not involve any financial transaction at the time of marriage; by pledging *mahr* and by writing it into the marriage contract, a husband merely undertakes to pay a certain amount of money to the wife upon her request. As a matter of form the phrase *'and-al-mutalebah* (lit. upon request) is always written next to the amount of *mahr* in marriage contracts, thus rendering it immediate. Although in law, a wife is entitled to claim the *mahr* whenever she wishes, in practice, she receives it only if she is divorced. A substantial *mahr* is often regarded as a restraint on the husband's right to unilaterally terminate the marriage and as an insurance for the wife in case of such an eventuality. In theory, a husband cannot divorce his wife without paying the *mahr* and a wife must forego the *mahr* if she seeks a divorce.[2] . . .

CHANGES IN MARRIAGE TRANSACTIONS

In recent years traditional marriage transactions have tended to be modified. This is more conspicuous in the village of Rudbarak, where the economic system has undergone a shift from subsistence agro-pastoralism to wage labour based on non-agricultural activities; in the iso-

lated villages transactions have retained their traditional features. . . .

Shirbaha has acquired a different function. In the past, it mainly served to provide for the celebrations at the bride's house. Consequently food staples constituted the bulk of *shirbaha* and the cash portion represented only a small fraction of its value. At present, however, there is a distinct tendency for a larger portion of *shirbaha* to be spent on providing a dowry for the bride rather than on feasting and celebration. Accordingly its cash portion has risen significantly. In some cases the entire *shirbaha* is demanded in cash; the bride's father then assumes the responsibility for providing the food staples required for the wedding festivities conducted in his house out of the cash he receives. If the groom's father does not have enough cash to pay for the agreed *shirbaha*, he undertakes to provide one or more items of the dowry later, upon receiving cash contribution of kinsmen. Thus the price of that item is deducted from the *shirbaha* but added to the list of the dowry. . . .

The changing content of *jahiz* explains the increase in the cash portion of *shirbaha*. *Jahiz* now contains the necessary furnishing for a new house; whereas in the past it mainly consisted of gifts for the bride with bedding and a carpet as the only household items. Fathers are claiming that even the present high amount of *shirbaha* is insufficient to defray all the expenses incurred in providing this newly required dowry for their daughters. In fact the sharp increase in the cash portion of *shirbaha* between 1978 and 1985 is due to the post-revolutionary inflation and the scarcity of goods in the market, as the prices of household items such as cookers have increased fivefold during this period. This rise—in order to defray black market prices—confirms . . . that this type of marriage payment in Kalardasht, is reimbursing the bride's father for his outlay in providing a dowry.

. . . In the past, *mahr* was not important. It was rarely specified in marriage contracts in these villages. If it was specified it was always a small amount. When older and middle-aged

[1]The immediate portion of *mahr* seems to have the same function as the cash portion of *shirbaha* in Kalardasht; it is spent on providing a dowry for the bride which remains her exclusive property. . . .

[2]It is not certain to what extent a substantial amount of *mahr* can provide security for women. The fact that women in Iran demand their *mahr* only in the case of a serious dispute with their husbands shows that it can be used as a threat either to prevent a husband from maltreating his wife or to buy a divorce. There is a saying among Iranian women to the effect of "let my *mahr* be forfeited but my soul be free" Tapper (1980:379) and Pastner (1978:442) believe it provides security for women in marriage and can be a real deterrent to divorce.

women (aged 40 years and above) were asked about the amount of *mahr* stipulated in their marriage contracts, they frequently replied: "nothing much, those were old days; women had no value.". . . In most cases, no *mahr* had been specified. The women, however, added that *mahr* had only gained importance in recent years. . . . A low *mahr* now reflects on the honour and the status of the woman and her family. . . .

At present in Rudbarak, as in the urban centres, *mahr* is related to the status and qualities of the woman and to the social standing of her family. *Mahr* is higher for an attractive, educated virgin-bride; the *mahr* of girls from wealthy families is always considerable (cf. Behnam and Rasikh,1960; Momeni, 1972). In Rudbarak, agreeing upon *mahr* has become as important as negotiating the *shirbaha*. In the past, and even now in isolated villages, reaching an agreement on the *shirbaha* was the major issue. In 1978, in Rudbarak, the average amount of *mahr* stipulated in marriage contracts was 50,000 tomans, which rose to 100,000 by 1985. This is a drastic rise in comparison to the *mahr* of a generation ago which was seldom higher than 100 tomans. . . . As marriages become less kin-oriented, fathers feel the need to safeguard their daughters' interests. As already mentioned a substantial *mahr* imposes limitations on the husband's unilateral right to divorce and provides the wife with compensation if the husband exercises his prerogative.

The financial arrangements of recent marriages among salaried and wages earning Rudbarakis is a clear indication of the increasing importance of *mahr* and *jahiz* at the expense of *shirbaha*. In urban centres, *mahr* and *jahiz* represent the only institutionalized exchange of wealth at marriage. The groom's family is directly responsible for wedding expenses and not by passing the amount to the bride's family for the purpose; while *jahiz* is provided by the bride's father without any financial aid received from the groom's side. However, the main reason for the changes lies in the ability of young

men to provide for their own marriage expenses which alleviates their total dependence on their elders for arranging their marriages. This economic independence has allowed young men a greater voice in the selection of their brides and enabled them to modify traditional criteria in the evaluation of a potential suitor. Now a young man's education and skill, which provide him with a means of acquiring a permanent income, has gained importance at the expense of his father's/kin-group support. I know of some cases in Rudbarak in which the groom did not pay any *shirbaha*, subsequently, the wedding festivities were extremely minimal and paid for by the groom himself. On the other hand, the amount of money pledged for *mahr* was very high. In all these cases, the choice of the bride was strongly opposed by the groom's household, and they refused to initiate the traditional marriage procedure.

These changes also allude to the growing importance of the conjugal family in comparison with the extended family during recent years. This is especially true of the educated Rudbarakis. . . . In recent years the availability of wage labour has enabled sons to gain their independence much earlier, and this has precipitated the break up of extended households (Mir-Hosseini, 1980 and 1987). The changed marriage transaction is compatible with this process. The *shirbaha* which is now almost entirely spent on buying a *jahiz* facilitates the establishment of an independent household. Interestingly, in the majority of cases of recent marriages, where the bride has taken her *jahiz* to the household of her father-in-law, she has not unpacked it but, kept it stored for later use in her independent household. . . .

At present, both the traditional and modified systems of selecting spouses and of conducting marriage ceremonies co-exist. While the new trends are gaining acceptance and are practised in Rudbarak, the traditional marriage rituals remain intact in the three isolated villages.

At the root of the changes lies the economic autonomy of young men. . . . The changes offer young men a much greater degree of independence from their fathers and their kin-groups. The increased importance of *mahr*, which does not involve any immediate exchange of wealth, and the possibility of replacing *shirbaha* by paying for the costs of a limited festivity, weaken the limitation on the choice of spouse and the dependence of individuals on the kin-group that are inherent in the traditional marriage transactions. The *jahiz* (dowry) that a girl brings into the marriage now provides a part of the material preconditions for establishing a new household. This is reflected in the newly-married women's perception of their *jahiz*; many of them keep it safely packed for their independent household.

The recent changes have affected men to a greater extent than women. In the matter of choice of a spouse, a girl still has virtually no say. It is only the men who have acquired economic independence, and men who have the right to initiate matters concerning their marriages. The recent changes have further enhanced male prerogatives without any corresponding advances for women.

Moreover, the changes described are mainly limited in their impact to those villagers who are educated, engaged in wage labour inside or outside the village or those who are migrants living largely in urban centres. . . .

REFERENCES

BEHNAM, J. & RASIKH, S. 1960. (1339) *Tarh-i Mughadamat-i J'am' ashenas-i Iran*, Tehran: Khayam Publication.

MIR-HOSSEINI, Z. 1980. Changing Aspects of Economy and Family Structures in Kalardasht, a District in Northern Iran. Unpublished Ph.D. thesis: University of Cambridge.

—— 1987. "Impact of Wage Labour on Household Fission in Rural Iran." Journal of Comparative Family Studies, forthcoming.

MOMENI, D. A. 1972. "Difficulties in Changing the Age at Marriage in Iran." Journal of Marriage and the Family 34:545–551.

PASTNER, M. Mc 1978. "The Status of Women and Property on a Baluchistan Oasis in Pakistan." Pp. 434–450 in N. Keddie & L. Beck (eds), Women in Muslim World.

TAPPER, N. 1980. "The Women's Subsociety among the Shahsavan Nomads of Iran." Pp. 374–399 in N. Keddie & L. Beck (eds), Women in Muslim World.

Introduction

In most countries of the world the only legally sanctioned marital relationships are between one man and one woman. Plural, group, or polygamous marriages are legal only in some countries. Yet, as we saw in Excerpt 7, polygamy continued to be widely practiced in a number of African countries up to a few decades ago. Some societies give more weight to the act of becoming married in a legally recognized ceremony than others. In Thailand and the West Indies (as you will see in the next two articles), common-law unions are relatively common.

This article asks how marriage patterns in Thailand have changed with social development. In Thailand, parents have less say in choosing marriage partners for their children than was the case in Bangladesh or Iran. Also, in Thailand, common-law unions are generally accepted and approved by Thai Buddhism. Marriage decisions in Thailand are affected most by whether people live in cities or rural areas, their family's wealth and the changing status of women (as, for example, indicated by their increasing level of education).

According to this study, most young people in Thailand choose their own partner. Although most couples choose a traditional marriage ceremony, if parents are not supportive, or if the family is poor the couple may elope, or simply live together. Doesn't this seem like the kind of thing young people might do in Michigan, Milan (Italy), or Malmo (Sweden), if faced with the same problems? How would you account for the similarity?

10

Variations in Marriage Patterns in Central Thailand

Andrew Cherlin
Aphichat Chamratrithirong

. . . One outcome of development may be the maintenance, or even enhancement, of diversity in marriage patterns. Contrary to theories of cross-national convergence in family patterns (Goode, 1963; Inkeles, 1980), the path of development in Thailand—and by implication in other developing countries—may reinforce differences in marriage among different socioeconomic groups.

Overall, our aim in this article is to present further evidence of the complexity of family change in a developing society—of the diversity of traditional patterns, the different directions of change, and the variations in current patterns. We seek to demonstrate that these variations are tied to such factors as a family's socioeconomic position and the amount of education attained by their daughters. The information comes from three settings in central Thailand: rural, rice-growing villages in the central plains north of Bangkok; established neighborhoods in Bangkok; and a large squatter settlement in Bangkok. It will be shown that several different forms of marriage coexist in these settings and that the dominant form is different in each. The determi-

nants of experiencing a particular marriage form will be analyzed, and some tentative conclusions will be offered concerning the relationship between national development and family change.

ↄ

DATA

Rural Sample. The data are from the Asian Marriage Survey in Thailand (AMS), conducted between December 1978 and April 1979 (Chamratrithirong, 1984). Personal interviews were conducted with ever-married women aged 15–44 in three settings. . . . The rural sample comprised residents of rice-growing villages in the central plains, most of whom were engaged in farming or farm labor. Nearly all were ethnically Thai and Theravada Buddhist, the dominant ethnicity and religion in the country. The community was not unaffected by social change: Eighty-four percent of the households had electricity; 12 percent of the respondents reported that they had lived in Bangkok; and all children were required to complete four grades at the community school. Still, the organization of family life and the ways of making a living were quite similar to earlier descriptions of central plains communities (e.g., Kaufman, 1960; Sharp and Hanks, 1978). Consistent with na-

Source: Cherlin, A. and A. Chamratrithirong (1988) "Variations in marriage patterns in central Thailand," *Demography,* 25, 3, August, pp. 337–153. Reprinted with permission of *Population Association of America.*

tional estimates (Limonanda, 1983; Knodel et al., 1984), cohort analyses of the rural data showed little change in average age at marriage.

Urban Samples. A second sample was drawn from the Master Sample of the Bangkok Metropolis, which was developed by the Department of Applied Statistics of the National Institute of Development Administration in 1978 (Suwatti and Saisaengchan, 1978). This provided good representation of the established, economically stable areas of Bangkok, and it will be referred to as the urban established areas sample. Many of the families can be described as relatively prosperous, though not wealthy. The selected blocks did not, however, cover residents of squatter settlements, which, in Bangkok as in many other cities in developing nations, contain large, economically marginal populations. Therefore, the AMS included a third setting—the squatter settlement sample—consisting of the residents of one of the largest and oldest squatter settlements in the city, known as Slum Klong Tocy. There was no running water in the settlement, though most dwellings had electricity; and sanitary conditions were poor. Most of the men sought work as porters, drivers, or similar kinds of unskilled laborers.

The two urban samples in the AMS are much more diverse than the rural sample. Fifty-nine percent of the respondents in the urban established areas and 78 percent of those in the squatter settlement reported that they had been born in rural villages and subsequently migrated to Bangkok. Twenty-nine percent of the women in the established areas and 44 percent of the women in the squatter settlement had not moved to Bangkok until after they were married. Though data on place of origin was not obtained, qualitative interviews suggested the migrants to the established neighborhoods came primarily from the central plains, but that the squatter settlement attracted migrants from the more distant north and northeast regions as well. Moreover, the established areas included a substantial minority of ethnic Chinese, whose families typically owned shops or trading businesses. . . .

To avoid an overrepresentation of women who married at an early age, our analyses are restricted to women aged 26 or older in the rural and urban established areas and 24 or older in the squatter settlement, these being the ages by which 90 percent of the women in the respective strata had experienced a marriage. The effective sample sizes are therefore as follows: 494 for the rural sample, 408 for the urban established areas, and 370 for the urban squatter settlement. The AMS also attempted to obtain interviews with as many of the husbands of the respondents as possible. . . .

In comparing these three samples, we are making the implicit assumption that the rural setting represents the kinds of marriage patterns that were common before substantial development occurred in central Thailand. The difficulty with this assumption, as with the synthetic cohort comparisons that demographers often make, is that contemporary rural villages also have been affected by development. To be sure, this is a limitation of our study and of many ethnographic studies of the rural family. . . .

VARIATIONS IN THE FORM OF MARRIAGE

Observers of rural central Thai society have noted several types of marriage, including the following: marriage with negotiations between the parents and a formal ceremony, elopement, and living together without ceremony. All three patterns were reported by the AMS respondents. The ceremonial marriage best fits the romantic ideal of Thai tradition (Riley, 1972). According to Kaufman (1960), the ceremonial form typically begins when a young man approaches his parents concerning a girl he wishes to marry. If the parents approve, they hire the services of a go-between, who negotiates an agreement with the bride's parents, including the payment of a bride price. . . .

As Riley (1972) noted, however, the villagers recognize and accept that not everyone can follow the romantic ideal. In particular, when a conventional ceremony is not possible because the parents disapprove of the match or because the cost would be too expensive, the young couple may run away together. This elopement pattern often follows its own elaborate ritual, in which the couple runs away to a nearby village only to return after a short stay of a few days or weeks. Then the young man begs forgiveness from the young woman's parents. The parents nearly always agree to forgive, and typically an abbreviated ceremony is held and a greatly reduced bride price is paid. Although the elopement is supposed to take place without the knowledge of the parents, in some cases it may be a convenient device for avoiding a ceremony that the families cannot afford. . . .

A third type of marriage is for the couple to simply live together without any rituals or ceremonies. This pattern is only rarely reported in village ethnographics (and is rare in the AMS rural sample). . . . Living together is an acceptable way of marrying, especially if the marriage is later registered with the civil authorities. Nevertheless, it does not follow the romantic ideal and does not allow the families to participate in or ratify the marriage.

A second dimension of the marriage process on which there is variation is the degree of involvement of the parents in the choice of spouse. . . .

In a national survey conducted in 1969 and 1970, married women were asked, "When you married who chose your spouse for you?" Seventy percent of the rural central plains women chose the response category "self-selection," 17 percent said "parental selection," and 13 percent said it had been relatives, friends, or others. In Bangkok, 55 percent chose self-selection, 37 percent chose parents, and 8 percent said others. The author concluded self-selection was the predominant pattern among Thai women. Moreover, cross-tabulations by cohort suggested declining parental influence over time, though this

trend was much more pronounced among urban than rural women (Limonanda, 1979).[1]

Marriage Forms

Table 1 presents evidence from the AMS on two dimensions of the process of entry into marriage—ceremony and parental involvement.

Bride Price

. . . Overall, the prevalence of a bride price and the amount paid tended to be higher among village women. More than one-third of the marriages among women in urban established neighborhoods and nearly one-half of the marriages among women in the squatter settlement in-

TABLE 1. Indicators of Marriage Form, by Stratum (%)

		Stratum	
Question and Response	Rural	Urban Established Areas	Urban Squatter Settlement
In your first marriage, by what method did you marry?			
1. Marriage ceremony	71	80	51
2. Ran away/eloped	21	5	14
3. Lived together	7	14	34
4. Other	1	1	1
n	494	408	370
How did you make the decision to marry?			
1. Parents' decision totally	8	10	6
2. Parents' decision with your approval	13	9	6
3. Parents' and your decision	6	4	3
4. Your decision with parents' approval	15	17	11
5. Totally your decision	58	59	72
6. Others' decision (relative, employer, etc.)	1	1	2
n	483	401	359

volved no payment of a bride price. Payments of 5,000 baht or more were rare, regardless of marriage form. Thus the payment of a bride price does not appear to be simply a function of parental wealth or status because the incomes of many of the urban families certainly were comparable or superior to those of the rural families. Rather, bride price payments appear to reflect a specific kind of transaction between families in which the groom gains rights to farm a part of the land of the bride's family. . . . When his exchange of money for rights in land is absent, as in Bangkok, either the bride price is ignored or a modest payment is made. . . .

The Effect of Socioeconomic Status and Education On Rural Marriage Patterns

The more education a woman had, the more likely was a ceremonial marriage. Among those who married ceremonially, women from white collar or landed farmer backgrounds had the highest probabilities of parental involvement, those from landless farmer backgrounds had a substantially lower probability, and those from laborer backgrounds were in between. . . . In general, then, women from more prosperous socioeconomic backgrounds reported more parental involvement.

Consider women from landed farmer backgrounds who were aged 26–34. The more education they had, the less likely they were to involve their parents in their choice of a husband. . . . Since a higher level of education was more common among daughters from prosperous families . . . the very families who had the greatest incentive to be "choosy" and "demanding" were educating their daughters in ways that produced (or at least reflected) a greater independence in the matter of spouse choice. As a result, a white collar family whose daughter had completed five or more grades of school was less likely to be involved in her choice of spouse than was a landless farmer whose daughter had completed fewer than four years of school.

In sum, the rural findings . . . show that socioeconomic background and education have effects on the marriage process that are sometimes reinforcing and sometimes cross-cutting. Women from families with access to land or white collar jobs were more likely to marry ceremonially, as were women who had more education. A family's access to land or a white collar position also increased the likelihood of parental involvement for rural women, but a higher level of education decreased the likelihood of parental involvement.

We attempted to conduct similar multivariate analyses for the urban samples, but data limitations made the analyses more problematic. . . . Though the results of the analyses were similar in general to the rural setting, we have less confidence in their validity and will not report them here.

DISCUSSION

What can be said about how the process of entry into marriage changes as development occurs? Our answers must be tentative because the Thai data are cross-sectional and because some assumptions must be made about the future course of development. We assume further development and internal migration in central Thailand will bring an increase in the population of both the relatively prosperous established areas of Bangkok and the relatively impoverished urban squatter settlements. If so, we expect a continuing and perhaps widening split between the marriage patterns that predominate among families in these two settings. The prevalence of nonceremonial forms such as elopement and living together is associated with families who have the least amount of economic resources and social status. Even in the village sample, women whose fathers were laborers were much more likely to marry by elopement or other nonceremonial means. In addition, women from the squatter settlement, who had a higher proportion of laborer backgrounds and a lower proportion of white collar and shopkeeper backgrounds than did urban women from established areas, had much higher reported levels of marrying by just living together.

Consequently, among rural families with access to land through ownership or tenancy, the existence of rituals such as the bride price and a marriage ceremony may remain important for reasons of economic exchange and social prestige. Similarly, for shopkeeper families in Bangkok, a ceremony may remain important for transferring rights to the family enterprise or because of the persistence of Chinese traditions. For urban white collar families, ceremonies may remain important for status considerations. It is among poorer families—villagers who do not have access to land, city dwellers who do not have access to steady, contractual employment— that the economic and status considerations that would lead to a marriage ceremony are weakest. If population pressures, the consolidation of land holdings, or patterns of urban economic development lead to continued growth of this latter group, then differences in marriage patterns within each setting and across settings could become more pronounced. Differences in age at marriage would also be maintained: In the villages and the urban established areas, women who had a marriage ceremony married about two years later than those who did not.[2] To the extent that marriage timing affects the number of children ever born, fertility differentials would also be maintained.

The Thai data also suggest the possibility of a growing tension concerning marriage patterns *within* families. Our findings from the rural sample suggest that if families become more prosperous and then use some of their resources to educate their daughters better, as seems likely, two contradictory developments may occur: the families may have a greater incentive to participate in the marriage process to make sure that their daughters marry a suitable young man, but the daughters may insist on choosing their own spouses. Put differently, an increase in parental resources appears to increase the likelihood of

parental involvement in the marriage process, but the associated increase in the personal resources of daughters appears to decrease the likelihood of parental involvement.

Finally, the large differences in educational levels, economic resources, and marriage patterns between the established areas of Bangkok and the squatter settlement remind us that family change is not necessarily uniform. Thus a last lesson to be drawn from this analysis is the theories of cross-national convergence in family patterns (Goode, 1963; Inkeles, 1980) are limited by their failure to consider the growth and persistence of populations in squatter settlements and, more generally, in the informal economic sector of contemporary developing countries. . . .

NOTES

1. Cross-tabulations of the AMS data by cohort also show modest declines in parental influence for rural women and women in the squatter settlement but no decline for women in the urban established areas.

2. The mean ages at marriage for each sample, by marriage form, were as follows: (a) rural—ceremonial, 22.3; nonceremonial, 20.6; total, 21.9; (b) urban established areas—ceremonial, 22.9; nonceremonial, 21.3; total, 22.6; (c) urban squatter settlement—ceremonial, 20.1; nonceremonial, 20.2; total, 20.2.

REFERENCES

CHAMRATRITHIRONG, A. 1984. Loosely-structured Thailand: The evidence from marriage culture. Pp. 223–274 in A. Chamratrithirong (ed.). *Perspectives on the Thai Marriage*. Salaya, Thailand: Mahidol University, Institute for Population and Social Research.

GOODE, W. I. 1963. *World Revolution and Family Patterns*. New York: Free Press.

INKELES, A. 1980. Modernization and family patterns: A test of convergence theory. *Conspectus of History* 1(6):31–62.

KAUFMAN, H. K. 1960. *Bangkhuad: A Community*

Study in Thailand. Locust Valley, N.Y.: J. J. Augustin. (Reprinted 1977. Rutland, Vt.: Charles E. Tuttle.)

KNODEL, J., N. DEBAVALYA, N. CHAYOVAN, and A. CHAMRATRITHIRONG. 1984. Marriage patterns in Thailand: A review of demographic evidence. Pp. 31–68 in A. Chamratrithirong (ed.), *Perspectives on the Thai Marriage.* Salaya, Thailand: Mahidol University, Institute for Population and Social Research.

LIMONANDA, B. 1979. *Mate Selection and Post Nuptial Residence in Thailand.* Paper no. 28. Bangkok: Chulalongkorn University, Institute of Population Studies.

—— 1983. *Marriage Patterns in Thailand: Rural–Urban Differentials.* Paper no. 44. Bangkok: Chulalongkorn University, Institute of Population Studies.

RILEY, J. N. 1972. Family Organization and Population Dynamics in a Central Thai Village. Unpublished Ph.D. dissertation, University of North Carolina at Chapel Hill, Dept. of Anthropology.

SHARP, L. and L. HANKS. 1978. *Bang Chan: Social History of a Rural Community in Thailand.* Ithaca, N.Y.: Cornell University Press.

SUWATTI, P., and U. SAISAENGCHAN. 1978. *Master Sample of Households in Bangkok.* Bangkok: National Institute of Development Administration.

THORNTON, A., M.-C. CHANG, and T.-H. CHAN. 1984. Social and economic change, intergenerational relationships, and family formation in Taiwan. *Demography* 21:475–499.

WHYTE, M. K., and W. L. PARISH. 1984. *Urban Life in Contemporary China.* Chicago: University of Chicago Press.

WOLF, A. P., and C.-S. HUANG. 1980. *Marriage and Adoption in China. 1845–1945.* Stanford, Calif.: Stanford University Press.

YODDUMNERN, B. 1981. *Premarital Use of Family Planning: Effects on Age at Marriage.* Report no. 50. Singapore: Southeast Asia Population Research Awards Program, Institute of Southeast Asian Studies.

Introduction

Consensual unions and "visiting" relationships have long been an alternative to formal marriage in the Caribbean Islands. Because the relationships between couples seemed far less enduring than mother-child relationships, anthropologists reasoned that these were matrifocal societies. This paper uses survey data to analyze marriage patterns in the French-speaking islands of Guadeloupe and Martinique. As you will see, the data described here challenge assumptions about the instability of Caribbean unions and extent to which the society can be described as matrifocal.

As we might predict, many couples begin a relationship in a visiting or common-law union that eventually leads to marriage. More than half the women over thirty were married at the time of the survey. While this is about 10% less than in the United States the difference is not dramatic. Nor is there much evidence of structural matrifocality. In other words, there are very few three-generational, female-headed households.

The author, a French social scientist, concluded that marriage patterns in the Caribbean increasingly resemble those in the West as a result of both modernization and westernization. This conclusion is one we keep stumbling on throughout the literature on family life.

11

Union Patterns and Family Structure in Guadeloupe and Martinique

Yves Charbit

This paper aims at investigating relationships between union patterns and family structure in two French-speaking Caribbean islands, each of a population of about 320,000. . . .

This paper is divided into three parts. First, a demographic analysis of union patterns is carried out to describe differences between the three types of unions: married, "common law," i.e., with cohabitation, "visiting", i.e., without cohabitation. It is shown that the degree of stability is a better criterion than that of legitimacy, and that, altogether, the whole system of union patterns is less unstable than might be thought, a result which is indicative of advanced modernisation.

The hypothesis of modernisation is confirmed on examination of the distribution of households, which are broken down by current union status: nuclear households are by far the most frequent (Part II).

In Part III, family relationships are examined: again nuclear models and stability characterise union patterns and family structures.

ↈ

I. UNION PATTERNS IN GUADELOUPE AND MARTINIQUE: LEGITIMACY AND STABILITY

A. Current Status

At any given time, the union status of a woman can be one of the following: married, common law, visiting, currently single. In a rather young population, it is however useful to distinguish a fifth status, that of women "never in a union," in which most young girls fall.

Stable unions, and especially marriage, become more and more frequent as age increases. More than half of the women above 30 were currently married at the time of the survey, a result which is revealing of the degree of westernisation of the population. The proportion of married women among all women aged 15–49 is at 35.5% higher than in Haiti: data collected in 1977 during the Haitian Fertility Survey indicate 17 per cent of the women aged 15–49 were currently married (J. Allman, 1978: T. 2). This proportion is also of about 20 per cent in Jamaica and among non-Indians in Trinidad (Roberts, 1975: 184).

Single women are also more numerous as age increases, most likely because a woman in her forties usually finds it difficult to start a new union, or is no longer willing to do so. Lastly, one should note that, contrary to what was a characteristic of the European marriage pattern in the 19th century (Hajnal, 1965), most women, by the age of 30, have entered at least one union, while one-fourth of young girls (15–19) are currently involved in a union.

B. Union Type Analysis

If data on current status suggest marriage is the dominant pattern after age 25 and that unstable unions tend to stabilise, the analysis of past unions experienced by each woman confirms that trend.

Source: Charbit, Y. (1980) "Union patterns and family structure in Guadeloupe and Martinique," International Journal of Sociology of the Family, Vol. 10, January–June, 41–66.

Reprinted with permission from International Journal of Sociology of the Family.

Since we know how long each union lasted, and how it ended, we can measure the proportion of unions of a given type which either turned into a union of another type or correspond to a real separation from the partner. . . .

This distinction is important because the relative importance of stabilisations and of ruptures among visiting unions is decisive when assessing the overall instability of the union system in the Caribbean.

If we classify all the unions of a given type by their duration, we can construct a life table. Thus, 18 per cent of visiting unions lasted less than one year as opposed to 5 per cent of common law unions. Only 26 per cent survived more than five years, as compared to 43 per cent of common law unions and 97 per cent of marriages. Practically no visiting union lasts more than twenty years. . . .

Except in the youngest age group, where the union may sometimes have been a simple "flirt," one-third of the visiting unions were turned into a more stable union. For common law unions, the ratios are slightly lower. . . . Illegitimate unions tend to stabilise and/or to turn into marriage, a feature noted by G. Roberts about Trinidad (1975: 132).

A question remains: do consensual unions correspond to a shorter life in union than marriages? If so, . . . these unions are "unstable" insofar as women find themselves confronted with much longer periods of loneliness.

If we concentrate on women aged 40–49 at the time of the survey, comparisons between the various forms of union become possible. . . .

For age (40–49), the average difference between women currently married and those currently engaged in a visiting union only amounts to 3, 4 years.

C. Union History Analysis

Older women currently involved in a "visiting" union have probably always been involved in such unions in the past. . . . But currently married or common law women, probably started their union life in a visiting union.

To measure correctly the mean time spent in union, another method therefore requires the reconstruction of the woman's union history.
. . .

Because of the size of the sample, comparisons are only possible for the average 40–49 age group. The mean duration of common law unions (21.1years) is comparable to that of marriages (21.0 years). This analysis, which is more rigorous than that based on current union status shows the contrast between stable and unstable unions is not as marked as is usually believed.
. . .

II. HOUSEHOLD STRUCTURE AND UNION PATTERNS

. . . Household structure and residential matrifocality can be thoroughly studied in a sample representative of the female population aged 15–49. . . . Our sample was composed only of women.[1]

TABLE 1. Life Table of Unions by Type (women 35–49)

Exact Duration in Years	Number of Unions Not Broken (per thousand)		
	Marriage	Common Law	Visiting
0	1000	1000	1000
1	1000	950	820
2	995	830	600
3	990	720	450
4	980	640	340
5	970	570	260
6	960	510	200
7	950	460	150
8	940	420	120
9	930	380	100
10	920	350	85
15	860	220	45
20	805	120	20
25	750	60	10
Median	—	6.2	2.5
Mean	—	9.0	4.2

---

[1] The sample consisted of 2,849 women aged 15–49.

Information on the union status and family relationships of the head of household was systematically picked up. It is therefore possible to isolate household structures which are matrifocal.

Households can be divided into five categories.

A. Matrifocal Households

Only 3.5 per cent of all households are matrifocal, if matrifocality is defined by the fact that three generations of women and children live together and that their union status is either "visiting" or not currently in a union. . . .

If matrifocality is so marginal in the population, one must either conclude that, when a young woman has a child, she tends to settle on her own and leaves her mother's household, or that very rarely do young women living with their mothers become pregnant because of occasional sexual relationships.

B. Quasi-Matrifocal Households

It seemed worthwhile examining if young couples were frequently put up by a single woman head of household. If such a category were frequent, it would be indicative of the part played by mothers at the beginning of marital life, for instance in helping with children. Here again, this category is very marginal, 0.3 per cent, a figure which is striking in contrast with the number of young women (15–24) currently married or common law: these women constitute 6.4 per cent of the sample.

C. Non-Matrifocal Non-Nuclear Households

This category reflects the incidence of the instability of unions. 18.6 per cent of all women fall into this category; most of them have children (16.7 per cent). . . .

Currently single women are not all representative of unstable Caribbean unions. A woman can be single because she is legally married but separated ("de facto") from her husband; she can also be divorced or a widow. Only a spinster can be assumed to never have been involved in a union specific to the Caribbean (visiting or common law). . . .

Only 10.6 per cent (instead of 18.6 per cent) of non-nuclear/non-matrifocal households can be regarded as the product of the instability of Caribbean union patterns.

D. Nuclear Households

By contrast, nuclear households representing 68.2% of all households, are by far the most numerous in the population. . . .

E. Other Households

9.4 per cent of all households cannot be classified in one of the four above categories. . . .

To sum up, residential matrifocality is marginal and nuclear households are by far the most important category, although the instability of unions in the Caribbean society is reflected in a noticeable proportion of single women living with their children.

III. FAMILY RELATIONSHIPS AND THE PARTNER

Even if matrifocality is only marginal, the Caribbean family may be different from the nuclear model if, for instance, the family network is tighter and if couples can rely more heavily on their kin. . . .

Two kinds of helps are examined hereafter. First, the woman can obtain help from her kin for the children living with her. Second, some children might be sent away to live with relatives. The partner's contribution will be assessed in the last part of this section.

A. Children Living with the Woman

The question asked of the woman was intentionally vague: "As for the children living with you, does anybody help you, and in which way?" Well-off women could then mention their maid, whereas destitute women benefiting from the help of a social worker could also mention this. Thus, another indication of the degree of westernisation was collected, insofar as these three types of help are competing and not simultaneous, which proved to be the case.

15.5 per cent of the women are helped by their family, 4.5 per cent have a maid, 2 per cent benefit from social help. The help received is either the custody of children while the woman is at work, or a contribution to household duties, or both ("not specified").

Married and common-law women cannot—or do not—rely on kin as much as those currently single or with a visiting partner, most probably because their partner contributes to the rearing of the children.

However, the proportion of women benefiting from family help is by no means indicative of strong traditional family networks. A nationwide opinion poll, undertaken in France in 1975 (INED, 1976), shows ... the proportion of French married women who can rely on family help is higher than that of married Caribbean women ... (17 per cent as opposed to 15.5 per cent).

It seems likely that Guadeloupe and Martinique are undergoing rapid social and economic changes which tend to dislocate traditional family networks: the rural exodus, changes in the status of women and a general trend towards modernisation (Charbit and Leridon, 1980; forthcoming) have nuclearised these societies, whereas family networks in France are far

stronger than is usually thought (Gokalp, 1978; Roussel, 1976).

B. Children Below 16 Living Outside the Household

More than half of the children below 16 are permanently kept by kin on the mother's line and mainly by the grandmother, but the father's line is far from negligible (all status = 28.1 per cent). Common law and married women are in a comparable situation, whereas children of women in a visiting union or currently single are very often kept by the father's line, a result completely contradictory to current beliefs on the functional relationships between unstable unions and family networks, and on the low contribution of fathers to family responsibilities. . . .

This might be due to the degree of modernisation reached by Guadeloupe and Martinique. . . . The proportion of children kept permanently by the grandparents, is lower than in France, where it amounts to 4 per cent (Roussel, 1976). For married couples in Guadeloupe and Martinique, the percentage is 3.0 per cent, and . . . fertility is higher than in France. . . .

C. Fathers and Partners

. . . Our data first lead to questioning the distinction between legitimate and consensual unions, whether from the point of view of family life or of couple relationships. Second, they suggest the part played by partners in the upbringing of children is very important.

Nearly all married, *and* common law, partners contribute to family responsibilities, and nearly six out of ten visiting partners do so. . . .

If we turn to couple relationships, those of married and common law couples are very similar. A common law partner is physically nearly as often present as a husband, whereas visiting unions are looser. . . .

These data are based on the current union of the women. It could be argued that women engaged in consensual unions might experience a succession of short-lived unions. If that were the case, unstability of traditional unions would not be disproved.

As has been shown above, the duration of visiting unions is somewhat shorter than that of other types. This could be a factor favorable to a high turnover of partners. But among older women, who have reached some stability in their union history, differences between current statuses, if real, are far from dramatic. And not all visiting or common law unions are fertile. Therefore, the image of women raising children of many different fathers is largely exaggerated since the mean number of fathers is significantly lower than that of partners. . . .

SUMMARY

. . . The major findings are as follows: marriage is the most frequent current union status (50 to 60 per cent from the age group 25–29), more than in other Caribbean islands. The proportion of married and of single women increases with age, at the expense of visiting unions.

On average, a visiting union is much shorter than a common law or a marriage. But, since some visiting unions turn into a more stable one, . . . the instability is only relative. . . . Common law unions are very comparable to marriages. Stability thus appears a better criterion than legitimacy, and seems to characterise the whole system of union patterns. . . .

Nuclear households are by far the most frequent situation. . . . Matrifocal or related forms of household are very marginal, which proves the independence between union types and family structure, and might be correlated to the high degree of modernisation reached by Guadeloupe and Martinique. . . . The assumed dependency of young girls on their mothers is most questionable.

. . . Contrary to current belief, family contributions to child-rearing, far from being important, are less than in France. The rapid modernisation which Guadeloupe and Martinique are undergoing would thus result in a dislocation of family links. By contrast, partners appear to be present and cooperative, even when only visitors; there is no difference between common law partners and husbands. If father roles seem rather intensively assumed, much the same can be said about partner roles. Married and common law women almost constantly see their partners. Visiting partners are seen three times a week. Lastly, the case of older women confirms the overall stability of the system of unions. Even among women currently in a visiting union, who are likely to have mostly experienced such a type of union, the turnover of partners during the whole of their reproductive life span is moderate. That of fathers is even less. . . .

REFERENCES

ALLMAN, JAMES. 1978. "Patterns of sexual union formation in Haiti," July, Mimeo.

CHARBIT, YVES and HENRI LERIDON. 1980. Transition demographique et modernisation en Guadeloupe et en Martinique. INED, Travaux et Documents, Cahier n° 88. Paris, France: Presses Universitaires de France.

GOKALP, CATHERINE. 1978. "Le réseau familial." Population 6 (November–December): 1077–1094.

HAJNAL, JOHN. 1965. "European marriage patterns in perspective." In Glass and Eversley (eds.). Population in History, pp. 101–143. London, G. B.: Edward Arnold.

Institut national d'études démographiques. 1976. Natalité et politique démographique. INED, Travaux et Documents, Cahier n° 76. Paris, France: Presses Universitaires de France.

ROBERTS, GEORGE. 1975. Fertility and Mating in Four West Indian Populations. Institute of Social and Economic Research, University of the West

Indies, Jamaica. Old Woking, G. B.: Unwin Brothers.

ROUSSEL, LOUIS with the collaboration of BOURGUIG-

NON, ODILE. 1976. La famille aprés le mariage des entants. INED, Travaux et Documents, Cahier n° 78. Paris, France: Presses Univesitaires de France.

Introduction

This excerpt is a review of research on cross-national marriages. International or cross-national marriages are a particular type of intergroup marriage. Intergroup marriages join couples of different religious background (interfaith marriages), different race (interracial) or different ethnicity (interethnic). Cross-national marriages may also be interfaith, interethnic or interracial. These have become more common in the second half of the twentieth century with the rise in international mobility.

Social scientists did not begin to study cross-national marriages until the 1950s. Then the trigger was the large number of war brides coming to the United States with returning servicemen. This excerpt reviews three types of cross-national marriage; colonial or war bride marriages, educated Western-non-Western couples and educated Western-Western couples.

The main theme in studies of marriages of war brides to American soldiers is isolation and alienation. War brides have typically experienced a great deal of upheaval in their lives prior to marriage. Both husbands and wives had idealized images of their spouse that the spouse could not possibly live up to. For example American husbands of Asian women tended to idealize (stereotype) Asian women as supportive and subserviant.

Since midcentury it has become increasingly commonplace for people to live and work or go to school abroad. So an increasing number of Western men and women have the opportunity to meet people from different countries, either at home or because they are travelling. Typically both are from privileged backgrounds and open to cross-cultural interchanges. One area of difficulty is adapting to non-Western attitudes to women, when these are more conservative than they have been used to. When two people from different Western countries marry there is less cultural difference to cope with. In these marriages the issues are related to language and culture retention for the next generation.

12
Cross-National Marriages

Ann Baker Cottrell

Intergroup marriages have occurred throughout history. One kind, the cross-national marriage, is a particularly modern phenomenon, reflecting a dramatic increase in international mobility since the mid 20th century. . . . Yet there has been very little research on cross-national marriages and no review exclusively of this literature.[1] This paper, based on a review of the few existing studies . . . draws some conclusions about cross-national marriage today.

AN OVERVIEW OF CROSS-NATIONAL MARRIAGE LITERATURE

. . . The studies of cross-national marriages reveal three general types of cross-national marriage. . . .

Colonial/War Bride Marriages

These marriages are the result of one nation's military or colonial presence in another. Most of these studies concern American soldiers and their Asian wives. . . . The presenting theme in these studies is isolation and disruption, alienation and anomie. The American husbands are described as alienated, loners, insecure, dependent, and disproportionately from families split by divorce, separation, or death. . . . They are reported to be threatened by the independence and strength of American women and conse-

quently to idealize Asian women as supportive and subservient. . . . Not all studies paint such a pathological portrait of the husbands—Strauss (1954) calls the men uncommitted—but all agree that they are from working or lower middle class backgrounds, and have, on the average, a high school education.[2]

Most of these wives had experienced significant disruption in their lives before marriage. Many Japanese and Korean war brides grew up in nations traumatized by occupation and war, and in families traumatized by death. . . . These women tended to idealize American men as kind, supportive, and financially secure. Because of social disorganization during the war, nearly all these wives had broken many of the cultural norms which traditionally constrained females; most were employed, many lived away from their families, and virtually all had become acquainted with a new and freer culture through contact with Americans. . . . In Korea many were prostitutes. . . . Asian wives were, on the average, from a somewhat higher socioeconomic background than their husbands; their families were generally lower middle to middle class. . . .

Most of these studies portray the couples as socially isolated. . . . This is especially true for wives in the U.S. who rarely work outside the home. Lack of communication between partners, and husband's inability or unwillingness to help his wife adapt in the U.S., contribute to isolation as well as to other dysfunctional behavior, including violence. These difficulties are compounded by the fact that neither partner lives up to the other's idealized image, or the

---

Source: Cottrell, Ann Baker (1990) "Cross-national marriages: A review of the literature," *Journal of Comparative Family Studies*, Vol. XXI, No. 2, Summer, 151–169.

[1]Barnett reviewed the literature on interracial and international marriages, but less than one quarter of the studies were of international marriages.

[2]Fritz (1950) points out that soldiers who married English speaking Europeans were apparently from somewhat higher socioeconomic status than those who married non-English speaking Europeans, and those who married Asian women were usually the lowest in status.

husband wants both subservience and independence. . . .

Not all studies present a uniformly bleak picture of the Asian-American war bride couples. Strauss (1954) and Schnepp and Yui (1955) identify reasons for relative lack of conflict in American-Japanese marriages, e.g. high consensus on division of labor.[3] Jones (1972) identifies many areas of satisfaction with the marriage, although she also finds a higher level of conflict among these couples than a control group of intramarried couples. Additional researchers found most couples rated their marriages as happy, or at least reported little conflict. . . .

Verbal reports of marriages between American technical personnel and host national women in the Middle and Far East suggest these couples fit the pattern described above. Likewise, what we know of the British soldiers and the women they married in the early colonial India also fits this picture.

Educated Western-Non-Western Couples

This type of cross-national marriage . . . involves highly educated individuals, usually male, who live abroad as students or in professional roles. . . .

In this type of cross-national marriage the husbands are usually from the non-Western nation, although the other combination also occurs. . . . Both partners are typically from middle to upper class families and have university or advanced degrees. . . . They are free from strict constraints of their own cultures. Most are not deeply committed to a religion, for example, and many have had some contact with foreigners before marrying. . . . Some have been so highly involved with international groups and friends that this marriage represents a consolidation of

this life style (Cottrell, 1973). Most, however, have not actively sought new associations or adventures, and most of the Western wives, had little or no understanding of their husband's culture when they moved to their husband's country. . . .

The theme in these studies shifts . . . to adaptation and marginality. All these studies report that Western wives in non-Western countries have to make significant adaptations on many fronts ranging from physical amenities to relations with the family and child rearing. These wives are less isolated than the Asian war bride wives because: most are employed in professional or semi-professional positions, there is less of a language barrier since many educated non-Westerners speak some English, and they have more personal and social resources to help them cope. Rather than isolated they feel marginal, and their difficulties stem from adapting to expectations of those with whom they associate. In response to the feeling of marginality, many of the wives in Japan, Nigeria, and Thailand turn to other Western wives for their primary friendships. This pattern is not as prominent in Cottrell's research in India; few of those wives had extensive association with other foreign wives, although this pattern was more common in India at an earlier time.

A prominent issue in the African, Japanese, and Thai studies is how women raised in one of the least patriarchal societies learn to live in and with traditional families in male dominant cultures. This is especially important because the Western wife does not know how to play her primary role in a traditional society, that of mother and wife. She does not know the heritage which is her responsibility to transmit to her children, and she does not understand the institutional arrangements for cultural transmission. Most of these women living in their husbands' countries, married while their husbands were still in the West. Thus, they also had to adapt to new relations with their husbands because of the high degree of gender segregation in traditional cultures. . . . When these couples live in the Western nation most of the wives do not

---

[3]The characteristics of Japanese-American couples Strauss (1954) cites as reducing conflict are precisely those which others use to indicate alienation. For example, Strauss says separation from peer group allegiance means there is no competition between rival premarriage friendship groups, thus little strain. Others see this as social isolation.

experience the same degree of difficulty adapting to a new culture.

Educated Western-Western Couples (near cultures)

This discussion is based on a single study of the American wives of Frenchmen by Varro (1988). . . . These highly educated partners are among the affluent, professional elite in France. Culture conflict is minimized because French and American cultures are not dramatically different and further, most of the wives had experienced French culture or were Francophiles by the time they married. . . .

The agenda for these American wives in France, then, revolves around fulfilling two types of personal needs. The first is their strong desire that something of their culture be preserved in the next generation. This is manifest in concern with their children's bilingualism. . . . Second, these women are concerned about fulfilling their career aspirations. These highly educated, often career oriented, women marry into a social class in which women traditionally have not been employed outside the home. Further, because often their American credentials are not acceptable in France they must settle for extensive retraining or for less challenging jobs, e.g., teaching English.[4] . . .

A FEW GENERALIZATIONS

In spite of gaps in the literature, certain themes show up in these studies with enough frequency to permit a few generalizations about cross-national marriages. . . .

---

[4]The importance of maintaining one's profession for the self esteem of some foreign wives is also a theme in Bhattacharyya's (1989) autobiographical analysis. In this the need for professional fulfillment is explored as one dimension of the "outsider wife" role, a manifestation of the conflict between cultures emphasizing individuality and group membership. Imamura (1987) also raises this theme, noting that more Western wives in Nigeria have jobs close to or above their training than Western wives in Japan.

(1) Resnik (1933) proposed that persons who intermarry are emancipated, rebellious, detached, or adventurous. With two additions described below "embracers" and "multiculturals", these characteristics apply to descriptions in most of the studies. . . .

Rebellion and detachment, suggest alienation from or rejection of, one's culture of origin, Strauss' description of the American soldiers as "uncommitted" illustrates detachment. "They had no strong institutional affiliations . . . their church attendance . . . is spotty or non-existent; they belong to few organizations; and their ethnic allegiances are generally nil or weak" (1954:101). In contrast, the detachment of many Asian war brides is due to the breakdown of much of the traditional social order. Their desire to marry an American may be seen, in many cases, as an effort to escape a war torn nation rather than a rejection of that culture. While rebellion is undoubtedly a factor in some cross-national marriages, the research gives no evidence that this is a primary factor in modern cross-national marriage. Rebellion is more likely to play a role in marriages which are defined as taboo rather than merely non-normative. . . .

Resnik's second two types, emancipated and adventurous, suggest moving beyond the culture of origin without rejecting it. . . ."Emancipated," best describes most of the participants in the studies reviewed . . . people not alienated from their own society and culture but not constrained by them. Adventure does play a role in some of these marriages, but this suggests the association with a foreigner and his culture is something new and different. In some cases it is; in many it is not.

Two additional types must be added to fully describe the people who marry cross-nationally today. Some are drawn to the positive features of another culture or society with which they are familiar, as were many American wives in France. These are embracers. . . . And some participants in cross-national marriages were socialized in a multicultural environment—as children of mixed marriages, in immigrant subcultures, or in a third culture. These are individuals for whom cross-national relationships may be the norm. Fritz (1950) reports that most of the men in his sample, especially those with non-English wives, are the children of foreign born or mixed-nationality parents. Sixty-nine percent of Cottrell's (1970, 1973) respondents in India were "internationally experienced" or "highly international" when they met their partners.

(2) The majority of couples wish to retain some degree of bi-cultural identity. No evidence is provided of individuals wishing to completely disassociate themselves from their backgrounds. The degree to which both cultures are incorporated in a family's life varies greatly, however. . . .

Bi-lingualism is only addressed by two authors (Nitta, 1989; Varro, 1988), thus generalization is difficult. Both, however, are studies of English speaking mothers who feel strongly about their children knowing English. It is possible that bilingualism is particularly an issue when: a) the mother is the foreigner, b) the foreign language is generally useful and/or prestigious as English is, or c) the family is committed to preserving the foreign partner's culture. Support for this generalization is found in the fact that none of the children of British mothers and South Asian fathers in Britain speak an Indian language, except for those committed to the Muslim or Sikh faith (Cottrell, 1977 a,b).

(3) Cultural practices and social patterns generally conform to the dominant culture in the country of residence unless there is a strong commitment to an alternative pattern such as to Islam in Britain.

(4) Adapting is easier when the couple lives in the wife's country, or a country with a similar culture. In her own country the wife has the cultural and social resources to fulfill her primary role as wife and mother.

(5) Cultural differences do not necessarily cause stress in cross-national marriage and degree of difference is not necessarily related to degree of stress. Much of the stress is related to society's tolerance of exogamy which, in turn, is manifest in attitudes of friends and family. The most stressful environments for children in the literature reviewed are Japan and Korea which place extraordinarily high value on racial purity. The fact that Nitta (1989) reports far less marginality of these children than either Hurh (1972) or Wagatsuma (1976, 1978) reflects change in Japan over the past 20 years. At the other extreme, several studies done in Hawaii, which has a high level of racial tolerance and a high level of outgroup marriage, indicate that children of mixed couples are well adjusted both socially and psychologically. . . .

It is often assumed that the greater the difference between cultures in a marriage, the greater the degree of cultural conflict and stress. That this is not necessarily the case is suggested by Kimura's (1956) and Imamura's (1987) observations regarding the difficulties experienced by Japanese war brides in Hawaii and black American wives in Nigeria. Further, Imamura (personal correspondence) points out that near-culture marriages between Japanese and Koreans are likely to be more stressful than marriages between Japanese and Americans due to attitudes developed over years of historical enmity between Japan and Korea. Similarly, several of Cottrell's Hindu respondents in India commented that their families preferred Western partners to Pakistanis or Muslim Indians.

Cultural differences do not necessarily mean interpersonal conflict either. Encountering a very different culture is usually stressful at first, but in the long run it is . . . personal rigidity regarding those differences which account for interpersonal conflict.

SUMMARY

This review of 33 studies identifies three different types of cross-national marriage in recent times, each with a dominant theme; the military or colonial—alienation and isolation, the educated Western-non-Western—culture conflict and marginality; and the educated "near culture" (Western-Western)—wife's personal fulfillment through bicultural children and career achievement.

Cross-national couples' lives generally reflect the culture of the country in which they reside, unless there is strong, usually religious, commitment to the foreign partner's culture. Even when there is little overt expression of the foreign partner's culture, couples desire to maintain a bicultural, or some transcending, cultural identity. Cultural differences are not, themselves, the source of conflict, but rather conflict reflects personal and social attitudes toward differences. Further, it is not necessarily true that the greater the cultural difference, the greater the conflict. Given the reality of different cultural practices and social attitudes, however, it appears that adjustment is easier when a couple resides in the wife's country. . . .

REFERENCES

BARNETT, LARRY. 1963. "Research on international and interracial marriages." Marriage and Family Living (February): 105–107.

BATTACHARYYA, DEBORAH P. 1989. Being Foreign and Female in Calcutta. Paper presented to the Association for Asian Studies.

COTTRELL, ANN BAKER. 1970. Interpersonal Dimensions of Cross-Cultural Relations: Indian-Western Marriages in India. Michigan State University: PhD Dissertation.

—— 1973. "Cross-national marriage as an extension of an international life style: A study of Indian-Western couples." Journal of Marriage and Family 35(4):739–41.

—— 1977a. Immigration and mixed marriage: British-Asian couples in Britain. Paper presented to the American Sociological Association.

—— 1977b. Children of British-Asian Couples in Britain: Attitudes and Identities. Unpublished paper.

FRITZ, CHARLES E. 1950. A Study of World War II International Marriages. University of Chicago: Masters Thesis.

HURH, WON MOO. 1972. "Marginal children of war: An exploratory study of American-Korean children." International Journal of Sociology of the Family 2(March): 10–20.

IMAMURA, ANNE E. 1987. Strangers in a Strangers Land: Coping with Marginality in International Marriage. Paper 152, Michigan State University: Women in International Development.

JONES, IRENE EIKO. 1972. Interracial Marriage: Japanese Women and American Men. San Diego State University: Masters Thesis.

KIMURA, VUKIKO. 1956. "War Brides in Hawaii and their in-laws." American Journal of Sociology 63: 70–76.

NITTA, FUMITERU. 1989. The Japanese Father-American Mother and Their Children: coming Bicultural Socialization Experiences in Japan. University of Hawaii: Ph. D. Dissertation.

RESNICK, REUBEN B. 1933. "Some sociological aspects of intermarriage of Jew and non-Jew" Social Forces 12:94.

SCHNEPP, G. J. and A. M. YUI. 1955. "Cultural and marital adjustment of Japanese war brides." American Journal of Sociology 61: 48–50.

STRAUSS, ANSELM. 1954. "Strain and harmony in American-Japanese war bride marriages." Marriage and Family Living 16(May): 99–106.

THORNTON, MICHAEL. 1983. A Social History of a Multiethnic Identity: The Case of Black-Japanese Americans. University of Michigan: Ph.D. Dissertation.

VARRO, GABRIELLE. 1988. The Transplanted Women: A Study of French-American Marriages in France. New York: Praeger.

WAGATSUMA, HIROSHI. 1976. "Mixed blood children in Japan: An exploratory study." Journal of Asian Affairs 2 (February): 9–17.

—— 1978. "Identity problems of black Japanese youth." Pp. 117–129 in Robert Rotberg (ed.), The mixing of Peoples. Connecticut: Greylock Publishers.

Discussion Questions

1. It has been argued that a relationship based on romantic love will inevitably begin to deteriorate at marriage. Do you agree? Are expectations of romantic love exaggerated in our culture?

2. Ask men and women in the class to brainstorm (separately) about the kinds of things they would like to see covered in a prenuptial agreement. How do the lists differ?

3. Are increases in cohabitation a sign of the declining importance of marriage: Does a half-hour marriage ceremony really make a difference?

4. Explain what Lee and Whitbeck (Excerpt 7) mean by saying "Families may become polygynous if they are wealthy, but they do not become wealthy if they are polygynous."

5. In Excerpt 8, Ahmed explains that in Bangladesh Muslim men may marry non-Muslims, but Muslim women may not. Why do you think this is so?

6. What "ripple" effects might you predict as more young couples throughout the world choose their own marriage partners?

Data Collection Exercises

1. Interview religious functionaries (for example ministers, priests, rabbis) from at least two different houses of worship about wedding rituals. Ask them to describe the rituals and explain their meaning. Ask them also about ways wedding ceremonies have changed over the past several decades.

2. Using microfiche copies of any newspaper you choose, do an historical comparison of (a sample of) wedding announcements over time. You might, for example, choose the first Saturday in June 1900, 1910, 1920, and so on. What patterns do you see in the descriptions provided? Or, use the periodical index to locate advice-to-bride-or-groom articles. Is there any evidence that responsibilities have shifted from the bride's parents to the couple?

3. Using any census unit you choose, track the age of first marriage for men and women for at least fifty years. Are there predictable "bleeps" that signal war, economic depression, or changing labor force participation of women?

4. Use your networks to find a cross-national couple to interview. Design an interview guide based on Excerpt 12. How do your findings compare with Cottrell's review of cross-national marriage?

Writing Exercises

1. Read one of the following two articles and, assuming a similar voice, write a 500-word description of a wedding you have attended. [Horace Miner, "Body Ritual Among the Nacirema," *American Anthropologist*, 58 (1956) 503–507. Robert

Jones "Myth and Symbol Among the Nacirema Tsicolocos." *The American Sociologist* 15 (November 1980) 207–212.]

2. Compare the financial responsibilities incurred by North American brides, grooms, and their parents before and after the wedding to the arrangements described in the articles in this section.

3. "The ceremonies associated with marriage are, in many respects the embodiment of norms and values attached to it." Use examples from the excerpts to explain (in 2–3 typed pages) what Mir-Hosseini (Excerpt 9) means by this statement.

4. Write a 4–5 page script of a discussion between two young people about to marry. One is marrying someone he or she met in a sociology class. The other is marrying someone his or her parents have chosen. Each argues that his or her way is the best possible way to begin married life.

Glossary

Endogamy—The tendency for people to marry partners very much like themselves in terms of race, ethnicity, and class.

Family life cycle—A model of family life depicting sequential stages of family development.

Joint family—Describes a horizontally extended family of married siblings living together.

Lucrilocal—Describes a residence pattern whereby a married couple lives with whichever parent can best provide needed resources such as housing or work.

Matrilocal—Describes a residence pattern whereby a married couple resides with, or very near the bride's parents.

Neolocal—Describes a residence pattern whereby a married couple establishes an independent household separate from either bride's or groom's parents.

Patrilocal—Describes a residence pattern whereby a married couple resides with, or very near the groom's family.

Polygamy—Marriage of more than one husband or wife to a spouse of the opposite sex.

Polygyny—Marriage of two or more women to one man.

Polyandry—Marriage of one woman to two or more men.

Stem Family—Describes a vertically extended family of three generations.

Suggested Readings

FLETCHER, RONALD. (1988) *The Abolitionists: The Family Under Attack.* London: Routledge. Fletcher looks carefully at three sources of criticism of "modern" families: 1) those who see family interaction as the root of mental illness; 2) Marx and Marxist feminists; and 3) liberal and socialist feminists.

GOLDTHORPE, J. E. (1987) *Family Life in Western Societies.* Cambridge: Cambridge University Press. This book is a critical analysis of Western family life which draws primarily on British research. It begins with a lengthy historical chapter; includes a chapter outlining the Parsonian influence on the development of sociological theories on the family, as well as chapters on socialization, women's employment, and divorce.

SUSSMAN, MARVIN B., and SUZANNE K. STEINMETZ. (1987) *Handbook of Marriage and the Family.* New York: Plenum Press. This book is the most complete resource available to students of the family. Over 800 pages in length, it contains 30 chapters, each a comprehensive overview of a subtopic in the area of family sociology and each written by an area specialist.

TREMBLAY, HELENE. (1988) *Families of the World: Family Life at the Close of the Twentieth Century.* Volume I: The Americas and the Caribbean. Camden East, Ontario: Old Bridge Press. For over two years Ms. Tremblay traveled in North and South America staying with families and sharing their lives. This book, written under the auspices of the United Nations, records her travels. It combines photographs, statistical snapshots, and lively descriptions of family life.

TROST, JAN. (1988) "Conceptualising the Family," *International Sociology,* 3, 3, 301–308. Jan Trost has established an international reputation through his insightful analyses of the Swedish family. In this article he tries to get past the definitional dilemmas regarding the family by considering both spousal relationships and parent-child relationships. He suggests that any group consisting of one or the other (or both) of these is a family.

WALTER, LYNN E. (1989) "Who are they? When is then? Comparison in Histories of the Western Family," *Journal of Comparative Family Studies,* 20, 2, 159–173. This article makes the very important points that we must be precise when making both we-they comparisons and then-now comparisons. Too often, comparisons are so loosely drawn as to be meaningless.

PART III

Reproduction and Childbearing

In this section we shall examine excerpts on the "value of children" in different societies, traditional fertility patterns in Nigeria and new ones in China, the role of contraception in Western population history, the reasons so many American teenagers get pregnant, and the relationship between marriage and fertility in Sri Lanka.

Concerns about childbearing are at the top of policy planning agendas in many societies today. In industrial countries, many consider the rate of childbearing too low. Low birth rates result in a shortage of workers and an aging population. In some places, like Quebec, people also fear low fertility will lead to cultural extinction. Concerns about childbearing are often at the top of policy planning agendas in less developed societies as well. There, many people consider birth rates too high. High fertility results in a large proportion of infants and children and requires a great deal of spending on primary education and child welfare.

In part because of changes in marriage, and for other reasons we will go into shortly, childbearing patterns are changing around the world. Increasingly women, not their husbands, boyfriends, or kin, are deciding whether and when to have children. What's more, the reasons for having children are also changing. Generally, children have less value to parents than they once did. Related to this, in many parts of the world we find a declining preference for sons over daughters.

Educational and work aspirations are playing an ever greater part in women's fertility decisions. Cheaper, safer, and easier contraception methods allow women to avoid or delay childbearing if they wish. Most important of all, new individualistic values encourage below-replacement fertility as people become more prosperous. These values encourage people to enjoy their prosperity and leisure, not bear and raise a large number of children.

The Old Way: Rural Nigeria

To see the way fertility is changing around the world, let's start with the contrasting case of rural Nigeria. (We have included in this section an excerpt on rural Nigeria by Alfred Ukaegbu.) In central Africa, fertility has changed very little in centuries. People here still behave in "the old way." Seeing how the old way works, and what motivates old practices, will give us a better sense of how much the rest of the world has changed in a century or less.

Ukaegbu's study of rural Eastern Nigeria surveyed over 1600 currently married women from sixteen villages to determine how cultural values influence childbearing. In this Igbo region of Nigeria, fertility "is regulated within marriage, and a high fertility is traditionally viewed as the goal of marriage, a justification for its existence, and a measure of its success." High birth- and death-rates (roughly 50 per thousand and 20 per thousand, respectively) yield a total fertility rate of between 7.3 and 7.9 children per woman.

Though this article is based on data collected in 1974, there has been little sign of a major fertility decline in the past fifteen years. That this is so is shown in an article by Sai (1988) about fertility throughout Africa. For Nigeria, Sai reports a total fertility rate, rural and urban peoples combined, of 6.9 children in 1985, and a desired family size of 6.3. Only 5% of married Nigerian women reported using contraception in 1984. We can assume that further change has been equally slow in the last nine years. Thus, little has really changed since Ukaegbu published his article on Nigeria.

In this region of high marital fertility and strong traditional values, young wives today bear almost as many children as their mothers before them. Generally, little time passes between successive births; in fact, an average of only 25 months among women 25–44 years old. Indeed, the intervals are even shorter (a mere 22 months) among women under 25 and recently married women, whatever their age. Even so, Nigerian women do not bear children at the biological maximum.

Louis Henry's (1976) research on natural fertility showed a strong connection between women's age at marriage and their completed fertility. The earlier a woman marries, the more children she bears in total, if she does nothing to limit her childbearing. Ukaegbu finds a somewhat different relationship between age at marriage and fertility in rural Nigeria. There, later-marrying women catch up on lost years of childbearing by shortening the interval between births.

No magic is required. It is simply that earlier-marrying women have restricted their prodigious fertility. Though they are bearing an average of seven or eight children in total, they could be bearing more if they wanted to. They restrict their childbearing mainly by means of prolonged breastfeeding and a lack of sexual intercourse after childbirth. Marital instability also reduces childbearing, as it does in our own society.

As Henry would have predicted, Ukaegbu finds that "marriage duration is the most important predictor of fertility. This is followed by the number of children reported dead to wives, and whether the women wanted additional children." Socioeconomic factors play little part in the fertility of these relatively homogeneous (mainly poor) rural people.

Women whose children die in infancy bear more children to replace them. High fertility is "a direct response either to forestall future losses or to replace deceased children," especially in the households of illiterates and peasants. And, despite declining infant and childhood mortality, "the traditional anxiety for child survival has not been modified to a significant degree."

The main influence on Nigerian childbearing is the wives' desire for additional children. Over two-thirds of wives sampled believe that couples with a large number of children are, or will be, rich. They also believe that (a) no amount of material wealth is superior to children; (b) the power or influence of any household depends upon large numbers of their male members; (c) children are gifts and blessings from God which are not given to everyone in need of them; (d) a large number of children earn a big income when they are grown up; (e) family responsibilities are made easier since they can be shared by everyone in a large family; and (f) the couples who have a large number of children will be guaranteed grand burial.

The author remarks that "Nowhere else in the world outside Africa is there such a reluctance as in Nigeria to cease childbearing." More factors in rural Nigeria favor high fertility than low fertility.

Because of frequent and continual childbearing, the Nigerian household is full of children of all ages, from infancy up through early adulthood. Most Nigerians marry and live most of their married lives in households full of children. By contrast, very few Americans, Germans, Australians, or Japanese people do.

The New Way: The Developed West

The developed West offers us a very different picture of adult life. There, a rejection of large families has increased the proportion of one- and two-person households. Fewer households contain any children at all. At the same time, single-parent families have increased to 1 in 5 in many countries. Such single-parent families used to be headed by widows and widowers, but now they are commonly headed by divorcees and never-married women.

Even when couples remain together (that is, do not divorce), they spend less of their adult lives in the company of children. Instead of bearing children over ten, fifteen, or even more years, as in earlier generations (and like rural Nigerians), North American women today bear children over a mere five years or less.

With this "compression" of the childbearing period, the number of years when any children are present in the home has dropped from thirty to twenty years, on average. Instead of spending almost no time alone with a spouse in an "empty nest," Western wives can expect to average twenty or thirty years alone with their spouses, if they remain married.

Now, a significantly smaller proportion of adult life is devoted to childrearing responsibilities. The median age at birth of the last child decreases dramatically from one generation to the next. So does the median age when a family home empties of children—the so-called empty-nest period. Beaujot and McQuillan (1986) show that this compression is due to a smaller total number of children, not closer spacing of the children born.

The mean number of years people live in an "empty nest" increases dramatically because parents now are much younger when their last child marries than average parents were a century ago. For example, in 1981, Canadian mothers were 55 years of age, as compared with 63 years of age in 1851 when the last child left home to live alone or get married. Again, this is primarily due to fewer children, not earlier marriage or childbearing.

So, childbearing certainly affects the lives of parents, and vice versa. What has not changed much at all is (most) adults' desire to have at least one child and do so early in life. Despite many dramatic changes, Gee (1986) finds certain continuities in parenting: notably "a continuing trend for married women who have children to do so early in marriage and to space their children closely. . . [There is] no discernible trend towards one-child families."

Most (though as we shall see, not all) demographers believe that the family, and family-related values, must change before childbearing rates will fall very far. When such reductions do occur, causes are usually to be found in the reorientation of emotional ties away from extended kin, toward the nuclear family. Also important is the erosion of traditional authority that gave males and the elderly all the power to make decisions within the family. In the developing world, fertility will decline as these (mainly male) family decision makers no longer gain a material advantage from high fertility (Cain, 1982).

In preindustrial societies like Nigeria, high fertility provides those controlling the family with three main benefits: old-age support by children, child labor, and insurance against risk. Wives, as well as husbands, may gain by producing many children (especially, sons). Where work is divided by gender, women are limited in earning power and independence and therefore have a strong incentive to bear many children. Since they depend economically on spouses and children, women do benefit from bearing many children in such societies.

The economic value of children is zero (or negative) in modern societies, but it is positive in preindustrial societies. In these societies, children provide their parents with security as caretakers and earners once the parents get old. The more children (especially sons) parents have, the more secure and prosperous their old age is likely to be, especially if the aged parents retain control of the land their children are working. In an excerpt in this section, Kagitcibasi examines the "value of children" with data from Indonesia, the Republic of Korea, the Philippines, Taiwan, Thailand, Singapore, Hawaii, and the Federal Republic of Germany. As expected, he finds that people in more developed countries—especially the United States, Singapore, and Germany—place less value on children as sources of security than people in developing societies do.

Because of these security concerns, family planning may succeed less than expected if planners pay too little attention to people's needs for insurance against risk. These needs may account for the widespread preference for sons wherever social security is otherwise unavailable. This preference for sons is also partly a result of traditional religious beliefs and social customs. It is found in many less developed countries and contributes to high fertility in all of them. For example, Das (1987) estimates that fully 13% of Indian fertility is due to women making repeated efforts to bear a son.

Changes in the economic role, and security value, of children have reduced fertility significantly in the West (see, for example, Caldwell, 1984). A great many other factors associated with modernization also lead toward smaller families. Where peer group pressure used to influence parents to have many children, it now influences them to have few. There is now a good public understanding of the emotional and economic costs of children—an understanding people may have lacked a generation ago. The women's movement may have also promoted lower fertility by revealing the links between frequent pregnancy, women's economic dependence, and male domination.

In the last fifteen or twenty years, the proportion of women ending up with fewer than two births has doubled in many developed societies. The trend has been away from large families. The Baby Boom of the 1950s seems to contradict this trend, but it doesn't really if we consider the family sizes people actually wanted. Many third and later births during the Baby Boom were unintended. Since the 1950s, improved contraception and access to legal abortion have reduced the number of unintended births. Another baby boom is therefore quite unlikely.

The Role of Contraception

Demographers are still debating the historic role of contraceptive technology in reducing fertility in the West. On one hand, some believe that motivation is everything. Once people want to reduce their fertility, they will need little in the way of knowledge or technology to do so, the thinking goes. On the other side are those who believe that contraceptive knowledge is everything, and a motivation to reduce births can be taken for granted. They believe that, once people know that they are able to limit their fertility, they will set about doing so.

Results from the European Fertility Study, excerpted in this section, tend to support the latter view. In so doing, these results raise serious doubts about the validity of the Demographic Transition theory. In particular, this research questions whether people living in preindustrial societies before the last century really exercised a choice in their childbearing. Perhaps they did not so much want children as got them without thinking about it.

This debate about contraception is complex, and all the evidence is not yet in. Be this as it may, the availability of contraceptives can have an important impact on fertility where people are already motivated to reduce fertility. The continued low (absolute) use of contraceptives in many countries—for example, Bangladesh (Ahmed, 1987)—suggests a need to increase availability and reduce the perceived costs (see Excerpt 8). Shortening the distance (in miles) to a family planning clinic increases contraceptive use in these countries. Increasing wives' educational and employment chances does the same thing. In other countries, Kuwait for example, contraceptives are available and used, but only to space children, not restrict their total numbers (Shah and Kamel, 1985).

Like contraception, abortion plays an important role in reducing fertility (Krannich, 1980). Women who want to end their pregnancies often do so, whether or not the laws limit their access to legal abortions. When abortion becomes legal, it becomes significantly safer for women, and more common. So, throughout the developed world, the legal abortion rate has increased a great deal since the mid-1960s as a result of more liberal abortion laws and easier access.

As a result, abortion in the United States and elsewhere is an increasingly common form of fertility control. The incidence of abortion is only likely to decline with an increased use of contraception—that is, with the prevention of unwanted pregnancies. Prevented pregnancies do not have to be aborted.

State policy, therefore, can play an important role in fertility reduction by promoting contraception. For example, data reveal a significant change in the demographic behavior of Chinese people in response to state efforts to reduce fertility (Chen, 1984; see Excerpt 16). Since the establishment of the People's Republic in 1949, China's fertility has fallen by 60 percent. China has achieved the goal of later, and fewer births through large drops in fertility among women of all ages. This fertility decline has come about through an extensive birth planning program which has made contraceptive, sterilization, and abortion services available to the entire population.

Excerpt 16 shows that an explanation of this change is not to be found in demographic transition theory, for socioeconomic development has not progressed very far in China. Huge numbers still live in what we would consider dire poverty, even if their conditions are better than forty years ago. In agricultural areas, children continue to bring more economic benefits and fewer costs than in our own society. So the explanation of lower fertility must lie in greater exposure to contraceptive information and technology; and in a change of values promoted by a state anti-natalist policy.

The Role of Values

In China, the state has linked fertility reduction with patriotism and social responsibility. To the extent people value these things, they will value and produce small families. In other societies with low or declining fertility, the dominant values are materialism and consumerism.

Materialism and high personal expectations (about career, leisure, and self-actualization) lead away from large families—perhaps even from marriage. There are often economic pressures on wives to work for pay since, in many countries, a single income is no longer enough to provide middle-class comfort. As well, most parents want better opportunities for the children they already have, and research shows that children from smaller families get further ahead in life than children from larger ones (see, for example, Pineo, 1985). Marital relationships also seem to benefit from fewer children (see, for example, Lupri and Frideres, 1981). Finally, modern contraception has made it easy for people to avoid having children without avoiding sex or prolonging breastfeeding as the Nigerians do.

It may be that couples in modern societies gain less pride and sense of achievement from raising a child than couples in preindustrial societies. Conversely, they find more of these rewards in work and leisure activities. Other factors affect childbearing as well. Wherever there are more job opportunities open to women and they receive more education, women postpone and reduce fertility.

Research by Rowland (1982) shows that Australian couples who postpone parenthood are like couples that limit childbearing generally or have no children whatever. They tend to be financially well-off, career-oriented city dwellers. Like an overall reduction in childbearing, a delay in childbearing is largely due to changing roles of women, higher educational attainment, the growth in women's job opportunities, and more labor-force participation. In short, women who have the chance to do so spend more of their lives away from childbearing and children than women did in the past.

Taken as a package, the changes in values that have brought very low levels of childbearing in the developed world amount to a mini-revolution: what van de Kaa calls a "second demographic transition." (See Excerpt 55.)

The Second Demographic Transition

The process van de Kaa is referring to began around 1965 and is characterized by an emphasis on the rights and self-fulfilment of individuals. Approval for working mothers with school-age children, acceptance of a couple's voluntary childlessness, and acceptance of couples who choose to cohabit with no intention of marrying, have all increased in the last two decades. Another important factor accounting for the fertility decline is a change in marriage practices, noted earlier. Since 1971, Europeans and North Americans have been waiting longer to get married. A growing proportion of people have rejected the idea of marriage altogether.

More people are choosing not to become parents at all; instead they choose a childfree lifestyle. These voluntarily childless couples place a great deal of importance on their relationship. This change may be part of a process that began in Europe at the end of the Middle Ages and saw a reorientation of emotional ties away from the extended family toward the nuclear unit. In this context, sex for pleasure, not procreation, is profoundly aided by new contraceptive technology (Whicker and Kronenfeld, 1986).

By the mid 1960s, the improvement in contraceptives and increased access to legal abortion and sterilization had made a significant impact on family size. Abortion also became more accessible in the early 1970s, and sterilization became an increasingly attractive option for women who wanted to avoid the risk of an unwanted pregnancy.

There is no doubt that the second demographic transition is well underway in many developed countries; yet, several exceptions to this rule can be noted.

One is the teenage (often unwed) mother. Rates of pregnancy remain high among teenage American women, and Excerpt 17 explores the reasons. This is a problem worth addressing seriously, for teenage pregnancy can interrupt a young woman's education and may even, with childbirth, put an end to it. This, in turn, is liable to lead to economic dependency on the state or a spouse and, in the latter case, a very high risk of marital breakup (Moore, 1989).

The young mother may also be unprepared to undertake the duties of mothering. The result may be child abuse. If the mother is on welfare, the child will probably live in poverty. If the mother is single, or divorced, the child will grow up without a father present. These, in turn, have negative consequences of their own for the child's development and happiness. So, we can think of many good reasons for discouraging teenage pregnancy.

Another exception to the antinatalist "second demographic transition" rule is the effort some couples make to achieve parenthood, despite difficulty. There are still many women who want a child but have trouble getting pregnant. Some of these couples are using new technology to stimulate fertility and increase their chances of childbearing.

No one can deny these changes in the contemporary family—especially to very low rates of childbearing—are the result of many historic forces. Whether we call it a "second demographic transition" or not, this trend is unlikely to reverse itself. For these reasons, fertility will probably continue to decline and remain low in the foreseeable future.

References

AHMED, U. A. (1986) "Marriage and its transition in Bangladesh," *International Journal of Sociology of the Family*, 16(1), Spring, 49–59.

BEAUJOT, R. and K. McQUILLAN (1986) "Demographic change and the family," *Canadian Journal of Sociology*, 21(1), Spring, 57–69.

CAIN, M. (1982) "Perspectives on family and fertility in developing countries," *Population Studies*, 36(2), 159–175.

CALDWELL, J. C. (1984) "Fertility trends and prospects in Australia and other industrialized countries," *Australia and New Zealand Journal of Sociology*, 20(1), 3–22.

DAS, N. (1987) "Sex preference and fertility behavior: A study of recent Indian data," *Demography*, 24(4), November, 517–530.

GEE, E. M. (1986) "The life course of Canadian women: An historical and demographic analysis," *Social Indicators Research*, 18, 263–283.

HENRY, L. (1976) *Population: Analysis and Models* Translated by E. van de Walle and E. F. Jones. New York: Academic Press. Chapter 7.

KRANNICH, R. S. (1980) "Abortion in the United States: Past, present and future trends," *Family Relations*, 365–374.

LUPRI, E. and J. FRIDERES (1981) "The quality of marriage and the passage of time: marital satisfaction over the family life cycle," *Canadian Journal of Sociology* 6(3): 283–305.

MOORE, M. (1989) "Female lone parenting over the life course," *Canadian Journal of Sociology*, 14(3), 335–352.

PINEO, P. (1985) "Family size and status attainment," Pp. 201–228 in M. Boyd et al., *Ascription and Achievement: Studies in Mobility and Status Attainment in Canada.* Ottawa: Carleton University Press.

ROWLAND, R. (1982) "An exploratory study of the childfree lifestyle," *Australia and New Zealand Journal of Sociology,* 18(1), 17–30.

SAI, F. T. (1988) "Changing perspectives of population in Africa and international responses," *African Affairs,* 87(347), April, 267–276.

SHAH, N. M. and S. M. KAMEL (1985) "Contraceptive use among women in Kuwait," *International Family Perspectives,* 11(4), December, 108–111.

WHICKER, M. L. and J. J. KRONENFELD (1986) "Men and women together: The impact of birth control technology on male-female relationships." *International Journal of Sociology of the Family,* 16(1), Spring, 61–81.

Introduction

For nearly fifty years, demographers—people who study population scientifically—have believed in the validity of "demographic transition theory." This theory is based largely on European history: on the way mortality rates, then fertility rates, fell during the nineteenth and twentieth centuries. It argues that preindustrial people have many children because children are economically valuable and cost little to raise. As societies modernize, the costs of raising children rise, the benefits of having (many) children fall, and more infants survive to adulthood. For all of these reasons, people set about having fewer children.

Let's examine this theory for a moment. Yes, large numbers of children *are* a benefit in agricultural societies. They do the farm work and spend little time in school, so they lose little time from their chores. In short, they cost little to feed, house, or raise. Since many children are likely to die young, it makes sense to bear many children.

Besides doing the farm work, children also provide care to aged parents. The more children (especially sons) parents have, the more secure and prosperous their old age is likely to be. This is especially true if the aged parents keep control over the family holdings. (Shakespeare's character King Lear was foolish enough to believe that this was unnecessary; he paid a high price for his mistake.)

This excerpt looks at the way people in a variety of countries judge the "security value" of their children. As expected, people in more developed countries—especially the United States, Singapore, and Germany—put less value on their children as sources of security than do people in less developed countries like Indonesia, the Philippines, and Thailand.

13
Old Age Security Value of Children and Development

Cigdem Kagitcibasi

This paper presents some of the findings of the cross-national "Value of Children Study" (VOC Study) pertaining to the perceived value of Children in providing old-age security to their parents. To what extent this value is attributed by parents to their children and what benefits are expected from children are assessed in the context of development.

𝕯

The Value of Children

How people value children, what satisfaction they find in them is of great theoretical and practical significance. An understanding of the values attributed to children by parents is a key to developing insights into family dynamics, sex roles, social norms and attitudes as well as fertility behavior. Thus the value of children symbolizes the motivations for childbearing and assumes an important role in any micro model of fertility. Within the past two decades the value of children for parents has been conceptualized within two different disciplinary frameworks, namely, economic and social-psychological.

The economic interpretation typically using a micro-economic framework views the individual as trying to maximize satisfactions, given a range of goods, their prices and his own tastes and income. In this context children are considered to be a type of good. Thus, the demand for children competes with other demands for alternative goods of the decision-making, rational individual. . . . Within the microeconomic framework social psychological dimensions such as motivation, needs and values are subsumed under tastes or preferences.

Within the social psychological framework, the value of children for parents assumes importance in terms of the motivational dynamics underlying fertility behavior. As the needs of individuals are emphasized, needs satisfied by children come to the fore. These needs and the corresponding values attributed to children range from economic to social and psychological. . . .

The VOC Project

The VOC Project is a nine-country comparative social psychological study focusing on motivations for child-bearing which has evolved through two main phases. The first phase was initiated by the East-West Center of the University of Hawaii in 1972 with a conference on the satisfactions and costs of children (Fawcett, 1972). Samples of 360 married couples were used in six participating countries, namely Japan, the Republic of Korea, the Philippines, Taiwan, Thailand and the United States (Hawaii).

Based on the findings of the first phase, nine countries participated in the second phase, namely Indonesia, the Republic of Korea, the Philippines, Singapore, Taiwan, Thailand, Turkey, the Federal Republic of Germany and the United States. Nationally representative samples of 2000–3000 married respondents were used in these countries except in Indonesia where two samples, Sundanese and Javanese were used. The Federal Republic of Germany joined the project at a later stage with a smaller female sample drawn from Munich.

Comparative analyses are now being carried out on the data drawn from these nine countries. The core-questionnaire comprising the main research tool was applied in each country

Source: Kagitcibasi, C. (1982) "Old age security value of children and development: cross-national evidence." *Journal of Comparative Family Studies,* 13, 2, Summer, 133–142.

at approximately the same time and utilizing similar interviewing techniques; nationally representative samples of similar sizes were drawn; and one basic comparative coding system was utilized. Thus the cross-national data at hand are truly comparable.

The core-questionnaire contained 103 questions necessitating lengthy in-depth interviews in the field. The majority of the respondents in each national sample were women, however, couple data were also obtained. As there was an upper age limit of forty for women respondents, the samples were in general somewhat young, in Turkey the mean age being twenty-eight for females and thirty-four for males.

In the VOC Study the value of children is conceptualized in functional terms as the sum total of costs and benefits that parents obtain from having children. Both the costs and the benefits are viewed as complex variables, including psychological, social and economic dimensions. Thus the VOC concept refers to the perceived difference between these benefits and costs. For the purposes of our present analysis we shall consider mainly the benefits of children and specifically their "old-age security value".

Old-Age Security

Both the first and second phase VOC findings point to the profound value children have for their parents as sources of security in old age.

In Turkey it is the most salient value among a number of values of children. This is a complex positive value including both economic and psychological dimensions. It appears to be a prime motivating factor for child-bearing and also for sex preference in children as in most societies male children have higher old-age security value for their parents.

The old-age security value attributed to children by their parents also reflects social norms and practices regarding informal family care of the aged.

In the VOC study various questions dealt with this value, and we shall now consider them comparatively. In two closed-ended questions nineteen and twelve reasons were given, respectively, for having children in general and for wanting another child. Respondents were asked to indicate how important each reason was for them. The percentages by sex of the respondent and country are given in Tables 1 and 2.

Two patterns of responses clearly emerge from Tables 1 and 2 differentiating the United States and the Federal Republic of Germany from the rest of the countries. Obviously, in the highly developed, post technological society "old-age security" provided by the child is not at all an important reason for having a child or for wanting another child. In these advanced social welfare systems formal institutions or functions have replaced the immediate family, especially children in providing security in old-age,

TABLE 1. Reason for Having a Child*

			Turkey**	Jav	Sun	Phil	Thai	Kore	Taiw	Sing	USA	Ger
"To have someone to depend on when you are old" (as reason for having a child)	WOMEN	Not important	8	1	0	2	3	19	7	13	73	68
		Somewhat important	15	6	2	9	18	27	14	36	19	24
		Very important	77	93	98	89	79	54	79	51	8	8
	MEN	Not important	8	2	1	3	6	33	11	17	75	—
		Somewhat important	15	9	5	11	23	27	17	39	18	—
		Very important	77	89	94	86	71	40	72	44	7	—

*All the figures in these and the following tables are percentages.

**The abbreviations for countries stand for (in order): Turkey, Javanese and Sundanese (Indonesia), the Philippines, Thailand, the Republic of Korea, Taiwan, Singapore, the United States of America, the Federal Republic of Germany.

TABLE 2. Reason for Wanting Another Child

			Turkey	*Jav*	*Sun*	*Phil*	*Thai*	*Kore*	*Taiw*	*Sing*	*USA*	*Ger*
"To be sure that in		Not important	38	8	6	10	5	64	37	15	73	79
your old age you	WOMEN	Somewhat important	14	10	9	12	24	18	15	37	18	17
will have someone		Very important	48	82	84	78	71	18	48	48	9	3
to help you" (as												
reason for wanting		Not important	50	15	23	10	10	74	33	18	75	—
another child)	MEN	Somewhat important	14	12	13	12	24	13	15	39	17	—
		Very important	37	73	64	77	67	12	53	43	7	—

thus reducing the old-age security value of children. . . .

In the less developed countries, however, "old-age security"is a highly significant value attributed to the child and underlies the motivation for both having a child and wanting another child. Some variations are noticeable among these countries which roughly parallel differences in their overall development levels, cultural traditions and deliberate government efforts in population planning. Specifically, in Singapore and the Republic of Korea where industrial development is progressing and where wide-spread population planning is under way, being very effective in Singapore, we find responses between the developed and the underdeveloped patterns in emphasizing old-age security as a reason for wanting a child (Table 1). . . .

Thus, it appears that in societies with low levels of technological development without widespread social welfare institutions such as social security systems, unemployment insurance, free health care, nursing homes and the like, their functions are undertaken by families and especially by the adult-age children. . . .

Consistent differences are seen in expectations of support from sons and daughters in almost all of the countries. A clear exception to this trend is seen in the American responses, where no difference exists between future expectations from sons and daughters, both being very low. In Singapore little difference in expectations from different sex children is apparent together with low levels of expectations in general. Especially in regard to emergency help, where high levels of expectation are seen throughout the countries, the lowest levels of expectations in Singapore are noteworthy. . . .

Singapore is often considered to be the most developed country in East Asia after Japan. Indeed, the responses to these questions demonstrate a pattern of development in which children are not seen as a guarantee of old-age security because there *are* other guarantees. Together with this objective social welfare situation probably go more subtle, values put on self-sufficiency and self-reliance, which, for example, have been pointed out as core cultural values in the United States (e.g. Hsu, 1961). Such values would preclude admitting dependency even on one's children.

Thus, it appears that a low level of expectations from children is closely associated with low differentiation of expectations in terms of the sex of the child, thus low sex preference. High levels of expectations from children, on the other hand, would entail more sex differentiation because males are usually the "breadwinners" and thus sons are more dependable as old-age supporters. Among other countries, differential expectations from sons and daughters are most marked in Turkey and secondly in Korea, countries in which boy preference is wide-spread. Thus, cultural values seem to be important in determining parents' expectations from children. Greater reliance on the son, compared with the daughter, is wide-spread. . . .

A final question dealt with the degree of expected old-age support from children. As very little support was expected in the United States, this further question was not asked there. The responses show that some of the people who would like to depend on their children for old-age support, do not expect to get any. However, this is only a small percentage.

Responses from Singapore again show lowest expectations, followed by expectations from daughters in Korea and Taiwan and fathers' expectations from sons in Korea. The same overall pattern of higher expectations from sons compared with daughters also apply here to the degree of expectations. . . .

Effect of Social Change

The comparative results of the VOC study provide insights into the relationships between the value of children and general levels of development. When we consider social change within one national context, we find parallels to what has been discussed cross-nationally. Specifically, in Turkey the relations between the salience and importance of old-age security value of children and some indicators of social change and development have been studied. The latter are the level of development of the area of residence and mobility.

In general there is a reversal in the values attached to children according to the level of development. Utilitarian-economic values (including old-age security value) are more prevalent in rural and less developed areas and psychological values of children are more prevalent in urban, developed contexts. . . . The citing of "general security in old-age" as an advantage of having children decreases in importance as we proceed from under-developed to the developed metropolitan areas. It is mentioned by 24% of the respondents from less developed areas; by 20% of those who live in intermediately developed areas; by 17% of those who live in developed areas and only by 11% of those in metropolitan centers.

. . . General psychological values (including children providing primary group ties, affection and love) is mentioned more and more as we proceed from a village to a metropolitan center. "Security in old age", on the other hand, is mentioned by 52% of nonmobile village residents but by only 35% of those who have migrated to a metropolitan center.

Among the agricultural non-cash income groups "security in old age" is very salient (71%) as these respondents live in rural areas where they have no social security. With increased income and social security, the prevalence of this value decreases. Similarly, the importance of "security in old age" decreases as education increases. Finally, importance of economic security in general relates positively to expectation of financial help from children and to ideal and desired numbers of children.

The above reported findings are in line with the results of other analyses conducted on the VOC data. They all point to the replacement of economic and old-age security value of children with love-oriented psychological values through the development process. In Turkey, education, rural to urban mobility and area of dwelling appear to be indicators of this process of development.

The implications of the above findings for fertility appear to be as follows: Economic values and old-age security value of children are closely associated with child numbers whereas psychological value of children is not. This is because, in the context of underdevelopment, children are an economic asset and the more children one has, the more likely that at least one will provide old-age security, or their combined contributions will provide support. Thus this is an "additive" value whereas psychological value of children is not. Accordingly, different numbers of children (existing and desired) are found to be associated with different values in the Value of Children study.

With development, the underlying values associated with children change, as demonstrated, together with changes in fertility levels. Thus, it may be proposed that changing expectations from children and values attributed to them form a causal link between development and fertility. In this context, the decreasing importance of the old-age security value of children appears to be a key process, which through social change and development, contributes to lower fertility levels as well as to the modification of values and practices concerning the care of the aged in society.

REFERENCES

FAWCETT, J. T. (ed.) 1972. The Satisfactions and Costs of Children: Theories, Concepts and Methods. Honolulu: East-West Center.

HSU, F. L. K. 1961. Psychological Anthropology. Homewood, III: Dorsey.

Introduction

The preceding excerpt noted that people in developing countries put more store by the security value of children than people in developed countries. However, there is a lot of variation among people in developing countries too.

Some people put a much more positive image on childbearing than others. The next excerpt shows that women belonging to the Ngwa Igbo clan (in rural eastern Nigeria) see children as a blessing from God. Their culture favors high birth rates on principle; births have a religious significance in their society. Within the Ngwa Igbo clan, all births are to married women, and married women want as many births as possible. Says the author, "High fertility is traditionally viewed as the goal of marriage, a justification for its existence and a measure of its success."

With a birth rate of 50 births per 1000 population per year, and a death rate of 20 per 1000, the population grows at a whopping three percent per year. At this rate, the population doubles its size every 23 years.

Ukaegbu believes fertility will remain high in these villages until women change their attitude about childbearing. But two other factors are even more important in keeping fertility rates high. They are (1) high rates of childhood mortality—women whose children die young are likely to bear more children to compensate; and (2) little knowledge about contraception. Many women may not limit their births because they do not know how. They may not even know that it is possible to do so. We shall say more about this issue in Excerpt 15.

14

Socio-Cultural Influence on Fertility in Rural Eastern Nigeria

Alfred O. Ukaegbu

This paper is intended to add to the scanty cross-cultural data on the subject of socio-cultural influences on the fertility of women in a West African region. The major socio-cultural influences investigated include:

(1) age at first marriage;
(2) the coexistence of monogamy and polygyny;
(3) the incidence of infant and childhood mortality;
(4) the value of numerous children.

. . . The source of data is a single demographic inquiry conducted in Ngwa Igbo clan of the Imo State of Nigeria from August to September 1974.

A three-stage cluster sampling with a fixed sample size was used to select 1,672 currently married women from 16 villages.

☙

The Survey Population

. . . Both the women in the sample and their husbands are largely illiterate (67% and 56% respectively). Hence they are very traditional in practically every aspect of their behaviour—in the type of marital unions, occupation, the use of maternal and other health facilities, and in their attitude towards family-size.

Fertility in Ngwa Igbo is regulated within marriage, and a high fertility is traditionally viewed as the goal of marriage, a justification for its existence, and a measure of its success. Both the birth and death rates are high (about 50 per thousand and 20 per thousand respectively).

The product of both factors is a growth rate of about 3 percent per annum.[*]

A remarkable feature of this high rate of population growth is that it has been more or less stable over the past twenty-five years . . . For example, at the beginning of the second half of this century, the total fertility rate was probably in the order of eight children. By 1974, it lay between 7.3 and 7.9 children, showing little or no sign of the incipient decline . . .

Results
Age, Age At First Marriage, And Marriage Duration

The expected positive relationship between maternal age and fertility is clear in the age groups 15–44 years. Beyond the age group 40–44 years however, the relationship becomes erratic partly because of memory errors, and partly because of genuinely lower fertility. There is some evidence that the older wives practised longer spacing between births than the younger mothers who are nowadays combining lactation with artificial feeding of their babies. . . .

Ngwa Igbo wives tend to practice short intervals between marriage and first births, and between successive births. Between the age groups of wives, there is a noticeable decline in birth intervals from about 27 months by the oldest

---

Source: Ukaegbu, A. O. (1977) "Socio-cultural determination of fertility: A case study of rural Eastern Nigeria," *Journal of Comparative Family Studies*, 8, 1, Spring, 99–115.

---

[*]Both the crude birth and death rates were computed in the conventional way from the total numbers of births and deaths reported in the 12 months preceding the survey. The rate of natural increase was also obtained by differencing both indices. See, A. O. Ukaegbu, 1975, "Marriage and Fertility in East Central Nigeria: A Case Study of Ngwa Igbo Women", Ph.D. thesis held by the University of London, Chapter 5 pp. 110–30.

women to about 22 months by the women under 25 years old.

The following question was asked of all fertile wives regarding their attitude towards birth spacing:

"Some couples nowadays like to have all their children early enough instead of spacing them out for several years as was customary some years ago. Which of these practices do you support?"

Over 90 percent of the women under 35 years old, and about 60 percent of those aged 35–44 years supported short spacing in contrast to only 15 percent of the oldest women. The commonest reason given by wives who preferred short spacing is that this was "necessary to allow time to fend for the children's wellbeing.". . .

Age, Marriage duration, and Socio-cultural Determinants of Fertility

In order to measure the relative effects of a number of socio-cultural and demographic variables on fertility, a total of twenty variables were selected. The mean number of children ever born was listed for each variable, and it was discovered that when each variable was dichotomised for descriptive purposes, they all discriminated. But in order to ascertain the relative importance of each variable, step-wise multiple regression was employed. . . .

Marriage duration is shown to be the most important predictor of fertility. This is followed by the number of children reported dead to wives, whether the woman wanted additional children and the age of the wives. . . .

The findings may be summarised as follows:

(1) Infant and childhood mortality, and the unwillingness to cease childbearing are the leading factors in the reproductive behaviour of the Ngwa Igbo women.

(2) All but two factors which are signifi-

cantly associated with fertility function to raise rather than to lower fertility.

(3) Apart from age and marriage duration, all other important predictors of fertility largely hinge upon the traditions and cultural practices of the area.

(4) Finally, the fact that a substantial proportion of the variance has not been accounted for by the variables in the regression equation suggests that there are other important factors which also affect the fertility of the Ngwa Igbo wives.

Differential by Numbers of Children Reported Dead

The findings of this investigation underlie the importance of the concern for children's survival in shaping attitudes of the Ngwa Igbo wives towards family formation. . . . Whereas the women of all ages who have lost none of their children have an average of three children, those who have already lost two have an average of just under seven live births (6.9), and those who have already lost at least four have had an average of nine live births. . . .

The influence of child-mortality begins very early among the young women, and persists through the reproductive period. Women under 30 years who have lost two children have already had an average of 4.3 children compared to 2.1 children for their age cohorts who have lost none of their children.

The causal relationship between child mortality and fertility is outside the scope of this study. But in an earlier study in rural Senegal, Cantrelle and Leridon reached the conclusion that childhood mortality plays its role through the intermediary of breast-feeding and post partum infertility both of which are shortened by an early death of a child. But the same study failed to show any direct influence of fertility on mortality (Cantrelle and Leridon, 1974). Another study Synder (1974) concluded that Sierra Le-one parents tend to replace or over-replace a lost child when they are in the early stages of family formation. . . .

The high incidence of child mortality may result from high fertility, especially under conditions of poor nutrition and inadequate medical care. The indication of the effect of socioeconomic status on the incidence of childhood mortality may be seen from Table 1. The data show that even though the experience of child mortality is well defused in all socio-economic categories the burden rests heavily upon the illiterate and peasant households. Whereas over half of spouses who have primary level education or above have had no experience of child mortality, over half of the illiterate spouses have lost, at least two of their children. Estimates of the expectation of life at ages 2, 3, and 5 do not indicate a uniquely heavy infant and childhood mortality. The area's infant mortality rate was estimated to be about 158 per 1000, by Nigerian standards, a comparatively light mortality (Myers, 1975). They would not, therefore, provide support for the anxiety of women concerning the numbers of their children likely to survive.

What seems likely is that the traditional anxiety for child survival has not been modified to a significant degree as a result of a declining infant and childhood mortality. Probably the women are not yet aware that more children are surviving nowadays to adulthood than was the case when they themselves were children.

Differential by Wives' Desire for Additional Children

The desire for additional children was the second best predictor of fertility of the Ngwa Igbo wives. The women desiring more children have on average two children less than their age and marriage cohorts who wanted to cease child-bearing.

There are several subjective reasons why the women desired for numerous children. . . . The Ngwa Igbo believed that the couples who had a large number of children were rich or at least would be potentially so. Over two-thirds of the wives held this view and claimed: (a) no amount of material wealth was superior to children; (b)

TABLE 1. Number of Wives per Thousand Who Have Lost Exact Numbers of Their Children by Selected Variables, Ngwa Igbo, 1974

Variable	Exact Numbers of Children Dead to Wives per 1,000					
	0	*1*	*2*	*3*	*4*	*5+*
WIVES' EDUCATION						
Upper primary & above	619	261	80	40	—	—
Lower primary	539	281	107	48	16	9
Never been to school	52	375	254	155	102	62
HUSBANDS' EDUCATION						
College	604	269	87	40	—	—
Upper primary	457	282	129	64	45	23
Lower primary	301	333	166	119	16	65[a]
Never been to school	243	308	207	117	73	52
HUSBANDS' OCCUPATION						
Farming	148	355	224	141	78	54
Skilled/semi-skilled	435	284	149	63	52	17
Clerical/professional	502	311	99	39	44	5
All wives at risk	275	328	188	105	67	37

Note: a. The result was affected by chance fluctuation of small numbers.

the power of any household depended upon large numbers of male members; (c) children were gifts from God; (d) large numbers of children earned a big income when they were grown up; (e) family responsibilities were made easier since they could be shared by a large family; and (f) couples who had a large number of children would be guaranteed grand burial. . . .

In addition to these subjective considerations, the reason for desiring numerous children is directly related to the number of surviving children. The unwillingness to cease child-bearing is more of a function of the number of surviving children especially sons, than of the age of women. In this example, it is remarkable that even when six children are surviving, the proportion of wives desiring to stop further child-bearing is less than a third. . . .

The data, therefore, tend to substantiate Ware's remark that "Nowhere else in the world outside Africa is there such a reluctance as in Nigeria to cease child-bearing (Ware, 1975:293).

Differential by Type of Marital Union

The result of the regression analysis further confirms the earlier studies in Africa which hold the view that polygyny in the African region tends to depress fertility (Dorjahn, 1959:87–112; Henin, 1968:147–61; Van de Walle, 1968:183–238; Romaniuk, 1968:214–24; Morgan, 1971: 2,3). But in the Ngwa Igbo sample, the degree of association between polygyny and fertility is by no means strong.

Elsewhere (Ukaegbu, in press) both the extent of and factors affecting the fertility of wives in polygynous union have been examined in some detail. We, therefore, give the summary of the findings here. The fertility of wives in polygyny was compared to those of their marriage cohorts in monogamy in terms of the number of children ever born as well as in terms of their current births. The completed family size of wives in polygyny was 6 children, and their total fertility rate, 5.9 children. On the other hand,

the completed family size of wives in monogamy was 8 children and their total fertility rate, 8.5. Both indicates show an average deficit of 2 children per wife in polygynous union.

In the study referred to above, the investigation of factors affecting the fertility of the women in polygyny showed that the differential was attributable mainly to a comparatively wider age disparity between the polygnists, and their wives. This is probably the result of a biological mechanism whereby the males' capacity to procreate declines with age. In the Ngwa Igbo sample, 78 percent of the polygynists were over 50 years old, and among those 50-year-olds, 27 percent of their wives were under 25 years, and the proportion of their wives under 30 years rose over 40 percent. . . .

SUMMARY AND CONCLUSION

The evidence examined in this paper shows that the fertility pattern of the Ngwa Igbo of Nigeria is uniformly high for all age groups of wives and all durations of their marriages and does not show any sign of an incipient decline. There are more factors favouring high fertility and they are more powerful than those tending to depress fertility. Among those tending to encourage high fertility, the best three predictors are: the number of children dead to wives, whether wife desires additional children, and age of wives. Other factors which probably contribute towards high fertility include: the practice of short birth spacing by all fertile wives, very low incidence of infertility or childlessness, long reproductive span, and virtual absence of any effective family limitation method.

Factors which tend to reduce fertility are polygyny, the number of previous marriages, and the age of wives at first marriage. But these factors have a weak correlation with fertility because they have not reached a threshold upon which they can exert a powerful depressive effect.

Available evidence thus leads to the conclusion that the level of fertility will remain high until the factors favouring high fertility have been counter-balanced by negative factors. However, considering the predominance of traditional attitudes and beliefs favourable to high marital fertility, (Ukaegbu, 1976) the probable factors which might exert strong negative pressure on fertility would likely be: (a) the spread of contraceptive knowledge and practice, (b) raising the level of education of females beyond the present primary grade, and (c) a substantial reduction in the incidence of infant and childhood mortality, and an accompanying awareness of the women of that reduction.

The combined effect of all other socio-cultural factors which have been investigated is overshadowed by the incidence of childhood mortality and the consequent desire of wives for more and more children.

The effect of infant and childhood mortality on fertility indicates the necessity to improve the health of the rural population in Eastern Nigeria. In particular, policies aimed at improving the health of pregnant mothers and children under five would likely have an important effect in reducing fertility by ensuring a greater chance of survival of infants and young children.

REFERENCES

CANTRELLE, P. and LERIDON, H. 1974. "Breast Feeding, Mortality in Childhood and Fertility in a Rural Zone in Senegal. In *Population Studies* 25(2) pp. 505–33.

DORJAHN, VERNON, R. 1959. "The Factor of Polygyny in African Demography." In *Continuity and Change in African Culture*. W.R. Bascom and William Melville Herskovits (eds.). University of Chicago Press, Chicago.

HENIN, R. A. 1968. "Fertility Differentials in the Sudan". In *Population Studies*. XII, (March): pp. 147–61.

MORGAN, ROBERT, W. 1971. "Traditional Contraceptive Techniques in Nigeria." Paper Submitted for the African Regional Population Conference, Accra. December 9–18, pp. 2,3.

MYERS, PAUL F. 1975. *1975 World Population Data Sheet*. Population Reference Bureau Inc. Washington D.C.

ROMANIUK, A. 1968. "Infertility in Tropical Africa". In *The Population of Tropical Africa*. J.C. Caldwell and C. Okonjo (eds.). Longmans, pp. 214–224.

SYNDER, D. W. 1974. "Economic Determinants of Family Size in West Africa." In *Demography*, 11(2) (November), pp. 613–29.

UKAEGBU, ALFRED O. (in press): "Family Size Preferences of Spouses in Rural Eastern Nigeria." In *The Journal of Development Studies*, (London).

UKAEGBU, ALFRED O. (in press): "Fertility of Women in Polygynous Union in Rural Eastern Nigeria." In *Journal of Marriage and the Family* (Helsinki).

UKAEGBU, ALFRED O. 1976. "The Role of Traditional Marriage Habits in Population Growth: The Case of Rural Eastern Nigeria." In *Africa: Journal of the International African Institute*, (4) (November), pp. 74–82.

UKAEGBU, ALFRED O. 1975. Marriage and Fertility in East Central Nigeria: A Case Study of Ngwa Igbo Women. Ph.D. thesis held by the University of London.

WARE, HELEN. 1975. "The Limits of Acceptable Family Size in Western Nigeria." In *Journal of Biosocial Sciences*. (7), pp. 273–96.

VAN DE WALLE, E. 1968. "Marriage in African Censuses and Enquiries." In *The Demography of Tropical Africa*. W. Brass et al. Princeton University Press. New Jersey, pp. 183–238.

Introduction

The previous two excerpts showed that when parents think children are valuable, they produce more of them. They may value children highly because they believe their children will take care of them when they get old. They may even believe that children are a gift from God, a blessing to any marriage and, even, the reason for getting married.

But is this the *real* reason people bear children, or merely an attempt to make sense of fate—a justification for something people do not know how to prevent? Some researchers think it is the latter. Results of the European Fertility Study—a reanalysis of European historical statistics at Princeton University—have led scholars to doubt the validity of the demographic transition theory, which places a great emphasis on values and motivations.

The Princeton-based researchers have raised doubts that people living in pre-industrial societies really choose how many children they will bear. People may want fewer children, but children just keep coming despite their wishes. And if people are *not* exercising a choice, their stated values regarding children and childbearing are unimportant. They are mere consequences, not causes, of fertility behavior.

The next excerpt draws this important conclusion from nearly twenty years of painstaking work on old censuses from almost every European country. The research casts serious doubt on the demographic transition theory. By doing so, it calls into question the prevailing belief that fertility cannot fall until mortality (especially child mortality) falls. In effect, (the old theory has said) there can be no slowing of population growth without prosperity. The new theory questions this premise. Both views, old and new, have great significance for social planning, and for theories about family behavior.

15

Policy Implications of Historical Fertility Studies

John Knodel
Etienne van de Walle

There has recently been a marked increase in the number of historical studies of European fertility. As a result, a more detailed picture of the historical record is available today. Two types of demographic studies have been largely responsible for the expansion of our knowledge of historical trends: European micro-level family reconstitution studies, which typically refer to village populations during the preindustrial and generally pre-fertility decline period; and macro-level studies of the secular decline of fertility on the national and provincial levels. The first type of study is based on the reproductive histories of individual couples reconstituted usually from the church registers of baptisms, burials, and marriages. Also in this genre are studies based on genealogies of special subgroups of the population, particularly social elites, for whom previously compiled genealogies are readily available.

. . . The second type of study is based largely on published census and vital statistics data on such administratively defined geopolitical units as districts, provinces, or states.

In addition our understanding of reproductive behavior in the past is also being increased by . . . studies based on literary evidence, including letters and novels, and on commentaries by contemporary observers such as nineteenth-century statisticians' interpretations of vital statistics and county and small-town medical doc-

Source: Knodel, John and Etienne van de Walle (1979) "Lessons from the past: Policy implications of historical fertility studies," *Population and Development Review,* 5(2), June, 217–245.

tors' reports on their patients and on local health-related conditions. These shed light on the extent of knowledge of birth control and attitudes toward reproduction and children in the past. . . .

Our reading of the historical evidence leads us to several observations:. . . .

1. Fertility declines took place under a wide variety of social, economic, and demographic conditions.
2. Family limitation was largely absent (and probably unknown) among broad segments of the population prior to the decline in fertility, even though a substantial proportion of births may have been unwanted.
3. Increases in the practice of family limitation and the decline of marital fertility were essentially irreversible processes once under way.
4. Cultural setting influenced the onset and spread of fertility decline independently of socioeconomic conditions. . . .

We wish to underscore that our discussion is based primarily on the European experience.

⟡

THE SOCIOECONOMIC CONTEXT OF FERTILITY DECLINE

The fertility transition in Europe occurred under remarkably diverse socioeconomic and demographic conditions.

Evidence

. . . Although the fertility decline began in England only after considerable urbanization and industrialization had taken place, it occurred at about the same time in Hungary, which was at a substantially lower level of development as measured by conventional socioeconomic indexes. Indeed, the first country to show signs of fertility decline was France, where birth rates started to fall around the time of the French Revolution. France could hardly be considered

advanced at the time in terms of any standard definition of development. . . .

Differences in the level of literacy were also considerable. And within each country, no consistent relationship has been found between education and fertility. Fertility itself varied greatly in pre-decline Europe. Not only did diverse combinations of birth and death rates make for a wide range of growth rates at the time of the transition, but also variations in the proportions married—typically low in Western Europe and high in Eastern Europe—influenced the pre-decline levels of overall fertility.

The decline of infant and child mortality has often been singled out as a decisive factor that influenced the perceptions of parents about the desirable size of the family. It has been argued that parents revise their demand for births downward when the supply of living children increases. Yet fertility declined under a wide variety of infant mortality conditions. . . . In most instances, the decline of child mortality (but not necessarily infant mortality) had started before marital fertility dropped. But before a causal link can be established, the extraordinary differences in the lags between the two declines will have to be explained. . . . At this stage, no definitive conclusion can be reached on the role of declining mortality in the fertility transition in the West. . . . There is little evidence that this fall has been sufficient in itself to initiate a drop in the birth rate.

Clearly, large genuine differences in the level of development also existed among European populations at the start of their fertility declines. It seems that no obvious threshold of social and economic development was required for the fertility transition to begin.

Outside Europe, countries undergoing the demographic transition since 1960 show a diversity in socioeconomic levels of development similar to that which characterized the western nations in the nineteenth century. Moreover, in some countries that are more industrialized and urbanized and have lower illiteracy and infant mortality than many nineteenth-century European countries, marital fertility has not yet started to decline. . . .

Implications

Although a high level of social and economic development may accompany a fall of fertility, it is not a precondition. Thus, the introduction of a family planning program in a developing country at an early stage of development does not necessarily foreclose its success. . . . Whether a family-planning program will meet with success will be determined by how receptive couples are to reducing their fertility once the knowledge and means of birth control are available.

Conversely, the attainment of a certain threshold of socioeconomic development appears an uncertain predictor of the trend of fertility. . . . Thus, the historical record provides little assurance that efforts to reduce fertility or hasten a decline through raising the level of development will meet early success.

PRE-TRANSITION FERTILITY BEHAVIOR

Three propositions are advanced concerning fertility behavior in Western Europe prior to the onset of decline: the practice of family limitation was largely absent; it was probably unknown to large segments of the population; and there was latent motivation for reduced fertility among substantial portions of the population before fertility began to fall.

Evidence

. . . Family limitation emerges among some groups of the population much earlier than among others and long before any urban-industrial transformation is evident. This is especially true among certain groups of social elites, such as the Genevan bourgeoisie or the French and Italian nobility. . . . The same populations

characterized by early family limitation also experience early fertility decline, and when the data extend back to the pre-decline period in these populations, signs of family limitation are lacking. . . .

Indirect evidence leads us to conclude family limitation was not known to the majority prior to the fertility transition period and thus was not a real option. Moreover, additional evidence suggests births were frequently unwanted, especially among women.

First, in pre-transition populations, couples did not adjust their reproductive behavior to their own experience with infant and child mortality (Knodel, 1978a, 1978c). Couples whose children all survived continued childbearing just as long as couples whose children had died early. Thus, couples who would seem to have had the greatest incentive to practice family limitation—those whose children all survived—did not do so.

Second, marital and nonmarital fertility declined more or less simultaneously in most European countries. (Shorter, Knodel, and E. van de Walle, 1971); and, so a plausible interpretation is that birth control practices were not widely diffused prior to the parallel declines in legitimate and illegitimate fertility and that the spread of the knowledge to avoid unwanted births enabled both married and unmarried couples to reduce their fertility simultaneously. . . .

Implications

If family limitation was an innovation in Europe at the time of the onset of the fertility transition and its diffusion contributed to the pace of fertility decline there, the same process can occur in developing countries today. Organized family planning programs that provide information and services, as well as propaganda efforts designed to legitimate family planning practices, may help initiate or accelerate the adoption of family planning practices. . . . Naturally, the success of a family-planning program depends on the receptivity of the couples to fertility reduction. But the absence of practice prior to campaigns to disseminate information and services does not necessarily indicate the lack of such receptivity. . . .

THE IRREVERSIBILITY OF FAMILY LIMITATION AND FERTILITY DECLINE

Increases in family limitation and the decline of marital fertility were largely coincident and, once under way, largely irreversible. . . .

Evidence

Throughout Europe once the practice of family limitation rose above minimal levels, it continued to increase until much higher levels of control prevailed. Likewise, once the level of marital fertility decline began, it continued until much lower fertility, typically well below 50 percent of the pre-decline level, was achieved. . . . The evidence from Taiwan, and an increasing number of other developing nations (most of which are at an earlier stage of their fertility decline), suggests the same experience is being repeated in present-day developing countries at a greatly accelerated pace (see Knodel, 1977b; Knodel and Debavalya, 1978). . . .

Implications

The steady decline in marital fertility may reflect a combination of increasing efficiency in the practice of family limitation and falling desired family sizes. Indeed, these two factors may interact. Only after the possibility of effectively limiting childbearing becomes a reality and its advantages become fully appreciated does it make sense to couples to aim for even smaller family sizes.

If our hypothesis is correct, the high and relatively constant fertility that characterizes predecline societies corresponds to a period in which it is not widely acknowledged that repro-

duction can be manipulated. Couples accept, in some cases reluctantly, as many children "as God sends.". . . In the absence of a choice, societies accommodate high fertility: large families are welcomed or at least unquestioned. . . . Once methods are on hand by which smaller and smaller family sizes can be attained by successive cohorts of couples, the norm about size starts to evolve downward.

The steady increase in family limitation and steady decline in fertility is indicative of a "diffusion process." Once some couples adopt the new behavior patterns, it becomes easy for other couples to imitate. . . .

THE INFLUENCE OF CULTURAL SETTING

Cultural setting influenced the onset and spread of fertility decline independently of socioeconomic conditions. Proximate areas with similar socioeconomic conditions but dissimilar cultures entered the transition period at different times, whereas areas differing in the level of socioeconomic development but with similar cultures entered the transition at similar times.

Evidence

Despite the diversity of their socioeconomic characteristics, the countries of Europe had one striking factor in common when fertility declined: time itself. With the exception of the forerunner, France, and a few stragglers, such as Ireland and Albania, the dates of decline were remarkably concentrated. . . . We see this as evidence that some diffusion of information on contraception as well as some communication of normative beliefs must have occurred within the larger European (or Western) cultural sphere. . . .

The experience of English-language countries overseas demonstrates the importance of language and culture in the fertility transition. The "extraordinary similarity between the course of birth rates in Australia and the United States, and the similarity between the fertility of these two societies over time and those of Britain, New Zealand, and English-speaking Canada" serve as one striking manifestation of "the diffusion of fertility control practices within single language groups" despite the quite different social and economic situations that characterize these countries (Caldwell and Ruzicka, 1978, p. 81). . . .

Implications

Cultural setting and tradition are likely to exert an independent influence on the response of populations to organized family-planning efforts as well as to general development. While family-planning programs may elicit a favorable response in some populations even at quite low initial levels of development, in others we might expect such efforts to be quite unsuccessful at higher levels of development. . . .

CONCLUSION

Although the European experience confirms a loose relationship between socioeconomic modernization and fertility decline, it also suggests there was an important innovation-diffusion dimension to the reproductive revolution that swept the continent. This suggests the introduction of family limitation (along with the means of effective fertility control), in combination with the diffusion of tastes of modern consumer goods, higher material aspirations, and an awareness of alternative roles for women, can have a substantial impact on populations today. Indeed, given the modern communications existing in much of the developing world today, the potential for rapid diffusion of birth control practice is considerably greater than it was historically in Europe. At the same time, the historical record does not suggest success will necessarily be immediate. . . .

One implication of our interpretation is that recommendations to shift the emphasis away from family-planning programs and toward development efforts as a means of reducing fertility should be viewed with considerable caution. . . .

REFERENCES

CALDWELL, J. C. and L. T. RUZICKA. (1978) "The Australian fertility transition: An analysis," *Population and Development Review*, 4(1), 81–103.

KNODEL, J. (1977) "Family limitation and the fertility transition: Evidence from age patterns of fertility in Europe and Asia," *Population Studies*, 31(2), 219–249.

—— (1978a) "European populations in the past: Family-level relations." In *The Effects of Infant and Child Mortality on Fertility*, edited by S.H. Preston, pp. 21–45. New York: Academic Press.

—— (1978b) "Natural fertility in pre-industrial Germany," *Population Studies*, 32(3), 481–510.

—— and N. Debavalya. (1978) "Thailand's reproductive revolution," *Internation Family Planning Perspectives and Digest*, 4(2), 34–49.

SHORTER, E., J. KNODEL and E. VAN DE WALLE (1971) "The decline of non-marital fertility in Europe, 1880–1940," *Population Studies*, 25(3), 375–393.

Introduction

In an earlier excerpt, we saw how rural Chinese women have struggled through generations of poverty and social change. The results of such a struggle are sometimes hard to see on a day-by-day, person-by-person basis.

Yet if we look at the larger picture—an entire society changing over many decades—we can see an enormous transformation in the last forty years. In a survey of over 300,000 Chinese women aged 15–67, Chen finds evidence of dramatic changes in family life. For example, Chinese young people today wait longer to marry than they did a generation ago. Since 1949, the average age at marriage has risen from 19 to about 23 years. Fertility is down too, as seven out of ten married women of childbearing age practice contraception. Chinese fertility fell by about 60% (from 6 births per woman to 2.5 births on average) during the 1970s; since then it has continued to fall. What's more, these changes in marriage, contraception, and fertility are not confined to a small educated urban group, as is the case in many developing countries. Chen finds them in every region, occupation, education level, and age group in the country.

We will not find the explanation of this dramatic change in demographic transition theory, for China has not modernized very much. Large numbers still live in what we would consider severe poverty, even if their conditions are better than they were forty years ago. Many traditional practices continue. And children in rural areas still bring their parents more economic benefits, and fewer costs than in our own society.

Lower fertility is a result of cultural change promoted by the state. Nowhere is this state effort clearer than in the successful one-child-per-couple campaign, implemented in 1971 with the slogan "Wan, xi, shao" (or, "later, longer, fewer"). It includes a strong antinatalist policy and wider access to birth control information and technology.

16
China's Other Revolution

Pi-Chao Chen

INTRODUCTION

On July 1, 1982, China launched its third national census since the founding of the People's Republic in 1949. Unlike the prior censuses of 1953 and 1964, this one involved long and careful preparation, and was undertaken with the assistance of the United Nations and several national governments. Publication at the end of 1983 of selected tabulations from the 10 percent sample of the census showed a total mainland population of 1.008 billion in mid-1982, a crude birthrate of 20.9 per 1,000 population, a crude death rate of 6.4 and, therefore, a rate of natural population increase of 14.5.[1] Two months after

the census was launched, the Birth Planning Commission carried out a large-scale national survey of fertility, known as the One in 1,000 Survey because it involved interviews with women in households which contained more than one million persons.[2]

This article summarizes the major findings of that survey.

꽁

MARITAL STATUS

Data from the 10 percent census sample, show that in recent years, women have by and large complied with the government requirement to delay marriage. . . .

The mean age at first marriage rose from less than 19 to about 23 between 1949 and 1981.

Source: Chen, P. (1984) "China's other revolution: Findings from the One in 1,000 fertility survey," *International Family Planning Perspectives*, 10, 2, June, 48–57.

The government began to promote late marriage in the cities in the early 1960s, and in the countryside in the early 1970s. However, the rise in marriage age over the last three decades has been slow and fairly steady and does not reflect a rapid response to a government campaign. The mean age at marriage was higher in urban areas early on, and continues to be so. . . .

Until 1981, the minimum legal age at marriage was 20 for men and 18 for women. However, following introduction in 1971 of its wan, xi, shao (later, longer, fewer) campaign, the government ever more strongly encouraged young men to wait for marriage until they were 25 and women until they were 23 (the "late marriage" age). The new law "raising" the legal marriage age to 22 for men and 20 for women was announced in 1980 and took effect in 1981. Following announcement of the new increased age for legal marriage, the actual age at marriage began to go down. One reason for this is that in 1981, the government prohibited local officials from interfering with young couples who wanted to get married so long as they met the new legal age requirements.

To evaluate progress in the promotion of late marriage, the 1/1,000 survey attempted to reconstruct the proportions of women who married at age 23 or later from 1949 to 1981. The proportion of late marriages rose steadily, from seven percent when the People's Republic was founded in 1949 to 51 percent in 1981 (down slightly from a peak of 53 percent in 1979 and 1980—again, apparently, because of the change in the legal age for marriage). In other words, about half of Chinese couples are conforming to the late marriage ideal promoted by the government. As with the decline in the mean age at first marriage, late marriage first gathered momentum in the cities and later spread to the countryside. . . . Although the late marriage policy appears to have had little effect on the slow but steady rise in the mean age at first marriage, it has worked to compress the marriage age to a narrow range, centering on age 22. . . .

FERTILITY TRENDS

The total fertility rate (TFR) during the decade preceding the establishment of the People's Republic in 1949 was well above five children per woman of reproductive age. During the wartime years, 1940–1945, it fluctuated between 5.0 and 5.3, averaging 5.2. Following the war, fertility began to rise—a trend that continued, with some fluctuations, until 1957. During those postwar years, the TFR averaged 6.1. . . .

During the next decade, the TFR declined dramatically—to 4.3 children per woman in 1959, 4.0 in 1960 and to an incredibly low 3.3 in 1961. Thereafter, it rose again, to 6.0 in 1962 and to an unprecedented high of 7.5 in 1963, and averaged about 6.1 between 1964 and 1968. . . . The explanation for the dramatic fertility decline during this period lies in the widespread disruption of normal marital and reproductive life and the severe famines that swept the country during the 1958–1961 period. Tens of millions of families were separated temporarily in the course of the major national construction projects in 1958, the launching of the Great Leap Forward campaign and the further forcible implementation of agricultural collectivization that occurred during this period. These campaigns combined with natural catastrophes to bring about widespread crop failures and famine between 1958 and 1961. The officially reported crude death rate rose from 12 per 1,000 in 1957 to 25 in 1960, and fell back to 14 only in 1962.[3] . . . The nadir in fertility (a TFR of 3.3) occurred in 1961, the year following the worst part of the famine. The famine apparently depressed fertility in urban as well as rural areas. . . .

The rapid rise in fertility in 1962, and the peak of 7.5 reached in 1963, may be interpreted as a catch-up phenomenon. Many couples who postponed marriage or childbirth or experienced infant or fetal death during the years of the food crisis rushed to make up for lost time. After 1963, fertility fell again; it fluctuated between 6.1 and 6.4 children per woman between 1964 and 1968 (except for 1967, when it dipped to 5.3).

Thereafter, it fell steadily, to a low of 2.2 in 1980. . . .

The rapid decreases that occurred after 1970 are the result of the vigorously implemented birth control policies beginning with the wan, xi, shao campaign in 1971, and culminating in the one-child-per-couple policy begun in 1979. Whereas in the 1968–1970 period, the TFR averaged 6.0 births per woman, in the 1979–1981 period, it averaged just 2.5 births—a decline of 58 percent.

What caused the TFR to rise from 2.2 in 1980 to 2.6 in 1981? As noted earlier, the change in

the marriage law announced in 1980 and effective in 1981, technically raising the age of marriage, in effect lowered it, because local officials were no longer allowed to require young couples to wait to marry until they reached the late marriage age. Many women aged 20–22 took advantage of the new law to get married. Among women aged 20–23, the total marriage rate increased from 57 per 1,000 in 1980 to 74 per 1,000 in 1981, a rise of 30 percent in a single year. The age-specific marriage rate for other age-groups hardly changed at all.[4] A baby boom soon followed the marriage boom—the result of a short-

FIGURE 1. Age-specific fertility rates per 1,000 women, China, 1965, 1975 and 1980

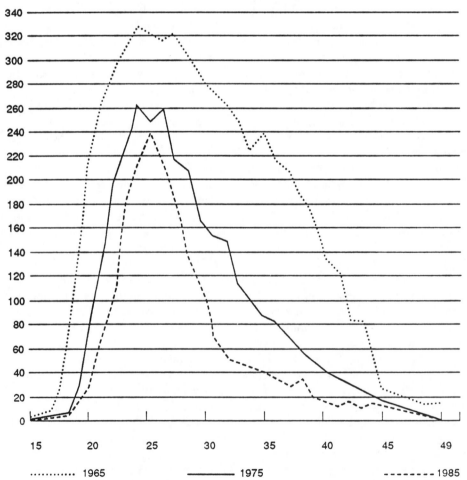

ening over the years of the interval between marriage and the first birth. Thus, 38 percent of couples who first married in 1957 had a first birth the same or the following year. This proportion rose to 63 percent in 1977 and to 67 percent in 1980.[5] Because of the frequent shifts in birth planning policies, few couples postpone childbearing once they marry, and some women even become pregnant before the wedding.

RURAL-URBAN DIFFERENTIALS

Fertility differentials between rural and urban women in China have existed historically and persist to the present. The average 67-year-old urban woman has had 4.5 children, and the average rural woman has had 5.3. This differential exists also for the number of children ever born to younger women, as is shown in Table 1.

In 1950 the TFR was 6.0 children per woman in rural areas and 5.0 in urban areas. Thirty years later, the rural TFR had declined to 2.5, the urban TFR to 1.1. Thus, despite dramatic declines in the fertility of rural and urban women, the TFR of urban dwellers remains less than half that of their rural counterparts. Rural and urban fertility trends exhibited the same fluctuations during the 1950–1980 period. However, not only did fertility decline among urban women begin several years before the decline among their rural counterparts, but the transition started from a considerably lower level among urban dwellers. Urban fertility began to decline in 1964. . . .

TABLE 1. Average number of children ever borne, by age and residence of mother

Age	Urban	Rural
35	2.2	3.6
40	2.9	4.6
45	3.6	5.5
50	4.3	5.9
55	4.7	5.9
60	4.6	5.6
67	4.5	5.3

Given the greater availability of contraceptive services in the cities, the greater capability of the government to regulate all aspects of daily life (including reproductive behavior) and the greater availability of pensions to replace the traditional dependence on sons for support in old age, it is not surprising that China's birth planning program has had a more immediate and profound impact on the urban women than on those living in the countryside. Starting from a much higher level, fertility in rural areas also fell precipitously during the 1970s, following initiation of the wan, xi, shao program. The government also expanded its program—initiated in 1965 as part of the Cultural Revolution—of bringing primary health care facilities, including contraceptive services, to the countryside. In 1968, the rural TFR was 7.0 children per woman. By 1980, it had fallen to 2.5, a decline of 65 percent. . . .

AGE-SPECIFIC TRENDS AND PATTERNS

China's fertility decline has involved substantial drops in age-specific fertility rates across the entire reproductive span. It is only in 1980, that the age-specific rates are clearly characteristic of a population in which contraceptives and abortion are consciously used to control fertility. The concentration of fertility in the mid-20s and its precipitous decline after age 25 were especially marked in 1980. In 1955, births to women aged 15–19 accounted for 7.2 percent of total births; by 1980, it had fallen to 2.2 percent. This decline reflects the steady rise in the age at marriage. . . . At the other end of the reproductive scale, births to women 35 and above accounted for 25 percent of total births as recently as 1965. By 1980, this proportion had fallen to just 3.6 percent. The current pattern of fertility suggests that women are having small families, having children soon after marriage in the mid-20s, and then using contraceptives, sterilization and abortion to prevent further childbearing.

Births to women in the peak childbearing years also dropped substantially. Thus, childbearing by women aged 20–24 declined by 50 percent between 1965 and 1980—from 289 to 142 births per 1,000 women in this age-group. . . .

EDUCATIONAL AND OCCUPATIONAL DIFFERENTIALS IN FERTILITY

In China, as in many other societies, better educated women tend to have fewer children. Thus, 50-year-old women who are illiterate have borne an average of 5.9 children each, compared with 4.8 children among primary school graduates, 3.7 among those who have completed junior middle school, 2.9 among the senior middle school graduates and 2.1 among those who have finished college. The same pattern is shown among younger women. . . .

· Fertility differentials are also apparent in China according to the woman's occupation. Cadres* have the lowest fertility (a TFR of 2.7 per woman), followed by workers (3.6) and "others," a miscellaneous category (4.8); peasants have the highest fertility (5.0). This pattern is distinct as early as age 35, and extends all the way to age 67.

From the time it initiated the wan, xi, shao program, the government has sought to enforce the norms of later, longer and fewer births ever more rigorously among the Han Chinese majority. The ethnic minorities were exempted from the two-child-per-couple norm. This policy, combined with cultural differences in attitudes toward reproduction, led to considerable differences in fertility between the ethnic minorities and the Han majority. As of 1980, minority women tended to get married at younger ages,

---

*"Cadre" refers to a person with education, skills, or administrative or professional responsibility, or someone who is in a leadership role. . . .

have their first birth earlier, stretch out their childbearing further and, therefore, have more children than the Han. . . .

CONTRACEPTIVE USE AND BIRTH PLANNING

By the beginning of the 1980s, the level of contraceptive use in China was as high as that found in the United States. Of the 170 million married women aged 15–49 at the time of the 1/1,000 survey in 1982, 70 percent—118 million—were current contraceptive users. By comparison, 54 percent of all women and 58 percent of those currently married were users in the United States in 1982.[6] Prevalence differed by urban-rural residence: Seventy-four percent used a method in urban areas, compared with 69 percent in the countryside. It should be noted that as recently as 1968, the TFR in rural China was 7.0 children per woman, indicating that there was little, if any, contraceptive use. Just 14 years later, nearly seven out of 10 rural women were practicing contraception; more than half of these were using the IUD, and nearly four in 10 had been sterilized. . . .

Starting in 1966, the Chinese government initiated the process of building an integrated primary health service in rural areas. By the end of the 1970s, a nationwide network of the three-tier primary health care system was in place. At the bottom of this system is the brigade cooperative medical station. Staffed by two to four barefoot doctors (trained paramedical workers), the station is responsible for providing preventive and simple curative health care as well as contraceptive services to a brigade with 1,000–3,000 persons. At the middle tier is the commune health center, responsible for the health care of a population of 15,000–50,000. It is staffed by college or vocational medical school graduates, laboratory technicians and other support personnel. It provides technical training, supports and supervises the barefoot doctors at the brigade level and treats cases referred from below. At the top, or county, level are the county (general) hospital, the maternity hospital and the epidemic control stations. Each of the three county-level units is responsible for providing training and technical support and supervision to the commune health centers.[7] In addition, there is a county birth planning office, responsible for implementing the wan, xi, shao policy and for coordinating training and provision of contraceptive services in the county.

By the end of the 1970s, each of the more than 2,000 counties had its own general hospital, maternity hospital and epidemic control stations; 55,000 communes, or about 90 percent, had their own health centers; and 700,000, or 90 percent, of the nation's production brigades had their own brigade medical stations. A total of 1.45 million barefoot doctors, are employed at these stations.[8]

The contraceptive service system has been built into this three-tier system. At least one barefoot doctor in each brigade medical station is a woman reportedly trained in IUD insertion and removal. Some of the women barefoot doctors are trained in aspiration abortion. At least one staff member at the commune health center is said to be trained in tubal ligation, vasectomy, IUD insertion and midtrimester abortion. . . .

Under this system, young people are persuaded or (until the new marriage law was implemented in 1981) sometimes required to wait to marry until they reach the late marriage age. Once they reach marriage age, they may apply for a permit to marry as well as for a birth permit. After the first birth, they must wait for at least three years to have a second birth. In the meanwhile, they are expected to use an effective method of contraception. Once the youngest of their officially approved children reaches five years of age, they are encouraged to undergo sterilization. . . .

In theory, the program offers all contraceptive methods to married couples. In practice, the local cadres encourage use of the IUD and,

where appropriate, sterilization. It is expected that unauthorized pregnancies, will be terminated by abortion. . . .

THE ONE-CHILD CAMPAIGN

In 1979, the wan, xi, shao campaign was replaced by the one-child-per-couple policy. Young people are asked to restrict the number of children they have to one in order to assist the government in reaching its goal of stabilizing the population at 1.2 billion at the turn of the century. . . .

About 21 percent of mothers of reproductive age had had only one child at the time of the 1/1,000 survey—33 percent in urban areas and 19 percent in rural areas. A total of 42 percent of women with one child had obtained a certificate—78 percent of those in urban areas and 31 percent of those who were rural.[9] . . .

The more education a woman has, the more likely she is to obtain a one-child certificate. Only three percent of illiterate women obtained the certificate, compared with 21 percent of those with a college education. The educational differential is found among rural as well as urban women. Cadres are most likely to sign up, followed by workers, especially those from urban areas. Peasants from the rural villages are least likely to obtain a one-child certificate. These differentials are to be expected in a society where social security allowances are almost nonexistent in rural areas, and where rural couples must depend on their children, in particular their sons, to take care of them in their old age. In the cities, on the other hand, workers and cadre can be assured of receiving pensions of 70–90 percent of their wages when they retire.[10]

The traditional preference for sons is apparent when one looks at the sex of the child of the certificate-holding parents: One-child certificate holders are 50 percent more likely to have a boy than a girl—78 percent more likely in rural areas,

and 21 percent more likely in urban areas.[11]
. . .

About six percent of certificate holders changed their minds and had a second child, although this meant giving back all the benefits they had received for signing up. It is notable that 98 percent of those who changed their minds were rural women.[12]

NOTES

[1]Population Census Office Under the State Council and Department of Population Statistics, State Statistical Bureau, eds., *Major Figures by 10 Percent Sampling Tabulation of the 1982 Population Census of the People's Republic of China*, Beijing, 1983.

[2]Editorial Board of *Renkou yu Jingji (The Population and the Economy)*, "Quan Guo Qian Fen Zhi Yi Ren Kou Sheng Yo Lu Chou Yang Diao Cha Fen Xi" ("An Analysis of the National 1/1,000 Sample Survey of Fertility"), special issue of *Renkou yu Jingji*, Beijing, 1983.

[3]Y. F. SUN, "Consolidate Statistics Work, Reform Statistics System," English text in Foreign Broadcast Information Service, China, Mar. 26, 1981, Original Chinese text in *Jingii Guanli (Economic Management)*, Vol. 2, No. 3, Feb. 1981.

[4]Editorial Board, 1983, op. cit., p. 169.

[5]Ibid., Table 1, p. 66.

[6]C. A. BACHRACH, "Contraceptive Practice: 1982," paper presented at the annual meeting of the Population Association of America (PAA), Minneapolis, May 3–5, 1984.

[7]P. C. CHEN, *Population and Health Policy in the People's Republic of China*, Smithsonian Institution Interdisciplinary Communications Program, Washington, D.C., 1976.

[8]P. C. CHEN and C. H. TUAN, "Primary Health Care in Rural China: Post-1978 Development," *Social Science and Medicine*, 17:1411, 1983.

[9]Editorial Board, 1983, op. cit., pp. 137, 141 and 143.

[10]D. DAVIS-FRIEDMAN, "Old Age Security and the One Child Campaign," unpublished manuscript, Department of Sociology, Yale University, New Haven, Conn., 1983; and——, *Long Life: Chinese Elderly and the Communist Revolution*, Harvard University Press, Cambridge, Mass., 1983, pp. 18–19.

[11]Editorial Board, 1983, op. cit., p. 139.

[12]Ibid., pp. 139–140.

Introduction

In developed societies like the United States, we assume that everyone has a good reason to limit childbearing (so says the demographic transition theory) and access to the means of doing so. Supposedly, people have only the children they want; it is hard to understand what could be meant by an "unwanted" pregnancy.

How, then, do we explain the high rates of teenage pregnancy in the United States when, in most countries, these rates are low or falling? Are these "wanted" pregnancies? And, whatever answer we may give to that question, do we as a society want to see a reduction in the number of teenage pregnancies? The authors of the next excerpt *do* favor a reduction in teenage pregnancy, and we can think of many reasons for supporting this. Teenage pregnancy interrupts a young woman's education and may even, with childbirth, put an end to it. This, in turn, is liable to lead to economic dependency on the state or on a spouse and, in the latter case, a very high risk of marital breakup.

The young mother may be unprepared to undertake the duties of mothering. The result may be child abuse. If the mother is on welfare, the child will be forced to live in poverty. If the mother is single or divorced, the child will grow up without a father present. These, in turn, have negative consequences of their own for the child's development and happiness.

So we can think of many good reasons for discouraging teenage pregnancy. This excerpt shows, through a comparison of the United States with dozens of other countries, that to succeed in reducing teenage pregnancy we will have to change the ways young people and their parents think about sex, sexual education, and contraception.

17
Teenage Pregnancy in Industrial Countries

Jacqueline Darroch Forrest
Noreen Goldman
Stanley Henshaw
Richard Lincoln
Jeannie I. Rosoff
Charles F. Westoff
Deirdre Wulf

. . . One policy implication to come from this study is the discrediting of certain beliefs that have tended to paralyze efforts aimed at reducing the high rates of pregnancy experienced by American adolescents. What are those beliefs?

- Adolescent pregnancy rates are higher in the United States than in Europe mainly because of the high pregnancy rate among U.S. blacks
- American adolescents begin sex much earlier and more of them are sexually active than their counterparts in other developed countries
- Teenagers are too immature to use contraceptives effectively
- Unwed adolescents want to have babies in order to obtain welfare assistance
- Making abortions and contraceptives available and providing sex education only encourages promiscuity and, therefore, increases teenage pregnancy
- As long as there is no clear path for unemployed teenagers to improve their economic condition they will continue to have babies as one of the few sources of satisfaction and accomplishment available to them

None of these beliefs explains the differences between teenage pregnancy rates in the United States and other developed countries.

LESSONS FROM THE 37-COUNTRY STUDY

The study of 37 countries was restricted to an examination of the factors affecting teenage birthrates. . . .

Six factors were important in their effect on teenage fertility. Those associated with low teenage fertility rates are:

- High levels of socioeconomic modernization
- Openness about sex
- A relatively large proportion of household income distributed to the low-income population (important mainly for younger teenagers)
- A high minimum legal age at marriage (important for older teenagers only)

Factors associated with high teenage fertility are:

- Generous maternity leaves and benefits
- Overall pronatalist policies designed to raise fertility

Although it is one of the most highly developed countries, the United States has a teenage fertility rate much higher than the rates observed in countries that are comparably modernized, and considerably higher than the rates in a number of much less developed countries. The inconsonance applies particularly to fertility among younger teenagers, where the U.S. rate falls between that of Romania and Hungary. The relatively high adolescent birthrate in the United States would suggest it has a pronatalist fertility policy (which it does not), high levels of maternity leaves and benefits, and a low minimum age at marriage. Maternity benefit policies on average are less liberal than those in most European countries (Kamerman, Kahn, and Kingston, 1983), and in most states women can marry on their own consent by age 18, an age similar to that in most of the countries studied.

The United States fits the pattern for high teenage fertility in that it is far less open about sexual matters than most countries with low teenage birthrates, and a smaller proportion of its income is distributed to families on the bottom rungs of the economic ladder. These findings suggest two factors are key to the United States' high teenage fertility: an ambivalent, sometimes puritanical attitude about sex, and the existence of a large, economically deprived underclass. . . .

In the 37-country study, the United States does not appear to be more restrictive than low-fertility countries in the provision of contraceptive services to teenagers; however, comparable data could not be obtained on the provision of contraceptives free of charge or at very low cost—a factor that appears to be important in terms of accessibility in the case studies. In this respect, the United States is more restrictive than the other 5 countries studied in detail—all of which have much lower adolescent fertility and pregnancy rates than the United States. The very high levels of religiosity reported for the United States is probably one factor underlying the low rating of the United States on openness about sex. It is also noteworthy that the United States scores relatively low among the countries studied on the measures of availability of contraceptive education in the schools.

Intercountry differences in teenage fertility and in teenage pregnancy are *not* mainly due to the fact that these rates are much higher among U.S. black than white teenagers. The birthrates of white American teenagers are higher than those of teenagers in any Western European country (Westoff et al., 1983). Similarly, U.S. pregnancy rates for those young teenagers are higher than those in all developed countries for which there are data.[1]

---

[1]Canada, Czechoslovakia, Denmark, England and Wales, Finland, France, Hungary, the Netherlands, New Zealand, Norway, Scotland, Sweden.

THE SIX COUNTRY CASE STUDIES

Two commonly held beliefs about teenage pregnancy are refuted in the case studies: teenagers are *not* precluded by their presumed immaturity from using contraceptives consistently and effectively; and teenagers in the United States are *not* more sexually experienced than adolescents in other countries with lower pregnancy rates.

With the possible exception of younger teenagers in Canada, national differences in the percentage of teenagers who have ever had intercourse appear to contribute little or nothing to the variations in teenage pregnancy rates. . . .

In the five countries other than the United States, contraceptive use, particularly the pill, appears to be greater than in the United States—among younger as well as older teenagers. Physicians and clinics in these countries encourage pill use among teenagers; and in some of the countries, there have been active campaigns addressed to young men to encourage the use of condoms. . . .

Does the availability of contraceptives, sex education, and abortion services in the United States encourage sexual promiscuity and thereby account for the higher teenage pregnancy rates in the United States? The findings suggest this cannot be the case, since availability is generally greater in countries with lower teenage pregnancy rates. . . .

Abortions are available free of charge in England and Wales and in France. The cost to the woman is low in Canada and Sweden and is small enough in the Netherlands not to be prohibitive. In more than two-thirds of U.S. states, the full price of an abortion must be paid by the woman, whether or not she can afford it; and, because abortion services tend to be concentrated in populous metropolitan areas, costs can include not only the fee for the abortion itself, but travel and hotel expenses. Access to abortion in some of the countries studied, however, is more restrictive than in the United States with regard to parental consent, gestational age, required waiting period, legally required overnight hospital stays, and required approval by an additional doctor or doctors or a medical committee. . . .

Sex and contraceptive education in the schools differs widely among the case-study countries. Sweden has by far the most extensive program. In the Netherlands, although there is little formal school sex education beyond the facts of reproduction, widespread public education via all the media is superior to that of any of the countries studied except, possibly, Sweden.

In short, teenagers living in countries where contraceptive services, sex education in and out of the schools, and abortion services are widely available have lower rates of adolescent pregnancy and do not have appreciably higher levels of sexual experience than do teenagers in the United States.

The findings from the 37–country study suggest generous maternity leaves and benefits are associated with higher fertility rates among older teenagers. . . . The United States does not have generous policies compared to other countries, even when private programs, as well as public subsidy, are taken into account (Kamerman, Kahn, and Kingston, 1983). Nevertheless, it has been suggested that U.S. Aid to Families with Dependent Children—a benefit largely limited to single mothers, a very high proportion of whom are teenagers—encourages out-of-wedlock fertility in the United States.

All of the countries in the case studies have more generous health and welfare provisions for the general population and for mothers than does the United States; and several, like the United States, provide special financial assistance for single mothers. Yet these countries all have lower teenage fertility rates than the United States. Differences in welfare assistance to mothers, or to single mothers, does not explain the differentials in teenage birthrates between the United States and the other countries and they do not explain the differences in abortion rates. . . .

Teenagers' prospects for economic improve-ment do not appear to be appreciably greater in the five case-study countries than in the United States; nor is the educational achievement of young people greater. However, more extensive health, welfare, and unemployment benefits in the other countries keep poverty from being as deep or as widespread as it is in the United States. The findings from the 37–country study suggest more equitable distribution of household income is associated with lower fertility among younger teenagers. The inequality of income distribution appears to be contributing to the differences between teenage birthrates in the United States and those in other developed countries. . . .

To summarize . . . : teenagers in these other countries apparently are *not* too immature to use contraceptives effectively; the availability of welfare services does *not* seem correlated with higher adolescent fertility; teenage pregnancy rates are *lower* in countries where there is *greater* availability of contraceptive and abortion services and of sex education; adolescent sexual activity in the United States is not very different from what it is in countries that have much *lower* teenage pregnancy rates; although the pregnancy rate of American blacks is much higher than that of whites, the white rate is still much higher than the teenage pregnancy rates in the other case-study countries; teenage unemployment appears to be at least as serious a problem in all the countries studied as it is in the United States, and American teenagers have at least as much schooling as those in most of the countries studied that have lower pregnancy rates. Because the other case-study countries have more extensive public health and welfare benefit systems, however, they do not have so extensive an economically deprived underclass as does the United States. However, the differences in teenage pregnancy rates would probably not be eliminated if socioeconomic status could be controlled. . . .

By and large, Sweden has been the most active of the countries studied in developing programs and policies to reduce teenage pregnancy.

Sweden has *lower* teenage pregnancy rates than have all of the countries examined, except for the Netherlands, although teenagers begin intercourse at earlier ages in Sweden. . . .

None of the five case-study countries has developed government-sponsored programs designed to discourage teenagers from engaging in sexual relations—even at young ages—a program advocated in the United States and rewarded through government subsidies. . . .

POSSIBLE APPROACHES

Several U.S. communities have instituted school-based health clinics that provide contraceptive services—usually in partnership with health, youth-serving, or other nonprofit agencies. In many cases, parental consent is required to enroll in the clinics (Dryfoos, 1985). Contraception, however, is only one of many health services offered, so the parent is not specifically informed when contraceptive services are being obtained. . . .

A complementary approach would be to enhance the current family planning clinic system . . . to provide free or low-cost contraceptive services to all teenagers who want them. . . . In fact, however, although the high unmet need for family planning services among teenagers in the United States is well documented, federal subsidies in real dollars have declined. Moreover, in many communities family planning clinics . . . tend to be stigmatized by teenagers who avoid them in the belief that they are restricted to very poor patients, that services are not confidential, that the surroundings are shabby and unclean, the services poor, and the treatment of patients disrespectful (Kisker et al., 1985). Advertising that portrays the clinic services as inviting, professional, confidential, and available to all segments of the community can counteract this negative image. In Planned Parenthood and some neighborhood health clinics, however, the trend toward charging a flat fee to all patients is likely to discourage teenage enrollment.

The growing reliance on health maintenance organizations (HMOs) to increase health coverage while reducing health costs provides another opportunity to extend family planning services to teenagers. There is no reason why HMOs cannot establish special adolescent clinics on the Swedish model to provide contraceptive services confidentially as part of a general health-care service. . . .

The U.S. federal government does not mandate or encourage the inclusion of sex education courses in public schools. . . . Although numerous public opinion polls show that American parents overwhelmingly approve of sex education in the schools, local school districts have tended to be timid about establishing courses because of fear of minority, but highly vocal, opposition. Although not all the countries studied put much emphasis on school sex education, the evidence from Sweden suggests comprehensive sex education programs can help reduce teenage pregnancy. . . .

The federal and state governments are in a position to influence the development and establishment of school sex education courses. By asserting that sex education is desirable, they could help to legitimate the inclusion of sex education courses in the curricula. Congress, by providing subsidies for the development of curricula, for teacher-training programs, and perhaps for some demonstration programs could further encourage such instruction. State governments can promote sex education by offering selected subsidies, and providing practical help in curriculum development.

In the United States . . . sex is treated far less openly and is surrounded by more ambivalence than it is in most of the countries in the case studies. In virtually all of the countries examined, for example, information about contraception and sexuality is far more available through the media than it is in the United States; condoms are more widely distributed; and advertisements for contraceptives are far more ubiquitous. . . .

The self-imposed restrictions on contraceptive advertising in the media are incongruous in an era when virtually every other product, including vaginal douches, sanitary napkins, and hemorrhoid preparations, is advertised everywhere and without protest. . . . It seems likely that if the restrictions were lifted, some manufacturers would develop effective advertising campaigns. . . .

There is also a need to disseminate more realistic information about the health risks of the pill (minimal for teenagers) and about its extensive benefits (Ory et al., 1983). Most Americans are badly misinformed on this subject (Gallup, 1985). It is probable that the development of new methods more appropriate for teenagers who have episodic sex—such as a once-a-month pill—could greatly reduce teenage pregnancies in the United States. Yet funds for contraceptive development have declined in real terms in recent years in the United States and research into a monthly pill is further hampered by governmental restrictions on abortion-related expenditures.

In general, American teenagers have inherited the worst of all possible worlds insofar as their exposure to messages about sex are concerned: movies, music, radio, and television tell them nonmarital sex is romantic, exciting, and titillating; premarital sex and cohabitation are visible ways of life among the adults they see and hear about; their own parents or their parents' friends are likely to be divorced or separated but involved in sexual relationships. Yet, at the same time, young people get the message (now subsidized by the federal government) that good girls

should say no. Little that teenagers see or hear about sex informs them about contraception or the consequences of sexual activity. . . . Such mixed messages lead to the kind of ambivalence about sex that stifles communication between partners and exposes young people to increased risk of pregnancy. . . . Increasing the legitimacy and availability of contraception and of sex education is likely to result in declining pregnancy rates, without raising teenage sexual activity rates to any great extent. . . .

REFERENCES

DRYFOOS, J. G. (1985) "School-based health clinics: A new approach to preventing adolescent pregnancy?" *Family Planning Perspectives*, 17, 70.

GALLUP ORGANIZATION, THE (1985) "Attitudes towards contraception," unpublished report to the American College of Obstetricians and Gynecologists. Princeton, NJ.

KAMERMAN, S. B., A. J. KAHN and P. KINGSTON (1983) *Income Transfers for Families with Children: An Eight-Country Study.* Philadelphia: Temple University Press.

KISKER, E. et al. (1985) "Teenagers talk about sex, pregnancy and contraception," *Family Planning Perspectives*, 17, 83.

ORY, H. W., J. D. FORREST and R. LINCOLN (1983) *Making Choices: Evaluating the Health Risks and Benefits of Birth Control Methods* New York: Alan Guttmacher Institute.

WESTOFF, C. F., G. CALOT and A. D. FOSTER (1983) "Teenage fertility in developed nations, 1971–1980," *Family Planning Perspectives*, 15, 105.

Introduction

The next article by John Caldwell and his Australian collaborators is a kind of detective story. It tries to answer the question, "Why did Sri Lankan women begin to marry at later ages than they had in the past?"

The obvious answer, "Because they were trying to limit their childbearing," has been under suspicion for nearly two centuries. It was then that Thomas Malthus, the first *demographer* (or scientific student of population) pointed out that late marriage is one way societies keep population growth under control. He called it a "preventive check" on population. (In the absence of birth control technology, this is a much better way of controlling population than "positive checks" such as famine and disease.)

So, when demographers today find a developing society in which late marriage is the norm, they suspect that people there are not practicing contraception, yet want (or need) to limit births.

In Sri Lanka, the authors show, the female mean age at marriage rose from 18.3 years in 1901 to 24.7 years in 1981. Was that change aimed at limiting births? No, the authors say, the change resulted from a loss of fear about some matters that had traditionally worried parents. These included teenage sex and pregnancy, the elopement of young lovers, and sexual contact between young people of different castes.

As these fears abated, for reasons the authors discuss, the need to marry young disappeared. At the same time, traditional values supporting early marriage disappeared with the collapse of Sri Lanka's agrarian society.

18

Marriage Delay and the Fertility Decline in Sri Lanka

John Caldwell
Indra Gajanayake
Bruce Caldwell
Pat Caldwell

Recent decades have witnessed rising ages at marriage for females and parallel or subsequent declines in female fertility in much of Asia . . . The question arises as to the motivation for change. And since most of the actors in these demographic dramas are still alive, it is possible to investigate these behavioral changes. Sri Lanka is an obvious laboratory for such work. Kirk (1969: 80–81) viewed it as a case in which late marriage had reduced fertility. . . . Certainly, changes in female marriage patterns have contributed to fertility decline, explaining, according to Fernando (1972), almost all the 1963–69 decline, and, according to Alam and Cleland

(1981), 59% of that in 1963–71 and 46% of that in 1971–75.

MARRIAGE TRENDS

The singulate mean age of marriage, as shown in Table 1, was, as early as 1901, 18.3 years. . . . It is probable, however, that the census data in 1901 and in the next two censuses overstated age at marriage because of a failure to include some unregistered marriages, which were not separately identified by the census until 1946 (ESCAP Secretariat, 1976: 110–111). . . .

By 1981 Sri Lankan women typically married at almost 25 years of age, comparable with most of the industrialized world. The average age at marriage had risen by almost 4 years in less than three decades, a period during which fertility

Source: Caldwell, John, Indra Gajanayake, Bruce Caldwell and Pat Caldwell (1989) "Is marriage delay a multiphasic response to pressures for fertility decline? The case of Sri Lanka," *Journal of Marriage and the Family,* 51, May, 337–351.

TABLE 1. Singulate Mean Age at Marriage, 1901–1975

Year	Males	Females	Average Annual Change for Females Over Preceding Period	Difference between Males and Females
1901	24.6	18.3	—	6.3
1911	26.5	20.8	+0.25	5.7
1921	27.0	21.4	+0.06	5.6
1946	27.0	20.7	−0.03	6.3
1853	27.2	20.9	+0.03	6.3
1963	27.9	22.1	+0.12	5.8
1971	28.0	23.5	+0.18	4.5
1975	28.2	25.1	+0.40	3.1
1981	27.9	24.7	−0.07	3.2

Sources: 1901–71: CICRED, *The Population of Sri Lanka* (Colombo: Department of Census and Statistics, 1974), p. 40; 1975: David P. Smith, *Age at First Marriage*, Comparative Studies, Cross-National Summaries, No. 7 (London: World Fertility Survey, 1980), p. 3; 1981: T. Nadarajah, "Marital Status," in Department of Census and Statistics, Ministry of Plan Implementation, *Census of Population and Housing 1981: General Report* (Colombo, 1986), p. 100.

Note: All figures are from the census except those for 1975, which are from the Sri Lanka Fertility Survey.

had fallen by over one-third. It was pertinent to ask whether the two phenomena were related. . . .

THE RESEARCH PROGRAM

The field work upon which this study draws was carried out in 1985 and 1987 in seven areas in Southwest Sri Lanka: two villages, two urban slums in inner Colombo, one squatter area in outer Colombo, a middle-class sector of Colombo, and a commuting area outside Colombo. . . . All sites were predominantly Sinhalese except for the inner Colombo slumbs, which were largely Moorish (Muslim). The research included participant observation and anthropological methods (cf. Caldwell, Reddy, and Caldwell, 1982), and surveys. The population studied consisted of 10,964 persons living in 1,974 households. . . .

AGE AT MARRIAGE FOR OUR SAMPLE

The singulate mean ages at marriage of males and females were 28 and 24 years, respectively, the male age approximating that of the 1981 census while the female age was a little lower. . . .

In common with World Fertility Survey analyses, our data show only small differentials in the age of female marriage by urban-rural residence (cf. McCarthy, 1982: 11; Trussell, 1980: 23), but significant although declining differences by education and religion. Women with schooling up to lower secondary exhibit median ages at first marriage about one year above the few who did not go to school, while higher education levels add at least another three years. The impact of education on male age at first marriage is similar but not as great. These differentials explain only part of the change in age at marriage since 1953. . . .

THE NATURE OF MARRIAGE

We asked, "When you married, did your parents make the arrangements about whom you should marry or did you make the arrangements yourself?" The findings are presented in Table 2.

Clearly, the modern Sri Lankan marriage pattern has not emerged recently, as one-quarter of prewar unions were love marriages. The distinctive recent change has been the near disappearance of differentials by education. . . .

Urbanization, education, movement up the

TABLE 2. Percentage of Love Marriages by Period of Wife's Education, 1913–1985

Period	n	None (%)	Up to 9th Grade (%)	Beyond 9th Grade (%)	All Marriages (%)
1913–1939	137	20	28	38	27
1940–1959	317	25	35	46	34
1960–1269	321	36	35	54	40
1970–1979	510	49	51	74	59
1980–1985	532	72	72	78	74
1913–1985	1,817	41	50	68	53

socioeconomic scale, being Sinhalese (either Buddhist or Christian), and the passage of time all tend to increase the proportion of love marriages. Nevertheless, it is not a simple case of an age conflict, for both the younger generation and their parents face gains and losses from either type of marriage. For the young, a love marriage means the freedom of their own choice and a greater chance of achieving compatibility, and nine-tenths of them give this as their first positive reaction to such marriages. Nevertheless, only one-fifth regard love marriages as having no disadvantages; two-thirds report love marriage means a weakening of ties with parents and other relatives. . . . The parental generation also reports two major gains: no obligation to pay dowry or meet wedding expenses, and freedom from the responsibility of making the right choice about a suitable partner. . . . The parental case against love marriages is more complex. One-fifth of the parents of unmarried daughters over 15 years of age were entirely in favor of such marriages, while another fifth were completely hostile and feared such freedom would result in cross-caste or cross-religion marriages. The rest worried about the weaker subsequent relations with children or the fact that a love marriage would prove their children had not trusted them to make the best selection of mates. Many thought the young would make unsuitable choices. . . .

The real situation is more complex than the attitudinal data might suggest, as was shown by

our examination of love marriages in the predominantly middle-class, area of the periphery of Colombo, where 60% of marriages were for love. Among all love marriages, the parents had agreed to accept the marriage before it occurred in 86% of all cases . . . and were subsequently reconciled in another 2%. Thus a complete break with parents occurs in only one-eighth of love marriages. . . . In the arranged marriages, 95% of wives expressed themselves as having fully approved of their parents' choice. One-sixth of all marriages (nearly all love marriages) were cross-caste and one-fifth cross-religion. . . .

The need for meeting dowry costs is commonly cited as a reason for marriage delay. We studied dowry and marriage costs in six of the research localities. Problems of dowry are increasing and dowry is being converted to onerous cash exactions.

Rapid marriage change has not yet led to a universal expectation of the newly married couple living on their own immediately after marriage. Only one-third did not live with their parents, and most of this group were not able to do so because they had refused an arranged marriage. . . . One-fifth of the couples moved out within a year, but the typical stay was 2 to 3 years. . . .

In one village and in the Colombo peripheral residential area, we explored the question of preferred marriage ages. The great majority believe the best age for a girl to marry is in the range of 22–25 years, and for a boy, in the 24–30 range.

Asked why women should not marry at a younger age, three-quarters of all replies were in terms of maturity and of being old enough for married life, to manage a household, and to be a capable mother . . . Interestingly, although no one ever reported that a marriage had been delayed in order to limit family size, one-quarter of those commenting on the disadvantage of younger marriages said the couple were likely to end up with too many children. The emphasis with regard to boys not marrying younger is on acquiring a secure job with sufficient income. . . .

THE DELAY OF MARRIAGE

The central question is which considerations delay marriage? Table 3 summarizes our findings.

Less than two-fifths of marriages were delayed by such problems, and on average they were postponed for only about two years. . . . There remains the question of delays before a specific coupling is suggested. The search for an employed bridegroom is an obvious example. Another is the feeling that couples should have enough saved to permit a successful marriage. . . . Nevertheless, there is some overlap here with the delays already measured, and we probably still have not explained as much as a third of the delay in female marriage since 1946. In an

TABLE 3. Factors Delaying Sri Lankan Marriages Where a Potential Partner Has Already Been Identified

Cause of Delay	Percentage of Marriages Affected	Median Delay to These Marriages
Horoscope problems	7%	2 years
Employment problems	7	2 years
Dowry problems	3	2 years
Child objecting to parents' choice	5	2 years
Parents objecting to child's choice	9	2 years
Waiting until older sibling married	5	4 years

effort to do this we focused on older women (those over 55 years). . . .

The Changes in the Marriage Market

This approach yielded near consensus from the older population. The core of the explanation is that girls in traditional society play a negligible role in their early marriage. . . . The driving force is the parental generation, and when parents relax their efforts, there is no counterbalancing pressure from the young women to maintain the early age of marriage. . . .

The traditional situation was that parents moved urgently to marry their daughters from the time of menarche. . . . The dominating fear of delay was premarital pregnancy or elopement. . . . The main apprehension was of cross-caste marriage. Then both parents and children would suffer because of the consequent estrangement. . . . If the parents did not break relations with their erring child, they too were ostracized by their relatives. . . .

There were mechanisms for facilitating early marriage. . . . Dowry more often took the form of transfer of land or promises of transfer. The worthy bridegroom came from a family that could provide him with access to family land or to a family business. There was less stress on his having employment and a secure income. There was also less shame in having an uneducated daughter and less difficulty in arranging a good marriage for such a daughter.

What changed was . . . social values and more important than any other factor was the decline in the importance of caste. . . . The caste system was eroded by urbanization, the growth of the nonagrarian economy, and the spread of education. The importance of caste lingers with regard to marriage, but what was once heinous sin is now closer to gaucheness and gracelessness. . . .

Three other factors allowed rapid change with regard to marriage. . . . The first is the education of girls. . . . Most Sinhalese parents have been prepared to educate daughters. . . . By 1971 girls were as likely to be in school as boys, even at age 15–19 (Wijemanne, 1976: 216). Pride in educational attainment competed with pride in the right marriage. . . . Education into adolescence not only mechanically displaced marriage but it implied the tempting prospect of some family financial return from subsequent employment. . . . When asked about the specific changes delaying marriage (as distinct from allowing its delay), nine out of ten older women made first reference to the education of girls. . . .

The second factor is the attitude toward premarital pregnancy and birth. . . . We researched all cases we could locate of premarital pregnancy or birth and the sequelae. Some young women were quickly married, others had jobs found for them elsewhere, and babies were adopted out. But, by regional standards, it was not a story of unrelieved tragedy, and not enough to give rise to the ever-present apprehension in the Middle East or much of rural India as to the disaster that might follow if postpubertal girls are not quickly married off. In Sri Lanka, women's position is relatively good and Buddhism does not preach that men are largely judged by their womenfolk's sexual morality.

The third factor is how easily households accommodate unmarried adult daughters. They and their mothers share jobs and converse easily. The atmosphere is not made tense by any dominating feeling that the only matter of importance is the marriage of the young woman. . . .

THE FAILURE TO MARRY OR TO REMAIN MARRIED

. . . In the locality where we followed up our earlier studies of never-married women and men, 8% of all women over 30 and 5% of men over 35 belonged to this category. Half of each group now believed they were unlikely ever to marry. Some of the problem was the belief that parents

and children should agree on desirable partners. In the case of the women, one-third had proposed a marriage that their parents refused, while half the parents had proposed a marriage the daughters refused. Among the men the refusals had all been on their side and had occurred with only one-quarter of them. In the case of a majority of unmarried daughters, parents are still attempting to find a spouse, but almost all the sons are now being left to make their own decisions.

About two-fifths of the unmarried women and two-thirds of the unmarried men said that they were not really interested in marriage. For about one-sixth of the women the reason was their careers, while an equal number reported unfortunate love experiences. Around one-tenth of both the unmarried women and men suffered from mental or physical handicaps sufficiently great to prevent marriage. One-third of the women, but no men, said it was just a matter of locating the right person, while one-eighth of the men said they had never been in an economic position to marry. . . .

Of the ever married, the divorced made up less than 0.5%, the separated only 4.2%, the polygynously married 0.2%, and the polyandrously married less than 0.1%.

THE NATURE OF THE MARRIAGE TRANSITION

. . . The first finding from our study is that there seems no evidence that rising age at female marriage was a response to pressure on family size. . . .

Very low age at marriage is essentially a parental response and not primarily the preference of the persons being married. . . . If there is no parental pressure, female marriage might be postponed for years after puberty without strong demand from the young women for marriage, provided that their peers are not all marrying, there is a place for them in the parental home and they are not made to feel they are a burden or abnormal, they have a role, such as, for example, the one provided by education and employment, and, finally, there is no emphasis on young women needing sexual relations. . . . All these conditions hold in Sri Lanka, and when society changed, there was a rise in the age at marriage.

What changed was the situation of the girls' parents. No longer did they have to arrange their daughters' marriages so early. No longer was it strictly necessary to arrange marriages at all. . . . Caste barriers fell, and cross-caste marriage was no longer so feared. Neither children nor parents were likely to be completely ostracized if it occurred. Love marriages and elopement became more acceptable. The good marriage itself was no longer the completely dominant aim for the parents of the daughters.

Once marriage ages could rise, there were reasons for the delay of marriage, such as the acquiring of skills, the finding of employment and the raising of dowries, and the possibility of making a "better" marriage if one were educated and employed; but these aims were possible only because marriage could be delayed. . . .

The aim is still universal marriage. The levels of bachelorhood and spinsterhood may rise, but this is not certain, and neither state may ultimately much exceed 5% of each age cohort. Furthermore, rates of divorce and separation remain low. What has occurred is the freedom of the age at marriage for females to rise from low levels. . . . The emphasis of the need for the husband to have secure employment explains why the age at first marriage rose and then fell during the 1970s and 1980s as unemployment rose and later fell. The proper timing for marriage does not depend on the ability to afford separate housing, as most Sri Lanka parents are prepared for the newly married couple to live with them. . . .

In the study of marriage in South India (Caldwell et al., 1983) we identified a growing emphasis on the need for wives and mothers to be mature, and a marriage squeeze, as two important elements in a rise to an age at first marriage that

is still far below that of Sir Lanka. The first is also an element in the Sri Lankan situation. The second, although foreseen in Sri Lanka, appeared by the 1980s to be a minor factor, partly because the age gap between spouses was rapidly narrowing. In Sri Lanka the timing of marriage change seems to be most closely related to social and educational change, the rise of the nonagricultural economy, and the capacity of that economy to provide employment. There seems no reason to ascribe marriage change to impersonal demographic forces; rather, parents and children have been reassessing their society and its economy.

REFERENCES

ALAM, IQBAL, and JOHN CLELAND. 1981. Illustrative Analysis: Recent Fertility Trends in Sri Lanka. Scientific Reports, No. 25. London: World Fertility Survey.

CALDWELL, JOHN C., P. H. REDDY, and PAT CALDWELL. 1982. "The causes of demographic change in rural South India." Population and Development Review 8:689–727.

CADLWELL, JOHN C., P. H. REDDY, and PAT CALDWELL. 1983. "The causes of marriage change in South India." Population Studies 37:343–361.

ESCAP SECRETARIAT. 1976. "Marital status." Pp. 110–122 in Economic and Social Council for Asia and the Pacific, Population of Sri Landa. Bangkok: United Nations.

FERNANDO, DALLAS, F. S. 1972. "Recent fertility decline in Ceylon." Population Studies 26:445–453.

KIRK, DUDLEY. 1969. "Natality in developing countries: Recent trends and prospects." Pp. 75–98 in S. J. Behrman, L. Corsa, and R. Freedman, Fertility and Family Planning: A World View. Ann Arbor: University of Michigan Press.

MCCARTHY, JAMES. 1982. Differentials in Age at First Marriage. Comparative Studies: Cross-national Summaries, No. 19. London: World Fertility Survey.

SMITH, DAVID P. 1980. Age at First Marriage. Comparative Studies: Cross-national Summaries, No. 7. London: World Fertility Survey.

TRUSSELL, JAMES. 1980. Illustrative Analysis: Age at First Marriage in Sri Lanka and Thailand. Scientific Reports, No. 13. London: World Fertility Survey.

WIJEMANNE, E. L. 1976. "Population growth and educational development." Pp. 208–233 in Population of Sri Lanka, ESCAP Country Monograph Series, No. 4, Bangkok: United Nations.

Discussion Questions

1. Knodel and van de Walle conclude that "Although the European experience confirms a loose relationship between socioeconomic modernization and fertility decline, it also suggests that there was an important innovation-diffusion dimension to the reproductive revolution that swept the continent." What do they mean? How would you apply their conclusion to China's experience with fertility decline?

2. Kagitcibasi finds that about one American woman in ten thinks it is very important to have a child "to have someone to depend on when you are old." Could this account for the teenage pregnancies Jones and her collaborators discuss in their article?

3. Ukaegbu finds child mortality plays a very important part in explaining childbearing in rural Nigeria. What is the relationship between child mortality and mother's fertility? Would Knodel and van de Walle agree with Ukaegbu's conclusion?

4. In a society in which almost everyone is a parent, not being a parent can cause people distress. Could this fact explain Kagitcibasi's finding that children are highly valued in countries where people bear a lot of children?

5. Judging by the data Jones and her collaborators provide, American teenagers seem very eager to bear children, compared with teenagers in other countries. Could this be because they hold the same values about childbearing as Nigerian villagers?

6. In the last few decades, Chinese parents have had to significantly scale down their childbearing, compared to past generations. How do you suppose this has affected their family life? Their work life?

Data Collection Exercises

1. What do Chinese teenagers know about, and think about sex? Collect information on teenager mating attitudes and practices in China and see if you can find a relationship with the level of teenage pregnancy in that country.

2. Knodel and van de Walle say that improved family-planning programs will do more to reduce fertility than the same amount of money spent on economic development. Choose any of the countries Kagitcibasi has studied and find out

PART IV

Parenting and Childcare

In most societies having a child is the "normal" expectation of marriage. Despite worldwide trends toward later marriage, the postponement of childbearing, and smaller family size, most women will become mothers. For both mothers and fathers, having a child is a bigger change than marriage, and it could be argued, initiates a more permanent relationship. The change is presumably more complicated for women than men, since women typically face a greater burden of responsibility for the care of children.

One of the things that distinguishes Western family life now from families in the past is the extent to which individuals can exercise choice over their family circumstances. Contraceptive technology and use has made parenthood, for the first time in history, a choice for the vast majority of women. According to recent statistics, 44% of married or cohabiting women in the less developed countries use contraception, compared to 74% in Canada and 68% in the United States (*The World's Women: A Profile,* Population Reference Bureau, Washington, D.C. 1985). Although the availability of contraception is limited by cost and constrained by religious belief, women generally have more reproductive control than ever before.

An increasing number of women in Australia, Europe, and North America choose to be childless. Nevertheless there are still strong pronatalist pressures to encourage childbearing. Attitude surveys find that childless women are consistently negatively stereotyped. Even the word "childless" suggests that something is missing. Pronatalism is much stronger in some societies than in others. For example, in the past in China "the most unfilial act of a son was being unable to produce sons to carry on the family name . . . for years it was permissible for a husband to take a second wife if his first wife did not bear sons." (Huang, 1982: 775)

Shifting Parental Responsibilities

Many share the view that pregnancy creates a unique bond between mothers and their offspring which has implications for the subsequent care of infants and children. Alice Rossi (1984) has made a persuasive argument in favor of what she calls a biosocial perspective on parenting. The biosocial perspective stresses the influence of physiological factors on sexual and parenting scripts. In Rossi's view, the relationship of a mother and her child through pregnancy, birth, and breast-feeding is fundamental to parenting. The ties established in these early stages will inevitably persist as the child grows. This for Rossi implies a great deal about the potential for men and women to ever have equal responsibility for the care of very young children. This is a contentious case to make at a time when mothers want and need (because of the economic necessity of paid work) far greater childcare commitment from fathers.

Whether or not we accept Rossi's argument, it is clear that much "mothering" behavior is historically and culturally specific. The notion of the mother's exclusive responsibility for childcare evolved in response to what Ehrenreich and English (1978) describe as the discovery of childhood at the end of the nineteenth century. A number of factors contributed to this discovery. Perhaps the most important was a decline in infant mortality and a subsequent drop in the birth rate. At the same time there was increased concern for child labor, and demands for compulsory education and public health reform.

The child-centered household and the ideal of full-time motherhood became entrenched in the first half of the twentieth century. Implicit in the idea of the motherhood mandate is the assumption that fathers in the past were not involved in childrearing. On the contrary, fathers in preindustrial North America were active parents—to their sons! As soon as a young boy was able to, he accompanied his father as he worked.

Why have Western fathers typically had such little involvement in the routine care of young children? Is it because fathers did not want to be involved, and because they had more power in the marital relationship, were able to avoid such responsibility? Or is it because they lack experience and are unclear about what to do? To some extent low involvement by fathers is a self-fulfilling prophecy. Fathers have very little preparation for the possibility of caring for infants or young children, are likely to feel awkward, and thus experience failure in their attempts to help.

Research investigating the interactions of fathers and infants suggests that men "tend to avoid high involvement in infant care because infants do not respond to their repetoire of skills and men have difficulty acquiring the skills needed to comfort the infant." (Rossi, 1984:8) For Rossi the solution is to teach fathers about parenting and thereby encourage their participation.

What about fathers who have sole responsibility for the care of young children because of death or marital breakdown? Risman (1987) predicted that men who become single fathers would act like mothers in their relationships with their young children. She compared a sample of single fathers, single mothers, and dual-earner couples on variables related to housework and parent-child interaction. The results supported the hypothesis that much of the variation in gender-typed behavior is a result of "situational exigencies and opportunities" rather than biology or socialization. Consequently, when situational factors change, "divorced, widowed, or even married fathers are capable of providing the nurturance that young children require despite their gendered socialization."

This research leads to a different conclusion regarding greater future involvement by fathers in nurturing their children. Whereas Rossi feels fathers will benefit from being taught nurturant behavior, Risman's research suggests more structural changes. Fathers will become more involved in parenting when structural constraints are reduced.

Childcare Issues

Two changes in family life have had a significant impact on children and childrearing. One is increased marital breakdown; the other is increased labor-force participation of mothers.

Since 1970 there has been a dramatic increase in the number of single-parent households in North America. In the United States half of all children will live in a fatherless household before the age of eighteen (Glick, 1984). Since women are more likely to retain custody of children at divorce and less likely to remarry, most single-parent households are female headed. In North America, the most pressing concerns of single mothers are financial. The financial inequities of no-fault divorce are discussed in Part Seven.

Throughout the world increased labor-force participation of married women affects both the practices and ideals of parenting and childcare. Over half of all women are in the labor force; this rises to over 60 percent in the more developed countries. In Western countries the most dramatic changes are in the employment of mothers of young children. Women's employment rates by age of youngest child for the United States and Canada are remarkably similar. Approximately 50 percent of all mothers of preschool children and over 60 percent of mothers of school-age children are in the labor force. It is predicted that by 1995 over three-quarters of school-age children and two-thirds of preschool children in the United States will have a gainfully employed mother. For preschool children, this represents a 35 percent increase from 1985 (Hofferth and Phillips, 1987:561).

In some European countries family policies have been designed to ease parental responsibilities, although most focus on maternity, not parenthood. While it is implicit that juggling paid work and family roles is a mother's problem, there is public support for both. For example, France has extensive out-of-home child care, while Hungary's policy has been to support new mothers by providing income maintainance and job protection. (Kamerman, 1979)

Because of the association of women with domestic work, and because of women's lesser power in the family, child care is usually thought of as a mother's, not a parent's responsibility. Men's greater economic opportunities reinforce this assumption.

Sweden is the only European country where family policy is based on the assumption that parenting is a responsibility shared by fathers and mothers. However, because of structured inequality in the labor force and continued stereotyping of parental responsibilities, Swedish fathers do not generally take advantage of parental leave. They are, however, far more active parents than men in other Western countries.

In most other Western countries and certainly in Canada and the United States, policy lags behind labor-force trends in providing support to employed parents. In the United States less than forty percent of employed mothers receive maternity benefits and these are usually over a very brief time period (Hofferth and Phillips, 1987:568). In North America demand far exceeds supply and there is a strong relationship between the adequacy of childcare arrangements and social class.

Although we tend to underestimate the importance of kinship ties in North America, relatives play a key role in providing childcare.

Cross-Cultural Experiences
of Growing Up

Cross-cultural comparisons help to identify ways our practices and ideas about childrearing are culture bound.

In large part, cross-cultural differences in language, customs, and values reflect differences in how we have been socialized. While recognizing that parents are individuals who have specific goals and expectations for their children, we can see that socialization takes place in a social and cultural context. The context of socialization includes class and ethnicity, family structure, and individual predisposition. How children are socialized will depend on a myriad of factors: where they live, the language they learn first, whether they grow up in a single-parent or multi-adult household, and so on.

Inferences can be drawn from such variables as age of mother at first birth, fertility, and longevity to suggest how parenting patterns vary from one generation to another and from society to society. Where life expectancy is short, marriages occur at a young age and childrearing is lifelong. Alternately, where men and women typically live long lives, the postparental period becomes a significant life phase.

Family structure and residence pattern have an important impact on parenting. In joint families (married siblings living together) or stem families (three-generation households), childcare will be shared by a number of adults. Nuclear families, particularly single-parent families, do not have this advantage. As you will see when you read Excerpt 35, the more childcare is shared, the less likely children are to be abused.

Family size and birth order are thought to be important determinants of children's academic success and personality. China (see Excerpt 21) is a particularly interesting test of this question because of the dramatic reductions in family size that have occurred recently. Population control policies, including the 1979 one-family-one-child policy, have in one generation successfully transformed China from a society of large families to a society of small families.

The first two excerpts in this section describe situations which challenge our thinking about childrearing. The first describes the philosophy of childrearing adopted by the Oneida community, a nineteenth-century American commune. The second excerpt describes the life of street children in a South American city.

Most children are raised by one or both parents, or in a familylike setting. Some experiments in communal living have tried to establish childrearing practices whereby all adults in the group "parent" all children. The Oneida community (see Excerpt 19) which started in the American Northeast in 1835 is an example. Oneida children spent most of the first year of their lives with their biological mothers. Parents were not monogamously married, but married to all adults in the community in what John Noyes the leader called a "complex marriage." After the age of one year, children increasingly became the responsibility of the commune. By age three they no longer lived with their mothers, but slept and ate with other children in the community. Oneida children were nurtured, schooled, and disciplined by all members of the community.

In contrast, the Hutterites, another North American commune, built the community around family ties. Although children were socialized by the community as a whole, they spent evenings and nonschool time with their parents. In Hutterite communities married couples and their children sleep in their own quarters but eat communally (Cavan, 1983).

Excerpt 20 is a fascinating account of the lives of street children in Columbia. These children are among an estimated forty million children living on the streets in South American cities. Surprisingly few of the children are orphans. Only sixteen percent of the children in this study could not locate at least one parent. For the most part they left home because life on the streets promised more. It also promised relief from the poverty, abuse, and neglect they experienced at home.

What makes these youngsters so remarkable is their resiliance and their self-taught survival skills. While we can admire their ability to cope, we can't help but wonder what the future holds for them.

Sex-Role Socialization

Three determinants of status in most cultures are gender, age, and class. For children, adolescents, and adults, gender identity is a fundamental aspect of the development of self-concept. People learn gender through a complex interweaving of experience, expectation, and predisposition. Although research on sex differences find male and female infants and children more alike than different, there are clear differences in adolescents and adults.

One of the reasons for this inconsistency is the pervasiveness of gender stereotyping. Gender stereotypes frame our understanding of the social behavior of males and females from infancy through adulthood. Small behavioral and attitudinal differences in childhood are reinforced through adolescence and become pronounced in adulthood. The process of gender socialization is complex. Children are exposed to many models of behavior and gain a sense of masculinity and femininity from a variety of sources.

The mass media and the schools are important influences. Hundreds of studies of media content have shown the extent to which women are underrepresented, stereotyped, and trivialized by the media. And because children spend more time watching television than they do in school, the media have a greater impact on subsequent self-concepts.

Now, more than ever, gender stereotypes have important implications for a young woman's future. At a time when most women—wherever they live—will likely spend most of their adulthood gainfully employed, early learning of occupational opportunities is very important. It is similarly important for young men to develop parenting skills in anticipation of this responsibility.

Excerpt 22 is about gender (or sex-role) stereotypes in school textbooks in Singapore. Textbooks used in grades one and five in Singapore schools display many of the same stereotypes found in American or Canadian texts. Quah found women were consistently presented as housewives; men in the husband-economic-provider role. She is disturbed about the implications of these stereotypes since the majority of women in Singapore act as if labor-force participation is an incidental matter. They work in low-status, low-paid jobs and leave the labor force at marriage—behaviors clearly not in their long-term best interest.

Adolescence and Beyond

Childhood, adolescence, and adulthood are social constructs that broadly define periods of social, psychological, and biological development. These are generally, but not absolutely, determined by age. Adolescence, as Campbell (1975) describes it, involves a period of unlearning as young people develop a sense of autonomy and independence, and prepare for adult responsibilities.

We generally think of adolescence as a period of rebellion and angst. Yet Daniel Offer's (1988) study of adolescence in fourteen countries found young people to be well-adjusted and content. Generally they shared their parents values. Excerpt 23 finds that young people in Poland also share their parents goals and values. While we might expect that rapid change would create a situation where parents try to preserve tradition and children try to rebel against it, this is not the case in Poland. There, it seems, parents and children alike value family and health above material success. Children want above all to be successful in school and well-liked by their friends.

According to Campbell (1975: 34), the most significant experience of adolescence is "the demise in relative influence of the family as a reference group and the central emotional pillar." However, other influences are tempered because parents continue to control important resources. Young people in Thailand seem to exhibit this dilemma (Excerpt 24). They need to leave their parents' rural households in order to find work and their parents typically hate to see them go. On the other hand, they return periodically to their parents' homes in a process referred to as circular mobility.

While longevity has increased the post-parental period, despite later age at first birth, other factors add to the responsibilities of parents to their older children. Job insecurities and unemployment add to parents' financial responsibility. When their jobs or marriages end, adult children may periodically return to the parental household. Such periods of dependence create a dilemma for both parents and children, as children approach adulthood, yet remain in many ways tied to parents' authority and influence.

Conclusion

The availability of contraception means that more and more women throughout the world are in a position to determine if and when they will have children. Some women will not marry, some will marry and not become parents, some will parent without marrying, and some will marry and parent. Of course there are many factors restricting choice today, so we can't assume that life circumstances necessarily reflect life choices. Not all families are the desired size; not all childless women are voluntarily childless.

Changing attitudes toward childbearing, the changing economic role of children, increased female labor-force participation, and the general availability of birth control have combined to influence declining fertility in the West (see Koo, Suchinran and Griffith, 1987). We can predict that as people in developing countries are affected by similar constraints and opportunities, and as they are increasingly influenced by Western values through the mass media and through education, smaller families will become the norm.

Children everywhere are increasingly valued for psychological reasons (Walters and Walters, 1980: 814). Financial costs may be a major reason for limiting family size, but are not generally considered a major disadvantage of having children. Comparative studies find that the reasons for desiring first children differ from reasons for wanting subsequent children. "The first birth tends to symbolize values relevant to the achievement of adulthood, fulfillment of the marriage, parenthood, and curiosity related motives like the opportunity to experience pregnancy and childbirth; to recreate another life and to witness the growth and development of one's own child (Callen, 1982: 388)." The main value of a second child is companionship to the first.

An important theme throughout this book is that there are similar changes in family living across different societies. Almost everywhere, households are getting smaller, fertility is declining, and marital disruption is increasing. In the West, fewer children will be raised to adulthood by both birthparents. Children now are much more apt to have stepsiblings, half brothers or sisters, stepparents and stepgrandparents. They have a different network of kin than was typical a generation ago, and will have to work out their own rules to govern these relationships.

References

CALLEN, VICTOR J. (1982) "How Do Australians Value Children?" *The Australia and New Zealand Journal of Sociology,* 18, 3, 384–398.

CAMPBELL, ERNEST Q. (1975) *Socialization, Culture and Personality.* Englewood Cliffs: Prentice Hall.

CAVAN, RUTH SHONLE. (1983) "The Family in Communes—An Overview," *International Journal of Sociology of the Family,* 13, (Autumn), 3–15.

EHRENREICH, BARBARA and DEIDRE ENGLISH. (1978) *For Her Own Good.* New York: Anchor Books.

GLICK, PAUL. (1984) "How American Families are Changing," *American Demographics,* (January), pp. 21–25.

HOFFERTH, SANDRA and DEBORAH PHILLIPS. (1987) "Childcare in the United States, 1970 to 1985," *Journal of Marriage and the Family,* 49, No. 4, 559–571.

HUANG, LUCY JEN. (1982) "Planned Fertility of One-Couple/One-Child Policy in the People's Republic of China." *Journal of Marriage and the Family* (August), 775–784.

KAMERMAN, SHEILA. (1979) "Work and Family in Industrialized Societies," *Signs,* 4, No. 4, 632–650.

KOO, HELEN P., C. M. SUCHINDRAN and JANET D. GRIFFITH. (1987) "The Completion of Childbearing: Change and Variation in Timing," *Journal of Marriage and the Family,* 49, No. 4, 281–293.

OFFER, DANIEL. (1988) *The Teen-Aged World.* New York: Plenum Press.

RISMAN, BARBARA. (1987) "Intimate Relationships from a Microsocial Perspective: Men Who Mother," *Gender and Society,* 1, 6–32.

ROSSI, ALICE. (1984) "Gender and Parenthood," *American Sociological Review,* Vol. 49, 1–18.

WALTERS, JAMES and LYNDA H. WALTERS. (1980) "Parent-Child Relationships: A Review, 1970–1979," *Journal of Marriage and the Family,* 42, No. 4, 807–822.

Introduction

The Oneida community was a nineteenth-century American commune. It was a religious community which, like the Shakers and Mormons, tried to purposely redefine family relationships. Both the Oneida and the Shaker communities rejected monogamous marriage and the idea of an exclusive bond between parents and children. The Shakers believed in and practiced celibacy, which in large part accounts for their demise. The Oneida community practiced what their leader John Noyes called "complex marriage," whereby adults considered themselves married to all members of the commune. Marital love or parent-child love was thought to work against the idea of the mutual love and commitment of all members to the group.

Oneida infants were cared for by their birthmothers for their first year, but by age three they were independent members of the larger community and lived apart from their parents. Caring for and disciplining children was the responsibility of the community as a whole.

At a time when schooling for most children in North America was sporadic at best, Oneida children participated in a full day of organized activity not unlike contemporary day-care programs. The point of the comprehensive program was to socialize the next generation of community members. Yet, as this article shows, the long-term effects of being raised in this kind of setting were not what Noyes anticipated.

19
The Children of Oneida:
Heirs to the Promised Land

Susan M. Matarese
Paul G. Salmon

One of history's most remarkable experiments in family organization is found in the Oneida Community, a religious utopia which flourished in northwestern New York State during the nineteenth century.[1] Its social structure and child-rearing practices represented a radical alternative to patterns of community organization based upon the nuclear family. Some of the community's children were the result of one of the earliest experiments in human eugenics. All were raised communally according to religious ideals which stressed cooperation and non-exclusive attachments among community members. The purpose of this essay is to provide a broad overview of the community's unique social organization and resultant child-rearing practices.

Founded in 1848 by radical theologian John Humphrey Noyes, the Oneida Community was based upon the doctrine of "Perfectionism" which held that through union with God, persons could live lives free from sin.[2] Noyes and his three hundred followers sought to emulate the primitive apostolic church in which "believ-ers possessed one heart and one soul and held all things in common."[3] These principles gave Oneida some of its most distinctive features: economic communism, communal sleeping and dining arrangements, government by mutual criticism and collective labour in agriculture, manufacturing and light industry.

The communal ideal extended even to sexual relations and resulted in the . . . controversial practice: "complex marriage."[4] Under this system, monogamous relationships were forbidden and adults . . . were encouraged to have sexual relations with a wide variety of partners. Central to the institution . . . was the practice of "male continence," a method of birth control which allowed the community to separate the propagative from the social functions of sex.[5]

During the first twenty years of the community's history, the number of births was intentionally limited, averaging fewer than two a year.[6] By 1868, however, Noyes had become mindful of the need to develop a new generation of Oneidans to carry out his ideals. He initiated an experiment in human breeding which he called "stirpiculture."[7] During the next ten

Source: Matarese, S. and P. G. Salmon, (1983) "Heirs to the Promised Land: the Children of Oneida," *International Journal of Sociology of the Family,* 13, 2, Autumn, 35–43. Reprinted with permission from *International Journal of Sociology of the Family.*

[1] For an excellent general work dealing with the beliefs and practices of the Oneida Community, see Carden (1969).

[2] Noyes (1849).

[3] Oneida (1867:11).
[4] Carden (1969:49–61).
[5] Noyes (1866).
[6] Oneida (1875:19).
[7] Noyes (1875).

years, fifty-eight children were born as a result of these selected pairings.

According to "Perfectionist" doctrine, children belonged to the entire community, and the women were exhorted to understand they produced children not for their own satisfaction, but for God and communism.[8] Noyes maintained the love of the community was superior to the "special love" engendered by exclusive child-parent bonding. The community's newspaper, the Oneida *Circular*, emphasized the need to "communize the children. . . . as completely as we have all other possessions."[9]

In keeping with this doctrine, the community assumed primary responsibility for child-rearing. . . . There were several reasons for this. First, Noyes wanted to ensure that socialization was standardized as far as possible. To this end, he appointed as caretakers a small group of his most loyal and trusted followers. Second, Noyes feared that an intense attachment between parents and children would threaten the system of complex marriage by encouraging exclusionary loyalties.[10]

Separating parents and children took place in stages.[11] During the first year of life, children were cared for by their mothers, much as in any traditional family. At the age of weaning, however, the community began to take a more active and intrusive role. . . . At this time, children were placed in the community's nursery during the day. This nursery was located in a special wing of the Mansion House, the main residence of the community's members. Here they encountered for the first time not only new caretakers, but other children of comparable age. The intent was to wean the child not only physically, but psychologically. This process was virtually completed when at age three they were moved into communal sleeping quarters which further curtailed the amount of maternal-child contact. Although parents and children were allowed time together during the day, this marks the point at which parental—especially maternal—influence ceased to have a decisive impact on the child's day-to-day behaviour. . . .

Since Noyes . . . opposed what he termed "philoprogenitiveness," that is, special loyalty or love for one's own progeny,[12] . . . it is, surprising that he permitted mothers and children virtually unrestricted access to each other during the infant's first fourteen months. Sustained contact of this duration allowed ample time for the formation of strong maternal child attachment. This resulted in powerful emotional ties that ran counter to the spirit of communal love. The subsequent separation of mother and child was apparently quite traumatic, especially for the mother.

Although the advantages of communal care were publicly supported by women's testimonials in the Oneida *Circular*,[13] memoirs of the community's children reveal considerably more ambivalence on the part of their mothers. For example, Pierrepont Noyes' autobiography poignantly describes weekly meetings in his mother's room in which she lavished affection upon him as though trying to make up for lost opportunity. He recalled she frequently interrupted his play to ask, "Darling, do you love

---

[8]Augusta E. Hamilton, for example, speaking at the dedication of the community's new Children's House stated:

> . . . We mothers, too are enabled by the thought that we bare (*sic*) our children, not for ourselves, but for the good of the church.

Oneida *Circular*, October 3, 1870.

[9]Oneida *Circular*, June 5, 1868.

[10]Barren and Miller, eds. (1875:282). An early community statement of "general principles" regarding the relationship of parents to children also declared that love between adult men and women was a "superior passion' to love between adults and children. Oneida *Circular*, January 29, 1863.

[11]For a detailed discussion of life in the Children's House, see Pierrepont Noyes (1937).

[12]Oneida *Circular*, October 5, 1868.

[13]Alice Ackley, for example, offered the following endorsement of communal child-rearing:

> I now realize . . . that the old way of each mother caring for her own child, begets selfishness and idolatry; and in many ways tends to degrade women . . . I appreciate the opportunity (community responsibility for child-rearing) affords me of not only joining in public work, but of self improvement and "going home" to God every day.

For this and other testimonials from community mothers, see Oneida *Circular*, June 23, 1873.

me?"[14] Yet toward the end of their visits, she became aloof if it appeared he would resist returning to the Children's House. To a young child, this abrupt change in demeanor must have been confusing. For the mothers, it created strong feelings of conflict. They needed an outlet for the love that had developed during the child's first year. On the other hand, they were aware of the community's practice of temporarily suspending visiting privileges between parents and children for displays of "special love."[15] . . . This is illustrated in Corinna Ackley Noyes' recollection of a chance encounter with her mother during a two-week enforced separation:

I caught a glimpse of (my mother) passing through a hallway near the Children's House and rushed after her screaming. She knew—what I was too young to know—that if she stopped to talk to me another week might be added to our sentence. Hoping, I suppose, to escape, she stepped quickly into a nearby room. But I was as quick as she. I rushed after her, flung myself upon her, cultching her around the knees, crying and begging her not to leave me, until some Children's House mother, hearing the commotion, came and carried me away.[16]

Between the ages of three and six, the children spent their days in the East Room, appointed much like modern-day nurseries. Toys and playthings were provided, which the children were expected to share in a non-possessive fashion.[17]

Although play was encouraged, Oneida's philosophy of child-rearing emphasized constant instruction and training. As a result, even young children's schedules were planned to allow ample time for many activities which were explicitly instructional. The young children arose at 5:35 every morning. After washing and dressing, they had a brief exercise period, breakfast and a session of Bible reading. At this point children participated in work, recreation and religious

training that filled most of the day. By seven o'clock, the youngest children were in bed; the older ones retired an hour later.[18]

At age six, children were moved to the South Room and formal education began. . . . Formal education was required of all children, and encompassed primary and secondary grades. Instruction was provided in a range of subjects, including reading, spelling, grammar, composition, arithmetic, algebra and Latin.[19] Although books and other instructional aids were available, students were encouraged to master these subjects through discussions and class reports rather than by memorization.[20]

A community University was planned but never materialized. Several young men received college educations subsidized by the community. They received training in applied areas, such as medicine, which they were then expected to practice within the community.[21]

In addition to their schoolwork, the older children were required to work in the community's agricultural and manufacturing activities. On an average day, children devoted approximately equal time to work and formal studies. In addition to . . . farming, carpentry, and housekeeping, children's jobs included the production of traps, boxes, and traveling bags.[22] Despite the community's stated belief in sexual equality, young women were most often channeled into traditional women's work including laundry, sewing and housekeeping services.

An important aspect of socialization concerns the manner in which a community responds to transgressions. At Oneida, . . . people other than biological parents played a significant role in socializing and disciplinary activities. Children were accountable not only to the community's adult members, but to God and their peers. Accountability to adults took the form of frequent "criticisms," a practice in which even

---

[14]Noyes (1937:65–67).

[15]Carden (1969:63–66).

[16]Corinna Ackley Noyes (1960:16).

[17]Oneida *Circular*, June 15, 1868.

[18]Oneida *Circular*, October 29, 1857.

[19]Robertson (1970:182–185).

[20]Oneida (1850:15).

[21]Robertson (1970:178).

[22]Noyes (1937:101).

young children were apprised of their flaws by a group of adults and provided with guidelines for rectifying their mistakes. These criticisms had religious overtones as well, for children were encouraged to "confess Christ" and thereby restore themselves to good standing in the spiritual realm. Children were also encouraged to monitor one another's behaviour, and to report transgressions to appropriate adults.[23]

Noyes had a liberal attitude toward discipline and discouraged corporal punishment.[24] Instead, efforts were made to talk and reason with young offenders. Adults were encouraged to use positive rewards and incentives to encourage behavior consistent with community norms. For example, one Children's House worker initiated a club known as the "Order of the O and F" (Obedient and Faithful), giving badges for good behaviour.[25]

. . . Descriptions of the children generally portray them as cheerful, energetic and well-behaved. Compared with children outside the community, they were perceived as highly cooperative and mutually supportive.[26] They were also physically robust: a medical report by Dr. Theodore Noyes revealed they were taller and heavier then a sample of children taken from a Boston school.[27]

Among the most controversial features of the community's child-rearing practices was sexual initiation. This occurred at a young age, in some cases predating puberty.[28] At the age of 10 to 12, children were considered to be adults and moved into individual rooms in the Mansion House. There their sexual initiation took place. Young boys were paired with women past childbearing age; girls were initiated primarily by Noyes himself. . . .

The practice of sexually pairing young and old members of the community was based upon

the doctrine of "ascending fellowship," a reflection of Noyes' belief that community members ranged in ascending order from those who were the least to those who were the most nearly perfect. He argued persons who were at lower levels of spiritual development should associate with their superiors; hence the term, "ascending fellowship."[29] In general, it was felt older persons were spiritually more advanced than their younger counterparts. When applied to complex marriage, this principle dictated younger persons should be paired with older persons of the opposite sex. This arrangement was buttressed by systematic segregation of young men and women between the ages of 12 through 25 to curb what Noyes termed "horizontal fellowship." This referred to the natural attractions of young people for one another.[30] Noyes believed children experienced "amative desires" when quite young, and apparently thought it best to channel such sexual energies in ways which promoted community solidarity.[31] Specifically, he wished to avoid the intergenerational conflict responsible for the demise of earlier communal efforts. . . .

Despite his best efforts, many of the offspring . . . grew dissatisfied with community life and thereby contributed to its dissolution.

Several reasons explain this unanticipated outcome. First, though raised under conditions that promoted social homogeneity, children of the Oneida community were not preselected for specific spiritual or moral values as their forebears . . . had been. This is true even of the stirpicults, who were presumed by Noyes to have inherited their parents' moral and spiritual commitment.[32] There is implied in this a perhaps un-

---

[23]Pierrepont Noyes (1937:51).

[24]Oneida (1850:13–14).

[25]Kanter (1972:14)

[26]Noyes (1937:148).

[27]Theodore Noyes (1878:2).

[28]Van de Warker (1884:789).

[29]Carden (1969:52–53).

[30]Oneida *Circular*, April 4, 1864.

[31]Van de Warker (1884:789)

[32]Parker (1935:264). Parker quotes Noyes as follows:

I can tell just when all this repeating of troubles is going to end. It will be when wisdom and righteousness are fixed in the blood, so that the lessons which the parents have learned by experience, the children will have in them when they are born. . . . Educating (children) is not going to do it, only as it helps the process of breeding. It is breeding that is going to finish the work.

founded faith both in the powers of environmental control and the mechanisms of heritability.

Educational factors contributed as well. . . . Children sent to college developed a perspective on life that transcended the community's boundaries. Those who returned often did so with criticisms of the existing social order.[33] Even those whose education took place within the community grew dissatisfied. For one thing, Noyes encouraged a spirit of scientific inquiry in the educational process that undoubtedly undermined the faith and obedience which had been fundamental to the Perfectionist creed.[34] Second, the children's teachers lacked the charismatic qualities that had aided Noyes in converting people to Perfectionism. Moreover, aside from his role in sexually initiating young women, Noyes appears to have been remote from the day-to-day activities of the children.[35]

Finally, despite Noyes' emphasis on "ascending fellowship," children developed strong peer attachments. They ate, slept, studied, worked and played together beginning at a very early age. This fostered solidarity vis-a-vis adults. They founded secret societies, resisted pressures to report on one another, and proved to be mutually supportive in the face of adult intrusions.[36] Despite frequent contact with older community members in . . . sexual encounters, they retained a loyalty to their own cohort.

The Oneida experiment came remarkably close to achieving a system of child-rearing in which environmental factors and heritability were successfully controlled. Under such highly regulated conditions, it may come as a surprise that the community was racked by internal dissent

and ultimately dissolved. This outcome attests to the difficulties in reshaping traditional family structure and insuring the continuity of the resultant changes from one generation to the next.

REFERENCES

CARDEN, MAREN LOCKWOOD. 1969. Oneida: Utopian Community to Modern Corporation. Baltimore: Johns Hopkins Press.

KANTER, ROSABETH. 1972. Commitment and Community. Massachusetts: Harvard University Press.

NOYES, CORINNA ACKLEY. 1960. The Days of My Youth. Utica, New York: Widtman Press.

NOYES, JOHN HUMPHREY. 1849. Confessions of John Humphrey Noyes, Part 1: Confessions of Religious Experience: Including a History of Modern Perfectionism. Oneida, New York.

—— 1866. Male Continence. Oneida, New York: Office of the Circular.

—— 1875. Essay on Scientific Propagation. Oneida, New York: Oneida Community.

—— 1875. Home Talks. Edited by Alfred Barron and George Noyes Miller. Oneida, New York: Oneida Community.

NOYES, PIERREPONT. 1937. My Father's House: An Oneida Boyhood. New York: Farrar and Rinehart.

NOYES, THEODORE. 1878. Report on the Health of Chidren in the Oneida Community. Oneida, New York: Oneida Community.

ONEIDA. 1850. Second Annual Report of the Oneida Association. Oneida, New York: Leonard and Co., Printers.

—— 1864–1879. The Circular. Oneida, New York: Oneida Community: Thirteen Volumes.

—— 1867. Handbook of the Oneida Community. Wallingford, Connecticut: Office of the Circular.

—— 1875. Handbook of the Oneida Community 1875. Oneida, New York: Office of the Circular.

PARKER, ROBERT ALLERTON. 1935. A Yankee Saint. New York: G.P. Putnam's Sons.

ROBERTSON, CONSTANCE NOYES. 1970. Oneida Community: An Autobiography. New York: Syracuse University Press.

VAN DE WARKER, ELY. 1884. "A Gynecological Study of the Oneida Community." The American Journal of Obstetrics and Diseases of Women and Children, XVIII: 785–810.

---

[33]Noyes' eldest son, Theodore, for example, was an avowed agnostic. See Carden (1969:96).

[34]Oneida Circular, January 4, 1869.

[35]Pierrepont Noyes apparently reflected the feelings of many of the community's children when he stated:

> I revered him, but he was much too far away, too near to heaven and God. He lived somewhere upstairs and, whenever I saw him, was usually surrounded by men . . . who were associated in my mind with the Apostles Pierrepont Noyes (1937:70).

[36]Pierrepont Noyes (1937:49, 112)

Introduction

One theme implicit in the articles in this section is the extent to which family environments prepare children for eventual independence.

The children described in this excerpt have established independence at a very early age. They, like an estimated forty million other Latin American children are urban street children. Yet the majority of these children are not orphans. Only sixteen percent could not locate at least one parent. Their street life is an adaptation to family poverty or abuse. Indeed, it may be that the street children are the more resourceful members of their families. They have left behind those unable to care for themselves.

These children have adapted well to the harsh reality of street life. They are able to get the money they need to eat and travel around the city by panhandling. Many have developed sophisticated cognitive skills. Tests administered to similar street children in Columbia found them to be both intelligent and relatively healthy in emotional and neurological terms.

In Columbia, street children are described by the media in contradictory ways. On one hand, they are thought of as victims of poverty or abuse. On the other hand, they are described as threats to "family." What lies at the bottom of this seeming contradiction? The author feels it is rooted in a threatened loss of power in upper-class patriarchal families.

20
The Rearing of Colombian Street Children

Lewis Aptekar

STREET CHILDREN OF COLOMBIA

UNICEF recently estimated that the crowded and busy streets of Latin American cities are home to 40 million children living without parental authority and surviving however they are able (Tacon, 1981; 1983). Although, the children are usually described as being abandoned by their families, an inevitable consequence of cruelty or poverty, they are not always perceived

Source: Aptekar, Lewis (1990) "How Ethnic Differences Within a Culture Influence Childrearing: The Case of Columbian Street Children," *Journal of Comparative Family Studies*, Vol. XXI, No. 1, Spring, 67–79. Reprinted with permission from *Journal of Comparative Family Studies.*

this way. Samper (1984), a well known Colombian journalist, referred to the children in the leading Bogota daily as a "plague" threatening the fabric of traditional family discipline. That the children were worthy of pity appealed to our common sense, but why they were perceived as a threat to family discipline seemed less certain. . . .

I was fortunate enough to have the opportunity of studying . . . Colombian street children and society's reaction to them. With a group of 12 Colombian University students I spent the better part of a year collecting ethnographic, psychological, and archival data. At first we met children in a private store front program that served them lunch. After we got to know them we were able to accompany them on the streets and to meet their friends. In order to get more information about their mental health we administered to 56 children, ages 7–16, three psychological tests.

We measured their intelligence by using the Kohs Block Design Test. Although, there were few cases of very high IQs, the mean score of all the children was within the normal range (88.38), and excluding the margin of error there were no more examples of mental retardation than what would be expected in the normative population. There were many reasons why our sample should have scored lower. The children came from homes where nearly one half of the fathers, and a third of the mothers were illiterate (Granados, 1976). They had many siblings, nonintact or one parent families, and lived in poverty. All these characteristics have been associated with low academic aptitude (Anastasi, 1982).

Given the poor and impoverished beginnings why did the children seem so intelligent? It may well be that street life, rather than taking away from cognitive growth, actually added to it. There were many daily activities that street children performed which were associated with improving cognitive skills, and in fact were often used in classrooms for such purposes. The children moved through a series of self managed, non supervised activities, initiating and completing tasks that involved enough social awareness of people to allow them to manipulate others into giving them alms. Their livelihood depended on it. They accomplished this in a complex urban environment, traveling around the city, often at great distances away from home.

Using the Bender Gestalt and the Human Figure Drawing Test gave us measures about their emotional and neurological functioning. About a quarter of the sample scored within the pathological range, but nearly half were clearly without pathology. The remaining children scored in an intermediary category. Cortes (1969) reported that the only study which compared street children with their siblings they left behind found the street children weighed more. This was not only a vital statistic in a less developed country, but spoke to the children's ability to organize their lives productively. . . . We compared our test scores across ages in order to see if the time spent on the streets made their mental health worse, as would be predicted since the children were allegedly smoking the highly addictive *basuko* which was a lethal residue produced by refining cocaine. Our results indicated that time on the streets did not lead to poorer emotional or neurological functioning.

Certainly, there was ample reason why the children in our sample should have demonstrated more pathology than they did. They had all lived on the streets for at least three months, many had been incarcerated, some came from homes where there was abuse, others had no homes, and they all knew first hand the effects of poverty. Why did they do as well as they did? It could be that a preselection factor existed. Having left a set of bad circumstances for an unknown future might have meant, contrary to public opinion, that the emotionally stronger children were the ones on the streets, while their weaker siblings remained at home. Once on the streets they joined a lively peer group that gave them a good deal of friendship and support. Many had benefactors. . . . Also, almost all of the children received an early training for independence that made leaving home less traumatic than the assumption of rejection or abandonment implied.

In order to understand people's reaction to the children we used structured interviews, read twenty years of newspaper reports about the children, and examined how they were perceived in the professional literature. We discovered attitudes toward street children were mainly directed toward their families. These perceptions could be summarized by characterizing the families of street children as being headed by mothers who were considered victims of their abusing male partners, the stepfathers (*padrastros*) of the children. The mothers endured the abuse because of their need for economic survival. As a result of being placed between the demands of the *padrastro*, and the love for her children there was severe tension in the home. Thus, the children were neglected, abandoned, or otherwise forced to leave. As we will show this commonly accepted scenario arose from important differences between the class dominant patrifocal family, and the lower social class matrifocal family. The street children coming from matrifocal families were being judged by patrifocal family standards. Because of the political struggle in Colombian society the power of the patrifocal system was being drained, and in defense they were striking back.

THE CHANGING CIVIC IDENTITY

On April 9, 1948, Colombians experienced *La Violencia*. On that day the dictatorial government of Ospina Perez was overthrown and the populist president-elect Gaitan was assassinated. Gaitan, a product of a poor *barrio*, had won the hearts of the people as well as the support of the political system. He thus instilled a sense of possibility in the populace. . . .

After *La Violencia* the country became more equalitarian and meritocratic which increased the individual's opportunity to participate in civic, social and political life. The possibility to be someone without having to rely on family name, or a family history, was born. . . .

Many scholars traced the origins of street children to the epoch of *La Violencia*. (de Mantilla, 1980; Munoz & Palacios, 1980; Neron, 1953; Pineda et al., 1978). It was at this time that the children were first labeled "abandoned". The emotional nature of this term implied that their families were remiss, irresponsible, and in need of restructuring. . . .

The expression, "losing the children to the streets" became a metaphoric flag which identified this deeper struggle. Such an expression indicated a nearly archtypal place of anonymity, where family name had no meaning, where family connections were worthless, but where one's personal merit to get the job done were paramount to survival. For a civic personage to come into existence, the families' hold on public life would have to wane.

MATRIFOCAL AND PATRIFOCAL FAMILIES

In Colombia there were two family structures, the patrifocal and the matrifocal, representing not only different family dynamics but also different amounts of power in the society. The typical Colombian patrifocal family was of the middle or upper class. . . .

The Colombian families of the lower socioeconomic status, of more Indigenous or African decent, had a matrifocal family structure. They had "male kin marginality" (Siegal, 1969) which meant men were marginal to these homes. When present and appropriate they were valued, and the economic products of their labor were used. When either of these two factors lost their value, the men were asked to leave. . . . The mother was the source of wisdom and her children turned to her when there were dangers. . . .

The boy child in the matrifocal family . . . was socialized to leave home and to be independent of his mother. This insured that by the time he reached puberty he would have many experiences on his own away from home and often with other children on the streets. As he reached puberty his welcome at home depended on bringing in money and thus contributing as an adult. . . .

In the middle and upper social classes where the dominant family tradition was Spanish and patrifocal both boys and girls were encouraged to stay at home far longer, and neither left without the blessings of both parents. . . . The streets were out of bounds. . . .

In the families that purportedly were producing street children (which we are postulating are matrifocal), men were only serial companions to the women until the woman reached middle age (Mintz, 1984). . . .

The matrifocal family reared girls and boys to expect that the relationship between husband and wife had less importance and was less necessary. . . . Girls were socialized to become independent of men, to look for their identity without being dependent on intimate relationships with men. This posed a threat to the integrity of the patrifocal family which saw the conjugal relationship as the basis of their families' ties, and the backbone which instilled and maintained authority and obedience within their families. The conjugal relationship was also important for the patrifocal family in defining the family publicly. . . .

Matrifocality was viewed as pathological . . . from an ethnocentric notion that a family other than one's own was not just different, but flawed. As the children of matrifocal families sought entry into society they created tension in the civic politic which contributed to the pejorative view of them and their families.

The children on the streets in their conspicuously dirty appearance, in their flirtation with the dangerous, and in their cunning thievery, all of which took place in full public view, were viewed symbolically, as a defiance against the power of men in the class dominant patrifocal family. Sensing that this role gave them power the children participated in the scenario. It was not hunger or family disintegration which impelled them to be so public in their displays, but rebellion against the inevitability of inheriting the lowest social status due to their being deprived of patrilineal favor.

At the heart of the pejorative attitude toward street children was the challenge they brought to the man's power in the patriarchal family, a power already waning due to the changes brought about by *La Violencia*. As long as this was the case children would be seen as dangerous, not pitiful. When they were described as "a

miniature *querrilla* band at large in the urban areas of Colombia (Gutierrez, 1972: 45)" it was because this image represented a more compelling reality than that of being pitiful. . . .

. . . The street children in our study were not without family. Only 16% in our sample were unable to locate at least one parent. What was being referred to as abandonment and neglect was a method of child rearing that was deliberate and helpful in training children for independence and self assurance. These skills help poor children make a living in an urban economy where there are few wage opportunities open to them.

A CROSS-CULTURAL COMPARISON

By describing the Qalander (Berland, 1982), a peripatetic group of entertainers in Pakistan who traveled from village to village performing animal acts and magic tricks for their audiences, we will be able to illustrate remarkable similarities between how the Colombian street children were raised and lived, and treated by the larger society. This will help us understand why the street children are said to be abandoned instead of, as we claim, living and coping adequately with their poor urban circumstances. . . .

Amongst the Qalander the word *berupia* was used to denote the actors, many of whom were child beggars. By age six the children had learned to dance in public, to control bears and monkeys, perform magical tricks, juggle, and do impersonations with appropriate sexual references. . . . They were not responding to economic hardships, but learning to be competent in their society.

Living as they did, always moving, the Qalander were constantly mingling with people who were stationary. We refer to these stationary people as having a sedentary culture. As these nomadic entertainers came upon a village, the children of the sedentary cultures ran to greet them. While their animals and magic tricks were viewed with interest and curiosity by the children, they were seen as alarming to their parents. . . .

In these sedentary cultures, families were composed of blood members. Keeping the family together, involved a relationship between parents and children where the lines of authority were clear, and where obedience toward parents was sacrosanct. Friendships between children were closely supervised so that peer relationships did not become too powerful.

CONCLUSION

The street children's early, but subculturally appropriate independence endangered the strict obedience that was part of the patrifocal family's child rearing. Leaving home at an earlier age than what the patrilineal and class dominant culture assumed legitimate, they often chose friendships with peers and lived with them on the streets without being abandoned, or receiving the parental abuse or rejection that was commonly associated with them. Matrifocal child rearing, and their nomadic entertaining way of life, which was needed to make ends meet in an impoverished economy, contributed to helping us understand that street children were in fact growing up in an orderly manner.

The matrifocal family created a large mass of children with less reverent attitudes toward men. . . . This contributed to the stress on men in patrifocal families since their power rested on an unlimited acceptance of the marriage contract, and an unquestioned respect for their authority within it. The reaction from men was predictable. They viewed matrifocal families with disdain. . . .

The streets represented a place that was outside of family control. Their public nature made people anonymous citizens, as opposed to being known members of a family group. After *La Violencia* patrifocal family control over the civil politic was . . . precarious. In this weakness, the ano-

nymity of the streets loomed as an on-coming truck, capable of flattening the vestiges of a world where one was known to everyone by one's family name. . . .

In Colombia where the division between those who were wealthy and those without any resources was large, the family as an institution of identity acted to deprive those outside of its boundaries from getting some share of the goods. It also caused them to be alienated from what they perceived to be their just benefits from their society.

It was therefore, . . . not the poor families who were in jeopardy by the presence of street children but, the wealthier families who had gained so much by maintaining "the family", merging it with state control, and access into material well being. The accusations made by the dominant society concerning the nature of these poor families; their irresponsibility, their lack of education, their disrespect for their spouses, and their cruelty toward their children, were merely reactions, politically defensive maneuvers on the part of the controlling families to provide special favor for their own children. The issue was not poverty, of which there was plenty, but the nature of the state and the family in it. . . .

REFERENCES

ANASTASI, A. 1982. Psychological Testing, 5th edition, New York: Macmillan.

BERLAND, J. 1982. No Five Fingers Are Alike. Cambridge: Harvard University Press.

CORTES, L. 1969. Temas Colombianas: La Metamorfosis del Chino de la Calle. Bogota: Editextos.

DE MANTILLA, N. 1980. "El Gamin; Problems social de la cultura urbana," Revista Javeriana 94:457–464.

GRANADOS, M. 1976. Gamines. Bogota: Editorial Temis.

GUTIERREZ, J. 1972. Gamin: Un Ser Olvidado. Mexico City: McGraw Hill.

LOMNITZ, L. 1977. "Organization of a Mexican shantytown," Pp. 135–155 in Wayne Cornelius and Frank Trueblood (eds), Latin American Urban Research, Vol. 4. New York: Sage Publishers.

MINTZ, S. 1984. Caribbean Transformations. Baltimore: Johns Hopkins University Press.

MUNOZ, CELIA, and PALACIOS, MARIA. 1980. El Nino Trabajador. Bogota: Carlos Valencia Editores.

MUNOZ, CELIA, and PACHON, XIMENA. 1980. Gamines: Testimonios. Bogota: Carlos Valencia Editores.

NERON, G. 1953. El Nino Vago. Madrid: Impreso de Espana.

PINEDA, VIRGINIA, DE MUNOZ, ELVIA, ECHEVERRY, YOLANDA, and ARIAS, JAIRO. 1978. El Gamin su Albergue Social y su Familia. Bogota: Instituto Colombiano de Bienestar Familiar.

TACON, P. 1983. Regional Program for Latin America and the Caribbean. New York: UNICEF document.

SAMPER, L. 1984. "Ressurge el 'gaminiso", El Tiempo, Bogota, (October 5): 1984.

SIEGAL, J. 1969. The Rope of God. Berkeley: University of California Press.

Introduction

Faced with the monumental task of forestalling crippling population growth, China introduced a number of population control programs. The one-couple-one-child policy was introduced in 1979. In a country where large families had been valued, the policy was remarkably successful. Now, the vast majority of children born in cities are first births. For example, ninety-eight percent of children born in Shanghai in 1985 were first births. The proportions are smaller in rural areas, but for the country as a whole the figure was sixty-eight percent. China has moved in one generation from being a nation where most people are raised in large families, to a nation of small families. Will only children raised in China be similar to only children raised in Western countries?

This study compares only children to children with siblings raised in both rural and urban settings. In Western countries only children are similar to children with siblings in their adjustment, sociability, and personality, but they perform better in intelligence and achievement tests. The most plausible reason for the difference is that parents of only children are more likely to give that child more attention and to expect more from the child than parents of larger families. Will Chinese parents behave similarly?

The results of this paper show that, indeed, being raised as an only child has similar advantages in China and the United States. Urban Chinese only children outperform children with siblings in school achievement. Interestingly, rural only children in China do not seem to have this advantage. Since the question of this kind of rural-urban difference has not been asked by North American researchers, we don't know if it also exists in the West!

21

The Academic Performance and Personality
Traits of Chinese Only Children

Dudley L. Poston, Jr.
Toni Falbo

The purpose of this article is to determine whether the intellectual and personality traits of only children in China are similar to those of children in the West. Numerous studies conducted by Western social scientists have compared single children with those with siblings. Of particular interest here is the finding from recent quantitative reviews of this extensive literature (Falbo and Polit 1986; Polit and Falbo 1987; Blake 1989) that only children in the West are not very different from those with siblings in terms of adjustment, sociability, and most personality characteristics. Falbo and Polit have shown, however, that only children tend to outperform those with siblings in intelligence and achievement.

About 10 years ago, China initiated a policy restricting families to one child only. Before the Chinese initiated this policy in 1979, families with only children were relatively rare and were found mostly among the urban elite. Now 10 years or so after its implementation, the policy has been judged relatively successful. . . .

Western researchers have conducted many analyses of the causes of the advantaged achievement and intellectual outcomes of only children. These investigations have pointed to two likely causes. First, only children in the United States are more likely than those with siblings to have parents with greater educational attainments (Blake 1981). Thus the advantaged academic outcomes of only children may well reflect the values and abilities of their parents. However, even when parents' educational levels have been statistically controlled, the advantages for "onlies" are maintained, suggesting there may be something about the relationship between onlies and their parents conducive to intellectual development (Blake 1989; Polit and Falbo 1988). To illustrate, parents of only children frequently report taking a more didactic approach in their communications with their children (Lewis and Feiring 1982), and have higher expectations for their children (Kammeyer 1967), than do parents of more than one child. . . .

Second, because the academic achievements of only children resemble those of firstborns, Falbo and Polit (1986) focused on aspects of the parent-child relationship that would promote academic abilities, namely, the enhanced opportunities for only children to gain attention and care from their parents. Firstborns are only children until the births of their first siblings. Before those births, they receive considerable attention from their parents. . . .

Chinese only children, however, may not share in these desirable circumstances. In urban areas, almost all the families formed since 1979 are one-child families. In urban China today, newlyweds know, their first child will probably be their only child. Such knowledge may lead some parents to overindulge or overprotect an only child. . . . Indeed a survey of Tianjin families (Bian 1987) indicated parents of only children reported devoting more time and income to their single children than they thought they should.

In rural areas, the economic status of the fam-

Source: Poston, Dudley L. and Toni Falbo (1990) "Academic performance and personality traits of Chinese children: 'Onlies' versus others," *American Journal of Sociology*, Vol. 96, No. 2, September, 433–451. Published by the University of Chicago Press. © 1990 The University of Chicago. All rights reserved.

ily is often an important factor in determining whether the family has only one child. Hardee-Cleaveland and Banister (1988) have reported that the more economically advantaged rural families can often afford to pay the fines incurred by having additional children; moreover, they can afford the costs of sending additional children to school. The economically disadvantaged families who have more than one child are frequently unable to pay the fees to send the additional children to school.

Another difference between Chinese and American children is that Chinese children have a greater opportunity to interact with other children. Even in rural areas, families tend to live in close proximity to one another, and it is commonplace for pre-school-aged children to be cared for in organized groups. . . .

Investigators have responded to the popular concern in China about the potential problems parents incur by having single children by conducting many studies comparing only children to those with siblings. Although the results are not entirely consistent, the predominant finding is that only children tend to outperform their peers with siblings in academic skills (Yang, Kao, and Wang 1980; Poston and Mei Yu 1985; Xiao and Zhang 1985). . . .

However, the Chinese literature is unclear about the personality outcomes of single children and those with siblings. . . . Jiao, Ji, and Jing (1986) used peer ratings to evaluate children ranging from four to ten years and living in Beijing. Their results indicated only children were at a severe disadvantage, regardless of age or urban or rural residence. Almost without exception, the comparisons between onlies and others ($N = 360$) indicated onlies had undesirable personality characteristics; specifically, they were found to be low in independent thinking, persistence, behavior control, cooperation with peers, and peer prestige, and high in frustration proneness and egocentrism.

In contrast, Chen (1985) obtained personality data from the children's teachers, parents, and peers. No consistent disadvantageous or advantageous patterns were found for only children. This study considered the collective orientations of 964 children from urban and rural primary schools and kindergartens in Beijing. . . .

SAMPLE AND RESEARCH DESIGN

Our study was undertaken in the urban and rural areas of Changchun, an industrial city in Jilin Province in northeastern China. In 1985 the city had a population of 5.8 million, with an urban component of 1.8 million (State Statistical Bureau 1985). . . .

Our study was undertaken in collaboration with demographers from the Population Research Institute of Jilin University. A pilot survey of 165 children was conducted from December 1986 to January 1987 and the full survey of 1,465 schoolchildren was conducted in June and July 1987.

The survey contained four parts, with the children's teachers and parents (usually the mothers) each completing two parts. The teachers provided information on the students' academic achievements (their scores on the most recent standardized tests in mathematics and Chinese); they next completed the teacher's version of the 31 Attributes Checklist. The students' mothers completed a detailed background questionnaire including information dealing with the size of the family, the educational attainments and occupations of both parents, household income, the long-range expectations of each parent for the child, and how often each helped the child in his or her studies. The mothers also completed the parent's version of the 31 Attributes Checklist. . . .

Eight schools participated in the survey, five in the urban part of Changchun (72% of the students in the survey), and three in the rural part (28% of the sample). . . .

The 31 Attributes Checklist was designed to assess the extent to which primary school chil-

TABLE 1. Component Factor of the Two Personality Dimensions of Virtue and Competence: Jilin Schoolchildren, 1987*

Virtue	Competence
Gentle	Competent
Concerned about being liked	Has definite views
Selfless	Makes decisions easily
Cares about others' feelings	Confident
Kind	Answers questions actively
Helpful	Competitive
Never willful	Acts as a leader
Respects property	Doesn't give up
Never aggressive	Brave
Respects elders	
Modest	
Never lies	
Obeys class discipline	
Never copies homework	
Shares belongings	

*Derived from 31 Attributes Checklist by factor analysis.

dren have acquired personality attributes that Chinese adults regard as desirable in children. . . .

RESULTS

. . . Among all the Changchun schoolchildren, only children uniformly perform better than all types of non-only children on standardized mathematics examinations, and on standardized Chinese language examinations. The finding that onlies perform better than non-onlies who are not firstborns is consistent with Western results, but the finding that onlies perform better than other firstborns is not consistent with Western studies.

With regard to the personality outcomes, however, the differences between onlies and non-onlies are considerably less. For instance, when the teachers rate the children's virtue levels, only children have significantly higher scores than firstborns and second-borns from two-child families and than children of third or higher birth orders. The differences between the average scores of onlies and all other types of non-onlies are not statistically significant. When mothers rate the children's virtue levels the differences between the mean scores of only children and non-only children are not statistically significant. Finally, there are no statistically significant differences between the average scores of only children and non-only children on the competence scales as scored by either the teachers or the mothers. . . .

In only three of 48 regression equations is the only-child variable significantly associated with an outcome variable, net of the other independent variables. In the larger sample (i.e., the sample comparing only children with all children with siblings), among urban first graders, being an only child is significantly associated with both mathematics and verbal achievement. And, in the larger sample, among urban fifth graders, being an only child is significantly associated with achievement in mathematics. In all three cases, only children outperform their peers with siblings. An only-child advantage is not found among rural children. Furthermore, when the comparison is restricted to single children and firstborns, no significant only-child advantages in achievement are found.

For the personality outcomes, the analyses yield no significant only-child effects. . . .

If being an only child is not consistently associated with children's outcomes, what is? . . . The most consistently significant predictor for academic achievement is parental education. In 12 of 16 regression equations predicting mathematics or verbal (Chinese) achievement, parental education is a significant predictor. For most of the Changchun schoolchildren, their scores on mathematics and Chinese-language examinations are positively and significantly associated with the levels of their parents' education.

In the virtue ratings, gender is a consistent and statistically significant predictor. Indeed, in all the 16 regression equations where virtue is the dependent variable, gender is a statistically significant predictor and often the most significant. Whether the girls reside in urban or rural areas or are in the first or fifth grade, they are consistently evaluated as more virtuous than the boys by both their mothers and their teachers. Furthermore, if the child attended nursery school before elementary school, he or she is often evaluated, particularly by the teachers, as more virtuous than the child cared for by relatives. . . .

When competence is rated by the teachers, the most consistent predictor is whether the child attended nursery school; when rated by the mothers, the best predictor is parental expectations for the students. . . .

CONCLUSION

The results of the study are remarkably similar to those of comparable studies in the West. In terms of academic achievement, urban only children were found to outperform their later-born peers, even after parental characteristics, gender, and nursery school attendance were controlled for. The consistency of this finding with Western results suggests that, in urban areas, only children are advantaged in their academic outcomes, and these advantages may not be entirely explained away as reflecting their parents' higher educational attainments.

This finding adds weight to the remaining explanation addressed by us concerning only children's advantages, to wit, the enhanced nature of the relationship of only children with their parents. Because parents of one child have more opportunity to spend "one-on-one" time with that child than do parents of children with siblings, this enhanced attention may facilitate intellectual development. . . .

The lack of advantages for only children in the rural areas challenges the parent-child relationship explanation. Presumably, rural parents with just one child have more time to spend with their only child than do those with more than one. Our results suggest the parents fail to do so or the children fail to benefit from the rural parents' attention. While rural parents of one child were found to have more years of education than parents with more than one, their ed-

ucational attainments were substantially less than those of urban parents with more than one child. Enhanced attention from less educated parents and grandparents may not be an advantage.

Furthermore, only about 50% of the rural children attended nursery school before primary school, compared with about 70% of the urban children. Recent research has demonstrated the importance of preschool in China in preparing children to meet prevailing academic and social standards (Tobin et al. 1989). And this variable performs well as a predictor of children's competence as evaluated by the teachers.

The finding that only children, as evaluated by both their mothers and teachers, do not differ significantly from others in terms of two personality dimensions representing childhood adjustment in China is also consistent with the results of Western studies.

Parental education was the factor most consistently related to children's academic outcomes. This is consistent with Western results.

Gender was most consistently related to the assessments of virtue, whether these were made by the mother or the teacher. As in the West, young females in Changchun are evaluated as more selfless, kind, and helpful (i.e., more virtuous) than males, and this difference is probably attributable to gender-specific socialization practices. . . .

Parental expectations and child-care status were the next most important predictors of the traits of Chinese children. Mothers who rated their children as more competent expected their children to acquire more prestigious jobs. And children who had attended nursery school were evaluated by their teachers as being more competent and more virtuous than children who had not. . . .

Overall then, our results indicate that many of the significant and consistent predictors of children's outcomes in China are similar to those that have been shown to be influential predictors of the same outcomes among children in the United States. . . .

REFERENCES

BIAN, Y. 1987. "A Preliminary Analysis of the Basic Features of the Life Styles of China's Single-Child Families." *Social Sciences in China* 8:189–209.

BLAKE, JUDITH. 1981. "The Only Child in America: Prejudice versus Performance." *Population and Development Review* 7:43–54.

—— 1989. *Family Size and Achievement.* Berkeley and Los Angeles: University of California Press.

CHEN KEWEN. 1985. "A Preliminary Study of the Collective Orientation of the Only Child." *Journal of Psychology* 3:264–69.

FALBO, T., and D. F. POLIT. 1986. "A Quantitative Review of the Only Child Literature: Research Evidence and Theory Development." *Psychological Bulletin* 100:176–89.

HARDEE-CLEAVELAND, KAREN, and JUDITH BANISTER. 1988. "Fertility Policy and Implementation in China, 1986–88." *Population and Development Review* 14:245–86.

JIAO, S., G. JI, and Q. JING. 1986. "Comparative Study of Behavioral Qualities of Only Children and Sibling Children." *Child Development* 57:357–61.

KAMMEYER, K. 1967. "Birth Order as a Research Variable." *Social Forces* 46:71–80.

LEWIS, M., and C. FEIRING. 1982. "Some American Families at Dinner." Pp. 115–45 in *Families as Learning Environments for Children*, edited by L. M. Laosa and I. E. Sigel. New York: Plenum.

POLIT, D. F., and T. FALBO. 1987. "Only Children and Personality Development: A Quantitative Review." *Journal of Marriage and the Family* 49:309–25.

—— 1988. "The Intellectual Outcomes of Only Children." *Journal of Biosocial Science* 20:275–85.

POSTON, D. L., JR., and YU MEI-YU. 1985. "Quality of Life, Intellectual Development, and Behavioural Characteristics of Single Children in China: Evidence from a 1980 Survey in Changsha, Hunan Province." *Journal of Biosocial Science* 17:127–36.

STATE STATISTICAL BUREAU. 1985. *Zhong Guo Cheng Shi Tong Ji Nian Jian: 1985* (City statistical yearbook of China: 1985). Beijing: Statistics Press.

TOBIN, J. J., D Y. WU, and D. H. DAVIDSON. 1989. *Preschool in Three Cultures: Japan, China and the United States.* New Haven, Conn.: Yale University Press.

XIAO FULAN and ZHANG QIBAO. 1985. "Guan yu xiao xue du shen zi nu jiao yu qing kuang de diao cha" (A survey of the primary school education of the only child). *Xinli Xuebao* (Psychological journal) 3:50–52.

YANG, H., H. KAO, and W. WANG. 1980. "Survey of Only Children in the Educational Institutes of Beijing City Districts." *China Youth Daily*, October 2.

Introduction

One of the early issues addressed by the women's movement in North America was sex-role socialization. Children learn sex-specific behaviors from a number of sources. The mass media, particularly advertising, and school materials are universally important as agents of socialization. In this article Stella Quah focuses on textbooks as a source of sex-role stereotypes for young girls in Singapore.

This study analyzed English language first to fifth grade readers used in Singapore schools. Quah found a systematic stereotyping of male and female roles. "The most frequently mentioned sex-role for females is that of housewife." The most common role for men is the husband-economic-provider role (HEPR). Girls are portrayed as being interested in dolls; boys are interested in becoming mechanics, firemen, doctors, or sportsmen.

Interestingly there were more references to females than males in the Singapore study. (American studies consistently find women and girls underrepresented). Quah finds this difficult to explain.

The very high rates of female labor-force participation in Singapore make these stereotypes particularly troublesome. In Singapore, as everywhere, women work in the lowest status, lowest paid jobs. There too, young women tend to leave the labor force when they marry. These patterns seem consistent with the two-role ideology or a "belief that home and work are incompatible spheres of activity for females." Clearly, accepting this belief is not in women's best interests.

22

Sex-Role Socialization in a Transitional Society

Stella R. Quah

... The purpose of this paper is twofold: firstly, to discuss the sex-role stereotypes children encounter in school textbooks. Secondly, to contend that the influence received during the first years of school, which emphasize traditional sex-roles, contradicts the latter social call faced by young women to join the labour force and may give rise to role conflict particularly among female workers who are wives and mothers. . . .

∂

FROM ANTICIPATORY SOCIALIZATION TO ROLE CONFLICT

... The typical example of a social situation where females face role conflict and role strain due to contradictory-role demands, is a society with the "two-role ideology" described by Bernard (1972:235–46). The two-role ideology exists when women are expected to "combine motherhood and the care of home with outside activities" (1972:237) particularly a formal job. Bernard uses the concept to describe the United States, Britain and some other European countries in the 1960s. . . . The next development

which Bernard already sees in those countries albeit in an incipient stage, is the "shared-role ideology" whereby both family and occupational roles are shared by men and women (1972:242).

The "two-role ideology" concept is useful in understanding sex-role stereotypes in nations of the Third World which are currently in advanced stages of industrialization. Singapore is one such nation. Two important characteristics come to light when the two-role ideology lens is used for analysis. Firstly, industrialization in the Third World does not necessarily bring a change in traditional values. . . . On the contrary, one may observe the coexistence of traditional values and beliefs together with modern ideas; the former are likely to predominate in family and primary group behaviour while the latter are implemented mostly in formal interactions including technology issues and transactions dealing with the production and distribution of goods and services.

Secondly, the two-role ideology may not give way to the shared-role ideology in Third World nations. It is not uncommon to find people who contend that women are called to take jobs—the two-role ideology—only as a temporary measure while the national economy stabilizes; once this is accomplished, legislators, the common man, or both, hope "to return things to normal" to put females back at home. . . .

The preceding concepts lead the way for the

Source: Quah, S. R. (1980), "Sex-role socialization in a transitional society," *International Journal of Sociology of the Family,* 10, 2, July-December, 213–231. Reprinted with permission from *International Sociology of the Family.*

twofold objective of this paper namely, (*a*) to test the assumption that schools contribute to the legitimization of sex-role stereotypes through textbooks thus providing formal anticipatory socialization for traditional female roles; and (*b*) to probe the proposition that young women socialized under this process face role conflict and role strain as the two-role ideology demands from them performance of two mutually exclusive—from a traditional viewpoint—sets of roles, family and job. . . .

FORMALIZING ANTICIPATORY SOCIALIZATION ON TRADITIONAL ROLES

One common finding appears in several analyses of children's books and sex-roles in the United States: the books systematically emphasize the male roles and play down or neglect the role of females. . . .

A content analysis of six reading textbooks[1] used in the first to fifth grades of elementary school in Singapore reveals similarities as well as differences with the above studies. The most important similarity is the emphasis given to traditional male and female roles. The most important difference rests on the fact that female roles are portrayed in higher proportions than male roles. . . .

The textbooks analysed here concentrate on a few sex-role stereotypes for males and females conveyed through written expressions, stories, exercises and/or through sketches or pictures. The most frequently mentioned sex-role for females is that of housewife. Children learn to put

---

[1]The procedure of selection of these six reading textbooks involved two steps. The first step was listing the ten most widely used reading textbooks in elementary school during the past three years. A preliminary analysis of these textbooks showed a great similarity in presentation and emphasis of sex-role stereotypes. Such similarity allowed the second step, the random selection of six of the ten textbooks using a table of random numbers. The smaller number of textbooks facilitated the content analysis. No textbook was found portraying equal roles for males and females.

letters and sounds together by reading sentences such as "mother cleans table," "the lady sweeps the floor," "mother does not want the boy in the kitchen," but "girls help mother in the kitchen.". . .

On the other hand, the Husband Economic Provider Role or HEPR, the label introduced by Gronseth (1972) for the traditional sex-role assigned to males, is not neglected in these textbooks. . . . Another example is this story found in a third grade's textbook:

Mr Lee gets up early . . . he goes to his shop in his car . . . (and after working all day) at six o'clock (he goes) home. . . . Every evening he has dinner at home and plays with his children. The children go to bed at eight o'clock. Then Mr Lee talks with his wife. (Cobb and Cheong, 1970:3).

This story is a typical example of the characterization of men in these textbooks. As said earlier, housewife is the most frequently found sex-role for females, followed by teacher and nurse and activities dealing with child care, buying clothes and personal care. Moreover, girls are portrayed as naturally more interested in dolls than in sports and even afraid of mice. Conversely, the typical sex-roles for males in addition to HEPR are that of mechanic, repairman, driver, fireman, policeman, doctor, dentist, sportsman and businessman among others.

Sex-role stereotypes go beyond determination of occupations. They involve norms on appropriate behaviour. . . . Girls are expected to wear dresses while "boys wear shirts and shorts." Recreational activities should be differentiated too; for example, "girls play with dolls, but boys don't. Do girls play football? No they don't" (Cobb and Cheong, 1970: 2). Girls in fact undergo anticipatory socialization through stories and phrases depicting girls playing with dolls and caring for their little brothers. . . .

In sum, there is a striking similarity in the use of sex-role stereotypes between elementary school textbooks in Singapore and those in some industrialized western countries. . . .

With reference to the major difference presented by school materials in Singapore, females far from being neglected are given more "coverage" than males. . . . In the six elementary school textbooks analysed here, the average proportion of references to females is 65 per cent, while only an average of 35 per cent deal with males. . . .

A tentative interpretation of the above finding may be given based on cultural values and traditions. Traditionally, the Chinese, Malays and Indians—the three major ethnic groups in Singapore—perceive the main goal of women as wives and mothers (cf. Ryan, 1971). Consequently, it is understandable that the purpose of schooling for girls be seen by textbook writers as a means to enhance these roles and provide further, more "formal" preparation for their implementation. On the same line of thought, the strong emphasis on traditional sex-roles for girls may counteract any harmful, modernizing effects of education. . . .

Basically, the first assumption probed in this paper is supported by the data. School materials do present stereotypes that reinforce the anticipatory socialization of girls for the roles of housewife and mother. . . .

FEMALE WORKERS AND ROLE CONFLICT

The percentage of Singapore's total female population aged 15–64 years in the labour force has increased from 31.5 per cent in 1971 to 42.3 per cent in 1978 (Department of Statistics, 1979b).

This increase however, is not evenly distributed in all sectors of the economy. The nature of economic development in Singapore is reflected in the concentration of the labour force into three major sectors i.e., manufacturing, commerce, and services including community, social and personal services. The distribution of male and female workers in the latter two sectors became almost equal in 1977. But there are higher proportions of females than males in the manufacturing sector. . . .

Singapore's female workers usually work for the bottom wage levels in the labour force. . . . This situation is typical in Third World nations. Another common feature in these nations is the systematic disparity in salaries given to males and females holding the same jobs. This occurs in Singapore throughout the occupational system but particularly in the lower ranks and among the daily-rated workers (Ministry of Labour, 1979: 45–53; Ong, 1979:14–15; Nain, 1979:6).

The preceding supports Gronseth's (1972) argument on the negative effects of the husband economic provider role (HEPR). Gronseth observes that the HEPR is conducive to discrimination against working women. Their salaries are perceived as "extra" income for the family and thus expendable while men, considered by employers to be main breadwinners, are given preference in job allocation, promotion and higher salary. . . .

The picture before us presents two key characteristics: (a) women are needed and called into the labour force out of national economic necessity and personal financial need; (b) concurrently, social values favouring traditional sex-role stereotypes remain highly influential. This picture may be completed by yet another trend of female labour in Third World nations. This is the female withdrawal from the labour force upon marriage or childbearing. The peak of female labour force participation in Singapore is reached between 20 to 24 years of age. A sharp and steady decline takes over from there on. This decline coincides with the average age of marriage for Singaporean females: namely 24.2 years (Ministry of Finance, 1979: Quah, 1979). . . .

The most likely interpretation of the withdrawal experienced in the female labour force in Singapore rests on the concepts of role conflict and role strain. Female workers face incompatible role demands and expectations in their daily lives. The degree of incompatibility may be lowest for single female workers; it increases for married female workers, and may be highest for working mothers as the latter are likely to have more of their time demanded by concurrent job, marital, child care and housework commitments. The role expectations generated from the role of worker or employee are incompatible with those from the housewife and mother roles in that the latter two are traditionally perceived as the major if not the only goals of women in society. The priorities are clear for females who have fully internalized the sex-role stereotypes transmitted through anticipatory socialization. They simply leave their jobs, if any, when one or both of these two roles are attained. For those who can afford to leave the withdrawal from their jobs is a "solution" to the problems of role conflict and role strain. . . .

The proportion of females over 25 years old who remain in the labour force suggests there is a small but steadily increasing number of women who either cannot leave their jobs due to financial need, have not solved their role priorities and/or are convinced that self-fulfillment goes well beyond marriage and motherhood. . . .

This group of women has the highest probability of undergoing stress trying to comply with contradictory role demands. The most important reason for the incompatibility of role expectations is the preponderance of a version of the two-role ideology.

In Singapore there is a common belief that home and work are incompatible spheres of activity for females. If one role is attained, the other will be neglected. The absence of comprehensive institutional arrangements to support working wives and mothers lends credibility to this belief in incompatibility. . . .

The Director of Manpower Planning of the Economic Development Board perceives problems of role conflict and role strain when he states that among married women "those who continue working suffer through considerable difficulties and divided loyalties. Those who leave do so with considerable regret" (Ong,

1979: 19). Indeed, even some educated working women have expressed their belief in traditional values and the stress generated by incompatible demands. . . .

At the national level, the call for solutions to solve the problems faced by working . . . wives and mothers, is becoming stronger. . . . Suggestions have been made by community leaders, private citizens and government bodies but the solutions do not come easily in a free-enterprise economy. Three major suggestions can be identified. The most popular appears to be "split-work shifts" or part-time jobs for married female workers (Loh, 1979: 36; NTUC, 1979: 57), which the Ministry of Labour has recommended to employers (*New Nation*, 1979a). A few factories have already established flexible working hours for women (*New Nation*, 1979b).

Another idea is the provision of prolonged unpaid maternity leave of one year (*Sunday Times*, 1979b; *Straits Times*, 1979b) or three years as suggested by a male pediatrician. . . .

The third major suggestion is the expansion of child day-care services (Loh, 1979: 36) and the establishment of full-day school (*Straits Times*, 1979d). The trade unions and the People's Association are expanding their day-care services (*Straits Times*, 1979e). However, there are indications of prejudice against institutional child care. . . . Working . . . women . . . seem to prefer the personalized care provided by relatives and friends (Quah, 1979).

In conclusion, the beliefs that the woman's main goal is family and motherhood; that she is unable to handle housekeeping and a paid job simultaneously; and that she should participate fully in the national economy, are all part of the Singaporean version of the two-role ideology. . . .

This paper has presented evidence which supports two propositions. Firstly, school textbooks give legitimization to traditional sex-role stereotypes of males as providers and females as housewives and mothers. These ideas . . . reinforce what children learn through socialization at home. The traditional sex-role stereotypes are thus carried into adult life as part of anticipatory socialization.

Secondly, real-life economic pressures, require . . . women to play alternative roles in the labour force. Yet, the social and cultural environment does not provide women with the means for a congruent working life. Family and children are still emphasized as the ideal . . . goal of women; the husband's sharing of household chores is a little known idea or if known, it is poorly accepted; discrimination in wages still exist. The two-role ideology is strongly embedded in the minds of Singaporeans of both sexes. . . . Some voices have been recently calling for a more equitable deal for working women. The changes may come but not before the two-role ideology has been left behind. . . .

REFERENCES

BERNARD, J. 1972. "Changing family life styles: one role, two roles, shared roles." In L. K. Hoke (ed.), The Future of Family, pp. 235–46. New York: Simon & Schuster.

COBB, D. and W. S. CHEONG. 1970. Looking Ahead with English 3. Singapore: Longmans.

Department of Statistics (Singapore). 1979b. Singapore Annual Key Indicators. Singapore: Department of Statistics.

GRONSETH, E. 1972. "The breadwinner trap." In L. K. Hove (ed.), The Future of the Family, pp. 175–91. New York: Simon & Schuster.

HOBBS, J. 1973. New Primary English Book 5. Singapore: Longmans.

LOH, M. 1979. "The social responsibilities of working women in the home and in society." In NTUC, The Responsibilities and the Aspirations of Working Women in Singapore, pp. 34–39. Singapore: NTUC.

Ministry of Finance (Singapore). 1979. Economic Survey of Singapore 1978. Singapore: SNP.

NAIR, C. V. D. 1979. "Opening address." In NTUC, The Responsibilities and Aspirations of Working Women in Singapore, pp. 6–7. Singapore: NTUC.

New Nation. 1979a. "Call for split shifts to lure housewives." 6 March, p. 5.

New Nation. 1979b. "The new breed factory workers." 6 March, p. 3.

NTUC (National Trade Union Congress). 1979. Seminar on the Responsibilities and Aspirations of Working Women in Singapore. Singapore: NTUC.

ONG, W. H. 1979. "The problems and prospects of working women in Singapore." In NTUC, The Responsibilities and Aspirations of Working Women in Singapore. Singapore: NTUC.

QUAH, S. R. 1979. "Child welfare and socioeconomic development: the Singapore experience." Indian Journal of Public Administration 25:815–27.

RYAN, N. J. 1971. The Cultural Heritage of Malaya. Singapore: Longman.

Straits Times. 1979a. "Religious class helps them face moral dangers." 22 October, p. 7.

Straits Times. 1979b. "Priority now." Editorial, 15 October, p. 16.

Straits Times. 1979d. "Full-day school: only 25 pc mums will seek jobs." 2 October, p. 1.

Straits Times. 1979e. "Plan to expand PA's child daycare service." 23 October, p. 15.

Sunday Times. 1979b. "Call to allow a year's unpaid maternity leave for women." 14 October, p. 6.

The New Syllabus. n. d. The New Syllabus English Book 4.

Introduction

Few European societies have experienced as much internal and external turmoil in the last century as Poland. In the middle decades of the century, Poland moved from being a primarily agricultural society to an industrializing society. This created expectations which could not be satisfied quickly. In the 1980s the world watched as Lech Walesa led the struggle for political and economic reform.

The transition to an urban, industrial society brought together people of very different cultural backgrounds. Industrialization also offered employment opportunities to women and greater educational opportunities for all. These changes had a subsequent effect on marriage and fertility. Now, approximately one quarter of all marriages are "nonhomogenous" in that husbands and wives are from very different cultural backgrounds. Family size is decreasing as more women enter the labor force.

This study of family values and interactions is based on interviews with families living in three different areas of Poland: a city, a rural area, and a transitional area. The researchers found the sexual division of labor to be less rigid now than in the past, and less rigid in urban than rural areas. Children are more involved in family decision making now, and have input regarding such things as major purchases. Even in this period of rapid change—or perhaps because of it—parents and children share a value system. Both give priority to family cohesion and health above money and material goods. Children want most to be good students and liked by their friends—much like children in any other industrial country.

23
Tradition and Modernity in the Polish Family

J. Bednarski and Z. Jasiewicz

HISTORICAL AND SOCIO-CULTURAL BACKGROUND

. . . [There have been] two periods in the post-war history of the family in Poland. The first lasts until the end of the 1950's and the second comprises the 1960's and 1970's. The first period brought profound social changes connected with the nationalization of the factories employing more than 50 workers and the expropriation of about 64,000 families who were owners of more than 50 hectares of land (about 25% of the arable land). . . . In this period family legislation

Source: Bednarski, J. and Z. Jasiewicz (1984) "The family as a cultural unit: Tradition and modernity in cultural activity within the family in Poland," pp. 281–344 in Manfred Biskup, Vassilis Filias and Ivan Vitanyi (eds.), *The Family and Its Culture.* Budapest: Akademiai Kiado, for the European Coordination Centre for Research and Documentation in Social Sciences.

in the whole country was unified and marriage was formally and legally secularized.

The law consistently emphasized the egalitarianism of the couple and State propaganda encouraged the reduction of the functions of the family. This model took little account of the emotional factor in married and family life. It also favoured youth as the carrier of progressive ideas and attributed an ideological character to the "generation gap". The second period is characterized by concern with the inner, private aspect of family life. Elements of a new propagandist model of marriage and the family, showing a tendency to acknowledge a wider range of its functions and to emphasize the equivalence of family and professional roles, were crystallized. . . .

Directly after the war the number of marriages as well as the birth-rate increased. In the early 1950's, the peak period for this phenomenon, the number of newly married people per 1,000 people above age 15 was the highest in Europe. For men this was 37.6 in the cities and 30 in the villages. From 1950 to 1955 the birth-rate in the cities reached 19 births per 1,000 and was equal to or higher than that in the villages, while the average age of newly-weds decreased. In the post-war period people started families more often and earlier than before the war, and they had more children, who also survived; and the differences between the city and the village in the frequency of marriages and the number of children born temporarily disappeared. . . .

Industrialization changed living conditions. The population of cities in Poland, which was 29.9% of the total population in 1938, increased in 1979 to 58.2%. The number of people employed in the non-agricultural sector increased from 52.9% in 1950 to 76.6% in 1978. . . . These migrations of the rural population to the cities caused an increase in the category of families which were non-homogeneous as far as their environmental origin was concerned. . . . The increasing socio-professional differentiation and the lowered barriers separating social classes and strata caused the establishment of a large group of socially non-homogeneous marriages: worker and peasant, worker and intelligentsia, and peasant and intelligentsia. . . .

We can also treat the changes in family structure as a result of industrialization and urbanization. Equal job opportunities and the elimination of unemployment created conditions for the emancipation of families from procreation. . . . The number of small families increased.

Women working outside the home created the conditions for egalitarian relationships in marriage, which, however, also resulted, in many problems in the family. Equipping the household with modern labour-saving conveniences as well as the transmission of culture increased the attractiveness of the family environment. The system of family values has been changed: values such as happy family life and free time have been consolidated. The low di-

vorce rate—0.5 per 1,000 inhabitants in 1960 and 1.2 in 1977 in the cities, and 0.2 and 0.3 respectively in the villages—is an expression of the stability of traditional cultural norms in the family.

The number of people with a university education increased from 2.1% in 1960 to 4.5% in 1978; the number with a grammar school education from 10.3% to 19.8%, with a secondary-technical education from 3.1% to 17.3% and with a primary school education from 39.3% to 45.6%. The number of illiterate people and those who did not complete their primary education both decreased. Education, recognized as the main factor in social mobility, turned out to be a new value in the life of many families. It is this factor which, next to membership in a socio-professional group, most strongly differentiates cultural needs and activity. Equality in education is one of the bases for the choice of a marriages partner or the aspiration to complete one's education in an already contracted marriage. As is evident from the data from 1972, the level of education of both partners was the same in 67.7% of all marriages. . . .

Organization of Family Life

Division of Roles Within the Family.
. . . The families investigated show the increasing independence of individuals within the family and a more partner-like arrangement. The division of various household duties into female and male chores is preserved in peasant families, but has disappeared in the intelligentsia. In the remaining types of families it depends on individual situations. . . .

In contemporary peasant families a clear division of chores in the household and on the farm—"My husband takes care of the cows and other difficult jobs, while I take care of the pigs, clean the house, wash the clothes, and cook meals. The boys help their father with his chores, and my daughter helps me with my housework"—does not result from tradition but from a rational division of chores.

If most of the families belonging to the intelligentsia have some division of jobs, it is not as strict, and members of the family can trade jobs if they desire: "Besides chores of a technical character, like repairing something, and those which require strength, there is no division into female and male jobs, ". . . When I have time I do some of the so-called female jobs, for example, I do the washing or cook our meals".

In the farm workers' families, workers' families and families in the commercial and service sector, the arrangement of chores depends on whether the mother goes out to work; if she works, the arrangement is clearly defined, and if she doesn't it is changeable, but, in general, more traditional: "The work is divided among the members of our family according to their schedule. Both my wife and I take turns in cleaning the house or doing the laundry; we don't have any trouble with washing clothes, because we have an automatic washing-machine.". . .

It is a general opinion that children helped around the house more in the past, and their family duties often interfered with their getting a good education, especially in the rural area: "I didn't go to school because I had to milk the cows and cried all the time I was doing it. Today children say, 'I can't', and they walk out the slam the door. They say this is the 20th century and times have changed". Children usually have clearly defined duties, often different for sons and daughters, but doing chores depends to a great extent on the children's completion of homework. . . .

Children help parents least often in families belonging to the intelligentsia and here they treat their help as obeying orders. In the rest of the families, children commonly express the opinion they are obliged to help. In families with a large number of children the obligation to help also concerns taking care of younger brothers and sisters. . . .

In extended families the grandparents' generation is included in the intra-family division of labour. Their help facilitates the mother's professional work, farm work, and in taking care of children. . . .

Decisions on educational matters are usually taken by both parents jointly in all types of families. In the intelligentsia there has been an increase in children's participation in these decisions; however, in farm workers' families and families working in the commercial and service sector the exclusive educational role of the mother has been preserved to the greatest extent. In the latter types of families the mother is also the main person who helps the children with their homework. . . .

Although the mother holds the purse-strings in most families, she makes decisions about expenses together with her husband. There has been an increase in children's participation in this kind of decision in families belonging to the intelligentsia, however, the mother still remains the decision-maker in farm workers' families. Children's participation in discussions on important family matters and the following of their advice depends primarily on their age: "As far as I am concerned, children from around 14–15 years of age can already make decisions together with their parents.". . . Most parents ask for their children's opinions: "Even when we don't agree with our children's opinions, we want to know what they think about a given matter." . . . In many rural families, parents take their children's opinions into account in buying furniture and arranging it in their homes. In all types of families it is also no longer only the parents who decide how the family spends its vacations. . . .

Everything that directly concerns the children's everyday life, the way they spend their free time, their choice of friends and, above all, their future usually belongs to the domain of the children's individual decisions. In these matters parents have a role which is primarily advisory. . . .

Leisure Time in the Family. . . . Free time for family members . . . is limited and formed by such activities as shopping, housework, preparation of meals, taking care of various business matters, taking care of children, helping children with their homework, studying, organizing intra-family life and professional work. In a lot of workers' families in which the schedule of professional work is changeable, as well as in some families belonging to the intelligentsia working in a non-standardized schedule of work, the category of free time is flexible. In peasant families, farm workers' families, as well as some families working in the commercial and service sector, the amount of free time depends on the seasons. In all types of families, the greatest amount of free time is on Sunday and holidays. Most have free time in the late afternoons and evenings. . . . In peasant and farm workers' families the free time has become separated from economic, productive, social and ceremonial activities. Free time is not synonymous, of course, with time spent on cultural participation. To a great extent it is used for relaxing. . . .

System of Values in the Family. . . . To the question "What do you value most in life?" from 58% to 80% of the parents in all categories of families answered that a happy family life was of the highest value: "Work is important, but the family is probably more important—the good of the family.". . .

It was commonly pointed out that family members' health is a basic condition for the achievement of any individual as well as family goals; and it is well illustrated by the following statement: "I value my health the most. Everything else takes care of itself. If a person is healthy, he can achieve anything. It depends on his work".

Applying a ranking order to the system of values recognized by parents, we can define their hierarchy of preference. High income takes second place in peasant and farm workers' families, while in the remaining family categories it is peace (which takes third place in the first two family categories). High income is in third place among workers' families, in fourth place among

families employed in the commercial and service sector, and only in the fifth place in families belonging to the intelligentsia. In this last category, third place is occupied by interesting work, but in families in the commercial and service sector it is free time.

Children are generally in agreement with their parents: "The most important thing in life is health and mutual understanding. What good is money if everything falls to pieces?". . . "Nowadays money means so much that if someone has it, he has just about everything; but no, probably the most important thing in life is health. If I weren't healthy I wouldn't be able to work."

. . . The greatest inconsistency between parents and children is found in peasant and in farm workers' families. In these families parents rate values connected with living conditions and material necessities the most highly; however, in families belonging to the intelligentsia, values connected with cultural activity play the greatest role. . . . Parents of peasants, workers' families and families belonging to the intelligentsia rate honesty most highly as an individual value, and next in line is diligence in work. This order is reversed in farm workers' families and families employed in the commercial and service sector. Third and fourth place in peasant families, families employed in the commercial and service sector and families belonging to the intelligentsia are occupied by citizens' responsibility and common sense, respectively, and, as before, this order is reversed in the two remaining groups. The values rated most highly by children in all categories of families are: being a good student, being honest and straightforward and having a lot of playmates and friends.

Preferred Model of Family. . . . People in all family categories preferred the nuclear family with a small number of children (becoming independent right after marriage), in which the mother does not work professionally, and which is based on a partner-like relationship between

TABLE 1.   Hierarchical System of Parents' and Children's Selected Group of Instrumental Values (Rank)

	Socio-Economic Structure*									
	1		2		3		4		5	
	P**	CH***	P**	CH***	P**	CH***	P**	CH***	P**	CH***
Better living conditions	1	1	1	1	1	1	1	1	1	2
Fashionable and elegant clothing	8	5	8.5	4	9.5	7	10	4	11	8
Colour TV	6	7	7	9	7	10	9	11	10	10
Good food	3	6	3	10	4	4	3	5	8	9
Car, better car	4	2	4	2.5	5	6	8	8.5	5	6
Better chance for cultural participation	9	10	8.5	8	8	8	4.5	8.5	3	5
More chances of going out	5	9	10	7	9.5	9	6	10	7	7
More modern household equipment	2	4	2	5.5	2	5	4.5	3	4	4
More comfortable furniture	7	11	5	12	6	11	7	7	9	11
A lot of books, records and tapes	11	8	11	5.5	11	3	11	6	6	3
Interesting vacations, trips	10	3	6	2.5	3	2	2	2	2	1
Expensive sports	12	12	12	11	12	12	12	12	12	12

*1 = peasant families, 2 = farm workers' families, 3 = workers' families, 4 = families employed in the commercial and service sector, 5 = families belonging to the intelligentsia.

**P = parents.

***CH = children.

husband and wife, as well as between parents and children. This model gives children significant freedom of choice of everyday behaviour. . . . The acceptance of this model of the nuclear family results mainly from personality inconsistencies of different generations, from desires to autonomize intra-family life and make it more private, and also from the disappearance of former economic dependence: "A family should live on its own; people aren't angels, older people already have their own habits and they don't want to change them. It may seem that there is help in a larger household, but it's better to work hard and be on your own.". . .

Introduction

One of the consequences of industrialization in Thailand is that rural villages can no longer offer opportunities for young people to earn a living. Consequently, young people move back and forth between parents' farms and cities like Bankok in search of work. This process is called "circular mobility."

In North America, young people seem to be given lots of opportunity to act autonomously. Yet researchers consistently find that parental attitudes have a relatively strong effect on the behavior of young people. Does the same hold true in Thailand? The answer seems to be no. How Thai parents feel about circular mobility seems to have little impact on the behavior of their postadolescent children. Thai children seem to make their own decisions about moving to the city regardless of how their parents feel.

This seeming contradiction is an interesting one to think about. We tend to assume that North American children are quite independent compared to children in traditional cultures who are perceived to follow their parents' wishes. Yet this study shows the opposite. Is the "generation gap" therefore greater in developing countries than in the United States?

24
Parental Influence in Thailand

Alan C. Acock
Theodore Fuller

THIS STUDY ASKS:

1. How much does the attitude of a parent influence the attitude and behavior of his or her children? Does a generation gap exist in a developing nation?

2. To what extent does attitude influence behavior? To what extent does behavior influence attitude?

3. How stable are attitudes and behavior in a developing nation experiencing rapid social change?

These questions will be addressed using a longitudinal study of circular mobility attitudes and behaviors which was conducted in 1978 and 1979 in a rural area of Thailand. A parent and a post-adolescent child were interviewed in each family in order to measure the attitude of the parent toward the child moving, the attitude of the child toward moving, and the circular mobility of the child. Circular mobility involves young adults from rural areas moving back and forth between cities and parents' farms. The young adults move to the city to work when farm work is slack. They return to the farm when their work is needed there.

Source: Reprinted with omissions from *Social Forces* 62 (4), June 1984. "The attitude-behavior relationship and parental influence: Circular Mobility in Thailand by Alan C. Acock and Theodore Fuller. Copyright © The University of North Carolina Press.

BACKGROUND

Our three research questions have received a great deal of attention in the U.S., but little attention elsewhere, especially in developing nations. This background section is divided into three subsections. The first subsection reviews literature on the relationship between parents' attitudes and those of their children. This is followed by a section dealing with the causal relationship between attitudes and behaviors and finally by a brief discussion of the stability of attitudes and behaviors.

Do Parents Influence Children?

. . . Rapid social change in a developing society can drive a wedge between generations, causing members of historically close generations to espouse substantially different philosophies and ways of life. Although a "generation gap" is often viewed as a modern phenomenon, it is perhaps during periods of rapid social and cultural transformation of traditional societies that we can observe the greatest divergence between generations. . . . In such cases the youth shape the social change (Lipset and Altbach, 1967). Similarly, Emmerson notes "The roster of governments whose downfall followed major student protests in the last ten years is long . . ." (390). In Thailand, students have had an important role in political change. University students, organized through the National Student Center of Thailand, were widely regarded as playing an instrumental role in toppling the military government in 1973; the NSCT has also been active in organizing labor unions and farmer organizations (Morell and Samuda-vanija).

Revolutionary change is dramatic, but it is not the only nor necessarily the most important source of social change, nor are students the only young agents of social change. Influences other than the character and the composition of the central government wield great influence. . . . In Thailand, where approximately 85 percent of the population is scattered across thousands of villages, the presence of young villagers who have lived and worked in cities may be a potent force for social and economic change (Goldstein). From this standpoint, circular mobility between rural and urban areas can contribute to modernization.

The profound social change in third world nations may render parental influence impotent. A prime example of this may be the circular movement of young adults. The attitudes of their parents toward this mobility may be far less important than the social and structural forces this new generation faces (cf. Aldous and Hill's work in the U.S.). If this is the case, . . . it would suggest the family is an ineffective socialization agent in developing nations.

The Causal Relationship Between Attitudes and Behaviors

. . . Schuman and Johnson correctly indicate that attitudes and behavior may have reciprocal and sequential effects. For example, your current attitudes may dispose you to behave in a certain way. If you behave according to your attitudes, this will reinforce your attitudes. If you behave inconsistently with your attitude, then you may change your subsequent attitude. While this formulation is intuitively appealing, it is difficult to identify separate effects of attitudes and behaviors. Longitudinal data are required.

Are Attitudes and Behaviors Stable?

If a person's attitude is constantly changing, it is doubtful that the attitude at Time 1 will predict the behavior at Time 2, even when the behavior at Time 2 depends directly on the attitude at Time 2 (see Alwin). One source of instability in attitudes involves measurement error. Research has shown that some attitudes measured in the U.S. are highly stable once measurement error is removed (Wheaton et al.). In general, the applicability of such work to developing nations, where social change is rapid, is unknown. Because we are dealing with a developing nation, we need to examine the stability of attitudes and behaviors as well as their interrelationship. . . .

DATA

The data presented in this paper were collected in six Thai villages during two waves of interviews: July–September 1978 and July–August 1979. The study area is a relatively poor part of Thailand marked by a high rate of circular mobility, much of it between the rural villages and Bangkok.

Villages ranged in size from just under 500 people to just over 1,000. A simple random sampling system was used to select households, with the proviso that selected households should have in residence at the time of the initial interview at least one person within the demographic groups from which the great majority of migrants are drawn: males 15–39 and never-married females 15–39. . . . Approximately 50 percent of the households in each village studied entered the sample, for a total of 356 households.

Two interviews were conducted in each household. The household head was interviewed, as well as one person in the above-mentioned demographic groups. . . . We are interested only in pairs of respondents consisting of parents and post-adolescent children, 114 pairs in all. . . . The mean age of the heads of household was 53.5 (based on first year data; median = 53.1). The mean age of the children was 21.2 (first year; median = 18.3).

Three sets of variables were utilized: parent's stated attitudes concerning the circular mobility of their children, children's stated attitudes concerning circular mobility, and children's reported circular mobility behavior.[1]

Three questions were asked to assess parental attitudes about mobility of their children. These asked the parent to indicate whether s(he) would discourage or encourage a child to move to town, if the child wanted to move. The questions presented hypothetical situations in which the duration of time the child would remain in town varied, and referred to whether the child would be available to help with farming. . . . For each item, the responses were coded as "discourage," "encourage," or, if volunteered, a middle category indicating a contingent response.

A second set of items measured the attitudes of young adults concerning circular mobility. One series of questions measured attitudes about circular mobility to provincial capitals, including Bangkok. A second series focused on Bangkok in particular. The two series are used as indicators of young adults' circular mobility attitudes.[2]

The final set of variables measured the mobility of children based on retrospective responses obtained at the time of the second survey. The study area is characterized by relatively high rates of circular mobility. . . . Time spent outside the village was used as an indicator of actual circular mobility. . . .

RESULTS AND CONCLUSIONS

Three main points emerge from the above analyses. First, parents' preferences concerning the circular mobility of their children have little impact on either the attitudes or behavior of postadolescent children. . . . The irrelevance of parents' attitudes on childrens' attitudes or behav-

ior may not be surprising in light of the lack of stability of parents' attitudes. . . .

Aldous and Hill's U.S. research suggests that less parental influence should be expected in those areas where the family cannot draw on organizational support. . . . One can speculate that in a rapidly developing nation, circular mobility is an example of an area in which family socialization has no organizational support. To the contrary, the social structure is providing dramatic incentives fostering circular mobility and works against parents' traditional rural attitudes. This contrast between the demands of a changing social structure and traditional familism may contribute to the irrelevance of the parental attitudes and the apparent confusion among the parents reflected in the current instability of their attitudes.

Our argument . . . finds support in the anthropological literature on Thailand. Klausner's observations indicate that while parents initially had ultimate authority in these matters, they now have remarkably little influence over the movements of their children. Klausner's conclusion, reached through a very different methodology, coincides with our own. Klausner writes: "The migration has gotten out of hand, and the parents do not seem to be able to control it any more . . ." (p. 86).

A different interpretation of the lack of similarity in circular mobility attitudes between parents and their children is possible. Inkeles found evidence that Russian parents actively influence their children to have a new set of values that would fit the needs of the emerging Soviet society even though these values were different from the values the parents held based on their experience in Tsarist Russia. It is plausible that the parents' attitudes are confused, and not correlated with the attitudes of their children because the parents are preparing their children for a new set of structural constraints. If this is correct, the parents are *allowing* their children to engage in behavior the parents may understand, but see as unavoidable.

Second, for post-adolescent children, circular

mobility behavior affects attitudes more strongly than attitudes affect mobility behavior. These results lend support to theoretical positions which argue that behavior causes attitudes, but they also confirm the merit of Schuman and Johnson's position, that the causal links between attitudes and behavior run in both directions. Third, circular mobility behavior is more stable than circular mobility attitudes.

Three criticisms can be anticipated. First, while it might be argued that either parent's attitude could represent "parental attitudes," one might argue that the stability of parents' attitudes in this sample was reduced because in some cases different parents were interviewed in different years. However, when the sample was limited to households in which the same parent was interviewed in each year, parental attitudes were no more stable. Thus, the fact that different parents were sometimes interviewed does not account for the low stability of parental attitudes.

A second potential difficulty is the substantial amount of attrition between the two interviews. Approximately 30 percent of the children in relevant households were absent at the time of the second interview. . . . Attitudinal information for children who were absent in the second year is not available, and these cases were omitted from the analysis.[3]

We evaluated the effect of attrition on the results by analyzing a modified model with child's attitude in year two removed. It is possible to analyze this model because information about the mobility behavior of the absent post-adolescent children is available, supplied by other members of the household. The number of cases available for analysis with this model is 175. The coefficients for the modified model are quite similar to the coefficients for the first model. Thus, while it would be desirable to know the current attitudes of those children who are absent, the results are substantially identical for those parts of the model which can be estimated with the full sample.

A third problem is the lack of stability of pa-

rental attitudes, a persistent problem in attitude surveys in developing countries (Knodel and Piampiti 1977). Critics may argue that the lack of stability of parental attitudes accounts for the lack of impact of those attitudes on their child's attitudes or behavior. We argue that the measures of parental attitudes possess reasonable face validity in terms of encouragement or discouragement of circular mobility behavior. . . . The pattern is consistent over time. . . .

We have focused attention on a group of young adults who have only recently reached a stage in their life cycle when they can begin to make independent decisions about a number of issues. Since the children still live in their parents' homes, the expectation might be that the children's decisions would be significantly influenced by parental desires. However, this was not the case. Parental preferences have essentially no effect on circular mobility behavior of these village youth. It is not clear whether parental preferences would be so ineffective with other issues. Nevertheless, it is clear that on the issue of circular mobility . . . Thai village youth are acting quite independently of their parents' desires and responding instead to other social and economic forces operating in that developing society. This is indicative of a level of social change—and a "generation gap"—which is more radical than has been documented in the United States.

NOTES

[1]Specifically, the three questions asked, "If one of your children wanted to move to town temporarily and would return to do farming each year in the rice farming season, would you try to persuade them not to go or encourage them?"; "If one of your children wanted to move to town, coming and going several times each year, and might not return to do farming, would you try to persuade them not to go or encourage them?"; "If one of your children wanted to move to town permanently, and would not return to

do farming, would you try to persuade them not to go or encourage them?"

[2]The questions for migration to provincial capitals began with "During the next five years, do you think you will go to live in Bangkok or any provincial capital anywhere?" Following the initial question, a series of questions was asked in order to classify the respondent into one of seven categories, indicating his or her expectations about moving to any city. The seven categories are: definitely will not move in five years; probably will not move in five years; definitely will not move in one year (but might move within five years); probably will not move in one year; not sure about movement in one year; probably will move in one year; definitely will move in one year. A similar series was asked about Bangkok in particular.

[3]There are a number of significant differences between young adults who were present in both years versus those who were absent at the time of the second survey. Those who were absent from the second interview were slightly but statistically significantly younger than those present for the second interview; the mean difference was less than two years. Not surprisingly, absent villagers had, at the first interview, expressed stronger expectations that they would move to some city; a nonsignificant difference was found for Bangkok. Absent villagers had more circular mobility in both years. Interestingly, there were no significant differences between attitudes of parents of those absent and present. . . .

REFERENCES

ALDOUS, J., and R. HILL. 1965. "Social Cohesion, Lineage Type, and Intergenerational Transmission," *Social Forces* 43:471–82.

ALWIN, D. E. 1973. "Making Inferences from Attitude-Behavior Correlations. Sociometry 36: 253–78.

EMMERSON, D. K. 1968. "Conclusion." In D. K. Emmerson (ed.), *Students and Politics in Developing Nations.* Praeger.

GOLDSTEIN, S. 1976. "Facets of Redistribution: Research Challenges and Opportunities." *Demography* 13(4):423–34.

INKELES, A. 1955. "Social Change and Social Character: The Role of Parental Mediation." *Journal of Social Issues* 11:12–23.

KLAUSNER, W. J. 1981. *Reflections on Thai Culture: Collected Writings of William J. Kalusner.* Bangkok: Suksit Siam.

KNODEL, J., and S. PIAMPITI. 1977. "Response Reliability in a Longitudinal Survey in Thailand." *Studies in Family Planning* 8(3):55–66.

LIPSET, S. M., and P. G. ALTBACH. 1967. "Student Politics and Higher Education in the United States." In S. M. Lipset (ed.), *Student Politics.* Basic Books.

MORELL, DAVID, and CHAI-ANAN SAMUDAVANIJA. 1981. *Political Conflict in Thailand.* Cambridge: Oelgeschlager, Gunn & Hain.

SCHUMAN, H., and M. JOHNSON. 1976. "Attitudes and Behaviors." In A. Inkeles, J. Coleman, and N. Smelser (eds.), *Annual Review of Sociology,* Vol. 2. Annual Reviews.

WHEATON, B., B. MUTHEN, D. ALWIN, and G. SUMMERS. 1977. "Assessing Reliability and Stability in Panel Models." In D. R. Heise (ed.), *Sociological Methodology 1977.* Jossey-Bass.

Discussion Questions

1. In North America we assume that an ideological gap exists between parents and children, and that parents are more traditional than their children. Yet the premise of the very popular television series *Family Ties* was just the opposite. Perhaps the generation gap pendulum swings back and forth. Discuss.

2. Are gender stereotypes more or less restrictive to women in the West than in other parts of the world?

3. John Noyes wanted to "develop a system of childrearing which would minimize divisive intergenerational conflicts." (See Excerpt 19) Why was his plan unsuccessful?

4. What changes in the organization of paid and unpaid work would pave the way for more involvement by fathers in childcare?

5. According to Poston and Falbo's findings (Excerpt 21) "Whether the girls . . . reside in urban or rural areas or are in the first or fifth grade, they are consistently evaluated as more virtuous than the boys by both their mothers and their teachers." How would you explain this finding?

6. Referring to the excerpts in this section would you say that parents generally help or hinder children's adjustment to rapid social change?

Data Collection Exercises

1. Take a poll of men and women in your school. Ask them about their expectations concerning the timing of marriage and parenting and the possibilities of remaining unmarried and/or childless. Do the results of your poll reflect current demographic trends?

2. Working in pairs, do a content analysis of sex-role stereotyping in books found in the children's section of your public library. Use Quah's study as a guide. Do you find significant change over time?

3. In Canada in 1987 there were 1.9 million children under the age of thirteen needing childcare because of parents' employment, but only 243,545 spaces. Find comparable data for at least five other countries from different world regions.

4. Using public opinion polls as a source of data find questions that would allow you to make comparisons with the attitudes measured in the Polish study (Excerpt 23). Are North Americans like the Poles in the strength of their family ideology?

Writing Exercises

1. Why has North America lagged behind European countries in providing publicly supported day care and other supports for employed parents?

2. Consider the effect of reproductive technology and surrogate motherhood on the way we think about parenting relationships and responsibilities. Summarize your conclusions.

3. A major theme in American studies of growing up is the idea of adolescent rebellion. Write a personal account of your own experience.

4. Using the references cited in Excerpt 19 as a start, try to find out as much

as you can about the decline of the Oneida community. Write a four- or five-page report explaining what went wrong.

Glossary

Biosocial perspective—American sociologist Alice Rossi's view that stresses the influence of physiology on parenting scripts.

Circular mobility—The movement of young people in Thailand between parents' farms and cities.

Complex marriage—The label given to the system of marriage in the Oneida community whereby all adult members of the community considered themselves to be married to one another.

Gender socialization—Or sex-role socialization is learning "appropriate" sex specific behavior.

Gender stereotypes—Assumptions made about the capabilities of people based on sex. Male qualities are inevitably higher status.

Generation gap—Refers to different world views of parents and children. In our society we assume the generation gap to be the result of parent traditionalism.

Motherhood mandate—The view that motherhood is women's primary responsibility to the exclusion of other activities.

Pronatalism—An attitude that encourages childbearing as a positive, expected life event.

Socialization—A lifelong process of learning appropriate social behavior.

Suggested Readings

EASTERLIN, RICHARD. (1982) "The changing circumstances of child-rearing," *Journal of Communication*, 32, 3, 86–98. This study outlines ways children today have very different home lives from what their parents or grandparents had. A big difference is the amount (an estimated 25% of their waking hours) of time children today spend watching television.

HOFFERTH, SANDRA. (1985) "Children's life course: Family structure and living arrangements in cohort perspective," in G. H. Elder (ed.), *Life Course Dynamics: Trajectories and Transitions, 1968–1980*, Ithaca, NY: Cornell University Press, pp. 75–112. Using American data Hofferth shows how decreasing proportions of children live in nuclear families. Most American children will experience living in a variety of family configurations and many will have a complex network of family ties including stepparents and stepsiblings, half brothers and sisters, and so on.

LEWIS, CHARLIE, and MARGARET O'BRIEN. (1987) *Reassessing Fatherhood: New Observations on Fathers and the Modern Family*, Newbury Park: Sage. This book is a three-part collection of papers which looks at the idea of "new fatherhood." Part One is an analysis of the constraints of fatherhood. Part Two looks at some attempts to change fathering patterns, including Sweden's family policies. The third section looks at the impact of traditional expectations on moments of personal or family crisis.

OFFER, DANIEL. (1988) *The Teenage World.* New York: Plenum Press. This study of 6000 adolescents from ten countries takes a new look at adolescent rebellion and teenage angst. Contrary to expectations, the study found that most adolescents were confident, well-adjusted, and making a smooth transition to adulthood.

WHITEHEAD, MARY BETH. (1989) *A Mother's Story.* New York: St. Martins Press. When Mary Beth Whitehead decided that she could not give up the baby she contracted to have for a childless couple she initiated a very fundamental controversy. Whatever side of the debate you support, Mary Beth's story raises disturbing questions about reproductive technology and the buying and selling of children.

PART V

Families and Work

🐦🐦🐦🐦🐦🐦🐦🐦🐦🐦🐦🐦🐦🐦🐦🐦🐦🐦🐦🐦🐦🐦🐦🐦🐦🐦🐦🐦🐦🐦

Since mid-century, there has been a dramatic increase in the labor-force participation of married women. Worldwide, the proportion of women in the labor force varies from a low of three or four percent to a high of eighty-five percent. Rates are lowest in some African countries and parts of Southwest Asia and highest in Africa, Scandinavia, Eastern Europe, and the former Soviet states. Sweden has the highest rate in this group. The United States and Canada are almost as high as Sweden. Table I shows the percentage of women in the labor force by world region.

In the West, rapid increases in female labor-force participation began in the postwar period. Since then there has been a gradual shift in employment patterns. At first, most employed women were single. When women married they generally stopped working for pay. Then in the 1960s it became increasingly common for married women to work for pay until they had children. When children went to school women reentered the labor force. In the 1980s, marital status and age of children stopped being good predictors of women's labor-force participation.

Postwar reconstruction, and the need to develop an industrial economic base made Eastern-bloc countries far more reliant on women's labor than was the case in the West where women were responding to employment needs in the service sector. In Eastern Europe it was necessary to create social supports such as day care for families with two wage earners. In the Third World there has never been a close relationship between fertility and female work patterns. "The prevalence of part-

TABLE 1. Percent of Women (Aged 15–64)
in the Labor Force; World Regions

World	47
More Developed Countries	59
Less Developed Countries	43
Less Developed Countries (excluding China)	38
Africa	44
Northern Africa	8
Western Africa	52
Middle Africa	49
Southern Africa	47
Asia	46
Asia (excluding China)	40
Southwest Asia	27
Middle S. Asia	36
Southeast Asia	48
East Asia	55
China	55
Japan	54
North America	60
Canada	59
United States	60
Latin America	30
Middle America	29
Caribbean	38
Tropical S. America	29
Temperate S. Amer.	31
Europe	52
Northern Europe	59
Western Europe	50
Eastern Europe	65
Southern Europe	41
U.S.S.R.	71
Oceania	53

Source: The World's Women: A Profile. Population Reference Bureau, Washington, D.C. 1985.

time, informal, home-based jobs for women means that frequently there is very little connection between the two variables." (Chant, 1987: 286)

Labor-force segregation is a universal aspect of employment. In the industrialized world women dominate in low-status clerical, sales, and service occupations. A second universal is pay inequality. Pay inequity is tied to occupational segregation and is deeply embedded in discriminatory practices. Western women who have graduated from universities earn about the same as men graduates of high school. Only about a third of pay differences can be explained by differences in education and experience. The remainder is due to discrimination (both intentional and systemic).

During the postwar period women's earnings have increasingly become a necessary part of family income. In North America, wives contribute approximately thirty percent of family income. This situation creates a double jeopardy for women. Women enter a segregated labor force to work in a job for which they receive low pay relative to men. Their wages augment their husbands' wages, but are insufficient to enable them to be self-supporting. So, although women make a concrete economic contribution to the household, universal pay differentials make it difficult for most women to be self-supporting, or to earn enough to support themselves and their dependents.

Industrialization and Dual Spheres

Work in preindustrial societies centered around self-sufficient households. Family members were economically dependent on one another. Typically there was a strict division of labor along age and sex lines, although men and women did different kinds of work in different societies. In preindustrial North America, women cared for infants and domestic animals and took care of the family's food and clothing needs. Women's labor, like men's, was necessary for survival.

In some respects, women in Botswana (see Excerpt 25) lead a life similar to pioneering women in North America. Like many wives in nineteenth-century Canada or the United States, women in Botswana tend the family farm while men go off to earn money elsewhere. Pioneer men took jobs fishing, hunting, or logging; men in Botswana leave their farms to work in the urban centers of Botswana or South Africa.

Predictably, this absence has a great impact on family life. There are high rates of singlehood and many children are born to unmarried women. Men rarely marry until they are in their thirties. Most children spend the first part of their lives with their mother in their maternal grandparents' home. Extended family ties are strengthened for women, but all family ties for men are weakened.

Throughout the world, industrialization has changed the economic responsibilities of husbands and wives. Wage labor has taken men away from home during the day, or in some cases for longer periods, leaving women responsible for home management and child care. Laslett (1977: 106) describes the absence of men from home during the working day as the single most important event in the history of the modern family!

The Victorian image of dual spheres was built on the assumption that men, as husbands and fathers, would perform wage-earning work and women as wives would be responsible for domestic maintainance. However, the private world of home and the public world of work were less distinct than the ideology suggested. Only the well-to-do could afford one breadwinner. Working class women may have believed in the ideal of full-time domesticity, but they needed to work or take in boarders in order to live.

The idealization of separate spheres remains an effective means of social control. In order to work, women everywhere have had to fight against the attitude that men are the family breadwinners, or that women should be available to young children.

Excerpt 26 describes low-income families in the Mexican city of Querétaro. Mexico has one of the lowest rates of female labor-force participation in the world. There are few opportunities for women in the industrial sector of Querétaro. Most employed women work in the "informal" economy. The informal economy describes "economic activities which are small scale,which operate outside the law, which are labor intensive, which use rudimentary technology and which are characterized by low and irregular earnings." (Chant, 1987: 282) The most common economic activity of the women in this study is making tortillas.

The cult of machismo is a strong deterrent to women's employment. "In general there is a sharp division between the sexes in Mexican society. Men are encouraged to be aggressive, dominant and "manly"; while women are supposed to be passive, retiring, and devoted to their homes, their children and the church." (Chant, 1987: 287) Husbands in the study did not want their wives to work for several reasons: they might be more successful than their husbands, others might think the husbands unable to support their families, and women might have more opportunities to be unfaithful.

Domestic Power and Spousal Relations

Sexual inequality is a universal aspect of human interaction. For this reason some characterize sexual inequality as part of the natural order. Others point to ways inequality is structured by economic power, religious practice, legislation, and policy. Excerpts 25 and 26 imply that men's power has an economic basis.

In Botswana, women have very few opportunities to earn money, although they contribute substantially to the household through their farm labor. The earning power of women in the Mexican city of Querétaro is effectively controlled by their husbands' attitudes, and the cult of machismo that these attitudes reflect. For women to earn money is to challenge men's power.

Is access to economic power the route to sexual equality? This is the question addressed in Excerpt 28. Warner, Lee, and Lee use data from the Ethnographic Atlas to test the relationship between women's contribution to the family economy and their relative power in marriage. Since income is not a relevant factor in all societies, Proportionate Female Contribution to Subsistence is used to measure economic contribution.

The authors found the relationship to be influenced by two factors: family structure and kinship structure. Wives have less power in extended families because of the rigid sexual division of labor. Nuclear families tend to be more egalitarian because spouses are more interdependent. Secondly, wives have some power advantage in matrilocal matrilineal societies or neolocal societies compared to patrilocal and patrilineal societies.

Excerpt 27 takes a more specific look at marital power. This study focuses on peasant couples in Southern Spain. Typically, married couples in this area establish their households very close to the wife's mother. As Gilmore describes it, *close* means within a five-minute walk! This proximity and the rigid sexual division of labor that characterizes this society gives women relatively greater domestic power. Indeed women make most of the decisions regarding household matters and the allocation of household income. Men seem to passively accept this authority structure.

Do men accept subordination in domestic matters because household work is too trivial to command their attention? Gilmore does not think so. Rather, he feels, in Spanish peasant society men are relatively powerless in both their public and private lives. Women at least have domestic power.

Women's Double Day

Housework is the shared experience of most women throughout the world. In pre-industrial households men and women did different kinds of household work, although both contribute to family survival. Industrialization created job opportunities outside the household, and created a distinction between household work and paid work. The Victorian idea of the home as haven reinforced the notion that domesticity was less akin to work than a reflection of women's nature. The continued association of domestic work with women, and its lack of remuneration contribute to the general perception of housework as mindless drudgery.

Now, most women do unpaid housework and paid work. Yet their employment has not changed what is euphemistically referred to as "the sexual division of labor" in the home. Housework continues to be defined as women's work, even if the women are gainfully employed. Women have adjusted to the necessity of working for pay, but there has been little reciprocal adjustment on the part of other family members. In most families, housework falls on women's shoulders. Either they do it themselves or they supervise a substitute. North American sociologists refer to this extra work as a double day or, as Hochschild (1989) calls it, the "second shift."

Much of the research and debate surrounding women's double day looks for solutions in two areas. The first is sharing domestic work; the second is a system of social supports, most notably child care. Excerpts 29 and 30 look at each of these solutions in turn.

Excerpt 29 turns the question of domestic labor on its head. It asks what happens to the division of household labor when one or other of a two-income couple becomes unemployed. Those sampled were educated, married Israelis.

Their responses to the questionnaire indicated a clear-cut sexual division of labor for housework. "The women seem to take the lion's share of meal preparation tasks, the cleaning tasks, and the child-care tasks, while the husbands perform most of the maintainance tasks." (Think of how often meals are prepared, children are cared for, and cleaning is done; compare this to how often maintainance jobs are done. Clearly, "division" of labor is a misnomer!)

Logically, we would expect unemployed husbands to do more housework. In fact this was not what the study found. Employment status does not affect the division of labor generally, although unemployed people do a little more housework than employed people. However the difference is not dramatic. Unemployed husbands do not take over the cooking, cleaning, and childcare tasks typically done by employed wives.

Does the fact that housework has traditionally been defined as women's work "protect" women from the negative psychological effects of unemployment? Are unemployed men who do housework similarly "protected," or does doing housework reinforce an unemployed man's failure as a breadwinner? This study found no relationship between sex, employment status, and psychological well-being. But women whose husbands share housework express greater psychological well-being than women who get little help. Hochschild's (1989) American study found the same thing. Couples were happier when husbands did more housework.

Policy Implications of the Double Day

With some exceptions, work structures and work cultures have been largely unresponsive to the needs of two-income or single-parent families. The five-day, forty-hour work week became the rule when few married women were in the labor force. Then it was a reasonable standard. Now, conventional work schedules place great strains on dual-income families, or on single-parent families when that parent is gainfully employed. They are even less reasonable when we consider that 40 hours is a minimum expectation in many jobs.

Career expectations typically confuse effort with success, and time at work with commitment. When commuting time is factored in, there is little time left over for family or leisure. In North America, work is conducted in an environment that generally ignores the family responsibilities of employees. Yet until recently there was little to challenge the assumptions that work came first, overtime and travel were necessary, dependent care was a family (not a work) problem, and so on. In short, "Corporations have done little to accommodate the needs of working parents, and government has done little to prod them." (Hochschild 1989: 267)

The assumption that work will take priority makes it hard for men and women to be both good parents and good wage earners. Both take job risks if they make employment decisions in terms of family priorities. Few work schedules allow parents to deal with the predictable requirements of tending to children's needs (doctor appointments, school conferences, and the like)—let alone emergencies!

Men's relationship to family and women's to job are two sides of a coin. There is increased evidence that many fathers regret the lack of time they have to parent. In the United States, ninety percent of male executives under the age of forty are fathers, but only thirty-five percent of their female counterparts are mothers (Brown et al, 1989: 82).

Marshall's study (1987:7) of Canadian women in male-dominated occupations concluded that for many women, unlike men, "the decision to pursue a career may mean limiting marital or parental options." Women who become parents face a no-win situation. Employed mothers are overworked; full-time homemakers are economically vulnerable.

The problems dual-earner couples experience are multiplied in single-parent households. Mother-only families are increasing in number in all advanced Western industrialized countries. In the past, most mother-only families were created by death. Now they are the result of increased marital separation and increased births to unmarried women. The United States has the highest rates of teenage pregnancy and birth in the Western world. Sweden has the highest rates of children born to cohabiting couples. Sixty percent of first births in Sweden are to unmarried women (see Excerpt 30). Few of these women are living alone and paternity is acknowledged in all but three percent of cases.

As Excerpt 30 shows, the European situation is very different from the American one. Single-parent mothers in Europe are not as relatively deprived as they are in the United States where poverty rates are high. Generally, there have been four different approaches to public policy regarding single parents in Europe. The first is the British approach whereby needy single-parent families are covered by the same social assistance available to needy groups generally. Single-parents are not encouraged to work for pay; both jobs and childcare are scarce. Despite the available assistance, single-parent mothers in Britain are becoming relatively poorer.

The second approach is to provide social assistance specifically aimed at single mothers. This is the strategy in Norway. Single parents in Norway receive the most generous social assistance of all European countries. They are covered by social assistance until the child is ten years of age. Then they are expected to find paid work.

The third strategy, used in France, is to provide universal benefits to all children. The French strategy is designed "to equalize the economic burdens of those with children and those without, to assure a minimum standard of living to families with children, to aid in the care and rearing of very young children, to make child-rearing comparable with employment for parents, and to encourage families to have a third child." French mothers can choose employment or full-time motherhood until children reach age three. Most (seventy-eight percent) of French single mothers are gainfully employed.

The fourth policy, adopted by Sweden, is to encourage both parenting and employment. Sweden seems to have taken the best of the other three strategies. Young mothers are encouraged to work, and most (83–85%) do. There is a generous social infrastructure that includes health care, childcare, and a one-year parental leave.

Europe is generally ahead of North America in introducing policies to provide income for divorced women and their children, and in providing support for employed mothers regardless of marital status. Health care, childcare, maternity and paternity benefits and leaves, and housing subsidies are well established in Europe. They are woefully lacking in the United States.

Conclusion

Thirty years ago text books did not include chapters on integrating family and employment. In the past, families were presumed to adjust to the employment demands of husbands and fathers. For the few wives and mothers who were employed, family responsibilities were unquestionably their first priority.

As more women enter the labor force, we are beginning to see a shift in attitudes and behavior. The rising cost of living, and labor-force and marital insecurities mean that wives and mothers will be gainfully employed for most of their adult lives. It is in the best interests of family members to support one another in meeting employment demands. And it is in the best interests of employers to make it easier for men and women to integrate family and work responsibilities. The individual, family, and social costs of failing to do so are high.

A decade ago Janet and Larry Hunt (1982) argued that unless increased support is provided for parents, we might expect the proportion of childless couples to increase as women make greater commitments to employment. Because of the extra pressure of combining family and work life, the Hunts predict an increased polarization of career-centered and family-centered lifestyles. They argue that the demands of careers for married women will be more apt to result in a decision to remain childless, because sharing domestic responsibilities is so problematic.

The Hunts' point is that, increasingly, family and career commitments are incompatible. Those whose main commitment is to a career will forego children and possibly marriage. Alternately, commitments to family life and children preclude involvement in highly competitive and demanding careers. According to the Hunts, an important consequence of this polarization will be a widening gap in the standard of living between parents and nonparents.

On a societal level too, the costs of workplace inflexibility are high. There are too many signs that children are not receiving the care they require. Statistics describing the number of children in self-care, and the incidence of suicide, obesity, poverty, and homelessness are chilling. We will describe some of these signs in Part Six.

References

BROWN, SCOTT, MELISSA LUDTKE and MARTHA SMILGIS. (1989) "Onward Women," *Time* (December), 4, 82–89.

CHANT, SYLVIA. (1987) "Family Structure and Female Labor in Queretaro, Mexico," in *Geography and Gender in the Third World*, eds., Janet H. Momsen and Janet Townsend. Albany: State University of New York Press, 277–293.

HOCHSCHILD, ARLIE. (1989) *The Second Shift: Working Parents and the Revolution at Home.* New York: Viking.

HUNT, JANET G. and LARRY L. HUNT. (1982) "The Duality of Careers and Families: New Integrations and New Polarizations," *Social Problems*, 29, No. 4, 499–519.

LASLETT, PETER. (1977) "Characteristics of the Western Family Considered Over Time," *Journal of Family History*, 2, 89–115.

MARSHALL, KATHERINE. (1987) "Women in Male Dominated Professions," *Canadian Social Trends* (Winter) 7–11.

Introduction

In North America the transition from a rural-agricultural to a cash economy was a gradual one. In the nineteenth century as the economy became more diversified, more families came to depend on wage labor. During this transition stage, which occurred first in the Eastern states, and later in the West, it was not unusual for farm husbands to be away for long periods of time earning money fishing, hunting, or logging. While their husbands were away, women added the responsibility of running the farm to their normal domestic jobs.

In the developing world, the pattern of development has been much more erratic. The pace of change has been far less gradual, and the impact on family life more dramatic. This article looks at the effect of migratory labor on family life in the African country of Botswana.

In the past, the economy of Botswana was based on subsistence farming. With the rapid industrialization of white South Africa, there was a greater demand for labor than could be satisfied by black South Africa. Young men from rural Botswana provided an additional source of labor both for white South Africa, and urban Botswana. The economy of Botswana became increasingly dependent on a system of migratory labor. Young single men left the rural areas of Botswana to work. Some men worked until they had saved enough to establish their own farms; others never returned.

Predictably, this outmigration has had a great impact on family life. Marriages occur later for men—they typically marry in their thirties—and fewer women marry. More children are born to unmarried women. Most children will spend the first part of their lives with their mother in her parents' home. Women have become increasingly dependent on their family of orientation (the family they were raised in), while men have become increasingly independent of any family ties.

25

The Impact of Male Labour Migration on Women in Botswana

Barbara B. Brown

... Labour migration is a common phenomenon today within the Third world. ... Yet, there has been little in-depth study of the effects of this migration on women. ... Evidence shows that high male outmigration has led to a modification in the structure of family life and has transformed women's social and economic position to their detriment.

This argument on women and migrant labour falls within the growing body of literature which holds that labour migration engenders underdevelopment. According to this argument,

Source: Brown, Barbara (1983) "The Impact of Male Labour Migration on Women in Botswana," African Affairs, Vol. 82, No. 328, pp. 367–388.

migration discourages local development by producing a 'low-level equilibrium trap' in which migrants and their families are maintained at or near subsistence level by the low wages received. Due to manpower shortages within the sending areas and the lack of capital, productivity of the rural areas remains unchanged or declines, thus spawning further dependence on the migrant labour system. ...

Other scholars argue that in southern Africa, including Botswana, a precapitalist rural sector continues to exist and is functional to the process of accumulation and growth in the capitalist sector. Subsistence farming permits employers to offer a wage lower than the cost of maintaining a worker and his family. As a result of the traditional sexual division of labour, much of the burden of social reproduction and agricultural production is borne by women. Men return to the rural areas only for rest or when they are too old to work.

The principal concern of scholars working in this vein has been to analyze capital accumulation in southern Africa. They . . . have not examined what changes in the family have occurred as a consequence of the migrancy. . . .

◙

LABOUR MIGRATION IN THE SOUTHERN AFRICAN CONTEXT

As the economy of South Africa grew, it required a large supply of cheap labour. The easiest way of obtaining such labour was to 'semi-proletarianize' a large segment of the black population, pushing rural dwellers into wage labour while not paying them enough or allowing them to settle permanently in urban areas. As a result, migrant workers had to depend on the rural areas for part of their subsistence and for family life. In this way capital would not be 'wasted' on the provision of wages and social services . . . to reproduce another generation of labour.*. . .

As South Africa itself did not have a population large enough for the kind of labour reserve needed, people from neighboring countries such as Botswana were drawn into the South African system. Since the end of the last century Batswana have gone to work in the mines, factories, kitchens and farms of white South Africa. However, since independence in 1966, the Botswana economy has undergone changes which have affected the size and direction of labour migration. With the discovery of copper, nickel and diamonds and the establishment of an administrative infrastructure to foster development, there has been a significant increase in demand for la-

bour inside the country. As a result, the labour flow shifted so that by 1976 two times as many migrant workers from rural areas were headed for Botswana's towns and mines as to South Africa.[1] . . . . As a result, the rural areas have been maintained as labour reserves, supplying South Africa and urban Botswana.[2] . . . In 1976 23 per cent of the national population were migrants.[3]

THE CASE OF BOTSWANA

. . . Isaac Schapera studied the effects of labour migration in Tswana life in the 1920's–40's. . . . In the 1940's labour migration became a major force in Tswana society. In 1936 6 per cent of the population were migrants; by 1943 the percentage had increased by 10 and since then has grown dramatically. In 1978 I carried out an intensive study of migrancy in Kgatleng district in southeastern Botswana. This study included the collection of detailed data from 210 households.[4] A comparison of this material with Schapera's data provides a clear picture of the impact of migration on women's lives. . . .

CHANGES IN MARRIAGE PATTERNS

Isaac Schapera found men and women married in their twenties, following a long engagement. Schapera was told 'in the old days' people wed when they were even younger.[5] In the 1920's families selected spouses for their children, al-

---

*See, inter alia, Bernard Magubane, *The Political Economy of Race and Class in South Africa*, New York: Monthly Review Press, 1979); Carmen Diana Deere, 'Rural Women's Subsistence Production in the Capitalist Periphery', *Review of Radical Political Economies*, 8, (1967).

[1]Government of Botswana, *National Development Plan, 1976–81.* (Gaborone: Government Printer, 1977) table 1–2.

[2]David Massey, 'The Changing Political Economy of Migrant Labor in Botswana', *South African Labour Bulletin*, 5, (1980), 5, pp. 4–26.

[3]Government of Botswana, *National Development Plan, 1976–81.*

[4]My colleague David Massey who was conducting similar interviews in Kgatleng in 1978 has kindly allowed me to aggregate some of his data with mine.

[5]Isaac Schapera, *Married Life in an African Tribe*, (Harmondsworth: Penguin, 1971), pp. 38 and 62–3.

though sons and daughters were consulted on their preferences. 'Extremely few people' never married, as marriage offered social status, companionship, economic cooperation and, for men, legal paternity of their children.[6] Cultural convention discouraged sexual relations before becoming formally engaged. While a woman might bear a child after her engagement, she would rarely have more than one until her marriage had been finalized.[7]

By the 1970s marriage patterns had altered dramatically, due primarily to high levels of outmigration. Marriage is now delayed until a later age. While migrant workers might come home between jobs or on vacation, they generally do not settle down until they reach their thirties. Until then, they continue working as migrants while they gather the financial resources to set up their own household.[8] Today, men marry when they are over thirty, ten years later than fifty years ago.[9]

Even though marriage may be delayed, courting relations and love affairs flourish. Before the final step of marriage takes place and, frequently, before an engagement has been formalized, most women have borne several children. This pattern is in contrast with the sexual relationships of previous periods, according to Schapera. . . . Before the European intrusion into Tswana life, few women bore children before marriage. If they did, they faced severe public humiliation.[10] By the 1920s and 1930s, more unmarried women were having children, and community attitudes had modified to the point where women were privately condemned but no longer publicly ridiculed. In 1943 Schapera

found 23 per cent of unmarried women of childbearing age (15 to 54) had borne children in Kgatleng district;[11] by 1978 the figure was up to 54 per cent. Today, an unmarried mother is generally accepted by her family and community.

Most children today will probably spend their first few years with their mother in her parents' home. Consequently, three generation households are common, with both young men and young women with their children remaining with their parents. As a result, individual households have increased in size. In Kgatleng today, the average number of people in a household is nine, while a study by Schapera in 1929 found five to six people.[12]

If a woman marries, she and her children will move into her husband's home. Until that time, the children are provided for by her family's income. . . . The young unmarried father usually offers only a small portion of his earnings to the mother of his children, as a token of his commitment to marry. Those men who do not intend to marry the mother of their children usually give nothing as support. In either case, the bulk of a man's earnings goes to his parents. . . .

Not all relationships can withstand the separation required by migrancy. Love affairs and engagements break off. Some women remain unmarried mothers, even though they would prefer to marry.[13] This situation occurs due both to a gap in the number of women and men of marriage age and to the decline of polygamy which could have permitted otherwise single women to marry.[14] The population gap is itself the result of

---

[6]Schapera, *Married Life*, p. 32.

[7]Schapera, *Married Life* and Schapera and Simon Roberts, 'Rampedi Revisited: another look at a Kgatla Ward', *Africa*, 45, (1975), pp. 258–279.

[8]In the 1978 Kgatleng study 84 per cent of the married men were living at home.

[9]Interviews in Kgatleng district, 1978.

[10]Isaac Schapera, 'Premarital Pregnancy and Native Opinion: a note on social change', *Africa*. 6, (1933), pp. 59–89.

[11]Isaac Schapera, *Migrant Labour and Tribal Life*, (London: Oxford University, 1947), p. 173.

[12]Schapera, *Married Life*, p. 86. A 1972 study in another district of Botswana obtained figures on household size similar to those from Kgatleng in 1978. D. F. Eding, A. A. J. Udo and M. S. P. Sekgomo, *Report on Village Studies*, (Gaborone: Ministry of Agriculture, 1972).

[13]Most women interviewed by the author wished to marry. The few women I knew who preferred to remain single (though not necessarily childless) were all financially self-supporting and secure.

[14]Schapera presented the following figures on the incidence of polygamous marriages in Kgatleng district: 1850–43 per cent, 1880–30 per cent, 1932–4 per cent. *Married Life*,

two factors. First, a number of male migrants are 'lost' to South Africa and never return home. Second, cultural norms and the delayed marriage age mean men marry in their thirties women who are in their twenties. . . .

For the survival of themselves and their children, most unwed mothers must rely on support from their immediate family. . . . Within their own family, however, women are able to contribute relatively little to the household's economic security. Though women perform vital economic and social functions (growing crops, raising children, caring for the sick and old, and seeing after the small stock) these activities offer few financial rewards. Yet while women's financial security is provided by family ties, these ties are undergoing major changes. Reciprocal obligations and cooperation are no longer as strong as in the past. The family, under its male head, is no longer the key production unit. People earn money and earn it separately from their families. This process of individualization increases the vulnerability of those with limited resources, such as women.

THE SITUATION OF FEMALE-HEADED HOUSEHOLDS

. . . The existence of households headed by single women represents a major change in rural Botswana. Isaac Schapera noted the emergence of this new type of household on the final page of his 1930s study of married life in Botswana.[15]

Today, 7 per cent of all households are headed by single women.[16] . . . In addition, a further 16 per cent of households are headed by widows, bringing the total of female-headed households to 23 per cent.[17] There are indications that the number of single women heading households is closely related to labour migration: Kgatleng district has the highest percentage of such households (15 per cent) and also the highest rate of outmigration. Moreover, within Kgatleng, the study of three different villages showed that the village with the highest level of migration also had the highest number of single women heading households (22 per cent). . . .

The data from Kgatleng show households headed by single mothers are significantly poorer than male-headed households. Women are disadvantaged as farmers, lacking equal access to land and cattle.

. . . Even when a family is able to plough at the right time, other obstacles to good farming remain. The family must be able to gather labour to hoe and to scare birds properly. This task is not necessarily easy when well over a third of the men over fifteen are away and most children are in school.[18] . . .

Widows, who account for 16 per cent of all households face difficulties similar to those of single women. . . . They also have limited resources for farming and obtain small harvests. Both types of female-headed households could benefit from kinship cooperation. In the past, redistributive mechanisms existed and the extended family was expected to assist those in need. Obligations toward widows were specified in Tswana customary law. While families continue to share responsibilities today (for example, people still help relatives to plough and old women often look after the children of their working daughters) the frequency and extent of cooperation has diminished. People share less and within a narrower family circle.

These changes have resulted principally from

---

p. 87. In 1978 there were no polygamous marriages in the sample.

[15]Schapera, *Married Life*, p. 321.

[16]Wendy Izzard, 'Preliminary Ideas on the Rural-Urban Migration of Female-Headed Households within Botswana', in Carol Kerven (ed.) *Workshop on Migration Research*, (Gaborone: Central Statistics Office, 1979), p. 74, citing preliminary figures from the National Migration Study, a national random sample survey of 3000 households.

[17]Izzard, 'Preliminary Ideas on the Rural-Urban Migration'.

[18]Government of Botswana, *1971 Population Census*, (Gaborone: Government Printer, 1972) and *National Development Plan*.

the commoditization of the economy. While wage employment has grown, so has the need for cash to buy goods and services. . . . The penetration of capitalist relations of production has altered old forms of cooperation and exchange. Goods formerly exchanged on the basis of kinship or need are now bought and sold for cash. Resource-poor households, male as well as female-headed, have been hurt as a result. . . .

THE IMPACT OF ECONOMIC DEVELOPMENT PROGRAMMES

In Botswana rural women work mainly in the least productive and most neglected economic sector: crop farming. . . . Today the development of the economy has propelled productive activities other than crop farming to the forefront. . . . Commercial cattle ranching has grown rapidly and the wage sector has provided new jobs. Because these changes are advantageous mainly to men, they have in turn meant a reduction in women's proportional contribution to household income. . . .

Many women have sought work in South Africa. In the Kgatleng district study, one-fourth of the women in wage employment were across the border, working primarily as domestics. Yet these jobs were becoming difficult to find, and keep, in the face of rising unemployment and a security crackdown on those migrating illegally. The 1971 Census showed 26 per cent of all adult men in Botswana were migrants to South Africa and 5 per cent of all adult women. Almost all of these women were working illegally, while men were able to obtain some work legally through the Chamber of Mines.[19] Women expressed grave reservations about working (or returning to work) in South Africa. . . .

Women are pushed out of the subsistence sector by their responsibility to provide for their children and by the low productivity of arable

_____
[19]Government of Botswana, *1971 Population Census*, table 13.11.

agriculture. Labour outmigration of rural women only got under way after World War I, some twenty years after men began leaving for South Africa. There were strong cultural and legal sanctions against female migration. Continuing at least through the 1940s, women's movements were restricted by customary law. . . .

In comparison with the 1940s, more women are working today; they are younger; and they are more likely to be single. The 1978 data reveals the majority (60 per cent) of the women who were migrant workers were unmarried mothers with children under fifteen years of age. These unmarried mothers are more likely to be working than single women without children. The mothers generally leave their children in the care of their own mothers. This relationship carries a number of benefits for both the urban woman and her rural family. The working woman is relieved of the problem of day care. With her child (or children) at home, she is likely to send money and goods regularly to her parents, thus helping them to manage. The grandparents benefit from this assistance and also from the children's help around the house. . . .

CONCLUSION

. . . Because women bear the primary responsibility for feeding their children, a woman's need for a family is more immediate than a man's. Moreover, her needs and his occur in different time frames. She needs financial support when she is raising her children. The man may be relatively independent during this time; he may find a job and only feel the need to establish a home and claim his children when he is in his thirties. . . .

Besides the fact that oscillating migration itself discourages men from settling down, marriage may also be delayed in Botswana because it does not offer any major economic rewards. In other countries, marriage offers immediate and important assets and rights to a man. In Lesotho, for example, land is a scarce commodity, and no man can apply for land unless he is married. In Botswana, however, land shortage is not yet serious and young unmarried men may acquire cattle and herd them with their fathers. Marriage is still attractive but mainly in the long run. As a man grows older, he will need to rely increasingly on his own children to earn wages and to contribute to household income. Marriage gives a man legal paternity of his children and is also important in cultural terms. It confers social status, designating a man as a member of the community who can take care of his own. . . . In sum, marriage is still important for men, but its economic return is less intense and occurs later in life than for women. . . . Both women and men depend on labour migration for survival. Yet most women in turn depend on men who are the primary income earners. The ties of support and cooperation between men and women and within families have weakened. Some women raise their children without help from the children's fathers. Assistance within families has declined. As capitalism penetrated Botswana, the whole society became distorted by and dependent on migrant labour. Migration became a necessity to insure the economic survival of the family, even while it undermined the family. Consequently, both women's and men's lives became structured by migrancy patterns. . . . Family ties and economic relationships have been so profoundly altered that it is no longer possible to consider the women and the migrant men as a unit. Women's relationship to migrant labour is largely mediated through men, and women's social and economic position has become less secure and more isolated, as their ties to these men have become more tenuous.

One striking manifestation of the process of decline in women's position is the feminization of poverty. An increasing percentage of the poor in Botswana are women. This is due to the decline in sharing and to the increased privatization of the means of production. . . . This feminization of poverty seems to be occurring at the international level as well, arising out of pressures causing a dissolution of family ties. . . . and out of a concentration in the ownership of the means of production.

Introduction

In the early postwar years in North America, rates of female labor-force participation were similar to the rates in Mexico today. Then, in Canada and the United States, most employed women were single and well-educated.

Over time, marital status, family size, and age of children stopped being good predictors of employment for women in these two countries. Attitudes toward the paid employment of women shifted accordingly. For example, public opinion polls showed a gradual shift towards increased acceptance of the idea that mothers of young children be gainfully employed.

In Mexico, domestic responsibilities and low education hamper women's employment opportunities. But, one of the greatest deterrents to women's employment is the cult of machismo. In Mexico, as in most of Latin America, men strongly resist wives' employment; they consider it emasculating. This attitude is strong enough to effectively create a strictly segregated labor force, where most female employment is confined to the home.

The most interesting part of this article concerns the relationship between family structure and attitudes toward women's employment. Most family scholars argue that "modern" nuclear families foster more egalitarian attitudes to women than are typical in "traditional" extended families. The opposite seems to be the case in Mexico. "In 'unconventional' family structures, albeit often through economic necessity, women have more freedom both to enter the labor force and also to choose the kinds of jobs they are going to do." The article explains this unexpected finding.

26
Family Structure and Female Labour in Querétaro, Mexico

Sylvia Chant

INTRODUCTION

. . . This chapter seeks to show the effects on female employment of household-related factors in three shanty towns in Querétaro—an industrializing city in Mexico. The data are derived from a 1983 survey of 244 low-income households selected randomly from lists of owner-occupiers. . . . It is suggested in the present study that a non-nuclear family structure maximizes a woman's opportunities to participate in economic activities outside the home. . . .

THE LABOUR MARKET IN QUERÉTARO

Rapid industrialization, much of it due to the investment of foreign capital, has fundamentally altered Querétaro . . . and in 1983 its population was about 350,000. . . .

Querétaro has become a key centre for industrial location under a nationwide programme of economic decentralization. . . . Industry employed 38 per cent of the workforce in 1980. . . . and an estimated one-quarter of the indus-

Source: Chant, Sylvia (1987) "Family structure and female labour in Queretaro, Mexico." Reprinted from Janet H. Momsen and Janet Townsend (eds.), *Geography of Gender in the Third World* (Albany: State University of New York Press), pp. 277–293, by permission of the State University of New York Press.

trial labour force were women (Meza 1982). However, women tend to figure more prominently in 'informal' occupations than in industrial employment. 'Informal' employment is a term used to describe economic activities which are small scale, which operate outside the law, which are labour intensive, which use rudimentary technology and which are characterized by low and irregular earnings (Bromley 1982; Gugler 1981; Lailson 1980; LACWC 1980; Moser 1978, 1981). The 'formal' sector is the converse of this, being distinguished by large-scale enterprises, foreign capital inputs, mechanized production and social and labour legislation. The informal sector itself is highly differentiated, and the term often acts as a catch-all for a variety of non-institutionalized employment; but it has often been seen as inferior to 'formal' sector work. . . .

EMPLOYMENT PATTERNS IN THE STUDY SETTLEMENTS

In the sample, . . . if we discount the 169 (69 per cent) who are full-time housewives, only 6 per cent of the female household heads and spouses at work were in manufacturing, 32 per cent are domestic servants and the overwhelming majority (55 per cent) are in commerce or in the hotel and restaurant trade. Traditionally these occupations have been associated with informal employment.... In Querétaro, two-thirds of the working male heads of household in the study settlements were in 'protected' employment, but only one-quarter of female workers. Although factory work was considered desirable by both men and women in the interviews, it was not the main occupation of working-class females. While 27 per cent of all employed male household heads in the study settlements worked in formal manufacturing enterprises, only 2 per cent of employed female household heads and spouses do so. Additionally, men in factory employment earned an average of 3586 *pesos* a week as manual workers, whereas women earned half this amount....

In the study settlements informal employment is most common in commerce and private services—in which women outnumbered men. ... The most common form of female commercial enterprise is the making and selling of *tortillas*, the Mexican staple foodstuff. In about one-third of these cases the wife makes them and the man sells them, otherwise women produce and sell direct to a specific clientele they have built up.... Women also produce other types of cooked food, or engage in small-scale manufacture of plant pots, dolls and soft toys. Net income in informal commerce for men amounted to an average of 3232 *pesos* a week, whereas their wives and female heads of household make an average of 1741 *pesos*. This is probably because women spend more time producing items than trading and thus earn less. Furthermore, women are more restricted in their choice of market locations. Women, therefore, are not only heavily involved in unprotected, non-unionized employment; they also rank low in the hierarchy of informal sector jobs, being in the worst paid activities with least status. Why do fewer women work than men, and why are they concentrated in different forms of economic activity?

Undoubtedly, this derives in part from the demand side. Querétaro industry is heavy, it produces many high-technology goods and parts for export, it is subject to state legislation, and it does not commonly employ home-based piece-

workers. Thus there is little opportunity for women to work in manufacturing, so they take up informal employment.... On the supply side, low levels of education, high fertility and a cultural formation emphasizing domesticity also decrease women's chances of getting out of the home.

HOUSEHOLD CONSTRAINTS ON FEMALE LABOUR

Age

... In the study settlements, the correlations between age and female employment accord with the results of previous studies—among women of working age and under 25 a total of 49 per cent are in paid work or self-employed; this is a much higher proportion than in any other age group. However, when these figures are controlled for marital status different results emerge: 66 per cent of unmarried daughters of all ages are in paid work, but only 10 per cent of married mothers. Among married mothers the highest rate of participation in the labour force is in the age group 40–44; about half the married women of that age work. The highest rate of employment for female heads of households ... is between the ages of 30 and 34, when children are probably too young to work and the mothers have no other option. So, age is interlinked with marital status: where there is a high frequency of marriage break-up, for example, women are far more likely to enter the labour force.

Family Size

... It is generally thought that women with smaller families are less bound to the home and more likely to engage in paid work.... However, in the Third World, the prevalence of part-time, informal, home-based jobs for women means frequently there is little connection between the two variables. . . . In the study settlements in Querétaro, women working outside the home in paid employment had the largest average number of children (5.4), compared with full-time housewives (4.1), and female workers in small family businesses (3.4). Logically this would also be affected by the age of the children, but no significant differences between age groups were found. . . .

Education

In Mexico, . . . in 1980, only 16.7 per cent of all men were recorded as illiterate compared with 21.3 per cent of all women. In the study settlements in Querétaro the discrepancy seems even more marked. One-quarter of the 211 male household heads had no education whatsoever, and the proportion rose to more than half for the thirty-three female heads. Only three female heads had completed more than four years of primary education. . . .

Educational requirements even for manual work in the formal sector, for example, exclude half the workforce from protected employment. In the study settlements, male and female factory workers had an average of six years' education (i.e., they had completed primary school). The men with least education worked in construction and agriculture (average of two to three years' schooling), the women with least education in commerce and private services. Most domestic servants had no education whatsoever. . . .

CULTURE AND THE SEXUAL DIVISION OF LABOUR

. . . Fieldwork in Querértaro indicated men had three main reasons for not wishing their wives to work. First, the wife might earn more than her husband and 'get ahead', though this is unlikely in practice. Second, it might suggest to other families that the husband is unable to fulfil his role as breadwinner and to other men that he is failing to exercise authority over his wife: in other words, that he is weak. And third, the greater freedom of movement accruing to working wives is viewed suspiciously by their husbands, who fear it may result in their spouses being unfaithful (Chant 1984a). This last explanation means women are less likely to be allowed to apply for jobs where they will work alongside men, and it may account for the concentration of women in occupations noted for their isolation, such as domestic service.

THE EFFECT OF FAMILY STRUCTURE ON FEMALE EMPLOYMENT

. . . Nuclear families represented 68 per cent (167) of the sample households. Single-parent families (headed by women) represented 9 per cent (twenty-two) of the total. Extended families (families residing with kin) constituted 23 per cent (fifty-five). (Four-fifths (forty-four) of this group were headed by males and one-fifth (eleven) by females. . . . One interesting feature emerging from the Querétaro data is that the prevalence of the nuclear family may be related to male authority. In-depth interviews with a sub-sample of forty-seven families revealed many women would welcome the opportunity of introducing a relative into the house, but there was much male resistance to this. As many as four-fifths of the male heads of nuclear families were unwilling to share their homes with a relative, for fear of losing exclusive ownership of the family's property, or because they feared lack of privacy, or were jealous that another man, even a brother-in-law, would share the same house. . . .

The structure of the nuclear family lends itself most easily to a strict sexual division of labour, the male partner earning a wage and the woman in the home doing the housework and looking after the children. That women bear children, and that men earn more in the Mexican labour market combine to favour the man's position as breadwinner, apart from cultural influences. This rigid division of male and female labour often results in a marked imbalance of power, with female subjugation to male authority reinforced by economic dependence. In as many as half the nuclear families in the Querétaro study, men regularly withheld half their wage packets from their wives and children. The amount and regularity of family privation varied according to the strength of the husband-father's commitment to his dependants. . . .

The husband's economic support was often negligible, yet if his was the only wage in the family and he was opposed to his wife working, she was on weak ground if she wanted to earn a wage of her own and thus raise the level of household well-being. In single-parent families and in extended families where there may be several adults under one roof, . . . the cultural norms may be sufficiently diluted to allow greater equality within the household and thus improve the women's status. The exigencies of life in low-income communities have been seen in the past as forcing certain families to seek alternative roles in order to survive (Nalven 1978; Lomnitz 1977): this appears in Querétaro to apply most to non-nuclear families. In 'unconventional' family structures, albeit often through economic necessity, women have more freedom both to enter the labour force and to choose the kinds of jobs they do.

Only one-third of the female spouses in nuclear families have paid work, compared with nearly half of the women in male-headed extended families and four-fifths of female heads. What explains this variation? Several authors assert the rise of the nuclear family in industrializing economies is accompanied by an improvement in the status of women. This is . . . not borne out by the data from Querétaro. There it appears to be the women from non-nuclear households who gain access to work in urban areas, and not those from nuclear families.

The organization of housework is one factor explaining why women in some families are

more likely than others to take paid employment. Domestic work is often seen as women's main obstacle to entering the labour force. Nowhere is this truer than in the study settlements, which lack many basic urban services such as piped water, sewerage, rubbish collection and paved roads, and where housing is of poor quality. Deficient housing and servicing make the domestic workload much greater for women in shanty towns than for their counterparts in more consolidated neighbourhoods, and it is therefore probably far more difficult for them to take up paid work in addition to their domestic chores. . . .

Family structure may reduce some of these problems by allowing housework to be shared. . . . In nuclear families the frequency and amount of help is considerably lower than in non-nuclear households, and often housework is done by the female spouse alone. The reasons are as follows. First, because the woman has no other role except her domestic one, it is assumed she can manage that labour in its entirety. Second, even where her husband encourages the children to help, they may be too young to do so. Third, there may only be male children, and in a culture which discourages male participation in 'female spheres', boys should not be seen to help their mothers. In non-nuclear families the help of both sons and daughters in single-parent households (movitated by the fact their mothers have full-time jobs), and of female relations in extended families, means there are often two, if not three, people to shoulder the burden of housework.

Another factor influencing female work-roles is the relative need for women to work. In many single-parent families, women obviously have to take up paid work, especially if their children are young. In extended households, because the housework is shared and because there are more people to support, there is less pressure on women to be in the home on a full-time basis and a greater need for them to earn money. In nuclear households women not only find it far more difficult to balance the two work-roles, especially if they have no daughters to whom they can delegate some of the domestic tasks and if they are rearing young children, but also, if the husband is earning, there is less apparent need for them to enter the labour force. They conform to a cultural pattern whereby the man alone provides for his wife and dependants. . . .

In single-parent households, sons and daughters help financially because women's earnings need to be supplemented. In extended families, the greater number of adults allows more people to enter the labour market. A notable finding of the Querétaro study was that in families where wage-earning was divided between two or more people there was a greater tendency to pool all earnings in a collective family budget and to allocate finance more equitably among the dependants (Chant 1984a). The built-in checks to egoism caused by sharing earnings could mean the family (and its male head where relevant) has a vested interest in sending as many members as possible out to work and maximizing potential income. In one in two of the nuclear households the husband-father does not share his earnings: and he feels he has nothing to gain if his wife goes out to work.

. . . Male authority is modified in non-nuclear structures. In single-parent households the absence of the male leaves the woman the freedom to decide whether to take up paid work (though she often has to). In extended households, the presence of several earners means no man has the position of sole provider and arbiter of expenditure. Women who are not dependent on one wager-earner alone are in a stronger position to press for the right to employment outside the home. Furthermore, the sharing of workroles, both paid and unpaid, appears to spread an ethic of equal participation in the strategies and benefits of family life: it makes it less easy to justify the division of labour on the basis of sex. For example, if one adult woman in the family has paid employment, it is difficult to substantiate an argument that another woman may not.

A final influence on the entry of women into the labour force is the support gained through having other women resident in their homes. For example, there is often more than one adult woman in the home in male-headed extended families; this contributes to female solidarity and strength and helps women challenge male authority. . . .

CONCLUSION

We have discussed the way household type and composition influence women's involvement in the labour force in Querétaro, Mexico. These 'supply' constraints include cultural norms, age and fertility, and the predominance of the nuclear family, in which few women are allowed by their husbands to enter the labour market. The nuclear family is conducive to a strict segregation between male and female roles, whereas other family patterns not only make it functionally more feasible for women to work, but also allow a degree of deviation from the standard ideology that a woman's place is in the home. Female heads, have the freedom to determine how they will organize the family's earning strategies. Female spouses in male-headed extended families enjoy a reduction in their housework burdens if these are shared by other family members, they have greater support for their claim to work from other female members, and the sharing of decision-making and finance among several adults means the male head has less of a prerogative in dictating what his wife will do and more of a vested interest in maximizing the earning potential of the household. . . .

REFERENCES

Bromley, R. (1982) 'Working in the streets: survival strategy, necessity or unavoidable evil?', in Gilbert, A. in association with Hardoy, J. E. and Ramirez, R. (eds.), *Urbanisation in contemporary Latin America: critical approaches to the analysis of urban issues*. Chichester: John Wiley, 59–77.

Chant, S. (1984a) *Las Olvidadas: a study of women,*

housing and family structure in Querétaro, Mexico, unpublished Ph.D. dissertation, University College, London.

GUGLER, J. (1981) 'The rural–urban interface and migration', in Gilbert, A. and Gugler, J., *Cities, poverty and development: urbanization in the Third World*, Oxford: Oxford University Press.

LAILSON, S. (1980) 'Expansion limitada y proliferacion horizontal. La industria de la ropa y el tejido de punto', *Relactiones del Colegio de Michoacán*, **1**(3), 48–102.

Latin American and Caribbean Women's Collective (1980) *Slaves of slaves: the challenge of Latin American women*, London: Zed Press.

LOMNITZ, L. A. de (1977) *Networks and marginality—life in a Mexican shanty town*, New York: Academic Press.

MOSER, C. (1978) 'Informal sector or petty commodity production: dualism or dependence in urban development?', *World Development*, **6**(9–10), 1041–64.

MOSER, C. (1981) 'Surviving in the surburbios', *Bulletin of the Institute of Development Studies*, **12**(3), 19–29.

NALVEN, J. (1978) *The politics of urban growth: a case study of community formation in Cali, Colombia*, Ph.D. dissertation, University of California at San Diego, reprinted by Ann Arbor: Michigan.

MEZA VARGAS, M. A. (1982) 'Desarrollo industrial en el estado', in PRI, *Consulta popular en las reuniones nacionales*: Querétaro, 22–24, Mexico City, PRI

Introduction

The community studied in this article is in southern Spain. Like other European peasant communities, this one is strictly segregated by sex and has a rigid sexual division of labor.

Men spend most of their waking hours outside of their home—either at work or at the neighborhood tavern. Women spend most of their time in their homes where they are the uncontested bosses. Couples invariably establish a household within very close proximity of the woman's mother. Men seem to accept both the authority and the ever-present mother-in-law.

Men explained their compliance as "part of the natural order," or in terms of expediency. They said that their wives would be better housekeepers if helped by their own mothers. Their general attitude was "no hay remedio" (there is no remedy for it).

The alliance between wives and their mothers is a strong one. Its power extends beyond the domestic realm. "For example many men complain plaintively that although they hate to emigrate to work outside of Andalusia, they are literally forced to go when faced with the fait accompli of a decision made by wife and suegra."

Wives make decisions regarding major purchases and they control the family purse. "One man . . . spoke of his wife seriously as the 'generalissima' of the household finances (using the feminine form of Franco's title)." Clearly this is a very different picture from the one usually painted of peasant life.

ical device that one encounters in so many male pronouncements concerning wives, mothers-in-law, and women's capacity to get their own way in general. Although this may reflect, in part, the usual male indifference to "feminine" preoccupations, it also seems to indicate a degree of moral surrender, as the issues concerned were indeed of importance to men and were often, as they knew, sources of dissatisfaction later. In this sense, we may characterize male abstention from such domestic matters as de facto, although ambivalent, recognition of uncontested female authority in domestic decision making.

The most important consequence of the husband's ambiguous acquiescence is that the *suegra* (mother-in-law) maintains a high profile in the man's life, often intruding into domestic arrangements and sometimes asserting the balance of power in marital disagreements. The powerful image of this invasive female scourge is found also among urbanites in western Andalusia (Press 1979). . . . Because of the associated structural preponderance of the domestic matri-core, the Andalusian husband often finds himself outmatched by the weight this fierce harridan throws in supporting her daughter, and his laments often evoke a revealing sense of masculine alienation before a female dyad elevated to domestic sovereignty. The *suegra* . . . (mother-in-law), and her daughter enjoy a moral symbiosis that the husband cannot match. Although he may have many friends, his male friendships are founded as much on competition as cooperation, and he cannot plead for help in domestic skirmishes without endangering his reputation as a "strong man." His own mother of course may intercede, but no man wants to have his mother fight his battles. So he acquiesces, maintaining a respectable façade of indifference before his peers. The husband knows that "trouble" with the *suegra* leads to marital discord, unless of course the wife is "strong" and prefers to mollify her husband while alienating her own mother (this is said to be rare). . . .

The alliance of wife and *suegra*, with the latter assuming the mythopoetic status as masculine nemesis, has achieved a kind of apotheosis in verse and poetry. In both Fuenmayor and El Castillo, the men sing *coplas* during Carnival to great acclaim and applause, reflecting common male concerns. What is most interesting about these verses is the formidable physical power ascribed to the *suegra* in metaphors and imagery, a tradition in which the male appears victimized and indecisive. This may reflect, as Driessen suggests (1983:126), deep-seated insecurity or cognitive dissonance about the power of women, which the "cover" of male indifference or self-abstention is meant to assuage. . . .

One man told me his *suegra* was a "dragon" who expelled him from "her house" (his too) whenever he disagreed with her. Other men described their *suegra* as a "brave bull," a "tomcat," an "armor-plated lizard," and other such scaly or vicious animals.

These pseudo-jocular laments are revealing because of the intimations of sex-role reversal and power inversion with their unconscious implications of sublimated male gender-identity insecurities. Also revealing is the sense of powerlessness . . . as a result of the man's tenuous connection to the home, which is, after all, haunted—sometimes owned outright—by his *suegra*. Even if the man lives neolocally, the *suegra's* intrusion is so all-encompassing that the man feels menaced in his own house. . . .

Faced with this powerful matri-core, the working-class husband often finds some of the most basic decisions in his life taken over. For example, many men complain that although they hate to emigrate to work outside of Andalusia, they are forced to go when faced with the fait accompli of a decision made by wife and *suegra*. . . .

Occasionally, a man may express the opinion that his wife cares more about her mother than her husband, a complaint that may convey a sense of injustice and affective exclusion. . . .

In addition to her dominance in economic planning, the non-elite Andalusian wife usually acts as the administrator of domestic finances. This is especially true among the rural proletarians in Fuenmayor and El Castillo, where the husband may surrender his entire day-wage to his wife each night. In return he expects the house to be run properly, and will himself be given a small "allowance" for his expenses at the bar and for his nightly card game. . . . Again, male acquiescence here may be seen as morally ambivalent. Men evade onerous responsibilities by giving the wife final authority, but there is a lingering self-doubt about it; as usual, this tension finds expression in self-deprecating humor. . . . The few women I spoke all seemed to agree that domestic control, though sometimes taxing, added to their stature and sense of self-importance. . . .

DOMESTIC POWER AND CLASS

This tendency to let the wife and her mother run the family's finances . . . correlates with class status. Among the wealthier peasants, most husbands retain rights over the domestic economy and play a more active part in allocating resources for the family. Among the gentry in Fuenmayor, most husbands . . . take a more active role in finances and may even control the family purse strings. . . . However, in the working classes, where surplus cash is a rarity and where the domestic economy is often managed on a credit or deficit basis (because of the vagaries of agrarian employment), the wife "rules" the household economy and the husband accepts this. . . . Again, working-class male remoteness here is a trade-off in which the man sacrifices control for a modicum of comfort. Conversely, in the propertied classes, comfort is assured through the practice of hiring servants; perhaps because of the above, the rich tend to live patrilocally or patrivicinally after marriage: the *suegra* is not "needed."

POWER AND SEXUALITY

Finally, there is the "power" exercised by wives through their ability to withhold sex, which is the same in all classes. . . . There is a general understanding that in marital relations, it is the woman who "uses" the strategy of withholding sex as a means of controlling or persuading. . . . According to informants—male and female—a husband never withholds sex purposefully in order to manipulate his wife. "He could not do that if he were a man," one man asserted firmly, adding this is an exclusively feminine weapon that would be humiliating for a man. It is also a weapon that carries more than psychological weight. For example, I was once talking to a couple of newlyweds . . . about . . . the importance of having a first child exactly nine months after the wedding. Husband and wife agreed that this is necessary to quell gossip about the man's potency. If a first child is delayed, people assume the husband has sexual problems and gossip about his manhood. They implied that since this is so, some brides are able to "lead the groom about by the nose" by threatening to withhold sex. The man has to placate her so that she quickly becomes pregnant. . . .

CONCLUSIONS

. . . If power is defined as personal autonomy and the ability to impose one's will regardless of the source of this ability, then . . . men have less of this ability than their wives . . . in the lower classes of these Andalusian communities.

. . . Although the lower-class men claim this imbalance is by design and that it "frees" them to concentrate on more important matters, I am inclined to regard this as Rogers seems to do (1975), as farcical face-saving, rather than an inverse "power" to evade work. Beyond the domestic realm, real power is a scarce commodity denied to most men. . . . Most Andalusian workers have little or no political power; nor do they exercise power in relations with their peers, all of whom start from the same point of equivalency in basically egalitarian relationships. They may have influence with their cronies, but few men can be said to have power, whatever its provenance—except perhaps over their sons, but even this is equivocal (Murphy 1983). In Andalusia, men rarely abuse or beat their wives. Andalusians abhor physical violence; wife-beaters in particular are scorned. Since working-class men have virtually no *alternative* sources of power over their peers in communities like these two, they are relatively powerless compared to women, whose domestic power is real and unqualified. Male dominance is indeed mythical in the lower classes. . . .

Finally, given the discrepancies in marital relations due to social class, it is hard to ignore a direct correlation between wealth and male control. Yet such a correlation, though pertinent in Andalusia and elsewhere in Spain (Lisón Tolosana 1971:258–259), seems too perfunctory and simplistic as a general rule. It obscures a host of intermediating psychological and ideological variables. While many rural Andalusians fail to achieve an unequivocal patriarchy, partly because of poverty, I do not see this local-level female superordination as characteristically Hispanic, or south European, or something narrowly associated with relative poverty. . . . Andalusia may represent one gradient on a complicated sliding scale of gender and power. . . .

REFERENCES

CARRASCO, PEDRO. (1963) 'The Locality Referent in Residence Terms. *American Anthropologist* 65:133–134.

CASSELBERRY, SAMUEL F., and NANCY VALAVANES. (1976) Matrilocal Greek Peasants and Reconsideration of Residence Terminology. American Ethnologist 3:215–226.

COUNIHAN, CAROLE M. (1988) Female Identity, Food, and Power in Contemporary Florence. Anthropological Quarterly 61:51–62.

DAVIS, JOHN. (1973) Land and Family in Pisticci. London: Athlone Press.

DRIESSEN, HENK. (1983) Male Sociability and Rituals of Masculinity in Rural Andalusia. Anthropological Quarterly 56:125–133.

FRIEDL, ERNESTINE. (1975) Men and Women: An Anthropologist's View. New York: Holt, Rinehart and Winston.

LISÓN TOLOSANA, CARMELO. (1971) Antropología Cultural de Galicia. Madrid: Siglo Veintiuno.

MURPHY, MICHAEL D. (1983) Emotional Confrontations between Sevillano Fathers and Sons: Cultural Foundations and Social Consequences. American Ethnologist 10:650–664.

PITKIN, DONALD. (1985) The House That Giacomo Built: History of an Italian Family, 1898–1978. New York: Cambridge University Press.

PITT-RIVERS, JULIAN. (1961) The People of the Sierra. Chicago: University of Chicago Press.

PRESS, IRWIN. (1979) The City as Context: Urbanism and Behavioral Constraints in Seville. Urbana: University of Illinois Press.

ROGERS, SUSAN C. (1975) Female Forms of Power and the Myth of Male Dominance: A Model of Female/Male Interaction in Peasant Society. American Ethnologist 2:727–756.

Introduction

This excerpt raises a question that has long puzzled those concerned with sexual inequality: Is domestic power related to economic power? In the West the question is phrased in terms of income. If women earn as much or more money than their husbands, will they have a power advantage compared to women who earn less?

This question comes out of an American theoretical perspective called resource theory. Does resource theory help to explain decision making in non-Western societies as well? This article looks for an answer in a large sample of preindustrial societies, characteristics of which are recorded in the Ethnographic Atlas and the Human Resources Area Files. These are arguably the most comprehensive sources of data available to social scientists.

True, some of the data were collected by anthropologists many years ago, and some of the societies for which data have been collected have since changed because they have been influenced by contact from outsiders. Nevertheless, if we accept that the relationship between money (or its preindustrial equivalent) and power is a universal one, these data sources provide a good sample.

28
Spousal Resources and Marital Power

Rebecca L. Warner
Gary R. Lee
Janet Lee

. . . This study is premised on the assumption that marital power structures vary, across societies as well as across individual marriages, even when cultural norms are patriarchal. Our objective is to ascertain the conditions under which wives may have greater or lesser decision-making authority in marriage. . . .

ⓩ

HYPOTHESES

We hypothesize that two factors affect wives' power in marriage. The first is family structure: wives are expected to have more influence in marital decision making in nuclear than in extended families. Second, we expect wives' power to be highest in societies with matrilineal descent and matrilocal residence, and lowest in societies with patrilateral descent and residence. We will assess the extent to which these aspects of family and kinship organization contribute to the explanation of cross-cultural variation in wives' power over and above the contribution

made by women's role in the productive economy.

METHODS

Sampling

The data for this study were obtained from the Standard Cross-cultural Sample (SCCS) (Murdock and White, 1969), and the Human Relations Area Files (HRAF). The Standard Cross-cultural Sample is a subset of the Ethnographic Atlas (Murdock, 1967), which contains data on 186 societies. Although it is not a random sample, it was designed to be representative of all nonindustrial societies and of all cultural and geographic regions. The societies in the sample were selected in such a way as to minimize the effects of diffusion or cultural borrowing on correlations observed between cultural traits (Lee, 1982: 37–39).

Although all of our independent variables are available in the SCCS, our dependent variable, marital power, is not. This variable was coded from the Human Relations Area Files, which contain written ethnographic information on 296 societies in the microfiche version available

Source: Warner, Rebecca L., Gary R. Lee, and Janet Lee (1986) "Social organization, spousal resources, and marital power: A cross-cultural study," *Journal of Marriage and the Family,* Vol. 48 (February), 121–128.

to the researchers. Our sample for this study is made up of the 122 societies that are included in both the SCCS and the HRAF.

Measurement

Our first independent variable is family structure. The relevant distinctions are those between nuclear, stem, lineal, and fully extended family types (see Lee, 1982: 107–114, for definitions). However, stem families, in which one child remains in the parents' household throughout life, are virtually indistinguishable from nuclear family systems in demographic terms (Berkner, 1972, 1977; Ring, 1979), since all children but one from each family of orientation form nuclear families of procreation. . . . Nuclear and stem family systems are therefore combined in this analysis.

The second independent variable is a combination of systems of residence and descent. . . . The combination was effected in three steps. First, postmarital residence was recoded into the categories of patrilocal, matrilocal, and other. Second, type of descent system was recoded into the categories of patrilineal, matrilineal, and other. Third, our reasoning led us to the conclusion that, in terms of their abilities to affect marital decision making, wives are advantaged by both matrilineal descent and matrilocal residence, but disadvantaged by their patrilateral counterparts. There is an insufficient number of cases in the sample to distinguish among all possible combinations of residence and descent systems, so a three-category variable was created. The categories are:

1. Societies with either patrilineal descent or patrilocal residence.
2. Societies with both bilateral descent and neolocal residence.
3. Societies with either matrilineal descent or matrilocal residence.

This scheme results in the successful classification of 107 societies into one of the three kinship/residence categories. Our theory suggests wives' power in marriage is lowest in the patrilineal/patrilocal case, higher in bilateral/neolocal societies, and highest in those with matrilineal/matrilocal systems.

Proportionate female contribution to subsistence (PFCS) is a control variable. It was calculated by multiplying each society's estimated proportional reliance on each of five modes of subsistence production (hunting, gathering, fishing, herding, and agriculture) by estimates of women's proportional contribution of labor to each activity (see Lee, 1979b; Lee and Petersen, 1983). Estimates of women's role in subsistence production [were made] for 116 societies.

With the focus of this paper on power in marriage, it may be clearer to operationalize contribution to subsistence as wives' contribution instead of female contribution in general. However, data on contribution to subsistence by family position are not available. Furthermore, in most nonindustrialized societies the proportion of adult women who remain unmarried is very small. Finally, we have no reason to expect the roles of married and unmarried women in economic production differ in these societies. Therefore, in most cases, we expect PFCS is an accurate estimate of the economic contributions of married women.

Marital power was coded from the Human Relations Area Files. Five coders were employed, with each society coded by two persons. The coders were randomly assigned to societies as individuals, so that no pair was disproportionately matched. Wives' power was defined as "the extent to which wives exercise independent decision-making authority with respect to their own behavior, and exert influence over the behavior of other family members, including husbands" (Lee and Petersen, 1983: 30). Ratings were made on a 5-point scale, with higher scores indicating higher power for wives. Sufficient information existed for both coders to make a rating of wives' power for 119 of the 122 societies in the sample. Six of these cases were dropped from the analysis because of disagreement of two or more scale points between coders, due in each case to a paucity of information. . . . To arrive at a final score the two ratings were summed, yielding a scale ranging from 2 (low power) to 10 (high power).

FINDINGS

Our first hypothesis is that wives' power is greater in societies with nuclear family structures than in those typified by extended families. This . . . hypothesis is supported. . . . According to our classification scheme, nearly half (46.3%) of the societies with nuclear or stem family systems are characterized by high levels of wives' power, while only 29.2% of the societies with fully extended families fall into that category. Societies with lineal family systems are intermediate. This relationship is not strong, but it is in the predicted direction (see Table 1).

The second hypothesis is that wives' power varies according to customs of residence and descent, and is higher in societies with matrilateral than patrilateral customs. Table 2 shows this hypothesis is strongly supported. . . . Only 32.5% of the societies with patrilocal residence and/or patrilineal descent are characterized by high levels of wives' power, compared with over 70% of the matrilocal/matrilineal societies in the sample. Societies with neolocal residence and bilateral descent are, as predicted, intermediate.

TABLE 1. Wives' Power by Family Structural Complexity (in Percentages)

	Family Structure		
Wives' Power	Nuclear/ Stem	Lineal	Fully Extended
Low	29.6	34.3	41.7
Intermediate	24.1	22.9	29.2
High	46.3	42.9	29.2
Total	100.0	100.1	100.1
N	(54)	(35)	(24)

TABLE 2. Wives' Power by Residence/Descent System (in Percentages)

	Residence/Descent		
Wives' Power	Patrilocal/ Patrilineal	Neolocal/ Bilateral	Matrilocal/ Matrilineal
Low	42.9	15.4	5.9
Intermediate	24.7	30.8	23.5
High	32.5	53.8	70.6
Total	100.1	100.0	100.0
N	(77)	(13)	(17)

In order to assess the impact of our organizational variables simultaneously on conjugal power, we regressed family structure, residence/descent patterns (COMB), and proportionate female contribution to subsistence (PFCS) on our scores for wives' power. . . .

Only PFCS and residence/descent have statistically significant impacts on wives' power. . . . Patterns of residence and descent have the largest independent effect on wives' power. This provides support for our contention that nonmaterial dimensions of . . . resources are important in marital power. However, our material measure, PFCS, does have a larger effect than . . . family structure.

DISCUSSION

. . . In research on marital power, most studies that utilize resource theory use material resources as independent variables—for example, education, occupational prestige, and income. Lee and Petersen (1983), recognizing that "income" is not directly relevant cross-culturally, operationalized the concept for wives as "proportionate female contribution to subsistence." We suggested, however, that nonmaterial dimensions of social structure may also operate as direct and indirect resources in determining marital power. Specifically, we hypothesized that family structure and rules of residence and descent would have independent effects on wives' power in marriage.

Resource theory was developed in a society characterized by a nuclear family system. Marital power was viewed as an outcome of a negotiation between husband and wife. Many societies, however, are characterized by nonnuclear family structures, and thus more family roles may be involved in the negotiation process. Those who have suggested that family structure has an effect on marital power have hypothesized that the more complex family structures will be associated with less power for wives (Conklin, 1979; Straus, 1975; Whyte, 1978). We found this to be the case. Wives also may be under more supervision in extended families, especially in patrilocally extended families (Ellis et al., 1978; Olsen, 1974). Also, development of hierarchies in larger families may take away some of the decision making from wives.

Nonindustrial societies also differ from Western industrial societies in the importance placed upon kinship. . . . The kin group one belongs to affects how one's life is organized. We found that kinship structure has a considerable impact on wives' power in marriage. In fact, it has the largest independent effect of all our variables. When descent is reckoned through the mother's line or a newly married couple lives with the wife's kin group, wives have more power in their marital relationships than if residence or descent is with the husband's kin group. Patterns of descent and postmarital residence, then, may provide a resource for wives by allowing them to become less dependent on husbands for survival and/or less dependent on the husband's kin groups for meeting their needs.

Wives' power falls between the two extremes (patrilineal/patrilocal and matrilineal/matrilocal) when descent is bilateral and residence is neolocal. In this situation, descent and residence do not provide a direct resource for wives but an indirect one in the sense that wives are not completely dependent on husbands for support, either material or emotional. Negotiation between husband and wife may play a larger role.

In sum, this paper suggests, as do Lee and Petersen (1983), that "resource theory" is more ap-plicable than previously thought. More specifically, we suggest that in using resources to explain cross-cultural variation in conjugal power, a rethinking of just what constitutes valued resources is needed. . . . Expanding our conceptualization of resources beyond traditional measures may allow for a better understanding of the decision-making process in marriage.

REFERENCES

BERKNER, LUTZ K. 1972. "The stem family and the developmental cycle of the peasant household: An eighteenth-century Austrian example." American Historical Review 77:398–418.

BERKNER, LUTZ K. 1977. "Household arithmetic: A note." Journal of Family History 2:159–163.

CONKLIN, GEORGE H. 1979. "Cultural determinants of power for women within the family: A neglected aspect of family research." Journal of Comparative Family Studies 10:35–53.

ELLIS, GODFREY J., GARY R. LEE and LARRY R. PETERSEN. 1978. "Supervision and conformity: A cross-cultural analysis of parental socialization values." American Journal of Sociology 84:386–403.

LEE, GARY R. 1979b. "Marital structure and economic systems." Journal of Marriage and the Family 41:701–713.

LEE, GARY R. 1982. Family Structure and Interaction: A Comparative Analysis (2nd ed.). Minneapolis: University of Minnesota Press.

LEE, GARY R., and LARRY R. PETERSEN. 1983. "Conjugal power and spousal resources in patriarchal cultures." Journal of Comparative Family Studies 14:23–38.

MURDOCK, GEORGE P. 1967. "Ethnographic atlas: A summary." Ethnology 6:109–236.

MURDOCK, GEORGE P., and DOUGLAS R. WHITE. 1969. "Standard cross-cultural sample." Ethnology 8:329–369.

OLSEN, NANCY J. 1974. "Family structure and socialization patterns in Taiwan." American Journal of Sociology 79:1395–1417.

RING, RICHARD R. 1979. "Early medieval peasant households in central Italy." Journal of Family History 4:2–25.

STRAUS, MURRAY A. 1975. "Husband-wife interaction in nuclear and joint households." In D. Narain (ed.), Explorations in the Family and Other Essays. Bombay, India: Thacker.

WHYTE, MARTIN K. 1978. The Status of Women in Preindustrial Societies. Princeton, NJ: Princeton University Press.

Introduction

In this article we approach the question of domestic labor from a slightly different angle. What happens to the division of household labor when one spouse is unemployed? Will unemployed husbands pitch in as much as unemployed wives?

This study uses a sample of Israeli couples, one of whom was unemployed at the beginning of the study. Husbands and wives were asked questions about who does what household tasks. The list of tasks included such items as planning and cooking meals, and handling bills. One of the problems with a list of this type is the difference in the amount of time each job takes. Taking out the garbage takes a few minutes a week. Meal planning and preparation takes many hours a week.

Anyone familiar with studies of household division of labor will not be surprised to find that among Israeli couples there is a clear division of labor. Women do most of the cooking, childcare, and cleaning; men do more of the repair and maintenance work. Interestingly, men tend to see the task distribution as more equitable than women do.

Unemployed partners do more than employed partners. On the other hand, unemployed men do not take over domestic jobs to relieve their employed wives. Unemployed men do little more childcare or meal preparation than employed men, and much less than employed women! These kinds of behavioral inequalities are very slow to change.

29

Unemployment and Household Division of Labor

Boas Shamir

. . . It is reasonable to predict that women who . . . become unemployed would increase their share of the performance of household tasks. This pattern is probably expected of them by their social environment. . . . In addition, such an increase might stem in part from the often reported guilt felt by employed women due to "neglecting" their families. Being unemployed may give them a chance to redress the situation. . . .

Source: Shamir, B. (1986) "Unemployment and household division of labor," *Journal of Marriage and the Family,* 48, 1, February 195–206.

Of more interest is the behavior of husbands who become unemployed. According to conventional wisdom, men do little in the family because of the demands of paid work. In accordance with this view and with the exchange rationale . . . their right to abstain from taking a full share of the family tasks depends on *satis factory* performance of the breadwinner role. . . . Nonperformance of this role combined with the financial implications of unemployment should lead husbands to assume greater responsibility and devote more time to . . . household tasks. . . .

Furthermore, . . . sex-role ideologies have become more egalitarian. On this basis alone we could expect that at least highly educated "modern" husbands would turn their time and energy to the family when unemployed. . . . The household task performance of highly educated unemployed men may therefore be regarded as a test both for the exchange view of family relationship and for the alleged change in sex-role ideologies. . . .

The literature on the psychological impact of unemployment would lead us to expect different consequences for men and women. Married women are known to suffer from the psychological effects of unemployment to a lesser extent than men (Warr and Parry, 1982). One explanation . . . is that . . . the return to the traditional role of housewife provides some time structure and sense of purpose and activity (Jahoda, 1982). We can therefore . . . hypothesize a positive correlation between the share of family roles performed by the woman when she is unemployed and her psychological well-being.

It is more difficult to derive a directional hypothesis in the case of men. On the one hand, . . . family roles can provide the time structure and activity enforcement, the lack of which is partly responsible for unemployment's negative consequences. . . . On the other hand, some of the ill effects of unemployment for men have traditionally been attributed to the "demasculization" involved in job loss. . . . On balance, we . . . predict positive correlations between household activity and psychological well-being among unemployed women and negative correlations between household activity and psychological well-being among unemployed men.

It is reasonable, however, . . . that the relationship between employment status and household division of labor and the relationship between household division of labor and psychological well-being would depend, to some extent, on the individual's level of work commitment. . . . Among women, high work commitment should decrease the expected positive correlation between contribution to household tasks and psychological well-being. Among men, high commitment to work is expected to in-

crease the predicted negative correlation between contribution to household labor and psychological well-being.

Two other issues will be examined in this study. . . . The first is the relationship between household division of labor and the duration of unemployment. The second is the relationship between household division of labor and the job-search intensity of the unemployed individual.

METHOD

Sample and Data Collection

The population studied included individuals with academic qualifications who registered as unemployed with the Employment Service of the Israeli Ministry of Labor and Welfare during a period of 7 months. Questionnaires were mailed to the population in two waves, 6 months apart. . . .

From this sample we selected . . . only married individuals (age 27–47). . . . Since the number of individuals whose spouse was also unemployed was small, we excluded them from the present analysis in order to hold the spouse's employment status constant. This . . . left us with 115 men and 170 women respondents. . . .

In addition to comparisons between unemployed and reemployed men and women at the first stage of data collection, some longitudinal analysis will also be presented. This is based on following up those individuals unemployed at the first stage and collecting data from them 6 months after the first data collection. By the second stage, 60% of the respondents had found a job and 40% had remained unemployed. These two groups will provide the basis for the longitudinal analysis. . . .

Measures

Family Task Sharing. The subject was presented with a list of 11 common household tasks. For each task he or she was requested to indicate how the task has been done in their household: by him or her alone, by him or her mostly, by him or her and the spouse equally, by the spouse mostly, or by the spouse only. The subject could indicate the task does not apply in their household. The tasks were: shopping for groceries; planning and cooking meals; cleaning the house; taking out the garbage; child care (including feeding, cleaning, etc.); playing with the children; assisting children with their homework; making minor household repairs; car maintenance; handling the bills; and deciding how money should be spent. Subjects responded to each task on a 5-point scale, with a lower score indicating a heavier share of tasks being done by the respondent.

In addition to the scores for each task, three combined indices were calculated for each respondent: (a) the proportion of tasks performed by self . . . (b) the proportion of tasks performed by spouse . . . (c) the proportion of tasks equally shared. . . .

Psychological Well-Being. This dimension is represented here by four variables indicative of the emotional state of the individual:

1. Self-esteem. We selected the Rosenberg Self-Esteem (RSE) scale (Rosenberg, 1965) to be included in this study. . . . The scale contains 10 items with which the subjects are asked to strongly agree, agree, disagree, or strongly disagree. . . .

2. Anxiety. . . . The question subjects were requested to respond to was: How much would you say you worry these days about . . . ? The items were: Not having enough money for everyday living; Your health; Your job situation; The world situation; and In general. Subjects responded to each item on a 5-point scale and their responses to the items were averaged. . . .

3. Depressive affect. The instrument used to measure this variable is the Depression Adjective Check List (DACL, Lubin, 1967). . . . The DACL is a brief self-administered instrument including 34 adjectives, 22 connoting depression

and 12 free of depressive connotations. The subject is asked to indicate the adjectives that describe his current feelings. . . . The respondent got one point for each adjective of depression he or she circled and one point for each nondepressive adjective . . . not circled.

4. General morale. We used one item for the measurement of general morale. The item was: On the whole, how is your general mood these days? The subjects were asked to respond on a 5-point scale ranging from "Good almost all the time" to "Bad almost all the time."

Job-search intensity. Our respondents were asked to indicate the frequency of using seven common job-search methods during the previous month on a 7-point scale ranging from "never" to "more than 20 times.". . .

Commitment to Work. This construct was conceptualized as the normative belief in the value of work in one's life. This definition follows Kanungo (1982), who constructed a scale to measure general work involvement (as distinct from involvement in a specific job). The scale contains six items. . . .

RESULTS

. . . There seems to be an agreement between men and women that decisions regarding expenditures are more or less equally shared by the two spouses in this population. In all other respects there are clear gender differences. The women take the lion's share of the meal preparation tasks, the cleaning tasks, and the child-care tasks, while the husbands perform most of the maintenance tasks. . . .

The women claim to perform 47.8% of the tasks mainly by themselves, while the men claim 33.9% of the tasks are performed mainly by themselves.

Employment status has a significant effect on . . . shopping for food, cleaning the house, taking out the garbage, and handling the bills. In these cases the unemployed report performing a larger share than the employed. . . .

The results . . . support the hypothesis that unemployment would be associated with increased participation of men and women in the performance of household tasks. The differences are not dramatic, but unemployed men and women take upon themselves a larger share of household tasks. . . .

The findings did not support our hypothesis that work commitment would moderate the relationship between employment status and family division of labor.

Further support for the effect of employment status on household division of labor is provided by the longitudinal analysis . . . of . . . two groups of subjects: those who were continuously unemployed at both stages of the study and those whose . . . status changed from unemployed to employed. . . .

In the small group . . . who remained unemployed there was no change in the household division of labor. Only one activity shows a significant change . . . —helping children with homework. In all other respects there is stability. . . . In contrast, the group whose employment status changed . . . reduced their share in meal preparation tasks and in handling the bills. More important, there is a clear and significant reduction in the proportion of tasks performed mainly by the respondent and an increase in the proportion of tasks performed mainly by the partner. Reemployed men and women reduce their participation in household task performance. . . .

The overall picture suggests . . . the individuals who found employment emerge as flexible and responsive to employment status, increasing their participation in household labor when unemployed and decreasing it when becoming reemployed. . . .

The only significant difference between the two groups at the second stage is in the proportion of tasks shared equally. This difference was "produced" by a slight increase in sharing among the reemployed individuals and a 5.5% decrease in the proportion of tasks shared by the continuously unemployed subjects. The relative stability in the contributions of continuously unemployed subjects to household labor over the 6-month period . . . suggests the duration of unemployment did not play an important role. . . . Among unemployed men, the duration of unemployment was not related to any of the scores. Among women, it was related only to the proportion of tasks performed equally. Longer duration was associated with reduced proportion of equally shared tasks. . . .

The only proportion that is significantly related to psychological well-being is the proportion of tasks equally shared, for unemployed women. The higher this proportion, the higher the self-esteem and the morale of the unemployed woman and the lower her levels of anxiety and depression. This finding is not surprising, and similarly low but significant correlations were found among employed women. . . . There was no support for our hypothesis that among unemployed men and women special relationships would emerge between indicators of household division of labor and psychological well-being. . . . The only exception was a positive correlation among unemployed men between their contribution to child care and psychological well-being. . . .

Are these relationships moderated by work commitment? No significant correlations were found between household division of labor and psychological well-being for men or women with high work commitment. Some significant correlations were found, on the other hand, among individuals low in work commitment. Among unemployed men with low work commitment, low self-esteem seems to occur when more tasks are being performed mostly by their wives. . . . Among unemployed women with low work commitment, self-esteem is negatively related to the proportion of tasks performed mostly by themselves . . . and positively related to the proportion of tasks equally shared. . . . The higher the proportion of tasks performed mostly by the woman and the lower the proportion of tasks performed mostly by her husband, the lower her morale and the higher her level of depression.

Finally, . . . for unemployed men there is a positive correlation between the proportion of tasks performed mostly by themselves and their job-search intensity.

DISCUSSION

. . . Men present a picture of highly egalitarian division of labor, with roughly a third of the tasks performed mostly by themselves, a third of the tasks performed mostly by their wives, and a third of the tasks equally shared. Women, on the other hand, report that they do about half of the tasks mainly by themselves, and their husbands do less than a quarter of the tasks mainly by themselves. . . . The data suggest that in addition to real gender differences . . . there are biases in perception.

More interesting from the viewpoint of the present study is . . . that employment status does not affect the division of labor in most of the tasks studied. . . . However, employment status influences the proportion of tasks performed mostly by the individual versus the proportion performed mostly by his or her spouse. Unemployed individuals do take some of the burden off their spouses' shoulders. . . .

. . . There is no indication of the "role reversal" described by several authors (Kaufman, 1982). . . . Unemployment may increase husbands' contribution to family tasks but not in a dramatic manner. . . .

The behavior of men and women in this area was not influenced by . . . their . . . commitment to the work role. Unemployed individuals with lower commitment were not more involved in household tasks than unemployed individuals with higher commitment. Nor was there any indication that investing time in household and family tasks represents "domestication" in the sense of withdrawing efforts from the labor market. Among women, job-search intensity was unrelated to their contribution to household tasks. Among men, there was even a positive correlation between the proportion of tasks

done mostly by the respondent and his job-search intensity. . . .

Among women, whether employed or unemployed, task sharing . . . is positively related to psychological well-being, though the correlations are low. Apart from that, there was no indication the relative contribution of an unemployed individual, man or woman, to household tasks is related to his or her psychological well-being. No support was found for the hypothesis that for women, investing time in household tasks may protect them from the psychological ill effects of unemployment, nor support for the hypothesis that among men, such an involvement would lead to further deterioration of their psychological state. . . . Among highly educated men the investment of time in household and family roles is no longer regarded as a sign of demasculization. The positive correlation found among unemployed men between child care and psychological well-being is worth mentioning in this context.

The degree of commitment to work did not moderate the relationships between household division of labor and psychological well-being in the expected direction. Clear relationships emerged only among women with low work commitment. For them, the larger the share of household tasks performed mostly by the woman and the lower the share performed by the spouse or shared, the worse the psychological well-being. This finding is contrary to our expectation of finding positive correlations between the degree of involvement in household tasks and psychological well-being among women with low work commitment. The only explanation we can suggest . . . is that if low work commitment means high commitment to the family . . . , then for women with low work commitment the organization of household tasks may be more important than for women with high work commitment, and hence the stronger relationships between household division of labor and psychological well-being. In any case, the results indicate that even among women with low work commitment, household tasks cannot provide some of the "latent functions" of work such as filling one's time or enforcing a level of activity.

In conclusion, . . . the present study joins previous studies that found the domestic division of labor to be relatively stable and unaffected by structural conditions. . . . The present study supplements this picture by showing that changes in the employment status of men and women have only limited (though statistically significant) effects on household division of labor, and that the strongly reported interest of men in their families (Pleck, 1983) does not lead them to immerse themselves in family tasks when unemployed. . . .

REFERENCES

JAHODA, MARIE. 1982. Employment and Unemployment. Cambridge: Cambridge University Press.

KANUNGO, RABINDRA N. 1982. "Measurement of job and work involvement." Journal of Applied Psychology 67:341–349.

KAUFMAN, HAROLD G. 1982. Professionals in Search of Work: Coping with the Stress of Job Loss and Underemployment. New York: John Wiley & Sons.

LUBIN, BERNARD. 1967. Depression Adjective List Manual. San Diego, CA: Educational and Industrial Service.

PLECK, JOSEPH H. 1983. "Husbands' paid work and family roles: Current research issues," Pp. 251–333 in H. Z. Lopata and J. H. Pleck (eds.), Research into the Interweave of Social Roles: Jobs and Families. Greenwich, CT: JAI Press.

ROSENBERG, MORRIS. 1965. Society and the Adolescent Self-Image. Princeton, NJ: Princeton University Press.

WARR, PETER, and G. PARRY. 1982. "Paid employment and women's psychological well-being," Psychological Bulletin, 91:498–516.

Introduction

As divorce and extramarital pregnancy have become more common in the last few decades, the number of female-headed, single-parent families has increased. In this excerpt, Kamerman and Kahn look to Europe to find out what governments there are doing about single-parent families. They wonder if American planners should adopt European solutions, and if so, which ones? The authors find that different European countries have adopted different strategies for dealing with single-parent families.

Some European countries provide for all mothers equally regardless of marital status. In France, all mothers receive assistance until children are three years old; in Denmark it is until children are ten. Most European countries try to make it easier for single parents to work for pay. This is most evident in Sweden where family and employment strategies are far more integrated than in North America. In Britain, as in North America, single parents are given assistance if needed—just as any other person in need—regardless of marital or parental status, or age.

Some European solutions work in the short-term but cause other problems in the long-term. For example, in Norway, single-mothers receive particularly generous aid. Few are obliged to work for pay. However, many have trouble entering the labor force after their benefits run out (when the child reaches age 10). Other countries focus on poverty, not family status, as the problem to be solved in a single-parent family. Some combine generous welfare benefits with training programs to help parents find work and day care. In their varied ways, these policies make single-parent families viable, if not ideal.

30
What Europe Does for Single-Parent Families

Sheila B. Kamerman
Alfred J. Kahn

THE INCREASE IN SINGLE-PARENT HOUSEHOLDS

Although all the European countries report an increase in the number and proportion of families headed by one parent, the size and composition of the increases vary substantially (Table 1).

In Austria, Britain, France, and West Germany, between 10 and 20 percent of families with children are single-parent families. About 85 percent of these families are headed by women. Divorced women constitute . . . almost half of the total . . . and unwed mothers have replaced windows as the second largest group among mothers heading families alone. About 20 percent of all mother-only families . . . are headed by never-married women. In the 1970s cohabitation increased primarily as a prelude to marriage, and couples would get married once children arrived. Nowadays, cohabitation is less likely to end in marriage, with or without children. Cohabitation is also becoming an acceptable alternative to remarriage in many places.

In the Scandinavian countries, an even more dramatic change in marital patterns is occurring. In Denmark, Norway, and Sweden, between 20 and 32 percent of families with children live with only one parent (the U.S. rate is about 26 percent); and almost 90 percent of these are headed by mothers. What makes the situation in Scandinavia unusual is that about half of these women have never been married. (The comparable figure for the United States is 29 percent.) In Scandinavia many of these unmarried mothers are living with the father of their child or with another man. . . . In Denmark and Sweden, out-of-wedlock births now constitute more than 40 percent of all births. (In the U.S., the 1984 figure was 21 percent.)

. . . Almost all Swedish couples who marry now have lived together previously. More importantly, cohabitation has become . . . an alternative to marriage. A growing number of young couples in Sweden are living together, having children, breaking up, and uniting again with another partner—all without ever having been legally married. In Scandinavia, the line between marriage and cohabitation is quietly being erased. . . .

Unwed teenage mothers are common only in the U.S., but their numbers are growing in several other countries, including Canada, Australia, Britain, France, West Germany, and especially Hungary. The modest increase (by American standards) in such young, unwed parenting is "explained" everywhere with a local variation of the same rationale—young women make a "career" of motherhood because they lack alternatives, and cannot find suitable males to marry, especially during a period of high unemployment. . . .

The general European demographic picture is like the American one: characterized by delayed

Source: Kamerman, S.B. and A.J. Kahn (1988) "What Europe does for single-parent families." Reprinted with permission of the authors from The Public Interest, 93, Fall, 70–86. Copyright © 1988 by National Affair, Inc.

TABLE 1. Single-Parent Families with Children under Age 18,[a] Various Years (Expressed as Percentage of All Families with Children)[b]

Country	Year	Total	Female-Headed	Male-Headed
Austria				
(Children under 15)	(1984)	13	12	1
Britain				
(Children under 16)[c]	(1985)	14	12	2
Denmark[d]	(1984)	26	23	3
Finland	(1984)	15	13	2
France[d]	(1981)	10	8	2
Hungary	(1984)	20	18	2
Italy	(1981)	6	5	1
Norway				
(Children under 16)	(1982)	19	18	1
Sweden[e]	(1985)	32	29	3
West Germany[d]	(1985)	13	11	2
United States	(1985)	26	23	3
	(1970)	13	12	1

[a]Or other ages, as specified.

[b]*Sources:* Country census or microcensus reports, and reports to 1987 meeting of European Council of Ministers Responsible for Family Affairs.

[c]To age 19, if in school.

[d]Figures include unmarried cohabiting couples.

[e]To age 19, if in school. The rates include cohabiting (but not legally married) couples. For 1985, 18 percent of families with children were headed by women living alone and 14 percent by cohabiting couples.

marriage, deferred childbearing, fewer children, the declining incidence of marriage and remarriage, increasing or high but level divorce rates, and increasing cohabitation. Beginning in the 1970s, divorce increased dramatically in all the countries that permit legal divorce. Illegitimate births have increased almost as dramatically, but for the most part only in the 1980s, and not with the large number of births to teenagers that characterizes the United States. Although divorce remains the single greatest factor in the rise of single-parent families in Europe and the U.S., unwed motherhood is a growing secondary factor; and as we have seen, it has become common in some Scandinavian countries and in Austria. Finally, the increase in nonmarital cohabitation even after children have arrived raises . . . questions about the future of marriage. . . .

EUROPEAN POLICY STRATEGIES

There is no uniform European policy response to the developments we describe. Some countries have addressed the single-parent question directly, while others have considered it as part of a larger poverty problem. Although these policies may not be fully realized, we have identified . . . four alternative models.[1]

1. *An anti-poverty strategy.* Here the policy is to . . . meet the general needs of the poor, and thus help the family headed by a single mother

---

[1]For details, see our "Mother Only Families in Western Europe," a report to the German Marshall Fund of the United States (New York: Columbia University School of Social Work, November 1987), and our earlier *Child Care, Family Benefits, and Working Parents* (New York: Columbia University Press, 1981).

as well. Britain is the best illustration of this model. A single mother in Britain may remain at home and receive a means-tested assistance grant until her child or children are 16 years of age. Although half of all single parents are assisted by Income Support, the program is unlike America's AFDC [Aid to Families with Dependent Children], because most recipients are two-parent families, the long-term unemployed, or the elderly. There is no pressure on single mothers to take on training or a job. The tax and welfare systems ... create a disincentive for part-time work; but full-time jobs are hard to come by, and mothers of very young children require child care that is largely unavailable or unaffordable. Single mothers who work at least twenty-four hours a week at low wages are eligible for a wage supplement. Nevertheless, most single mothers stay home with their children. Mother-only families are also helped by child allowances, the national health service, and priority access to public housing.

Despite this assistance, the situation of these families has become worse. In 1979 the average gross income of a one-parent family was about 51 percent of that of a couple with two children. By 1984 the figure was down to 39.5 percent. The value of the child allowance has not kept up with inflation, while the income of two-parent families has increased. The proportion of single mothers supported by public aid has increased substantially, from about 38 percent in 1979 to more than half in 1985.

2. *A categorical strategy for single mothers.* Here the policy is one of providing special financial aid to single mothers ... so they can remain home with their children. (This was once the mission of AFDC in the United States.)

Norway ... is the most generous country in supporting these families, and it clearly expects most single mothers to stay home until their children are ten years old. The Transitional Benefit, an income-tested cash benefit, is available to a woman in a cohabiting relationship as well, as long as the couple does not have a child together. The benefit has a tapered phase-out: 60 percent of earnings may be kept until wages equal three times the grant. It supplements the child allowance (provided for all children), the guaranteed minimum child-support benefit (provided if the non-custodial spouse does not pay), a housing allowance, medical care, and various tax considerations. The special financial assistance provided to single-mother families is sufficient to eliminate poverty for these families but not enough to maintain them at the level of husband/wife families. One result is that single mothers have far lower labor-force participation rates than married mothers; they find it hard to enter the labor force when their children reach age 10 and the Transitional Benefit ends.

3. *A universal young-child strategy.* Here the policy is to provide cash benefits for all families with children, in particular those with children under age 3, so that a parent may remain at home during the child's first years. Single mothers may have add-ons, but they are mostly aided by the overall family policy.

French family policy is designed to benefit all families with children. Its main instruments are an elaborate system of both universal and income-tested (but non-stigmatized) family allowances, including a basic family allowance, family-allowance supplements, housing allowances, maternity and paternity leaves, and special allowances for mothers of very young children. The objectives of French family policy—as enunciated in the ninth national plan (1985)—are to equalize the economic burdens of those with children and those without, to assure a minimum standard of living to families with children, to aid in the care and rearing of very young children, to make child-rearing compatible with employment for parents, and to encourage families to have a third child. . . .

French policy offers all mothers of children under age 3 a choice of whether to work or remain at home; it provides a transitional benefit conferring modest support for one year to poor single mothers with children over three. Once children reach age 3, parents . . . are expected to work if they are in financial need. . . .

4. *Combining labor-market and family policy to permit a successful combination of parenting and work.* Here the policy is to provide . . . cash benefits and policy supports for families with children. Young mothers are encouraged to enter and remain in the work force, . . . instead of being supported at a low standard, at home, by public income-transfer payments. . . .

Sweden has implemented social policies that stress the importance of full employment. . . . Like Norway, Sweden provides a special benefit for single parents; however, this benefit is designed only to help maintain the children, and not to support the mother and full family at home. . . . Like France, Sweden provides assistance to all families with children, in particular those with very young children; but much of what is done is designed to support parents in their efforts to balance work and family life. . . .

Wages are viewed as the fundamental source of family income in Sweden. . . . Transfer payments—social benefits—are at best transitional (and very short-term) or supplementary if and when earnings are low. Work—the prevailing pattern for both married and single mothers—and parenting are supported by a generous social infrastructure that includes health care, childcare services, and a variety of benefits designed to ease the tension between work and family life. . . .

LEARNING FROM
THE EUROPEANS

One big difference between the U.S. and Europe is that European countries have moved . . . to develop new social policies in response to the increase in divorce. All the Nordic countries (Norway, Sweden, Denmark, Finland, and Iceland) have established some form of guaranteed child-support payment, paid for by the government when non-custodial parents fail to pay or pay inadequately. A government agency assumes responsibility for collection from the non-custodial parent. These benefits are available to all custodial parents, regardless of income. Where they exist, they add significantly to income from earnings. More importantly, receipt of adequate child support, provided by the guaranteed minimum, protects women and children from needing to claim a stigmatized social-assistance benefit, while also providing incentives to work.[2]

. . . In effect, divorce is being redefined as a social rather than an individual risk, which has negative economic consequences for women and children and warrants protection through the public income-maintenance system. This has not occurred in the U.S., but is being discussed; one experiment in Wisconsin guarantees child support—if not from the absent husband, then from the state.

In most countries, single mothers are already expected to work. . . . However, if mothers are to work, an adequate social infrastructure must exist. Here European countries are far ahead of the U.S., in providing basic social services like health insurance, child-care services, maternity and parenting benefits and leaves, and housing subsidies.

. . . In most countries single mothers are likely to work full-time. Part-time work is not remunerative enough when income-tested social benefits are lost as a consequence. But for many, especially when their children are young, full-time work is not feasible, because of time and child-care problems. No country has yet resolved the problem posed by the need for a full-time wage coupled with the inability to cope with the time pressures of a full-time job. Currently the extent to which work is expected of single mothers is in part a function of unemploy-

[2]See our *Child Support: From Debt Collection to Social Policy* (Beverly Hills, CA: Sage Publishers, 1988), and Irwin Garfinkel, "Child Support and Public Policy," paper prepared for the OECD meeting "Lone Parents: The Economic Challenge of Changing Family Structures," December 1987.

ment rates. Britain is still supporting single mothers at home, while Sweden, Finland, Denmark, Germany, and France expect them to work. . . .

The policy of giving special support to parents with children under age 3 is designed to promote numerous policy goals: to improve the labor market (by lessening the pressure on it when unemployment rates are high), to increase the population (by making it easier for women to have more children), to reduce public expenditures (by providing less government-financed child care), and to further equality between the sexes (by making it easier for women to work while still being able to bear and rear children). These policies involve extending paid and job-protected maternity/parenting leaves with supplementary leaves and cash benefits, the latter usually at a lower level than the immediate post-childbirth benefit. In some countries (Sweden, Finland, Austria), these benefits are contingent on prior work, and therefore create strong incentives for early labor-market participation and strong disincentives to adolescent parenting. By assuring job protection, the policies facilitate a return to work for women who might otherwise find it difficult to get jobs. . . .

Americans rightly worry about the unanticipated consequences of policies. But European . . . analyses consistently arrive at this reassuring conclusion: women do not have babies in order to qualify for social benefits, and couples do not break up to get benefits. Social policies do not cause these developments. But once an unwed mother has a baby, and once a couple divorces, social benefits make the single-parent family possible in various ways, depending on the policy.

In both the U.S. and Europe, single-parent families with children face economic difficulties, because families cannot manage financially with only one wage-earner. The difference between the U.S. and Europe, however, is that the European countries have understood this and have addressed the problem; the U.S. has not. As a consequence, the European countries provide extensive child-related income supplements for all families with children (child allowances, tax credits, child-allowance supplements, etc.), while the U.S. does not. The European countries have a far more extensive social infrastructure for children and families than does the U.S. (consisting of things like health-care coverage and public preschools). The European countries provide income-tested benefits (rather than stigmatized, means-tested aid) that are likely to help single-parent families (especially with supplementary cash and housing support), while the U.S. does not. The European countries increasingly provide guaranteed minimum child-support (in part by collecting from the absent parent); the U.S. still lacks such a policy, despite active discussion and the Wisconsin experiment. In addition, the Europeans have gone much further in making work viable for parents (by providing maternity and parental leaves, flexible work time, leave to take care of a sick child, etc.). The result is that most single-parent families are better off economically in Europe than in the U.S. . . .

Discussion Questions

1. Does the status of women improve with industrialization? Discuss with reference to readings in this book.

2. Where would you choose to live as a single parent—assuming you had your choice of country? Why?

3. Gilmore (Excerpt 27) argues that male dominance is "mythical" among lower-class Spaniards. Do you agree with his argument?

4. Some have argued that men would spend more time with their children if only they weren't so pressured by work. Yet studies of the household division of labor consistently find that men do not use their nonwork time for childcare or housework. How do you explain this inconsistency?

5. Resource theory predicts that husbands will usually be dominant because they bring more resources to a marriage. Is this argument circular? Explain why or why not.

6. Will the household "division of labor" become increasingly egalitarian over time? Why or why not?

Data Collection Exercises

1. Using United Nations data for age of marriage for men and women, and births to unmarried women, see if you can predict which countries of the world supply migrant labor. (See Excerpt 25 for some hints.)

2. Using the periodical index, locate articles from the 1950s and 1960s on the topic of maternal employment. Make a list of the pros and cons that are described. Are there signs of a shift in attitude since that time?

3. Reproduce the list of household tasks found in Excerpt 29. Add columns for respondents to indicate whether the job or decision should be joint, husband primarily, or wife primarily. Then add appropriate "face sheet" variables (age, sex, marital status, etc.). Administer the questionnaire to at least 15 married people and analyze the results.

4. Interview at least six married people about the determinants of power in marital relationships. Write a report addressing the following questions. Who has more power—husbands or wives? How is power exercised? Does power shift over time?

Writing Exercises

1. How did the demand for wage labor that accompanied industrialization affect North American families? Compare these to the current situation in Botswana in a brief (500-word) essay.

2. Anthropologist Michelle Rosaldo is quoted in Excerpt 27 as saying "We have plenty of data 'on women' . . . What is needed is not so much data as questions." What do you think she means by this? Outline and explain two or three "big picture" questions raised by the excerpts in this section.

3. Why don't men do more housework? In a brief essay, answer this question in terms of the structural constraints placed on men by the social environment. How do we go about removing these barriers?

4. Is male power in North America—like male power in Spain—a sham? Write a dialogue between two men who disagree about the answer. Document their opinions with examples.

Glossary

Breadwinner trap—A term used to describe the dilemma men experience regarding the conflicting demands of paid employment and involvement in family life.

Domestic or marital power—The capacity to prevail in decisions within the context of a marriage.

Dual spheres—The idea that men should be wage earners and women be responsible for domestic work and childcare.

Informal employment sector—A term used to describe economic activity outside of the formal economy. These activities are typically small scale, labor intensive, use low technology, and provide low earnings. Women make up a large part of the informal employment sector in the Third World.

Labor reserve—Men from rural areas in the Third World provide a source of labor to capitalist development in urban areas or other countries.

Machismo—The idea of male superiority embodied in displays of male strength and prowess.

Systemic discrimination—Employment practices that result in different job futures for men and women.

Underdevelopment debate—The debate over whether large scale labor migration contributes to Third World underdevelopment by discouraging local development.

Suggested Readings

GALINSKY, ELLEN. (1990) "The impact of human resource policies on employees: Balancing work/family life," *Journal of Family Issues*, 11, 4, 368–383. This article is based on interviews with five Fortune 500 companies and universities to gain an understanding of the problems employees face and the employers' response. The major family-related problems are childcare, elder care, work time and relocation.

HOCHSCHILD, ARLIE. (1989) *The Second Shift: Working Parents and the Revolution at Home.* New York: Viking. This book reads like a novel yet is an insightful and well-researched account of how American couples negotiate housework and parenting. Interestingly, those who distribute the work most equitably are most satisfied with their relationship, although both spouses had to make sacrifices at their paid jobs.

HUNT, JANET, and LARRY HUNT. (1982) "The dualities of careers and families: New integrations or new polarizations," *Social Problems*, 29, 5, 488–510. An early and insightful article showing the fallacy of the assumption that dual-career households are symmetrical regarding the distribution of nonpaid work. In addition the Hunts show the consequences of women's overwork in the difference in standard of living between households with children and those without.

KAMERMAN, SHEILA. (1989) "Family policy: Has the United States learned from Europe?" *Policy Studies Review,* 8, 3, 581–598. A comparison of American and European family policy that finds the United States somewhat lacking. One of the inhibitors to a comprehensive family policy in the United States is the longstanding hesitation to avoid intruding into what are assumed to be individual concerns.

ONTARIO WOMEN'S DIRECTORATE. (1991) *Work and Family: The Crucial Balance,* Toronto: Queen's Park. This book is a readable and practical introduction to what Canadian companies have done to help men and women integrate their family and work responsibilities.

WILSON, S. J. (1991) *Women, Families and Work* (3rd ed.), Toronto: McGraw-Hill Ryerson. An historically grounded analysis of changing family and employment responsibilities for Canadian women with a chapter on the women's movement as a catalyst for change.

PART VI

Crisis and Conflict in Family Life

ᘓᘓᘓᘓᘓᘓᘓᘓᘓᘓᘓᘓᘓᘓᘓᘓᘓᘓᘓᘓᘓᘓᘓᘓᘓᘓᘓᘓᘓᘓᘓᘓᘓᘓᘓᘓᘓ

Few would disagree with the notion that family life is stressful. Families are under stress for a variety of reasons. Millions of families throughout the world live in the shadow of political upheaval, war, poverty, famine, and natural disaster. Even in the relative prosperity and tranquility of the West, few families will avoid the stress created by the ill health or death of a family member, financial trouble, job loss, or marital breakdown.

Indeed, it would be impossible to catalog all the disruptive situations families deal with. The articles in this section touch on some of the many sources of stress for families. The first three articles describe ways families cope in the face of social environments that are extremely stressful: acute poverty, war, and homelessness. The last three focus on interpersonal relationships, and the use of violence as a means of interpersonal control.

Are families now under more stress than families in the past? Has conflict increased or decreased? Is there more violence in our society now than in the past? These questions are very difficult to answer. The mass media make us constantly aware of the everpresent threats to peace, to the environment, and to global health. We are certainly more conscious of the extent and the consequences of world conflict than in the past, and more fearful of the future.

One undeniable sign that things are getting worse and not better is the appallingly high number of children who are not protected from poverty, war, disease, and violence. The statistics are grim. Every day thousands of children die of starvation and disease. Childhood deaths amount to one-third of all deaths worldwide, but one-half to two-thirds of all deaths in developing countries. In Europe and America, children account for two to three percent of all deaths. Almost as many children die annually as the total death toll for the duration of World War II. Even in the United States, more children have died of neglect than people have died in combat (Kent, 1991). Millions more children are abused and neglected and hundreds of millions are undernourished.

Most of the deaths, the abuse and the neglect are linked to poverty. Children die, or are sold, abandoned, or orphaned because their parents are poor. Neither the local community, nor the international community has provided a safety net. While Westerners grow (quite literally) fat, women and children in developing countries have insufficient food. The problem, of course, is not only the inequitable distribution of resources between rich and poor countries. Within Western countries children regularly go to bed hungry. In cities across the United States thousands upon thousands are homeless.

In Part Four we looked at some ways families influence the course of their children's future. In ideal situations parents provide material and emotional comfort and encourage children to grow physically and psychologically so that they will become independent adults and make their way in the world. The Columbian street children (Excerpt 20) did not have such advantages. They, like independent children in refugee camps, runaways, or child prostitutes, fend for themselves—often with dire consequences to their physical and emotional well-being.

Millions (estimates vary from 50 to 150) of children work to support themselves or help support their families. They work in "adult" jobs, for "adult" hours, but do not receive "adult" pay. Often they work in conditions reminiscent of the mines and sweatshops of Western history books. Child workers are employed in agriculture, manufacturing, food service, drug trafficking, and prostitution. The demand for child labor is not confined to newly developing countries. An estimated one million Mexican children are employed in the United States. (Kent, 1991) Children everywhere work because they are poor, their families are poor and the community has failed to protect them through education or legislation.

In the United States more than half of all black children are born to women who are not married. Black or white, young unmarried mothers in the United States live in poverty. But black female-headed families will likely stay poor. As Edelman explains in Excerpt 31, they stay poor because they have the economic support of neither family nor community. Young black pregnant women do not marry because young black men face such bleak futures. They have little chance of meaningful employment and face a high risk of being involved in violence or substance abuse. Edelman concludes that "the key to bolstering black families, alleviating the growth in female-headed households, and reducing black child poverty lies in improving education, training, and employment opportunities for black men and women."

Compare the plight of single parents in the United States to single mothers in Sweden. In Sweden, almost half of all children are born to women who are not married, although the majority of the mothers cohabit. The concept of illegitimacy has no meaning in Sweden. Swedes do not differentiate children according to the marital status of their mothers.

As Excerpt 30 pointed out, Sweden provides extensive social benefits to all parents. All are guaranteed a one-year paid parental leave after childbirth. When parents return to work (about eighty-five percent of Swedish women are in the labor force) there are extensive public health and childcare services available. Single parents who do not receive child support from the noncustodial parent receive a generous support payment from the government.

National and International Conflict

While it is true that there are fewer wars now than in the past, "modern" wars are more violent. More lives are lost and the devastation is greater. One thing that distinguishes current wars from wars in the past is the large number of civilian losses now compared to the past. Inevitably families living in societies affected by war suffer multiple loss. They experience the death or separation from family members, loss of home and material possessions, and loss of livelihood. Most importantly perhaps, they suffer a loss of future.

Excerpt 32 is a study of family adjustment to relocation occasioned by the Iran-Iraq war. Those surveyed were Iranian war migrants. In spite of the loss of their homes, their communities, and their farms or their businesses, public pressure opposed their move. They were unwelcome at their destination because they had resisted the government's plan to remain at the front to forestall invasion. "They were referred to as cowardly, not patriotic, and unfaithful to Islam."

In 1988 an estimated twelve million people lived in refugee camps. Most refugee camps, at least in the Third World, are peopled primarily by women and children. Many of the children are orphans who are left to fend for themselves. All will carry the effects of their experience for a lifetime.

The sense of social disorganization of camp life inevitably leads to marital conflict and violence. Women are particularly vulnerable. "There are multiple reports of rape . . . ; women being forced into sexual favors in order to obtain food rations; hastily arranged marriages in the hopes of finding protection; and horrific sexual abuse and abduction." (See Excerpt 33)

Family Violence

Given the prevalence of global violence, the extent of interpersonal violence between family members should not come as a surprise. Many people argue that stress and conflict are inherent in family life. Our image of a golden age when families were a source of comfort and support is largely false. As social historians are now finding, family life in the past was likely as disrupted and as violent as family life today. The fact that we are now more aware of child abuse, wife battering, or incest is because these are just beginning to be recognized as problems—not because they are new. In all likelihood there were some families in the past who lived up to the "Little House on the Prairie" stereotype, just as some families today are loving and supportive. Then, as now, there were also families where abuse was frequent.

Violence, or the threat of violence, is the ultimate source of social control for individuals or societies. In the past, the use of physical force by husbands and fathers was accepted as necessary on occasion. Our acceptance of male authority, particularly in family matters has amounted to a tacit acceptance of aggressive male behavior including violence.

> The absence of clear-cut legal prohibitions and penalties for intrafamily violence throughout our society's history is a major reason for our present attitudes and relative lack of interest in punishing wife beaters. . . . Attitudes that tolerated and perpetuated the abuse of women remained long after the laws permitting assault were repealed." (Propper, 1990:281–82)

Our ignorance of family violence is also related to the notion that family relationships are private, not public matters. It was not until the 1960s that social scientists even began to study child abuse, and not until the 1970s that wife battering was identified as problematic. Women and children are the most usual victims of violence; men the usual perpetrators.

So extensive is family violence that Levinson (Excerpt 35) was led to conclude that it "is something that is witnessed or experienced by most human beings at some point in their lives." Most evidence points to the fact that violence between family members is learned behavior. Family members who are victims of violence, or who observe violence between other family members may go on to become violent themselves. Many parents who are abusers, were themselves abused. MacLeod (1987) found half of battering husbands and one-third of battered wives were beaten as children.

In Part Two we said that female infanticide was connected to polyandry (the marriage of one woman to more than one man). In such societies killing infant girls helps balance the sex ratio. Killing unwanted children is one of four reasons Levinson found for infanticide. The two most significant reasons were illegitimacy (as a result of rape or adultery) and deformity. Some societies sanction infanticide in the case of twins or other unusual births.

Violence against children is often disguised as punishment for the child's own good. The label *battered child syndrome* was used by an American researcher who uncovered repeated X-Ray evidence of physical abuse against children too young to speak. Many Western children were raised on the spare-the-rod-and-spoil-the-child principle. Parents have a great deal of leeway in determining how rigidly or loosely they choose to discipline their children.

Levinson found the physical punishment of children to be almost universal. However only a few societies in Levinson's sample used physical punishment regularly and most use mild forms.

The idea of violence against children by related adults contradicts our most fundamental expectations about parent-child interaction. Ironically the strength of the contradiction helps to perpetuate the problem. Many people are reluctant to believe that it is widespread. Indeed, we don't really know how extensive child abuse is in the West. In the 1960s, after child battering was identified as a social problem, there were attempts to gather information about frequency of occurrence. It seems clear that the number of reported cases has much to do with public awareness. In 1970, Florida reported seventeen cases of child abuse. In 1971 after a telephone hot line was set up and widely publicized, there were 19,120 reported cases (Moorehead, 1990).

Child abuse takes many forms from neglect, to physical violence, to sexual violation. Internationally, child prostitution—involving children as young as five years of age—is very big business. Although we may think of child prostitution as a problem confined to Southeast Asia, it thrives in most countries. In North America, child prostitutes work in all major cities. Here, most are runaways. In Asia, children are driven to, or sold into prostitution because they are poor. Tourists are the main "clients" and tourism is very important to the economies of countries where child prostitution is most entrenched: the Philippines, Thailand, Indonesia, and South Korea.

The sexual abuse of children is not confined to prostitution. Children are abused in their homes, in day-care centers, in churches, in schools—indeed everywhere they interact with adults. Sexual abuse of children amounts to adult abuse of power. Estimates of the numbers of children so abused are one in three or four girls and one in ten boys. However, most abuse is unreported so it is impossible to be precise. Underreporting of child sexual abuse is effectively accomplished by abusers who bribe, cajole, or threaten children into silence. Silence is also maintained by other adults who refuse to believe the child.

Sexual abuse may or may not involve violence; it will always involve coercion, however implicit. Although Western children are well-schooled in tactics for avoiding the approach of strangers, relatives and friends are far more likely to be sexual abusers.

The traditional definition of incest is sexual intercourse between relatives. Most societies have strong sanctions against incest, although it is known to occur almost everywhere. In the last decade, an alarming number of adults in North America have identified themselves as victims of unwanted childhood sexual advances by parents, relatives, or other trusted adults.

Now therapists define incest as the sexual violation (including fondling or fellatio) of children by older or adult family members. What sets incest apart from other forms of child abuse is that the perpetrator is a person both trusted and powerful in the child's eyes. It is the violation of trust that makes incest so personally devastating and recovery so long-term.

Wife Battering

Levinson found wife abuse to be the most common form of family violence throughout the world. It occurred at least occasionally in 84.5 percent of the societies in his sample. Levinson found three explanations for wife beatings: as a response to adultery, as general punishment, and willful beatings that are part of a husband's prerogative.

Western estimates suggest that at least one woman in ten is physically abused. Macleod estimates that each year one million Canadian women are beaten by their husbands. In a November 1988 Gallup Poll twenty-three percent of Canadians said they were personally aware of serious incidents of physical abuse of wives by husbands.

MacLeod's study of wife battering in Canada (Excerpt 36) conceptualized wife abuse in broad terms. According to her definition, wife battering includes physical violence, as well as psychological, sexual, verbal, or economic abuse. According to MacLeod's analysis, neither batterers nor their victims fit a psychological or sociological profile. Nevertheless, women who have lived with abuse suffer low self-esteem, isolation, and guilt.

Why do women stay in abusive relationships? The most obvious reason is that they literally have nowhere else to go. (Most of the abused women who stayed at battered-women's shelters in Canada were poor.) But they also stay because they are ambivalent about the relationship. As MacLeod found, they do not want to live with abuse, but they may not want to end the relationship. Until social service agencies recognize this ambivalence, they will not be in a position to provide a useful service to violent families.

A very high proportion of murders are between family members. A British study found most women murder victims to be murdered by husbands, boyfriends, or relatives. Eighty percent of victims in suicide-murder cases are immediate family members. (Goldthorpe, 1987:82) In Canada in 1988, 143 people were killed by an immediate family member. Half of these were women killed by their husbands. (Women in Canada, 1990:155)

Typically marital homicide is related to wife abuse. Wives kill husbands in self-defense. Husbands kill wives because they have taken habitual abuse one step too far. That marital homicide is inevitably preceded by other acts of violence makes early intervention crucial.

Conclusion

This discussion has just touched the surface of the range of internal and external stressors affecting families today. Poverty, war, revolution, and famine are interrelated problems that touch more and more lives. We have not talked about the way AIDS has, and will continue to affect families throughout the world. Many of the turning points in family living described in other parts of the book—infertility, unemployment, divorce, widowhood—are also areas of stress for families. Excerpt 34 describes one of these stressful turning points—marital infidelity.

Compared to the stressors described in the other five excerpts in this section, marital infidelity may seem to be a small complaint. Yet infidelity is the root of much interpersonal conflict and much distress. Internationally, adultery is the most common cause of divorce (Betzig, 1989) What infidelity and abuse have in common is the violation of trust.

Marital infidelity is probably as old as marriage, and the double standard as old as extramarital affairs. While this may seem to some to be evidence of men's greater need for sexual variety, its roots lie in the notion of women as men's property. Now, it is also a practical issue. Women have more to risk if a marriage ends and so are less apt to risk this through extramarital liasons.

As you will see in Part Seven, labor-force inequality and the fact that women usually retain custody of children mean that most women suffer a significant drop in standard of living at divorce.

References—Part Six

BETZIG, LAURA. (1989) "Causes of conjugal dissolution: A cross-cultural study," *Current Anthropology*, 30, No. 5 (December), 654–676.

GOLDTHORPE, J. E. *Family Life in Western Societies* (New York: Cambridge University Press, 1987).

KENT, GEORGE. (1991) "Our Children, Our Future," *Futures* (January–February), 32–49.

MACLEOD, LINDA. (1987) *Battered, But not Beaten . . . Preventing Wife Battering in Canada.* Ottawa: Canadian Advisory Council on the Status of Women.

MOOREHEAD, CAROLINE. (1990) *Betrayal: A Report on Violence Towards Children in Today's World.* New York: Doubleday.

PROPPER, ALICE. (1990) "Patterns of Family Violence," in *Families: Changing Trends in Canada,* 2nd ed. Maureen Baker (ed.), Toronto: McGraw-Hill Ryerson, 272–305.

Statistics Canada. (1990) *Women in Canada: A Statistical Report,* 2nd ed. Ottawa: Minister of Supply and Services.

Introduction

Perhaps the most significant source of stress in families around the world is poverty. Forty percent of the world's population live in poverty. More than ten million people die of starvation annually. Worldwide inequalities are reproduced within Western countries where poverty levels, particularly for children, are appallingly high. In the United States at least twenty percent of children are poor. A disproportionate number of these children are black.

In this article, Marion Edelman describes the plight of black families in America today. Black children in the United States are more likely to be poor now than they were a decade ago. A black child born in a female-headed household has a two in three chance of being poor. If the child's mother is under twenty-five, the chances are four in five! More than half of all black children are born to women (or teenagers) who are not married.

Why is it that young black pregnant women are less apt to marry than in the past? Why are they less apt to marry than young white pregnant women? Edelman's argument is that marriages don't occur because black men have worse employment opportunities now than in the past. As she argues, the focus of reform should be to increase future employment prospects for young blacks.

31
The Black Family in America

Marian Wright Edelman

A 1985 Children's Defense Fund (CDF) study, *Black and White Children in America: Key Facts*, found that black children have been sliding backward. Black children today are more likely to be born into poverty, lack early prenatal care, have a single mother or unemployed parent, be unemployed as teenagers, and not go to college after high school graduation than they were in 1980.

Compared to white children, we found that black children are

twice as likely to
- die in the first year of life
- be born prematurely
- suffer low birthweight
- have mothers who received late or no prenatal care
- see a parent die
- live in substandard housing
- be suspended from school or suffer corporal punishment
- be unemployed as teenagers
- have no parent employed
- live in institutions;

three times as likely to
- be poor
- have their mothers die in childbirth
- live with a parent who has separated
- live in a female-headed family
- be placed in an educable mentally retarded class
- be murdered between five and nine years of age

- be in foster care
- die of known child abuse;

four times as likely to
- live with neither parent and be supervised by a child welfare agency
- be murdered before one year of age or as a teenager
- be incarcerated between fifteen and nineteen years of age;

five times as likely to
- be dependent on welfare; and

twelve times as likely to
- live with a parent who never married.

We also found that:
- Only four out of every ten black children, compared to eight out of every ten white children live in two-parent families.
- Births to unmarried teenagers occur five times more often among blacks than whites, although birth rates for black teens, married and unmarried, have been *declining*, while the birth rate among white unmarried teens has been *increasing* in recent years.
- In 1983, 58 percent of all births to black women were out of wedlock. Among black women under the age of twenty, the proportion was over 86 percent. For thirty years these out-of-wedlock ratios have increased inexorably. They have now reached levels that essentially guarantee the poverty of many black children for the unforeseeable future.

Whether black or white, women under the age of twenty-five who head families with children are likely to be poor. The poverty rates in 1983 were 85.2 percent for young black female-headed families and 72.1 percent for young white female-headed families. But black female-

Source: For permission to photocopy this selection please contact Harvard University Press. Reprinted by permission of the publishers from Edelman, Marian Wright (1987) "The Black Family in America," *Families in Peril: An Agenda for Social Change*. Harvard University Press, Cambridge. © 1987 by the President and Fellows of Harvard College.

headed families are much more likely to stay poor. In female-headed families with mothers aged twenty-five to forty-four, there is a 20 percentage-point gap between black and white poverty rates.

Today black children in young female-headed households are the poorest in the nation. While a black child born in the United States has a one in two chance of being born poor, a black child in a female-headed household has a two in three chance of being poor. If that household is headed by a mother under twenty-five years of age, that baby has a four in five chance of being poor.

Black teens are having fewer rather than more babies: 172,000 births in 1970; 137,000 in 1983. The proportion of black women under twenty who have given birth has been falling steadily since the early 1970s. . . . However, the percentage of those births that were to unmarried teens soared from 36 percent in 1950 to 86 percent by 1981. Among black women reaching their twentieth birthday between 1945 and 1949, 40 percent had given birth. Among black women reaching their twentieth birthday between 1975 and 1979, 44 percent had given birth—an increase of only 4 percent. From 1947 to 1977, however, the marriage rate for pregnant black fifteen- to seventeen-year-olds dropped about 80 percent; and for black eighteen- and nineteen-year-olds the marriage rate is down about 60 percent.

Today's young white population also is less likely to let pregnancy lead to marriage, but the decline is nowhere near as great. Seven percent of white teen births were out of wedlock in 1960, 17 percent in 1970, and 39 percent in 1983. Among pregnant white fifteen- to seventeen-year-olds, the proportion marrying before birth fell from 62 to 43 percent during the same thirty year period (1947 to 1977), while the proportion of pregnant eighteen- and nineteen-year-olds who married fell from 52 to 50 percent. The current white prenatal marriage rates are still much higher than the corresponding black rates were even back in 1950. . . .

It is important to identify why the proportion of out-of-wedlock teen births is rising. The cause among black teenagers is a drop in marriage rates. . . . Among white teens the cause is more babies coupled with a decrease in marriage among those who become pregnant.

In 1970 teens accounted for half of all out-of-wedlock births. In 1983 almost two-thirds of the babies born to unmarried women were to women twenty and over. This is true for whites and blacks (63.4 percent white; 63.0 percent black). Again, while the share of out-of-wedlock births occurring to adult women has been going up for both blacks and whites, the reasons for the increase are different. Birth rates for white unmarried women (aged sixteen to forty-four) have been going up (19.3 per 1,000 in 1983) because more unmarried white adult women are having babies. Birth rates for unmarried black women have been going down (95.5 per 1,000 in 1970; 77.7 in 1983), but fewer young black women are getting married, and married black women are having fewer babies. . . .

The crux of the problem facing the black family today is that young black women who become pregnant do not marry nearly as often as they used to. Nor as often as young pregnant white women do. *Why young black marriages do not form is thus central to our concern about the proportion of black children in female-headed families.* That is especially true since the *whole* of the increase in the proportion of black children in female-headed families over the last decade is accounted for by the increase in those who live with unmarried mothers, and not by the increase in the proportion who live with divorced or separated mothers.

In 1981, among the infants born to fifteen- to seventeen-year-olds, 48 percent of those born to white teenagers were out-of-wedlock, compared to 94 percent of those born to black teenagers. CDF research staff used data to determine what would happen if black teen girls had behaved as white teen girls had. In general the white young women were less likely to be sexually active, more likely to abort if they did become preg-

and an increase in the service industries where black female employment grew.

Some black males . . . balked at accepting entry-level jobs that probably would not lead to better things. As more immigrant groups passed blacks by, the message being received by many black youths was that poor blacks were not going to make it, even if they tried. Overnight, it seemed, jobs in restaurants, hotels, and office buildings—jobs that might lead to a way out and up for newcomers—became the property of new, often illegal immigrants. Did young black men experience real exclusion or were they the ones who turned away for lack of opportunity or perceived lack of opportunity to move ahead?

There is no doubt that when there is greater unemployment and underemployment those with the poorest education, the greater proclivity to experiencing discrimination, and the poorest personal and work skills have the worst time.

If their own attitude compounds their problems, should we be surprised?

We must continue to try to understand why this accelerated deterioration of black male joblessness in the 1970s occurred. To the degree that it arises out of lack of jobs and from job discrimination, government and the private sector must take immediate steps to remedy it. To the degree that it results from a ghetto lifestyle, lack of individual initiative, and poor work habits, a concerted effort by black families, community leaders, and agencies to resurrect strong work and family values is imperative. . . .

. . . As important as black self-help is, it is not enough. Teenage pregnancy and parenthood and the growth of female-headed households are intimately intertwined with poverty and lack of economic opportunity which flow from governmental policies or abdication of responsibility for some of its citizens. . . .

Introduction

This article is a study of Iranian families dislocated by the Iran-Iraq War of the 1980s. Over 2.5 million Iranians moved away from the front during the war. Many came from rural areas or villages to settle in camps on the outskirts of southern cities. There they faced overcrowded housing, inadequate services, and resentment from established residents.

It would be hard to imagine a more difficult situation for families to endure. In many cases the move was precipitated by the death of a family member. Many families were forced to flee, leaving money and jewels behind. Nor were they welcomed by their new communities. Public opinion held that by leaving the war zone, people were making it easier for the enemy to advance.

Predictably families experiencing such severe disruption are more likely to suffer other symptoms of family breakdown. At the same time, a society at war is in the worst possible position to provide support and services to needy citizens.

32
War and Migrant Families in Iran

Akbar Aghajanian

INTRODUCTION

On 22nd September 1980, the Iraqi army invaded Iran along a front of 1,352 km, penetrating at certain points as deep as 80 km into Iranian territory. In less than a few weeks 14,000 km of Iran came under Iraqi occupation. Five out of 24 Iranian provinces came under Iraqi attack. . . . These provinces are densely populated and most of the ethnic minorities live in these areas. . . . The short run damages of the war have been huge in terms of (1) human loss; (2) damage to settlement systems; (3) material destruction; (4) and huge financial budgetary losses. Human losses included many thousands who have been killed, disabled, or disappeared, at the war front. The unofficial figures for human loss is about a million.

Damage to human settlements has been devastating. Although only 5 provinces were involved in the war, a number of neighboring provinces, the adjoining four in particular, have suffered from missile attacks and bombs. This damage increased with Iraqi's air raids and use of medium range missiles against big cities including the capital city of Tehran and the large city of Isfahan, in 1987 and 1988. Hence more than 51 cities and 4000 villages have been damaged.

According to government sources, the total monetary damages amounted to 234,782.6 million rials (almost equal to 33 billion dollars) until 1985. The damage to production has been estimated to be about 40 percent of the national

Source: Aghajanian, Akbar (1990) "War and migrant families in Iran: An overview of a social disaster," *International Journal of Sociology of the Family,* Vol. 20 (Spring), 97–107. Reprinted with permission from *International Journal of Sociology of the Family.*

product. There was an 80 percent decline in the production of oil which has been the main sources of the government revenue in Iran (Alnasrawi, 1986; Chubin and Tripp, 1988). . . .

Over 2.5 million population were forced to migrate to war-free zones where they lived in refugee camps or self-prepared shacks. As a consequence . . . , the population of some cities in the war-free zone increased significantly. . . .

This paper focuses on the prevalence of certain social problems such as unemployment, divorce, mental illness, school dropout among the war-migrant families. . . .

ᘒ

MARGINALIZATION AND SOCIAL DISORGANIZATION OF WAR MIGRANTS

War migrants . . . were uprooted from their community of origin where the family had a long history of respect and recognition. These communities usually were small villages and towns where life was interactive and interdependent. The economy and family were not separate and familial reputation was very important. . . .

In the villages and small towns where they lived, they had significant social economic exchange with the extended family. . . . This network was destroyed after the forced migration. . . . Many families of the same kin group and village were living in different camps and in different cities after migration. Furthermore, many families reported loss of immediate members and relatives in the first 3 months of the war before they were forced to move out. . . .

The majority of the war migrant families depended on self-employment in small businesses and segregated into crowded and lower quality schools. These children . . . were frustrated and sometimes aggravated by fighting native children. Under such conditions, it is natural to expect a high rate of drop-out. Out of all families studied, 28.5 percent reported they have had at least one school drop-out since they migrated. This is a . . . higher rate of school drop-out than for native children in . . . Shiraz. The rate is on the average about 15 for the native families. After controlling for socio-economic factors, the war migrant families still had a rate of 24.3 for school drop outs.

SUMMARY AND DISCUSSION

One consequence of the imposed Iraq-Iran war was the redistribution of a population of about 2.5 million from the villages and small cities of the provinces of the war front. Considering the size of this . . . population and the period of 3 months in which they had to move out, the crisis situation of this forced redistribution is evident. The huge economic cost of such sudden change and disruption is also of considerable importance in calculating . . . the damages of the war.

While it is possible to measure the economic damages, social and psychological damages are less amenable to calculation. . . . But they are significant. A large number of studies of migration have dealt with the relationship between migration and symptoms of alienation, delinquency, family disorganization, mental illness, unemployment and poverty. These studies have shown that migrant population have a higher frequency of all

these . . . problems (Packard, 1972). These problems are not . . . characteristic of migrants, but are rather imposed on them by the social setting and the social relations in the process of moving out of the place of origin and settling in the place of destination. These social relations and settings could be favorable or unfavorable to the emergence of such phenomenon. In case of the war migrant population in Iran, all forces from the origin and at the destination were favourable to more deviant behavior. . . .

REFERENCES

ALNASRAWI, A. 1985. "Economic Consequences of the Iraq-Iran War," Third World Quarterly 8(3): 435–450.

CHUBIN, SHAHRAM and TRIPP. 1988. Iran and Iraq at War. (London: Tauris Inc.).

HODGES, V. 1968. "Non-attendance at School," Educational Research (11-12):5661.

Iran Statistical Center. 1980. Report of the 1976 Census of Iran, (Tehran: Iran Statistical Center).

—— 1983. Statistical Yearbook of Iran, 1982, (Tehran: Iran Statistical Center).

—— 1984. Statistical Yearbook of Iran, 1983, (Tehran: Iran Statistical Center).

—— 1986. Statistical Yearbook of Iran, 1985, (Tehran: Iran Statistical Center).

PACKARD, V. 1972. A Nation of Strangers. (New York: David McKay).

Plan and Budget Organization. 1986. Report of the Imposed War up to 1985, (Tehran: Plan and Budget Organization).

ROBINSON, V. 1979. "The Achievement of Asian Children" Educational Research (22):148–150.

Introduction

Excerpt 32 described some of the consequences of wartime migration for Iranian families. In the aftermath of the 1991 Persian Gulf War, people around the world received daily news reports of the appalling reality of day-to-day life for Kurdish refugees. We were shown people stripped of all that might give material or psychic comfort, facing starvation, disease, harsh weather, and death. This paper, which was published before the Persian Gulf War, is an extensive review of what social scientists have been able to learn about what happens to family life in these situations. The focus of the article is on the ways people cope with life in a refugee camp.

As Williams explains, the fabric of family life begins to change before the family migrates as members deal with the precipitating crises. In many cases husbands and/or sons are obliged to leave home first. Many of these men die or are killed. Consequently, women and children make up the majority of refugee camp residents.

The exigencies of camp life create a new set of stressors. Camps are typically ill-equipped and overcrowded. Food is rarely sufficient, and health care inadequate. The communication of disease is a constant problem. It is not surprising that familes show signs of disintegration under these conditions.

33
Families in Refugee Camps

Holly Ann Williams

OVERVIEW OF REFUGEE EXPERIENCE

Although the focus of this paper is to describe how families react in a camp setting, it is important to view the camp experience within the milieu of the total refugee experience. The decision to flee one's country is fraught with pain, sadness, fear, and a host of other disturbing emotions. While each refugee situation is created by unique circumstances, common reasons for flight include war, social disorganization, political persecution, natural disasters, and economic insufficiency. Refugees leave a situation that has become intolerable in the hope of reconstructing a normative social environment in a place of safety. Once thought to be a spontaneous decision, it appears that the decision to flee is a conscious action reflecting thoughts to the consequences (Allen and Hiller 1985). . . .

Source: Williams, Holly Ann (1990) "Families in refugee camps," *Human Organization,* Vol. 49, No. 2, 100–109. Reproduced by permission of the *Society for Applied Anthropology.*

How families respond to the refugee experience can first be examined by looking at the process of flight.

The pre-flight process involved material, social, and psychological preparation, relying intensely on social ties to assist in this process. People collectively attempted to redefine their situation and to determine appropriate acts, making rational decisions as to who should go or who should stay behind. As such, migration became a family oriented project, although the family may not be able to leave as a unit (Allen and Hiller, 1985). . . .

. . . I propose that the fabric of family life begins to be dramatically altered during pre-migration periods, with serious repercussions to all involved. For varying amounts of time, the family has been exposed to detrimental factors, such as war or famine. Because of these pressures, family units may begin to break down, or begin to alter their familiar patterns. Families may be physically separated due to the father seeking employment options outside of the community, or due to military involvement. Absent family members may re-enter the family for abbreviated periods of time. However, the family as such is generally enmeshed in a local social network system that provides social support and possible access to resources. When the home situation is no longer tolerable, migration becomes an option, whether it is internal migration, migration across national boundaries to a camp, or spontaneous settlement in another country. . . .

How families respond to the migration and re-location will be discussed in the next section. . . .

☜

THE EFFECT OF REFUGEE CAMPS ON FAMILIES

. . . If the family is fleeing war, some fathers or sons may stay behind to be resistance fighters. Other families experience multiple deaths or separations during migration. The notion of an "intact" family migrating together may not be realistic for many families.

. . . The majority of the current Third World refugees in camps are women and children (Hutchinson 1985, Calloway 1986). These estimations may not count for refugee men who are away from the camps, such as those who become labor migrants. . . .

The changes in family structure are a major element in the shifts and re-organization that occurs within the camp setting. An assumption has been made in the literature that the separation of family members is always . . . negative. While it . . . may hold true for the majority of families, in some situations the placement of women and children in the camps may be seen as a purposeful device in order to secure material goods for other members of the family. For example, the Thai-Kampuchean border has several camps where the women and children live in the camps and obtain rations. Their soldier husbands visit . . . for rest, clothing, food, and drugs (Jackson 1987). . . .

LOSS

The overwhelming emotion that confronts individuals and their families is reported to be one of loss; loss which is multifaceted and in direct correlation with the feeling of being uprooted (Allmen 1987, Baker 1983, Barudy 1987, Eisenbruch 1988, Hitchcox 1988a, Roe 1987). Losses include actual family members, home environments, material possessions, status, culture and language, employment, a sense of the future, and most importantly, human rights. With each loss, there is an individual and collective loss. For example, there is unique and solitary grief felt by each member on the loss of another member. In addition, the texture of the family unit is also dramatically altered, both in actual numbers of the family and in the sense of how the survivors now envision "family." The losses will continue to affect relationships, but the family responses to the losses will alter over time. If the loss involved violence, there may be "psychic numbing"; seen as apathy, detachment, or an inability to feel or relate, which makes family life almost impossible (Krumperman 1983). Because of the circumstances of being refugees, many families have been unable to manifest grief (Baker 1984). . . .

Is . . . there any positive aftermath to the loss? Do the accumulated losses serve any cohesive function? In studying Vietnamese refugees in camps, Hitchcox (1988b) surmised a sense of collective strength from the losses, a recognition of everything they had experienced and survived. In my own field work as a Head Nurse in pediatrics in Khao I Dang, (1981–82), my Khmer workers would discuss their losses in terms of a national pride, a unity that the Khmer survivors of Pol Pot shared. . . .

The social disorganization of life is dramatically altered within the context of a refugee camp. . . . Traditional leaders are absent; refugees may be forced to share space with strangers, even those who are considered traditional enemies; and there is a noticeable lack of any political connections to the host government, which host citizens can enjoy (Clark 1985). Bousquet (1987), in describing Vietnamese in camps in Hong Kong, called this time a "liminal period." Despondency, a loss of initiative, and a sense of dependency were particularly seen in families where there was no hope of resettlement. . . . Hitchcox (1988a) noted that the longer the time spent in camps, the more dire the psychological consequences. Reynell (1986) found the serious problems of marital conflict, violence with children, conflicts with neighbors, decreased morality, and a sense of hopelessness in the Thai/ Khmer border camps.

. . . Hitchcox (1988a) noted that refugees may confuse or deliberately mislead their interviewers in a hope to "better their chances." In my own experience at Khao I Dang, I had refugees who altered their life histories. . . . Many did not want to admit to having served in the military, for fear of rejection on that basis alone. When they were rejected for resettlement, the sentiments expressed were of confusion and bitter self-regret for their actions. The personal despair and remorse certainly could contribute to deepened depression and loss of hope. Additionally, individuals who are socially undesirable or in some way impaired (e.g., drug addicted, alcoholic, mentally retarded, criminal history) are less likely to be chosen for resettlement. The potential influence of these sub-groups of the refugee population needs to be considered when evaluating the psychological consequences of remaining in the camps for an extended stay.

The emotional sequelae described in previous paragraphs appear to be directly related to a loss of a sense of future. A study was done by Knudsen (1983) of Vietnamese in five refugee camps located in the Philippines, Hong Kong, and Japan. The . . . refugees interviewed described camp life as time-wasting, meaningless, and pacifying, with a loss of right to influence their own situation. . . .

In spite of the stress experienced within the family, the family itself becomes the base for reestablishing new social networks. Families are a key to the past with shared memories and a hope for the future with unification in a country of resettlement. . . .

FAMILY UNIT DISINTEGRATION

. . . Families may not all be supportive. . . . While some individuals draw closer together within their marriages, other marriages have been broken with divorces or desertions in the camp setting (Palmer 1981). The couples may simply be too exhausted to sustain support for one another (Lin 1986). Of most concern is the repeated reports of increased family violence, particularly directed to women (Bonnerjea 1985, Chan 1984, Krumperman 1983, Lin 1986, Reynell 1986). . . .

ROLE CHANGE AND VULNERABILITY OF WOMEN

Family adaptation is reported to depend heavily on the ability of the mother to adapt (Allmen 1987, Bonnerjea 1985). . . . In addition to maintaining traditional roles, many women are pushed into assuming primary economic activities, particularly during resettlement. . . .

One . . . advantage refugee women have in contrast to refugee men is a continuation of roles such as childbearing and food preparation. In the Vietnamese camps in Thailand, Hitchcox (1988a) found that women coped better than men on a day-to-day basis, organizing their day around household tasks that had earned them respect in the Vietnamese community. During my time at Khao I Dang, this pattern repeated itself with Khmer refugee women. In addition to family and household tasks, women gained satisfaction from organizing a morning market, selling pastries and food items to expatriate hospital staff. Suffering from status inconsistency and being denied their traditional role of breadwinner, refugee men suffered from depression and apathy (Hitchcox 1988a, Ye-Chin 1980).

Considering the large number of women and children alone in the camps, women are forced to take on primary decision-making responsibilities, yet some are vulnerable in this role due to lack of literacy, skills, or training. These women are attempting to learn the new tasks required for family maintenance, while at the same time, still assuming the bulk of the domestic and child-care responsibilities (Palmer 1981). . . .

During migration, women are often separated from extended family ties and other forms of traditional support systems. Most feel isolated, particularly if at home they were discouraged from socializing with non-family members (Allmen 1987, Bonnerjea 1985, Goitom 1987, Palmer 1981).

Women are subject to personal violence throughout the process of becoming a refugee, and in the camps. There are multiple reports of rape in the camps; women being forced into sexual favors . . . to obtain food . . . ; hastily arranged marriages in the hopes of finding protection; and horrific sexual abuse and abduction of women fleeing in the South China Sea (Bonnerjea 1985, Hutchinson 1985, Indra 1987, Palmer 1981, Reynell 1986).

As a consequence of such trauma and the accumulated effects of her multiple roles, the health of women in camps tends to be marginal at best (Bonnerjea 1985, Hutchinson 1985, Sundhagel 1981). Frequently women receive less food than men at a time when they are pregnant or breastfeeding, which is precisely when they need supplemental calories. This practice may reflect camp policies that issue rations to men, and/or cultural prescriptions which have men eating prior to women. In 1986 in the Khmer border camps, only women and girls over age 8 received regular rations to prevent guerilla soldiers from receiving aid. In spite of this, the men did receive food when they came to the camps for "rest periods." Food deficiency was serious as the daily rations only provide 1850 kcal/day, 500 kcal over what is needed to sustain life (Reynell 1986). Malnutrition then affected not only the women, but also the children in the family.

Other common problems seen in refugee women include menstrual disorders and infertility, both of which are compounded if the woman is grieving over lost infants (Sundhagel 1981). Due to cultural restrictions, women may hesitate to use medical facilities if they are staffed by men and hence, not receive the type of care that is needed. . . .

Perhaps the most insidious form of abuse that occurs to women [is] . . . the lack of status, the lack of participatory management in camp organization, and the loss of protection. . . .

Because women have been seen as dependent on men, in many situations they have been denied access to major decision-making positions within the camp situation (Calloway 1987). The accumulated stress of adapting to shifting societal roles and family expectations, coupled with generally having less power personally to affect changes to ease this transition, leaves women exposed to possible debilitating psychological effects. Yet women are functioning, . . . families are being maintained. . . .

CHILDREN IN AN ADULT WORLD

. . . Attempting to cope with the disruption is taxing to anyone, but children are in a more precarious situation due to their developmental needs. . . . The children are exposed to the intra-family tensions caused by the redistribution of the roles and tasks of the parents. Particularly in the case where the father is absent, the child must assume tasks and responsibilities beyond their years (Barudy 1987). Unable to comprehend the violence and rapid changes in their families and communities, the child may be unable to develop or maintain a sense of what constitutes "normality" (Barudy 1987, McCallin 1986). . . . Children born and raised in camps may never learn the adult value of self-sufficiency (McCallin 1986). . . .

Overall, growth and development is severely hampered in refugee camps. Malnutrition will

not only stunt physical growth, but will impair cognitive functioning, as demonstrated by language delays and learning problems (Carlin 1986). Insecurity may be manifested by an immature sense of self, and other problems such as insomnia, bedwetting and night terrors (Roe 1987). . . .

Children exposed to violence, or children who have been forced to participate in violent acts, are more susceptible to psychological trauma. Male children who lacked family protection on the Thai border fell victim to recruitment from Khmer resistance armies (Boothby 1986). Boothby, from extensive field work with unaccompanied children, and children in war, has concluded there is a far greater amount of psychological disturbance seen in children who perpetuated violence than in children who were its objects. From experience as a psychiatrist working with refugee children, Carlin (1986) noted that refugee children and adolescents carry vivid memories of atrocities, fear, and terror. For younger children, pre-verbal memories may be manifest as night terrors or nightmares at a later date.

. . . Evidence is reported that children do better in the company of known adults. Regardless of age, a child's security and sense of adjustment is influenced by the presence or absence of an accompanying family member (Carlin 1986). . . . Parents are the primary source of emotional security for children, and assist them in learning ways to cope with the changes in their environment. . . .

Children may carry residual effects of the flight and camp situation into resettlement, and possibly into their adult years. Having assumed adult roles, the child may not be willing to return to the role of the child, creating conflict with the parents (Barudy, 1987). Intergenerational conflicts may occur if the child, exposed to new norms and values at school, begins to assimilate in ways that the parents fear. As a result of learning a new language quickly in school, the child may become the family interpreter and culture-broker. All of these situations may strain the existing roles and relationships and lead to family conflict (Carlin 1986, Nguyen, 1982). . . .

REFERENCES

ADEPOJU, ADERANTI. 1982. The Dimension of the Refugee Problem in Africa. African Affairs 81:21–35.

ALLEN, REBECCA and HARRY HILLER. 1985. The Social Organization of Migration: An Analysis of the Uprooting and Flight of Vietnamese Refugees. International Migration XXIII 22:439–451.

ALLMEN, EVA. 1987. The Refugee Woman and Her Family. Refugees 6:8.

BAKER, RON. 1984. Is Loss and Crisis Theory Relevant to Understanding Refugees in Africa? Paper presented at Refugee Studies Programme, Oxford, England.

BAKER, RON, ed. 1983. The Psychosocial Problems of Refugees. Luton, England: L & T Press, Ltd.

BARUDY, JORGE. 1987. The Therapeutic Value of Solidarity and Hope. Paper presented at a joint meeting of the International Catholic Child Bureau and the Refugee Studies Programme, Oxford.

BONNERJEA, LUCY. 1985. Shaming the World: The Needs of Refugee Women. London: World University Service.

BOOTHBY, NEIL. 1986. Children and War. Cultural Survival Quarterly 10:28–30.

BOUSQUET, GISELE. 1987. Living in a State of Limbo: A Case Study of Vietnamese Refugees in Hong Kong Camps. In People in Upheaval. S. Morgan and E. Colson, eds. Pp. 34–53. New York: Center for Migration Studies.

CALLOWAY, HELEN. 1986. Refugee Women: Specific Requirements and Untapped Resources. In Third World Affairs. Gaunar Altaf, ed. Pp. 320–325. London: Third World Affairs Foundation.

CARLIN, JEAN. 1986. Child and Adolescent Refugees: Psychiatric Assessment and Treatment. In Refugee Mental Health in Resettlement Countries. C. Williams and J. Westermeyer, eds. Pp. 131–139. Washington, DC: Hemisphere Publishing Co.

CHAN, KWOK. 1984. Indochinese Refugees and Social Support: The Theoretical Importance of the Family

and Social Networks in Research and Social Intervention. *In* Refugee Resettlement: Southeast Asians in Transition. R. Nann, P. Johnson, and M. Beizer, eds. Pp. 125–132. Vancouver: Refugee Resettlement Project.

CLARK, LANCE. 1985. The Refugee Dependency Syndrome: Physician, Heal Thyself. Washington, DC: Refugee Policy Group.

COOK, JANE. 1986. Children: The Battleground of Change. Cultural Survival Quarterly 10:1–4.

DAVIDSON, SHAMAI. 1983. Psychosocial Aspects of Holocaust Trauma in the Life Cycle of Survivor-Refugees and Their Families. *In* The Psychosocial Problems of Refugees. Ron Baker, ed. Pp. 21–31. Luton, England: L & T Press, Ltd.

EISENBRUCH, MAURICE. 1988. Uprooting and Cultural Bereavement: Loss of Past and Self among Cambodian Youth Without Families. Unpublished manuscript.

GOITOM, EYOB. 1987. Systems of Social Interaction of Refugee Adjustment Processes: The Case of Eritrean Refugees in Khartoum, Sudan. *In* Refugees: A Third World Dilemma. John Rogge, ed. Pp. 130–142. Totowa, NJ: Rowman and Littlefield.

HITCHCOX, LINDA. 1988a. Vietnamese Refugees in Transit: Process and Change. D.Phil. thesis, University of Oxford.

—— 1988b. Personal communication.

HUTCHINSON, MARIA. 1985. Women Refugees and the U.N. Decade for Women. Refugee Abstracts 4:3–5.

INDRA, DOREEN. 1987. Gender: A Key Dimension of the Refugee Experience. Refugee 6:3–4.

JACKSON, TONY. 1987. Just Waiting to Die? Cambodian Refugees in Thailand. Oxford: Oxfam House.

KNUDSEN, JOHN. 1983. Boat People in Transit. Bergen, Norway: University of Bergen Department of Social Anthropology.

KRUMPERMAN, ANDRE. 1983. Psychosocial Problems of Violence, Especially Its Effect on Refugees. *In* The Psychosocial Problems of Refugees. Ron Baker, ed. Pp. 14–20. Luton, England: L & T Press, Ltd.

LIN, KEH-MING. 1986. Psychopathology and Social Disruption in Refugees. *In* Refugee Mental Health in Resettlement Countries. C. Williams and J. Westermeyer, eds. Pp. 61–73. Washington, DC: Hemisphere Publishing Co.

McCALLIN, MARGARET. 1987. The Non-Material Needs of Refugee Children. *In* Third World Affairs. Gaunar Altaf, ed. Pp. 1–6. London: Third World Affairs Foundation.

NGUYEN, SAN. 1982. The Psychosocial Adjustment and the Mental Health Needs of Southeast Asian Refugees. The Psychiatric Journal of the University of Ottawa 7:26–34.

PALMER, INGRID. 1981. Advancement Preparation and Settlement Needs of Southeast Asian Refugee Women. International Migration Review 19:94–101.

REYNELL, JOSEPHINE. 1988. Socio-Economic Evaluation of the Khmer Refugee Camps on the Thai-Kampuchean Border. Oxford: Refugee Studies Programme.

ROE, MICHAEL. 1987. Central American Refugees in the U.S.: Psychosocial Adaptation. Refugee Issues 3:21–30.

SUNDHAGEL, MALEE. 1981. Situation and Role of Refugee Women: Experience and Perspectives from Thailand. International Migration Review 19:102–107.

WALDRON, SIDNEY. 1987. Blaming the Refugees. Refugee Issues 3:1–19.

YE-CHIN, JAY. 1980. The Refugee Experience: A Resume. Egham, England: Minority Rights Group.

Introduction

In the first three articles of this section we looked at how family members deal with acute external sources of stress. In this article the stress is of a very different kind. Here it is occasioned by marital infidelity.

The following excerpt is taken from an ethnographic study of women conducted in the Norwegian city of Bergen. *Kitchen-Table Society* focuses on a small group of working-class mothers and their interactions with their husbands, their children, their own parents, and perhaps most particularly each other. The study is interesting for two reasons. First, there have been very few ethnographies of Norway available to English-speaking scholars, so this study provides much rare insight. Secondly, the author is a feminist who lets the women speak for themselves. As she says in her introduction (Gullestad, 1984: 12):

> I used an empirical discovery procedure, taking as the point of departure problems female friends often and explicitly express and discuss among themselves. In this way I hope . . . to make visible and tangible not only their problems, but also their resources, their problem-solving abilities, and the dignity of their lives.

Because of their stage in life, relationships with husbands are the focus of much of the women's kitchen-table talk. This excerpt, which focuses on the marital troubles of Benny and Sissel, shows how Sissel relies on both family and friends for advice and support. Female friends in a sense mediate between the private and public worlds that frame their lives.

34
Kitchen-Table Society

Marianne Gullestad

When women sit together in the morning drinking coffee, smoking and looking after their children, or meet in the *klubb* (the sewing circle with or without sewing) in the evening every other week, they talk about . . . their lives as wives, mothers, employees, customers, daughters, daughters-in-law, etc. Some anthropologists have . . . taken an interest in such talk, . . . and have shown how it expresses important ideas and values in the culture. . . . Women's talk may be analyzed as a moral discourse about what is right and wrong. Their talk includes rightness and wrongness in child-rearing practices, in division of labour between spouses, in relationships with parents and parents-in-law and other relatives, issues surrounding work, issues raised in films on the TV or picture magazines, etc. . . .

Their relationships with men are the focus of an intensive interest. . . .

↺

MORAL DISCOURSE

. . . A gap between moral rules and the application of them in practice often occurs. People stick obstinately to some ideas and rules that do not quite work, but are all the same important to them. . . . They stick to values of monogamous love and faithfulness while . . . testing the limits of these rules. When chatting they make constant intellectual efforts to harmonize opposing values and conflicting experiences. This debate takes many . . . forms from criticizing others' misdeeds to admitting one's own. The following example of the moral discourse . . . about a marriage crisis . . . makes explicit some of the informal rules, notions and assumptions about male/female relationships. . . .

Source: Gullestad, Marianne (1984) *Kitchen-Table-Society,* pages 220–257, 346. Oslo: Universitetsforlaget.

Example

Sissel and Benny had been married for almost 6 years. They were both about 25 years old and had two children aged 5 and 2. Benny was a sales clerk. Sissel cleaned classrooms in a school every afternoon. They seemed to have a happy marriage. One day something happened that changed everything. Sissel called me early one morning from a telephone booth. "I need somebody to talk to. Benny has found himself another woman." I went to see her, and she told me the whole story:

"I have felt for a long time that something was wrong. There has been something in the air. My stomach has been upset. Yesterday I made a lot of fuss (*maste veldig*), and he admitted it. He is in love with somebody else. It has lasted one month. He has not gone to bed with her. Benny is not the kind of man who only wants one thing. They have been kissing and smooching . . . in the car. He says that he does not know which one to choose, me or her. He wept yesterday evening and this morning. We sat up and talked until five. Then he went to sleep. I was sitting here, smoking and thinking. They have decided not to see each other again until after Easter. He says that I am much prettier and have a much better figure than her. I believe she is married too. I looked in his notebook to find out, and I found a telephone number on a cigarette paper, put away under the cover.

The worst thing is that this has happened before, 4 years ago. I found a love letter to a 17-year-old girl. She was not in love with him, however. My father was so angry, then. So I do not want to tell my parents this time. It took such a long time before they forgot. They were so curt when talking to him. . . . He was so embarrassed.

He said yesterday that he wanted to relax and see how things arrange themselves during Easter and then perhaps choose me. But I was thinking when he slept . . . I must have some pride. I must show him that he can't do whatever he wants to. Therefore I said this morning that he has to move over to his mother's. . . . I packed his suitcase and told him to choose her or me, and change his place of work. I do not want this to happen over and over again. He started to cry. What if he was not allowed to stay with his parents? I could not put him on the street. . . . He said he is so fond of me. He patted my cheek and asked me to lie on his arm in bed.

I am so anxious about how things will work out for me alone, what money we shall live by. He said he would give me money, but . . ."

Benny . . . moved over to this parents' place that day. He gave Sissel 300 kroner before he left. . . .

The day after I went to see Sissel again. . . . At her place I found Tore, the husband of Benny's sister. "Sissel has just gone on an errand with Ellen", he explained. . . . (Ellen is Sissel's neighbour, childhood friend and *klubb*friend.) . . .

Sissel and Ellen had been to talk to the woman Benny is in love with. Through a friend they found out her name and where and when she usually worked.

The first thing they both exclaimed is "she looked shabby (e.g. rural). She was not very pretty. . . . Her coat looked like a sack. Her pants were too wide and too big for her. When she sat down there were lots of pleats over her bottom. She had no make-up at all on her eyes, and her eyelashes were completely white."

Ellen and Sissel are themselves both pretty and fashionable. Both are relatively tall and slim. Sissel has long dark hair, big grey eyes and a pretty face. Ellen has short, dyed, blond hair, blue eyes and a pretty face. Both use make-up on their eyes and perhaps a little lipstick and rouge on the cheeks. They wear very tight blue jeans, fashionable blouses, tight tweed sport jackets, and high-heeled boots.

They then proceeded to tell what happened. When they arrived at Benny's workplace, Sissel approached the other woman and asked: "Are you Kari Nilsen?" The other woman nodded. "I am Benny's wife", Sissel then said. "We are about to be separated. He has moved over to his mother's. My little boy is very upset because of this. He cries and trembles because the father has moved." "My goodness", Kari answered. "Has it gone that far!" Then she had told them that she and her husband had had a crisis, but had now found . . . there was, with two children, too much to lose. Sissel then asked her not to see Benny any more, to come to her work after Benny had gone home. "I think I did the right thing", Sissel said to us afterwards. "Now I have all the best cards. What matters now is to play them well."

Around the kitchen-table they continued to discuss what else Sissel ought to do. Ellen condemned Benny's acts: "There is no excuse for Benny's acts. He deserves not to get things too easy." Tore agreed: "He knew what he did. He has gone into this with his eyes open.

Tore and Ellen strongly advised Sissel to separate officially from Benny: :You must secure the kids and yourself economically. You cannot be dependent on him giving you money. What if he one day just says he has no money for you?". . .

In the ensuing period Benny stayed with his parents. . . . His parents have . . . strong moral convictions against divorce. They . . . partly blamed their daughter-in-law. ("She is not a competent mother." "Her children are dirty and badly kept.") Partly they solved the problem by helping Benny to find a new, smaller, apartment. When he was no longer under their roof, they felt less responsible for his acts.

The happenings that led to Sissel and Benny's separation demonstrate how . . . relatively innocent events . . . quickly escalate into a serious crisis. . . .

Both Benny and Sissel codified the situation as a crisis. Sissel's perception of crisis seems to some extent to be derived from Benny. He has experienced strong emotions of being in love and is insecure about what these emotions mean and what he ought to do about them. According to the rules of marriage, such feelings should be reserved for one's spouse. . . . He therefore, according to Sissel, immediately feels he has to choose between

his wife and the new woman. . . . The choice is between the two women. That he eventually loses home and children at the same time as he loses his wife is implied but not expressed by Sissel. He wants, however, some time to reflect and think things over, she says.

Sissel calls on allies and confidantes to help her sort things out. . . . One of the first things she does is to approach the other woman direct, to find out about her interests and present her own. She presents herself as Benny's wife, and brings in the feelings of the children. . . . The other woman has different interests, but Sissel obviously counts on her being the same sort (a woman) and thus on her ability to identify with her own situation. She does not approach her alone, but together with a confidante, a witness and moral support. The other woman reacts exactly the way Sissel hopes. She recognizes Sissel's problems. She has the same problems herself, and has chosen marriage because of the children.

Sissel has turned the problem into a conflict between adversaries who are equal and identical. It is an honourable conflict, where the adversaries are able to identify and recognize each other's good qualities and different resources. Attractiveness is one kind of resource. The first thing Ellen and Sissel report on, when they come back, is her attractiveness (beauty, decoration, fashion). What they see does not threaten Sissel's identity as an attractive woman. Ellen's comment ("I would have wrung her neck") suggests that less honourable conflicts are also possible. In this situation Benny is a helpless onlooker to the women's discussion. For him the situation has got completely out of hand. . . .

The emotional bond is closely related to the economic . . . and legal bonds as defined in Norwegian law. Ellen and Tore advise her to separate officially. . . . The matter will then not only be their private concern, but also a concern for the authorities, and accordingly more serious. They advise her to give priority to her own independence. The value of autonomy is thereby brought inside the household. . . . Their reason for suggesting that she should prioritize her independence is that they judge Benny not trustworthy.

When he lacks control over his emotions, how can he control his money? Autonomy and individualism are better than dependence on a man who has proved to be out of control. Also inside marriage the value of autonomy thus makes itself felt. When a crisis happens one easily thinks of dissolving the corporation into two autonomous units. Very quickly their whole marriage and communal household are at stake, and Sissel is at last left with the choice between very radicalized alternatives.

MORAL SUPPORT
FROM FEMALE FRIENDS

When together on their own, young women develop informal common understandings about how to handle their lives, including their husbands or menfriends. They support each other, but also give each other warnings and apply sanctions. The shared understandings that they develop are the source of some strength in their relationships with their husbands.

Their moral discourse demonstrates some of the basis for identification and conflict both between women and between women and their husbands/boyfriends. During a crisis friends are mobilized and informal rules are made more explicit than in everyday life. There are similarities and differences between segments of Norwegian society in the way such crises are codified and solved, by routinized practices and solutions. In the social circles described in this book women are very influential concerning moral matters and the family networks. The husband/wife relationship is ideologically dominant (Hsu 1971).[1] "The husband comes first", then the friends. This is symbolized by always finishing coffee klatches in due time to tidy up the house and fix *middag* (dinner) before he is home. The *middag* is the most compelling

reason for finishing a coffee klatch. . . . But . . . loyalty to husbands in this milieu does not . . . prevent the wives from seeking advice and support in some matters.

Through their discussions and sociability women get more "private" information than men. They tell humorously how their husbands try not to show how eager they are to hear the latest news when, for instance, they arrive home from the *klubb*. They try to hide compromising information about their own best friends from their men, even if they criticize a friend among themselves for the way she has behaved. A husband might use this information as an argument . . . : "See what she did. Therefore I don't want you to go out alone!", or he might just feel their marriage threatened. Information control is not completely effective, however. . . . They do not conceal information about . . . women with whom they are not . . . close friends.

Female friendships are thus ideologically secondary to marriage, but . . . expectations of loyalty are . . . high, and disappointments over disloyalty equally strong. "How could a woman friend do such a thing!"

There are, however, limitations to moral support. The women . . . keep some . . . secrets from their men, but they do not give each other moral support to break moral rules that are regarded as important. One cannot confess and expect support about having a lover. One may at most confess that one is in love but not . . . doing anything about it. . . .

CONCLUSIONS

The moral discourse of the young mothers is . . . concrete and personal. They never discuss moral problems *in abstracto*. . . .

They give each other warnings, support, sanctions, advice about how to handle their sexuality. Sexuality is important to them, and they are at the stage of life when one is sexually most active. They are also relatively young and do not feel as confident about love, sex and attraction as they will perhaps later become. . . .

---

[1]Here the husband-wife relationship is ideologically dominant in contrast to, for instance, the Middle East where the father-son relationship is dominant (Barth 1971) or East London in the fifties (Young and Wilmot 1957) or the Bahamas (Blom 1970) where the mother-daughter relationship, in different ways, seems ideologically most important.

Some matters are not talked about or only problematized in certain ways. The personal feelings of love, attraction and sexuality remain basically very private, and each person is left alone with her eventual feelings of insecurity.

Their ethic seems to be more normative than situational. Actions and their relations to each other are examined, whereas motives are to a large extent taken for granted. Their ethic is one of norms and assumed consequences of breaches of norms, presuming, often, one meaning for each act. . . .

Their dilemma is, to some extent, to reconcile two different worlds—hearth and home and going out. Female friends may . . . be mediators between those two worlds, as escorts, allies and confidantes. The women in this study are . . . striving to create an integrated whole of their lives, to integrate diverse and conflicting roles and experiences. In so far as they insist on pursuing conflicting interests, they also work hard intellectually to integrate these interests. Life as an integrated whole is the ideal, not life as a hotchpotch of different colourful roles. Contradictions and ambiguities are not accepted. They constantly try to solve the contradictions inherent in pursuing both identities as attractive women and identities as decent and morally responsible persons. The ideal of being whole, integrated and autonomous persons seems to be a specific theme in Norwegian culture.

Connected with these underlying ideas about the whole person is their way of viewing problems in relationships in terms of there being something wrong with the persons involved. What is at stake in cases of jealousy, then, is to some extent, self-esteem. This is . . . why some of these cases are so emotionally disturbing and dramatic that relatively innocent (from an outsider's perspective) actions escalate into a crisis and a choice between radicalized alternatives in one step.

Their concrete way of discussing moral problems is connected with their position as working-class women having relatively little formal education. The image one gets of women trying to control their own and men's morality confirms other descriptions of strong working-class mothers, both from Norway and from England, for instance Young and Wilmot (1957). Control is one key concept here. The emphasis of control is related to identities as "decent ordinary folk", as stable working class as opposed to different stigmatized categories, and to women's particular role to achieve this for her family. A man needs a woman who controls that he goes to work regularly and who keeps his urges for women and alcohol at bay. Being morally responsible is an important part of female identity, it means something different for them than for men. There is a cognitive division along gender lines between "them" and "us". "We think of the kids. We drag ourselves home." "Men are so irresponsible." "Men are so egoistical. They get things so easily." "Men are really like big children", are common refrains. . . . There seems to be a mutual ascription of attributes between women and men. Women find men irresponsible. Men, on their side, find women fussy, gossiping, nagging and so on.

Men are probably not less moral then women, but they apply more of their energy to different realms of life than personal relationships. They talk about other things when together and do not in the same way debate personal relationships. To some extent women have understandings . . . that are not shared by men, and to some extent they are the ones who are debating, maintaining and changing cultural ideas and values about love and personal relationships. In these realms of life men . . . appear muted and women . . . appear articulate and influential.

REFERENCES

HSU (Ed.). *Kinship and Culture.* Chicago: Aldine, 1971.

YOUNG, MICHAEL AND WILLMOTT, PETER, *Family and Kinship in East London.* (First published, London, 1957). Reprinted in Pelican books, 1962.

Introduction

This and Excerpt 36 look at issues of power and submission within families. In an alarming number of families throughout the world, conflicts between members are settled with the use of violence. This excerpt is from an extensive cross-cultural study of family violence. The author, an American anthropologist named David Levinson used the Human Relations Area Files to study the patterning of family violence throughout the world. According to this study, violence between family members occurs in about eighty-five percent of all societies.

> The factors that predict low or no family violence include monogamous marriage, economic equality between the sexes, equal access to divorce by men and women, the availability of alternative caretakers for children, frequent and regular intervention by neighbours and kin in domestic disputes, and norms that encourage the nonviolent settlement of disputes outside the home. (David Levinson, 1989)

The two most common forms of violence between family members are wife beating and the physical punishment of children. Not surprisingly, adult women are the most frequent victims.

35

Family Violence in Cross-Cultural Perspective

David Levinson

INTRODUCTION

. . . In this book, I examine this worldwide reality of family violence by means of worldwide comparative study. Worldwide comparative studies . . ."test or develop a theory through statistical analysis of data on a sample of ten or more small-scale societies from three or more geographical regions of the world" (Levinson and Malone, 1980: 3). Worldwide comparative studies . . . use . . . secondary data culled from ethnographic reports and . . . are truly comparative since they sample a large number and broad range of societal types. . . .

Source: Levinson, David (1989) *Family Violence in Cross-Cultural Perspective*, pages 9–38. Frontiers of Anthropology, Volume 1. Newbury Park: Sage Publications.

METHODOLOGY

. . . The sample used here is composed of 90 small-scale and peasant societies selected from the HRAF Probability Sample Files (PSF) sample (Lagace, 1979). The PSF sample is a stratified probability sample of 120 societies presumably representative of the 60 major geographical/cultural regions of the world. . . . Only 90 societies are used here since systematically organized data are not yet available for all 120 societies. Two types of societies are included in the sample. First, small-scale (primitive, kin-based, nonliterate) societies that are defined as cultural units with no indigenous written language. Second, peasant (folk, traditional) societies that are defined as cultural units whose members share a common heritage, who produce at least 50% of their own food, and who are under the control of a nation state. . . .

FAMILY VIOLENCE
IN LIFE-SPAN PERSPECTIVE

Infancy

Infants are an infrequent target for other family members. Sale of infants for sacrifice and the binding of body parts are limited practices that, while causing pain to the infant, are usually considered acceptable, if not expected, behavior of the parents by other members of the society. . . .

Infanticide is . . . usually carried out by the mother (60% of societies) or another relative (17% of societies). In addition, it is almost always the family who decides infanticide must be performed. This does not imply infanticide is . . . taken lightly or performed easily. Rather, it is often performed with great pain by the mother who has no other choice. There is often no other alternative, because infanticide is a mechanism through which societies dispose of infants whose birth or condition makes them a liability to the family or to the entire group. This point becomes obvious when we consider the major reasons for infanticide. Four reasons stand out: First, when the infant is considered illegitimate, because of unknown or irregular paternity, such as through rape or adultery, about 50% of societies allow or require infanticide under these circumstances. Second, when the infant is deformed, with about 50% of societies permitting infanticide for this reason. Third, when the birth is unusual, often evidenced by the birth of twins. In about 40% of societies one twin might be sacrificed in this situation. Fourth, because the infant, despite being normal and the product of normal conception and birth, is unwanted. More often than not it is unwanted because it is the wrong sex (16% of societies), with female infanticide more common than male infanticide. . . .

Female infanticide has drawn special attention as a form of population control, particularly in polygynous societies as a means of balancing the sex ratio.

Childhood

. . . As with violence directed at infants, most types of violence directed at children tend to occur in only a few societies. In fact, the only types with widespread distribution are the use of physical punishment in child rearing and fighting between siblings. . . .

I found that physical punishment is regularly used in only 13.3% of the 90 societies, frequently used in 21.1%, infrequently used in 40% and rarely or never used in 26.5%. In addition, many techniques other than punishment are also used, both apart from or in conjunction with actual punishment. . . .

The majority of societies do not rely on physical punishment as their major child-rearing technique. Rather, as the data from Barry et al. (1980) suggest, most parents around the world rely on a variety of techniques, with physical punishment most often used to stop current misbehavior rather than to inculcate specific behaviors or values. Setting an example, rewarding through gifts and ceremonies, and lecturing are often far more important than is physical punishment in shaping behavior and values. . . .

Our data suggest violence between siblings is not especially common in societies around the world. It is reported as present in only 43.7% of the societies in our sample. However, since I could find information on sibling violence for only 48 of the 90 societies in the sample, there is some question as to whether sibling violence is underreported because it is often overlooked by ethnographers (perhaps because it is so common in Western societies) or whether sibling violence is not mentioned because it does not occur. . . .

Sibling violence may be relatively infrequent in non-Western societies for two reasons. First, in some societies siblings are segregated by age, and in many societies by sex. Thus the opportunity for violence between older and younger siblings or brothers and sisters . . . is considerably reduced. Second, in many societies, older siblings play a central role in helping care for their younger brothers and sisters. In this role, they often follow the lead of their parents or other adults in the child-rearing techniques they use. Since, in many societies physical punishment is used infrequently and is less important than other techniques, it follows that sibling caretakers will tend not to punish physically siblings in their care.

Adolescence

. . . Initiation ceremonies are a formal social recognition that the child is passing into the next stage in the life cycle, either adolescence or adulthood, and often, though not always, occur at or after the biological changes associated with puberty. Initiation ceremonies occur in about 55% of societies, with more societies having ceremonies for girls than for boys (Schlegel and Barry, 1980). Both our data and Schlegel and Barry's indicate that painful procedures or pain inflicted during genital operations occur in about 47% of the societies with ceremonies. Painful procedures include scarification, tattooing, tooth extraction, and the like to change the child's appearance; and whippings, cold baths, forced starvation, and the like as part of the ceremony or training program leading up to the ceremony. Genital operations, generally conducted without anesthesia, include circumcision and subincision for boys and clitoridectomy for girls. These procedures as well as the ceremony are carried out by adults in the community, with the support of the child's immediate family, but usually without their active participation. Thus pain infliction during initiation ceremonies is violence directed at children or adolescents by adults with the approval of the child's family. . . .

Adulthood

. . . Wife beating is the most common form of family violence around the world. It occurs at least occasionally in 84.5% of the societies in our sample. It occurs in virtually all households in 18.8% of societies, in a majority of households in 29.9%, in a minority of households in 37.8%, and never or very rarely in 15.5%. Wife beatings severe enough to kill or permanently injure the wife are reported in 46.6% of all societies in the sample—that is, in 58% of societies in which wife beating is present. Wife beating is discussed in more detail in the following section. . . .

Husband beating occurs in 26.9% of the societies in our sample, or in about a third of the societies with wife beating. In about 6.7% of societies husband beating occurs in a majority of households, and in a minority of households in the other 20.2%. Husband beating occurs only in societies in which wife beating also occurs. Not only is husband beating less common cross-culturally, but it occurs less often than does wife beating in those societies in which both are present. . . .

However, in some societies with wife beating, there are circumstances that empower the wife to beat her husband, with evidence of adultery being the most common. Among the Tikopia of Polynesia, for example, a husband who stays out all night is greeted by a stick-wielding wife who beats him on the legs and pinches him to draw blood, a punishment he must endure in silence for fear of awakening the other residents of the household (Firth, 1936: 133).

Alice Schlegel (1972) has brought to our attention the practice of adult brothers beating their adult sisters in societies with matrilineal descent systems. Schlegel categories the societies in her sample in terms of the degree of control brothers or husbands exert over their sisters or wives. In societies in which brothers dominate, sister beating is tolerated, but husband beating is not. Where husbands dominate, both wife beating and sister beating are tolerated, although wife beating is more common. In societies in which brothers and husbands share control, wife/sister beating is uncommon. . . .

Fighting between co-wives in polygynous societies is another form of family violence largely unknown in the Western world. Co-wives . . . often live in the same family compound or dwelling with the husband and their children. . . . That violence between co-wives will occasionally break-out is not surprising given the role complexity in polygynous family households. Not only are there two or more co-wives who share the same husband and must cooperate in economic matters, but there are their children who share the same father and are related to one another as half siblings. Thus there are often conflicts over sexual access to the husband, distribution of wealth, and disciplining of the children. Among the Siriono of Bolivia, for example, older wives sometimes fight with younger wives over sexual access to the husband (Holmberg, 1950: 50). However, aggression is not always directed at the other co-wife, as among the Kapauku of New Guinea, where sexual neglect might lead a wife to either attack another co-wife or destroy her husband's garden (Pospisil, 1958: 136).

. . . Fighting between co-wives appears to be part of a general pattern of women in polygynous societies settling disputes through violence. Our data suggest physical aggression between women occurs almost exclusively in societies with polygynous marriage, with much of it motivated by sexual jealousy. . . .

The other forms of family violence listed in Table 1 are sparsely distributed around the world, either because they occur in only a few societies (raiding for brides, for example), or because, while they do occur in many societies, they occur very rarely (matricide, for example).

TABLE 1. Family Violence in Life-Span Perspective

Infants
  infanticide
  sale of infants for sacrifice
  binding body parts for shaping (head, feet, and so on)
  force feeding
  harsh disciplinary techniques such as cold baths
Childhood
  organized fighting promoted by adults
  ritual defloration
  physical punishment (beating, kicking, slapping, burning, twisting ears, and so on)
  child marriage
  child slavery
  child prostitution
  drugging with hallucinogens
  parent-child homocide/suicide
  child labor
  sibling fighting
  nutritional deprivation
  corporal punishment in schools
  mutilation for begging
Adolescence (puberty)
  painful initiation rites (circumcision, superincision, clitoridectomy, scarification, cold baths, piercing, sleep deprivation, whipping, bloodletting, forced vomiting)
  forced homosexual relations
  physical punishment
  gang rape of girls
Adulthood
  killing young brides
  forced suicides by young brides
  wife beating
  husband beating
  matricide
  patricide
  forced suicide of wives
  wife raiding
  marital rape
  parent beating
  co-wife fighting
  sister beating
Old Age
  forsaking the aged
  abandonment of the aged
  beating of the aged
  killing the aged
  forcing the aged to commit suicide

Old Age

. . . In the 1980s, elder abuse has become a major focus of attention. Perhaps the most reliable data come from Glascock's (Glascock and Wagner, 1986) study of the treatment of the aged in 60 societies. Their data put to rest the notion that the elderly are routinely left behind to die in small-scale societies. While this does occur in some societies, it seems confined mainly to a few nomadic groups and the practice is used only for those elderly who are too ill or weak to travel with the group. The elderly in most small-scale societies are treated with respect and cared for by their families and the community. However, there are exceptions: . . . in 12% of societies some elderly people are thought to be witches; in 12% of societies the elderly must give up their property; in 21% some elderly are not allowed to live with the main social group; and in 21% some elderly are killed because they are old. . . .

WIFE BEATING

. . . People around the world believe wife beating occurs or should occur for three main reasons. First, people in 17 societies believe wife beating occurs primarily as a punishment for adultery or because the husband suspects his wife has been unfaithful. . . .

The second type of wife beating I call wife beating for cause; that is, people in 15 societies believe that a husband may beat his wife, so long as he has a good reason. What constitutes a good reason is commonly understood by men and women alike and often involves the wife's failure to perform her duties or to treat her husband with the . . . respect he expects. . . .

The third type of wife beating is wife beating at will, since people in the 39 societies in which this type predominates believe that it is the husband's right to beat his wife for any reason or for no reason at all. This is by far the most common type of wife beating. . . .

A number of studies suggest that alcohol use may be directly or indirectly related to family violence (especially wife beating) in American families. . . . In the sample I found seven societies in which wife beating occurs mainly in association with alcohol consumption by the husband, one society in which it occurs usually when both the husband and wife are drinking, and five societies in which both alcohol- and nonalcohol-related wife beating are reported.

In all other societies, alcohol use apparently plays no or only a limited role in wife beating. . . .

Based on the data at hand, it seems that alcohol use is of little or no importance in family violence events in most societies around the world. At the same time, however, there are a few societies in which alcohol use is a key component in the sequence of events leading up to wife-beating incidents, with the supposed disinhibiting effects of alcohol used to excuse behavior that would not otherwise be tolerated by the wife, her family, or the community. . . .

REFERENCES

BARRY, H., III, L. JOSEPHSON, E. LAUER, and C. MARSHALL (1980) "Agents and techniques for child training: cross-cultural codes 6," pp. 237–276 in H. Barry, III and A. Schlegel (eds.) Cross-Cultural Samples and Codes. Pittsburgh: University of Pittsburgh Press.

FIRTH, R. W. (1936) We, the Tikopia: A Sociological Study of Kinship in Primitive Polynesia. London: Allen & Unwin.

GLASCOCK, A. P. and R. A. WAGNER (1986) HRAF Research Series in Quantitative Cross-Cultural Data. Vol. II: Life Cycle Data. New Haven, CT: HRAF.

HOLMBERG, A. R. (1950) Nomads of the Long Bow: The Siriono of Eastern Bolivia. Washington, DC: Government Printing Office.

LAGACE, R. O. (1979) "The HRAF probability sample." Behavior Science Research 14:211–229.

LEVINSON, D. and M. MALONE (1980) Toward Explaining Human Culture. New Haven, CT: HRAF.

POSPISIL, L. J. (1958) Kapauku Papuans and Their Law. New Haven, CT: Yale University Department of Anthropology.

SCHLEGEL, A. (1972) Male Dominance and Female Autonomy. New Haven, CT: HRAF.

SCHLEGEL, A. and H. BARRY III (1980) "Adolescent initiation ceremonies: a cross-cultural code," pp. 277–288 in H. Barry, III and A. Schlegel (eds.) Cross-Cultural Samples and Codes. Pittsburgh: University of Pittsburgh.

Introduction

The cross-cultural study of family violence described Excerpt 35 found that wife beating is the most common form of family violence around the world. The following excerpt is from a study of wife battering in Canada. Here the focus is on understanding and preventing this kind of violence. What makes this such a difficult task is that wife abuse occurs in virtually every type of family situation.

As the author explains, wife battering is a complex social dynamic. It is rarely a clear demonstration of male power. Indeed, women who have experienced abuse may see their husbands as weaker and less powerful than themselves—except in physical terms.

Why do women stay in abusive relationships? Because battering occurs in relationships that are otherwise healthy, women may excuse early incidents—especially if the abuse is relatively "mild". Women may not see themselves as battered until a pattern is recognized, and by then they are enmeshed in a self-destructive cycle of violence.

MacLeod's argument is simply this: unless we understand the ambivalence women feel toward their spouses, we will not be able to offer the kind of help many battered women will find useful.

36

Wife Battering in Canada

Linda MacLeod

OUR GROWING UNDERSTANDING OF WIFE BATTERING

. . . Battered women and batterers come from all walks of life. They may be working outside the home or in the home. They may be unemployed or have a steady job. They may be rich or poor, well-educated or illiterate, of any nationality or race, young or old, with or without children. . . .

Despite the difficulty of understanding wife battering, two major types of explanation have . . . been widely used to respond to battered

women, their children, and the men who batter them. . . .

Power-Based Theories

. . . These theories explain that violence against women is perpetuated by society's power structure which makes men dominant over women through the creation of separate and unequal roles for each gender. This dominance is reinforced through institutional rules and structures based on male supremacy.

As staff members of the Women's Research Centre in Vancouver have . . . stated:

Wife assault is a reality in our society because men have the socially ascribed authority to make the rules in marriage: and because violence against their wives

Source: MacLeod, Linda (1987) Battered but not Beaten: Preventing Wife Battering in Canada. Ottawa: Canadian Advisory Council on the Status of Women.

is accepted in the eyes of society, as an appropriate instrument of control. The social and economic structure of marriage as an institution in which women are dependent on men, requires this assignment of authority to men.[1]

Power-based theories of wife battering emphasizing sex-based inequality and the patriarchal structure of society . . . have gained . . . acceptance by policy-makers and service-providers in this field. This explanation for . . . wife battering appears in most writings on the subject and helps guide intervention . . . services for battered women, their partners, and their children.

Research on the power dynamics in battering families also asserts that power is more highly valued . . . in battering families than in non-battering families. On the surface, this power may not always overtly rest with the man. However, research findings suggest that, in families where the woman is dominant in terms of decision-making or earning power, or where the woman is perceived to be superior in some other way, violence is often used by the man to shift the balance of power. . . . Many counsellors reported that many men resort to physical violence when they feel their wives are more articulate than they are. These men frequently complain that they can't win an argument with their wives, so they "shut them up" by the use of force. . . .

In power-based theories, the acceptance and social reinforcement of violence in the family is a means to establish and to maintain the male in a dominant relationship over his wife.

Because male roles are socially created as dominant over female roles,

Wife assault arises out of the socio-cultural belief that women are less important and less valuable than men and so are not entitled to equal status and respect. Thus central to the task of dealing with the problem of wife assault is the need to recognize that wife assault is a social problem experienced by many Canadian women each year rather than an isolated interpersonal problem between two particular spouses.[2]

Learning Theories

Learning theorists argue that witnessing or suffering violence teaches people to use violence to try to solve problems or deal with stress . . . [3] This argument is supported by research and by statements from service-providers which reveal that many batterers come from families where their mothers were battered and/or where they themselves were physically, sexually, or psychologically abused as children.[4] These findings are corroborated by the statistics collected for this study. Sixty-one per cent of the partners of the women who stayed in transition houses in 1985 had been abused as children. Thirty-nine per cent of the battered women reported being physically abused as children, 24% reported being sexually abused, and 48% reported being emotionally abused as well. . . . Of the women who said they physically abused their own children, 69% said they had themselves been physically abused during their childhood.

Learning theorists also argue that the use of violence as a discipline tool can teach violence. In this vein, researchers report a "strong relationship between parental punishment and aggression" and suggest,

. . . increasing evidence indicates that a high price is paid for maintaining order in the family through violence. The norms that legitimate violence assure a family institution and a society characterized by violence for years to come.[5]

---

[1]Helga Jacobson, Co-ordinator. A Study of Protection for Battered Women (Vancouver: Women's Research Centre, 1982). p. 5.

[2]Marion Boyd, ed. Handbook for Advocates and Counsellors of Battered Women (London, Ontario: London Battered Women's Advocacy Clinic Inc., 1985), pp. 12–13.

[3]Anne Ganley, "Causes and Characteristics of Battering Men", in Wife Assault Information Kit (Victoria: Ministry of the Attorney General. April 1986), pp. 68–69.

[4]Research supporting this hypothesis is summarized in Straus and Hotaling, The Social Causes, pp. 14–15.

[5]Ibid., p. 15.

Learning theorists also frequently explain the perpetuation of violence . . . by stating that victims, friends, and society as a whole unintentionally reinforce the violence. . . .

The victim after the beating, may indeed do as he insists; others may treat him with more respect and often he feels more in control. Even if he feels remorseful or guilty about her injuries he (and sometimes the victim herself) tends to blame the victim for 'causing' him to 'lose control'. He denies responsibility for the negative behaviour. Due to the tacit acceptance of family violence in society and to the lack of clear messages that his violent behaviour must stop, his violence is rarely punished.[6]

Finally, learning theorists suggest that witnessing violence vicariously . . . can teach some men to use violence . . . within or outside the family. This . . . tenet has created . . . concern about pornography as a teaching tool for violence. . . .

These types of explanations, one based on the structure of power in our society, the other on learning theory, have clarified our understanding of wife battering, and have helped to guide intervention efforts. Yet many shelter workers and other service-providers lamented that . . . "these theories that seem so clear to us just don't seem to ring true for too many of the women who come to us". . . .

HOW DO BATTERED WOMEN UNDERSTAND THE BATTERING?

Battered women . . . speak of a shifting, ambiguous . . . power. They spoke sometimes of feeling powerless against their . . . partners. They also spoke of their power in the relationship and of the powerlessness of their partners. Many . . . believe . . . women are more powerful than men, as the quote below elucidates:

I can't quite make sense of what the women here [at the shelter] are saying about the patriarchal structure of society and about power and society making men more powerful and all that. When I was growing up, my mother was for sure stronger than my Dad in every way but physically. She was smarter, could do more, and more people respected her. I think it's the same with my husband and me. There's no way he's stronger than me, except physically, and that's why he hits me, because he feels so low.

Other women elaborated this theme in terms of a mother-son model of relationships between themselves and their partners.

My husband and all the men I've ever known are like little boys. We're really like their mothers, underneath. Everyone keeps telling me to leave him; they say he'll destroy me. But they don't know how strong I am and how weak he is underneath.

Others spoke of the power they feel in the relationship.

Sure I feel sorry for him. He says he would have nothing without me and the kids. I know he's pretty rotten sometimes. But he really needs me. I guess that's why I keep going back. He makes me feel important.

Still others spoke of their partners as victims or losers in society.

You can talk about men being powerful in our society if you want, but you're not talking about my husband. My husband's never had any power in his whole life. He's never had a chance. He was born poor. He was born Indian. He's never felt better than anyone. He's never felt better than me. It's because he's so low that he hits me.

. . . Many battered women do not feel like powerless victims, and will not respond positively to services which treat them like victims instead of survivors.

These experiences remind us of the complexity of the realization of power in individual relationships. They also remind us that power in our society is not just gender-based; it is also class-, race-, and age-based.

---

[6]Ganley, "Causes and Characteristics", p. 70.

Many battered women also understand battering as something that "got out of hand", as an extension . . . of a normal part of a normal relationship. Many battered women feel their relationship started out much like any other relationship and, in fact, some emphasize that they feel they had an unusually loving, intense, and close relationship. . . .

Intimate relationships, by definition, generate a wide range of emotions. . . . The image of romantic love idealized in our society is characterized by highs and lows. Being "in love" is living "on the edge", participating in a kind of emotional aerobics. . . . The socially accepted use of drugs, the preoccupation with "having it all", with creative stress, the fitness craze, and even our social addiction to soap operas and violent television shows emphasize high energy and intense emotional highs and lows.

For these reasons, wife battering at the outset is often difficult . . . to prevent, or even to identify, because some violence (rough sexual play and psychological games intended to elicit jealousy) is intertwined with our . . . ideal of "being in love" (isolation and possessiveness). In different socio-economic groups, this violence may be more or less psychological, or more or less physical, but the romantic desire to be alone together in a private world and the desire to have constant physical contact with your loved one are simply the "positive" faces of the jealousy and isolation which become part of most wife-battering experiences.

Battered women often talk of the intensity of their love for the batterer. Throughout this study, many battered women made the following kinds of statements: "I've never had better sex with anyone", "I just can't believe he'd hit me. I know he really loves me as much as I love him", "No one's ever loved me the way he does". Battered women also speak of the highs and lows of the relationship:

You know, life was a roller-coaster with Bill. In the end, of course, that became unbearable—all the ten-

sion. But in the beginning, it was just so thrilling. I never wanted to come down.

Many battered women . . . are guilty of no greater "weakness" than being in love with being in love. It's their attempt to stay in love, to retain an idealized vision of their partner, that often prevents many battered women from realizing they are being battered until the battering has become a part of life.

Women who are battered do not generally define themselves as battered . . . the first time they are battered. In fact, because wife battering includes emotional, verbal, and financial battering, as well as physical and sexual battering, it may be difficult to define when the first incident actually occurred. . . . This ambivalence is evident in the words battered women use to describe their early experiences with the batterer. It is not uncommon for battered women to say:

I was flattered by his jealousy at first—I thought it meant he loved me.

He said he would rather stay home, just with me, than go out with friends. I loved the attention and closeness at first. I thought he was the most romantic man in the world.

Even the first case of physical abuse is not always clear-cut. In many cases, the woman is "just pushed". While pushing can result in severe injuries, depending on the location of the push—down the stairs, over a chair, into a pot of boiling water on the stove, etc.—the push itself can be easily re-interpreted by the batterer and by the woman who is battered as something minor. The results of the push . . . can be viewed as an accident. . . .

I was just baffled the first time he hit me. It wasn't really a hit you know, not like a punch or even a slap, he just pushed me really hard. I broke an arm, but it was from falling backward over a chair, not from his push.

Another woman's statement mirrors these sentiments:

I couldn't believe my husband had hit me. I just kept asking, is this the same man who loves me so much that he can't stand it if another man talks to me? It was really easy for me to accept his explanation that he'd had a hard day at work and a little too much to drink. I couldn't see anything else without having to ask if he really did love me, and that was just too painful. It wasn't until much later, years of violence later, that I could see that the way he loved me—his jealousy, his possessiveness—were also part of the violence.

Is this . . . "illogic" really so different from the logic . . . which we call compromising, or "forgiving and forgetting", when it does not involve identifiable . . . violence? . . .

While violence almost always escalates, it may not do so . . . for months or years. The result is that women accept the violence as unpleasant but bearable . . . , given the good things about the relationships (and most battering relationships do still provide sporadic periods of closeness during the honeymoon phases of the violence) . . . until they are so enmeshed in the cycle of violence and so demoralized and trapped by it that they can't "just leave".

Many service-providers, and even women who have been battered, counsel that leaving or calling the police "the first time it happens" is the most effective way to ensure it won't happen again. However, given that it may be hard to define "that first incident", especially since definitions of intolerable violence are culturally relative and since most women have a lot of emotional and practical investment in their relationships, this advice frequently has an unreal, hollow ring to it. . . .

American author Susan Schechter points to the "normalcy" of the early reactions of most battered women, at least in terms of the current "rules" of intimate relationships, in her comment: "Most people feel ambivalent when ending a long-term relationship. Major change is always difficult, often slowly and haltingly undertaken".[7]

There is growing evidence that leaving provides no guarantee the battering will stop and may even escalate the violence. In the present study, 12% of the women were separated or divorced. Anecdotal information suggests the majority of these women were battered by their ex-husbands, some by new partners. Michael Smith, in his telephone survey of 315 Toronto women, found that, while the rate of abuse for all women interviewed was 18.1%, for women who were separated or divorced, the rate jumped to 42.6%.[8] . . .

The reactions of most battered women . . . are often strong and logical and must be . . . treated this way if we are to reach out to battered women and provide services for them which "ring true", will be helpful, and will be used by a greater number of battered women. It is easy . . . to scoff at, or be discouraged by, the astonished response of many women to the suggestion that they leave their violent husbands: "But he's my husband, and the father of my children. . . . I can't just abandon him". It's easy from an outside vantage point which assumes that the batterer, the battered wife, their relationship, or all three are defective, to dismiss as misguided sentiment the woman's heroic attempts to keep her marriage together, to keep her children from knowing about the violence, to insist that she loves her husband. The woman's actions and statements are easy to dismiss as long as we assume the battered woman, along with her partner and their relationship, are somehow . . . different from us . . . in terms of the basic personality of the man and woman and in terms of the initial quality of the relationship.

However, as this study has established repeatedly, research shows that battered women do not fit one psychological or socio-economic mould. Few common characteristics which are not the direct result of the battering have been

---

[7]Susan Schechter, *Women and Male Violence: The Visions ~d Struggles of the Battered Women's Movement* (Boston: ~th End Press, 1982). p. 20.

[8]Michael D. Smith, *Woman Abuse: The Case for Surveys by Telephone.* The LaMarsh Research Programme Reports on Violence and Conflict Resolution. Report #12 (Toronto: York University, November 1985), p. 29.

cited. In fact, in the one study known to the author where the personality traits of battered women **before** the violence were discussed, Lenore Walker found women who are battered "perceive themselves as more liberal than most" in their relationships with men[9]—a far cry from the stereotype of the battered woman as a traditional woman totally oppressed by, and dependent on, her partner.

It is **after** prolonged battering, as a result of the battering, that battered women begin to display certain similar psychological traits. After prolonged battering, women suffer from low self-esteem and isolation. They are emotionally dependent on the batterer, are compliant, feel guilty, and blame themselves for the violence, and yet demonstrate great loyalty to the batterer. Not only do they want the relationship to continue, they state they are staying for the sake of the family. They believe the batterers' promises to change and frequently believe the violence would stop if only their partners would get the one lucky break they've always wanted.[10]

. . . To understand the actions and perceptions of battered women, it is important to think of how we all act in relationships, what we want, and the extent to which many of us will go to preserve a relationship. As one shelter worker poignantly said:

Relationships are hard to come by. Sure we should help women know that they have worth outside their marriages, but a marriage isn't just status and a piece of paper . . . it's warmth, belonging, and a future. Battered women don't always get these good things out of their relationships, but most of them did in the beginning, and they just keep hoping it will come back. People will go to any lengths to feel loved, and love is not just waiting around the next corner for every battered woman who leaves her batterer.

Even the majority of women who report the violence do so out of hope—that, by reporting the violence, she and her partner will be helped to return to their pre-violent state. Of course, she may also hope she will get attention and be listened to because she is frequently lonely and unnurtured as a result of the isolation most batterers impose on their victims. She may also hope he will be punished or "get his just deserts". But behind it all, she often just wants them to be happy again. The importance of these hopes should not be diminished.

Unfortunately . . . many of the services which have been created for battered women and for their partners have been built on the assumption that . . . the relationship is not worth saving and ignore or belittle the woman's hopes to save and rekindle it. The hope of the service-providers is most often to save or protect the woman as an individual or to help or change the batterer as an individual in some way. This well-intentioned, institutional hope often buries the woman's pleas for a different kind of help. This . . . discrepancy between the battered woman's hopes and the hopes of the service-providers renders many of the initiatives taken inappropriate and frustrating for the women who are battered and contributes to the burnout and despair of the . . . people who try to help the women, their children, and their partners. . . .

[9]Walker, "The Battered Woman Syndrome Study", p. 8.

[10]Alberta, Social Services and Community Health, *Breaking the Pattern: How Alberta Communities Can Help Assaulted Women and Their Families* (Edmonton: November 1985), p. 17.

Discussion Questions

1. Ask people in your class who have lived with a chronically ill or disabled family member to describe the effect of this illness (or disability) on other family members and how they get along.

2. Gullestad, the author of *Kitchen-table Society,* describes her approach as

explicitly feminist. What do you think she means by this? How would you differentiate a feminist perspective from a nonfeminist perspective?

3. Cast the issue of child labor in a framework of international trade. Check the labels in the clothes you are wearing to see where they are made. Is it possible that your clothes were made by children? Do we as a society care more about animal rights on an international level than child rights?

4. Advocates of an analytical approach to business decisions suggest a technique called "the five whys." This is a deceptively simple process of probing for underlying causes by repeating the question, "why?" It is a useful way to probe beyond the obvious. Use the five whys to ask why fifty-eight percent of black children in the United States are born to unmarried mothers. See if you can carry the argument further than Edelman has done in Excerpt 31.

5. Levinson's cross-cultural study of family violence found that violence is least likely in societies where relationships between men and women are more equitable and where there are a number of alternative caretakers for children. Family violence is also less common in societies which discourage violence outside the home. If these findings are generalizable to the West, what would you predict about the amount of family violence in our society?

6. What cultural blinders prevented North Americans from identifying family violence as an important social issue until the mid-1970s?

Data Collection Exercises

1. What resources does your community have to help family members who have been victims of violence? Interview a knowledgeable practitioner in your community to find out both the extent of the problem and the sources of help. (Compare the findings of different members of the class to determine whether there is general agreement among law enforcement officers, social workers, and so on.)

2. In Excerpt 31, Edelman gives an overview of black families in America. She compares white and black marriage rates, birth rates by marital status, and employment rates. Extend this comparison to native Americans.

3. Brainstorm to create a scale to measure sources of stress for students at your institution. Pretest the scale, then administer it to fifteen students. Include a number of "face sheet" variables such as sex, race, and age and analyze the results.

4. What do you think is the most serious problem facing families today? Support your answer to this question with primary data.

Writing Exercises

1. Imagine that you have been asked to write a thousand-word feature story on homeless children for your school paper. Focus on any society, jurisdiction, or subissue you choose.

2. Why are single-parent families likely to be poor in the United States and as well off as two-parent families in Sweden? Probe beyond the obvious legislative differences. What cultural differences account for the two approaches to family problems?

3. Keep a journal for a month, paying particular attention to situations that create stress in your life and the means you use to alleviate the stress, or its source.

4. Read (and write a five-hundred-word review of) Sue Miller's novel *Family Pictures,* about a family coping with an autistic child. Evaluate the book in terms of the insights you gain, rather than its literary merit.

Glossary

Child abuse—Any act of commission or omission which adversely affects the physical, mental, or emotional well-being of a child.

Child sexual abuse—Using physical power or influence to involve children in sexual activity.

Incest—Sexual abuse by a father, mother, stepparent, or older sibling.

Infanticide—The purposeful killing of infant children.

Infidelity—Also referred to as adultery or extramarital sexual activity. Cross-culturally, adultery is the leading cause of marital dissolution.

Marital homicide—Murder of a spouse.

Wife battery—Includes physical violence as well as psychological, sexual, verbal, and economic abuse.

Suggested Readings

ALLEN, CHARLOTTE VALE, (1981) *Daddy's Girl,* New York: Wyndham Books. A personal account of incest survival by novelist Allen.

BASS, ELLEN, and LOUISE THORNTON. (1983) *I Never Told Anyone.* New York: Harper Collins. This is a collection of writings by adult victims of child sexual abuse. While the experiences are chilling, bringing them to the surface is part of the healing process.

EDELMAN, MARION WRITE. (1987) *Families in Peril.* Boston, Mass: Harvard University Press. Excerpt 31 is taken from the first chapter of this book. The rest of the book is highly recommended for its unusually good balance. Edelman manages to convey the extent of the problems facing black families today, yet leave us with the sense that the situation is far from hopeless.

GILMOUR, ALAN. (1988) *Innocent Victims: The Question of Child Abuse.* London: Michael Joseph. A description of the nature and extent of child abuse in Britain written by the Director of the National Society for the Prevention of Cruelty to Children.

KENT, GEORGE. (1991) "Our children, our future," *Futures,* (January/February), 32–49. Kent provides an overview of the situation of children throughout the world. Kent blames not poverty, but the priorities of the powerful for the problems children face.

MOOREHEAD, CAROLINE. (1990) *Betrayal: A Report on Violence Toward Children in Today's World.* New York: Doubleday. This book is made up of eleven reports by journalists from around the world describing different aspects of the hidden world of violence against children. The chapters tell the stories of and the statistics behind child prostitution, homelessness, and abuse.

PART VII

Marital Disruption and Divorce

In this section, we examine excerpts on marital disruption and divorce. They include historical works on divorce in nineteenth-century America and Japan; contemporary studies of divorce in (Hindu) India and (Moslem) Libya; and the economic effects of divorce on American women today.

As an overview to this section, we can note several main trends in divorce. Around the world, easier divorce laws are making divorce more common. More women are divorcing their spouses as they become able to earn a living wage. Cohabitation is increasing the rates of dissolution of formal and informal unions. Lower fertility is contributing to higher rates of divorce: people without children are more likely to split up. And finally, more people—adults and children alike—are feeling the consequences of separation and divorce.

The reasons people give for breaking up are similar wherever we happen to look. An excerpt in this section finds that spouses in India end their marriages with complaints that are very much like the ones people express in our own society. These complaints about their marriages—cruelty, quarrelsomeness, failure to provide income, or use it wisely, and so on—are probably as old as marriage itself.

Divorce lets people escape from relationships they find deeply dissatisfying. More and more, divorce is replacing other ways of dealing with marital dissatisfaction. In Libya, men have traditionally ignored the unsuitability of their mates, or handled the problem through polygyny. Polygyny (more than one wife per husband) tends to favor husbands, but it may take some of the pressure off dissatisfied wives too. It gives the husband a greater chance of having at least one wife he wishes, and the wife fewer demands by an undesired husband.

One might say that polygyny is a good solution to problems caused by arranged marriage. It is a solution that Moslems have practiced for a thousand years. However in Libya, according to an excerpt by Khalidi in this section, divorce is gradually replacing polygyny as the solution to this age-old problem of incompatibility between mates.

This change to easier divorce is meeting with resistance in some quarters. People who value, or stand to gain most from, the old patriarchal ways tend to resist easier divorce laws. Some cite the explosive rise of divorce rates over the last few decades as evidence of the "decline of the family." That divorce rates have risen in most parts of the world, and especially the West, is undeniable. What is less clear is the meaning of this trend. Has the family "declined," improved, or merely changed?

Before drawing any conclusion about the meanings of a higher divorce rate for the future of the family, we need to know who is getting divorced, and why. If we understand why, we will be better able to judge the future of divorce and its likely impact on the family in years to come.

How Divorce Rates are Changing

A vast amount of research on divorce has yielded some commonly agreed-upon facts. First, divorce is more common in the United States than in many other countries (except Scandinavia), due to "a preexisting tendency toward a voluntaristic form of marriage" (Furstenburg, 1990: 381). Everywhere, divorce rates have increased as people have come to view marriage as a pairing of people for companionship, not an economic relationship between kin groups (Burgess, 1948). Nowhere is this companionate, romantic ideal of marriage stronger than in America.

Paradoxically, a romantic outlook on marriage guarantees a higher divorce rate, because the chances of disappointment with a spouse are that much higher, and more important. In this sense, divorce may be the inevitable result of a marriage system that emphasizes romance and a free choice of mates, on the grounds of romantic love.

Viewed from this perspective, divorce allows people to correct their earlier mistakes in choosing an unsuitable marriage partner. People are no longer expected to stay with a mate who no longer pleases them, simply because they chose that mate at some earlier time. Indeed, there has been a gradual shift in marital standards from "one which required couples to remain married even if they were not in love to one which virtually demanded divorce unless they remained in love." (Furstenburg, op. cit.)

Shifting cultural standards in marriage also reflect a shift in the economic basis of marriage. With more women working for pay, spouses depend less on one another. Particularly, wives depend less on their husbands for income. For their part, husbands depend less on their wives for domestic and child-raising services. They can easily buy domestic services (for example, cleaning and laundry services, take-out food) outside the home, and there are fewer children for a wife to look after, given the decline in fertility we discussed earlier. So husbands (indeed, households) have less need of full-time wives and mothers than in the past.

As we see in another section of this book, scholars continue to debate the inequality of domestic work: how great it is, whether it is declining or standing still, and so on. At the very least, it seems clear that women continue to do the lion's share of domestic work whether they are working for pay and whether there are young children in the household. From this standpoint, husbands seem to get more out of marriage than wives do.

Such domestic inequality is nothing new. In fact, it is a pale remnant of the inequality that marked nineteenth-century marriages, as we learn from an excerpt in this section by Clark. No wonder women fighting for more liberal divorce laws in the mid- to late nineteenth century compared themselves to slaves, and their fight for easier divorce to the fight for an abolition of black slavery! They wanted the same freedom as men, and thought reforming the divorce laws would provide them with this freedom. The divorce debate tapped traditional American concerns about the inalienable rights of the individual. Ever since, there has been a link between high divorce rates and a high value placed on individualism.

Individualistic values may explain high divorce rates in the United States even today, but they do not always explain high divorce rates elsewhere. For example, an excerpt in this section shows that Japanese divorce rates were high even before Western values, women's labor force participation, and romantic love-matching took hold. Indeed Japanese divorce rates were higher in 1880 than they were in 1980. Since Japan was certainly not as Westernized or individualistic a century ago as it is today, we must search elsewhere for an explanation of these high divorce rates.

Kumagai puts forward a variety of explanations which are more or less compatible with one another. Divorce rates in the past were high due to poverty and the rural nature of the area. There was little to lose through divorce, which held little moral meaning anyway. Concubinage and polygyny were generally not options. Unsatisfactory marriages through parent selection could also be remedied by divorce and remarriage.

After 1880 the divorce rates fell for over half a century, presumably as marriage traditions broke down and prosperity increased. However in Japan as elsewhere, Westernization set off a new rise in divorce rates after 1940. It is this phase of high divorce rates that may be explained by using theories of modern companionate marriage.

If industrialization, individualism, and romance are to blame for high divorce rates, these rates should continue to rise without stop in the future. Yet what we are seeing in many Western countries is an apparent leveling off of these rates. This may be due to the fact that young people, whose marriages have been more apt to end in divorce, are now cohabiting rather than marrying. Rates of cohabitation go unrecorded, so it is hard to know how many common-law marriages break up.

Divorce rates are also affected by changes in the age composition of the married population. Younger, more recently-married people are generally the most likely to divorce. The longer a couple has been married, the less likely they are to get a divorce. (The reason for this seems to be that the longer they have been married, the more "marital capital" spouses have invested, and the harder dissolution becomes.) This helps to explain why people who married in the 1950s and early 1960s were a lot less likely to divorce than people who married in the 1970s or 1980s, when divorce laws had become much more liberal and divorce was more socially acceptable.

With population aging, there are simply fewer high-risk (young, recently-married) people around, so fewer marriages are at high risk of divorce. As a result, demographers and sociologists disagree as to whether divorce is really leveling off or just appears to do so.

They disagree less about the long-term results of today's high divorce rates: all see a very high proportion of people passing in and out of marriage through their lifetimes. For example, Norton and Moorman (1986) and Castro-Martin and Bumpass (1989) estimate that nearly two thirds of all American first marriages made in the 1980s will end in separation or divorce. Does this continued pervasiveness of divorce signal the "decline of the family," as some have suggested?

Does More Divorce Prove The Family is in Decline?

Answering that question forces us to ask other questions. Is easier divorce an inevitable part of family change, and family change an inevitable part of social change? Is society as a whole in decline? Is social life on this planet getting worse and worse, better and better, or neither?

It is easy to show that easier divorce *is* an inevitable part of family change, and in turn, family change is an inevitable part of social change. In modern times, two main forces have led to a restructuring of family ties and a redefinition of the family: industrialization and urbanization. These processes have transferred the production of goods and services from the family to the market, and from households to stores, offices, and factories. In this way, they have reduced the importance of the family as an economic unit.

In turn, this change has helped to individualize people's lives. Over the past few centuries, people have increasingly come to see themselves as distinct from their families. They have developed and expressed needs and desires that often conflict with those of other family members.

It is no longer the case that what is good for the family as a whole is good for each of its members, and vice versa. Few people in modern societies believe otherwise, though they feel great fondness for their parents, siblings, and children, and pay lip service to the social importance of "the family."

One way of dealing with this clash between individuals and families has been to redefine the family. We have already noted that family formation has come to be a voluntary act. From that perspective, what's done can be undone. Since spouses are not as closely tied to each other economically as they once were, they can opt out of marriages that do not meet their earlier expectations. On this score, Moore (1989: 341) concludes that "[t]he rise in divorce may not mean the decline of the marriage institution so much as the failure of [people's] new expectation" of emotional and psychological growth within marriage.

In general, more and more people have come to define their lives in terms of "choices," and their relationships in terms of "contracts." This is true at school, at work, and in the family too. If we accept the notions of choice and contract as essential to modern life, we must accept them for family life; if we accept them for family life, we must accept free choice in divorce as much as in marriage and childbearing. Thus, the rise in divorce rates represents the full flowering of a choice-and-contract civilization, not the decline of the family.

By this reckoning, people with the most to gain and least to lose from divorce, and people who have been most thoroughly socialized into the choice-and-contract culture of family life, *should* be the most likely to divorce. This is what we indeed find when we examine data on the kinds of people who are most, and least, likely to divorce.

Who Divorces, and Why?

As we have already noted, divorce risks or probabilities are highest for young, recently-married people. The younger people are when they get married, the more likely they are to get a divorce at some time in the future. The reasons: younger people are less likely to have been exposed to many different experiences. As a result, they are less able to make a wise choice of marriage partners. Also, people's personalities are not fully formed when they are young. Once married, people may find their personalities, tastes, and interests changing in ways that make them less compatible with their partners.

As well, young people have invested little time or money in the marriage and stand to lose little by ending it. They stand to gain more by finding a better lifelong spouse than someone with fewer years to live. And they have grown up exposed to more recent versions of the choice-and-contract cultural outlook.

We find an association between early marriage and a high divorce risk in many different societies. For example, Amoateng and Heaton find the same relationship in Ghana. The authors note that "for each year that a woman delays entry into marriage, her chances of getting divorced are reduced by about 3 per cent."

We find an apparent exception to this rule in Iran (Aghajanian, 1988). There, the younger a wife is when she marries, the *less* likely a couple is to divorce. Iranian women are socialized to submit to the authority of their fathers and husbands. They are married off at a young age precisely so that they can be "broken in" by their mothers-in-law. By contrast, women who manage to put off marrying until they are older are less willing to tolerate domination by their husbands' families. They are also more likely than average to divorce their mates.

However the reader who has been following carefully should be able to show that our choice-and-contract theory works in the Iranian case too. (Try working it out for yourself!)

Besides early marriages, second marriages also carry high risks of divorce. Different researchers offer different explanations of this finding that second marriages have a higher risk of divorce than first marriages. For example, Bohannon (1985) argues that remarriages are strained by the presence of children from first marriages who may have trouble accepting (and being accepted by) their parent's new mate. And, as Cherlin (1978) notes, most people are still unclear about the rules and expectations that should guide such families. Along these lines, White and Booth (1985) believe that the uncertainty built into stepfamily roles interferes with bonds between the husband and wife.

Other explanations focus on the divorce-proneness of people who are likely to enter into second marriages. Halliday (1980) notes that people who enter second marriages have (often) shown themselves willing to leave an unhappy relationship. Because they proved capable of choosing divorce once, they are more likely than average to choose it twice.

Even where choice is not a factor, people who divorced once may be more vulnerable to divorce than others. For example, Castro-Martin and Bumpass (1989) remark that some people who were vulnerable to a first divorce because of little formal education—the result of a premature first marriage—remain vulnerable to a second divorce for the same reason. The message of this finding for divorced people is clear enough: don't enter a second marriage under the same conditions (unintended pregnancy, economic dependency, or impulsive decision) that you entered your first (failed) marriage. If you do, the result is probably going to be the same: divorce.

Socio-economic Factors in Divorce

Studies from around the world show a surprisingly high degree of agreement on which socioeconomic factors are significant in predicting divorce. Beside age at marriage, the most important factors are a wife's level of education, her labor-force participation, and the presence of children.

The number of children present in a family is almost always negatively related to the likelihood of a couple divorcing (see, for example, Canabal, 1990). Women with children, particularly children under the age of six, are much less likely to get a divorce than are their childfree counterparts. (On the other hand, a couple that marries because of an unintended pregnancy is also *more* likely to get a divorce than other couples, other things being equal.)

There are a number of possible explanations for this relationship between divorce and an absence of children. Perhaps, couples who cannot have children get divorced because they cannot satisfy their marital desires for children in the current union. Or, happy marriages are more likely to produce children, and people who are unhappy in their marriage put off having children and end up getting a divorce.

The most likely reason for this relationship between an absence of children and divorce is that people are less willing to consider divorcing when young children are involved. Children are very likely to be hurt, emotionally and financially, by their parents' separation. A decision to divorce is easier to make when children are not in the picture, as fewer people will be affected. On the other side, it is often hard for fathers to give up frequent contact with their children, as often happens in the event of a separation.

Stated in our earlier terms of choices and contracts, divorce is harder when children are present because the psychological and economic costs of choosing divorce are higher; there are more "contracts" (parental, as well as spousal ones) in danger. It is hard to dissolve a marital contract without violating, or seeming to violate, the unspoken rules of the parent-child "contract."

Another practice that has significantly increased in recent years—cohabitation—also increases the risk of divorce. Studies (for example, Blanc, 1987) show that premarital cohabitation predicts a higher risk of divorce after marriage. Dissolution rates in the first two years of marriage for women who *had* cohabited are over three times those of women who had not. In sum, cohabitation, an increasingly common adult experience, is a less stable form of union than marriage. Whether a history of cohabitation de-stabilizes marriage, or simply selects in favor of more divorce-prone people is yet to be determined.

Another factor that predicts the likelihood of divorce is household income. The higher a husband's earnings (or potential earnings), the lower is the likelihood of divorce. When a family's income is high, the family suffers fewer of the financial difficulties that cause so much conflict and stress in poorer households. At the same time, economically well-off people stand to lose more by choosing divorce, since they have more to lose.

Generally, women with higher levels of education are slightly less likely to divorce than women with less education. In part, that is because women with a higher level of education are more likely to have married later and been able to choose their own mates (rather than acquiesce in marrying the man her parents had chosen). A woman who is well educated and chooses her own mate is also more likely to choose him in light of a good deal of experience in the "marriage market." She will be in a better position to make an informed choice, for she will know what she wants and what she can realistically expect to get (given what is "out there"); and she will make her decision accordingly.

Much less ambiguously, women who work for pay are much more likely to get a divorce than women who do not work for pay. Working for pay empowers women to choose divorce if they have to, for they are not dependent on their husband's income.

Or is it because women working outside the home de-stabilize their marriages? In Puerto Rico, for example, it is not only labor-force participation that raises the chance of divorce, as the economic theory would suggest (Canabal, 1990). It is also a *change* in employment status that signals, or causes, marriage dissolution. Women who have never worked before, and begin working when married, run a higher risk of divorce than women who continue working after marriage.

All of the above variables significantly influence the likelihood of divorce. However, at least in the United States, "socioeconomic variables such as education and income which have been regarded as discriminating predictor variables have become less discriminating" with the passage of time (Norton and Glick, 1976: 17). There is more "idiosyncrasy" in people's lives: people are living more differently from one another than ever in the past (Jones et al, 1990.) There is one important similarity, however: divorce is becoming a more common alternative to an un-happy marriage for people from a wide variety of socioeconomic backgrounds. The choice-and-contract culture has come to prevail in all parts of American society, and is sweeping through the developed world (see, for example, van de Kaa, 1987).

As nineteenth-century debaters expected, divorce rates have risen as divorce laws have liberalized, making divorce easier to attain. When divorce laws are re-strictive, divorce rates go down; and vice versa (Stetson and Wright, 1975). Changes in divorce laws since about 1970 (when no-fault divorce was instituted in California) have attempted to institutionalize fundamental social changes in family patterns (Weitzman and Dixon, 1986). Such new legislation often alters the definition of marriage, the relationship between husbands and wives, and the economic and social obligations of former spouses to each other and to their children after di-vorce.

In keeping with a choice-and-contract ethos, modern divorce laws eliminate the fault-based grounds for divorce and the adversary process. Financial aspects of divorce are now to be based on equity, equality and economic need, rather than sex roles or the identification of fault. Unfortunately, a key assumption of these new laws is, often, that a woman can become immediately self-supporting upon divorce.

Of course, this is no more true of many ex-wives than it was of many black ex-slaves a century ago. People who have lived in a state of dependency, without marketable job skills, cannot suddenly lead independent lives when they are given their freedom. In practice, ex-wives have a great deal of difficulty supporting them-selves and their children after a divorce.

Consequences of Divorce

As we have seen, a wife's labor-force participation predicts a higher probability of divorce. Women who have the financial means to free themselves from an un-happy marital situation usually choose to do so. However, the financial position of many divorced women declines, typically because they get custody of the children.

Women are economically disadvantaged by divorce in most cases. This disad-vantage is a result of many factors such as discrimination in the labor force, poor child-care availability, and little state support for women with dependent children. Even when women are employed outside the home, they work primarily in the low-paying service sector. Cumulatively, the disadvantage leads to what people have called the "feminization of poverty." An excerpt in this section by Arendell describes the process by which divorce impoverishes women and not men in mod-ern American society.

The numbers of children exposed to divorce is increasing. At the turn of the century, children were more likely to lose a parent to death than divorce. According to Uhlenberg (1983), about a quarter of all children lost one or both parents by age fifteen a century ago. With desertion and divorce added in, a third of all children would have spent some time in a single-parent home by their mid-teens. As the twentieth century progressed, loss of a parent due to death decreased, but loss through divorce increased.

Current estimates of children experiencing a single-parent family range widely. Hofferth (1985) estimates that three-quarters of all American children being born today will be born to single parents or lose a parent to divorce. Bumpass (1984) and Glick (1984) put the estimate at three out of five. According to Furstenburg (op. cit., 383), "44% of all children will live in a single-parent household by age 16." The estimates are highest for black children, with fewer than one in five "born in the 1980s spend[ing] their entire childhood with both of their parents."

Children living in one-parent families are disadvantaged in comparison to those living in two-parent families. For example, on average, Dutch children in single-parent families reach lower levels of educational attainment than those in two-parent families (Bosman and Louwes, 1988). It is not the absence of the father per se that hinders the educational success of children. In some cases, it is the way that absence is defined. Children of divorce still face a serious stigma in many societies. Such stigmatization may lead to less encouragement in school than other children receive.

As we have noted, divorce also means less available income and the consequences of living in poverty. Children who experience divorce or separation often experience a deterioration in their health. In the United Kingdom, reported illnesses are higher for children in families that have experienced separation than for those who have not (Blaxter, 1990). This is due either to a reduction in family income and parental attention, or to stress associated with the family breakup.

The divorced parents also experience negative consequences. Both men and women suffer significant increases in depression upon divorce. People who remain divorced for a long period of time are likely to experience more, not less, depression (Ahrons, 1980). This is largely due to people's decline in social integration upon divorce: a loss of social roles. This recalls Durkheim's (1951) finding a century ago that divorced and other unmarried men run the highest risks of suicide, because of their lack of social integration.

Of course, such a loss of social roles affects people differently, depending on their other social characteristics. But in general, unmarried (especially divorced) people suffer emotional and economic disadvantages. This continues to be true despite their increased numbers and the decreased stigma attached to their status. Such "costs of divorce" help explain why so many people rush to cohabit or remarry after a divorce.

References

AGAJANIAN, A. (1986) "Some notes on divorce in Iran," *Journal of Marriage and the Family*, 48(4), November, 749–755.

AHRONS, C. R. (1980) "Divorce: A crisis of family transition and change," *Family Relations*, 29, October, 533–540.

AMOATENG, A. Y. and T. B. HEATON (1989) "The sociodemographic correlates of timing of divorce in Ghana," *Journal of Comparative Family Studies*, XX(1), Spring, 79–96.

BLANC, A. K. (1987) "The formation and dissolution of second unions: Marriage and cohabitation in Sweden and Norway," *Journal of Marriage and Family*, 49(1), February, 391–400.

BLAXTER, M. (1990) *Health and Lifestyles*. London: Tavistock Publications.

BOHANNON, P. (1985) *All the Happy Families*. New York: McGraw-Hill.

BOSMAN, R. and W. LOUWES (1988) "School careers of children from one-parent and two-parent families," *Netherlands Journal of Sociology*, 24(2), 117–131.

BUMPASS, L. (1984) "Children and marital disruption: A replication and update," *Demography*, 21, 71–82.

BURGESS, E. W. (1948) "The family in a changing society," *American Journal of Sociology*, 53, 417–421.

CANABAL, M. E. (1990) "An economic approach to marital dissolution in Puerto Rico," *Journal of Marriage and the Family*, 52(2), May, 515–530.

CASTRO-MARTIN, T. and L. BUMPASS (1989) "Recent trends and differentials in marital disruption," *Demography*, 26, 37–51.

CHERLIN, A. J. (1978) "Remarriage as an incomplete institution," *American Journal of Sociology*, 84, 634–650.

DURKHEIM, E. (1951) *Suicide: A Study in Sociology*. Translated by J. A. Spaulding and G. Simpson. New York: Free Press.

FURSTENBERG, F. F. (1990) "Divorce in America." In W. Richard Scott and Judith Blake (eds.), *Annual Review of Sociology*, 16, 379–403.

GLICK, P. (1984), "Marriage, divorce and living arrangements: prospective changes," *Journal of Family Issues*, 5(1), March, 7–26.

HALLIDAY, T. C. (1980) "Remarriage: the more complete institution," *American Journal of Sociology*, 86, 630–635.

HOFFERTH, S. L. (1985) "Updating children's life course," *Journal of Marriage and the Family*, 47(1), 93–115.

JONES, C., L. MARSDEN and L. TEPPERMAN (1990) *Lives of their Own: The Individualization of Women's Lives*. Toronto: Oxford University Press.

MOORE, M. (1989) "Female lone parenting over the life course," *Canadian Journal of Sociology*, 14(3), 335–352.

NORTON, A. J. and J. E. MOORMAN (1986) "Marriage and divorce patterns of U.S. women in the 1980s." Presented at the Annual Meeting of the Population Association of America, 4 April.

—— and P. C. GLICK (1986) "One parent families: a social and economic profile," *Family Relations*, 35, January, 16.

STETSON, D. M. and G. C. WRIGHT (1975) "The effects of laws on divorce in American states," *Journal of Marriage and the Family*, August, 537–547.

UHLENBERG, P. (1983) "Death and the family." In M. Gordon (ed.), *The American Family in Social-Historical Perspective*, New York: St. Martins, pp. 169–178.

VAN DE KAA, D. J. (1987) "Europe's Second Demographic Transition," *Population Bulletin*, 42(1), March. Washington, DC: The Population Reference Bureau.

WEITZMAN, L. J. and R. B. DIXON (1986) "The transformation of legal marriage through no-fault divorce." In A. S. Skolnick and J. H. Skolnick, eds. *Family in Transition*, 5th ed. Boston: Little Brown, pp. 338–351.

WHITE, L. and A. BOOTH (1985) "The quality and stability of remarriages: the role of stepchildren," *American Sociological Review*, 50, 689–698.

Introduction

"'Til death do us part"—the recipe for wedded bliss or a lifetime sentence to slavery?

Feminists wrestled with this question in mid-nineteenth-century America as they debated the liberalization of divorce laws. Opinions varied widely. Many men, and some women opposed the feminist cause altogether. Some women supported the feminists' goals but found their rhetoric and methods unacceptable. And some women supported the theory and method of feminism but feared that more liberal divorce laws would have unexpected and undesired effects on the family, and on women.

The struggle to abolish black slavery, going on at about the same time, gave both supporters and opponents something to think about. On the one hand, the anti-slavery struggle provided a powerful metaphor that could be used in the fight for easier and fairer divorce rules: the metaphor of marriage as slavery and liberalized divorce as abolition. "How could anyone support the abolition of black slavery, yet stand in the way of women's rights (including the right to easier and fairer divorces)?" supporters asked.

On the other hand, the metaphor of marriage as slavery also fuelled fears that family life, and women's lives, were in for hard times if divorce laws were changed too much and too quickly. That spouses were locked in a mortal struggle for power was hard enough to bear, given nineteenth-century sentiments about the home and family. What if families were to break up more easily? What would happen to women and children, suddenly released from the bondage of traditional marriage by easier divorce. How would they support themselves? How would they fit into a society founded on male power and male-dominated families?

Answers to these questions were as slow in coming as those about the place of freed black slaves in a post-Civil War America. In both cases, Americans found that, for vulnerable people, freedom has to be more than a mere absence of chains.

37

Slavery and Divorce in Nineteenth-Century America

Elizabeth B. Clark

MARRIAGE AND SLAVERY IN THE POST-WAR PERIOD

In the post-Civil War period, the rhetoric of divorce changed dramatically as the language of rights replaced that of duty to God or children.

Source: Clark, Elizabeth "Matrimonial bonds: Slavery and divorce in nineteenth century America," *Law and History Review*, Vol. 8, No. 1, 25–54

For feminists, . . . the wrongs of brutalized wives served as a catalyst for early consciousness of individual rights . . . Earlier, divorce had been understood as an act of self-defense; now it became an issue of personal liberty. The idea of the right to one's body and to one's labor was a critical tenet of post-war political theory; liberal feminists adapted this "rights" definition to their own ends.

Slavery had ended, but slavery/freedom became the ruling paradigm through which liberal feminists conceived and developed their vision of rights within marriage. The analogy between marriage and slavery was natural and powerful. . . .

After the war, liberal feminists' use of slavery imagery took on a new directness, serving to describe the actual physical and emotional relations between husband and wife. Slavery imagery gained dominance and new meaning, and bondage became the metaphor of choice for pro-divorce feminists. . . .

In gross terms, middle-class women who compared themselves to bondswomen may seem melodramatic and self-aggrandizing. But feminists felt themselves in both acute physical and spiritual bondage. The slavery/freedom dichotomy helped articulate common apprehensions of the illegitimacy of male and masterly authority, as well as women's genuine outrage at a marital servitude that many felt keenly was as degrading as actual bondage. In describing bad marriages, women spoke of being crushed, dwarfed, broken, crippled—a language of assaults on the body that resonated wildly in the immediate aftermath of the slavery contest. Stories abounded of wives who pictured themselves as "legalized slaves" to "masters" who meted out brutal treatment unchecked and unprovoked. . . .

Women's writing made frequent literary use of the escape scene inspired by fugitives from the South. Diatribes against the laws of parental custody were laden with descriptions that drew on the Eliza story from *Uncle Tom's Cabin*, the slave mother escaping with her child, hounds baying at her heels. Such mothers, escaping their oppressive husbands, asked, "but he will follow me, will traduce me, and take my baby away from me, and the law won't give me my freedom, will it?"[1]

This sentimentalized presentation of marital enslavement and its consequences among all classes of society is portrayed vividly in *Fettered for Life, or, Lord and Master*, written in 1874 by the prominent suffragist Lillie Devereaux Blake. . . . Antebellum divorce and anti-marriage rhet-

oric had pictured all women as potential victims of a husband's drunken violence without acknowledging hurts or rights special to any group. But in *Fettered for Life*, women of different classes are at risk in different ways, and follow out particular patterns in their marriages. . . .

MARRIAGE AND FREEDOM OF CONTRACT

Slavery's antithesis in nineteenth-century political discourse was freedom, and feminists' equation of marriage and slavery compelled their audiences to contemplate divorce through its obvious analogy, emancipation. The traditional marriage was undergoing its own Reconstruction. . . . In the view of a growing number of liberal feminists led by Elizabeth Cady Stanton, its most important tenets were self-ownership within marriage and a right to divorce if the marriage became degrading. . . .

In this attempt to reconstruct the nature of obligation, liberal feminists moved naturally toward legal concepts. Seeking to recast the marriage relationship on more nearly equal terms, they groped for language that could express their vision in ways harmonious with mainstream thought. Contract was an obvious choice. The contractual ideal was pervasive in nineteenth-century society, so much so that to speak of feminists invoking contract as a "strategy" is misleading; it was the common coin of intellectual life, spreading far beyond its legal bounds to influence notions of reciprocity, obligation, and personal and business relations. Use of the slavery paradigm brought the issue of freedom of contract into play: In effect, the condition of slavery had less to do with disfranchisement than with a slave's more immediate inability to sever old work ties and form new ones and to bargain for a fair wage—powers that acquired almost mystical importance in the years around the Civil War. In addition to its more general civil status, then, "freedom" took on a narrower definition in the ability to make and break agreements at will.[2] Contract provided women both with a theory of equal and reciprocal duties within an ongoing relation and also with a model for breaking that relation when the bargain went sour. . . .

For Stanton, the concept of contract represented largely the *deregulation* of marriage, the noninterference of church and state in the private realm.

Stanton did give some credence to the power of government to regulate the initial formation of contracts, including marriage. Citing the need for safeguards like minimum age, competence, and full disclosure, she encouraged legislators to remedy "the absence of form and dignity in the marriage contract which is unknown in any other civilized nation" with a strict set of prior conditions.[3] But this list also reads as a set of contractual defenses, setting out grounds on which she thought divorce should be more easily granted or marriages annulled. Stanton pointed out that in other civil contracts, failure to comply with the conditions of entrance "vitiates the contract, and it is annulled by the mutual agreement of both parties. But in the marriage contract, which the state allows to be formed so thoughtlessly, ignorantly, irreverently, the parties have no control whatever, though ofttimes in its formation and continuance all laws of decency and common sense are at defiance. . . .[4] Stanton sought tough entry and easy exit, but felt that stricter regulation of the creation of a marriage contract would cut down on failed marriages.

The notion of free contract served as a blueprint for remodeling the marriage relationship as well as for ending it. A part of the liberal project on marriage entailed demystifying it by applying to it the everyday terms of bargain and exchange, which governed arms-length agreements for services. Feminists used contractual analogies to describe faithful adherence to their marital terms, despite men's repeated violations of their own. Many men refused to perform their own obligations while insisting that women meet theirs, thus moving the agreement from the realm of contract into slavery.[5] . . .

Stanton . . . sought to establish marriage as an affective relationship based on a romantic love that was voluntary, ephemeral, spontaneous, and unresponsive to legal coercion. She looked to the "highest good of the individual. It is the inalienable right of all to be happy. It is the highest duty to seek those conditions in life, those surroundings, which may develop what is noblest and best.[6] . . .

Clearly, a marital relation that existed only through the rigor of the law and not the mutual love and ongoing consent of the parties was not conducive to the highest human development, and the furthering of happiness and human growth became the new standard by which social and political functions were judged. Utilitarianism combined with the developing creed of liberal Protestantism to produce a new rationale for institutions from the state down to the family. It was to accommodate this new vision of the family as constituted by the ongoing consent of the parties rather than by legal forms that Stanton sought to recast the marriage bond to eliminate any element of irrevocability or coercion from outside. She denied that marriage vows were anything but a voluntary, temporary mutual agreement for the benefit of both. . . . By 1870, Stanton declared that in the Protestant world the question was no longer whether marriage was a sacrament or a contract, but, as a contract, for what reasons it might be dissolved.[7]

Stanton envisioned the family as reforming along the lines of the republican state: it would consist of free and independent individuals, voluntarily contracting for a corporate existence during the pleasure of the parties, each protected in its own autonomy by inalienable individual rights.[8] . . .

PROTECTIONISM AND LIBERALISM

. . . In addition to applying the forms of contract to marriage, divorce reformers sought to tighten the correspondence between rights in the family and the civil realm by using constant analogies from other areas of law and public policy, which they brought to bear on the law of the family as well. To this end, Stanton . . . drew on analogies from liberal economic theory, free labor and free trade ideology, and the constitutional guarantees of freedom of conscience and separation of church and state to sketch in a new model of family law. . . . Reformers were working to make the regulation of families of a piece with broader principles at work in areas of public and private commercial law. At heart, the problem in all areas was the same: to secure the removal of an external structure of laws to allow natural governing forces to assert themselves. . . .

Stanton also analogized religious tolerance to liberal (non-regulatory) family laws, seeking to extend the established principles of freedom of conscience and of theological persuasion to cover unorthodox sexual relations as well. . . . Stanton heartily concurred that the rigid enforcement of the Christian ideal of lifelong monogamous marriage represented undue influence by church and state in the private lives of individuals.

Stanton's own repeated advocacy of free labor, free trade, and free currency shows that she extended her belief in deregulation to the economy; and that there was more than a superficial affinity between her views on marriage, her philosophy of government, and classic liberal notions of laissez-faire.[9] . . . Stanton's liberalism was based firmly in a liberal Protestant creed that celebrated the innate goodness of human nature and its ability to find its own right course once external regulation was lifted. . . .

Stanton's composite writings and pronouncements tended toward the disaggregation of the family as well, an outcome she found personally, socially, and politically desirable. . . . Politically, she classed the patriarchal family with "despotic governments (and) infallible churches. . . . Every new step in civilization tends to individual awareness, dignity, responsibility, alike in the church, the state, and the home."[10] Clearly, the democratic reorganization of the family required that each individual be accorded full status and

rights: Stanton denied that the "representative" theory of the family as a "unit" was acceptable. Government should deal with individuals, not with families, or with certain of its members as representatives of others.[11]

Inherent in the push for the disaggregation of the family was the recognition that, like slavery or the harem, the protection offered by family membership was often at the price of liberty. For slaves, being "'a part of the family'" had "protected" them from the onus of taxation, as well as denying them a civil voice: leaving the "family" changed both.[12] Any physical obligation that owed its existence to a code or rule was similarly discredited: . . . the liberal feminists equated the safety of marriage with the harem, paternalism, and slavery, claiming "protection is the leech that preys upon the heart of liberty." "Protectors" take on a sarcastic significance in Stanton's work as those who rape and seduce women.[13]

In fact, discussions of the marriage question both within and without organized feminism also centered on another set of issues—economic protection and the consequences of easy divorce for wives and mothers. In 1860, Stanton's . . . optimistic beliefs in the potential for the liberated and energetic woman to achieve economic parity allowed her to ignore the problem of dependence.[14] A decade later, some feminists were more skeptical. . . .

Writers for the *Woman's Journal*, the paper of the American Woman Suffrage Association (AWSA), found Stanton's rhetoric naive and disingenuous in its assumption that free divorce would primarily benefit women. How many mothers, under the circumstances, could afford to sweep grandly out and set up housekeeping on their own? They intimated that "freedom" for a divorced mother of six should be known as its other names, immiseration and abandonment. For the suffragists of the AWSA, divorce was at best an unfortunate necessity in cases of chronic spousal abuse, but free divorce in Stanton's terms represented "practically, freedom of unworthy men to leave their wives and children

38
Divorce in Hindu Society

S. Pothen

... The Hindu Marriage and Divorce Act of 1955 ... for the first time, offered equal opportunity to the wife and husband to separate from each other or to terminate their marriage legally. The present researcher has analysed 200 cases where either an actual decree of divorce was granted or a decree of judicial separation was obtained, and the parties have lived separately for more than five years, so that the marital bond can be considered as irretrievably broken. A Hindu is governed by the Hindu Marriage and Divorce Act of 1955, with subsequent Amendment in 1976. Relief is granted to the parties according to the provisions of this law. The area of study was mainly Indore city, a major urban centre of Central India. ...

In every country, there are laws governing marriage and divorce. According to the Hindu Marriage Act of 1955, the grounds for divorce are, (i) adultery (ii) cruelty (iii) desertion for two years, (iv) conversion to another religion, (v) incurable lunacy or leprosy, (vi) venereal disease in communicable form, (vii) renunciation, (viii) missing for seven years, (ix) no resumption of cohabitation even after one year of passing of a decree of restitution of conjugal rights, or judicial separation, and finally (x) mutual consent (new provision according to the Marriage Law Amendment Act of 1976).

... In practice, the actual complaints of husbands and wives against each other are very different from the legal grounds on which the divorce was granted. ... Except in cases of impotency or unsound mind, ... no ... single factor has led to marital crisis. A combination of factors worked together to build up tensions and conflicts which culminated in divorce. ...

A detailed analysis of some of the important complaints revealed valuable ... information regarding factors instrumental in disorganizing families (see Table 1).

Cruelty was the complaint of highest frequency of females. Physical cruelty was common in the lower class followed by the middle class. Though cruelty was not directly alleged by husbands, many complaints put forward by them amount to ... cruelty. Interference by in-laws is another serious complaint by both the partners. In the traditional joint family situation, a bride has to get along with a number of relatives of the husband. The tolerance and forebearance of young Indian women for which they were lauded in the past is definitely vanishing due to ... factors like modern education, employment and ideas of equality and freedom. Extramarital relations definitely undermine ... marriage. In the present study, there are many allegations of extramarital relations both by husbands and wives. But, ... in many cases, they were ... allegations to degrade the other party and to justify one's own actions. However, there were several cases in which the husband or wife actually indulged in illicit sex. Mental disorder is a legal ground for divorce, and 3% of the respondents secured divorce on this ground. In most cases, mental disorders existed prior to the marriage, and the fact was concealed. Hasty and unplanned marriage also has brought about catastrophe. ... They were usually arranged by elders. Sociologists all over the world agree that economic hardships tend to create and aggravate family problems. In the present study this was true. Authors like Rama Mehta (1975) and Fonseca (1966) have observed that women of India no longer like to occupy a subordinate posi-

Source: Pothen, S. (1989) "Divorce in Hindu Society," *Journal of Comparative Family Studies*, 20, 3, Autumn, 377–392.

TABLE 1. Showing the Complaints of Husbands and Wives against Each Other

Complaint of Husband	Frequency	Complaint of Wife	Frequency
Poor management of income	90	Cruelty	99
Insufficient income	68	Insufficient income	99
Wife Nonadjusting	52	Interference of inlaws	83
Interference of in-laws	50	Husband quarrelsome	81
Wife quarrelsome	50	Squanders money	67
Interested in other men	45	Husband not affectionate	54
Incompatible nature	39	Husband's vices	45
Wife not affectionate	39	Husb. interested in others	43
Wife goes off to parents	34	Husb. demands dowry	36
Wife extravagant	33	Desertion	35
Wife Nagging	30	Incompatible husband	32
Desertion	29	Suspicious	30
Wife wants to break away from joint family	27	Husband unemployed/lazy	28
Poor education/intelligence/manners	21	Husb. not interested in home	27
Wife misbehaves with parents/relatives	21	Husband stingy	26
Wife too much interested in her own work	18	Husb. misbehaves/insults	25
Sexual maladjustment	17	Lack of freedom	25
Wife unsubmissive	16	Objectionable friendship	22
Objectionable friendship	15	Selfish & inconsiderate	21
		Inferior intelligence, status & education of husband	20
Poor looks	11	Sexual maladjustment	20
Immorality	10	Fraud	16
Mentally unfit	7	Husband unsocial/illmannered	15
Poor health of wife	6	Husb. comes home late	14
Wife barren	6	Interference in hobbies	11
Illegitimate pregnancy of wife	5	Poor looks	9
Undisclosed physical defects	3	Forced to lead immoral life	7
Fraud	3	Polygynous	4
Wife suspicious	3	Mentally unfit	4
Tried to murder	2	Much older	4
Alcoholic	1	Tried to murder	4
Forced marriage	1	Threatens suicide	2

tion in the family. At the same time, the males in India are more or less traditional . . . and try to treat their womanfolk as inferior. . . . This is becoming a point of conflict in many Indian homes. . . . Sexual dissatisfaction is fatal to any marriage. In the present study, . . . several spouses complained of sexual dissatisfaction. There were several cases of impotency in males and structural malformation of the female genitalia, which made consummation of the marriage impossible. . . . Child marriage is still widely practiced in India, especially in rural areas. Though the study was in the urban area, . . . 60% of the females and 12.5% of the males had their marriage before the age of 21. In sev-

eral cases, it was explained that as the couples grew up, differences between them became too obvious and they could not get along. Incompatibility is not accepted as a ground for divorce in . . . India. . . .

Unhealthy habits like squandering money, smoking, drinking, and gambling were observed mainly in men. When such traits become chronic, they pose serious adjustment problems. Desertion was a frequent problem, mainly in the lower classes. Men deserted their families more often than women did. Wide disparity in academic achievement or intellectual capacity can lead to incompatibility. In India, this . . . might occur frequently because as a whole . . . Indian parents do not provide equal opportunity to female children in education. In cases of child marriages especially the girls are not educated after their marriage, whereas boys continue their academic pursuits. . . . Dowry is a serious problem in business communities like Banias and Jain, as well as in some Brahmin sub-castes. Lack of affection . . . was also a major complaint. . . . A good number of wives complained of an associated problem, that is, lack of consideration, and understanding from their male partners. Several husbands, especially those of the lower strata of society, spend the money on their own comforts and luxuries, and virtually leave the families to starve. Similarly several wives felt that the husbands do not take interest in the home. . . .

. . . Many people waited . . . years to approach the court even after the marriage had broken down. Fear of social stigma, uncertainty about future, lack of legal knowledge, emotional upheavals, etc. were the main reasons for this delay. Men and women approached the court to file the petition for divorce almost in equal number. Before the passing of the Marriage Amendment Act, 1976, divorce suits took . . . 5–8 years. But, after the Amendment of the marriage laws in 1976, provision for divorce by mutual consent is added and most couples use this provision and get the . . . divorce within a year. In the present study, 45.5% of wives received alimony during the period of trial and 12.5% were granted Department alimony. An analysis of the court files showed . . . few petitions for divorce up to 1970. The period between 1970 and 1976 showed a gradual rise in the number of divorce applications. The number suddenly shot up in 1976, and continues to rise every . . . year.

[Fortunately] 65% of the men were in the age-group of 26–35, and 67.5% of women belonged to the age group of 21–30, at the time of divorce. This is positive . . . because the divorcés were still young at the time of divorce, and hence, have better chances of remarriage and readjustment. Women were subjected to more severe economic and emotional problems. Most of the women were economically dependent, and, this added . . . to their sense of personal failure. Frustration, shyness, feelings of inferiority, loneliness, insecurity and uncertainty about the future are some of the problems enumerated by the divorcées. . . .

. . . Divorce did not influence the male partners' level of education. Among the females also, the uneducated females' level remained status quo whereas the less educated groups have completed their education and many became graduates or postgraduates. Similarly, there was no substantial change in the occupation of the male partners after . . . divorce. At the time of marriage, only 16.5% of women engaged in gainful employment, whereas at the time of interview, 58% of the women were working outside the home. . . . Divorce created an economic crisis and most of these women had to fend for themselves and . . . were compelled to seek employment. 35% of the male divorcés and 21.5% of female divorcées expressed tender or at least cordial feelings for their ex-partners whereas the remaining expressed bitter and antagonistic views. . . .

58% of the couples of the present study had no children . . . mainly due to the short span of congenial relations of cohabitation between the spouses. 18.5% of the couples had one child each. . . . The researcher also felt that . . . childlessness also was a . . . factor which enabled the couples to seek divorce without much hesitation. . . . Children usually remained with the mother.

In two-third of the cases, the mother and her people supported the children. . . . At least 50% of the fathers did not try to . . . contact their children. Several fathers wished to be in touch with their children, but could not do so, because they could not face their ex-wives, or, they had deep-rooted guilt-feelings. In 64% of the cases, children are aware of the divorce . . . and . . . 55% of the children are upset about their disorganized home. 21% seem reconciled to the situation and are happy and well adjusted. . . . Although the picture of the children seemed bleak, . . . several children are extraordinarily successful young people, more mature and responsible as compared to children of normal homes. . . .

One . . . solution to . . . divorce is remarriage. In India, remarriage of a woman was . . . until recently, . . . not sanctioned. The impact of these traditional beliefs can be noticed in the Hindu society even now. At the time of the study . . . 75.5% of the divorced husbands had already remarried whereas the percentage of remarried female divorcees was only 35. Divorced men could get single girls of their choice, whereas, divorced females . . . married widowers. . . .

For female divorcées, the presence of children was an important hindrance for remarriage whereas for male divorcés, it was not so. Similarly, female divorcees who had children through the first marriage had fewer children, or no children through the second marriage, whereas male divorcés had children in the second marriage irrespective of the number of children born earlier. . . .

The . . . majority of the remarried males and females are happy or at least somewhat happy. Only a minority said that they were again unhappy or separated. Western sociologists like Goode (1965), O'Mohony (1959), Burgess & Locke (1950) have also concluded that remarriages are more successful as compared to the first marriage. The . . . majority of the male single divorcés were contemplating remarriage, whereas, the majority of the single female divorcées said they had no interest in remarriage. Improbability of getting a suitable partner, shock and bitterness due to the first marital failure, etc. are some of the main reasons for the disinterest of female divorcees to get remarried. . . .

. . . The rate of divorce is increasing. . . . A close relationship exists between the type of legal provisions for divorce and the number of divorces taking place . . . in India. . . . Under . . . the Hindu Marriage and Divorce Act, 1955, it was very difficult to obtain a divorce and it took several years of court proceedings. As a result, the number of divorce decrees was very small. With the Amendment of Marriage Laws in 1976, the procedure . . . has become simple . . . and quick resulting in a sudden rise in the divorce rate. . . .

Divorce usually results from the cumulative effect of a number of pressures working together. Though divorce is a personal tragedy for both males and females, it poses greater problems and difficulties for the Indian females. Remarriage of divorcé males is relatively easy while it is not so for divorcée females. In India, the mother-child relationship seems to be extremely strong even today. In a vast majority of the cases, the children remained with their mothers after divorce. Though divorce can precipitate many crisis situations for children, it need not disorganize them. Children can . . . adjust and adapt better than adults can.

A few . . . theoretical conclusions may be arrived at, which may be relevant in the Sociology of the Family:

1. Even traditional societies are touched by . . . social change and modernization.

2. In traditional societies, changes are met with greater social resistance.

3. In patriarchal societies, changes in the status and role of women are met with extreme resistance.

4. Modern education has brought about different changes in males and females. Males, though modernized in many respects, want to perpetuate the traditional roles and value systems regarding females, whereas women awakened by the wave of modernity and education are . . . eager to . . . discard completely the relics of the past. This gap in view points is a major point of friction. . . .

5. . . . Tradition is so deep-rooted that even after going through . . . social change . . . a society is not able to discard several age-old

patterns. Some of these old customs are enforced with a greater zest. . . .

6. Increased awareness gives birth to greater expectations and consequently greater frustrations. . . . With increased knowledge, ego is inflated and tolerance decreases. When this happens in marital partners, it can become a threat to marriage.

7. . . . Divorce is the product of a number of factors working together for a period of time. Wide variations are possible in social situations and the effects each situation produces on each individual is extremely variable. Hence, . . . each divorce is a unique . . . response to a social situation.

8. Marital disruptions, though . . . distressing to a child, need not disorganize him. Traditional societies offer children the advantage of the support of the kinship group of at least one parent.

9. Remarriage seems to be the best solution for . . . divorce.

10. Divorce is a deep human problem. . . . Everyone involved in the trauma should receive equal consideration, sympathy and assistance. This should come from the family, community and society in general.

REFERENCES

BURGESS, E. W. and H. J. LOCKE. 1950. The Family, From *Institution to Companionship*. New York, American Book Co.

FONSECA, M. 1966. Counselling for Marital Happiness. Bombay, Mankatala & Sons.

GOODE, W. J. 1965. Women in Divorce. New York, Free Press.

MEHTA, R. 1975. Divorced Hindu Woman. New Delhi, Vikas.

O'MOHONY, J. (Ed.). 1959. Catholics & Divorce. London, Thomas Nelson.

Introduction

A previous excerpt from India has shown the typical pattern: an increase in divorces with modernization. The next excerpt, from Japan, shows a similar pattern too. As before, rising divorce rates are attributed to "industrialization and urbanization, the Westernization of lifestyles, and the growing autonomy of women in society."

But this is not the whole story. The excerpt also shows that divorce rates in Japan were higher in 1880 than they were in 1980. Since Japan was certainly not as industrialized, urbanized, or Westernized a century ago as it is today, we must search elsewhere for an explanation of high divorce rates.

The author puts forward a variety of explanations which are more or less compatible with one another. Chiefly, Kumagai suggests that divorce rates were high in 1880 because a great many people were poor and lived in rural areas. They stood to lose little through divorce, attached no moral meaning to it, had little opportunity for concubinage, and saw divorce and remarriage as ways of remedying a bad parental choice of mates. If this explanation is correct, the divorce rate should start to rise as people become less poor and stand to lose more through divorce (property splits); attach new meanings to divorce (perhaps through Westernization); have more chance for extra-marital sex; and marry for reasons of love, not parental pressure.

All of these things happened, with the result that the divorce rate declined steadily between 1880 and 1940 (or so). Then it began to rise again. This time, we suppose, it was modernization to blame.

39
Changing Patterns of Divorce in Japan

Fumie Kumagai

THE HISTORY OF DIVORCE IN JAPAN

... The changing trends in marriage and divorce rates from 1882 to 1979 are shown in Figure 1. ... It may be appropriate to present an overview of the six periods into which the past one hundred years can be divided: 1882–1897, 1898–1899, 1900–1943, 1947–1950, 1951–1964, and from 1965 to the present.

The First Period: 1882–1897.

Japanese society was transformed by the Meiji Restoration beginning in 1868 (Meiji Era: 1868–1912), and the people enthusiastically took part in laying the foundations of modernization. Official statistics on divorce became available in 1882. During the early part of the Meiji era, the divorce rate was extremely high, from a peak of 3.39 in 1883 to a low of 2.62 in 1892, the average being 2.82 for the fifteen years from 1882 to 1897. A divorce rate of 3.34 is equivalent to that in the USSR today, and it is only since the 1970s that such a high divorce rate has been attained in the United States (United Nations Demographic Yearbook, 1978). The divorce rate in the United States between the years 1882 and 1892 was somewhere around 0.6; only after 1915 did it exceed 1.0 (U.S. Bureau of the Census, *Vital Statistics of the United States*, 1980). In fact, the

high divorce rate in Japan surpassed that of any other nation at the time. ...

There are various explanations for this. Goode argued that in Japan, the traditional family system was originally a "high divorce" system, and that once the traditional family system began to be undermined, the divorce rate would fall (Goode, 1963). Others such as Kuwahata (1956:26) and Ohshio (1956:61–69) attributed these high rates mainly to the then existing custom of expelling a wife from the traditional Japanese family, the so-called *ie* system.[1] The majority of divorces during this period, however, occurred among the common people—farmers, fishermen, and merchants—who made up approximately 80 percent of the total population. The members of the upper strata consisted of the samurai warriors, landowners, and noblemen. Goode contended that in a system which permits rather free divorce, the lower strata will have a higher divorce rate than the upper strata (Goode, 1963).

There are three major reasons for a low divorce rate among the people of the upper strata. First, the husband who married a woman from such a family background was reluctant to divorce her, being constrained by her family and his in-laws. Second, concubinage was practiced among people of the upper strata at this time;

---

[1]The phenomenon of expelling the wife is called *yome oidashi*, in which the wife was driven out of the household mainly by the in-laws. When the in-laws disliked the son's wife they could expel her, and she was not allowed to resist. Confucian filial piety was the basic moral code of the traditional Japanese family.

Source: Kumagai, F. (1983) "Changing divorce in Japan," *Journal of Family History*, 8, 1, spring, 85–108.

FIGURE 1. Marriage and divorce rates in Japan; 1882–1979.

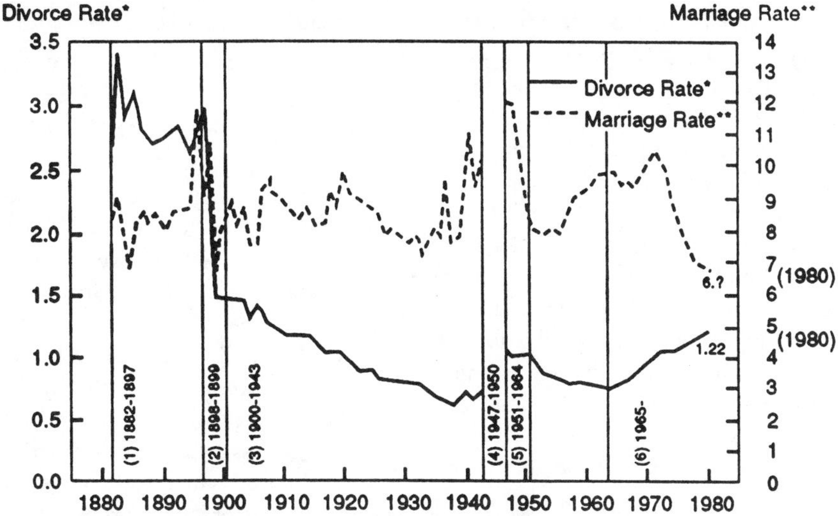

Sources: 1882–1899 Prime Minister's Office, Bureau of the Census, *Nihon Teikoku Tokei Nenkan* (Tokyo, 1915).

1990–1979 Ministry of Health and Welfare, *Vital Statistics: 1979, vol. 1* (Tokyo: Health and Welfare Statistics Department, 1980).

1980 Estimations of the Health and Statistics Association (Tokyo, 1981).

*Rate per 1,000 population.

**Rate per 1,000 population.

that is, a husband who did not feel affection for his legal wife had tacit public permission to possess a concubine. Therefore, it was not considered adultery if the husband had sexual relations out of wedlock. Third, a woman in an upper strata family was strictly socialized to prepare herself to become a good housewife; complete submission of the wife to the husband was the ideal. For these reasons, divorces among families of the upper strata were quite rare.

On the other hand, divorce among the lower classes and in rural areas occurred frequently, and it is these which contributed to the high overall rate. In addition to those reasons discussed by Goode, Kuwahata and Ohshio, three other explanations for this phenomenon are possible. . . . First, all five prefectures in the Tohoku region . . . , the northern part of the main island Honshu, primarily the farming areas, exhibited high divorce rates. Marrying young was common in the Tohoku region. The average age

at first marriage in these five prefectures in 1882 was below 21 for males and 18 for females, and in the case of Iwate prefecture, 17.07 for males and 14.09 for females—about five years younger than the national average (Prime Minister's Office, 1886). The aim of early marriage was to force the young bride to surrender to the groom's family by taking advantage of her immaturity. The farming households in northern Japan possessed larger farms than those in western Japan and regarded the bride as valuable labor. However, when the young bride did not meet the expectations set forth by her husband's family, she was simply expelled. Lacking any influence in the situation, she had no other course than divorce.

Second, there were three times as many matrilineal marriages in the Tohoku farming region and the fishing villages in Hokkaido, the northernmost island as in Kyushu, the southernmost island. In the matrilineal system, the relation-

ship between husband and wife was considered to be an employment contract in which the groom agreed to supply his labor to the bride's family in exchange for a guaranteed livelihood. If the work of the groom turned out to be unsatisfactory to the bride's family, he was . . . divorced. It is likely that matrilineal marriage itself could create a high divorce rate. In a traditional male-oriented society, . . . such nontraditional marriage tends to be regarded as a deviant family system and would most likely create frustration in the male partner in the marriage, and conflict within the family. It was possible for the dissatisfied bride's family to use divorce as an effective means to resolve conflicts in marriage.
. . .

Third, there was a casual attitude among the common people toward marriage and divorce; both the divorce rate and the remarriage rate were high. Arichi pointed out the four most frequently cited reasons for divorce at the time (Arichi, 1977:32–38): the lack of deliberation at the time of marriage, financial problems, the persisting authority of the in-laws and the husband, and the simplicity of attaining divorce and remarriage. Marriages were frequently based on a forced arrangement by parents or relatives, or else by the temporary emotion of the partners. As a consequence, the break-up of the marriage occurred early in . . . marital life. The dominant attitude toward marriage, that is, the lack of a strong commitment, might be influenced by the absence of the concept of the companionship marriage in the traditional ie system. On the other hand, the persisting authority of the in-laws and the husband in marriage reflected the institutionalized marriage of the traditional family system in Japan. These contrasting aspects of the traditional ie system, that is, the stringent impact of the family on the institution of marriage and the lack of an interpersonal relationship, affected each other, and perhaps resulted in the high divorce rate. Aside from the traditional institutional aspect of the ie system, somewhat loose social, as well as moral controls of the institutions of marriage and divorce during

the early years in Meiji era also existed. These were mainly due to the abolishment of the feudal system, i.e., the Meiji Restoration, as well as to the introduction of Western ideas.

The Second Period: 1898–1899

There was an abrupt drop in the divorce rate in 1899, one year after the Meiji Civil Code was put into effect.[2] Within two years the divorce rate decreased by half, i.e., from 2.87 in 1897, and 2.27 in 1898 to 1.50 in 1899. The enforcement of the Civil Code required that marriages as well as divorces be reported to the kocho, or headman, if they were to be valid. In addition, it became necessary to submit in writing the reasons for divorce, which was contrary to the "no-reason" divorce practiced previously. As a result, people's attitude toward divorce changed; that is, there was more deliberation before marriage and divorce. . . .

The Third Period: 1900–1943

The rate of divorce during the third period shows a gradual decline. Occasional upward fluctuations in the rate are all attributable to the impact of specific events: Japan was involved in three wars, namely, the Russo-Japanese War (1904–5), World War I (1914–18), and World War II, which shaped the years from 1931 to 1945. This period is also remembered in connection with such grave events as the Great Kanto Earthquake of 1923 and the economic crisis of 1929 and 1930.

Divorce rates in the years immediately after the above-mentioned events usually increased over those of the immediately preceding years. The general trend, however, was a decline, i.e.,

---

[2]Although both husband and wife were granted the right to divorce under the Meiji Civil Code, the reality was far different. The wife's right to divorce was considerably restricted. It was only after the enactment of a new Japanese Civil Code in 1947 that the wife was accorded an actual right to divorce.

the rates decreased from 1.46 to 0.68 per thousand population from 1900 to 1943. During these years there was remarkable progress in education while the initial stages of industrialization and urbanization were achieved. These factors contributed to the increase in divorce rates in Western societies, whereas in Japan they lowered the rates.

Yuzawa discusses possible reasons for this decrease (Yuzawa, 1974:345). On the one hand, the forced divorce in the institutional ie system gradually lost its dominant power due to the influence of modernization and the individualistic orientation of the West. On the other hand, a newly emerging type of family in Japan, the conjugal family, in which the wife was expected to be submissive to the authority of the husband, contributed to the enhancement of the traditional sex role of women—that is, to be considered a good wife and mother, a woman had to stay in the home. . . .

The Fourth Period: 1947–1950

Statistics for the divorce rate during the years between 1944 and 1946 were unavailable due to the turbulence of World War II. . . . The new Japanese Civil Code of 1947 made various changes in the family and household, such as the abolition of the ie (house) system, the redefinition of marriage as based on individual choice instead of parental permission, and the equal distribution of inherited property among spouse and children.

In the Civil Code of 1947, modifications were also made in the reasons for judicial divorce, which were reduced from ten to five.[3] In addition, three new legal principles were set forth: First, the equality of the right to divorce the

spouse was established. Second, freedom from the ie system was guaranteed by prohibiting abusive conduct on the part of relatives and kin. Third, a "breakdown" provision was included, i.e., if it were no longer possible to maintain the marital relationship, the law allowed divorce by mutual agreement. This provision makes it *possible* to obtain a divorce based on the mutual agreement of both spouses, and without regard to fault, if the marriage has become insupportable because of discord, or if the conflict of personalities destroys the legitimate ends of the marriage relationship. . . . This breakdown provision in 1947 was regarded as a significant innovation. . . . Marriage in Japan now emphasized the personal happiness of the spouses based on mutual affection rather than the consideration of family lineage and family harmony.

In both the old and the new Civil Code of Japan there are two types of divorce—by agreement and by judicial procedure. Divorce by agreement can be obtained simply by filing a notification with the official in charge of family registers. As for divorce by judicial procedure, under the new civil code all cases must be handled by the domestic courts established in 1948, where conciliation is compulsory.[4]. . . Divorce by agreement has always been the dominant type in Japan (about 90 percent or more of all cases). . . .

The sharp increase in the divorce rate during this period (from 0.68 in 1943 to 1.02 in 1947) might have been caused by the following factors: the state of confusion caused by radical social change and the legal policies of the occupation after the defeat of World War II; the postponed marital dissolutions which were at last actualized; and the termination of remarriages due to the discovery that former husbands had not been killed in the war. . . .

---

[3]The five reasons for divorce in the new Civil Code are: 1. adultery, 2. malicious desertion, 3. separation for more than three years, 4. malignant mental illness, and 5. serious reasons for not being able to maintain matrimony. (This last item, no. 5 is so broad and vague as to include all the reasons omitted in the old Civil Code.

[4]There are three types of judicial divorce under the new Civil Code, i.e., divorces by arbitration, divorces by judgment of domestic counselors, and divorces by court decision. . . .

The Fifth Period: 1951–1964

The divorce rate during the next fifteen years showed a steady decline from 1.01 in 1950 to 0.74 in 1964. During this period Japanese society experienced further social change due to rapid economic recovery and growth. The small nuclear family became the dominant family pattern.[5] Through the mass media people were increasingly exposed to liberal attitudes regarding heterosexual relationships. Despite the steady decline in divorce rates, marriage rates increased consistently from 7.95 in 1951 to 9.91 in 1964 (see Figure 1).

While such factors contributed to divorce in the West, they did not in Japan. It may be assumed that married couples adhered to the historic upper-class ideals of Japan. Divorce was still considered a disgrace, and the stigma assigned to divorced individuals made it difficult for them to regain their social status. Resocialization of divorced women, in particular, was extremely difficult. One might speculate that unhappy marriages, so-called "latent" divorces, were numerous. . . .

The Sixth Period: 1965 to the Present

In the most recent period, the divorce rate in Japan has shown a gradual yet consistent increase since 1965, i.e., from 0.79 in 1965 to 1.22 in 1980. The marriage rate, on the other hand, has revealed a peculiar trend. That is, the rate increased continuously from 9.72 in 1965 to 10.5 in 1971, but has been declining sharply since then (6.7 in 1980) (see Figure 1).

During this period every sphere of Japanese society has been influenced by the still rapidly growing economy and the degree of industrialization. As a consequence, remarkable changes have naturally occurred in family life. With the

---

[5]Nuclear family households as a percentage of all households in Japan are as followers: 54.0 (1920); 60.2 (1960); 62.6 (1965); 63.5 (1970); and 63.9 (1975) (Ministry of Health and Welfare, 1980b).

benefit of technological advancements, the geographical distance between Japan and other countries, especially the West, seems to have shortened drastically. Through cultural diffusion, modern life in urban areas in Japan resembles that in the West, at least on the surface. It is conceivable that not only the outward but also the inward aspects of life in Japan now resemble their Western counterparts. Personal relationships are more strongly emphasized than lineage. Marriages and divorces in recent years are perhaps motivated more by traditional reasons such as personal happiness than by traditional reasons, i.e., the interests of the house.

The years since 1965 have seen the longest period of an uninterrupted increase in the divorce rate in modern Japanese history. . . . Therefore, it could be said that, for the first time, a similar trend has emerged in Japan as in industrialized societies in the West. That is, industrialization has increased the divorce rate in contemporary Japanese society. . . .

FUTURE OF DIVORCE IN JAPAN

. . . People in postwar Japan have somewhat different lifestyles from those of the past: They take the initiative in divorces. They have grown up with material abundance and have enthusiastically adopted Western lifestyles, especially those imported from the United States. Not only surface behavior, but also values and attitudes have shifted from traditional to modern. Therefore, one would expect the emergence of divorce patterns in Japan similar to those in the United States.

Although Japanese society is highly industrialized today, the hierarchical-vertical social structure (Nakane, 1970) is still at the core of human relationships. The normative structure of male supremacy in society has yet to be altered, and the traditional nature of sex role identification persists. The autonomy of Japanese women has increased gradually owing to the continuing efforts of various organizations and to the mass media. An increasing number of women are also demanding equal treatment in society. These liberated women . . . will perhaps become another major force in the alteration of divorce patterns in Japan.

Finally, we can predict that in spite of all the socioeconomic similarities, the level of divorce in Japan will never become as high as in America. Tradition in Japan is still strong and the . . . modern liberal impulse to pursue divorce might be suppressed by the weight of tradition.

The reality of a relatively low divorce rate, however, does not guarantee that married couples in Japan are happier than their Western counterparts. It is possible . . . there are a high proportion of latent divorces in Japan. It may no longer be a virtue for a Japanese woman to submit quietly to the authority figure in the family at the expense of her personal happiness. . . .

REFERENCES

ARICHI, TŌRU. 1977. Kindai Nihon no Kazoku-kan: Meiji Hen (The Modern Japanese Family: The Meiji Era). Tokyo: Kōbundō.

GOODE, WILLIAM J. 1963. World Revolution and Family Patterns. New York: The Free Press.

Health and Welfare Statistics Association. 1981. Kokumin no Fukushi no Dōkō (Social Welfare and Social Policy in Japan). (Special issue of the Kosei no Shihyō [Social Welfare Indicator], vol. 28, no. 11). Tokyo: Health and Welfare Statistics Association.

KUWAHATA, YŪKICHI. 1956. "Rikon no jittai" (Realities of Divorce). In Eiichi Isomura, Takeyoshi Kawashima, and Takashi Koyama, eds., Rikon (Divorce), 7–38. vol. 5, Modern Families. Tokyo: Kawade.

Ministry of Health and Welfare, The. 1980a. "Jinkō dōtai shakaikeizaimen chōsa hōkuku: rikon-1978" (Socioeconomic Statistics on Divorce in 1978). Tokyo: Health and Welfare Statistics Association. 1980b Vital Statistics of Japan, vol. 1. Tokyo: Government Printing Office.

NAKANE, CHIE. 1970. Japanese Society. Berkeley and Los Angeles: University of California Press.

OHSHIO, SHUNSUKE. 1956. "Rikon no imi" (The Meaning of Divorce). In Eiichi Isomura, Takeyoshi Kawashima, and Takashi Koyama, eds., Rikon (Divorce), vol. 5, Modern Families, 39–97. Tokyo: Kawade.

Prime Minister's Office, The. 1886. "Official Bulletin: January 4, 1886." Tokyo: Government Printing Office.

TSUBOUCHI, YOSHIHIRO, and REIKO TSUBOUCHI. 1970. Rikon: Hikaku Shakaigakuteki Kenkyu (Divorce: Through Comparative Sociological Perspectives). Tokyo: Sōbunsha.

YUZAWA, YASUHIKO. 1974. "Rikon-ritsu no suii to sono haikei" (The History of Divorce Rates in Japan). In Michio Aoyama, Wataru Takeda, Tōru Arichi, Itsuo Emori, and Haruo Matsubara, eds., Kōza Kazoku, vol. 4: Kon＝in no Kaishō (Marriage and the Family, vol. 4: Dissolution of Marriage), 331–350. Tokyo: Kōbundō.

Introduction

In the last excerpt, we noted the difficulty in distinguishing modern and traditional causes of divorce. This suggests that a high (or rising) divorce rate may not be as good an indicator of modernization as many have believed. Nor, as good a measure of "a crisis in the family," as conservatives in our own society seem to believe.

Take the case of Libya, described in Excerpt 40. Like many countries in North Africa, Libya is an Islamic country. When first conceived, the Islamic religion gave women many more rights than they had enjoyed in tribal Arab countries, and in the large (especially trading) cities of Islam women actually came to practice these rights. But in rural peasant areas, Islamic women gained no more rights than they enjoyed in Hindu society or feudal Europe. As Khalidi says, "the initial marriage takes place against a background of compulsion and inconsistency of expectations between the two sexes." Marriages are divorce prone, yet divorce has not been common in the past.

Historically, a lack of compatibility between spouses has been ignored and submerged, or handled through polygyny. Polygyny—more than one wife per husband—takes some of the pressure off each dissatisfied spouse. It gives the male spouse a greater chance of at least one wife he wishes and the female spouse fewer demands by the undesired husband. Not a perfect solution by our romantic standards, but an improvement perhaps!

Today, people are replacing polygyny with serial monogamy (a series of divorces and marriages) that continues until, one hopes, each person finds a compatible mate. This practice satisfies both traditional norms of family control over (first) mate selection and modern notions of compatibility between spouses.

40
Divorce and Polygyny in Libya

Musa S. Khalidi

This critical commentary looks at role changes in Libyan marital relations. More specifically it is concerned with the phenomenon of divorce in Jabal el-Akhdar. Comments and observations are primarily based on Fattah's book (1981): *Divorce in Libyan Society: A Field Study of the Divorce Phenomenon in Jabal el-Akhdar*, as well as on later field work conducted during a research project on marital relations in collaboration with Fattah.[1]

☉

FATTAH'S WORK ON HIGH INCIDENCE OF DIVORCE

Fattah's work (1981) based on a non-random sample of 500 divorced males, and a stratified random sample of 500 divorced females, is a pio-

neering descriptive study of data obtained by the interview method. . .[2] What prompted his study is the high rate of divorce in Libya, and the lack of reliable data in this field. . . .

In Jabal el-Akhdar, Libya, divorce can be viewed as a lesser crisis than a marriage which was initially undesired. Divorce, therefore, becomes a safety valve when incompatibility occurs.

HOMOGENEITY OF BACKGROUND VERSUS BRIDE PRICE ARRANGEMENTS

. . . Fattah's data (1981) on . . . divorced couples shows that most first marriages are endogamous, matching in education, family status, religion,

Source: Khalidi, M.S. (1989) "Divorce in Libya: a critical commentary," *Journal of Comparative Family Studies*, 20, 1, Spring, 118–124.

[1]In 1978–79. Dr. M.S. Fattah, in collaboration with Dr. Omar S. Ahmad and the author, surveyed random samples of 500 married men and 500 married women in a subsequent

research project in the same area entitled: "Marriage and Marital Relations: Perspectives, Methods, and Reality in Jabal el-Akhdar, Libya." Results of relevant replicated questions were comparable to Fattah's earlier study of divorce. Unfortunately, statistical data could not be retrieved at the time of the author's departure from Libya in 1980.

[2]In the case of divorced males, the absence of reliable records from which to draw a random sample necessitated

and other variables. The only exception is an observed average differential of 9.5 years between older male and younger female divorcees. . . . The Sunni Maliki sect in Libya . . ."insist that even an adult woman must be contracted in marriage by her guardian" (Anderson, 1970:496). Subsequently, the payment of a high bride price and the cost of lavish ceremonials are prevalent for the preferred first betrothals of females. According to Libyan tradition, the bride price is paid upon contracting the marriage with no requirement for a delayed dowry. . . . Hence if marital dissolution occurs, the husband is not obligated to pay any alimony to his wife after proclaiming his third and final divorce (talaq), except for the care of an infant child if the baby is too young to be separated from its mother. According to the Islamic law (Shari'ah) a divorced woman receives only her personal property, and children go to the father (Lutfiyya, 1970:525, Tomeh, 1982:41).[3]

A MALE-FEMALE DICHOTOMY OF PERSPECTIVES ON MARRIAGE

Fattah (1981) reconfirms . . . that in Moslem societies women have little freedom to determine their first marriages or select their mates. However . . . Fattah's data (1981) show a wide gap exists between Libyan males and females in their expectations of marriage. Many more males than females feel their marriages are essential for stability and preservation of the family institution.[4] . . . Many more females than males express . . . feelings that necessity, chance, fortune, and family wishes influenced their decisions. Their responses reveal capitulation to pressure . . . in their marriages. Women's responses are also in sharp contrast to those of males, who insist on the need to maintain institutionalized arrangements in the family. This evidence tends to confirm the . . . dichotomy between the social worlds of males and females as noted by Nelson (1973:44) and Abu-Laban (1980:28), as well as the yearning by women for independence which seems associated with divorce-prone marriages as observed by Cohen (1971:171). The initial marriage takes place against a background of compulsion and inconsistency of expectations between the two sexes, without due regard for the personal complementarity of newly-wedded couples. These variables cannot be ignored . . . when important factors in divorce are investigated.

EMERGENT NEOLOCAL HOUSEHOLDS

. . . Studies show a substantial number of independent households being established in Jabal el-Akhdar for married couples and their children (Al-Nouri, 1980, Fattah, 1981, Khalidi, 1985). . . . Extended family controls upon newly-weds subside considerably when control becomes more remote. If then the need of divorce arises, the pressure more likely comes from one or both of the spouses themselves. This conclusion is supported by Fattah's data (1981:67–70) which reveals that, in at least half the cases of dissolution, divorce was desired by either the husband or the wife or both. Although the . . . freedom to divorce rests far more in the hands of husbands, wives (Tomeh, 1982) are not entirely helpless. . . . Informal initiation of divorce is not the sole prerogative of males. More importantly, family controls appear to be on the wane when compared with their initial decisive influence upon first marriages. Hence when initially either a male or a female is compelled at a vulnerable

---

acceptance of a non-random sample for comparative purposes.

[3]For more specific material on the concepts of property and inheritance in Jabal el-Akhdar, see Chapter 7 in Behnke's work (1980): *The Herders of Cyrenaica.*

[4]Male responses were as follows: 1) Essential for family situation: 12.7 percent as compared with 0.0 percent for females, 2) To have children: 22.8 percent as compared with 3.0 percent for females, 3) Essential for stability: 25.6 percent as compared with 9.0 percent for females, and 4) To satisfy a religious requirement: 14.4 percent as compared with 1.8 percent for females (Fattah 1981, 63-64).

young age to mate with a partner for whom no love is felt, that person is freer to create all sorts of marital tensions as an excuse for reaching the conclusion that divorce would be the best solution, regardless of the views of the extended family. . . .

COPING WITH DIVORCE

. . . Normally, problems revolve around the custody of children and the possible economic burdens to be borne by husbands and wives. If children are present, the resolution, as pointed out earlier, lies in the Islamic law (*Shari'ah*) requirement that they become wards of their father's household unless they are very young. Moreover, since more than half the male and female samples in Fattah's study (1981:65) remained married for no more than three years, the number of children born in such unions . . . is small. . . .

Divorced women, whether childless or relieved of the custody of children, have future opportunities for marriage. They are assured a basic salary by the State if they are not employed. Similarly, the presence of children acts for males as an incentive to remarry so as to provide female care for the children. Moreover, since males are not encumbered with alimony . . . , seeking another wife with negligible costs become desirable. If a . . . male seeks remarriage to a virgin, the costs are prohibitive. However, a second marriage to a young divorcee is alluring since neither a large dowry nor a delayed one is required. . . . Pressure from relatives, being less effective from a distance, allows more freedom for divorced husbands and wives in the new selection process.

NEW PATTERNS

a. Waxing Serial Monogamy. . . . In numerous cases remarriage is repeated by divorced couples perhaps until each finds a compatible mate. It is not surprising, therefore, that serial monogamy has become popular. . . . Fattah's data (1981) is revealing. . . . In 87.4 percent of male divorces, remarriage occurred from two to six times compared with an occurrence of 45.2 percent among female divorcees.[5] In addition, more than half the female divorcees under 50 years of age were desirous of getting remarried . . . (see Table 1). No stigma is attached to divorce in Libya (Fattah, 1981: 31). . . .

b. Waning Polygyny. . . . In about one-fifth of the cases investigated by Fattah (1981:33), another wife was maintained at the time of the divorce. . . . This element can further facilitate divorce where couples are childless. And while polygyny is not uncommon, the practice of serial monogamy, of which divorce is an inseparable component, might help eventually to reduce the need for polygynous marriages as informal pressure and formal forces by the state increase. As noted by Abu-Laban (1980), Al-Nouri (1980), and Ziadeh (1987), the trend is in the direction of lesser polygyny, if not elimination, due to reform laws introduced in several Arab states, and the pressure exerted by women's organizations. . . .

CONCLUDING NOTES

. . . The ease with which divorce is obtained lies in the structural conditions of the household. Forced endogamous marriages are initially preferred and encouraged. Yet first marriages to single females have become expensive events. There is also a wide gap between males and females in their reasons for getting married. . . . Avenues in the Islamic Law (*Shari'ah*) are utilized for ending undesired marriages. Children become wards of the husband's household, and di-

---

[5]The noted difference in remarriage rates between male and female divorcees is probably a function of age differentials, whereby females are divorced at a much younger age than their male counterparts, and may have more years in which to remarry.

TABLE 1. Frequency of Marriage for Divorced Men and Women in Jabal el-Akhdar, 1981[1]

No. of Times Married	Men (N = 500)		Women (N = 500)	
	Percent	Accumulated	Percent	Accumulated
1	10.6	10.6	54.4	54.4
2	55.6 ⎤	66.2	30.4 ⎤	84.8
3	19.2 ⎟	85.4	9.0 ⎟	93.8
4	8.0 ⎬ 87.4%	93.4	4.0 ⎬ 45.2%	97.8
5	2.8 ⎟	96.2	1.8 ⎦	99.6
6	1.8 ⎦	98.0	—	99.6
7	0.4	98.4	0.2	99.8
8	0.8	99.4	0.2	100.0
9	0.4	99.6	—	100.0
10	0.2	99.8	—	100.0
11	—	—	—	100.0
12	0.2	100.0	—	100.0

[1]Adapted from Fattah (1981:107–108)

vorced wives are easily absorbed into the households of their kin, even with monetary support from the State. Prospective husbands and wives from the divorced population are then allowed more freedom in a wider selection from the field of eligible mates. . . .

REFERENCES

ABU-LABAN, B. 1980. *An Olive Branch on the Family Tree: The Arabs in Canada.* Toronto: McClelland and Stewart.

AL-NOURI, Q. N. 1980. "Changing Marriage Patterns in Libya: Attitudes of University Students," *Journal of Comparative Family Studies.* 11 (Spring), pp. 219–232.

ANDERSON, J. N. D. 1970. "The Islamic Law of Marriage and Divorce," in A.M. Lutfiyya and C.W. Churchill (eds.), *Readings in Arab Middle Eastern Societies.* The Hague: Mouton.

BEHNKE, JR., R. H. 1980. *The Herders of Cyrenaica.* Studies in Anthropology (12). University of Illinois Press.

COHEN, R. 1971. *Dominance and Defiance: A Study of Marital Instability in an Islamic African Society.* Anthropological Studies No. 6, Washington D.C.: American Anthropological Association.

FATTAH, M. S. 1981. *Divorce in Libyan Society: A Field Study of the Divorce Phenomenon in Jabal el-Akhdar,* (in Arabic). Benghazi: University of Garyounis Research Center.

KHALIDI, M. S. 1985. "Dilemmas of Rural Development in Cyrenaica, Libya," in *Studies in Comparative International Development.* Vol. 20, No. 2, Georgia Institute of Technology.

LUTFIYYA, A. M. 1970. "The Family," in A.M. Lutfiyya and C.W. Churchill (eds.), *Readings in Arab Middle Eastern Societies.* The Hague: Mouton.

NELSON, C. (ed.). 1973. *The Desert and the Sown: Nomads in the Wider Society.*, Research Series 21, Institute of International Studies. Berkeley: University of California.

ZIADEH, F. J. 1987. "Permanence and Change in Arab Legal Systems," *Arab Studies Quarterly,* Vol. 9, No. 1, Winter, 1987.

Introduction

The conventional wisdom on divorce compares traditional societies with modern societies. In the former, women are (supposedly) victimized by mates they do not want, and in the latter, women have greater autonomy. From this standpoint, modern marriage is perceived as a romantic choice by both mates. Modern divorce is also the result of a choice, by both, to terminate an unsatisfying relationship.

As we have seen, divorce in traditional societies is often followed by remarriage. There is simply no place—socially or economically—for single people, especially single women. In modern societies, there *is* a place for single women. This fact lowers the psychological and economic costs of divorce. With lower costs (and high possible benefits), divorce rates rise in modern societies. At least, that is how the theory goes.

Yet, if we examine the economics of divorce in the United States and other Western countries, we see that the prospects for women are not really as rosy as all that. In fact, women are seriously disadvantaged economically by divorce. This disadvantage is a result of many factors such as discrimination in the labor force, poor child-care availability, and little state support for women with dependent children. Divorce leads to what people have called the "feminization of poverty."

The next excerpt, by Terry Arendell, describes the way divorce impoverishes divorced women, and not divorced men in modern American society. Faced with poverty, women who are dissatisfied with marriage are right to wonder whether they have any real choice about remaining in their marriage.

41

The Economic Impact of Divorce on American Women

Terry J. Arendell

. . . Divorce is a primary contributor to the increase in the number of impoverished women. Most married women, whether working outside the home or not, are economically dependent on their husbands. . . .

Divorce typically discontinues the redistribution of income from the husband as breadwinner to his wife and children. Divorce thus terminates most women's access to the financial resources and economic status that were available to them in marriage through their husbands.

The inequality between men and women in marriage is magnified in divorce as women's standard of living declines and men's rises. Men leave marriage with their earning abilities and social statuses intact. The Panel Study of Income Dynamics found that men's standard of living actually improves after divorce.[1] . . . Several other studies confirm that socioeconomic decline shapes women's—not men's—postdivorce experiences.[2]

[1]Mary Corcoran, Greg J. Duncan, and Martha S. Hill, "The Economic Fortunes of Women and Children: Lessons from the Panel Study of Income Dynamics," in *Signs: Journal of Women in Culture and Society* 10, no. 2 (Winter 1984): 232–48.

[2]Lenore Weitzman, "Economics of Divorce: Social and Economic Consequences of Property, Alimony and Child Support Awards," *University of California, Los Angeles Law Review* 28 (1981): 1181–1268, and *The Divorce Revolution*; David Chambers, *Making Fathers Pay: The Enforcement of Child Support* (Chicago: University of Chicago Press, 1979).

Source: Arendell, T.J. (1987) "Women and the economics of divorce in the contemporary United States," *Signs: Journal of Women in Culture and Society,* 13, 1, 121–135.

Divorced women's economic decline . . . is further evidenced by the fact that they spend significantly less on food, recreation, clothing, and discretionary items than do divorced men.[3] Such differential spending is not surprising considering divorced women's significantly lower incomes. Housing, food, and child care were the three greatest expenses for sixty divorced California women studied in 1982 and 1983 who described themselves as having had during marriage middle-class life-styles with a relatively broad range of discretionary spending.[4] Many single-parent families move three or more times in the course of two or three years in order to reduce their housing expenses.[5] . . .

Women with children are especially harmed by divorce. "Should marital disruption occur, women with children, regardless of their previous economic circumstances, are usually poorer after the marriage fails.[6] Indeed, the total family incomes of most divorced women and their children is less than 50 percent of their family incomes prior to divorce. Yet the custodial parent needs approximately 80 percent of the income prior to divorce to maintain the family's standard of living.[7]

Women's position in a gender-stratified labor force, as well as their traditional family roles, make it difficult for them to recover economically from divorce. . . . Women . . . work primarily in the expanding, lower-paying service sector. Pigeonholed in this "pink-collar" sector, they are paid low wages and receive few benefits so that many women live below or near the poverty level even though they are employed.[8] . . . Even when women enter male-dominated occupations, their wages are lower than men's, primarily as a result of wage discrimination.[9] . . .

Women who do not work outside the home while they are married, especially those who are mothers . . . run a higher economic risk following divorce than do women who are employed during their marriage. Rainwater found a direct relationship between women's economic recovery after divorce and their work histories prior to divorce. To the extent that wives become more regular labor force participants, they increase their possibility of having stable and somewhat higher incomes should they become heads of their own families. For example, by the fourth year that they headed their own families, women who had worked regularly before heading their families had family incomes equal to 80 percent of their average family income while they were married. Women who had not worked had incomes slightly less than half that of their last married years.[10]

. . . Displaced homemakers, defined as women over age thirty-five who have been out of the job market for extended periods of time, confront an employment and wage system that undervalues their . . . domestic work experience and discriminates against women on the basis

[3]Thomas Espenshade, "The Economic Consequences of Divorce," *Journal of Marriage and the Family* 41, no. 3 (1979): 615–25; George Masnick and Mary Jo Bane, *The Nation's Families: 1960–1990* (New York: Auburn House Publishing Co., 1980); Terry Arendell, *Mothers and Divorce: Legal, Economic, and Social Dilemmas* (Berkeley and Los Angeles: University of California Press, 1986).

[4]Arendell.

[5]Cheryl Buehler and Janice Hogan, "Managerial Behavior and Stress in Families Headed by Divorced Women: A Proposed Framework," *Family Relations* 29, no. 4 (1980): 525–32; Arendell; Masnick and Bane.

[6]USCCR (n. 4 above), 11.

[7]Chambers. Policymakers in other nations, such as Sweden, have indicated it . . . costs more to maintain a single-parent family, owing to such added costs as child care and mother's work transportation. Thus they have legislated supplemental allowances to female heads of households.

[8]Louise Howe, *Pink Collar Workers: Inside the World of Women's Work* (New York: Avon Books, 1977).

[9]Catherine MacKinnon, *Sexual Harassment of Working Women* (New Haven, Conn.: Yale University Press, 1979); Corcoran et al. (n. 9 above); Leo McCarthy, *The Feminization of Poverty: Report of the Lieutenant Governor's Task Force on the Feminization of Poverty* (Sacramento: State of California, January 1985); Rachel Kahn-Hut, Arlene Daniels, and Richard Colvard, *Women and Work: Problems and Perspectives* (New York: Oxford University Press, 1982); Francine Blau, "Women in the Labor Force: An Overview," in *Women: A Feminist Perspective*, ed. Jo Freeman (Palo Alto, Calif.: Mayfield Publishing Co., 1984), 297–315.

[10]Rainwater, 78.

of age.[11] . . ."The dramatic increase in divorce, especially in the marriages of long duration, predicts an increase in the number of older women living alone and in poverty in the next generation."[12]

The economic impact of divorce affects children also. . . . Census data show 23.7 percent of all children live with only one parent because of divorce or marital separation. Over 90 percent of children living in single-parent families live with their mothers; there has been no change since 1960 in the proportion of children living with a single-parent father (2 percent).[13] Thus, women's economic decline as a result of divorce directly affects their dependent children as well.

Divorce may also affect children older than age twenty-one. Though research on this issue is still in preliminary stages, evidence suggests that after divorce, some women . . . cannot financially assist their older children and may themselves become dependent on their offspring.[14]
. . .

FOUR FACTORS AFFECTING DIVORCED WOMEN'S EARNING POTENTIAL

Continuing Caretaking Responsibilities

. . . Because women's role as primary caretaker continues after divorce, women's employment options are limited after marriage. . . .

Mothers of young children confront both a discriminatory labor market and the inadequate availability and high cost of quality care for their children.[15] Child care is a huge expense for most mothers employed outside the home; for single mothers supporting families, it can be prohibitively expensive. Unmarried mothers who work outside the home must also confront the logistical difficulties of, for example, the need to be both at work and at home to care for a sick child.

As . . . the aged live longer, women, who are the primary caretakers of the dependent elderly, will be faced with increasing caregiving responsibilities for the frail elderly. Particularly for divorced women who must rely on their own earnings, the demands of such responsibilities are a burden that is extremely detrimental to their already difficult economic situation.

Wage Discrimination Against Women

. . . More than three-fourths of divorced mothers with custody of their children are employed; 88 percent, full-time. Divorced mothers constitute the largest proportion of employed women. . . . Most divorced and separated mothers work instead of depending on public assistance to compensate for the loss of family income as a result of divorce.[16] However, because most divorced women occupy low-paying positions that offer few opportunities for mobility or flexible schedules, they have neither the time nor the resources to pursue advanced training or education or to seek better jobs. Thus, "studies generally conclude that even great effort on the part of female heads of families does not help to

[11]Laurie Shields, *Displaced Homemakers: Organizing for a New Life* (New York: McGraw-Hill Book Co., 1981); Nancy King and Mary Marvel, *Issues, Policies, and Programs for Midlife and Older Women* (Washington, D.C.: Center for Women Policy Studies, 1982), esp. 44; Sara Rix, *Older Women: The Economics of Aging* (Washington, D.C.: Women's Research and Education Institute of the Congressional Caucus for Women's Issues, 1984); Coalition on Women and the Budget, *Inequality of Sacrifice: The Impact of the Reagan Budget on Women* (Washington, D.C.: National Women's Law Center, 1984).

[12]King and Marvel, 9, 11.

[13]USBC, *Statistical Abstract of the United States, 1985.*

[14]Arendell (n. 11 above).

[15]USBC, *Current Population Reports: Child Care Arrangements of Working Mothers: June 1982*, Series P-23, no. 129 (Washington, D.C.: Government Printing Office, 1983).

[16]Rainwater (n. 10 above); Arendell; Weitzman, *The Divorce Revolution* (n. 2 above); Lee Rainwater, *Welfare and Working Mothers* (Cambridge: Joint Center for Urban Studies, 1977).

reduce poverty and dependence."[17] Esther Wattenberg and Hazel Reinhardt concluded: . . . ."To reverse the pauperization of female-headed households will require sustained attention to discrimination in the labor market, and will require a redefinition of unemployment in recognition that a woman's work within the home is essential."[18]

Inequities Under the Law

. . . In 1981, 81 percent of divorced and 66 percent of separated women with children had child-support orders.[19] However, most fathers do not fully comply with child-support orders. Only about 20 percent of fathers are in full compliance . . . ; another 15 percent pay irregularly.[20] Only 47 percent of all divorced and separated fathers made any child-support payments in 1981.[21]

. . . Few child-support orders include provisions for automatic cost of living increases. Even fewer recognize that child-rearing costs increase as children grow older. Also, the noncustodial parent has no legal obligation to provide for a child once he or she reaches age eighteen. . . .

Although women who obtain their divorces in community-property states generally receive better settlements than those who divorce in common-law states, they are not compensated for the less tangible acquisitions of a marriage that are not legally considered marital property, such as advanced education, professional or career development, degrees and licenses, and future earnings resulting from joint marital efforts.[22] Because it is typically women who forgo these acquisitions in order to support their husbands' educations and to care for the home and family during their husbands' careers, women are most harmed by the law's failure to recognize a more comprehensive definition of marital property.

Frequently, a divorced woman has no rights to her former husband's retirement pension . . . and has no pension in her own right because she did not work outside of the home or had only intermittent employment. . . . Divorce courts typically award women less than one-half of the couple's property, according to Norma Harwood:

One or more of the following frequently occurs in the trial court: income-producing property is granted to the husband; the husband is granted all the property and is permitted to pay off the wife's interest in prolonged installments, thereby using future deflated dollars, and the wife is forced to spend these property pay-off dollars for daily living due to her low income level and/or inadequate alimony award; pension plan contributions and the future benefits remain the husband's and the value is not included in marital assets and business interests simply remain the husband's. When one realistically looks at what has been acquired during the marriage, the wife's property award may be as little as 10 percent.[23]

. . . Despite media attention to a few divorces in which women received high alimony pay-

[17]Esther Wattenberg and Hazel Reinhardt, "Female-headed Families: Trends and Implications," *Social Work* 24 (1979): 460–67.

[18]Wattenberg and Reinhardt, esp. 464.

[19]USBC, *Statistical Abstract of the United States, 1985* (n. 3 above); and *Current Population Reports: Households, Families, Marital Status, and Living Arrangements*, Series P-20, no. 382 (Washington, D.C.: Government Printing Office, 1983).

[20]USBC, *Current Population Reports: Households, Families, Marital Status and Living Arrangements*. For further discussion of noncompliance with child-support orders, see Weitzman, *The Divorce Revolution*, *The Marriage Contract*, and "Economics of Divorce: Social and Economic Consequences of Property, Alimony, and Child Support Orders"; Chambers (n. 11 above); Carol Bruch, "Developing Normative Standards for Child-Support Payments: A Critique of Current Practice," in *The Parental Child-Support Obligation*, ed. Judith Cassetty (Lexington, Mass.: Lexington Books, 1983).

[21]USBC, *Statistical Abstract of the United States, 1985*.

[22]Barbara Babcock, Ann Freedman, Eleanor Norton, and Susan Ross, *Sex Discrimination and the Law: Causes and Remedies* (Boston: Little, Brown & Co., 1975); Halem; Fineman. For discussion of community-property advantages in divorce, see Weitzman, *The Marriage Contract*; Carol Bruch, "Management Powers and Duties under California's Community Property Laws: Recommended for Reform," *Hastings Law Journal* 34, no. 2 (1982): 769–92. Harwood, 67.

[23]USBC, *Statistical Abstract of the United States, 1985*.

ments, spousal support was awarded in just 17 percent of all divorces in 1982. It was actually received in fewer than 6 percent of cases.[24] . . .

Inadequacy of Public Assistance

. . . Only a minority of divorced women depend on welfare, and those who do, do so primarily for temporary assistance.[25] Furthermore, "among those who do not receive welfare assistance in the first year after the dissolution of their marriages, only 5 percent receive welfare assistance thereafter."[26]

. . . In no state does welfare provide enough assistance for a family to live above the poverty level. . . . Also, benefit levels have not kept pace with inflation. . . . Since 1970 there has been about a one-third loss in purchasing power for families on public assistance.[27] . . .

Women who are poor and whose children are grown do not qualify for Aid to Families with Dependent Children. Nor does the loss of their positions as homemaker-wives, as a result of divorce, entitle them to unemployment compensa-

tion since the government does not recognize their work as an occupational category. Unless they are age sixty-two or older, were married for at least ten years, and have a former husband who has retired *and* is eligible to collect social security benefits, these women qualify for no or only minimal spousal social security benefits. . . . For most displaced homemakers who find paid work, prospects for substantial advancement are slim; most will accrue few retirement funds, if any. . . .

In summary, . . . economic hardship is the essence of many women's postdivorce experiences. Furthermore, . . . divorced women as a group remain poorly represented in the public sphere and have limited access to the political and legal resources necessary to make their predicament the subject of public debate. Programs and policies that should be addressed by this debate fall into six broad categories: income supplements, housing, health care, child care and care-giving support services, legal reforms in divorce laws, and retirement pension coverage. Without widespread changes in public policy in each of these realms, marriage is destined to become for women an institution that they cannot afford to support and cannot afford to dissolve.

---

[24]USBC, *Statistical Abstract of the United States, 1985.*

[25]Rainwater, *Welfare and Working Mothers* (n. 16 above), 5.

[26]Children's Defense Fund.

[27]King and Marvel; Coalition on Women and the Budget (n. 11 above).

Introduction

In many ways, sociological research on divorce leads to a single, inescapable conclusion: we are in the midst of a worldwide divorce revolution.

The reasons for this are not hard to see. In many parts of the world, as in nineteenth-century America, marriage is (and has been) a lot like slavery for women. For them, divorce represents an escape from domestic slavery. In India, divorce also offers an escape from the mistakes parents made selecting their children's mates. In America, it offers an escape from the mistakes young people made in selecting their own mates. Escape from an unhappy marriage is particularly crucial where the relationship is to be a companionate union based on love and friendship, and where only one mate is allowed at a time. No wonder then, that divorce rates increase as the practice of polygamy decreases (as in Libya).

Yet, easier divorce is not really an escape from slavery if it means falling into poverty. Then, divorce may mean the exchange of one kind of slavery (household domination) for another (wage slavery). We cannot be certain that divorce always means more freedom for women, even when they can participate in the labor force.

The next excerpt shows that, across a wide variety of societies, there is a curved relationship between divorce and (1) socioeconomic development, and (2) women's labor-force participation. In every society's history, there will be a period when divorce rates slow down, then speed up to a gallop. In this sense, the Japanese case we examined earlier is not the exception—it is the rule.

42
What Determines Divorce Rates?

Katherine Trent
Scott J. South

In this study, we use the most recent divorce data available for a sample of 66 developed and developing countries. The net effects of socioeconomic development, women's labor force participation, sex ratios, and religion on the divorce rate are analyzed.

☑

DATA AND METHODS

... The sample includes countries from all inhabited continents, although lesser-developed countries are proportionally underrepresented. ... Figure 1 lists the countries included in the analysis.

The dependent variable is the crude divorce rate, that is, the number of divorces per 1,000 population (United Nations, 1982: Table 33). The year in which the divorce rate is measured varies slightly across countries but is usually between 1976 and 1982. In our sample, the divorce rate ranges from a low of .02 in Malaysia to a high of 5.08 in the United States. The mean divorce rate is 1.36. ...

Sources: Trent, Katherine and Scott J. South (1989) "Structural determinants of the divorce rate: a Cross-societal analysis," Journal of Marriage and the Family, 51 (May), 391–404

The crude divorce rate is, of course, sensitive to the age and marital status composition of the population (England and Kunz, 1975; Shryock and Siegel, 1976). ... While prior cross-national research has also used the crude divorce rate (Cole and Powers, 1973; Pampel and Tanaka, 1986; Semyonov, 1980), our results, as well as those of earlier studies, should be interpreted cautiously.

... The official divorce rate reflects not only the volume of divorce seekers but also each nation's laws and customs regarding divorce. For most countries, the official divorce rate does not include annulments and separations. ... The official granting of a divorce has important consequences, of course, including the possibility of a legal remarriage. In addition, the laws involving divorce are likely to be influenced considerably by the number of people desiring a divorce. But it should be recognized that the divorce rate used here is implicitly affected by both the size of the population seeking divorce and the legal structures regarding the opportunity to obtain one.

The principal independent variable is a measure of each nation's level of socioeconomic development. We performed an exploratory factor analysis of four common development indica-

FIGURE 1.   Cross-Tabulation of the Divorce Rate with the Development Index for 66 Countries

Divorce Rate	First Sextile	Second Sextile	Third Sextile	Fourth Sextile	Fifth Sextile	Sixth Sextile
High	Egypt Liberia	Dominican Republic	Cuba	Czechoslovakia Hungary Puerto Rico	Austria Federal Republic of Germany Finland German Democratic Republic New Zealand United Kingdom	Australia Canada Denmark Iceland Netherlands Norway Sweden Switzerland United States
Medium	Tunisia	Guyana Iraq Jordan	Costa Rica Fiji Guadeloupe Reunion Romania Uruguay Yugoslavia	Bulgaria Greece Israel Martinique Poland	Belgium Kuwait Luxembourg Singapore	France Japan
Low	Ecuador Guatemala Honduras Iran Nicaragua Peru Thailand Turkey	Jamaica Malaysia Mauritius Mexico South Korea Sri Lanka Syria	Panama Portugal Venezuela	Barbados Cyprus Trinidad and Tobago	Italy	

tors—gross national product per capita . . . the infant mortality rate, life expectancy at birth, and percentage of the population which is urban (Population Reference Bureau, 1983) . . . to create an index of socioeconomic development. . . .

Our measure of women's labor force participation is the percentage of adult women defined as economically active by the International Labor Office (Population Reference Bureau, 1981). In this sample, the women's labor force participation rate ranges from a low of 4.0 in Iraq to a high of 73.0 in Thailand, with a mean of 37.9. . . . The conceptual and methodological difficulties in measuring women's labor force participation are not trivial . . . and this particular measure . . . is probably best considered a rough indicator rather than a highly reliable measure.

The sex ratio is measured by the number of males per 100 females at ages 15 to 49 (United Nations, 1982: Table 7). Hence, a high sex ratio indicates a relative scarcity of women, while a low value indicates a relative surplus of women. The sex ratio ranges from 90.3 in Reunion to 137.1 in Kuwait, with a mean of 101.2. . . .

It is considerably more difficult to operationalize the extent of religious affiliations of various populations. We have attempted to do so with two variables. First, we have used the World Christian Handbook's (Kurian, 1979) estimates of the percentage of the population identified as Roman Catholic. Given the Catholic church's proscription of divorce, we expect this variable to be inversely related to the divorce rate. Second, we include as an independent variable a dummy variable representing predominantly Muslim nations.[1] . . . We anticipate that, all else being equal, Muslim countries will have a higher incidence of divorce.

Finally, we include as a control variable the average age at marriage for females (Population Reference Bureau, 1981).[2] There are several reasons for expecting an inverse relationship between this variable and a divorce rate. First, individual-level studies consistently document higher rates of dissolution for marriages contracted by young people (Booth and Edwards, 1985; Morgan and Rindfuss, 1985; South and Spitze, 1986). Presumably, individuals who marry early are less mature and spend less time in the marital search; both are factors that might precipitate divorce. Perhaps a more fundamental reason for anticipating an inverse association between age at marriage and the crude divorce rate is that countries with a young average age at marriage are also characterized by widespread marriage (Dixon, 1971) and, thus, a larger population at risk of divorce. To some extent, then, this control variable may serve to refine the crude divorce rate.

REGRESSION ANALYSIS RESULTS

. . . The relationship between the development index and the divorce rate is U-shaped; at low levels of development, the divorce rate decreases as development increases, while at higher levels of development, divorce increases as development increases. . . .

Both an older average age at marriage and a high sex ratio tend to reduce the crude divorce rate, with the sex ratio having a slightly stronger effect. As with the development index, the two labor force participation terms indicate a curvilinear relationship with the divorce rate. The form . . . is also U-shaped, the divorce rate at first decreasing and then increasing, along with increase in the female labor force participation rate. Taken together, the independent variables . . . explain well over 40% of the cross-national variation in the crude divorce rate.

When the two religious affiliation variables are added to the equation, . . . the coefficients for these variables are in the expected direction—negative for percentage Catholic and positive for the Muslim dummy variable—but neither coefficient is statistically significant and

both are quite small. The inclusion of these religious indicators does little to alter the effects of the other variables.

It should be noted that the surprising failure of the percentage Catholic variable to register a significant association with the divorce rate could . . . reflect sample selection bias (Berk, 1983). . . . Several countries with large Catholic populations proscribe divorce entirely and therefore do not report divorce statistics. These countries are excluded from our samples, but had they been included, the relationship between percentage Catholic and the divorce rate may have been strengthened considerably. What can be inferred from our results, however, is that among those countries permitting a legal divorce, the relative sizes of Catholic or Muslim populations do not seem to have a great influence on the divorce rate. . . .

Net of the other independent variables, the curve describing the relationship between the development index and the divorce rate begins downward, reaching its nadir when the development index is approximately one and one-third standard deviations below its mean (see Neter, Wasserman, and Kutner, 1983, for computational formulas). Representative countries at this stage of development, all of which have divorce rates below the mean, include Ecuador, Guatemala, Thailand, and Sri Lanka. . . . As the level of development rises from this point, the effect of development on the divorce rate becomes increasingly positive.

As a way of illustrating this relationship more concretely, Figure 1 shows the location of each country in a cross-tabulation of the divorce rate (in thirds) with the development index (in sextiles). The generally positive association between the two variables is clearly apparent, with countries in Asia and Latin America having low divorce rates and low development scores, and countries in Western Europe and North America having high divorce rates and high levels of development. It appears that the initial downswing in the development/divorce relationship is attributable largely, though not exclusively, to five Arabic countries: Egypt, Liberia, Tunisia, Iraq, and Jordan, whose divorce rates are comparatively high for their levels of development. At the other end of the spectrum, Italy appears to be something of an outlier, with a lower-than-expected divorce rate, given its developmental stage. . . .

Computations describing the curvilinear effect of the female labor force participation rate on the divorce rate show that when the labor force participation rate is less than 40%, the effect of women's labor force participation is negative. However, among countries with high rates of women's labor force participation, its effect on the divorce rate is increasingly positive. This U-shaped curve reaches its nadir when the female labor force participation rate is 39.3, or about at the sample mean. Countries having approximately this rate of women's labor force participation and divorce rates below the mean include Italy, Malaysia, and Panama. . . .

Figure 2 shows a cross-tabulation of the divorce rate with the female labor force participation rate. The more even distribution of countries here, compared to Figure 1, suggests a weaker relationship between women's labor force participation and divorce than between development and divorce. . . .

DISCUSSION AND CONCLUSION

. . . Four variables have been shown to bear a significant relationship to the crude divorce rate. Both a high sex ratio, indicating a relative undersupply of women, and a late average age at marriage for women are associated with lower divorce rates. Two other variables, a multi-item index of socioeconomic development and the female labor force participation rate, are significantly, but nonlinearly, related to the divorce rate. Both variables exhibit U-shaped associations with the crude divorce rate, with the level

FIGURE 2. Cross-Tabulation of the Divorce Rate with the Women's Labor Force Participation Rate for 66 Countries

Divorce Rate	< 21%	21%–29%	30%–38%	39%–47%	48%–54%	> 54%
High	Dominican Republic Egypt	Cuba Puerto Rico	Netherlands Norway	Australia Canada Iceland Liberia New Zealand	Federal Republic of Germany Sweden Switzerland United Kingdom United States	Austria Czechoslovakia Denmark Finland German Democratic Republic Hungary
Medium	Fiji Iraq Kuwait Tunisia	Costa Rica Reunion	Belgium Guyana Israel Luxembourg Singapore Uruguay	Greece Guadeloupe Jordan	France Martinique Yugoslavia	Bulgaria Japan Poland Romania
Low	Guatemala Honduras Iran Mexico Syria	Ecuador Mauritius Nicaragua Peru Portugal Sri Lanka Venezuela	Italy Malaysia Panama	Cyprus South Korea Trinidad and Tobago	Barbados Jamaica Turkey	Thailand

of development exerting a stronger influence than women's labor force participation.

Because of the cross-sectional nature of our data, . . . inferences about the secular trends in divorce among any group of countries must be made cautiously. Nonetheless, the historical dynamics of divorce in both Arabic Islam and Japan, described by Goode (1963), appear to fit the pattern uncovered in our data. In both of these populations, an initially high rate of marital dissolution fell during the early stages of industrialization. Among more advanced nations, increasing divorce rates accompanied economic modernization.

There is very little theory, aside from Goode's, that addresses the curvilinear relationship between socioeconomic development and divorce uncovered here. However, . . . Caldwell (1976: 352) argues that modernization entails "the import of a different culture," occurring through the infusion of mass education and the mass media. To the extent that the importation of Western culture erodes traditional patriarchal customs conducive to high divorce rates, it might be expected that countries having initially high divorce rates would experience a decline, or hold steady, in the face of industrialization. Western culture's emphasis on the nuclear family may also play a role here, insofar as it reduces the influence of kin in conjugal matters. . . .

It is also interesting to note that controlling for the rate of women's labor force participation does not reduce appreciably the observed influence of socioeconomic development on divorce. We suspect two processes are at work here. First, industrialization may elevate women's status in ways other than increasing their paid employment. These other dimensions of women's status might include educational opportunities, the *type* of work women do, and the ability of women to maintain separate households following divorce. Second, socioeconomic development may affect marital stability in ways only tangentially related to women's status. For example, industrialization may reduce the size of families and, hence, increase the likelihood of divorce, independent of its effects on women's social position. . . .

Although theoretical frameworks for explaining cross-national variation in marital instability exist or can be developed from more general comparative theories of family structure, relatively few studies have attempted to examine these perspectives empirically. The analysis presented here suggests that prior theory and research may have oversimplified the influences of socioeconomic development and women's labor force participation, underemphasized the role of imbalanced sex ratios, and overemphasized the effect of religion.

NOTES

[1] The countries in our sample with large Muslim populations are Egypt, Iran, Iraq, Jordan, Kuwait, Malaysia, Syria, Tunisia, and Turkey. The designation of Muslim countries follows Mauldin and Berelson (1978).

[2] We employ the average age at marriage for females because data on the average age at marriage for males were missing for several countries in our sample. We repeated the analysis using both male average age at marriage and the age at marriage for both sexes for a small sample of countries. The results were virtually identical to those reported in the text.

REFERENCES

BERK, RICHARD. 1983. "An introduction to sample selection bias in sociological data." American Sociological Review 48:386–398.

BOOTH, ALAN, and JOHN N. EDWARDS. 1985. "Age at marriage and marital instability." Journal of Marriage and the Family 47:67–75.

CALDWELL, JOHN D. 1976. "Toward a restatement of demographic transition theory." Population and Development Review 2:321–366.

COLE, CHARLES, and EDWARD A. POWERS. 1973. "Industrialization and divorce: A cross-cultural analysis." International Journal of the Family 3:42–47.

DIXON, RUTH. 1971. "Explaining cross-cultural variations in age at marriage and proportions never marrying." Population Studies 25:215–233.

ENGLAND, J. LYNN, and PHILLIP R. KUNZ. 1975. "The application of age-specific rates to divorce." Journal of Marriage and the Family 37:40–46.

GOODE, WILLIAM J. 1963. World Revolution and Family Patterns. New York: Free Press.

KURIAN, GEORGE THOMAS. 1979. The Book of World Rankings. New York: Facts on File.

MAULDIN, W. PARKER, and BERNARD BERELSON. 1978. "Conditions of fertility decline in developing countries, 1965–75." Studies in Family Planning 9: 89–148.

MORGAN, S. PHILLIP, and RONALD R. RINDFUSS. 1985. "Marital disruption: Structural and temporal dimensions." American Journal of Sociology 90: 1055–1077.

NETER, JOHN, WILLIAM WASSERMAN, and MICHAEL H. KUTNER. 1983. Applied Linear Regression Models. Homewood, IL: Richard D. Irwin.

PAMPEL, FRED C., and KAZUKO TANAKA. 1986. "Economic development and female labor force participation: A reconsideration." Social Forces 64:599–619.

Population Reference Bureau. 1981. Fertility and the Status of Women Data Sheet. Washington, DC: Population Reference Bureau.

Population Reference Bureau. 1983. World Population Data Sheet. Washington, DC: Population Reference Bureau.

SEMYONOV, MOSHE. 1980. "The social context of women's labor force participation: A comparative analysis." American Journal of Sociology 86:534–550.

SHRYOCK, HENRY S., and JACOB S. SIEGEL. 1976. The Methods and Materials of Demography. New York: Academic Press.

SOUTH, SCOTT J., and GLENNA SPITZE. 1986. "Determinants of divorce over the marital life course." American Sociological Review 51:583–590.

United Nations, Department of International Economic and Social Affairs. 1982. Demographic Yearbook, 1982. New York: United Nations Publishing Service.

Discussion Questions

1. In the United States today, is the escape from an unsatisfactory marriage like the escape from slavery? When answering, consider what Clark and Arendell have to say on the topic.

2. Research suggests that both the Islamic and Catholic religions make divorce difficult, especially for women. Do all religions have this effect?

3. Are the consequences of divorce likely to be similar in India and the United States? Why, or why not?

4. Research cited by Khalidi shows that, among divorced people in Jabal el-Akhdar (Libya), nearly ninety percent of the men and fifty percent of the women have been married twice or more. (In fact, fifteen percent of surveyed men have been married four times or more!) Do you suppose these rates are higher or lower than one would have found in preindustrial Japan? How about the United States today? Explain your reasoning.

5. Pothen concludes from his study of divorce in India that, "Remarriage seems to be the best solution for the intricate problem of divorce." Why would he

think so? Would his conclusion apply as well to North America as to India? (Refer to relevant excerpts in this section when answering.)

6. In nineteenth-century America, feminists adopted the dramatic metaphor of "slavery" to force a liberalization of divorce laws. In nineteenth century Japan, there were liberal divorce laws without, apparently, any need for dramatizing women's problems. What do you make of this difference? For example, does it prove that women are, and have always been, freer in Japan than in America?

Data Collection Exercises

1. Twentieth-century Puerto Ricans (Catholic and therefore committed not to divorce) divorce at a very high rate; nineteenth-century Americans (mainly Protestant and therefore not opposed to divorce in principle) divorced at a very low rate. Find one or two other cases like these that go against what you would expect to find.

2. Arendell concludes that "despite a dramatic increase in the number of households headed by divorced women . . . , social institutions—the labor market, the legal system, public assistance and health care systems, and the . . . family itself—have not adapted to accommodate the needs of divorced women." Collect some statistical information from Libya (or another Arab country) to determine whether the situation there is the same, better, or worse.

3. Collect historical data on divorce in a Latin American country, going back to at least 1900, to find out whether the preindustrial divorce rates in that country were higher than the rates today.

4. Stephen Pearl Andrews, a nineteenth-century anarchist and free-lover, argued for more liberal divorce laws, saying "The great lesson for the world is that *human beings do not need to be taken care of*. What they do need is such conditions of justice and friendly cooperation that *they can take care of themselves*." (cited by Clark, 1990: 48) Do you agree? Collect some data to test whether this "great lesson" is true or false. (Hint: Be very clear on what the research question is before you start gathering "facts.")

Writing Exercises

1. Write a brief (five-hundred-word) essay explaining why nineteenth-century American wives were probably better off (or worse off—you choose) than twentieth-century Libyan wives.

2. Write a brief (five-hundred-word) script of an imagined encounter between Arendell, Trent, and South. Have these researchers discuss the reasons why women who work for pay are more likely than other women to get divorced.

3. The ruler of Og is a fundamentalist committed to the traditional teachings of his religion, but he also wants his people to be happy. He hires you to plan a social program for Og that would achieve three goals: (1) maintain the practice of arranged marriages; (2) reduce the demand for divorce; and (3) make people happy with their spouses. Write a brief (five-hundred-word) summary of your response to the ruler of Og.

4. Commenting on current divorce trends in Japan, Kumagai writes "A sincere attempt to improve communication between husband and wife could eventually restore the stability of the family." Referring to one or more of the excerpts in this section, write Kumagai a brief (five-hundred-word) reply.

Glossary

Cohabit (cohabitation)—A stable, sexually intimate living arrangement that is not legal marriage.

Dissolution (of a union)—The ending of a spousal (marriage or cohabiting) relationship through separation, divorce, or death.

Divorce-prone—The characteristics of a set of people who are more likely than average to divorce their mates.

Feminization (of poverty)—The impoverishment of large numbers of women; the greater likelihood that women, rather than men, will experience poverty. Single mothers and aged women are particularly likely to suffer from poverty in North America.

No-fault divorce—A type of divorce law that allows people to divorce without determining who is "at fault" in the breakdown of the marriage. California was an early jurisdiction to try this kind of law.

Polygamy—A form of marriage in which one mate (of either sex) is wedded to two or more mates of the opposite sex; polygyny is a type of polygamy, where one man is married to two or more women.

Remarriage—The legal marriage of a divorced person.

Single-parent family—a family in which one parent—usually a separated or divorced mother—lives with one or more of her children.

Suggested Readings

BETZIG, L. (1989) "Causes of conjugal dissolution: a cross-cultural study, "*Current Anthropology,* 30, 5 (December), 654–676. A cross-cultural research that argues people marry to produce descendants, not for economic or other reasons. In this context, divorce is most likely when it fails to produce (legitimate) offspring. This theory helps to explain sexual biases in the divorce laws of many societies and the reason why lower fertility is associated with less marriage and more divorce.

FURSTENBURG, FRANK. (1990) "Divorce in America." In W.R. Scott and J. Blake (eds.), *Annual*

Review of Sociology 16, pp. 379–403. A thorough, up-to-date review of divorce facts and theories in the United States by a well-known family researcher. This is the place to start looking for a review of the literature.

MOORE, MAUREEN. (1989) "Female lone-parenting over the life course," *Canadian Journal of Sociology,* 14 (3), 335–352. Using data from Canada's Family History Survey (1984), Moore traces the typical sequences that create and dissolve three kinds of female single-parent families: those formed by nonmarital childbearing, divorce, and widowhood. Many more people pass through such families, as spouses and children, than we would expect.

VAUGHAN, DIANE. (1987) *Uncoupling: How Relationships Come Apart.* New York: Vintage. A sensitive and revealing account of the steps by which marriages come apart. Central to the process is the secret imagining, then creation, of an alternate life by one of the mates. By the time the other mate catches on, it is too late to catch up. An open exchange of thoughts may not be easy, or even save all marriages; but, by this account, it is likely to make things better for everyone.

WEITZMAN, LENORE T. (1985) *The Divorce Revolution: The Unexpected Social and Economic Consequences for Women and Children in America.* New York: Free Press. A discussion of no-fault divorce in America and how it reflects our current thinking about marriage and gender equality. It reminds us that liberty, or freedom from constraint, is only half the battle; *real* freedom means having the resources (chiefly, financial) to live as one wishes. Many divorced women and children lack these resources.

PART VIII

Aging

Throughout the book demographic changes have been the backdrop against which changes in family life have played out. The most important of these changes have been declining fertility and greater longevity. Earlier sections described universal trends toward smaller families and households, more unmarried people, and more people living alone. This section focuses on the effect of these changes on the quality of life of older people.

There is a tendency in popular literature about aging to describe family life today as less supportive of older members than families in the past. It is said that geographic and occupational mobility leave little time or occasion for interaction between adults and their parents; children and their grandparents. According to Goode (1984: 58)

> The industrial system has little place for the elderly, and the neo-local, independent household with its accompanying values in favour of separate lives for each couple leaves older parents and kin in an ambiguous position. The job ceases with retirement, and neither the economy or the family has developed any secure position for such people.

Others (see Goldthorpe, 1987; Nydegger, 1983) question that industrialization brought about the change, or that extended family living would really be a better option. On the other hand few would argue that retirement presents a turning point, or that social provisions for older people are lacking.

The introduction to Part Eight is divided into three sections which include the following topics: aging trends, different approaches to care issues, and the family roles of older people.

Aging Trends

The demographic transition has been simply described as the sequential processes of falling mortality and falling fertility. During the early stages of the demographic transition death rates decline. Because more babies live to maturity, growth rates increase substantially. As fertility begins to decline, growth slows and the population begins to age. When we say societies are "aging" we really mean that the proportion of older people in the population is increasing.

European countries were the first to age, and they remain the oldest. Although most countries in Asia, South America, and Africa are still relatively young, they too, are aging rapidly. Indeed, more than half of the world's older population live in the Third World. In China, there were almost fifty million people over the age of sixty-five in 1982 and these numbers are expected to increase by at least fifty percent in the 1980s (see Excerpt 45). "China contains as many persons aged 65 and over as constitute the total populations of all but 17 countries in the world." (Goldstein and Goldstein, 1986: 180.)

When do people become old? Industrialized countries tend to define age 60 or 65 as the onset of age because this is when people typically retire from the labor force. (In Eastern Europe retirement is typically at 55 or 60. Many countries have earlier retirement ages for women.) As life expectancy increases, and people remain healthy and active well after retirement, they may not think of themselves as old until much later.

Westerners will typically become grandparents in their mid-forties, long before they retire from the labor force. And they can look forward to many active healthy years after retirement. It is actually a very small segment of the older population who need extensive care. For this reason, some analysts prefer to separate the young-old (up to age 75) from the old-old (over 75), but these categories too are problematic. Given individual differences, where do we make the cutoff? Wouldn't age 70 be as good a dividing line as age 75? If we agree with those who argue that aging is a process that begins at birth and ends with death, any cutoff points are arbitrary.

In the end, we accept chronological age as our measure because there is no better alternative—especially for cross-cultural comparisons using aggregate data.

Westerners place far more importance on awareness of chronological age than people in other societies. We literally celebrate each anniversary of our birth. Age milestones of 30, 40, and 50 have become significant occasions for celebrating. Compare this to the situation in Nigeria (see Excerpt 46). When Ekpenyong and

Peil (1985) interviewed older Nigerians, many respondents did not know their age. The researchers estimated age by the respondents' memories of past events.

One of the most interesting consistencies regarding aging is the disproportionate number of older people who are women. Universally women outlive men; most older people in the world are women. In the West, this was not always the case. For example, in Canada at the turn of the century there were more men over 65 than women.

Some analysts predict a gloomy future based on aging trends. The question of whether the relatively smaller proportion of employed people can finance the health and social needs of such a large group is echoed around the world. Countries with social-security systems in place are finding the costs prohibitive and the needs of the elderly unmet. In developing countries there are few services to support the rapidly increasing older population.

Less than a century ago, most people in Europe or North America worked until they died or became unable to work. Indeed, in an economy dominated by agriculture, there is no option for most people. It was only as more people became dependent on wages that the issue of retirement surfaced. Universal retirement did not become the norm until after the Second World War. Since life expectancy was just over 60 years at the time, relatively few people lived to benefit from the system. Now of course, people live longer and spend a much longer period "retired."

The association of age with retirement reinforces negative stereotypes of older people as nonproductive. In Excerpt 43 Covey analyzes English words to describe older people. The English language has a long history of negative descriptions of aging and the old. Some of Covey's references date to the twelfth and thirteenth centuries.

Although some people like to think that there was a time in the past when older people were treated respectfully, Covey did not find evidence of this. What he found was "consistent ambivalence," although there are more derogatory references now than there were in the past. Perhaps our association of age with a loss of productivity encourages this.

Covey found interesting differences in the words used to describe old men and old women. "Terms used for old men tend to be focused on them being old-fashioned, uncouth, conservative, feeble, stingy, incompetent, narrow-minded, eccentric, or stupid. Terms for women are focused on mysticism, bad temper, disagreeableness, spinsterhood, bossiness, unattractiveness, spitefulness, and repulsiveness." (Covey, 1988: 291.) Ironically, although women live longer than men, they are labeled old at a younger age (typically at menopause) than men.

Cross-cultural Differences in Elder Care

How to best orchestrate the care of the growing number of older people is a pressing question in most societies. In the past the relatively few who lived to a dependent old age could be cared for in their own household by family members. Those who could not rely on the family had to rely on community charity. Care of the elderly has never been wholly a family concern in the West.

For centuries the community has shouldered part of the responsibility. The early Christian church cared for the poor and needy, both old and young (Goldthorpe, 1987: 26). This tradition was born of necessity. Nuclear-family residence patterns and a high number of single people in the population meant that there were more older people in need.

In the mid-twentieth century, many industrial countries adopted policies of universality with regard to social security, pensions for those retiring from gainful employment, and health coverage. The increasing size of the populations served is now straining the systems in many countries. Many question whether we can afford such policies in the future.

The way most societies finance social security means that as populations age, proportionately more older people depend on proportionately fewer younger people. As the old-age dependency ratio (the proportion of those over 65 to those of working age) increases, a greater financial burden is placed on the working population. Expectations about retirement created during more prosperous times may be difficult to satisfy today.

Where three-generation households have been the norm, as in Southern and Eastern Europe or Asia, there is more reciprocal care giving between generations. The oldest generation provides financial help and child care when they are able, and are cared for if they become sick or infirm. In Asia, there is a strong tradition of filial piety reinforced by Confucianist and Buddhist traditions.

But changing living circumstances make it harder for families to continue to meet the needs of older members. Greater longevity, smaller family size, and the increased labor-force participation of married women mean that fewer children have longer-term responsibility for parental care.

Should the state be responsible for elder care? Can children cope with the increased demands of providing for elderly parents? Most of the excerpts in this section touch upon this issue in one way or another.

Excerpts 44 and 45 focus on two societies with strong traditions of filial piety: Korea and China. The ideal of filial piety is based on the assumption that older people deserve both respect and care. Children are taught that they should return the care they have received throughout their lives. Traditionally filial piety is generalized to all older people.

In Korea (Excerpt 44), the value of filial piety is reinforced by the mass media and by school. "Typical ideals reflected in the stories are: showing respect for parents; making physical and financial sacrifices for parents; fulfilling responsibility to parents; repayment of debts to parents; devotion to parent care; sympathy and affection for parents; deep concern for the well-being of parents; making parents happy and comfortable; and carrying out difficult or unusual tasks for parents." (Sung, 1990: 611.)

The Korean Filial Piety Prize was established to recognize exemplary instances of filial piety in practice. People can be nominated by their communities and most nominees receive recognition. As many as 380 prizes are awarded annually. Excerpt 44 is based on a content analysis of the nomination submissions. Most of the prize winners were low-income women who sacrificed both time and money to care for aging parents or in-laws.

China too, has a strong tradition of filial piety. But as Excerpt 45 shows, the success of the one-child policy makes it difficult to fulfill obligations to parents. Nevertheless children (and, indeed, grandchildren) are required by law to care for aging parents. Two only children who marry will potentially have longer-term (because of greater longevity) responsibility for four aging parents. In the past, parental responsibility was shorter term (because people did not live as long) and shared among a large number of siblings.

Yet there is no comprehensive social security system, so children are the frail elderly's only resource. The Chinese government is beginning to fill the gap by providing for the social security needs of its older citizens.

The tradition of filial piety is eroding among Asian immigrants to North America. Chen (1982) found a gradual shift in filial responsibility to health and social service providers among a cross section of Asian immigrants.

Because the West has a tradition of community support in helping to care for older people does not mean that families play an unimportant role. On the contrary, there is often much interaction between generations, particularly between mothers and daughters. Many older people are cared for by their middle-aged offspring. The term *sandwich generation* has been aptly applied to this group who juggle the needs of parents, children, spouses, and jobs.

Third World adults are much more likely now to have living parents than in the past. The absence of social services means that aging parents must look to family members for help with housing and health care needs. But smaller families mean fewer siblings to share the financial and time demands of caring for older parents. As in the West, young wives and mothers are far more apt to be gainfully employed, so are less available to provide care. These middle-aged adults also become a sandwich generation.

Housing

Many people have suggested that one solution to the care of the elderly is to replicate the past by encouraging more three-generation households. As you read in Excerpt 1 by Peter Laslett, it is a myth that people in the past lived in three-generation households. In the first place, few people lived long enough to see their grandchildren. Extended-family living, including three-generation households were never common in the West. Nor is it clear that older people (now, or in the past) necessarily want to live with their offspring. Coresidence seems to be used as a slightly more palatable alternative to institutionalization for the disadvantaged. It does not seem to be a preferred living arrangement (Roland, 1984: 81).

In a recent comparison of living arrangements of older people in Europe, Wall (1990) found that most live independently. Few (less than 10%) live in institutions and few live in three-generation households. There are more three-generation households in Southern and Eastern Europe than in Western Europe. In France, less than two percent of households are three generational. Imagine how different is the experience of growing older in Korea (Excerpt 44) where over eighty percent of elderly parents live with their children.

Australia has introduced an interesting solution to the problem of housing for the elderly. "The granny flat is a form of housing that allows elderly people and their families to live close enough to each other for the family to provide necessary services but far enough apart for privacy and separate life styles." (Lazarowich, 1990: 171.) Granny flats are portable units, about the size of a two-car garage. They contain a living room, bedroom, kitchen, and bathroom. They can be attached to the family home or not. The units are rented, and relocated when no longer wanted.

Older People and Their Families

The idea of a family life cycle is based on the assumption that we experience predictable transition points in relationships with family members as we age.

In the twentieth century, greater longevity has radically altered the timing of family related life events. In the West people marry earlier, have fewer children, and women complete childbearing at a younger age. If couples remain together their post-parenting phase will be twice as long as the time spent in active parenting. Post-parenting will also overlap with other important transition points in family and work lives: grandparenthood, retirement, widowhood, and perhaps remarriage.

Now, parents typically become grandparents in their mid-forties, and may become great-grandparents before leaving the labor force. Even though more women remain childless, most people will become great-grandparents; some will become great-great-grandparents. Four-generation families are typical and five-generation families not unusual.

The stereotyped image of the elderly is of people who are in need of care; people who have become a responsibility, if not a burden to their families. But most older people are healthy, vibrant, and independent. Many provide considerable financial and practical help to their children, particularly in times of family or job crises. Older women in Nigeria (Excerpt 46) are more apt than men to live with their adult children because they are more apt to provide needed services such as housekeeping and babysitting.

Because of sex differences in longevity and the tendency of men to marry younger women, widowhood is typically a woman's experience. Most men will live out their lives in family settings—most likely cared for by a younger, healthier spouse. Most women face old age alone.

In Nigeria, far more older men than women are married. Most Nigerian men have at least one (often considerably younger) wife. In the West, widowed men are four times more likely than widowed women to remarry. Few elderly widows remarry, simply because there are fewer similarly aged men (and it is still unusual for women to marry younger men) and most of these men are married. On the other hand, women may have less incentive to remarry. They may be exhausted by the experience of caring for an ill and dying spouse (Matthews, 1987).

For women, financial worries increasingly overshadow the positive anticipation of age. The economic consequences of sex-ratio imbalances among older people are certain. Older women face a high risk of poverty, particularly if they have had little labor-force experience.

The Jamaican women described in Excerpt 47 face the problems of widowed women everywhere. Like most married women their age, they are wholly or partially dependent on their husbands' income. Even if they are or were gainfully employed, pay differentials mean that they will experience a significant drop in standard of living without a second income. The situation in Jamaica is made worse by a voluntary pension scheme and very high rates of unemployment. So if Jamaican widows are not employed, or if they or their husbands did not contribute to the National Insurance Scheme they will not receive a pension.

The case studies in this excerpt show how precarious is the financial situation of these women. As in Nigeria, there is no comprehensive pension scheme and no universal old-age security in Jamaica. Children are an unreliable source of financial assistance. Indeed, one of the widows interviewed was providing a home for twenty-seven people. Eight were her children, seven of whom were unemployed; nine were grandchildren.

Unmarried Older People

Studies of family relationships often overlook people who do not marry and do not have children. Yet it is clearly wrong to suggest that the never married or childless do not have close family ties. Interestingly, some of the respondents in Rowland's (1982: 28) study of childfree couples in Australia expressed the concern that they did not know any elderly childfree couples, "so could not get a sense of what aging outside the family context involved."

The final paper in this section is a retrospective comparison of the family lives of women who married and lifelong single women. The sample were all born into working-class families in the early years of the century. They reached adulthood during the Depression and were in their seventies when interviewed.

The key factor in determining whether the women married, was the extent to which they were needed at home at the time other women in their age group were marrying. Most of the never-married group lived at home to help support their families. Typically, the one who stayed home was the youngest or only daughter. In short, family responsibility determined whether women married on time, married late, or never married. "Their lives were shaped by influences of historical circumstances, social class, family composition, and gender." (Allen and Pickett, 1987: 523.)

All of the women, whether married or single, had strong family feelings. "Never-married women maintained their families in a variety of roles through their relationships with ancestors, lateral kin, and younger kin. They were caretakers of parents, aunts, and uncles. They were companions and caretakers of siblings. They served as surrogate mothers to the descendants of siblings. They were also the bearers of the family history by maintaining the family heirlooms and weaving into their own life histories the stories about their ancestors." (Allen and Pickett, 1987: 524.)

Conclusions

An implicit theme of many of the excerpts in this section is the division of responsibility for dependent elderly. Is dependent care a family or a social responsibility? With universal trends to increased longevity all societies are experiencing some social pressure to provide services for the elderly. Many European countries established pension and health care programs in the postwar period. However, the increased numbers of older people, and recent economic downturns have made these provisions prohibitively expensive. Most societies cannot afford to provide adequate coverage for senior citizens.

Some societies rely on family support more than others, but universal trends towards smaller families, labor-force participation of married women, and marital disruption make this an increasingly unreliable option. As more people live longer, the number of potential related caregivers declines.

Another important theme in this chapter is the issue of ageism. Our image of older people as needy and frail is simply incorrect. Most older people are healthy and vibrant. Given current marriage and childbearing patterns in North America, you may be a great-grandparent before you retire! It is a challenge to find the middle ground in our thinking and in our social policies.

References

ALLEN, KATHERINE and ROBERT S. PICKETT. (1987) "Forgotten Streams in the Family Life Course: Utilization of Qualitative Retrospective Interviews in the Analysis of Lifelong Single Women's Family Careers," *Journal of Marriage and the Family,* 49 (August), 517–526.

CHEN, PEI (1982) "Eroding Filial Piety and Its Implications for Social Work Practice" *Journal of Sociology and Social Work,* 9, No. 2 (September), 511–523.

GOLDSTEIN, ALICE and SIDNEY GOLDSTEIN. (1986) "The Challenge of an Aging Population," *Research on Aging,* 8, No. 2, (June), 179–199.

GOLDTHORPE, J. E. (1987) *Family Life in Western Societies.* New York: Cambridge University Press.

GOODE, WILLIAM J. (1984) "Individual Investments in Family Relationships over the Coming Decades," *Tocqueville Review,* 6, No. 1, (Spring-Summer) 51–83.

LAZAROWICH, MICHAEL. (1990) "A Review of the Victoria, Australia Granny Flat Program," *The Gerontologist,* 30, No. 2, 171–177.

MATTHEWS, ANNE MARTIN. (1987) "Widowhood as an Expectable Life Event," in *Aging in Canada: Social Perspectives,* 2nd ed. Victor Marshall (ed.), Toronto: Fitzhenry and Whiteside, pp. 343–366.

NYDEGGER, CORRINE. (1983). "Family Ties of the Aged in Cross-Cultural Perspective," *The Gerontologist,* 23, No. 1, 26–32.

ROWLAND, ROBYN. (1982) "An Exploratory Study of the Childfree Lifestyle," Australia and New Zealand Journal of Sociology, 18, No. 1, 17–30.

ROWLAND, D. T. (1984) "Old Age and the Demographic Transition," *Population Studies,* 38, 73–87.

Sung, Kyu-Taik. (1990) "A New Look at Filial Piety: Ideals and Practices of Family-Centered Parent Care in Korea," *The Gerontologist,* 30, No. 5, 610–617.

Wall, Richard. (1990) "The Living Arrangements of the Elderly in Europe in the 1980s," in *Becoming and Being Old: Sociological Approaches to Later Life,* Bill Bytheway, Teresa Keil, Patricia Allatt and Alan Bryman, eds. London: Sage, pp. 121–142.

Introduction

The awareness of age, and its negative connotation have a long history in English-speaking societies. In this article Covey describes the origins of dozens of words used to refer to old age and describe older people.

References to age and aging are found as early as the twelfth and thirteenth centuries. Many words describe the physical and mental decline of age. The changing meaning of these words gives an indication of how our feelings about aging and the aged have changed over time. Although there are now more negative references to older people than in the past, there is little evidence of a simple shift from respect to denigration. There were many references to the negative aspects of aging in the past and there are many positive words widely used today.

In every age it seems, there has been some ambivalence about older people, and this ambivalence is reflected in the language. Readers may be surprised to learn that some expressions used to describe older people have been around literally for centuries. For example, the expression *no spring chicken* dates to the early eighteenth century. *Senior citizen* has been used since the sixteenth century.

The English language has a long history of distinguishing older men from older women. Most of the words used to describe older women have a negative connotation. Even the earliest references to older women were negative, possibly because of the association of women with evil and witchcraft.

43

Historical Terms Used to Describe Older People

Herbert C. Covey, PhD

. . . Over time word use has proven a good indicator of the complimentary and disrespectful perceptions about older people (Butler, 1975; Fischer, 1977; Walker, 1985). Traced and reviewed were the evolution and development of certain terms referring to older people and to old age. A preliminary source was the *Oxford English dictionary* (OED). . . .

Additional sources . . . were also used. . . .

⊃

THEMES PRESENT IN THE TERMINOLOGY OF OLD AGE AND AGING

Although this limited history of terminology restricts the conclusions that can be drawn, it is possible to propose some central themes which correspond with other research.

First, gender appears to be a critical factor in the selection of terminology for the old. The English language has a long history of separating old men from old women. . . .

Secondly, there has been considerable attention paid to the negative consequences of old age. . . .

Third, . . . as the roles of older people changed over time, so did some of the words used to characterize them. The aged became defined as useless and incapable of functioning in the rapidly changing society which helped the young to eliminate the old as competitors for work, wealth, power, sex, and other socially desired objectives. The terms used to characterize older people paralleled these perceptions.

Fourth, one message gathered from the history of terminology is ambiguity. Terms applied to old age range the full gamut of positive to negative connotations. . . .

True, the old have been venerated and honored, but only as long as their wisdom was valued and their faculties were unimpaired. When these declined, the old became the target of disrespect and ridicule (see Haber, 1983; Stone, 1977a). This duality is suggested by the coexistence of respectful and derogatory terminology found in this review. . . .

OLD

The word *old* is of Indo-European origin and is related to the word *alere* which means *to nourish*. *Old* has also carried the connotation of prolonged experience; hence it has been used to imply skill and wisdom (Shipley, 1955). . . . By the year 1205, *old* was used to denote old age, or an advanced period of life. Another term was *oldly* (1382), which was for verging on old age. Around this same period, *old* was used in conjunction with *man* to represent a man advanced in life, as in *old man. Old man* and *old woman* were used by the year 1375. . . . In American slang, *old woman*, has been used to mean wife and mother. Contemporary use of *old man* and *old woman* may have little to do with old age, but rather marital relationships, as in *my old man* representing spouse and also parental relationships.

. . . According to Stearns (1978), *old* has never been an insult by itself. When *old* has been used with other words, it has often had negative meanings. When used with other words, *Old* has

Source: Covey, Herbert C. (1988) "Historical terminology used to represent older people," *The Gerontologist*, Vol. 28, No. 3, 291–297.

also had positive meanings and has been used with affection. For example, *old* was used in names such as *Old Bright* or *Old Hickory* without negative connotation (see Demos, 1979). In 1340 it was combined with *wife* to represent an old woman. In 1530 *old* was combined with *maid* to form *old maid*, which referred to an unmarried woman well beyond the typical age of marriage. In contemporary times, *old maid* is also . . . a name for a card game in which the loser was left with the *old maid*. . . .

Other terms from the late 18th through 19th centuries were *old womanish* (1775), *old buzzard* (1800), *old coot* (1800), *olden* (1827), *old womanism* (1828), and *old stager* (1780), a British usage for an experienced person. Late 19th century usage also included such British terms as *old gang* (1870–1900) for uncompromising old men, *old guard* (1880) for aged corrupt politicians and older reactionary members of society, *old salt* for retired or experienced sailors, and *old bird* (1877) for an experienced person. Late 19th century American usages were *old goat* for an elderly unpleasant person and *old timer* for an older person. Other late 19th century terms were *old duffer* for an incompetent person, *gay old dog* for a lively older person, *old crock, old fogey, old hag, old gal* for a wife, *old folks home* for nursing home, and *oldster* (1884). Other terms . . . such as *dirty old man* and *little old lady* were and are used for older people. . . .

The word *old* has been historically associated with denotation for the devil. In American and British use, the devil is referred to as *Old Harry, Old Splitfoot, Old Nick, Old Scratch,* and the American usage *Old Sam Hill.* The reference to *Scratch* probably was derived from the Norse word for devil, *skratti* (Morris & Morris, 1977; Palmer, 1969). *Old Nick* has been linked to *St. Nick* by some and to Machiavelli by others (Morris & Morris, 1977).

During the early 20th century, unlike many of the other *old*-based words, the word *old* itself carried a negative connotation and signified contempt. Note that most earlier uses of the word *old* lacked the negative connotation under-

stood today. There is little evidence that *old* was a pejorative in early usage. Ironically, contemporary older people do not like to use the word *old* in describing themselves or their membership groups. Many of today's elderly do not think of themselves as old (Barrow & Smith, 1979). . . .

AGE AND AGED

. . . By 1440, the word *aged* came into use and took on a meaning similar to today's usage. It was used to mean having lived or existed for a long time. In 1489, *age* meant a distinct period of life. In 1509, *age* was used for the physical effects or qualities of old age, such as senility. Other related terms such as *agedly* for after the manner of an aged person, and *agedness* (1530) for the quality of being aged began to appear. *Age* was used in 1588 to mean belonging to, or characteristic of old age. Much later, in the 19th century, *ageing* or *aging* would be used. The meanings of these 19th century terms were virtually the same as their meanings today, that is, becoming aged or old. Finally, in 1968 Robert Butler coined the term *ageism* (Butler, 1975) to mean a systematic stereotyping of or discrimination against people because they are old. . . .

Among the slang phrases was *no chicken* used in the year 1720 to mean old age, and to which was later added *spring* as in *no spring chicken. Chicken* also carried the additional meaning of cowardliness. The 19th century witnessed the coining of several slang expressions for old age including *mouldy* (1864), because the heads of old people were grey like mold. *Mouldy* was also used in American slang to represent old-fashionedness and worthlessness. Some 19th century British expressions were *dodo* (1891) for an old person, *come out of the ark* for being very old, and *over the hill, dizzy age, gay old dog* for old person, and *chair days* for old age. American terms from the same period were *fossil,* college slang for an old-fashioned person or old person, *ancient* for an old person, and *fungus* for old age. Other period terms were *has-been* (1870) for older people of forgotten fame, *gummer* for loss of teeth, *to get on* for becoming old, *gaga* and *one foot in the grave* for feeble and senile older people. Early 20th century expressions included *looking around the clock* (1900), American for showing old age and *run to seed* (1903) to mean the individual was old and worn out. . . .

The word *senior* was used as a noun in 1380 to refer to a person worthy of respect because of age. . . . *Senior citizen*, which seems a relatively new expression for older people, is actually very old. In the early 16th century, it was used to mean older people. . . .

Senile was derived from the earlier terms *senilis* and *senex* for old man. In 1661 *senile* was used to mean belonging to, suited for, or incident to old age. *Senectude* (1756) and *senectitude* (1796) were used in the same sense. The related term *senility* was used in 1791 to mean a state of being senile, old, or mentally and physically infirm due to old age.

By 1823, the term *senilize* was used to mean to make or become senile. by 1848 *Senile* connoted weakness. Carole Haber (1983) noted that by the late 19th century *senility*, once merely an expression for being old, had become a term in pathology (see Achenbaum, 1985) and was used solely for age-related ailments and diseases. Earlier, *senile* did not carry negative connotations, but with the new use became increasingly negative. Old people were increasingly viewed as being feebleminded or diseased. Contemporarily, *senility* is criticized for its broad application to the old (Spicker, 1978). Spicker criticized its general use as evidence of the lack of medical effort and interest in older people. . . .

In antiquity, *gera* and *geron*, from which the word *gerontology* is derived, referred to those of great age who for some reason were afforded respect and honor. The words referred to the privileges of age and the rights of seniority. *Gerocomical* or *geroncomy* was used by J. Smith in 1666 to refer to the treatment of the aged. It was based on the Greek *geras*, for old age, and *komia* for tending (Shipley, 1955). Several other related terms such as *gerontocracy* (1836) and *gerontar-*

chial (1884), for government by old men, and *gerontic* for of, or pertaining to, old age came into use later. In 1909, Nascher used the term *geriatrics* in a medical publication (see Achenbaum, 1974; Haber, 1983). According to Morris & Morris (1977), *geriatrics* refers to the study of the problems of aging people.

WORDS RELATED TO FAMILY RELATIONS

. . . *Grandparents, grandfather, grandmother,* and related terms describing the parents of parents can be traced back to the early 13th century. The oldest form of these words related to *grand* are *grandame* and *grandsire*, the former being traced back to 1225. *Grandame* was later (1550) used to mean an old woman who was a gossip. *Grandsire* and *grandame* developed new meaning by the end of the 16th century. In 1596 *grandsire* was used for a man of grandparental age or an old man. In 1620 *grandame* was used to refer to a descendant of Eve. About this same period *grandchildren* came into use along with *grandson* (1586) and *grandchild* (1587). . . .

In 1663, Dryden used an expression similar to *granny* or *grannie*, in a contemptuous manner to denote grandmother. *Granny* was also used at that time to mean an old woman who was a gossip. In 1794 *granny* came to mean a nurse or midwife. *Granny* was also used through the mid-nineteenth century to refer to a *weak old man* (Achenbaum, 1978). In contemporary use, *granny* refers solely to old women and not to old men.

Other forms of or modifications to *grandmother* were *grandmamma* (1763), *grandma*, and *grandmammy*. In the 18th century, *beldam* also meant grandmother, but later developed a meaning similar to *hag* (Fischer, 1977). A late 19th century British expression *teach one's grandmother to suck eggs*, meant to give advice to an older, wiser person in their area of expertise. Older peoples' expertise based on experience has been acknowledged and appreciated, as long as it was not perceived as old-fashioned or impeding progress.

Grandfather also took on various forms. Some of them were colloquial substitutes for *grandfather*, such as *grandada* and *grandaddy* (1698), *grandpapa* (1753), *grandpa*, *grandpappy*, an Americanism, and *granddad* (1819), an affectionate term for *grandfather*. By the 19th century, other forms of *grandfather* and *grandmother* appeared. Some of these forms were *grandparent* (1830), *grandmotherhood* (1846), *grandmotherly* (1846), and *grandparental* (1844). Not all terms were complimentary, as *granny* was used in 1887 to mean a stupid old woman. *Gramps* has also been used, possibly since the 19th century, with negative connotations but also, at times, with affection. . . .

OF OLD WOMEN

The bulk of words associated with older women have had a decisively negative bias. This tradition of negativism occurred much earlier in the English language for old women than for old men. One of the oldest non-slang expressions, with Greek and Egyptian origin is *hag*. In its Greek form, *hagia*, *hag* originally meant a *holy one* (Walker, 1985). The word *hag* was used in Greek and Roman mythology. Following its early religious and honorific use, the word evolved into a negative term similar to witch. . . . By 1337, *hag* meant an ugly, repulsive old woman. Two centuries later the word referred to ghosts and spirits (1538). During the mid-fifteen hundreds, the word was used to represent a female demon. About the same time, it connoted a woman with dealings with Satan, or a witch. This development corresponded with the witch hunts of the 15th and 16th centuries. Finally, by 1632, the word was used to mean a nightmare. . . .

Crone is another non-slang word with meanings and applications similar to *hag*. Neither word is commonly used in contemporary society but each was used in the past. In 1388, Wyclif used the term, without negative connotation, to refer to a woman of advanced years, but Chaucer, 2 years earlier, used it negatively to refer to a wicked old woman. In the middle of the 17th century, *crone* was used as meaning an old, worn-out man. Generally its meaning has run parallel to that of *hag* and *witch*. *Crone* does have additional meanings related to spiritual power, authority, death, childbirth, and wisdom (Walker, 1983; 1985). In contemporary society *crone* is little used, but a related word, *crony*, is used. Used by Pepys in (1665) to refer to an intimate friend or associate, it now is used with *old* to form *old crony*. In general, British use of *crony* refers to friend or long-time and trusted companion of either sex.

. . . The 18th and 19th centuries used several words and expressions for old women. Examples of British slang and expressions were *old trout*, for disagreeable old woman, *fairy* for a debauched, hideous old woman, *harridan*, possibly derived from *harried*, meaning a worn-out, withered old woman, *goose berry pudden* (1859) for old woman or wife, *tea bottle*, middle-class usage for *old maids* and their usual drink, and *tabby* or *tabs*, theatrical terms for old, aging women. This latter term was based on a strong association of old women and cats in the 18th and 19th centuries, and later was extended to all women in the 20th century. Around 1900 *Cat* was also used in British slang to mean a spiteful woman. *Old hen* was an Americanism for an old, disagreeable woman. For a period in the late 19th and early 20th centuries the British used the slang expressions of *delo namow* for old woman and *delo diam* for old maid. These were simply words spelled backward. *Bag* has not only meant to capture, but also means an unattractive and disagreeable woman past her prime, as in *old bag*. *Quail* (1920's) was American for old women viewed as easy marks by tramps. In contemporary times, most of these words and expressions have been replaced with new ones, such as *old bitch*, *old biddy*, *old crow*, and *old cow*.

OF OLD MEN

As with old women, old men have also been subjected to unkind names and expressions. In 1386 the word *grey* was used by Chaucer to refer to an old man. It is thought that the use of *grey* was due to changes in the physical appearance of the old. . . . *Baldhead* (1565) was a pejorative for old man and in 1575 *gaffer* was used for old man. . . .

In 1704 the word *presbyte* was used to mean old man. *Codger* was used as a friendly British term of address (1760) and, in 1796, was used to refer to a stingy, mean old man. In British usage *codger* also meant companion. But in American slang *codger* was also used to mean an old fellow or peculiar person.

A 19th century expression for old men was *gramps*, which may or may not have referred to a grandfather. In contemporary use, *gramps* is most likely to be used contemptuously. Some 19th century British terms were *pigtail* (1840) for an old man wearing his hair in 18th century fashion, *scarecrow* and *ally sloper* (1870) for a dissipated old man with a swollen nose, *old wigsby* for a crotchety, narrow-minded, and elderly man who sees no good in modern things, and *buffer* for an incompetent and old-fashioned old man. Americanisms were *druid* for old man and *galoot* for an uncouth old man. Other terms were *old cornstalk* (1824) for an ineffectual old man, *griffin* (1840) for an elderly and unattractive chaperone of either sex, and *pops* (1884).

Yet other British terms were *old put* for a pretentious, stupid, but gentlemanly old man, *buffer* (1870) for any man, but when combined with *old* meant elderly man and which was often used in friendly contempt to imply incompetence and old-fashionedness. The British also used *old moustache* (1880) for a vigorous, mustachioed old man, *old bean* for old man, *old goat* for a disliked old man, and *gummer* for a toothless old man. *Baldy* (1820) was an Americanism for old man, as was *poppy guy*. A common term for old men was *geezer* when used with *old*. . . . The British used *bits of grey* (1880) to denote single old men, and sometimes old women, at dances or weddings and *delo namo* (19th century) for old man. Americans used *father-time, bottle-nose* (1900) a scornful focus on old men's noses. *Gink* meant an old eccentric and *fuddy-duddy* an old-fashioned and unimaginative person. By the

20th century, *sugar daddy* (1918), American for an old man who buys gifts for young women to gain sexual favors . . . came into use.

The word *fogey* appeared in 1780 and referred to someone with antiquated notions. According to Phythian (1976), the British use the word to refer to a person with old-fashioned or fixed tastes, views, and attitudes. In addition, in its early form it referred to old, backward fellows. About the same time, *fogey* came to be used for invalid soldiers. A half-century later related terms such as *fogyism* (1839), *fogydom* (1859), and *fogyish* (1873) appeared. As slang, the word was used contemporaneously to mean military peacetime service. By the mid-19th century, *foozle* (1850) and *fossil*, developed negative connotations in reference to old men. . . .

CONCLUSION

. . . The perceptions about aging and about the old implicit in this evolution in terminology have definite patterns. One such pattern is the decline in status of the elderly and the increased focus on the debilitative effects of aging. It is suggested by the results of this review that perceptions of the old, as reflected in terminology, depend on other factors. As Haber (1983) and others (see Gratton, 1985; Laslett, 1976; Van Tassel & Stearns, 1986) have observed, other socio-economic factors than age play critical roles in determining status in the community. . . .

REFERENCES

ACHENBAUM, W. A. (1974). The obsolescence of old age in America, 1865–1914. *Journal of Social History*, 8, 45–64.

ACHENBAUM, W. A. (1978). From womb through bloom to tomb: The birth of a new area of historical research. *Review in American History*, 6, 178–183.

ACHENBAUM, W. A. (1985). Societal perceptions of aging and the aged. In R. Binstock & E. Shanas

(Eds.), *Handbook of aging and the social sciences.* New York: Van Nostrand Reinhold.

BARROW, G., & SMITH, P. (1979). *Aging, ageism, and society.* St. Paul, MN: West.

BUTLER, R. (1975). *Why survive? Being old in America.* New York: Harper and Row.

DEMOS, J. (1979). Old age in early New England. In D. Van Tassel (Ed.), *Aging, death, and the completion of being.* Case Western Reserve University of Pennsylvania Press.

FISCHER, D. (1977). Growing old: An exchange. *The New York Review of Books, 24,* 47–49.

GOODY, J. (1976). Aging in Nonindustrial societies. In R. Binstock & E. Shanas (Eds.), *Handbook of aging and the social sciences.* New York: Van Nostrand Reinhold.

GRATTON, B. (1985). *Urban elders: Family, work and welfare among Boston's aged, 1890–1950.* Philadelphia: Temple University Press.

HABER, C. (1983). *Beyond sixty-five: The dilemma of old age in America's past.* Cambridge: University Press.

LASLETT, P. (1976). Societal development and aging. In R. Binstock & E. Shanas (Eds.), *Handbook of aging and the social sciences.* New York: Van Nostrand Reinhold.

MORRIS, W., & MORRIS, M. (1977). *Morris dictionary of word and phrase origins.* New York: Harper and Row.

Oxfoard English Dictionary. (1933). Oxford: Clarendon Press.

PALMER, A. S. (1969). (1882), *Folk-Etymology.* New York: Haskell House.

PHYTHIAN, B. (1976). *A Concise dictionary of English slang and colloquialisms.* London: Hodder and Stoughton.

SHIPLEY, J. T. (1955). *Dictionary of early English.* New York: Philosophy Library.

SMITH, S. R. (1976). Growing old in early Stuart England, *Albion, 8,* 125–141.

SPICKER, S. F. (1978). Gerontogenetic mentation: Memory, dementia, and medicine in the penultimate years. In S. F. Spicker, K. M. Woodward, & D. D. Van Tassel (Eds.), *Aging and the elderly: Humanistic perspectives in gerontology.* Atlantic Highlands, NJ: Humanities Press.

STEARNS, P. N. (1978). Toward historical gerontology. *Journal of Interdisciplinary History, 8,* 737–746.

STONE, L. (1977a). Walking over grandma. *The New York Review of Books, 24,* 26–29.

VAN TASSEL, D., & STEARNS, P. (Eds.) (1986). *Old age in a bureaucratic society: The elderly, the experts, and the state in American history.* New York: Greenwood Press.

WALKER, B. (1983). *The woman's encyclopedia of myths and secrets.* San Francisco: Harper & Row.

WALKER, B. (1985). *The crone: Woman of age, wisdom and power.* San Francisco: Harper and Row.

WENTWORTH, H., & FLEXNER, S. (1968). *Dictionary of American slang.* New York: Pocket Book.

Introduction

Filial piety is an important value in Korea, as in other East Asian countries. Children are taught from an early age to accept the responsibility of caring for their parents in old age. About eighty percent of elderly Korean parents live with one of their children. In Europe and America, three-generation households are far less common, and it is far more common for elderly people to live alone.

In Korea, responsibilities to parents (spelled out in Confucianist teachings) continue as a social ideal despite internal changes in the family. Since most care givers are daughters, elder care in Korea will presumably be affected by increased labor-force participation of married women. What does filial piety mean in practice?

To reinforce filial responsibility, the Korean government awards Filial Piety Prizes to people who demonstrate particularly exemplary behavior. Hundreds of prizes are given annually to candidates nominated by their communities. This article analyzes the background stories provided about nominees to see how filial piety is practiced now.

Most of the prize recipients were low-income women who provided personal care to infirm parents. They did so because of respect for their parents, and because they felt it was their responsibility. Children of the award winners echoed the attitudes of their parents, which, as the author points out, shows the importance of socialization in developing filial attitudes among children.

44
Filial Piety and Care of the Old in Korea

Kyu-taik Sung, PhD

In recent years, national efforts in Korea to preserve the traditional values associated with the care of elderly people have been made under joint public and private auspices. The . . . "Filial Piety Prize System" is an example of such efforts.

The moral ideal underlying the drive to establish such social institutions is that elderly people should be respected and cared for as they are the ones who suffered to raise a new generation and who contributed to their family and society in past years. It is thus felt that when parents . . . can no longer take care of themselves . . . they should be cared for by those whom they themselves have raised. . . .

In recent years, the forms of respect for the aged have slowly been changing in these nations, including Korea, as the female labor market expands, multi-generation households decrease, and the young tend to emphasize an individualistic life style (Korean Institute for Population and Health, 1985). However, . . . in Korea respect for the aged has strong roots in the nation's culture and the values based on filial piety have not yet been undermined (Park, 1983a; Lee, 1985). . . .

What then is the de facto interpretation of

Source: Sung, Jyu-taik (1990) "A new look at filial piety: Ideals and practices of family-centered parent care in Korea," The Gerontologist, Vol. 30, No. 5, 610–617.

filial piety by Koreans today? Specifically, what are the kinds of care and services that filial persons should provide their elderly parents? What motives lie behind filial conduct? What should be emphasized most often in parent care, and what are the consequences of such practices? How does one carry out filial duties in relation to other family members? And finally, is there an ideal form of filial piety toward which Koreans are aspiring?

This study was conducted to answer these questions based on data about Koreans who have exemplified filial piety and have been awarded the Filial Piety Prize (Korean Institute of Gerontology, 1986). . . .

THE PRIZE AND THE STORY

The Filial Piety Prize . . . was established in 1973 and is maintained by the Ministry of Health and Social Affairs of the Korean government. The prize is awarded as one of the major events of the "Respect for the Elderly Week," held in May each year. The nomination of prize recipients takes place nationwide. Nominees are recommended to the Bureau of Family Welfare of the Ministry of Health and Social Affairs during the year preceding the award. . . . A committee appointed by the ministry reviews the nominees, but almost all of them receive a prize.

Through this process, the ministry has been awarding the prize to 150–380 filial persons annually. . . .

STUDY METHOD

The sample for this study consisted of 817 filial persons . . . selected at random from about 2,000 persons who received the prize . . . during a 10-year period (1975–1985). . . .

In the first phase, the contents of the stories of the 817 persons . . . were analyzed. The stories were compiled by the Korean Institute of Gerontology (1986). Each story illustrates the pious conduct of the winner of the Prize (hereafter called a "filial person"). The content analysis method, appropriate to the analysis of such unstructured material (Denzin, 1970; Altheide, 1987), was applied by 10 social work graduate students. . . .

In the second phase . . . 130 persons were selected at random out of the 817 filial persons. A 56-item questionnaire was sent to them to obtain their direct responses to important findings from the first phase; 106 responded. . . . The findings from the content analysis were validated by the findings from the questionnaire survey.

ANALYSIS AND FINDINGS

Social Characteristics

Of the 817 filial persons . . . in the first phase, 67% were female; 51% had less than 9 years of schooling, 22% had completed high school, and 16% had college degrees. The standard of living of 62% of them was fairly low to low. In terms of occupation, 35% were housewives, 21% farmers, 9% laborers,and 35% "other." The average length of time of the filial service to parents for

which they had been nominated for the prize was 12 years.

Of the parents served by the filial persons, 65% were female and 79% were 59 years or older. The majority (65%) had lost their spouse. Almost all (93%) were members of the filial persons' families. Parents-in-law (mother-in-law, 42%; father-in-law, 34%; some of these were couples) numbered more than parents (mother, 37%; father, 25%; some were couples). The number of the filial persons who served grandparents was small (5%). A bare majority of nominees (53%) served two or three elderly persons, whereas 47% . . . served one elderly person.

Care and Services Provided

. . . The 29 types of care and services provided to parents can be grouped into: personal care for parents (18 types); support for the family (six types); and services for the community (five types).

Personal care and services might further be classified into three tiers: primary services (e.g., housekeeping services, laundry work, serving meals, giving baths, caring for incontinent parents, nursing care); secondary services (e.g., accompanying on outings, carrying one's parents, respecting parent's wishes, providing pocket money); tertiary services (e.g., reading books, engaging in conversation, providing educational opportunities). . . .

All 29 types of service required both "feeling concern" and "performance of services."

Relationships between Filial Persons and Others

About 71% of the filial persons had unidirectional relationships with their parents, wherein the dominant flow of aid went from the adult child to the parent. The rest (29%) had reciprocal relationships with the parents, . . . wherein both sides supported each other as need and opportunity dictated. The parents reacted to the filial children gratefully, with sympathy, and by repayment. Support from parents usually consisted of babysitting, housework, providing information and advice, moral support, and financial aid.

Spouses of the filial persons were cooperative and sympathetic with their spouses. There were a few cases, however, in which the filial person was deserted by his wife. To relatives, the filial persons extended support in the form of visits, caring, living together, and material support. And to neighbors they paid respect, kept friendly relations, and provided services. Thus, filial piety covered . . . activities beyond the family unit. Up to 50% of the filial persons . . . maintained helping relations with their relatives and neighbors.

Motives for Filial Piety

. . . Motives were compared based on the frequency with which they were cited . . . Respect for parents stood out among all other motives, which was followed by filial responsibility. (Respect was indicated by: treating the parent with unusual deference and courtesy, showing exceptionally earnest and sincere consideration for the parent, showing extraordinary honor and esteem for parent. Filial responsibility was shown by: delaying marriage or education or withdrawing from social activities to be fully devoted to parent care; giving pious care to a parent-in-law after the death of one's husband or to a mother after the death of a father; supporting a large family along with an aged parent.) Family harmony emerged as the third most outstanding motive, and filial self-sacrifice the fourth. In order, these are followed by desire to repay, family continuity, filial sympathy, community harmony, compensation, religious belief, and lastly, saving family face.

To determine whether the motives for filial piety varied by social characteristics, an analysis was performed. The results did not reveal any

statistically significant predictor of the motives. . . .

To explore the underlying dimensions of the filial motives, a . . . factor analysis of the motives was conducted based on the questionnaire responses. . . . Three factors were extracted. . . . The motives for filial piety . . . have three dimensions: value commitment, service commitment, and emotional commitment.

Emphasis Given in Performing Parent Care

. . . Of the eight types of emphases given by the filial persons in carrying out their filial duties, . . . four are related to direct care for parents, two are about maintaining the family, and the rest concern services to the neighborhood. Findings suggest a greater emphasis was likely to be given to filial duties by those who had a lower standard of living, a lower education level, and a larger family.

Consequences of Filial Piety

Table 1 shows eight types of rewards and their rankings based on percentage sizes. . . . High rankings were given to harmonized family relations, award of a prize or letter of recognition, and praise from neighbors. These were followed by pious treatment by own children, so-

TABLE 1. Consequences of Filial Piety

Type of Consequence	1st Phase[a] (N = 817)	
	Ranking	%
Harmonized family relations	3	26
Award of prize/letter	2	36
Praise from neighbors	1	76
Filial piety by own children	6	6
Providing education to children	—	—
Recognition from society	4	23
Recovery of parents	—	—
Satisfactory family life	5	17

[a]Ranking based on the percentage.

cial recognition, and satisfactory family life. In return for their filial piety, the filial persons were rewarded with these . . . results. . . .

Sacrifice Endured for Parents

Three types of sacrifice—physical, financial, and social sacrifice—were identified. . . . Physical sacrifice ranks first in terms of the extent of sacrifice. *Physical sacrifice* means providing care through hard work, disregarding one's own comfort and good life. *Financial sacrifice* was determined from such acts as paying for medicine for parents without regard for one's own material needs. *Social sacrifice* was determined from the quitting of a job or loss of it, or missing a normal social life due to the time given to parent care. . . . Filial persons who were women and of a lower standard of living were more likely to endure greater sacrifices.

SUMMARY AND DISCUSSION

. . . Women were the major source of filial care (see also Choi, 1983; Waerness & Ringen, 1987). Sons provided emotional and financial support and resources outside the family, but they were less likely to help with instrumental, hands-on services. . . .

The filial persons were involved in . . . interpersonal relationships with elderly parents and others in the family support network (see also Sung & Park, 1988; Shanas, 1979). Obviously, the extent of filial piety was contingent upon positive interpersonal relationships between family members.

In Korea, 80% or more of elderly parents live with their children. . . . (Sung & Kim, 1988). Throughout the history of Korea, it has been a preferred cultural pattern for elderly parents and adult children to live together. . . . A family-centered practice of filial piety for one's own parents was often extended to the neighborhood and the community as a whole.

Respect for parents emerged as the most outstanding motive for filial piety. In the traditional and contemporary teaching of filial piety, respect for one's parents is the point most frequently mentioned and stressed. The next outstanding motive was filial responsibility or the responsibility of children for parent care. This finding has implications for social policy as well as for individual and family adjustment, . . . in terms of reinforcing adult children's obligation to care for and support their needy parents (Schorr, 1960; Seelbach & Sauer, 1977; Kosberg, 1986; Blust & Scheidt, 1988). . . .

The majority of the prize-winning filial persons were low-income people. The more affluent must practice filial piety as well, but their practice was less visible and was perhaps not so publicly praiseworthy because they could more easily provide such care without . . . as much sacrifice. . . . The critical factors that bring a filial person to social recognition would then be sacrifice and a sense of responsibility, which transcended the threshold of ordinary people.

The filial persons gave emphasis to the harmony of the family. Family harmony implies combining members of a family into an orderly whole whereby agreement in feeling, action, and interest can be attained. . . .

Rewards received by the filial persons were mostly psychological. Overwhelmingly, the filial persons felt that their filial piety resulted in the stabilization of the family and social recognition of their pious conduct. Impressively, their own children, who had learned how one should treat parents, acted the same to the filial persons. This suggests the importance of socialization for the development of filial attitudes. . . .

Categories for filial motives include: respect for parent, filial responsibility, harmonizing the family, and filial sacrifice. Categories for emphases given are: Harmonizing family for parent care, making sacrifice for the parent, and filial piety in the midst of poverty. These categories may . . . be reduced to four fundamental dimensions . . . : "respect," "responsibility," "family harmony,"and "sacrifice."

In short, *by putting their household in order, the filial persons cared for their parents with respect and responsibility while making sacrifices for their parents.* The four . . . dimensions above would thus seem to portray the ideal form of filial piety.

REFERENCES

ALTHEIDE, D. L. (1987). Reflections: Ethnographic content analysis. *Qualitative Sociology, 10,* 65–77.

BLUST, E. P. N., & SCHEIDT, R. I. (1988). Perceptions of filial responsibility by elderly Filipino widows and their primary caregivers. *International Journal of Aging and Human Development, 26,* 91–106.

CHOI, S. D. (1983). The elderly and the family. In *Modern society and the welfare of the aged [Hyundai Sahoe-wa Noin Bokji]* (pp. 229–241). Seoul: The Asian Social Welfare Foundation.

DENZIN, N. K. (1970). *The research act: A theoretical introduction to sociological methods* (pp. 219–259). Chicago: Aldine.

KOREAN INSTITUTE of POPULATION and HEALTH (1985). *A study on the aged population of Korea [Hankook Noin-Inkoo-ae kwanhan Yunkoo].* Seoul: Korean Institute for Population and Health.

KOREAN INSTITUTE of GERONTOLOGY (1986). *Documentaries of filial piety in Korea [Hankook Hyo-haeng Sil-lok].* Seoul: The Korean Institute of Gerontology.

KOSBERG, J. I. (1986, May). Family care of the aged in the United States. In *Social service and aging policies* (pp. 98–103). Taipei Conference, International Exchange Center on Gerontology at the University of South Florida, A Multi-University Consortium.

LEE, W. J. (1985). The ideal of filial piety and respect for elders in the traditional Korean society. In *Aging and welfare for the aged: Cross-cultural evaluation.* Daegu, Korea: Yungnam University and The University of Michigan.

PARK, C. H. (1983a). Historical review of Korean Confucianism. In *Main currents of Korean thoughts. The Korean National Commission for UNESCO.* Seoul: The Si-Sa-Yong-O-Sa.

SCHORR A. L. (1960, June). *Filial responsibility in the modern American family.* Washington, DC: Social Security Administration, U.S. Department of Health, Education, and Welfare.

SEELBACH, W. C., & SAUER, W. J. (1977). Filial responsibility expectations and morale among aged parents. *The Gerontologist, 17,* 492–499.

SHANAS, E. (1979). The family as a social support system in old age. *The Gerontologist, 19,* 169–174.

SUNG, K. T., & KIM, G. S. (1988). A study on the well-being of the elderly. *Journal of Korea Gerontological Society, 8,* 69–88.

SUNG, K. T., & PARK, Y. R. (1988). Study of social support networks of the elderly in Korea. *Social Welfare [Sahoe Bakjil], 34,* 16–47.

Introduction

China is the most populated country in the world. While the index of aging (the proportion of those over 65 to those under 65) is less in China than in many other countries, a large percentage of the world's elderly live in China. There are more older people in China than the total population of most countries. Only seventeen countries in the world have more people than China has older people!

China's one-child policy has effectively reduced the number of Chinese children born. However, because of very high birth rates in the 60s and 70s in China, it will be some years before the population will reach its peak and begin to shrink. During this period, which will last until the beginning of the twenty-first century, the number of older people will increase to four or five times their present number. Clearly, planning for such an increase is a monumental task in both practical and financial terms.

Part of the difficulty in China is that the policies to control fertility and to accommodate the needs of a planned economy, challenge what were once strong traditions of filial responsibility. In the past, older Chinese people could expect support from their children and grandchildren. Such an expectation works well in a society where families are large and there is little geographical mobility. When the majority of children are only children, and where job placement may be far from the parental home, the burden is far greater. When two only children marry, they face the eventual responsibility of four older people.

While the government is beginning to provide economic security programs including pensions, these are in the very early stages of development.

45

Meeting the Challenge of an Aging Population in China

Alice Goldstein
Sidney Goldstein

. . . China's current population policy envisages an eventual stable population of about 700 million. Before then, if the one-child family policy is fully successful, the population is expected to reach a peak of 1.2 billion by 2010. It is projected to fall below 1.2 billion only by 2040. Until then, the large cohorts already born will move through the age hierarchy to swell the absolute number of aged persons. Because of concurrent reductions in the number of births, the aged proportion of the total will also rise. . . .

◐

THE TRADITIONAL AND LEGAL POSITIONS OF THE AGED

The aging of China's population must be considered within the context of the traditional position of the elderly in Chinese society, a position

Author's Note: This research was carried out in China during March-May 1983. It is based primarily on discussions and interviews with officials, policymakers, and scholars and on observations during visits to various urban and rural locations. The research was funded by an Award for Advanced Study and Research from the Committee on Scholarly Communication with the People's Republic of China of the National Academy of Science. . . .

. . . that in many respects remains today. In the traditional Chinese family . . . the aged held particularly high status (Yang, 1965). Such a position is understandable in a primarily illiterate society where experience rather than formal education is the main source of knowledge. . . .

The communist ideology promulgated since . . . 1949 has had considerable influence on these traditional attitudes. . . . Because the young formed a dynamic element in the establishment of the new regime and in spreading its doctrines and policies, young people assumed roles of political importance. Furthermore, a stress on the capacity of all Chinese to be productive implies the young are to be as respected as the old. This attitude was emphasized by the restructuring of the work unit in rural areas under the commune system, which deemphasized the family as the basic unit of production and thereby also weakened the position of its older members. In urban areas, where education and modern technology became . . . widespread, the

Source: Goldstein, A. and S. Goldstein (1986) "The challenge of an aging population: The case of the People's Republic of China," *Research on Aging*, 8, 2, June, 179–199.

young also held an advantage. Nonetheless, although they no longer exercise authoritarian power within the family, the elderly continue to command a high degree of respect (Tien, 1977), and the traditional patterns of interdependence between generations have been largely maintained (Davis-Friedmann, 1983).

Legally, the position of the aged is defined by the Constitution of 1982 (Chinese Documents, 1983: 27): "Children who have come of age have the duty to support and assist their parents." The Marriage Law of 1980 . . . goes further to stipulate, "When children fail to perform the duty of supporting their parents, parents who have lost the ability to work or have difficulties in providing for themselves have the right to demand that their children pay for their support" (Beijing Review, 1981a). The Marriage Law even carries the burden of support to the next generation; grandchildren are also enjoined to support grandparents if the parents have died. Failure to meet these obligations is punishable under China's Criminal Code (Beijing Review, 1981b: 23). . . .

China is clearly attempting to reinforce and take advantage of the traditional obligations of children toward their parents. . . . In the absence of any national social security system, such support is undoubtedly seen as especially essential in rural areas, where 80% of China's population lives. The provisions therefore shift the primary burden of support onto the family rather than onto the government, the commune, or the work unit. . . .

POLICIES INDIRECTLY AFFECTING THE AGED

The One-Child Family Policy

. . . China's one-child family policy not only subverts traditional values favoring large families, but . . . jeopardizes the system of social security that depends on children's support of elderly parents. The problem is exacerbated by the still widespread custom of patrilocal residence after marriage. A couple, especially in rural areas, whose one child is a daughter can likely look forward to an old age without grandchildren or a child close by. . . .

The one-child policy is also eroding one of the traditional roles of the elderly—that of child care. Even if grandparents live in the same place with their offspring, they will have a few grandchildren to care for. . . .

Moreover, although children are supposed to care for their parents, it is difficult to assess either how adequate such care is or how much of a strain it places on the younger persons. If one couple must support four elderly people . . . the costs may be excessive (Du, 1984). . . .

Job Assignment Policies

. . . Upon graduation from secondary schools or universities, students are . . . assigned jobs wherever the government believes they are needed. Although a majority may be placed close to their family homes, many are not. . . . The situation may be particularly acute if rural-born youth are given urban job assignments . . . as China's strict policies to control urban growth generally preclude other family members from joining the urban resident. Therefore, even if an aging couple has . . . children, these children may be in distant places and unable to provide the physical or psychological support older persons need. . . .

The New Economic Responsibility System

In rural areas, the . . . individual responsibility system has placed a premium on intensive labor in the fields, so as to produce surplus crops that individual families can sell. Such . . . hard work is likely to bypass the aged who no longer have the stamina to spend long hours in the field. . . . In addition, the proliferation of small-scale light industry, which is also . . . part of the new economic development, is geared to the absorption of the younger segments of the rural population. . . .

A third aspect of the . . . responsibility system does, however, offer opportunities for the elderly. The system . . . encourages the cultivation of private plots and private raising of livestock. Produce from such enterprise can be sold in the . . . free markets. . . . Such enterprise has traditionally occupied elderly peasants and has helped to contribute to household income (Davis-Friedmann, 1983: 16–22). . . .

PROGRAMS FOR THE ELDERLY

Retirement Policies

China's retirement policies, although designed to apply to the rural as well as urban population, are adhered to more in urban places. As a result, relatively more individuals fall into the "aged" . . . category in cities and towns than in the countryside. Male factory workers and cadres retire at age 60; female workers and cadres at age 55, unless they are engaged in heavy work, in which case they retire at 50. Intellectuals and cadres may . . . work up to age 65. . . .

Among nonagricultural workers, a child may take over the job of a parent upon the parent's retirement. With about 4 million urban young people entering the labor force ages annually, a labor surplus exists. . . . Most young people can expect to wait a year after graduating . . . before receiving an assigned job. They can avoid such a delay if a parent retires and the child thereby "inherits" the job. Considerable . . . pressure may, as a result, be exerted by the young on parents in their early 50s to retire . . . earlier than necessary under law. The pressure is especially great for mothers to do so. . . .

The Childless Elderly

. . . The childless elderly . . . have been promised "Five Guarantees"; food, clothing, medical care, housing, and burial expenses (Beijing Review, 1984). Rural brigades that are developing retirement policies may provide extra services to the childless. Such policies are designed not only in recognition of the particular needs of the childless aged, but to prove that having only one child need not lead to misery in old age. The press now often reports how young people organize themselves to help the childless elderly—doing household chores, shopping, running errands, or just visiting (e.g., Beijing Review, 1982b; Jian, 1983). In addition, some administrative units (such as municipalities or provinces) now provide old age homes for those without children or close relatives. . . .

Pension Systems

. . . Formal retirement programs or facilities specifically for the rural aged are rare, but a few brigades have rudimentary pension systems. . . .

Moreover, production-team-sponsored retirement plans are likely to undergo change because of institution of the responsibility system. Under this new system, individual families negotiate directly with the brigade for the amount of cultivation to be undertaken and are responsible directly to the brigade for delivery of their crop quotas. The production team has thereby had its functions and sources of income curtailed, and programs for social welfare are becoming the responsibility of the brigade or commune (see Beijing Review, 1982b). . . .

For urban residents, a more widespread pension system is in place. According to the Constitution, "The state prescribes by law the system of retirement for workers and staff in enterprises and undertakings and for functionaries of organs of state. The livelihood of retired personnel is ensured by the state and society" (Chinese Documents, 1983: 26). This provision translates, in part, into pension systems developed and administered by individual factories or work units. . . .

Other Programs for the Aged

The . . . urban aged who are not eligible for pensions . . . fall primarily into two groups: (1) those who left the labor force before a pension system was instituted by their work units or after having worked for less than 10 years in a unit with a pension system; and (2) those—mainly women—who never were members of the labor force. As indicated above in principle, and as mandated by the Constitution, these aged are to be cared for by their children. . . . Only the childless aged become the state's responsibility. Figures released by the State Labor Bureau (Beijing Review, 1981b) suggest only about 45% of urbanites above retirement age are covered by pension systems. . . .

The state also recognizes the need to supplement income for persons not eligible for pensions and . . . allows such individuals to engage in small-scale private enterprise. This most often involves setting up a stand for the sale of clothing or small dry goods. . . .

Licenses for such stalls are typically issued by the city's Industrial and Commercial Bureau for a one-time fee of Y5. . . . Only persons without employment in the formal sector, or support from that sector in the form of pensions, can apply. . . .

With the advent of springtime in China, still another segment of the elderly population enters the informal sector, as ice cream (popsicle) vendors appear on almost every street corner. Most commonly older women, the vendors are licensed by the city and buy their products from state shops. . . .

Such economic avenues for older people with no direct, official support have met several important needs. Not only do they provide some income for the elderly, but the variety of merchandise made available thereby to the masses also fills a need for more color and variety in consumer goods. . . .

Several other ways have been found to utilize the elderly population. . . . Older men may direct traffic in congested neighborhoods. Men and women help enforce regulations in free markets. . . . Older persons sit on the Neighborhood Committees, help to ensure neighborhood sanitation, help enforce family planning regulations, and generally see that the neighborhood functions properly. Others may act as mediators in disputes or as after-school counselors (Wu, 1984).

Because highly skilled workers are at a premium in China, the elderly skilled are used . . . to teach others. Thus, a factory may ask a technician to stay on . . . after retirement to help train younger workers. Other retired workers may go "on loan" to factories in other cities or towns, and such a sojourn may last 2–3 years. . . .

Despite all these efforts, however, large numbers of older people are left with essentially nothing to do. . . . As one Chinese social researcher interested in the problems of his nation's aged commented, "Many are just waiting to die."

CHALLENGES FOR THE FUTURE

In many respects, the elderly in China are better off today than in the past. Family solidarity continues to provide a support system for the aged, whereas at the same time government policies are beginning to provide economic security independent of the family's role. . . .

In rural areas, the welfare of the aged is closely tied to the economic well-being of the communes . . . but, increasingly, also to the ability of individual households to realize higher incomes under the responsibility system. . . . As the rural population . . . ages dramatically over the next 50 years, the changing balance between labor force participants in their prime productive ages and the aged, . . . may have a serious negative impact on the well-being of the aged. A key determinant of continued agricultural productivity will be the extent to which China will by then have been able to modernize agriculture.

In urban areas, where ever larger proportions

of the retired population are covered by pension systems, the oldest segment of the aged are the most disadvantaged as they are in large part not covered by retirement benefits. This disparity should . . . disappear as the aged segment of the urban population comes to be constituted almost entirely by persons who have worked most of their lives in state enterprises. . . .

The welfare of the aged is thus inextricably related to the degree to which China is able to modernize and to continue to increase its output value of agricultural and industrial products. Such development is, in turn, predicated on achieving success in the nation's overall population control programs, including family planning and rural-to-urban migration. . . .

Traditional values about family solidarity . . . are likely to be put under considerable strain as family size and residential patterns change. New ways of expressing and maintaining family ties will have to be found. The programs beginning to be developed . . . for the aged will have to be greatly expanded in the future, and their cost is likely to be high. The very decentralized mechanisms by which they are currently being funded will likely also require alteration. In addition, other social welfare programs will need to be instituted both to meet the social needs of the elderly and to utilize their energies and expertise to the fullest extent possible. . . .

REFERENCES

BEIJING REVIEW. 1981a "China's Marriage Law." March 16: 24, 24–27. 1981b "Growing old in China." October 16: 24, 22–28. 1982a "Five-guarantees households in the countryside." March 1: 25, 9. 1982b "Support and respect the elderly." May 3: 25. 1984 "Old people—a new problem for society." January 23: 27, 10.

CHINESE DOCUMENTS. 1983. Fifth Session of the Fifth National People's Congress. Beijing: Foreign Language Press.

DAVIS-FRIEDMANN, D. 1983. Long Lives: Chinese Elderly and the Communist Revolution. Cambridge, MA: Harvard Univ. Press.

DU, R. 1984. "Old people in China: hopes and problems." Beijing Rev. 27 (April 16): 31–34.

JIAN, C. 1983. "Volunteer service shows improving social mores." Beijing Rev. 26 (December 12): 24–25.

TIEN, H. Y. 1977. "How China treats its old people." Asian Profile 5 (February): 1–7.

WU, Y. 1984. "A new look in gerontology." Beijing Rev. 27 (April 16): 34–35.

YANG, C. K. 1965. Chinese Communist Society: The Family and the Village. Cambridge: MIT Press.

Introduction

Excerpt 46 is a study of the housing arrangements of older people in Nigeria. In the past, people who came to urban areas to work expected to return to their rural birthplace when they stopped working. Now, because urban migration has been so extensive, there may be no one left in the village to care for them or to live with. Changing population patterns mean that more and more people, including older people, live permanently in urban areas.

Nigerian children expect to care for their older parents. As in most of the Third World, children are the most important source of support to the elderly. Indeed, in the absence of social services, it is the childless person who is worst off.

The authors describe several ways older people can cope with the changing demands of old age. Men who are relatively wealthy can marry a younger wife. Widows may move in with sons, and reciprocate by caring for grandchildren. Some women return to natal homes to live with siblings. Some move temporarily to urban for medical care. There is no comprehensive social security or retirement system in Nigeria. In fact, retirement is not particularly salient in an economy where most people are self-employed.

46
Old People's Housing in an African Town

Stephen Ekpenyong
Margaret Peil

. . . Long-term and permanent migration as well as the tendency of elderly widows to join their children in town have resulted in an increasing number of old people in African cities. While the young ones (under age 65 or 70) tend to be independent and self-supporting, older men and women are less so, and the need for housing and services from children, relatives, and/or the state increases. Governments are increasingly being urged to provide for the elderly, although their resources are already fully stretched (Brown 1984; Hampson 1985). Young adults today are much more likely to have living parents than was the case in the past, and these parents expect support; demands are likely to be particularly heavy at a time . . . when the need for money for school fees for their own children is also heaviest (Caldwell 1976; Peil 1988). The lack of relatives at home who are willing and able to look after elderly women is partly responsible for their movement to the cities, where sons who are already in crowded housing must find room for them.

What are the effects of the presence of an increasing number of elderly people on housing and health services? In what conditions are the elderly living, and how are these conditions likely to change as the aged population increases and as economic problems multiply? Our study was designed to answer these and other ques-

tions about the . . . elderly in . . . cities and villages. . . .

Surveys were carried out in 1984 and 1985 in three cities in southern Nigeria: Abeokuta, Ijebu Ode, and Port Harcourt. . . . The first two have a long tradition of sending out migrants who return in old age, whereas the third is a colonial creation with a largely in-migrant population and fewer old people than the "traditional" cities. Of the 533 urban residents over age 60 who were interviewed, 353 were men and 180 were women. The rural samples included 315 men and 156 women living in 22 villages within 30 km of the selected cities.

Port Harcourt, with a population of about 911,000 (Salau 1984) was the largest city studied. Founded in 1912 by the British as a major port and railway terminal . . . it is an ethnically heterogeneous industrial town and the capital of Rivers State. Its very rapid growth in recent years as a result of the oil boom and its administrative expansion have produced a . . . housing shortage (Ogionwo 1979), although most migrants expect to return home in old age. . . .

Abeokuta was founded in 1830, and Ijebu Ode is much older. Both are ethnically homogeneous Yoruba cities. Abeokuta is the capital of Ogun State, with a population of about half a million. It has very little industry, and many educated people migrate to Ibadan or Lagos for work (Peil 1981). Ijebu Ode is about half the size of Abeokuta and is mainly a marketing and educational center. . . .

Local knowledge was used in each case to ob-

Source: Ekpenyong, Stephen and Margaret Peil (1985) "Old age in town: Implications for housing and services," *African Urban Studies,* 21 (Spring), 15–24

tain samples which were as large as possible in the time available, using several widespread clusters to enhance the representativeness of the samples. . . .

HOUSING

As long as most migrants intend to return home eventually, it makes sense as well as being normative for Africans to build a house at home if they can afford to do so. With the rapid rise in urban land values, the profitability of urban housing, and the longer stay of most migrants in towns, urban house ownership has become both a symbol of success and a key to an independent old age. Ownership of a house makes continued stay in town feasible because one can live off the rents. . . .

Studies in several cities (Peil 1981) have found very few cases of urban landlords retiring to a village and leaving their houses in the care of their children or a relative. This tends to be an either-or choice; very few people can afford to build in both places, and wealthy urban residents tend to build . . . in town. . . . In our sample, more than half the elderly men in the towns but only one in eight of the women were owners and ownership varied considerably with migration experience and between cities. Women often lived in houses owned by their husbands, family, or sons. Indigenes who had never left home and returnees are more likely than in-migrants to live in their own houses; some of the latter may have houses at home to which they plan to return. Abeokuta returnees in particular tend to be living in family houses, but returnees have also acquired the resources for house-building through . . . work away from home. In this case, "home" is a city rather than a village.

. . . Ownership is highest among men in Abeokuta and among women in Port Harcourt. These latter are largely indigenes; some have inherited family houses, while others have inherited from their husbands. There tend to be too many members of extended families living in Abeokuta and Ijebu Ode for women to inherit houses, but most do have access to a room in a family house. More than one-quarter of the elderly women in these cities are tenants, however, dependent on their own resources, spouses, or kin for rent. They may be living in the household of a nonowner son or may have their own room, with rent paid by a child who has no space in his/her own household.

Many tenants were still working; the pressure to return home will increase as they grow older, and most will have a house or at least a room in a family house at home. The large number of male tenants in Ijebu Ode was unexpected; since 77 percent of them are in-migrants and virtually all are under age 75, they are probably still trading there without having the permanent commitment symbolized by owning a house. Ownership is lower in all three sample areas, for both men and women, in the cities than in the surrounding villages, but it is probably higher than it will be for later cohorts of elderly people. Rapidly rising land values and building costs make it increasingly difficult for ordinary people to acquire urban houses. . . . This will raise problems for those with nowhere else to spend their old age.

As between men under and over age 75, ownership increases from 50 percent to 72 percent, since many men return home in their 60s and early 70s. The proportion of women living in a house owned by a relative increases fairly regularly with age, from 53 percent for those under age 66 to 81 percent of those over age 85. Tenancy decreases with age for both men and women; only two women and no men over 85 were still paying rent. Thus, some men acquire a house in their old age . . . whereas women are increasingly accommodated by their children.

Owners may rent out only one or two rooms and often keep only one or two for themselves so as to maximize income (Peil 1981; Schwerdtfeger 1982). Many elderly landlords/ladies in Port Harcourt play an active role as compound heads. Resident owners are often preferred to distant ones who have rents collected by an agency, as is common in Lagos. Traditional family houses, with no tenants, are more likely in the Yoruba cities than in Port Harcourt.

In general, living conditions for these old people were typical of their neighborhoods as far as crowding, facilities, and housing conditions were concerned; . . . they do not appear to be suffering undue disadvantage. About one in seven lived in conditions rated poor by the interviewers. . . . The proportion increased with age and was most notable among women in Abeokuta and men in Port Harcourt. In about 75 percent of the houses, two or more families were sharing facilities (kitchen, bath, and toilet). Electricity and pipe-borne water were far more common than in the villages, and a large majority of urban houses had the former. Port Harcourt houses were best off, and Ijebu Ode houses were least often provided with water. Carrying water from a public standpipe is problematic for the elderly, but most have young people available to do it for them. Wells are often polluted because they are too close to the compound privies. Water tanks have become increasingly common in the cities in recent years; those who have them may sell water to neighbors.

Women are about twice as likely to be living in a single room and living alone as are men. This is partly due to marriages which break down after menopause; only 29 percent of the women were living with a spouse, compared to 78 percent of the men. Most men have one or more wives (often considerably younger than themselves) and children in their households, who provide the domestic services which the elderly women provide for themselves. However, many of the old women living alone in Abeokuta live in family houses, so there are relatives nearby to help if they need it. Median household size appears to increase slightly with age; the oldest are most likely to be living in three-generation households, but households of more than seven people are rare except in Abeokuta. They were more common in the villages around Port Harcourt (where many young adults were waiting for jobs to open up in town), but less common in the Abeokuta villages than in the city. . . .

ECONOMIC PROVISION

. . . While industrialized countries have developed elaborate social welfare systems to care for the needy, children remain the most important source of help for the elderly in Nigeria as in most Third World countries. Family bonds remain very strong in Nigeria, in daily life as well as in times of need. Given the absence of a comprehensive national welfare policy, the elderly are still the responsibility of their families (Brown 1984). So far, only about 3 percent of the urban population can be classed as elderly, but numbers are growing as health care improves.

Nigerian government policy on . . . social welfare and community development have a minimal effect on the elderly. The regulations on retirement, pensions, and gratuity are salient to only about 5 percent of the population and do not affect the large majority who are self-employed. For the few who earn a pension, it is often small and must be collected personally, requiring continued residence in the city of dispersal. Most elderly Nigerians therefore work as long as they are able; ill health is the major reason for leaving the labor force, although more urban than rural men are subject to compulsory retirement at age 60. Women tend to stop work earlier than men and often leave voluntarily because their children are prepared to support them, but many carry on domestic tasks into old age (Peil and others 1985).

Generally, economic activity continues at a high level into the 70s for most urban males. Some men in our sample were still supporting young children. Men who find farming or unskilled laboring too much for their failing strength may become watchmen or do small-scale trading. . . . Many in our samples avoided the impression of complete dependency through the roles of house owner, advice giver, and dispute settler.

. . . Elderly women can continue as petty traders from the house or concentrate on domestic tasks and looking after grandchildren. This is often very welcome to daughters or daughters-in-law, who find it difficult and expensive to obtain reliable child-minders. Thus, a woman is seldom completely dependent, even if she suffers considerable disability. . . .

As expected, women have considerably less disposable income than do men, and income declines with age. The Abeokuta men are relatively well off, as might be expected in a population which often has done well in wage and/or self-employment and whose children are often in well-paying posts. Men living in Port Harcourt come next; they were slightly more likely to be still working than were the Abeokuta interviewees. Ijebu Ode is clearly the least affluent; a large majority of its elderly were still in the labor force, many are tenants, and they tend to have less disposable income than the villagers. . . .

Very few women over age 75 have enough money to feed or house themselves; rural women appear to be better off than urban women in this respect. This may not matter insofar as they have children to provide for them, but childless women are often in a desperate situation. Almost all of the people who reported no income at all were childless women. Only 2 percent of the men, compared to 6 percent of the women, had no living children. These women often have no living siblings either, and they may be accused of witchcraft unless they have a personality which can overcome these afflictions. . . .

Insofar as economic activities and rents from tenants are insufficient for the needs of daily life, the elderly are dependent on their children or relatives for support. The reports of those in our sample on the help they received from children, siblings, and other kin show considerable financial and physical support is given, although not always as much as is needed. Because fertility rates are high, most old people have children to

look after them. Problems tend to be greatest when the children all live elsewhere, but this is . . . more common in villages than in cities. . . .

Various strategies are available to cope with the needs of old age. Men may marry a young wife. . . . Widows may move to the city to live with their migrant sons, which often means leaving the labor force and taking up the role of resident grandmother. . . . Other women move back to their natal homes if siblings there are willing to help them. Elderly people in need of medical attention often go to live with their urban children temporarily to obtain treatment, which constitutes a significant addition to the demand for medical care in cities. The cost and availability of medical care are an important political issue for large numbers of the elderly and their children (Ekpenyong and others 1987).

CONCLUSION

While the position of elderly people in African cities is not as desperate as is sometimes suggested, there obviously will be an increasing need for housing and for economic and social support for the elderly who choose to spend their old age in town. Some will have grown up in cities, and others will have decided that conditions in town are sufficiently better than in their home villages to make continued urban residence worthwhile. Others simply may have no place to go because they have lost land rights through long absence or government reorganization (as in Tanzania). Housing conditions are generally better in the cities, and there is a greater likelihood that some of one's children and grandchildren will be living nearby.

The social norm of caring for one's parents is still strong in Nigeria. While there have been homes for the aged since the beginning of the century (Iliffe 1987, p. 83), these have provided only a few places for those without family support. Large numbers of urban men own the houses in which they are living, and many receive a regular, if small, income from renting rooms. Children give to their mothers if at all possible, and many provide accommodation, not only out of filial piety but also for the reason that elderly women continue contributing to the household in a way that elderly men seldom do. . . .

Inflation and consumerism are taking their toll of support for parents but less than might be expected. It is largely the childless who lack support. . . . It is unlikely that pensions or other forms of social security will fill the gap for a long time to come, because most of the population is still self-employed and because any surplus which can be used for welfare remains small. However, government policies that encourage families to help their own (such as deductions from income tax for family support) could positively benefit the elderly. Expecting all old people to go back to the villages is unrealistic and may deprive many of help from urban-based children.

REFERENCES

BROWN, C. K. 1984. "Improving the Social Protection of the Aging Population in Ghana." *Population Studies* 19:183–99.

CALDWELL, J. C. 1976. "Fertility and the Household Economy in Nigeria." *Journal of Comparative Family Studies* 7:193–253.

EKPENYONG, S., O. Y. OYENEYE, and M. PEIL. 1987. "Health Problems of Elderly Nigerians." *Social Science and Medicine* 24:885–88.

HAMPSON, J. 1985. "Elderly People and Social Welfare in Zimbabwe." *Aging and Society* 5:39–67.

ILIFFE, J. 1987. *The African Poor: A History*. London: Cambridge University Press.

OGIONWO, W. 1979. *A Social Survey of Port Harcourt*. Ibadan: Heinemann Educational Books.

PEIL, M. 1981. *Cities and Suburbs: Urban Life in West Africa*. New York: Holmes and Meier.

—— 1988. "Family Support for the Nigerian Elderly." A paper presented at a conference of the Association of Social Anthropologists, London, April.

—— S. EKPENYONG, and O. Y. OYENEYE. 1985." Retirement in Nigeria." *Cultures et Développement* 17: 665–82.

—— 1988. "Going Home: Migration Careers of Southern Nigerians." *International Migration Review* 22.

PEIL, M., A. BAMISAIYE, and S. EKPENYONG. 1989. "Health and Physical Support for the Elderly in Nigeria." In G. Clare Wenger, ed., *Culture, Health and Ageing: Comparative Perspectives*. Holland: Reidl Publishing Co.

SALAU, A. T. 1984. "The Oil Industry and the Urban Economy: The Case of Port Harcourt Metropolis." *African Urban Studies* 17 (Fall-Winter): 75–84.

SCHWERDTFEGER, F. W. 1982. *Traditional Housing in African Cities: A Comparative Study of Houses in Zaria, Ibadan, and Marrakech*. Chichester: John Wiley.

Introduction

In most countries a disproportionate number of older people are women. Sex differences in longevity and the tendency for women to marry men older than themselves means that most women who stay married will become widows. Widowhood is largely a female experience. In Jamaica, more than half of the population over 65 are women. And, at every age over 20, the number of widowed women far exceeds the number of widowed men.

This article is based on a combination of survey data describing Jamaican widows and a number of case studies. The case studies give a sense of what individual women face when they are widowed, and their sources of support. As you will see when you read through the case studies, some widowed Jamaican women get help from their children; others provide for their children and grandchildren.

Like most married women of this age group, these Jamaican women had been wholly, or partially dependent on their husbands' income. In Jamaica, pensions are tied to both age and employment, and contributions are voluntary. Unemployment is very high. If wives were not themselves gainfully employed, or if husbands did not contribute to the National Insurance Scheme, wives will not receive pensions. Like widows everywhere the greatest concerns of widowed Jamaicans are financial.

47
Widowhood in Jamaica

Joan M. Rawlins

. . . For the purpose of this paper, a widow is defined as a woman whose husband had died. Those women who have lived all their adult years in a common-law union and whose partners have now died, are not included in this discussion. . . .

The national census (1982) for Jamaica indicates there were 37,644 widows in a population of 693,741 women age 15 and over. This means 1:18 women in that age group was a widow. . . . The life of the Jamaican widow needs to be explored to determine the extent to which her life is changed by widowhood.

METHODOLOGY

The study concentrates primarily on data on the widowed population obtained from the 1982 Jamaica census. . . . Further information . . . was obtained from twelve case studies . . . researched in 1987 in two communities near the Jamaica Campus of the University of the West Indies; one a working class area and the other a middle class area. . . .

Source: Rawlins, Joan M. (1989) "Widowhood in Jamaica: A neglected aspect of the family life cycle," *Journal of Comparative Family Studies,* Vol. XX, No. 3, Autumn, 327–339.

WIDOWHOOD IN JAMAICA THE STATISTICS

Widowed Population

Data from the 1982 Census of Jamaica show . . . 1,926 widows in the 15–44 age groups; 12,265 in the 45–64 and 23,453 who were 65 years and over. Widowhood . . . is essentially a phenomenon of elderly women.

In every age interval except for the 20–24, the number of widows greatly exceeds the number of widowers.

It is important to compare the widowed population with specific groups because some of these relationships . . . indicate opportunities for re-marriage and male companionship for widows.

The numbers of widowed females to widowed males, age 15–64, . . . (3,424 to 14,191) highlight the smaller number of men, which ensures many widows will not be able to find new husbands or other male companions from the considerably smaller group of widowed males.

Widows . . . may also look to divorced men and men previously unmarried. Experience however shows that only small numbers of widows in Jamaica re-marry. This might relate to the fact that the average age of widowhood is 61 years, and that the potentially eligible men . . . prefer to marry younger women.

Economic Concerns of Widowhood

An important area of concern for widows is that of financing themselves without the income previously provided by their husbands. . . .

The women in the case studies did not benefit from life insurance policies on their husbands. Some stated their husbands had had no such policies. Some received widow's benefits (provided by the Ministry of Social Security through the National Insurance System). All complained of its inadequacy ($15 per week) and most were concerned about financing themselves in the future. . . .

Widow's Benefit

Those eligible for widow's benefit are:
(a) A woman whose husband is dead
(b) A woman whose . . . common-law . . . partner is dead.

The Qualifying Conditions

The deceased husband/partner must have paid a minimum of 221 weekly contributions with an annual average of at least 13 contributions or he must have been a National Insurance pensioner. If he had been a pensioner, the contribution conditions are considered satisfied.

A full flat rate pension is payable where the deceased partner has an annual average of 39 or more contributions. A reduced rate will be payable where the annual average falls between 13 and 39 weekly contributions per annum.

To qualify for benefits the widow must satisfy at least one of the following conditions at the date of her husband's death. She must:

(1) be married to her late husband, or had been living with her late partner in a common-law union for at least three years, and she must be 55 or older;
(2) be pregnant by her late husband or partner;
(3) be married for at least three years and be perma-

nently incapable of work because of a specific disease or mental or physical disablement.
(4) be caring for a child of their family. Such a child must be under 18 years.

If the particular widow satisfies none of the four conditions but she was married for at least three years, she may received a pension for one year.[1]

Some widows might not be eligible for widow's benefit but might be eligible for the old age benefit. The old age benefit may be paid to a man age 65 or more or a woman age 60 or more who has made the required National Insurance contributions and retired. If the contributor remains in full-time employment, the benefits will not be paid until age 70 for a man and 65 for a woman.

The benefits available to a widow vary depending on whether . . . her husband had been employed in the government or the private sector. . . .

CASE STUDIES

Case No. 1

Mrs. E. is 61 years old and has been a widow for 9 years. Her husband died of a heart attack at age 55. They had been married for 24 years but had lived together for years prior to their marriage. Together they had ten children who range in age from 24 to 40 years.

Mrs. E. is now retired but had been employed at the local University as a laboratory attendant for 21 years. Her husband had been "a good mason", she says, and had built their own house, and "many other big houses in the neighborhood".

Mrs. E. owns her house, although she owes the bank $1,000 in connection with the house.

---

[1]Source: of information on Widow's benefit—Pamphlet: All about National Insurance. Ministry of Social Security, Kingston, Jamaica.

The house has eight bedrooms, but is in . . . disrepair. She is the head of her household and provides "shelter" for eight of her children, seven of whom are unemployed. These children together have seventeen children, and nine of these live in Mrs. E's house. Other occupants of her house . . . are one female tenant and her four children, three children (non relatives), and the "baby-father" of her youngest daughter. Twenty-seven persons reside in Mrs. E's house.

All but one of her children has received less than 5 years of education. The youngest attended high school for 3 years up to the time of her father's death.

Mrs. E's sources of income are a pension of $40 per fortnight and occasional rent from the tenant. "I have one tenant but rarely get any money from her". Her children she says are of no help as seven are unemployed and the others have their own families to mind. She worried about the future, "life is very hard and we struggle each day. If only I had some money I would fix up the house and rent out a bigger part".

She says she did not grieve for "long" when her husband died because she was still employed and "the people at work were especially good to me". She says her involvement in the church also helped. The fact that her children depend on her for . . . support also helped her to "return to normal".

Mrs. E. passes her day by "minding" nine of her grandchildren, and sometimes some of the other children who lived in the house. She says she is in good health apart from her varicose veins, and although thin, looked healthy.

Case No. 2

Mrs. A. is 65 years old and has been a widow for 13 years. Her husband, a messenger at a local high school had died 13 years previously of "heart problems" at the age of 62. They had been married for 12 years, had no children together, but she had a son, now 40 years old by a previous association.

Mrs. A is now retired but had worked as an office attendant for 17 years, up to the time of her retirement. She is the head of her household, and owns the small house in which she lives. She rents two rooms to people "who can hardly pay the rent most of the time".

She very rarely hears from her son who had been living in England almost twenty years. He is married but sends her nothing. She commented on the ingratitude of some children, especially male children. . . .

She had received no financial benefits as a result of her husband's death. Her only sources of income are $30 per fortnight as a widow's pension and the rent she receives from the two rooms. Her main worry . . . is the high cost of living. Because of this, she rarely leaves her house as she cannot afford the bus fares.

She stated that she was very worried about how widows managed on the meager pension and that most be very worried about the future. She says, "before my husband's death, I did not know what loneliness was, now I know what it is". She missed her husband very much in the first two years after his death and had overcome her loneliness because of her church and a few friends. . . .

Case No. 3

Mrs. D. is 70, and has been a widow for 19 years. She had married her husband after the first three children were born and they continued to live together for 30 years until his death. Mrs. D. is now retired but had worked as an assistant cook at the local University for most of her working life. Her husband had worked as a handyman at the University. She says she received no financial assistance . . . on his death as "he had always worked as casual labourer".

Mrs. D. and her husband, had four children, "all girls". One daughter lives in Canada while the others reside in Jamaica. They range from 30–40 years. The youngest is . . . unemployed, has four children and shares the house with Mrs. D.

Mrs. D. is the head of the household and her sources of income are:

(1) a widow's pension of $30.70 every other week
(2) occasional remittances from her daughter in the USA.

. . . Mrs. D. says she missed her husband tremendously, at first. "I was very lonely; you know how you get used to seeing people and then to not have them there, is something very hard to understand". She also misses her husband because he was "handy" around the house and she now has to do many of the things he would normally do. She said however, that because she was still at work when her husband died, her grief was minimized. Her work, her children and the church helped her to overcome her loss. She also visited the daughter who lives in the USA. . . .

Mrs. D. says she is very worried about the future. "Times are so hard now, I don't see how they could possibly get harder. The Pension ($30.70) is no good, as one trip to the supermarket for one day's meal would finish it". She complained a little about having to render financial assistance to her unemployed daughter, and says she wonders some days, what they will eat. . . .

DISCUSSION

The population age 65 and over increased from 100,875 in 1970 to 151,427 in 1982, with the majority (82,189) being women. (Social and Economic Survey, 1984). The population over 60 years in 1982 represented 10.8% of the total population. With this increase in the aged population, we will . . . see an increase in the number of widows. . . .

In Jamaica large numbers of women work outside of the home. The labour force figures show a labour force participation rate of 46% for 1985. (Economic and Social Survey, 1985), but this figure does not address . . . the large numbers of females employed in . . . hustling activities. It is estimated that in the urban areas 13,000 persons are employed in higglering (vending) and petty trades. (Taylor, A., LeFranc, E., and McFarlane, D., 1986). Therefore, among the working classes, Jamaican widows do not face the problem of returning to work on the event of widowhood, but are more concerned about coping with the loss of . . . economic contribution the husband had made to the household. . . .

The women in the case studies mentioned numerous financial problems they encountered. . . . Not all widows receive a widow's pension, as this is related to the husband's contributions which had been paid into the National Insurance Scheme, which also pays the widow's benefit. Not all widows receive an old age pension. . . . The old age pension is related to the widow's employment and the contributions she had made to the National Insurance . . . as an employee. It is therefore possible to find destitute widows who receive neither widow's pension nor an old age pension. These persons are . . . totally dependent on . . . relatives and friends.

Given the current economic problems of Jamaica, in which there is 25% general unemployment and 40% for Women (Economic and Social Survey, Jamaica 1985) . . . these widows might not receive assistance from relatives. . . .

Another problem these widows face, is that they are left to care for themselves, unaided. Having rendered nursing-type service to their spouses . . . they might have no one to give to them the care they had given to their husbands.

Additionally, some elderly widows have to take on the care of their elderly siblings or even aged parents. One widow, a 61 year old, who was interviewed for the case studies, had sole charge of her 86 year old mother. This situation is not uncommon and sometimes these widows, who might be in less than perfect health have to provide shelter and support to elderly, often senile relatives.

The issue of pension is emotive as even the

most highly paid government retired employee is not likely to get a pension . . . adequate to his needs. Retired teachers obtain a pitiful pension, which . . . leaves many faced with a life of embarrassment in their old age.

Women in Jamaica, frequently defend their large families by stating it is insurance for the future. . . . These widows however voiced opposite views having experienced the reality of problems caused by large families.

Some widows . . . stated that having children was no guarantee one would have companionship or receive financial assistance from them in later years. . . .

The widows with whom discussions were held . . . were emphatic that male children were less likely to render assistance to their parents in later years. . . .

In Jamaica, some widows can expect to receive financial assistance from their children. This would vary depending on the economic circumstances of the children as well as . . . other factors. . . . The case studies (essentially working class persons) do not indicate widows are dependent on such. . . . Most were dependent on the widow's pension and their own initiatives. . . .

The need for companionship was stressed by all the widows. Few seemed to dwell on the loss of their husband and most appeared to have overcome their bereavement in a . . . short time. Some added though "you never really get over the loss". Those who appeared to have been most affected by the loss of their husbands were those who now live alone, and who had been living alone with their spouse at the time of his death. It appears the main issue here is . . . the loss of companionship and the consequent loneliness.

SUMMARY AND CONCLUSIONS

Widows in Jamaica now represent a significant portion of the population, with one in eighteen adult females being a widow. . . .

. . . The widow's economic situation causes many to fear for their future. Many were heads of households and like other female heads of household (Massiah 1983) experienced poor living conditions. Many complained about the inadequacy of the widow's benefit and the old age pension. . . . The benefits are perhaps so minimal because one pays a small contribution into the respective fund during one's working life. The benefits . . . could perhaps be more realistic if the contributions were more realistic.

The need for companionship was stressed by all the widows and the alleviation of that need . . . , they suggest, played an important part in their return to normal life after the death of their husband. These women pointed to . . . family, church, and friends as assisting them in their return to normal life. . . .

REFERENCES

1980 ALL ABOUT NATIONAL INSURANCE (Pamphlet), Ministry of Social Security, Kingston, Jamaica.

1982 Demographic Statistics, Department of Statistics, Jamaica.

1982 Economic and Social Survey, Statistical Institute of Jamaica.

MASSIAH, J. 1983 Women as heads of household in the Caribbean. UNESCO Publications. 1970 Population Census of the Commonwealth Caribbean, Jamaica. 1974 Recent Population Movements in Jamaica. CIRCRED Series, World Population Year.

1984 Social and Economic Survey, Planning Institute of Jamaica, Kingston. 1985 Social and Economic Survey, Planning, Institute of Jamaica, Kingston. 1982 Statistical Yearbook of Jamaica, Department of Statistics, Kingston, Jamaica.

TAYLOR, A., LEFRANC, E. and MCFARLANE, D. 1986. "The Informal distribution network in the Kingston Metropolitan area". Unpublished Population council Paper.

Introduction

In the opening pages of this book we talked about the difficulty of describing precisely what social scientists mean when they refer to "families." In Part Two we talked about the marriage ceremony as a cultural signal of a new family. Because most people do marry, it is logical to think of marriage as a beginning point. Conceding this should not suggest that unmarried or same-sex couples, single parents and their children, or single adults and their kin have less reason to see themselves as families.

While much that is written about family life assumes an orderly progression from a family of orientation to a family of procreation, such a progression is only part of the story. As this article shows, lifelong single women maintain close ties to their families throughout their life. Understanding this relationship is especially important because it presents such a clear contrast to the usual assumption that gives primacy to maternity.

Lifelong single women born in the second decade of the twentieth century were interviewed for this article. Their stories were compared to those of widows of the same age. All of the women entered adulthood during the Great Depression. Their reasons for marrying or remaining single were largely circumstantial. Far from controlling their own destinies, the lives of these women were "shaped by influences of historical circumstances, social class, family composition, and gender." They, too, had significant family lives. Nevertheless, regardless of marital status, these women described the significance of family interaction in their lives.

48

The Family Life Course of Single Women

Katherine R. Allen
Robert S. Pickett

. . . The research question guiding this inquiry is: What similarities and differences in the family life course may be identified by never-married and widowed women from the 1910 birth cohort? To answer this question, the analysis compares similarities and discontinuities in the women's lives during three broad periods: childhood, the transition to young adulthood, and adulthood. . . .

In this study, we begin with a theoretical model of normative female life cycle experiences based upon national census data (Glick, 1977; Uhlenberg, 1974). The innovation offered here is to flesh out the model with data . . . gathered by interviewing women about their own experiences. . . .

🔁

THE SAMPLE

The sample consisted of 30 women. . . . They were white, native-born, working-class women, born between 1907 and 1914, and in their seven-

Source: Allen, Katherine R. and Robert S. Pickett (1987) "Forgotten streams in the family life course," *Journal of Marriage and the Family*, 49, August, 516–517.

ties at the time of the interviews. . . . Fifteen women were widowed at the time of the study. They had married only once, had at least one child who survived to adulthood, became grandmothers, and became widowed after a marriage that lasted 20 years or more. The other 15 women did not marry and did not bear children. These two groups represented the most typical and the most atypical of women aged 65 and over, respectively (Glick, 1977).

The interviews were conducted by the first author from January to June 1984 in a metropolitan area in upstate New York. . . .

PROCESSES AND TRANSITIONS IN THE FAMILY LIFE COURSE

The life course approach used in this analysis reveals the importance of family connections in women's lives. . . . The historical, social, economic, and political contexts into which women of the 1910 cohort were born set the stage for their socialization and later development. Their life stories highlight the centrality of family connection and responsibility—a theme . . . common enough and strong enough to be . . . woven into the present reconstruction of their lives. . . .

First, their childhood experiences reveal . . . a shared foundation of the familistic ideology they internalized and carried with them throughout the 20th century. Second, . . . the familistic ideology coincided with their individual circumstances by allowing or denying women the opportunity to marry. Third, the interdependence of the female life course and the family life course is revealed through the variety of caretaking roles they performed throughout their lives. Caretaking responsibilities, although a lifelong involvement, were especially evident during adulthood. . . .

Harsh Realities of Life during Childhood

. . . At the time these women were born, people sacrificed their personal desires and . . . placed their families first, as dictated by the prevailing . . . familistic ideology (Hareven, 1977). Older members of the working class had insecure employment, were employed in hard physical labor, and had few work-related benefits to cushion disability, injury, or the death of the main wage earner (Katz, 1983). As daughters of working-class families, the women in this sample also endured hardship by being subjected to the social-historical effects of immigrant status. Nineteen women were the children or grandchildren of European immigrants, primarily from Italy, Germany, and Ireland. Their sense of ethnic identity . . . reflected the insecurity of their early years, as the daughter of Italian immigrants noted:

Those days when we were kids, they were all from their own country, and they all followed their own race, how they lived. They didn't bother with nobody else. . . . We were brought up in such a different era. We were all just white people. All different races of whites. The Germans didn't like the Italians, and the Irish didn't like the Germans, and they were all fighting among each other.

As working-class females, their educational and occupational opportunities were severely limited. They experienced the working conditions and precarious opportunities that plagued their elders:

In my time, there were only three things I could have been that I know of. One was a teacher, one was a nurse, and one was a secretary. . . . Most of the girls got married. Men could do other things, but there weren't all the things that there are today, like lab technicians. . . . Your average people like my brothers who went to a country school, only a few would go on to do something.

Another major factor shaping the life course of these women was the early experience of loss.

As children, six of the never-married women and three of the widows survived the death of a parent. In addition, two widows lost contact with their fathers when their parents divorced. Physical and mental illnesses were common in the families of all the subjects, . . . The familistic ideology operated as a safety net by providing kinfolk as substitute caretakers for children whose parents died, divorced, or were institutionalized. As a consequence, . . . the women described close relationships with grandparents, aunts, older siblings, nuns, and other adults, most of whom were female. One widow explained,

My mother and father separated for a while, never legally, and we all lived together in this rooming house. Then, my mother got TB when my sister was born, and she had to go up to the sanitarium for a year. So, my grandmother had to take care of us. My aunt took my sister because she was ill, and my grandmother took my brother and I. I was only 8 and my brother was 11. She had to run the rooming house besides, and she took care of us, and we kinda looked up to her, as a mother really.

Being cared for by women in times of family hardship was a lesson these women learned early in life. They carried forth this lesson of family commitment and caregiving into their adult lives, when the single women became caretakers of aging parents, siblings, nieces, and nephews, and the married women cared for their husbands, children, and grandchildren.

Discontinuities in Family Responsibilities during Young Adulthood

. . . Two factors were critical in . . . the transition to adulthood that kept the never-married women at home and led the other women to . . . marriage. . . . The first factor was . . . the Great Depression . . . of the 1930s. . . . The second was . . . the relative need for involvement in the family of orientation at a time when their peers were marrying. The women who married differed according to the timing of marriage: 10 married between age 18 and 24; the remaining 5 married late, between age 26 and 30. During the transition to adulthood, then, three patterns were evident: early marriage, delayed marriage, and permanent singlehood. . . .

The effects of the Depression on individuals and families were not uniform. Elder (1974) . . . found that coping with unemployment in the Great Depression depended on the cumulative impact of previous life experiences, personality, family backgrounds, and the availability of other resources. Similarly, for the women in our sample, . . . the intersection of historical, family, and individual time allowed or denied the opportunity to marry. The Depression was one factor in ruling out marriage for the lifelong single women, whose labor was needed by their families. . . . The following examples reveal the expectations placed on young unmarried women. . . .

When you are the oldest and there are little kids in the house, you had to go to work. . . . And especially during the Depression when there was nothing, I did housework. I lived at the places where I worked a great deal of time, and I worked for one family for about 10 years.

I started to work in the Depression. . . . My father wanted my money. That's how come we moved, so he could pay for the house.

The Depression was a factor, as well, in delaying . . . marriage for the five widows who married late, as typified in the experiences of a woman who married at age 30 in 1939:

I went with him when the Depression was on, and after a couple of months, he asked me to marry him. I would have, but we both got out of a job at that time and then, three years later, he got back. He worked in a steel mill then. So we got married.

In addition to economic considerations, . . . the second factor that explains . . . delayed marriage and permanent singlehood is the women's perception of their responsibilities to their parents. . . .

I brought the children up, and I used to take care of the house and the kids, make up the beds. See, my mother was never too well. She had very serious operations. I thought we were going to lose her so many times. . . . That is why I stayed home so much. . . . She didn't like to go anywhere because she would say I would be left alone at home. . . . That was her excuse so she didn't have to stay anywhere because she just wanted to stay with me.

In addition, being the only daughter left at home to care for a widowed mother was common among the never-married women:

I had to take my mother into consideration. No, I couldn't do anything. She had to be my prime concern. . . . So there was just no question about it. . . . It was my responsibility because my older brother was married, and my other brother was in school, so I was elected.

. . . One never-married woman considered her own needs pale in comparison to those of her parents:

My parents were my whole life. . . . She was quite bad when I was in high school, and that probably contributed some to the fact that I didn't go on. See, I told you I wasn't very well when I was young. . . . They were basically years when I was just sort of stuck with my mother, and I didn't have too many young friends.

During much of their young adulthood, the five widows who married late paralleled the lives of the permanent singles. They described themselves as "almost old maids" because . . . responsibilities kept them at home. For four of these women, marriage followed the death of a parent. In the fifth case, a woman who married against her parents' wishes. . . .

She didn't want me to get married. But see, I was 30, and I thought if I don't marry this guy, I mean everybody should get married, and I liked him immensely. . . . I think at this late date I should have married the guy I went with before I met my husband. But he was divorced, maybe 12 years before, and (my mother) didn't go for that.

This passage reveals . . . the implicit . . . understanding that there is a point when it is appropriate to marry—if one plans to do so at all.

By contrast, widows who married in their teens and early twenties did so because of opportunity and expectation. . . . They recalled their early marriage as a time when their friends were getting married:

Like all my friends got married, because we all hung around together. I was the first one in my group to get married. And, then, they all spoiled my baby. They used to come to the house, and I was the only one with a baby. But, then, eventually, they got children, too, so our lives were all the same.

Another widow who married on time described the beginning of her marriage as a "liberation" from her mother's home. . . .

With my large family and there wasn't much money in the house, we had to do everything ourselves, and I was the one who had to do most of it. I never resented it, but I didn't realize until I got married what I did do before. It was an entirely different type of life for me. . . . Somebody now tried to do things for me.

. . . Although marriage was an attempt to escape the requirements of helping in large families, the reality of establishing one's own family of procreation was far from an escape. . . .

I had all these kids, and there was never any money. My husband was not educated and just made it to the eighth grade. He was a trucker when I married him. He worked on a nursery. He ran a gas station and did whatever there was to do. He hauled milk from the farmers to the dairy. So, he was struggling all the time to put a roof over our heads and clothes on our backs and food in our mouths, so life was not easy.

Responsibility to the family was a lesson . . . driven home to all members of the sample, regardless of . . . marital status. . . . Both groups of women exercised the mandates of the familistic ideology and became caretakers of their families. To explain permanent singlehood as a deviant lifestyle in comparison to the . . . normative patterns of marriage (Uhlenberg, 1974) does not capture the essential commonality of caretaking in women's lives. . . . Differences in family careers during adulthood reflect the variation in the way women were expected to fulfill their responsibilities rather than indicating who was normal and who was deviant. . . .

Discontinuities in Family Caregiving

Both widows and never-married women described their lives in terms of the caretaking roles they performed in their families. Widows . . . cared for husbands, and extended their family roles to descending generations as they became mothers, grandmothers, and great-grandmothers. As one widow remarked,

My grandson is the most important person to me. It used to be my son, but he moved away, so his son has taken his place for me.

The experience of caring for aging parents was not common for widows in this sample; only four did so. Of the four, only one assumed major responsibilities for the care of her parents. . . .

In contrast, . . . twelve never-married women took care of aging parents until their parents' deaths. . . . Fourteen of the never-married women functioned in a surrogate-mother role to their nieces and nephews or within an occupational capacity as a baby nurse or housekeeper. . . . As caretakers for aging parents and as surrogate mothers to their siblings' children, they provided support . . . to their extended families. As one woman noted,

I believe I was born for a certain purpose here on earth. . . . My purpose has been to take care of all these kids that have come along. Of course, they call me their second mother. I'm not as close as they would have been to their real mother, but I take care

of those kids. . . . If my sister wanted to go out someplace, she just called me and I'd usually stay with them.

Never-married women . . . were also the "bearers of the family history" by maintaining the family heirlooms and weaving into their own life histories the stories about their ancestors. . . .

The role of the unmarried daughter who took care of aging parents and provided surrogate caretaking to others was characteristic of families historically (Watkins, 1984). Typically, the one who remained at home was the youngest or only girl in the family. Five of the never-married women in this sample were the youngest child in the family and another four were only daughters. With one exception among the widows, an only child, all the widows had sisters and were the oldest or middleborn child. . . .

CONCLUSION

Every student of the family recognizes the significance of the . . . concepts of the family of the orientation and the family of procreation. The traditional treatment of these concepts is evident in the family life cycle model, which presumes a linear progression from the family in which one is born to the family one establishes by marrying and becoming a parent. Subsequent relationships with one's first family are dealt with in the separate realm of kinship networks and interactions. . . . Immediate family ties take precedence when "family" is considered.

Our data reveal, however, . . . that the linear progression from a family of origin to a family of procreation . . . characterized in the family life cycle concept reveals only one stream in the family life course. The experiences of lifelong single women reveal another. Although they did not establish their own families, awareness of their experiences broadens the notion of family life to include lifelong participation in the family of orientation and emphasizes, as well, the centrality of family in women's lives.

REFERENCES

ELDER, GLEN H., Jr. 1974. Children of the Great Depression. Chicago: University of Chicago Press.

GLICK, PAUL C. 1977. "Updating the life cycle of the family." Journal of Marriage and the Family 39: 5–13.

HAREVEN, TAMARA K. 1977. "Family time and historical time." Daedalus 106:57–70.

KATZ, Michael B. 1983. Poverty and Policy in American History. New York: Academic Press.

UHLENBERG, Peter. 1974."Cohort variations in family life cycle experiences of U.S. females." Journal of Marriage and the Family 36:284–292.

WATKINS, SUSAN C. 1984. "Spinsters." Journal of Family History 9:310–325.

Discussion Questions

1. Ask people in the class with knowledge of a language other than English to give examples and explanations of words used to describe older people and aging. Does the same ambivalence discovered by Covey hold for other languages? Are there male/female differences?

2. The Korean government awards several hundred Filial Piety Prizes annually (see Excerpt 44). Would such a prize be welcomed in North America?

3. Should the state be responsible for care of the elderly? Can children cope with the increased demands of providing for elderly parents? Can children who do not accept this responsibility be made to do so?

4. If you were an older woman, in which non-Western country described in the excerpts would you choose to live? Why? Would your opinion change if you were an older man?

5. In Jamaica, contributions to the National Insurance Scheme are voluntary (see Excerpt 47). There is no universal old age security system. What can countries like Jamaica do to lessen the financial problems of older citizens?

6. What images come to mind when you think of spinsters? Why do you think the word has such a negative connotation? Do the spinsters in excerpt 48 fit the stereotype?

Data Collection Exercises

1. Using United Nations data create a table of societal aging showing the percent of the population over 65 for as many countries as you can. What patterns are there among societies with higher or lower proportions of older people?

2. Plot the proportion of single men and women in a population over time. Use census data for any province, state, or country you are interested in. Are proportions stable over time? What inferences can you make from the data?

3. Interview spokespersons in your community about services for the elderly. What needs are well met? What are the gaps?

4. In the 1960s, one of the main concerns of the women's movement was media stereotypes of girls and women. Using one of these earlier studies as a guide, do a content analysis of the television portrayal of older people.

Writing Exercises

1. Write a short (750-word) essay about your relationship with an older relative or friend.

2. Working in a group, create a pamphlet describing organizations, services, and opportunities for older people in your community.

3. Write a thousand-word essay on some aspect of the Grey Liberation Movement.

4. Imagine that you are a Nigerian (or Jamaican, or Chinese, or Korean) immigrant to North America. Write a letter to your parents explaining why (or why not) they should retire in North America.

Glossary

Ageism—Stereotyping of, or discriminating against people on the basis of age.

Filial piety—The value of respect and care of older parents; based on a sense of duty to reciprocate for care received by children.

Gerontology—The study of the social aspects of aging.

Index of aging—The percentage of the population over 65 years old, or a ratio of the population over 65 years to the population under 15 years.

Longevity—Average life span.

Mortality—Death rates in a specific population; often expressed in age-specific terms.

Old age dependency ratio—A ratio of those over 65 to those of working age (15–65).

Pay-as-you-go pension schemes—Most pension schemes are based on a system whereby those currently in the labor force "pay" for those currently retired.

Sandwich generation—Middle-aged adults (usually women) caring for aging parents and growing children.

Suggested Readings

COHEN, LEAH. (1984) *Small Expectations: Society's Betrayal of Older Women.* Toronto: Mc-Clelland and Stewart. This is an expose of society's failure to address the consequences of age and sex discrimination. It is largely based on interviews conducted in Canada, the United States, and Great Britain. While the book is very critical, it ends on a positive note outlining a program for change.

DORESS, PAULA BROWN, and DIANA LASKIN SIEGAL. (1987) *Ourselves Growing Older.* The Midlife and Older Women Book Project, New York: Simon & Schuster. This wonderful collection of articles of interest to everyone whatever their chronological age is similar in format to its forerunner *Our Bodies Ourselves* (Boston: The Boston Women's Health Book Collective). The book is a practical, positive, and empowering collection of pictures and articles.

HAMILTON, GARY. (1990) "Patriarchy, patrimonialism, and filial piety: A comparison of China and Western Europe," *British Journal of Sociology,* 41, 1, 77–104. This article compares the origins of patriarchial authority in China and the West. The author argues that in order to understand China, one must understand both patriarchy and filial piety.

NYDEGGER, CORINNE N. (1983) "Family ties of the aged in cross-cultural perspective," *The Gerontologist,* 23, 1, 26–32. This is a humorous poke at several myths that dominate our thinking about aging. Nydegger explains that there is no evidence to support the beliefs that 1) the aged were better off in the past (the Golden Age myth), or 2) older people are better off in other societies (the Golden Isles myth).

RUBIN, LILLIAN. (1979) *Women of a Certain Age: The Midlife Search for Self.* New York: Harper and Row. This timeless book was recently (1990) reissued and so should be more generally available. It is a wonderfully written, thought-provoking, candid discussion of the 'what next' feelings women face when the job of childrearing is behind them.

SILVERMAN, PHILIP. (1987) *The Elderly as Modern Pioneers.* Bloomington: Indiana University Press. This well-researched discussion of the changing nature of aging in America includes a chapter on age in cross-cultural perspective.

PART IX

The Family
as a Public Issue

ɔɔɔɔɔɔɔɔɔɔɔɔɔɔɔɔɔɔɔɔɔɔɔɔɔɔɔɔɔɔɔɔɔ

In this section, we examine excerpts on population policy in Africa; family law and policy making in the former USSR, China, and New Zealand; compare the ways the United States handles day-care problems with the ways European societies do; and consider who has more power over children—the family or the state—in France.

These excerpts reveal a growing belief that the state has a crucial, but difficult, role to play in family life. A great many people have worried about the changes in family life that are taking place today. In responding to these concerns, policy makers try to ground their decisions in knowledge about what family forms are possible, probable, and preferable. However, social science is currently in the middle of a major controversy over the family: what the family is, how it is changing, and why. As we have noted, this definitional problem makes planning even more difficult than it would otherwise be.

Another difficult problem in planning is the misguided belief of many that the golden age of the family is buried somewhere in the past. Expecting the modern family to care for all its members' needs is related to the belief that many social issues ought to be dealt with privately—what people have called the "privatization" of social issues. This view holds individuals, or their families responsible for solving a wide range of problems many people face. Yet many doubt that issues such as child poverty or care for the elderly are any more private than, say, racial equality.

In this brief introduction, we will consider a few of the problems that are bound to arise when governments attempt to make policies about family life.

The Parameters of Policy-making

You may have gathered from earlier sections of this book that families are not without their problems. Take the example of domestic task sharing. There can be little doubt that wives do the lion's share of domestic work, whether they hold *no* paid job outside the home, a part-time job, or a full-time job. They do most of the domestic work whether there are *no* children in the home, infants, young children, or adolescents. And, they do most of the work whether their spouse is working full-time, part-time, or is unemployed.

Now this situation certainly seems unfair to most women. Further, the unfairness will probably cause resentment and conflict. The work overload may lead to problems of physical or mental health, and the conflict may generate domestic violence or marital breakdown. From the standpoint of the State, these are all undesirable outcomes, especially where dependent children are involved—for they are the blameless, helpless victims of the problem.

Yet, how should the State attempt to deal with this problem? Should it adopt a policy at all? And if so, what policy should it adopt? Asking this question, in relation to a problem that (to our knowledge) no state has attempted to solve, reveals some of the basic features of the policy process:

(a) For every policy effort, there must be a clear goal;
(b) Achieving the goal must lie within the means of the policy-maker; and
(c) The policy process must deal with interested parties who are likely to oppose the new policy.

How easy or difficult is it for the State to make family policy, in relation to each of these three parameters?

(a) A clear goal?

In the example we just looked at—unfair work sharing at home—we can see the first problem policy makers are likely to encounter: they may not have a clear goal. After all, does "fair" work sharing necessarily mean "equal" work sharing? Equality is relatively easy to achieve. If we are seeking precise equality in the household, it should be possible to divide up all tasks equally between the spouses (or, among all competent family members). We could rotate the tasks so that each spouse is responsible for a given task as often as the other spouse.

However, one spouse may be very good at a particular task (let's say, cooking) and very poor at another (for example, home repairs.) In that case, we may be willing to allow a specialization of functions, but require that the spouses do jobs of comparable worth and difficulty around the home. These notions of "comparable worth" (and "comparable difficulty") are not easy to put into effect, as employers have already come to realize. But in principle, it should be possible to operationalize these ideas.

However, this policy may have unexpected and irrational results. For example, suppose one spouse can charge $200 per hour for his or her time as a lawyer; but is obliged, instead, to spend five hours a week cleaning the kitchen—a job someone else could be paid to do for, say, $65. Will our policy allow spouses to "buy back" their time by paying someone else to do their share of the household work? Is it not more rational to conserve one spouse's $1000 earning potential by spending $65, than to mechanically oblige each spouse to spend an identical 5 hours scrubbing the broiler?

Well, that does sound more rational. On the other hand, if one spouse has an earning potential of $200 per hour and the other spouse, an earning potential of $20 per hour, then we are simply justifying domestic inequality. The latter spouse will always have to do ten hours of domestic labor for every hour the former spouse puts in. And, since women suffer sex discrimination in the paid work force, this virtually ensures that wives will end up working more hours than husbands—precisely the problem we set out to solve.

Perhaps, then, our goal should be to eliminate income discrimination against women; by this reasoning, equal work sharing in the home would follow naturally. Or, perhaps spouses should be expected to rethink their outlook on work sharing. If spouses cannot agree to an unequal split, based on unequal earning potential, then they should be obliged to reach an agreement based on other principles. Human relations don't always need to be economically rational. After all, if we were always economically rational, we might never get married in the first place; or, give birth to children, or try to be a good spouse, parent, and/or child to our family members.

So, perhaps our policy goal should not be to achieve equality in domestic work, it should be to gain consent from all concerned parties; and gaining consent may require irrational or nonrational behavior. Spouses may have to give up important earning opportunities to fulfil their household obligations, *not* because they could not find someone else to do them for pay, but in order to signify their willingness to sacrifice income for family solidarity.

Now, this may sound complicated and idealistic, and it is. We still have trouble defining our policy goal; what's more, we are starting to see that there will be enormous problems in putting a policy like this into practice. How will family members measure "comparable worth" or "equality"? How will they reach agreement in the event of different views? How will one spouse enforce compliance on the other? How will the State monitor whether the goal is being achieved or not?

Obviously, the State will have to consider what means it has at its disposal for making this policy work. Otherwise, the policy will be worthless; at best, a symbol of good intentions—at worst, a mockery of people with a problem to solve.

(b) Do policy-makers have the means?

It may have already become clear, in the example we have developed, that enforcing a family policy is no easy matter. In fact governments are not, by and large, equipped to intervene in domestic affairs. In many ways, they are prevented from doing so.

Just imagine how difficult and costly it would be to have government officials get around to every household in the nation to find out whether the workload was being shared equally! There are already enormous difficulties in getting people to fill out a census form once every ten years, or getting them to honestly calculate and pay their taxes. What makes us think we would do better finding out about their marital arrangements in relation to work sharing?

Often, at this point, the policy planner takes a different tack. Instead of asking, "Can I find the means to achieve a desired goal?" (in this case, to achieve domestic work equality), the planner may ask, "What worthwhile goal can I reasonably hope to achieve, with the means at my disposal?"

So, for example, it may be easier to banish workplace income discrimination against women than to banish economic rationality at home. And we have already noted that, conceivably, if women earned as much as their husbands, they might share the domestic work more equally. Therefore, planners might decide to opt for an attack on workplace discrimination *instead of* an attack on domestic inequality.

Or, they might decide it was easier to deal with the effects of domestic inequality on wives (physical exhaustion and stress, for example) than to deal with the causes. So, they might devise a policy of supporting more and better day care, or cheaper domestic services, or better transportation to and from work (cf. Michelson, 1985)—all with an eye to reducing the strain on overworked wives. (Of course, they could also consider subsidizing tranquilizers or paid vacations!)

In general, these kinds of solutions are easier to put into practice than many others. They simply throw money at the problem; a tried-and-true method of dealing with social problems. They do not threaten either husbands or bosses with the need to change their ways. So, if methods like this appeal to the taxpayers, they are likely to go ahead. If the taxpayers reject even these methods of dealing with the problem, the planner may be out of luck.

And this brings us to a third, very thorny, aspect of the policy process: how to deal with interested parties.

(c) What about the interested parties?

Interested parties are people who, often have an interest in things staying pretty much just the way they are, that is, in preventing or avoiding change. To bring about new policies, you have to take these people into account; either persuade them to cooperate, or overcome their opposition.

We have already noted that husbands and bosses have an interest in the present system of domestic inequality. Husbands get many domestic benefits without doing their share of the domestic work. Bosses get the workplace benefits of a devoted female work force without having to pay the wages men would demand (and get) for the same work. So neither bosses, nor husbands are going to readily change their ways. They have a stake in keeping things just the way they are.

We have already noted that taxpayers are also interested parties here, insofar as solutions to the problem of domestic inequality may require spending public money. To get change would require persuading taxpayers—many of whom are overworked women—to pay higher taxes.

Other stake holders are bureaucrats and/or private parties who have a stake in the way public money is currently being spent. If no additional taxes were raised, it would be necessary to shift tax dollars out of old programs into the new one; but obviously, people who benefited from the old programs would resist this change mightily.

Again, there are only so many ways to overcome objections or, more generally, to mobilize people for change. In his classic book, *The New Utopians: A Study of System Design and Social Change,* Robert Boguslaw (1965) describes several key types of policy planning: "formalist designs, heuristic designs, operating unit designs, and ad hoc designs."

Formalist designs are extremely detailed and specify not only the expected outcome, but also the assumed (stable) characteristics of all the units—the institutions and individuals—that will play a part. They are very popular with planners who use mathematical models of reality, because they seem so rigorous, exact, and objective.

For a variety of reasons, they are rarely appropriate for planning family policy. First, these planning styles assume a level of knowledge about social systems which is rarely justified. Second, they assume that people and situations will remain the same, in important ways, over long periods of time. This assumption is certainly unwarranted.

The *heuristic* approach "uses principles to provide guides for action . . . even in the face of completely unanticipated situations and in situations for which no formal model or analytic solution is available." (Boguslaw, 1965: 13.) The Golden Rule is an example of such a heuristic rule. If people obeyed the Golden Rule with some degree of dedication, it *might* solve the problem of domestic inequality.

However, you can easily see the advantages and disadvantages of basing a social system on a single heuristic principle, or even a few. Even among people with the best intentions, there is a problem of reaching agreement about how to interpret the decision rule (or heuristic). This may explain why, invariably, religious systems and codes of law evolve from simple documents (the Ten Commandments, the Napoleonic Code) into enormous, complex systems of decision rules.

By contrast, the *operating unit* approach "begins with people or machines carefully selected or tooled to possess certain performance characteristics . . . The various systems that get developed through the use of this approach are, to a considerable extent, based upon the range of flexibility possessed by the operating units." So, for example, we could attempt to socialize all children to believe in, and work for, domestic equality; then simply let them go at it.

However, this method raises certain problems. First, can you engineer human beings to have the very characteristics you require them to have? And, if it were possible, would it be desirable? Would it run the risk of horrible despotism? Second, is there any reason to think that people created in a certain fashion would know how to invent or use social institutions in a way that would accomplish their programmed goal?

It is easy to see that there are serious problems with the formalist, heuristic, and operating unit designs. That is probably why *ad hoc* designs—or, as we shall call them, "incremental policy making"—are the most common where family policy is concerned.

According to Boguslaw, the *ad hoc* approach is very useful in getting the system to change, by using people and resources as they become available. It is a very result-oriented, pragmatic approach. Indeed, "The ad hoc approach may also be used when the designer has no clearly perceived view of the future system." Still, the approach is likely to keep the customer, user, or public happy by giving the impression of effort and change. It is a type of "muddling through, a seat of the pants technique, or simply being practical."

According to Boguslaw, the shortcomings of this ad hoc, or incremental, method are the following:

1. The relative absence of predictability.
2. The tendency to regard environmental conditions as fixed . . . [as in] "That's all the public will stand for."
3. The tendency to perpetuate temporary arrangements beyond their period of usefulness simply because they were at one time perceived as . . . necessary for success.

As we examine a small sample of policy issues in this section, we will see many of these problems emerge. It cannot be said that family life is an area in which planners have made dramatic inroads.

What Family Policy Planners Have Done

To reiterate the theme of this book, family life has always been varied and changeable. History shows it has never been free of problems and injustices. We are dreaming if we think families ever provided most, or many, people with the love, companionship, and parenting one would ideally wish for. So, we must first enter into policy making with a willingness to accept historical fact, not myth, as the basis for our plans. We must know what human beings have been capable of doing in the past if we are to minimize mistakes in the future.

Second, we must truly understand the reasons for changes in family life that critics of the modern family decry: the reasons why more couples divorce, more women work for pay, more people cohabit than in the past, and so on. Families have changed for very good reasons, not the least of which is a greater concern with the rights and needs of women and children. Not content to be treated as objects—household possessions—more and more family members have come to claim their due as full-fledged members of society.

In fact, "the family" is not, and cannot be, a haven in a heartless world. In part, that is because all of life, family life included, suffers the influence of economic and political uncertainty. Family life cannot be a stranger to the stresses of work, the dangers of international affairs, or the rage of poverty. It cannot prevent these things or make them go away. If we want better family life, we are going to have to make a better world. We must deal with public issues in the public arena, not try to banish them to the private "havens" of family life.

Beyond that, all of life is made up of people with diverse, changing needs and views. Conflict is inevitable in human affairs. If people cannot avoid or resolve their conflicts, they may have to end their relations with each other. That is why spouses divorce and children choose to live away from their parents. It does no good to deplore the inevitable or brand people "narcissists," or "selfish," if they have to change their lives. We are all responsible for our own lives, as much as we are for the lives of those we love. Family living has to take this fact into account.

For this reason, we cannot assume our families will stand still and provide us with complete certainty and security. There is no denying the psychological value of certainty. But neither is there reason to think certainty is attainable in a society where people have the freedom to choose their private lives. To repeat, the family today meets no economic functions for the most part, and varies in its ability to meet emotional needs and fulfill child-raising functions. In truth, the family's most important role in a stressful, changing, varied world is to provide a place where people can cooperate to work out their own destinies.

In this context, most policy planners tend to be cautious and work gradually. They try to help as many people as they can while hindering the fewest, and make no unwarranted assumptions about a single grand plan for family life. Their policies aim at helping people pursue their own particular conceptions of the best possible family life, given their needs and values at the time. They avoid policies or plans which presuppose one "best" form of family life. In these respects, most policies are what Boguslaw would call ad hoc policies.

Many of the excerpts in this section—especially those from the West—reflect this gradual, ad hoc or incremental approach to family life as a social issue. They show an awareness of the many problems besetting family life around the world today. They also show awareness that a single grand plan—whether elaborately formalistic, or based on a central heuristic—is undesirable or impossible to carry out, even if desired.

Incrementalism has less often been the way communistic countries such as the former USSR and China make social policy, for a variety of reasons. First, these countries have claimed to follow Marxist-Leninist principles—a grand social and political vision of the future—in setting their social policy. Second, these countries have historically adopted central planning strategies. They have shown little responsiveness to regional variation or competing interest groups.

In such societies, then, people who make family policy have *not* had to reconcile competing interest groups. They *have* had to formulate family policy that accorded with socialist ideology. In some cases, they designed family policy to accord with a formal plan driven by economic goals. More often, family policy was shaped around certain conceptions of the desired "operating unit"—the socialist personality and so on.

Chinese planners have also had to fight against ancient family traditions rooted in Confucianist philosophy and religion. Every change in family life has meant reforming the way people think about many aspects of society and culture. With so much planning to do, there is a great need for research on family-related issues. Yet China's research capability is limited, for a variety of reasons. Poverty is one. A lack of the tradition of free inquiry is another. The systematic destruction of intellectual life during Mao Tse-tung's "cultural revolution" a generation ago is a third.

In some instances, ad hoc policy making is more dangerous than any of the alternative strategies. For example, incrementalism is probably not the best way to deal with the population problems facing sub-Saharan Africa. There, drastic solutions are needed in a hurry. Already, huge numbers of people are suffering from famine and war. Epidemics of disease are commonplace, and an AIDS epidemic that may kill huge portions of the world population is underway there. Reduced childbearing will not automatically solve all these problems. But all these problems will be easier to solve when there are fewer people straining a nation's supply of food, shelter, medicine, and social welfare.

Elsewhere, ad hoc policy making is relatively successful. Countries with smaller problems to deal with can afford to deal with them piecemeal. So, for example, different European countries have adopted different strategies for dealing with single-parent families. Their solutions have only one thing in common: one-parent or mother-only families rarely receive a lot of attention on the public-policy agenda. Some solutions work in the short term but cause other problems in the longer term. In their varied ways, these policies make single-parent families viable, if not ideal.

Increasingly, the governments of modern societies have been intruding on family life, usually on the side of the wives and children. So, as an excerpt in this section shows, some social policies are aimed at strengthening the rights of women and children in the event of a divorce. (More also needs to be done to strengthen these groups in the event there is *not* a divorce!)

The modern state also has a vested interest in shaping and protecting the next generation, often against their parents. Yet the interests of parents and the State are not always opposed. Parents have many reasons for turning to the government for help, and day care is one of them. Throughout the modern world, there is a "day-care dilemma." Many parents need high-quality, low-cost child care that will permit them to work for pay. Some countries are much farther along that others in providing high-quality day care to all children (and parents) who need it. In this respect, the United States is far behind Scandinavia.

As we see, the State has a difficult role to play in family life today. In responding to people's concerns, policy makers try to ground their decisions in knowledge about what family forms are evolving and what citizens will accept. For its part, social science will have to do better in defining and understanding what the family is, how it is changing, and why.

References

BOGUSLAW, R. (1965) *The New Utopians* Englewood Cliffs, NJ: Prentice-Hall.

LASCH, C. (1979) *Haven in a Heartless World: The Family Besieged.* New York: Basic Books.

MICHELSON, W. (1985) "Divergent convergence: the daily routines of employed spouses as a public affairs agenda," *Public Affairs Report*, 26(4), August, 1–9.

Introduction

Family life is often about the procreation and care of children. Not only has this role belonged to families through all of human history, but every other form of intimacy and dependency has, by now, found a variety of other forms. In most societies, a great many people enjoy sex outside of marriage, get needed economic support from the State, and base their social lives on friendship, neighborhood, or occupational ties rather than on the family.

Yet, though the procreation and care of children remains a central concern of family life, it has also become a central concern of the State. Like the family, the modern state has a vested interest in shaping and protecting the next generation. Children will become the next generation of citizens, workers, and taxpayers. As such, they are the future of the society, and the State must protect this future by monitoring and sometimes taking control of children's education, health, and welfare. Sometimes it means protecting the child's interest against those of his or her parents and community. Always it means setting limits to what families can do with their children.

Over the twentieth century, this has meant setting more limits and enforcing them more strenuously. Necessarily, state involvement has meant a shrinkage in the power of "family" (read "parents") over their children. In this article, Pitrou suggests this development is undesirable. She considers what French parents can do about their shrinking power, and examines efforts to expand that power.

49
Who Has Power Over Our Children—
The Family or the State?

Agnes Pitrou

Societies are rarely disposed to suicide and seek above all to perpetuate themselves. This is why societies give priority to the reconstitution and assimilation of their capital of children which is a guarantee of the future.

Nevertheless, the biological reproduction of this human capital demands a voluntary action on the part of the couple who, whether officially united or not, bring children into the world. Normally at least one member of the couple wishes to take responsibility for the child.

This responsibility is the basis of the family's social power. It is in the name of this same responsibility and at the cost of continuous development and adaptation, that the family has until now weathered all social, economic and political contingencies. The political power is

Source: Pitrou, A (1982) "Who has power over our children? A dialogue between the Family and the State," *Journal of Comparative Family Studies*, 13, 2, summer, 171–183.

only interested in the couple and the relationship between men and women in so far as it effects biological and social reproduction and the transmission of wealth and values from parents to children. Even though children in industrial societies are less and less the source of wealth for their parents they once were, they still provide families otherwise stripped of economic power social prestige with a means of returning a measure of power.

POWER SHARED ACCORDING TO POLITICAL CONCEPTS

This potential power in fact occupies an increasingly preeminent, if not unique, position as the status of the family develops in the industrialized countries. As certain historians of the family, like Aries (1960) and Shorter (1975) have shown, the family has gradually realized that children are the basis of its existence, especially since in modern societies its economic power has been reduced both as producer and consumer. The State in principle recognizes the responsibility of parents for the education of their children which should give them a certain power of decision and even allow them to bring pressure to bear, yet the division of responsibilities between the State including more or less dependent institutions, and the family, is the object of a fundamental ideological debate fed by all sorts of religious, ethical, philosophical or political considerations, which create cleavages in theory and practice.[1] Among these cleavages the opposite extremes often curiously resemble each other.

CHILDREN AS BELONGING TO THE FAMILY

The family is the basis of society and must be vested with exclusive authority over the education of children. This is the position still maintained by the conservatives and traditionalists, who are often among those who oppose Vatican II and politically right-wing if not extreme right-wing. They believe that the family should be strong, that it should be responsible for its children, that these children should be numerous, that the father should be listened to, as a compensation for his role as a good worker and that mother should be respected as a compensation for her maternal and domestic functions.

As a corollary, the family has certain duties. It must inculcate into children respect for the established norms and transmit traditional values. For the State, the family therefore seems to constitute a good relay unit for influencing successive generations even if the family refuses power-sharing.

Although apparently discreet, the State in

fact controls and prescribes the right manner of conduct, like the divine right industrialists who controlled all aspects of family life during the boom period of industrial development. The establishment retains the right to decide which are the "good" and the "bad" families according to their own conception of what is good for children.

Family rights can also be asserted by those of opposite political opinions. The left-wing protest movement strongly opposes the repressive normalizing role of the State in its dealings with the family. Repressive social control is spoken of particularly in connection with the activity of social workers and the increasing tutelage of the family especially among the financially and culturally underprivileged.

These ideological positions are sometimes translated into reality by refusing to carry out obligations imposed by the State (such as vaccination or schooling) or by replacing official institutions with spontaneous organizations, e.g. the creation of day-nurseries and "free" schools organized by the parents.

Nevertheless, unlike the traditionalists the holders of this opinion are not profamily. Although, they defend the right of families to dispose of themselves and their children, this right applies not only to traditional families but to any individual who has brought a child into the world (the individual's right to bring a child into the world or not being freely recognized). Everyone must have the freedom and right to be a parent and spouse according to his own conception. This is why children's rights are, when necessary, opposed to the arbitrary power of parents, and why a claim is made for "children's power" (Rochefort, 1976). In fact, . . . the assertion of the family's power tends to deny an oppressive and normalizing state power.

THE CHILD SEEN AS BELONGING TO THE STATE

Whereas the opinions described above are devoted to safeguarding parental autonomy, in the name of very different principles, we shall now

---

[1]This recognition of family right has led some totalitarian countries, such as Franco in Spain to confer family suffrage to the heads of families.

examine the inverse position, i.e. the demand for a more or less absolute state power in the organization of children's education. This claim is no more the exclusive privilege of a homogeneous political movement than the last, since Fascist revolutionary and post revolutionary governments have supported this claim and put it into practice.

The family is no longer considered to be the State's sure and effective ally but is . . . the object of . . . hostility, since the family can only be the bearer and transmitter of harmful and outdated principles, or at least contrary to the new "order". . . . Only a government . . . is capable of defining the education required to train the new men which the regime needs.

Educational directives should . . . predominate over family education, at the most leaving parents a few intervals during the day and the year in which to exercise their influence on condition that this remains a strictly private matter. Beyond that, the child should be completely removed from the parent's control by the institutions which look after them. Sometimes children even . . . play the role of the police when they are ordered to "re-educate" or even denounce cases of ideological deviation or opposition dissident behaviour.

No industrialized society has yet persisted in the long term experiment of totally substituting a collective education for the family environment[2]. For example, the post-revolutionary Soviet Union having attempted to undermine the family in countries under its control, has returned to a very classical conception of matrimony and the role of parents as well as the rights and duties of the family, while continuing to promote collective education. . . .

When one makes a synthesis of these conflicting policies, it would seem that the criteria which guide governments in sharing educational responsibility with the family, fall into three categories:

1. From the economic standpoint, does the family produce an education in optimum financial conditions which prepares designated place in society and provides them with the attitudes which the authorities deem appropriate to their society? Or is it not more efficient economically that . . . other specialized and more competent adults give children the necessary social education?

2. From the standpoint of the inculcation of norms and values do parents have the right doctrinal bias and are they capable of exerting a real influence?[3]

3. From the standpoint of socialization, what type of distribution of positions in society . . . does the family offer in guiding its children? Does the family tend to reproduce class stratifications, or is the family the agent of mobility transforming the order of the preceding generation? Does the family maintain the social hierarchy, for example by stimulating or obstructing the ambition of the young?

The interplay of the powers conceded to the family [and required of it] and the powers which the family has tried to win and maintain, make the family appear as a social regulator endowed with a great persuasive force because it is a unique institution and therefore difficult to replace, and because it is a long-term force with a power of inertia and passive resistance which allows it, . . . to counteract the fluctuations and excesses of the central power. The dispersal of the family into numerous cells difficult to mobi-

---

[2]The Nazi experiment (an odious attempt at "controlled" reproduction in forced prostitution centres) has fortunately never been repeated. As for the present kibbutzim experiment, the evidence is too diverse and fragmentary to allow us to draw conclusions for society as a whole.

[3]The most virulent critics of the family recognized the effectiveness of its inculcation and protest against it precisely because of its repressive and normalizing role. Cf. Reich (1968): "The family is a centre for the conservative ideological atmosphere. . . . The family is a factory producing authoritarian ideologies and conservative mental structures".

lize or even control can have unforeseen consequences in the case of authoritarian State action.

THE SCEPTICISM OF PARENTS ABOUT THEIR OWN POWER

. . . Contrary to the accusations of resignation made against them, parents of all backgrounds are quite convinced that they still have an important role to play in the education of their children, and, marginal cases excluded, they use all the means at their disposal and are greatly concerned to give them whatever may be necessary. But they are increasingly sceptical, on the one hand, about the real possibilities of modifying the State policies concerning schooling, future employment, etc. which greatly influence the future of their children. On the other hand, they are sceptical of their power to block the autonomy of their increasingly precocious children. Among the upper classes this autonomy is appreciated and recognized as an irreversible and even desirable tendency in modern education. Among the working classes, there is greater nervousness about the authorities, because of their strong desire that their children should succeed, and also because what is deemed "the right education" provides a criterion by which parents will be judged by their neighbours and especially the representatives of social institutions.

The main tendency therefore is to make repeated demands on the State to increase family benefits, as though it were a tutelary power. However it is not always properly realized that the State's coercive power and power of control will increase as it takes on more and more responsibility for the young.

In addition, the effect of administrative measures and the authorities is to strengthen the conviction among parents of their own guilt particularly when there is State supervision and the judicial system is put into action. Whether parents are simply taken to task for the misdeeds of their children or whether, in extreme cases, they

are stripped of their educational role, this is always in the name of parental power unwisely exercised. Conversely when the child is unusually successful, the parents are praised officially or unofficially as the coauthors of the success.

Attached as they are to the appearances of the micro powers which punctuate their daily lives, families in general show a deep scepticism concerning their capacity to influence their children's future. There is no contradiction between these two attitudes. Since they are not in command of the essential controls they try to reassure themselves by the daily exercise of their often illusory choices. However when . . . they see the future of their children, they allow their doubts to affect the realization of their hopes and plans, even when their children are still young and nothing has yet been decided about their lives.

REAL FAMILY POWER IS HIDDEN

The analysis of powerlessness, which deeply affects families at certain periods, does not result in criticism of the State power which is certainly ill-identified. Even though in general French families continue to defend their rights over children's education against a rather mythical "collectivist" offensive, they do not reproach the State for depriving them of a specific power because they find it difficult to locate. The means by which the authorities extend their influence are not obvious to them. Perhaps here and there, there still exists the hope, more or less well-founded that they will always be able to find a way to circumvent any law which encroaches on their autonomy. The prohibition of contraception and abortion is a striking example in this respect; for a long time a large part of the population managed to limit the number of their progeny despite the dangers for women. This explains the difficulty of establishing a collective family strategy in opposition to the State.

This use of passive resistance constitutes an intangible but important power in face of governmental injunctions and recommendations. With respect to children, the most striking effect of this—long before schooling—is the refusal to procreate and the desire to limit the number of one's progeny. . . .

A less striking example . . . is the decision of the family concerning the vocation of their children. This constitutes a masked opposition to predictions and planning. Whatever the outlook for the job market, families continue to put the highest value on long years of study and non-manual employment. . . . The State has not succeeded in channelling young people towards manual apprenticeship in sufficient numbers for a healthy state of employment. The same may be said in relation to the . . . schooling of infants of 2 or 3, which has never been encouraged by the authorities. . . . The authorities nevertheless had to . . . respond to this limited, but urgent, demand.

These examples show what might happen if families realized their collective power as reproducers of human capital. Feminists have sometimes indicated the reprisals they might carry out in response to alleged State repression. Yet, families in general, especially among certain social groups, feel ill-equipped for an explosive conflict. They are too dependent on the State benefits to which they are accustomed. Moreover, it is difficult to imagine what . . . might provoke such a crystallization of the isolated family cells.

Conclusion

. . . In societies as complex as those of the industrialized countries, there are too many intermediary powers which prevent the family and the State from seeing each other face to face. There is the power of employers, for instance, who control the family income of their employees and also control their life-style by means of the consumer expenditure they promote or impose. There is the power of the media which convey educational norms and modify their ori-

entation. There is the power of religions and professional groups who disseminate their idea of social roles. All this results in compromise or dependence on a dominant group. The central power then either makes use of these groups or attempts to exercise its own direct influence on the education of future generations by means of its own institutions.

Furthermore, it appears to be increasingly complicated to introduce a strict division of labour in the field of education. The tendency, which only allows parents power at a sentimental level, has endured not only for economic reasons, but also because it is increasingly obvious that feelings need a material support and that they cannot easily be limited to a specific area.

The increasingly precarious development of independence among the young ultimately appears to parents and public opinion to be a greater threat to parental power than the rigid control and prescriptions of the State. This results in the paradox—in marginal cases, it is true—that parents turn to the authorities . . . for assistance when they are no longer able to exercise the necessary authority over their children. Like every other type of power, the family is only worth the means at its disposal: today one is obliged to conclude that it is a hidden power on the defensive despite public declarations about "the family as the basic cell of society".

REFERENCES

ARIES, P. 1960. L'enfant et la vie familiale sous l' Ancien Régime. Paris; Plon.

BERTAUX, D. 1977. Destins personnels et structure de classes. Paris. PUF.

DELEUZE, G. 1976. "Introduction", in J. Donzelot, La police des familles. Paris: Editions de Minuit.

DONZELOT, J. 1976. La police des familles. Préface de DELEUZE (G). Paris; Editions de Minuit.

GISCARD D'ESTAING, V. 1975. Discours de la Bourboule.

—— 1976. Discours a l'occasion du 30ème Annives-

DONZELOT, J. 1976. La police des familles. Préface de DELEUZE (G). Paris; Editions de Minuit.

GISCARD D'ESTAING, V. 1975. Discours de la Bourboule.

—— 1976. Discours a l'occasion du 30ème Annivesaire de l'Union Nationale des Associations Familiales. Paris.

LORY, B. 1979. Rapport de synthése a la Conférence de l'Union Internationale des Organisations Familiales. Paris. UNESCO.

PITROU, A. 1978. Associations familiale et jeu social. In Informations Sociales, n° 6–7/1979.

—— 1978. Vivre sans famille ? Toulouse; Privat.

REICH, W. 1968. La revolution sexuelle. Paris, Collection 10/18.

ROCHEFORT, C. 1976. Les enfants d'abroad. Paris, Grasset. Cf "La Charte des Enfants" propounded by BOULIN (B.), 1977, and MENDEL (G.), 1974 "Pour dècoloniser l'enfant", Paris ; Payot.

SHORTER, E. 1977. The making of the Modern Family, New York; Basic Books.

Introduction

The preceding excerpt noted that parents have less and less power over their children all the time. In part, this is because the state is becoming more powerful. Families are also becoming less able to control or assist their children in what they have to do. When this happens, parents often ask "the authorities" for help.

However parents have other reasons for turning to the state for help, and daycare is one of them. Throughout the modern world, there is a "day-care dilemma." Many parents need high-quality, low-cost childcare that will permit them to work for pay. As Wolfe says in this excerpt, "one should never forget . . . that day care is provided primarily to serve parents and only secondarily to serve children."

Some countries are much farther along than others in providing high-quality day care to all children (and parents) who need it. In this respect, the United States is far behind Scandinavia. Does this mean that the United States should adopt Scandinavian methods? Research on day care in Denmark, Norway, and Sweden raises questions about the long-term effects on children. The effect on parents is more certain: a great many feel dissatisfied and guilty about leaving their children in day-care facilities through much of their childhood.

Like Pitrou, Wolfe suggests that the state ought to spend money advancing the family, not simply sloganeering about it. Perhaps everyone would be better off if more parents could work part time and care for their children part time. Maybe no one really needs more day-care spaces so that more parents can work more hours per day. On the other hand, can parents really afford to give up a third or half of their household income to care for their own children? And would they all want to?

50
A Scandinavian Perspective on the Day-Care Dilemma

Alan Wolfe

... Nowhere is the public commitment to child care more extensive than in Scandinavia. Sweden and Denmark have both committed themselves to providing full-time institutional care for children from the age of three months until they begin school (typically at age seven).

According to a recent study by the quasi-official Social Research Institute of Denmark, only 5 percent of Danish children under the age of six are being raised full-time by their mothers at home; fewer than 20 percent are being watched at home by working parents on shifts, mothers on pregnancy leave, unemployed parents, or parents who work at home. Twenty-one percent are in private day care and 55 percent are in public day care. In Sweden fewer children are in public day care, in part because of more generous maternity leaves. (The Swedish Social Democrats recently committed themselves to full maternity benefits for eighteen months, a policy that would greatly lower reliance on public day care for infants.) ... About a third of Swedish children remain at home with their mothers, but that minority will probably continue to shrink. ...

Enthusiasts for public day care rightly point out that there are few latchkey children in Scandinavia, and that children in day care are better nourished and more self-sufficient than children who stay at home. If the American and Scandinavian ways of raising children were the only ones from which to choose, the latter would be preferable by most criteria. Yet one should never forget, especially when turning to Scandinavia for lessons relevant to America, that public day care is provided primarily to serve parents and only secondarily to serve children. ...

DAY CARE'S EFFECT ON CHILDREN

... There is no unambiguous answer to the question of whether extensive public day care is better for children than the "traditional" family. ... Bengt-Erik Andersson, a Swedish educational psychologist, carried out a longitudinal study of 119 Stockholm and Gothenberg children from their first to their eighth years. He found that age of entry into public day care was a consistent predictor of success later on: children who began attending day care earlier fared better when they reached school.

Andersson and Lars Dencik (who has studied the lives of small children in Scandinavia) both conclude that the day-care system works well. Yet the matter is far from settled. A governmental commission on the status of children in Denmark, contradicting more optimistic studies, wrote in 1981 of a "closed child's world" cut off from adult life. Echoing that report, the National Association of School Psychologists found:

It is becoming more common that children who are beginning school are antisocial, loud, and confused. They are uncertain, unhappy, and badly in need of contact. They do not have the awareness that early beginners in school once had and they are missing moral conceptions. They have no respect for elders and are untrained in using their body and their hands. Many are passive or aggressive and they do not understand ordinary reprimands.

Ultimately, however, no amount of empirical research can resolve all the questions about day care. ... And even if the experts unanimously supported day care, nearly all Scandinavians—especially women—would still feel guilty about relying extensively on government to watch

Source: Wolfe, A. (1989) "The day-care dilemma: a Scandinavian perspective," *The Public Interest,* 95, Spring, 14–23.

their children for them. Most people know that specific children have specific needs, and that parents are in the best position to know what those needs are.

Even in an ideal world, where parents could be sure that the strangers who cared for their children nonetheless loved them as their own and spared no expense in helping them, leaving one's children in the care of others would probably still cause guilt. And the Scandinavian system . . . is far from ideal. Though Swedish taxpayers pay approximately $10,000 per year for every child in public day care, a series of problems plagues day-care institutions—nearly all of them having to do with money.

CONFLICTS OF EQUITY AND OBLIGATION

. . . Waiting lists abound for public day care in Scandinavia. In Denmark, which has the most extensive system of institutionalized care, two-thirds of the counties have waiting lists. A child growing up in Aalborg may not obtain a place in public day care until it is too late to use it. Rural areas (in Norway, for example) tend to have longer waiting lists than urban areas.

The most serious distributional imbalances, however, are . . . class-related. Middle-class people in all three Scandinavian countries rely on public day care more than working-class people. Day-care centers are open only during the day, making them unavailable for those who work nights and weekends. They are often not trusted by immigrant men, who are afraid . . . their children will become assimilated and their wives more conversant with their rights. Middle-class users know how to gain and keep access to public day-care institutions and are far better organized to take advantage of available services than working-class users.

As a result . . . the moral solidarity of the welfare state is cracking, if only slightly. Rather than symbolizing equal treatment for all and fostering collectivity, public day care reinforces the growing tendency of individuals in welfare states

to calculate which programs provide enough benefits to compensate for the taxes imposed. Using day care is a way in which middle-class people use the state to hire others to perform tasks they once did themselves.

A second series of problems faces those who . . . obtain places for their children. Bengt-Erik Andersson's study emphasized that good day care can work well. Not all public day care is good, however. The most serious problem is the rate of job turnover in day-care institutions. Many day-care workers are young women who have recently joined the labor force and are willing . . . to put up with the low pay. They leave when marriage or a new job beckons. If a child enters a day-care . . . at age three (all the Scandinavian countries have separate institutions for those under three and those over), it is likely that all the original workers will have left by the time the child starts school. The only way to correct this problem is to increase the pay and status of day-care work, but given fiscal constraints, that would decrease the availability of day care.

"Good" day care also falls victim to bureaucratization. Nothing horrifies Scandinavians more than the stories of child abuse coming from the United States, where day care is poorly regulated. (For that reason alone, the Scandinavian system is superior.) But overregulation can also cause problems. Government provision of a service comes complete with relatively inflexible rules, an overemphasis on procedures, and discussions framed by an emphasis on rights, often to the exclusion of obligations.

Many day-care workers are mothers of small children. These women are often idealistic and caring . . . but tend toward the left politically and are highly aware of their trade-union benefits. Insistent on their rights—such as periodic vacations, routine coffee breaks, and regular working hours—they often feel torn between solidarity to their colleagues and concern for the children in their care. Women who raise children at home must balance their obligation to themselves with their obligation to their children. Women who raise the children of others as a career have far more obligations to balance: to themselves, to their colleagues, to their own children, and to the children they are watching. As obligations proliferate, the children's needs may get lost in the shuffle.

PROVIDING SERVICE AND RESTRICTING CHOICES

If there is a consensus among the experts on children in the Scandinavian countries, it runs as follows: public day care can help build a child's healthy feelings of autonomy—but only if care is limited to about twenty hours a week. Less than that, and children become withdrawn. More, and they tend to become aggressive. Common sense, then, would suggest that children spend part of their time in public day-care facilities, and that parents work only part-time when their children are small.

Common sense, however, has not won out. Part of the reason is economic. Rapidly changing economic conditions have made it enormously difficult for Scandinavians *not* to exercise their right to full-time day care. Inflation and tax rates of 50 percent or more have combined to decrease the typical family's ability to live on one or one and one-half incomes. Knowing that day care is available makes it possible for employers to keep wages down, for the state to keep taxes up, and for husbands to encourage their wives to work without taking on additional child-care responsibilities themselves. As a result, most couples have little choice but to work full-time and send their children to day care.

In addition, the bureaucratization of a public service like day care makes it difficult to accommodate part-time users. Part-time work tends to be opposed by many women's organizations, which are committed to the idea of full equality for women in the labor market. Day-care workers themselves . . . support full-time work to protect the integrity of their jobs. Once day care is brought into the public sector, with its strong unions and firm rules, it loses much of its flexibility. Efforts by parents to play a greater role in

the governance of day-care centers, for example, are often opposed by a variety of entrenched interests. . . .

Studies of public opinion indicate continued support for . . . public day care. But subtle shifts have taken place. Instead of arguing that day care is a positive good, recent research suggests it does no harm. Surveys indicate that women want to work part-time when their children are very small. . . . Day care, in short, is an imperfect solution to the conflict between the needs of parents and those of their young children. Given one goal—equality between the sexes in the workplace—Scandinavians support public day care. Given another—doing what is best for their own children—they try to find ways to limit their reliance upon it.

SERVICE FOR "THE HARRIED LEISURE CLASS"

One of Sweden's most respected economists, Staffan B. Linder . . . once wrote a book called *The Harried Leisure Class*. The book . . . describes trends that affect most Scandinavians. . . . In all the Scandinavian countries people are working longer hours than ever before. Scandinavians lead busy lives. Both parents have jobs. Store hours in Denmark and Norway are highly restricted, and so most Scandinavians must do all their shopping in the last half hour of the day or in three hours on Saturday morning. And even though Scandinavians now have fewer children, they still have some, whose needs must be met as well.

. . . The pressures of work and family life make nearly everyone touchy and make feeling guilty a national pastime. . . . Fathers have always spent too little time with their children. Now mothers have joined them. The state has filled in because somebody has to watch children when everyone else is busy.

Recognizing that public day care has been advanced in the interest of parents would help to improve it. So long as people assume that children will be better off because of public day care, they will be likely to rely upon it too much. But the dissatisfaction and guilt felt by many Scandinavian parents indicate that parents . . . realize government ought to support families, not replace them.

How should Scandinavians reform their day-care policies? Berkeley professor Neil Gilbert . . . has suggested the period when parents have small children ought to be viewed as a special phase in the life cycle. Parents who stay home serve not only their own children, but society as well, by reducing the cost to others. Such parents ought therefore to be given credit. Gilbert suggests mothers who raise their own children could be given preferential treatment when applying for civil-service employment after their children have grown older, or perhaps advanced standing at educational institutions. In Scandinavian societies, proposals have been advanced, usually by . . . conservative and religious parties, to pay mothers who . . . stay home with their own children, since almost any such program would cost less than public day care.

Nearly all of these proposals are opposed by unions, women's organizations, and the Social Democratic parties. The logic of the modern welfare state stresses universalization and equality; it is consequently reluctant to admit the need for exceptions. Given these political realities, reforms are more likely to come in the form of new targeted benefits, such as extended parental leave. An eighteen-month parental-leave policy, at full pay with job guarantees, would enable parents to stay at home with their infants without sacrificing their careers.

. . . Governmental wage supplements would let couples decide for themselves how to allocate their responsibilities. Each parent could work three-quarter time while the children were young, or one could work full-time and the other half. It would even be possible for one to work time and a half while the other stayed home. Government would insure that families were paid the equivalent of two incomes—since families with small children tend to have high expenses—while leaving parents enough time to

rely on public day care only twenty hours a week and to care for their children the rest of the time. At the same time, struggles over gender roles would be left to individual wives and husbands, since they would have to negotiate their own agreements about who is to spend more time with the children. Most important, the wage-supplement program . . . would probably cost less than the universal provision of public child care. . . .

LESSONS FOR THE U.S.

. . . America has not yet made any serious public commitment to day care, relying instead upon a hodgepodge of solutions that is worse than Scandinavian programs for both parents and children. But patterns of American family life have changed; two-career families are here to stay. There is a positive role for government to play in offsetting the costs of the change.

It is clearly unwise, however, to turn the problem of raising the children of two-career families entirely over to government. In dealing with the intimate concerns of family life, strict rules and bureaucratic procedures work less well than intuition, common sense, and flexibility. Part-time work may conflict with the goal of equal pay for women, but it makes sense for children. Voucher schemes—which the Bush administration is likely to propose—should be designed to give parents flexibility. User fees for public day-care are not inappropriate; those who have resources ought to pay more so that those who lack resources can benefit.

There is little chance, given American conservatism and the limits on our fiscal resources, that we will soon establish a system of universal day care subsidized by government. Instead of bemoaning that fact as evidence of backwardness, we Americans ought instead to appreciate the advantages that being backward provides. A society that loves children will use the state to provide for them, but will also allow parents the time to be with them.

Introduction

One means by which the State can regulate family life is through the legal system. For example, by regulating the conditions under which adults form, maintain, and dissolve relationships, it sets limits to the harm people can suffer as spouses. The State is not concerned about whether people are kind and loving to one another in their family lives; but it is concerned about whether they are cruel, abusive, or dangerous.

That is not to say that the State has a complete picture of the downside of modern family life, for it does not. There are undoubtedly thousands of instances of cruelty, abuse, and danger that remain hidden for every instance that comes to light. Yet, when instances of domestic violence or child abuse *do* come to light, the State most certainly takes an interest.

Increasingly, the governments of modern societies have been stepping into family life on the side of the historically suppressed, namely, wives and children. This is largely to rectify the historic and continuing imbalance of power in families; children are always less powerful and independent than parents; wives are usually less powerful and independent than husbands.

Of course, wives have gained greater independence as they have entered the labor force and earned incomes of their own. Yet Excerpt 41 by Arendell has shown that in the event of divorce, women continue to bear heavier costs than men due to labor force discrimination (among other things). Domestic violence also remains a serious concern. What can the State, through family law, do about the danger and unfairness that women face in family life? That is the question this excerpt seeks to answer.

51

A Feminist Perspective on Family Law

Vivienne H. Ullrich

Family law in New Zealand affords equal rights to women as parents and as spouses. But the experience of many women using this law is one of disadvantage and injustice. These difficulties arise . . . from the notions of procedural justice deeply entrenched in our legal system, and from power structures embedded in the administration of the system. . . .

Source: Ullrich, V. H. (1986) "Equal but not equal: A feminist perspective on family law," *Women's Studies International Forum*, 9, 1, 41–48.

Because law is dispute-oriented . . . the legal system confronts social realities in the form of a two-sided debate between individuals. It is not regarded as just to resolve issues between individuals by imposing a solution designed to redress the biased valuing which is endemic in the entire social system. Ms Jones should not be allowed a greater share of the matrimonial property merely because she is less educated than her husband, or because her nursing job has paid less than her husband's work as an airline pilot. She can receive an equal share of the assets which recognises her equal labour input but not a greater share which redresses an inequality outside her relationship with Mr Jones. . . .

It would be regarded as very radical to suggest that in dealing with marriage break-up, courts should assess the future command over resources of each party and distribute assets accordingly. . . .

The 'clean break' principle which is now used to determine the distribution of economic resources on marriage break-up looks entirely to the past. The assets which the parties have already accumulated are to be divided on the basis of past contributions and from thence forward the parties should be economically independent of each other with ongoing maintenance being awarded for one spouse only in exceptional circumstances and usually for a limited time. This principle has caused problems when the matrimonial home is the only asset and is needed for the children but the backward-looking clean break is still advocated wherever possible.

The courts do look to the future when making decisions concerning the children of a marriage. In this area the welfare of the children is seen as overriding any justice between the two parents. . . . So a woman may have to share childcare arrangements with her ex-husband to a far greater degree than was ever the case before the divorce but at the same time fund her (probably major) share of the childcare from a vastly reduced resource base.

Even where the substantive family law affords formal equality to each party, women may still be disadvantaged by the administration of the system because they have less support with the power structure and less command over resources than men. The Family Courts Act 1980 and the Family Proceedings Act 1980 have instituted new procedures for dealing with family related matters which include many opportunities by way of counselling, mediation and assessment for family disputes to be resolved outside the courtroom. These less adversarial procedures have . . . ensured that the woman's point of view has a better chance of being presented but

women remain at a disadvantage in the Family Court environment. The Family Court system is administered by men. The only major input from women is in the counselling area where the system uses marriage guidance counsellors who are volunteers and therefore mostly women. Currently one judge out of the total of twenty-four is a woman. Under the Family Proceedings Act the judge chairs the mediation conference which takes place before any matter proceeds to a defended hearing (Family Proceedings Act 1980: s. 14). The aim . . . is to attempt a settlement of outstanding issues so orders can be made by consent (s. 15). The judges receive no training in mediation skills and stories from participants in mediation conferences suggest that some of them are very directive in their chairing role (Leibrich and Holm, 1984). As only 10.7 per cent of law practitioners are women, a woman is most likely to be represented by a man and may therefore be in a position of being asked to make decisions in a totally male environment. If one party to the marriage is determined to fight to the bitter end, the final decision will be made by a judge after a full adversarial hearing. . . .

One factor preventing informed debate on these issues is the difficulty of discovering what is happening in the Family Court system. The mediation conferences and the full hearings are held in private and therefore the only direct information is from witnesses, lawyers acting in the case, and from the parties themselves. This information is anecdotal and difficult to assess objectively. . . . The rules which . . . protect the privacy of parties in individual cases prevent a comparative assessment of the way cases are conducted. . . .

A further problem for women in . . . the Family Court system is in being able to afford good help. Under the New Zealand scheme civil legal aid is available for all proceedings ancillary to divorce . . . and the applicant chooses her own lawyer (Legal Aid Act 1969: ss. 15, 16). A woman receiving a domestic purpose benefit would always qualify for legal aid unless she had assets other than her home, contents and a vehicle, but because the disposable income and capital limits have not been increased since the Act came into force in 1970 a woman on other than a very low income will be ineligible. As average male incomes are higher than those of women, men are generally in a better position to . . . hire more expensive lawyers.

Against this background this article addresses three areas of family law . . . the economic aspects of marriage break-up covering property and maintenance; parenting including guardianship and custody; and domestic violence.

THE LAW AND ECONOMICS OF MARRIAGE BREAKUP

. . . The 1976 Matrimonial Property Act makes a categorical statement about the division of assets between spouses. The system can best be described as one of 'deferred community' in that each spouse controls his or her property separately unless they make a contrary agreement (s. 21) or ask the court for a ruling (s. 23). Although an agreement or application to the court can be made at any time (ss. 23, 24) most divisions of property come about because the couple separate. If the court is asked to make a ruling, the value of the matrimonial home and family chattels are to be divided equally between the husband and wife unless there are extraordinary circumstances rendering equal sharing repugnant to justice (ss. 11, 14). All other property acquired since the marriage is deemed to be matrimonial property and will be divided equally unless the contributions of one spouse to the marriage partnership have clearly been greater than that of the other spouse (s. 15). Contributions to the marriage include such things as childcare, housekeeping and emotional support as well as monetary contributions (s. 18).

Property acquired before the marriage and property acquired by gift or inheritance will be regarded as separate property not subject to sharing unless it has become part of the matrimonial home and family chattels (ss. 8, 9, 10).

. . . It seems to have become generally accepted that ultimately an equal division of the matrimonial home, its contents, and the family car is . . . appropriate. The main difficulties . . . over which legal battles tend to be fought, are the occupation of the matrimonial home when there are children to be taken care of, and the division of items of property which are perceived as having been acquired exclusively as a result of one spouse's individual efforts or circumstances. Such property includes the business which has been built up by the particular efforts and skills of one spouse, the farm which has been passed on from an earlier generation, or the superannuation fund to which one spouse has contributed out of his or her earnings. As sex-role stereotyping remains strong in New Zealand society these sorts of assets will tend most often to have been built up by a husband. . . .

In the majority of marriage break-ups the only assets . . . will be the matrimonial home and the family chattels, so if the assets are divided and sold both parties will be left with very little. There is power under the Act to determine shares but defer sale (s. 33), and to make an order granting one spouse the right to occupy the family home (s. 27). While some judges have been willing to give occupation orders to the spouse who has custody of the children, there has been a strong tendency to support the 'clean break' principle (*Doak* v. *Turner* [1981]). . . .

The . . . bias towards the clean break . . . sends the husband and wife out into the world with their respective shares of the matrimonial property but to vastly unequal economic futures.

. . . The maintenance law between spouses is little used. Where both spouses are earning, independence would generally be assumed. Where one spouse is not earning because he or she is caring for children then he or she is eligible for a social welfare benefit—domestic purposes benefit (Social Security Act 1964: s. 27B). Under the social security law the parent without custody is deemed a liable parent and a contribution is collected from the liable parent by means of an administrative procedure (Social Security Act 1964: ss. 27I–27ZI). . . .

As more women than men have custody of children after separation they are more likely than men to end up as social welfare beneficiaries. . . . Even if women are employed after the breakup of a marriage their household income is likely to be far lower than that of a household headed by a male solo parent. . . .

WOMEN'S RIGHTS AS PARENTS

. . . A woman is always the guardian of her child whether or not she is married to the father. A man only becomes a guardian of his child if he is married to the mother, living with her at the time of the birth, subsequently marries her or applies to the court for guardianship having proved he is the natural father (Guardianship Act 1968: s. 6). There is still a presumption at law that a child born to a married woman is the child of her husband but that presumption can be rebutted (s. 5).

Where parents of a child are not married to each other the mother can prevent the father's name from being entered on the birth's register, and unless he can prove his paternity by court proceedings, she can continue to deny his fatherhood (Births and Deaths Registration Act 1951, as amended 1969: s. 18).

The Status of Children Act 1969 abolished the legal distinction between legitimate and illegitimate children so that if paternity is proved or acknowledged the father has the same legal obligations towards his child whether born within or outside marriage (s. 3). But he is not given rights over his child in the sense of controlling her upbringing, religion or education unless he is also a guardian.

The right to custody of a child is normally an incident of guardianship which is fine so long as the parents are living together (Guardianship Act, 1968: s. 3). Obviously, when parents separate arrangements have to be made for the care of the children. . . .

Women can no longer assume . . . they will gain sole custody of their children so long as they are adequate and loving parents. . . . There has been a move to ensure that men are involved as fathers when families split up. . . .

The law treads a difficult line in trying to ensure the welfare of the children. Research indicates that most children benefit from continuing contact with both parents (Wallerstein and Kelly, 1980). The child's needs may not be best served by catering to the mother's needs. . . .

The theory . . . seems right but every so often a chink appears in the 'welfare of the child' front, and the conservative anti-woman views of some . . . judges are revealed. Take for example the following statement from a judgment in a custody case by the Principal Family Court Judge P. J. Trapski D.C.J.:

'Both parents appear to be convinced that the present access is unsuitable and must be changed. If it is then that means that there is one further night which [the mother] will not be at home while she is doing her Life Link Counselling or she must give up that activity, and all against the background of the changes that she has made in her life with such resoluteness, the courses she has undertaken, and generally her dynamic background more particularly over the last five years. I am not at all certain that she would opt for the latter or that if she did she would continue. I think she would find that unsatisfying. Indeed when she says she would be satisfied with her motherhood I do not agree. She has proved that was not satisfying to her in a marriage. How can it possibly be as enveloping and satisfying now that she is a solo parent. We are not talking here about a normal average woman. We are talking about a woman who has found independence as an individual who has become aware of herself and her abilities who has an intelligence which she has developed in many many directions and I believe that development would continue.' (A. v. A. (1983): 9).

These remarks were preceded by statements that the mother who was not in paid employment would be out two nights a week, one night at a Rape Crisis Centre and the other at Life Link Counselling. The judge described the husband as 'conservative, steady, solid and rigid'.

According to this judge normal women are not intelligent or independent and are much more likely to be satisfied as mothers while in harness with a conservative steady, solid and rigid husband. Also, the desire to spend two evenings a week away from her children is an indication of her dissatisfaction with motherhood.

One wonders in how many other cases these views were not made explicit but nevertheless strongly influenced the outcome. . . .

DOMESTIC VIOLENCE

The most recent family legislation in New Zealand seeks to deal with the problem of domestic violence. . . . The Domestic Protection Act 1982 . . . applies to men and women who are or have been living together whether legally married or not (ss. 4, 13(2), 19). . . . Although the Act is non-sexist and envisages both male and female victims of violence I will refer to women as the victims.

A victim of violence can apply for a tenancy order or an occupation order which will entitle her to remain in the family home and have her partner excluded (ss. 19, 24). These orders can be made in the first instance without the partner having received notice of the proceedings so that the application itself does not give cause for further violence before a remedy is available (ss. 20, 25). Non-molestation orders which prohibit the violent partner from coming on to the victim's property without consent and prohibit other types of harassment such as 'watching and besetting' are available in the same way (ss. 14, 16). For those who continue to live with a violent partner, a nonviolence order is available which, if breached, results in the violent partner being imprisoned for twenty-four hours (s. 9). In practice, in order to obtain any of these orders a victim must be able to produce evidence of previous violence. Once such an order has been made there is a good chance of having it enforced by the police if a copy is deposited with the local police station. . . .

The procedures set up under the Family Proceedings Act 1980 have not always worked satisfactorily for the victims in violent relationships. There have been complaints that women who are in fear of their husbands have been brought into contact with them through counselling referrals or at a mediation conference. The feelings of powerlessness which this has engendered has tended to favour solutions . . . advantageous to the husband. The attitudes of some . . . judges have also given cause for concern. One judge . . . has stated that one must be wary of women asking for these orders even when they show bruises caused by their husbands because it is possible that the attack may have been 'provoked'. Women who are involved in women's refuges are also angry that in some situations where violence has clearly been directed only towards the woman, joint non-molestation orders have been made so that both the husband and wife are prohibited from molesting each other. . . .

Legislation can never solve the problem of domestic violence, it can merely provide an ambulance at the bottom of the cliff. As a society we need to be educated away from our present social conditioning as to what is appropriate male behaviour. In the meantime organisations such as women's refuges need to be funded so as to give women the opportunity to get out of violent relationships. . . .

CONCLUSION

There is a limit to what the law can achieve. The task is to challenge the whole social structure. In the meantime the law must provide for those still locked into present structures in a way which does not militate against alternatives. . . . More women lawyers and judges would assist women going through the Family Court system and ultimately . . . would help change attitudes. Education for Family Court judges in facts about women in our society, as well as training in human relationship skills and mediation skills would help to correct the male power bias as it manifests through the present system.

REFERENCES

(a) *Cases*

A. v. A. (1983) unreported judgment Rotura Family Court. 14 January 1983. FP 95/82.

Doak v. Turner [1981] *New Zealand Law Reports* 18 (CA).

(b) *Books*

BRIDGE, CAROLYN. 1983. The division of farms under the Matrimonial Property Act. *N. Z. Law J.* 20.

LEIBRICH, JOLIE and SUZETTE HOLM. 1984. *The Family Court: A Discussion Paper.* Department of Justice, Wellington, New Zealand.

WALLERSTEIN, JUDITH S. and JOAN B. KELLY. 1980. *Surviving the Breakup—How Children and Parents Cope with Divorce.* London.

Introduction

Earlier excerpts in this section have dealt with problems that are confined to particular members of a family, or to particular kinds of family. Excerpt 52 deals with a public issue that affects everyone: overpopulation.

In sub-Saharan Africa, populations are growing at an enormously high rate. This is because death rates are falling while birth rates are not falling very much, if at all, for reasons similar to those described in Excerpt 14: namely, most African parents want lots of children. (You may want to take another look at the excerpt by Ukaegbu to recall the reasons why.) In fact, African women want and bear many more children than women in Asia, the Pacific, or Latin America.

The results are staggering. Huth shows that, even under the most optimistic assumptions about mortality and fertility, Africa's population will continue to grow at nearly 2.4 percent per year through 2020. The population will be doubling in size every 29 years, *if not faster.* Such rapid growth means a continued shortage of capital for investment in industry and agriculture; and, in turn, more famine and disease, and the need for continued financial assistance from the developed world.

African countries have approached the problem in various ways. Some have an official policy on family planning, and others do not. "Designing effective population policy must be a highly individualized process," says Huth. More important still is persuading the leaders and people alike that such a policy is, indeed, in their own best interest.

52

Population Policies for Sub-Saharan Africa

Mary Jo Huth

Despite significant progress in sub-Saharan African countries during the 1960s and 1970s—improved living standards, a substantial decline in mortality rates, impressive expansion of educational opportunities, and continued urbanization . . . —the fertility rates in this part of the world remain at extraordinarily high levels. It is not surprising, therefore, that the pace of economic and social development has already slowed down considerably; and . . . that, since fertility rates are expected to remain high throughout the remainder of this century, prospects for a resurgence in the rate of development within the near future remain bleak. . . .

☋

DETERMINANTS OF FERTILITY

Fertility rates in sub-Saharan Africa have declined . . . more slowly in response to increases in per capita income than in any other region of the world. Indeed, the recent World Fertility Survey of twenty-nine developing countries, which examined total fertility rates (defined as the average number of children per family), revealed . . . Africa averages 6.7 children per family—this compared to an average of 4.5 children per family in Asia and the Pacific, and 4.7 children per family in Latin America. In part, this can be seen as a reflection of the fact that the average desired number of children per family in Africa is 7.1; whereas in Asia and the Pacific it is 4.0 and in Latin America 4.3 (see Table 1).

What factors explain Africa's unusually high fertility rates and the prevailing preference for

large families? . . . From . . . the socio-anthropological literature, two working hypotheses are suggested. First, the notion exists that in fragmented, traditional societies—whose governments have not yet established rule by law and an effective police force . . . —large numbers of people in a family or clan may be the only guarantee of security. Thus, as Caldwell suggests, the fact that African societies have many—and frequently conflicting—tribes may have strengthened the norm of unrestricted fertility. Moreover, because sub-Saharan Africa's family institution is characterized by strong descent lineages rather than by close conjugal ties, land (the principal form of wealth) is usually communally owned. Hence, power and fortune have been derived almost solely from control over a large number of people.[1]

In the second hypothesis, Africa's high fertility is interpreted in terms of the predicament of its female population. Boserup points out that during Africa's pre-colonial history, the distinctive characteristic of its women was the dominant role that they played in agriculture. This he ascribes to several factors; namely, concentration on subsistence food crops, low population density, the widespread practice of shifting cultivation, and minimal technology.[2] Subsequent European colonial policy, however, did not cater to the prevailing female farming system in Africa. Instead, some males were recruited for wage-jobs on European-owned plantations, whilst others were encouraged to grow cash crops for export to Europe on their own small

---

Source: Huth, Mary Jo (1986) "Population prospects for sub-Saharan Africa: Determinants, consequences and policy," *Journal of Contemporary African Studies*, Vol. 5, No. 1/2, (April/October), 167–181.

[1]See Caldwell, J.C., "The Mechanisms of Demographic Change in Historical Perspective", in *Population Studies* (Vol. 35, No. I, 1981), pp. 5–27.

[2]See Boserup, E., *Women's Role in Economic Development*, St. Martin's Press, New York, 1970.

TABLE 1. Actual Fertility and Desired Number of Children

Region/Country	Actual Fertility (Total Fertility Rate)	Average Desired Number of Children per Family			
		All Women	Women 15–19	Women 45–49	Percentage of Women Who Want No More Children
Africa					
Kenya	8.0	7.2	6.5	8.6	17
Lesotho	5.9	6.0	5.7	7.2	15
Senegal	7.1	8.9	8.8	8.7	—
Sudan (North)	5.7	6.4	5.4	6.5	17
Asia and the Pacific					
Bangladesh	5.9	4.1	3.7	4.9	—
Indonesia	4.3	4.3	3.3	5.4	39
Sri Lanka	3.5	3.4	2.6	4.8	61
Thailand	4.3	3.7	2.9	4.4	61
Latin America					
Columbia	4.5	4.1	2.7	5.7	62
Mexico	5.9	4.5	3.8	5.8	57
Peru	5.3	3.8	3.1	4.6	61
Venezuela	4.3	4.2	3.0	6.0	55
Costa Rica	3.5	4.7	3.5	6.1	52

Source: Lightbourne, R. (Jr.), Singh, S. and C.P. Green, "The World Fertility Survey: Charting Global Childbearing", in Population Bulletin (Vol. 37, No. 1, 1982).

plots. This results in an increasing gap developing between the output of food and cash crops; and, of course, between the productivity of female and male farmers. For, while men acquired cash to improve their cultivation of export crops, women continued to use traditional, low-input, low-yield methods for their food production—a trend which led to a deterioration in the relative position of women. Eventually colonists appropriated all the best lands for the cultivation of cash crops, thus leaving women responsible for domestic food production on inferior lands while their sons and husbands left home to gain an education or to earn wages in the modern sector. However, because women failed to produce enough food on their plots, they became increasingly economically dependent on their husbands' cash earnings. Furthermore, their already considerable workload was increased thereby: in addition to child-rearing, and domestic and food-growing duties, women were expected to take over the responsibility for cash-crop production from their absent sons and husbands.[3]

The damage that the status of women suffered in colonial Africa has unfortunately not been redressed during the two and a half decades of socio-economic development since independence. After the mid- and late-1970s, agricultural productivity—both in terms of cash and food crops—has slowed down, as the internal terms of trade have shifted in favour of the cities. Waves of men migrated to urban areas in search of more lucrative job opportunities, while women increasingly head farm households. Nevertheless, the dominant role in family decision-making is still played by the male.[4]. . .

Kenya . . . provides a good illustration of the predicament faced by women in sub-Saharan ru-

[3]See Safilios-Rothschild, C., "The Role of the Family: A Neglected Aspect of Poverty", in Knight, P.T. (ed.), Implementing Programmes of Human Development (Staff Working Paper No. 403), World Bank, Washington, DC, July 1980, pp. 311–372.

[4]See Kossoudji, S. and E. Mueller, The Economic and Demographic Status of Female-Headed Households in Rural Botswana (Discussion Paper No. 81–49), World Bank, Washington, DC, 1981.

ral Africa today. Kenyan women are subject to strong social pressure to marry and produce children in order to extend the kinship network; unmarried and childless women are severely censured. Most Kenyan women therefore marry at . . . puberty—a fact which contributes to their dependence upon their husbands, and to their weak power position relative to the families into which they marry. Not only do they lack knowledge of birth-control methods but, because nearly 25 percent of Kenya's rural households are headed by women, their heavy workload induces them to produce many children as potential sources of labour and support. Moreover, as Faruqee points out, women in Kenya do not usually inherit land, but are merely granted the right to *use* land belonging to their husbands, fathers or sons. Consequently, since women lack security of land tenure, they are especially desirous of bearing sons.[5] . . .

MAJOR CONSEQUENCES OF RAPID POPULATION GROWTH

. . . The rapid population growth which has already occurred in sub-Saharan Africa portends a marked acceleration in the size of the labour force, and serious employment problems. . . . If African development policy fails to accommodate such unprecedented expansion in the labour force, economic instability and social demoralization will . . . ensue. . . . While such a large labour force can be an economic asset if it is healthy, well trained and fully equipped with capital requirements and infrastructure, this is not likely to be the case given the prevailing financial and management constraints and the formidable obstacles to institutional reform in most countries of sub-Saharan Africa.[6]

---

[5]See Faruqee, R. et al., *Kenya: Population and Development*, World Bank, Washington, DC, July 1980.

[6]See Faruqee, R. and R. Gulhati, *Rapid Population Growth in Sub-Saharan Africa: Issues and Policies* (Staff Working Paper No. 559). World Bank, Washington, DC, 1983.

That the challenge posed by rapid population growth in this part of Africa has not yet led to a commensurate government response in the form of technological or organizational progress, is evidenced in the area of basic needs services, where the . . . problem of "keeping up" the quantity and quality of existing coverage has compounded the long-standing problem of "catching up". Despite considerable progress in recent years in the provision of clean water, as well as nutritional, health and educational services, the situation is still unsatisfactory. . . . Infant and child mortality remain at fairly high levels; the coverage of primary education has risen to an average of 70 percent, but that of secondary education remains very low at 9 percent; and sanitary water supplies are available to only 20 percent of the population.[7] The relevance of the fertility issue to a government's ability to satisfy the basic needs of its population is well illustrated in . . . Kenya, which allocated 32 percent of its budget to education, health, housing, and water supplies during . . . 1975 to 1980. . . . If fertility continues at about the current rate (51 per 1,000), Kenya will have to increase its expenditures for these services by 878 percent up to the period . . . 2015 to 2020—just to maintain present coverage and quality. . . .

POPULATION POLICIES: PRESENT AND FUTURE

In 1981, the United Nations Economic Commission for Africa conducted a study of population policies in forty-two countries of sub-Saharan Africa. . . . Only eight of the countries (or 19 percent) . . . have an official policy to reduce their population growth rate. These are Botswana, Kenya, Lesotho, Mauritius, South Africa, Uganda, Ghana, and Senegal. Twenty others (or 48 percent) have an official policy supporting family planning for health reasons

---

[7]See *ibidem*.

but not for demographic purposes. The remaining fourteen (or 33 percent) neither have an official policy to reduce their population growth rate, nor do they support family planning for health reasons. . . . Therefore, the great majority (81 percent) of sub-Saharan African countries do not have any official policy to restrict rapid population growth. Moreover, those which do have such a policy are not strongly or consistently committed to its implementation.

Kenya, for example, was the first sub-Saharan African country to adopt an official family planning programme, but—while this was done in 1967—the programme has received substantial financial support only during the Third Five-Year Plan (1975 to 1979). A 1977/78 Kenyan fertility survey revealed that, although 42 percent of the sampled ever-married women knew of a place to secure family planning services, only 12 percent had ever visited such a facility and a mere 5 percent of women in the reproductive age group were practicing family planning. Two major factors explain this situation. First, 80 percent of Kenya's women would have to travel over 4.8 kilometres to reach the nearest facility offering family-planning services, and most of them either lack access to, or cannot afford, the necessary means of transportation. Second, because medical centres are overburdened with demands for therapeutic treatment, because their preventive services are underdeveloped and because their outreach programmes are poorly co-ordinated, many women of reproductive age remain outside the health delivery system. Furthermore, due to staff shortages, family-health field educators reach only a small percentage of these women.[8]

. . . Other factors which explain sub-Saharan Africa's . . . negative or ambivalent posture towards the control of population growth are . . .: first, low population density in most countries contributes to the widespread perception of vast

amounts of empty space and unutilized natural resources; second, since concern about Africa's population problems comes mainly from the technologically advanced . . . West, it is dismissed as politically motivated; third, religious and tribal beliefs and customs make population control an extremely sensitive issue; fourth, newly independent African governments have been giving top priority to nation-building and economic development via foreign aid; and finally, the increasing financial difficulties of African governments in recent years have diverted the efforts of policy-makers towards . . . urgent, short-term problems, rather than longer-term ones such as population growth.[9] Consequently, a prerequisite for strengthening or introducing population-control policies in sub-Saharan African countries is a recognition by their own opinion-formers and policy-makers that such efforts are in their respective national interests.

Furthermore, designing effective population policy must be a highly individualized process—one which identifies and assesses factors conducive to changing fertility patterns, as well as those contributing to the *status quo* in each country. This process would involve asking . . . : how does the system of land tenure affect women's sense of security?; does the intra-family division of labour impose an onerous burden on women?; do agricultural extension services, credit agencies and co-operatives discriminate against women?; are women deprived of income-earning opportunities?; do norms regarding family size differ by sex and by generation?; what kinds of individuals, households, kinship groups and social organizations are trying to break away from traditional values and norms?; and what is the nature and extent of opposition to deviant behaviour? In addition—since a key factor affecting the use of family-planning services is *accessibility*—it may be desirable to supplement existing clinic-based programmes, linked to the public health delivery system, with programmes offered through . . . other outlets, such as com-

---

[8]See Faruqee, R. and R. Gulhati, *Rapid Population Growth in Sub-Saharan Africa: Issues and Policies* (Staff Working Paper No. 559), World Bank, Washington, DC, 1983.

[9]Ibid.

munity self-help schemes, commercial channels, women's organizations, and rural development agencies. New instructions for propagating the family planning message should also be utilized, including nation-wide adult literacy campaigns and youth recreation programmes, family-life education courses in secondary schools and colleges, and the mass media.[10]

------
[10]Ibid.

Thus, building enthusiasm for, and commitment to, population control in sub-Saharan Africa will not be easy. It will require a thorough grasp of the underlying economic, social and political issues, the ability to project the case for government policy-making in a difficult area, and the capacity to define what is acceptable intervention—taking into account the range within which social and cultural change is feasible in each country. . . .

Introduction

The next excerpt is about family policy in the former Soviet Union, and it is based on research conducted in the early 1980s before the Soviet Union passed into history. It reflects a planning process that was already in the midst of change to a much more "American-style" approach to "human service delivery programs." As such, it tells us little about the traditional communist approaches to planning. (For this, see Excerpt 54 on family planning in China.)

Nor can it tell us much about the more recent changes in policy making since the break-up of that Union. These changes, still in the making, reflect both regional conflicts and ideological conflicts about the best way to change a society.

What is interesting in this excerpt is the evidence that, even before the break-up, assumptions about the family in this part of the world were very similar to Western assumptions. For example, people already seemed to believe that strong, intact families are good for society, that a rising divorce rate is a problem, and that women choosing to have "illegitimate" babies is shocking. Many Americans would willingly subscribe to these views, suggesting that such views are quite independent of a person's economic and political ideology (whether that person is communist or capitalist, for example).

At least one interesting difference does show up, though. American culture portrays men as dynamic achievers and women as helpers or sex objects. In this excerpt and in other recent works (see, for example, Francine de Plessix Gray's (1989) book on Russian women), the pattern is quite different. Russian culture recognizes women as steady, yet dynamic, achievers and men—including boys at school—as underachievers, if not victims.

References

GRAY, F. DU PLESSIX (1989) Soviet Women: Walking the Tightrope. New York: Doubleday.

53
Family Policy in the Soviet Union

Salvatore Imbrogno

CHANGES IN FAMILY STRUCTURES

A. Emerging Role of Women

Equal rights for all USSR citizens are guaranteed in Article II, Chapter 6 of the Constitution in providing women with opportunities equal to those of men: (1) in receiving an education and vocational training, (2) in labor remuneration and promotion, (3) including, as noted, special measures to protect women's labor and health; and finally, (4) creating conditions enabling women to combine labor and motherhood:

1. Legal protection and maternal and moral support for mother and child;
2. Granting of paid leave and other benefits to pregnant women and mothers of young children;
3. Gradual reduction of working hours for women with small children.

These provisions . . . reflect the traditional notion that women and not men assume primary responsibility for child rearing.

Equality between the sexes in the USSR has increased women's opportunities to decide on their own personal growth and development, and has made it possible for them to participate in the socioeconomic and political decision making process. The obvious result is a woman who is well-educated . . . engaged in an increasingly higher level of economic independence and who can now, through the acquisition of a new self-awareness and self-esteem control her life in ways she alone perceives as desirable. This places

Source: Imbrogno, S. (1986) "Family policy in the Soviet Union," International Journal of Sociology of the Family, 16, 2, Autumn, 165–180.

the Soviet women in a strategic position to acquire increasingly more political leadership and power as evidenced in the fact that one third of the members of the Supreme Soviet are women.

B. Sexual Disparities in Education

For the USSR as a whole, in 1970 more women than men aged 20 to 29 had at least a secondary general education; . . . This disproportion was most pronounced in the rural population (for every 100 women aged 20 to 29 with a higher education, there were only 59 men with that much education). . . .

Such a substantial lag in men's educational level makes educationally heterogeneous marriages inevitable, particularly in rural areas. At the same time, the widely held . . . view that the wife should not be better educated than the husband acts to discourage marriage (Roosson, 1984). Recent studies have shown that a major source for family conflicts is due to the fact that young men are lagging substantially behind women of their own age in education and apparently in overall cultural upbringing as well. Many Soviet women with higher education are married to men with only secondary education or less. . . . This has been considered as a major cause for family conflicts and divorce in the Soviet Union.

C. Household Responsibilities

Women's participation in the work place necessitates major shifts in traditional family roles. For 80% of all married couples under study, . . . quarrels over housework were commonplace, since women . . . spend two and a half to three times longer in household activities.

TABLE 1. Percentage of Husbands Who do Housework, by Husband's Age

Husband's Age	% Who Do Housework
25–29	83
30–34	78
40–44	58

. . . The younger age group is more readily accepting new . . . marital roles, that impact on traditional decision patterns. Z. Yankova concluded: "the psychological atmosphere in the family depends in part on the organization of housework." (Yankova, 1982).

D. Divorce

. . . The pre-1965 divorce procedures were clearly at odds with social equality. Women, as well as men, are no longer legally compelled to remain in troubled marriages or in marriages in name only. The USSR . . . , by proclaiming the legal freedom of divorce and abortions, . . . establishes that marriage and family are a matter of personal choice that should be based on the individual's own perceptions of sex, love and mutual respect. The increase in individual freedom of choice, as argued by some academicians, will lead to stronger family ties and interpersonal relationships among families that survive divorce.

Articles abstracted from news media, written by authorities and citizens' reactions to events and occurrences between 1982–1984, reveal . . . two major . . . developments in family structure. . . .

1. A continuous high rate of marriage dissolutions and divorce with a corresponding increase in marital conflicts and discords; and
2. A decrease in the number of marriages and a concomitant decrease in the number of children in the Russian Soviet Federated Socialist Republic, the Ukraine and Beylorussia, with an increase in the number of abortions and premarital and extramarital sexual experiences.

. . . The potential of legal reform . . . to strengthen the institution of marriage, reduce the divorce rate, and inculcate a sense of family responsibility in each citizen has not been realized. . . . Divorce rates have sharply risen . . . since the revision of complicated divorce proceedings in 1965. . . . The number of broken marriages has increased by 45% since 1970.

The following . . . statistics highlight the social changes in complex technological societies: (Sysenko, 1984).

1. 50% of all men in 1981 who were divorced and 40% of all women remarry. 40% of all men who were divorced and 48% of the women were no older than 29. The median age for men was 28.5 and 26.7 for women.
2. In 1979, about 20% of all divorces occurred in cities with populations of over one million.
3. Following are the 1980 divorce statistics relative to length of marriage and ages of men and women who were divorced: These statistics demonstrate . . . divorce is becoming a common and acceptable practice.

TABLE 2. Percentage of Marriages Ending in Divorce, by Length of Marriage

Length of Marriage (years)	% of Divorces
0–4	36.0
5–9	27.3
10–19	23.2
20 years or more	12.6

E. Family and Child-Rearing

Today, married couples in the USSR no longer consider children as one of life's greatest blessings, with the exception of Armenia, where 90% of women polled called children the greatest value in life. In other parts, particularly in Russia, Ukraine and Byelorussia children are considered a burden, both financially and psychologically. . . .

Continuous and widespread use of surgical abortion exists as a means of family planning.

Some of the reasons given by married women having one or more abortions are:

1. Jobs and housework are too time consuming. . . . The average time needed for a family to shop is two and a half hours per day, a task usually performed by women.
2. Apartments are scarce and poorly designed to accommodate a number of children. (Although there is an apartment shortage, 92% of those studied had their own apartment.)
3. Shortage of space in kindergarten, day care centers and the small number of schools with extended day care centers. . . .

Sixty eight thousand one hundred and seventy-eight (68,178) illegitimate births were registered in 1970 in the cities of the Russian Republic and 50,000 in the rural areas, of 5.6% and 7.2% respectively of the total number of births. In 1978 the number of children born out of wedlock in the same republics had doubled. . . . This is . . . affirmation that a new lifestyle for childbearing and childrearing might be emerging. . . .

Four out of five women who have a child out-of-wedlock choose to do so. . . . Whereas the peak age for single mothers used to be 17 or 18 now there is a new peak age from 30 to 40. There are similar developments in the USA. . . .

F. Femininity and Masculinity

. . . Dr. Chuprinin surveyed the treatment of relations between the sexes in fiction that appeared in Soviet magazines in 1984. . . . He . . . considered all instances of relations between men and women, . . . whether central or tangential to the main plot of a given work of fiction. The idea that the Soviets are witnessing the development of a matriarchy is gradually taking hold, and the notion of a reversal in the traditional roles of men and women has been showing up in fiction as well as nonfiction (Chuprinin, 1985).

SOVIET RESPONSES TO EMERGING CHANGES

A. Structuring Policy Problems

Individual and family problems are perceived as an intricate web of interdependent relations within the family, . . . community, and society and as interlocking parts that comprise the socialist system. Substantive problems areas are described and explained as interdependent and central to . . . the collective family. This can be exemplified by a statement of findings in recent social research:

1. Childhood neuroses are attributed to long drawn out marital conflicts: rejection of the child and/or parental upbringing and the climate and atmosphere of the home.
2. Neglected, dependent and delinquent children are attributable to "troubled families" requiring of the state and public officials earlier diagnosis of these families.
3. Excessive alcoholic consumption is responsible for a large number of marital discords and divorce and has recently emerged as a problem in juvenile alcoholic abuse.
4. The family situation in its totality is seen as both cause for and means by which to prevent juvenile crime.
5. The mental health of children is a condition responsive to collective environments. Treatment of illness requires the whole family to be in mental hygiene clubs.

This . . . conceptualization—where problems in one substantive area affect and are affected by family problems in other areas creates a "system of problems.". . . This view accounts for the Soviet propensity not to isolate any substantive problem area from the whole system. . . .

B. Direct and Concrete Services to Families

While Soviet scholarship searches for causal explanations there has been a rush of ad hoc expedient . . . social programs, services and activities . . . such as more benefits to families; family counseling services, more recreational and leisure activities, confidential helping, get-acquainted services; "Nikita Clubs" for newlyweds; "We" for problems in raising children and "Let's Make Friends Today". . . for the over forty age group. . . . A host of professional services have emerged: all of which are known in the west. These developments suggest a movement from a scientifically oriented, well-structured problem approach (i.e., medical model) to a . . . conception in which the preferred ends to the collective family are accepted, but there now exists uncertainty as to how best to realize these ends. . . .

There is a growing awareness of the importance of applied social sciences, derived from a Marxist sociological perspective. The CPSU [Communist Party of the Soviet Union] mandated in its June 1984 Central Committee's Plenary Session that sociology . . . broaden its . . . analysis . . . to include economics, law, social psychology, pedagogy, demography and statistics. There is virtually no sphere of significance that has not become an object of sociological study. However, based on available literature and in-person interviews with Soviet academicians, and . . . experiences in the U.S.A., there is no indication that an interdisciplinary and multidimensional approach is being realized.

Educational programs and information services are established in a variety of governmental health and education agencies whose responsibility is to disseminate information on demographic changes, family hygiene, child rearing and public health with an eye on enhancing and strengthening the collective family as the carrier of the "highest moral values of a socialist society." Proposals have been advanced by the Nedelya Public Council on the Family for specific programs to strengthen the family, such as:

"the first one is the creation (in major cities for a start of family, marriage and get acquainted services of the sort that have been created in Moscow). Evidently, they should operate along several lines; educational work on a mass scale and the preparation of young

people for family life; individual counseling on all family problems, child rearing, sexological, psychological, medical and genetic, and get acquainted services." (Pravda, 1982).

For the past 11 years, 13 counseling services with a psychosocial approach have been operating in Moscow. . . . A "confidential hot line" service, introduced as a "new concept" was reported to be very successful. Telephone calls are made by women (60%) and center on common family problems: conflicts between spouses or between parents and children, the threat of family breakup or the problem of loneliness once a breakup occurred. Thirty percent of those calling the hot-line are people between the ages of 20–30, and approximately 35% range in ages from 45–60 (Zhilyayeva, 1984).

DISCUSSION

By proclaiming the legal freedom for divorce and abortions and by creating a more accepting climate, . . . the Soviet State has inadvertently modified the concept of the collective family. The USSR responded to the . . . social changes brought on by divorce and abortion by enacting laws to strengthen family life primarily through the implementation of material benefits. The USSR now realizes that public law, public policy and its implementation through ministries must be complemented through a variety of human services that encompass sociological research and a psychological therapeutic component.

A study of social research in the USSR is giving rise to "many questions" . . . regarding the causal explanations for social changes and the solutions offered by the state. Although ideologically and conceptually the preferred ends to the collective family are claimed to be known and agreed upon, differences are arising regarding the means by which these ends "ought" to be realized. Hence, the Soviets are now compelled to resort to a system of human service delivery that evolved in the United States as one means of reaching their ideological goals.

REFERENCES

CHUPRININ, S. 1985. "Ladies Tango", Literaturnaya Gazeta. No. 1, January, p. 6.

ROOSSON, A. 1984. "Changes in Family Makeup in the Estonian Republic," Sotsiologicheskiye Issledovania. No. 1, January-March, pp. 94–97.

SYSENKO, V. 1984. Moscow State University, Economic Division Center for the Study of Population Problems (Statistical Monograph).

USSR Constitution Chapter 6, Article 66. 1977.

YANKOVA, Z. 1982. Problems of the Big City. Moscow: Navkia Publishing House.

ZHILYAYEVA, V. 1984. "Confidential Hot-line," Sovetskaya Rossia, May 13, p. 6.

Introduction

The evidence we have examined in this part of the book—especially the evidence from France, New Zealand, and Africa—has shown varied efforts at change through "incrementalism." Incremental change tries to correct social (in this case, familial) problems through a gradual hit-or-miss combination of small experiments. Typically, no grand social or political vision informs these efforts. Rather, all policies are aimed at finding a compromise between competing ideologies and interest groups. The result is far from elegant or complete; but there *is* a result, and it bears some relationship to observable reality.

The next article is about responses to family problems in China—a country whose official Marxist-Leninist ideology makes incremental change very difficult. Indeed, systems of government based on Marxist ideology have often attached more importance to ensuring their policies are ideologically *correct* than to seeing that they work in practice.

A central problem arises from the view, fundamental to Marxism, that social problems we are familiar with in the West (among others, high rates of divorce, family violence, delinquency, drunkenness, and so on) are due, ultimately, to capitalist exploitation. These problems should therefore all disappear under communism. But, in fact, they don't. So communist governments have historically veered between two equally difficult positions. On the one hand, they have tried to deny these problems exist; on the other hand, they have looked for explanations of these problems that would not challenge Marxist theory.

In China, the policy-making process has also been hampered by a shortage of social researchers, an official rejection of sociology (for several decades), and a generalized fear of asking and answering questions which, though relevant to policy-making, might disagree with ideologically acceptable views. This seems hard to defend since Marx himself, the founder of communism, was a social scientist who did research on social issues.

54
Responding to Chinese Family Problems

Wei Zhangling

FAMILY PROBLEMS IN CHINA

The new Marriage Law promulgated on September 10, 1980 (taking effect on January 1, 1981) is based upon the old Marriage Law, thirty years of practical experience, and the newly developed situation and problems.

The replacement of the old Marriage Law . . . indicates the Chinese government is attempting to deal with new family problems. . . . Many problems in marriage and family relationships . . . have to be solved. For example, parental arrangement of marriage for young people, mercenary marriage and other kinds of interference with free marriage, extravagant marriage ceremonies, etc. still exist, particularly in the countryside. The government had to promulgate a new Marriage Law as a legal weapon to cope with those troublesome problems and clear the way for progress through the Four Modernizations.[1]

If we compare the new Marriage Law with the old one, we can easily find differences. First, the minimum legal marriage age is raised from 18 to 20 for the female and from 20 to 22 for the male. This reflects the tendency toward later marriage. Second, the restrictions on divorce are relaxed. This shows the tendency toward individual freedom. Third, the 12th article of the new Marriage Law stipulates that both the husband and wife have the obligation to take family planning into practice. This conveys the strong emphasis on birth control throughout the whole country.

In regard to the different policies of the Chinese government toward marriage and the family, we can divide the years (since the Revolution) into three periods:

1. From 1949 to 1963 there was a high tide of marriages and a high rate of fertility. . . .
2. From 1964 to 1977 the government advocated that young people marry at a later age and begin to control fertility.
3. From 1978 up to the present, . . . the government has continued to advocate later marriage and has encouraged couples to bear one child. The slogan runs as follows: "To bear one child is best."

Generally speaking, before the 1960s the average marriage age for the rural female was 18, while for the urban female it was 20; but now the ages have changed to 23 for the rural and 25 for the urban female. . . .

Taking the country as a whole, the family planning effort is rather successful. In 1973 there were 53 million married couples performing family planning. They constituted 60% of the couples who were of childbearing age. In 1977 the number rose to 89.11 million (84%). Since 1970 the fertility has gone down because the rate of contraceptive use has risen. In 1971 the natural increase rate of the population was 23.4 per thousand; in 1978 it was reduced to 12.05 per thousand (Zhang, 1981). In Sichuan (the largest province), the rate of the natural increase was 31.26 per thousand in 1971 but dropped to 6.06 per thousand in 1978 (Zhang, 1981). Through such trends the authorities became convinced that the main method for population control was family planning.

Both family planning and later marriage are in direct conflict with the old Chinese traditions. Their implementation has caused not only a profound revolution but also numerous family troubles. . . . For example, the policy "to bear

Source: Zhangling, Wei (1983) "Chinese family problems: Research and trends," *Journal of Marriage and the Family,* November, 943–948.

only one child" will bring forth a lot of problems: the problems of old people will increase in the future; family planning procedures sometimes will cause health troubles to women, the policy of "only one child" will raise concerns over spoiling children.

The new China has won magnificent achievements in dealing with . . . family and social problems; but still, unnumerable troubles are emerging every day. For example, a large population is a critical challenge. By the end of this century, our population will be 1200 million, but the optimum population of China 100 years from now is 650 to 700 million, according to a recent report made by a group of ten population specialists, sponsored by the Chinese State Council.

Before the Revolution, the average life expectancy in China was 35 years; since 1949 the level has nearly doubled. The average life expectancy for males has reached 66.95 years, and for females 69.55, according to statistics for 1978 released by the Chinese Ministry of Health ("The average . . . ," 1981).

The mortality rate for China has been reduced from 25 per thousand before liberation to below 7 per thousand now ("The average . . . ," 1981). For the United States the mortality rate is 8.9 per thousand; for the Soviet Union it is 9.3 per thousand. Since the mortality in our country is very low, the task for birth control is very heavy.

Feudalistic influences still prevail in China. This kind of social phenomenon is more severe in the rural areas than in the urban areas. What we mean by feudalistic remnants are the following: early marriage, marriage to close relatives, mercenary marriage in disguised form, the idea of being well-matched in social and economic status for marriage, the old idea of regarding sons as superior to daughters, and so forth. Besides, the inequality between husbands and wives still exists in modern China and exercises its influence in many respects.

In modern China many family problems come from political instability and economic dif-ficulties. As Alexander Eckstein wrote in *China's Economic Revolution* (1977), the middle-level salary of an American worker is 25 times that of his Chinese colleague. The American purchasing power for food is seven times greater than the Chinese; for textiles, clothing, shoes and stockings, it is 11 times greater; for durable family goods it is 53 times higher. In addition, the household work is too strenuous for Chinese women, and housing-supply problems are pressing in China, especially in big cities. The financial difficulties of families cause quarrels between family members; crowded housing conditions cause discord between neighbors; material dissatisfaction enlarges the generation gap.

Social problems, such as inflation, unemployment, juvenile delinquency, social chaos, the inequality between men and women, maltreatment of women and old people, the new problems of only one child for a family, etc., also bring forth a lot of troubles in family life. In Beijing, for example, 75% of the criminals arrested are youths and teenagers. There are 456 middle schools altogether in Beijing; among them there are 389 schools that have had students arrested for criminal acts (Lei, 1980). In recent years . . . juvenile delinquency has become more serious. . . . With the attendant social chaos, this will undermine family socialization; inflation and unemployment will bring poverty to some families; the inequality between men and women in society will influence the status of women in the families. There are many social organizers and mass association workers who have done research work on this subject in many cities. They often investigate the families in order to analyze the roots of social problems. . . .

FAMILY RESEARCH AND TRENDS IN CHINA

After the Revolution, during the period of Land Reform, a lot of work teams were sent to the countryside. Many teachers and students of the social sciences in the universities took part in the work teams and did ... investigations of peasants' political positions, economic conditions, routine life, rural customs, etc. The sociologists, faculty members and students of sociology departments also went to the rural areas and accumulated valuable materials. Indeed, sociological research flourished. ...

Regrettably, in 1952, all departments of sociology in all ... universities were ordered to stop teaching and research. So any ... sociological subfield including family research also ceased to exist then. Nevertheless, while sociology as an independent discipline stopped its activities, rich and varied research and investigation work continued to exist under other names. The family life of workers, peasants, soldiers, and people of all walks of life were investigated; family histories and family trees of capitalists, landlords, as well as workers and peasants, were collected. In regions with minority nationalities, the democratic reform campaign went on in a mammoth movement during the 1950s. Thousands of minority-nationality specialists and research workers went to those districts and areas to do surveys and interviews. ... Articles and works on the marriage and family life of minority nationalities sprang up like mushrooms. In collaboration with Beijing Film Studio, the Institute of Nationalities in Beijing successfully produced documentary films on the marriage customs and family life styles of some minority nationalities. In recent years articles on ... the marriage and family life of minority nationalities, published in social science journals have been drawn out of these source materials, which were gathered in the 1950s and 1960s.

Although sociology as a discipline was proscribed for a long period, social research ... still existed. ... Trade unions, the Women's Federation, and the Youth League paid great attention to ... research on social phenomena, including family problems. Under the leadership of the State Council, many ministries (such as Civil Administration, Justice, Labor, and Public Security) established their own research sections and investigation bases. Their incessant work ... ac-

cumulated abundant valuable materials. Since China is a highly organized society, it is not difficult ... to do investigations and gather materials. ...

Since 1969, political movements have been carried out one after another. University teachers and students in the social sciences often are invited to do investigations and research. ... For example, in the movement for the "Four Cleanups" and the "Five Anti" in the early 1960s, millions of reports on family histories of workers, peasants, former capitalists and landlords, etc. were collected. A large number of publications, mostly internal, resulted from these campaigns.

In short, during the past 30 years in new China, a lot of significant work has been done in family research; but the contents and methods are quite different from those in ... Western countries. ... Research work on the family problems of China contains special characteristics, of which the main ones are:

1. These investigations ... serve the aims and interests of proletarian politics. They exercise strong influence on policy making and provide guidance for political movements.

2. Chinese Communist Party cadres ... employ these investigations ... as a weapon to strengthen proletarian dictatorship and educate the people (especially young people). For example, ... case studies of family history have been taken as teaching materials to expound the theory of class and class struggle.

3. For many years the methods of mass movements were widely promoted and deeply strengthened in doing ... research. None of the ... researchers were labeled as sociologists; but millions of cadres, social organizers, teachers and students of social sciences in all kinds of colleges and universities were involved in the work. Only a portion of the results were published in academic journals.

In 1979 the Chinese Sociological Research Association (CSRA) was established. It marks the restoration of sociology as a scientific discipline and the rehabilitation of former sociologists in China. In 1980 the Chinese Sociological Research Institute in the Chinese Academy of Social Sciences began to work. . . .

Sociological associations and institutes have been widely established in Shanghai, Tianjin, Heilongjiang, Jilin, Hubei, etc. In Beijing University, Fudan University (Shanghai), Nankai University (Tianjin), Zhongshan University (Guangzhou), The Chinese People's University (Beijing) sociological departments or subdisciplines have been established. The subjects for teaching and research include urban planning, population, marriage, family problems, youth employment, juvenile delinquency, and other topics ("Speed up . . . ," 1981).

Sponsored by the CSRA, new social research bases have been established in Beijing, Shanghai, Tianjin, and Guangzhou. . . . Many kinds of social problems are under consideration: population, housing, employment, income, marriage, family, fertility, youth, children, morality, occupational prestige and satisfaction, etc. . . .

In Beijing, Wuhan and . . . other big cities several research associations on marriage and family problems have been established. In collaboration with Beijing Children's Health Association, the Beijing Family Education Association has organized a lot of beneficial activities. . . . Its main activities are:

1. To investigate . . . family education in those families with a single child or with a delinquent teenager. . . .
2. Together with Beijing People's Radio Station, to conduct special programs on "how to educate a single boy or girl.". . .
3. In coordination with the Beijing Textile Printing and Dyeing Industrial Corporation, to hold "marriage, family and family education" seminars . . . ;
4. In collaboration with the Beijing Municipal Administration, Beijing Women's Federation and other organizations, to conduct several seminars on population eugenics, child psychology, preschool education, children's eyesight health, how to cure eye diseases of children, how to take precautions on children's teeth, and so forth.

Currently, the Beijing Family Education Association has organized people to edit books, such as *Lectures on Family Education* and *One Hundred Cases for Family Education*. It also cooperates with the Chinese Central Television Station to produce family education telefilms ("Beijing . . . ," 1981).

Since the All-China Women's Federation has established its own Family and Marriage Research Association, local associations will be established and developed on a massive scale. Usually the family research associations in big cities are under the leadership of the municipal women's federations. . . . Many undergraduate students in the social sciences used to do social surveys during their summer vacations of their own accord. The Beijing branch of the Chinese Democratic Alliance, one of China's democratic parties, has conducted a lot of family education lectures for mothers, including moral education, intellectual education, physical training, and aesthetic education ("All circles . . . ," 1981).

Often teachers and students of Chinese philosophy, history, and literature also take part in the social surveys on family problems. At Yunnan University the teachers and students in the philosophy department investigated the moral behavior of youth for four weeks in . . . 1981. The respondents were . . . workers, soldiers, students, and unemployed youths. The interview topics were mainly divorce problems of youths and juvenile delinquency. After their investigation and research, the teachers and students wrote more than 30 articles ("Investigation . . . ," 1981).

. . . Family research is strongly influenced by the Party's policies and in turn gives strong influence to policy making. For example, before the issuance of the new Marriage Law, some relevant departments of the government organized investigations on marriage and family problems. The Central Committee of the Chinese Communist Youth League distributed thousands of questionaires in Beijing concerning the problems of the proper age for marriage. . . . The All-China Women's Federation also did . . . investigations on marriage and family problems before the promulgation of the new Marriage Law. They paid close attention to investigations of family planning, marriage with close relatives, handicapped children, congenitally retarded children, juvenile delinquency, and so forth. Those investigations . . . also paved the way for practice in these areas.

Chinese family research has focused on practical family and marriage problems instead of on theoretical problems. This is also the tendency for future research. In Neijiang city of Sichuan, the local Women's Federation did successful investigations on juvenile delinquency. They found out that many wrong doings of teenagers had a direct connection with family education. Some parents spoiled their children with excessive accommodation and sheltered their bad behavior even when they violated the law. Some parents were themselves so selfish and greedy to obtain advantages over others that they never educated their children to obey the law and sometimes even supported their unlawful behavior. Some parents showed very poor morality themselves, so they influenced their children, and made them fly away from home and drove them into crime. Some children had no father or mother and, therefore, lacked family education and were tainted with bad habits. . . . The Niejiang Women's Federation summed up rich experience on educating children for their parents: (a) the parents must set good examples for their children in moral behavior; (b) the parents should not only praise and encourage their children's good points but also patiently correct their shortcomings and wrong behavior; they must not shield the children's faults; (c) the parents must help the children to form good habits and fine character from childhood; (d) family education must be closely combined with school education and social education; and (e) the parents must adopt a correct attitude toward social problems such as unemployment, the scarcity of opportunities for young people to enter universities, etc. The Federation held more than 50 meetings for exchanging experiences in educating children and selected model parents to pass on their experiences at such meetings. Many parents drew lessons from the past and obtained good results in socializing their children. In 1980, 761 teenagers who had gone astray then overcame their mistakes and returned to the correct path ("Going . . . ," 1981). . . .

In conclusion, I would like to summarize . . . the trends in family research in China today. They are:

1. . . . More and more family research associations and institutions will be established in the next few years. . . . The field of Chinese family research will grow and flourish. However, professional sociologists will guide only a small portion of this research.

2. . . . Chinese family research will offer advice to the policy making of the Party and government. Conversely, the development of Chinese family research is determined by the Party's policy to a considerable extent; that is to say, it must conform with the interests of the Four Modernizations program.

3. Chinese family research will develop an applied and practical orientation. It will attach primary importance to population, marriage, family planning, and family education. In regard to the theory and methodology of Western family research, their adoption will be slow, and a long course will be needed to put them into practice. . . .

NOTES

[1]The "Four Modernizations" refers to the modernizations of industry, agriculture, science, and national defense.

REFERENCES

"All circles in Beijing do good for the children." 1981 Guangming Daily (May 16).

"The average life expectancy has nearly doubled since Liberation." The People's Daily [or] Guangming Daily (February 15).

"Beijing Family Education Association and Children's Health Association vigorously launch activities." The People's Daily (May 26).

ECKSTEIN, A. 1977. China's Economic Revolution. New York: Cambridge University Press.

"Going into deep investigation and research, doing its best to persuade the parents, Neijian Municipal Women's Federation has redeemed the delinquent teenagers and has gotten obvious achievements." Guangming Daily (February 16).

HU SISHENG. 1981. "To establish the sociology of new China: an interview with Professor Fei Xiaotong." The People's Daily (February 9).

"Investigation on the state of morality among the youth and children." Guangming Daily (May 30).

LEI JIEQIONG. 1980. "It is the responsibility of the whole society to strengthen education among the youth." The People's Daily (September 13).

"Speed up the development of sociology and promote the Four Modernizations." Guangming Daily (June 17).

ZHANG LIZHONG. 1981. "Birth control, later marriage and the decline in the population growth rate." The People's Daily (February 3).

Discussion Questions

1. Is it possible to improve some aspects of family life while ignoring others? Or must planners always view the family as a small social system in its social context, and change it as a whole? What do you think? How do you think Imbrogno would answer?

2. "Families, not individuals or governments, are the basic elements of any society." Who do you think is more likely to agree with this statement, Pitrou or Ullrich? Give the reasoning behind your answer.

3. Are single-parent families likely to become a problem in China as they have in Europe and North America? Are the Chinese likely to deal with them in the same way?

4. Do most societies deal with family issues (for example, day care and laws regarding marriage breakup and family violence) inadequately because men usually make the most important decisions?

5. "Whatever they may say, governments usually weaken families, not strengthen them." Compare the views of Pitrou and Zhangling on this issue.

6. "Part-time work may conflict with the goal of equal pay for women, but it makes sense for children." Why does Wolfe hold this view, and do you agree with it? Is this view likely to find support in Russia, given what Imbrogno has told us about family policy in that part of the world?

Data Collection Exercises

1. Think of a way to measure whether the State has more power over children than the family does. Then, find out whether the family has (relatively) more power over children in France or Russia.

2. What do sub-Saharan African societies do for single-parent families? How does the treatment there compare with Europe and the United States?

3. Identify a family issue that is particularly pressing in China. Now, find out whether the same issue is equally pressing in one other communist country (for example, Cuba or Albania) and one noncommunist country.

4. The excerpt by Wolfe shows the usefulness of studying family issues in America by comparison with other countries. Take another family issue, for example, the handling of domestic violence, and collect data that allow you to compare how the United States and at least one other country deal with the issue.

Writing Exercises

1. A. S. Makarenko, a Soviet theoretician cited by Imbrogno, has applied for a large research grant. His purpose is to prove that "large families are the place where a great deal of emotional maturity, intellectual activity and social interaction takes place, all necessary conditions for rich early childhood experiences and training in later collective living." Vivienne Ullrich has been asked to evaluate the research proposal. Now, imagine you are Ullrich and write a brief (500-word) assessment, indicating why you think the research should, or should not, be funded.

2. As President of a sub-Saharan African state, write a brief (500-word) letter to the head of the World Bank explaining why you do not intend to support family planning without a $1 billion loan to support industrial development in your country.

3. "Some family problems are uniquely women's (that is, wives') problems and some are not women's problems at all." In a brief (500-word) essay, indicate whether you agree or disagree with this view. Where relevant, refer to excerpts in this section.

4. Agnes Pitrou writes "Societies are rarely disposed to suicide and seek above all to perpetuate themselves. This is why societies give priority to the reconstitution and assimilation of their capital of children which is a guarantee of the future." Pretend you are Alan Wolfe and write Ms. Pitrou a brief (500-word) letter outlining your views on the statement she has made.

Glossary

Companionate (marriage)—A marriage that is based primarily on emotional ties such as romance or friendship, not instrumental ties such as an interdependent division of labor.

Feminism (feminists)—A doctrine that argues women are systematically disadvantaged, and they should be guaranteed opportunities that are equal to men's.

Functionalism (functionalists)—A perspective on social life than explains social relations, or activities, in terms of their consequences for the operation of particular social institutions, or society as a whole. For example, the statement, ''People form families in order to bear and raise children; if they didn't, society would cease to exist. So, families are functional to society; they *must* exist,'' is a functionalist statement.

''Haven in a heartless world''—The title of a book by historian Christopher Lasch, this concept captures the idea that family life can, and should, protect people from the cruelty and thoughtlessness of non-family members.

Incrementalism—An approach to policy making which is practical, ad hoc or piecemeal, not determined by a single, consistent vision of a desirable society.

Relativism (relativistic)—A moral or theoretical outlook that holds that all social practices must be understood, or judged, in their social context—not against absolute standards of right or wrong.

Sociobiology—An approach to understanding social relations by referring to genetic characteristics and population (or environmental) limitations. In effect, it is an attempt to understand human behavior by focusing on the animal origins of human beings.

Suggested Readings

EICHLER, MARGRIT. (1988) *Families in Canada Today: Recent Changes and their Policy Consequences,* 2nd ed. Toronto: Gage Publishing Company. A brilliant analysis of the family literature, identifying common sources of bias in family research and their consequences for policy making. Traces changes in legal and governmental policies in relation to marriage, parental roles, child care and new reproductive technology, among others.

GORDON, LINDA. (1988) *Heroes of thier Own Lives: The Politics and History of Family Violence.* New York: Penguin Books. An important feminist analysis of the trouble reformers faced in making sense of, and changing policies related to child abuse, child neglect, wife beating, and incest. Examines the way class and gender issues intertwine in family policy making.

HOTALING, GERALD T., DAVID FINKELHOR, JOHN T. KIRKPATRIC and MURRAY STRAUS, eds. (1988) *Coping with Family Violence: Research and Policy Perspectives.* Newbury Park: Sage Publications. An up-to-date collection of research papers on various aspects of family violence research and policy making, with an emphasis on methodology and statistical analysis. Includes discussions with the victims as well as the roles police, medical care givers, researchers, social services and courts play in handling them.

KAGAN, SHARON L., DOUGLAS R. POWELL, BERNICE WEISSBOURD, and EDWARD ZIGLER, eds. (1987) *America's Family Support Programs: Perspectives and Prospects.* New Haven: Yale University Press. Examines the history and current practice of a variety of support programs, including day care, child abuse, home-school linkages, parent support groups, and income supplements, noting how needs vary across racial and ethnic groups. Follows the policy process from problem, to design, to implementation.

KOTLER, PHILIP, and EDUARDO L. ROBERTO. (1989) *Social Marketing: Strategies for Changing Public Behavior.* New York: Free Press. Examines the ways in which, increasingly, mass marketing techniques are being used to change public attitudes towards social issues and social policies (for example, towards family planning and contraception, and child education).

OKIN, SUSAN MOLLER. (1989) *Justice, Gender and the Family.* New York: Basic Books. An extended discussion of the philosophical issues behind family policy. It asks, ''What is justice?'' and, ''How can we achieve justice within families, given gender inequality in the society as a whole?'' The book shows how the inequality women face in the ''public'' sphere of the market, politics, and the workplace reinforces inequality they face in the ''private'' family setting; and vice versa.

PART X

The Future of Family Life

ଌଌଌଌଌଌଌଌଌଌଌଌଌଌଌଌଌଌଌଌଌଌଌଌଌଌଌଌଌ

The articles in this book have tended to point to one conclusion: Around the world, family life is often at odds with private or personal life. The result is that, when they can, people are changing their family lives. Extended families are becoming rarer, and nuclear families are becoming the norm. More people are living alone or in temporary relationships. And, as a result of more migration and divorce, along with less childbearing, people generally have fewer kin available to them than in the past.

Another result is that many traditional family functions, such as child care, are being performed by government, business, or the community. More important is the fact that, around the world, there is growing uncertainty about how people *ought* to perform their family roles: what rights husbands and wives have, and what responsibilities go along with them; what rights parents and children have; and so on.

This uncertainty has had important effects; for example, it has reduced people's willingness to marry. On the other hand, when people *do* marry, they have more freedom to select their mate than they did in the past. Today they are able to choose across what used to be rigid boundaries of religion, ethnicity, and social class. And, more often than in the past, they are marrying for love—not for practical reasons, such as a spouse's ability to earn money or keep house.

Now, many people are alarmed at the speed with which the family is changing. Some think these changes in the direction of freer choice prove people are more selfish than ever—less willing to sacrifice themselves, the way they imagine people did in the past.

Yet it seems likely people have *always* been selfish and chosen the path that was in their best interest. It is simply that, in the past, the family and community were all-powerful. The individual counted for nothing. So people *had to* participate—to be a good family member, an upstanding member of the community—if they were to survive. But industrialization takes control out of the hands of the family, and in this way it weakens people's commitments to other family members. Also, urban-industrial life offers new possibilities for satisfaction and new challenges.

For many reasons, investing in family life today may not pay as well as it might have a century ago. This is because of the shorter average duration of modern relationships, the smaller investment other family members are ready to make, and the possibility of getting more by "investing" in a new family than by reinvesting in the present one. In fact, the same investment in friendship, career, or self-development might pay better (see, for example, Goode (1984), on this topic.)

In view of all this change and uncertainty, does "the family" have a future? And if so, is there only one likely future or many? Let's start to answer these questions by examining the future of marriage.

The Future of Marriage

As we have seen, marriage is changing dramatically and its future is by no means certain. Yet some things have not changed very much in the last century (or longer), and they may not change very much in the next century either.

For example, most people still marry at least once in their lives and almost everyone has at least one spousal relationship, whether legally married or not. And most people still have their first spousal relationship in the second quarter of their lives: currently, between ages 20 and 40.

But what about the future? Suppose people lived to be 160 years of age and had to complete twice as much formal education as they do now. By extrapolating, we predict that people would start cohabiting around the age of 40 or 50, being too busy with education and travel before then to settle down. And putting off marriage that long would pose no problem, if people continue to separate marriage from sex and procreation, as they have been doing for the past few decades. So this marriage scenario is quite plausible.

At the same time, divorce rates are likely to stay high in the foreseeable future. There is no sign of a drop in the divorce rates and, indeed, we may see even higher rates of divorce in Scandinavia than in North America. The divorce rates are high because divorce is easy to get, because people dream of the perfect mate, and because the social costs of divorce are falling. For example, divorce is less stigmatizing today than it once was and breaks up fewer friendships than it used to.

So in the 21st century people are likely to spend about the same *proportion* of their adult lives in spousal relationships as they have in the past. However they will spread their time over a larger number of relationships, both legal and common law [on this, see Cherlin and Furstenburg (1983)].

Now these are the "constants" of married life, but many other things are changing. For example, cohabitation is becoming more and more popular; but it also is a pretty unstable relationship. If this pattern continues, people will have an increasing (average) number of spouses over their lifetime. Women and their children will form the basic family unit—the nuclear family of the future—and male spouses will flow through a great many female-headed households.

People will also spend more of their lives as "singles" in the future. As we all become more self-sufficient, more people will escape from unwanted economic and kinship responsibilities. That means more people will live singly as bachelors and spinsters (before their first marriage), and as divorcees and widows/widowers (after their first marriage) than in the past.

In fact, we may have to invent new words to adequately describe the many varieties of single status—whether short-lived or long-lived, intentional or unintentional, following a legal marriage or informal cohabit, and so on.

Already this change amounts to a "singles revolution." North Americans are already nine times more likely to live alone than to cohabit, and the reason is simple: Single life is easy and getting easier all the time. Singlehood is becoming a better option than many of the alternatives, including marriage.

Yet *lifelong* singlehood is likely to remain uncommon in the future. Instead people will move between singlehood, cohabitation, and marriage over the course of their lives. Neither singlehood nor cohabitation has emerged as a lifelong alternative to marriage in any Western country.

For its part, cohabitation is merely another stage in the process of courtship and marriage for most people. For middle-aged people, it is more and more often a resting place between first and second marriages. Though some people fear it may, cohabitation does *not* seem to spoil marriage prospects for anyone. People may be delaying marriage in favour of cohabitation; but their pool of eligible mates remains large. That's because other people are also delaying marriage or getting divorced. So cohabitation does no harm to marriage chances and makes it easier for everyone to get information about potential mates before marrying them. It seems likely to continue serving as a useful and popular living arrangement before first and second marriages.

What about the future of parenthood—traditionally, the central role of family life and the main social function of families?

The Future of Childbearing

In future, parenthood is likely to change in dramatic ways. All the Western countries have seen a steady decline in childbearing over the last one hundred years, and a great many other countries have shown signs of starting the same decline. From this standpoint, the "baby boom" of the 1950s and early 1960s was nothing but a brief departure from the long downward trend. And the introduction of oral contraception in the late 1960s has made this worldwide fertility decline absolutely certain, if it was ever in doubt.

So, unless there are dramatic, unforseen changes, people will continue having fewer children in the future, and large families will become a thing of the past. Most people will still choose to experience parenthood at least once. However one- or two-child families will be even more common than they are today, and three- or more child families, relatively rare.

In this way and others, children will stop being central to family life in the next century. Adults will spend a much larger portion of their lives with no children around at all. This is because women will bear few children and will bear them within a short space of time—as they are already doing. Other things being equal, this will mean fewer years until the youngest child leaves the family home.

Offsetting this trend slightly is a continued growth of child dependency, due to the lengthening of formal education; and the return home of older children who need renewed economic support. So far economic recession, not a belief in the traditional family, proves to be the strongest force keeping parents and children together.

Economic recession is the best friend of high fertility, since it encourages "fatalism"—a sense that people have no control over their own future, so why not have lots of babies? For example, poor North American teenagers will continue to ignore birth control until they recognize they have a stake in the future—especially, an educational and economic future that makes teenage pregnancy costly.

Other factors may also encourage high fertility for a time. For example, certain religious and social movements will try to encourage higher fertility. And ethnic minorities that are afraid of assimilation, or gender equality, will try to encourage higher fertility. But in the long run, all of these efforts will fail.

The historical evidence argues that most Western women will bear only a few children, and these early in life. Throughout the world, fertility will continue to fall wherever women have other activities open to them.

We can also see an increasing estrangement between parents and children. This is not occurring because of conflict (as it did in the past, during periods of rapid social change) but simply because parents and children have fewer common interests—a smaller communal investment—in the family than ever before. It seems likely that, with every passing decade, both parents and children will feel less committed to the family as a collective enterprise. They are ever more likely to calculate whether it is really worth their while maintaining an allegiance to it.

Already, parents spend much less time with their children today than they did in the past. We are not suggesting that parents of the past spent a lot of time playing with their children; but they did spend lots of time in each other's company, often in home production.

That is not the case today. Today, the time adults spend making money at work outside the home is time *not spent* at home investing emotionally in the family. Time spent at work means less time spent in family interaction. And as time pressures increase at work, parents and children spend less time together, enjoy less intimacy together—indeed, live more independent lives than they did in the past. As a result, they are less tied emotionally than in the past, just as they are less tied materially.

The decreased rate of childbearing proves that people are less willing to invest in children than in the past. Indeed, if our culture continues to discourage people from childbearing, parenthood may eventually become the activity of a select few who produce children for the many. And new biogenetic breakthroughs may also hasten this specialization of activities.

Consider the possibilities: We can imagine the life span doubling and female fertility extending into the sixties. New technologies can already separate conception from gestation; so in future, motherhood can become specialized. Some women will be able to conceive many children without having to provide for them, while others will take on the job of raising the children. Frozen sperm banks already provide men with a means to immortality. Knowing the donors will permit women to select distinguished genetic origins for their children—origins based on demonstrated male achievement.

The separation of sex, marriage, and procreation allows women without partners to have children. This, in turn, takes away a prime reason for marriage and may well make the heterosexual married couple a much less common family arrangement than in the past. As more people use the new technologies, there will be new legal and social questions to answer: For example, who shall we legally define as the mother of the child, where different women provided the egg, carried the fetus, and raised the child? They will also raise questions about who will decide on sex ratios, once it becomes routinely possible to select the sex of a child in uterus [on these and related themes, see Keller (1971)].

However, it is difficult to know how women will use this reproductive technology in the future. For example, we do not know what effect sex selection might have on the fertility rate. In many parts of the world, the birth of sons still seem to hold marriages together better than the births of daughters. However, sex preference is weak among North American parents, and it is unlikely many women will use the new technologies simply to ensure the birth of a son.

Nor do we know how much the new technology will lengthen women's childbearing period. It seems doubtful many women will want a longer reproductive period. Finally, we do not know when a male oral contraceptive pill will be invented and what effect *this* will have on decisions about fertility. So new reproductive technology raises the possibility of new parenting decisions, but the result may be far less dramatic than many people believe—because there is no evidence that people want to make parenthood a more important part of their lives.

In the past, most societies held procreation to be an unquestionable social goal of adult life. It was this belief that led the society to socialize males and females differently. Distinct sexual identities were important for childbearing and childraising—or, at least, people thought so. But with recent biological advances and a loss of interest in childbearing, sexual identities may blur. Heterosexuality itself may become only one of several forms of sexuality. In fact, one sex may even become superfluous or obsolete.

Of course, this is all speculation. Less speculative are the likely consequences of a continued high divorce rate. As repeated divorce and remarriage become a common lifestyle, there will be a widespread problem of balancing responsibilities between previous and current families. Divorce and remarriage will amount to a kind of "childswapping" from one marriage to the next—as though people were saying to one another, "You care for my children and I'll care for yours." That's fine as far as it goes. But, in practice, the complexity of the change means changes in family law and income security will be needed to make sure that everyone is being cared for properly.

The Future of Kinship

With all this coming and going, most children will have more than two living parents, even if the people occupying the roles of "mother" and "father" change from time to time. The number of *possible* uncles, aunts, and grandparents is astronomical. What's more, relatives will be "available" to their children for many more years, due to increased longevity. So children can expect to get more person-years of parenting in the future than they did in the past.

This is a good thing, because children need more and more parenting. The need is particularly great in times of economic recession when unemployment is high and the costs of education, food, and rent are also high.

In a sense, children are going to be better off than their parents. That's because, in the future, parents are going to have fewer children available to them, since they bore fewer children. On the other hand, their children are all living longer, so they will be available to their parents for a longer time. Indeed, by age 70, parents may have as many living children as they would have a century ago, when parents were bearing twice as many children who lived half as long.

For their part, parents will live longer too. Indeed they will be physically and economically strong for a longer period of time than parents in the past. However, like their children, they will also live more years in economic dependency—after retiring from the workforce—than people did in the past. And in the end, they will need all the "parenting" that their (fewer) children will provide.

Now, because of lower fertility, people living today have fewer brothers and sisters than in the past. This means, in future, there will be fewer siblings to help parents take care of their younger children, and fewer siblings to take care of their aged parents. And because their own parents did not have many brothers and sisters, people will grow up with fewer uncles and aunts. In turn, they will produce few cousins for the children of their siblings. In all: a complicated chain of kinship changes.

The result? We can forsee a shortage of lateral extended kin at every age: a growing shortage of uncles, aunts, cousins, nephews, nieces, and so on. The *vertical* extended kin group may persist, through a long survival of parents, grandparents, and even great-grandparents. But the *lateral* extended kin network may disappear from social significance. Kin terms like "cousin" and "nephew" may lose their practical meaning, in that they no longer form the basis for kin support.

Perhaps other social practices will make up for this loss of kin support. They may include adoptive caring roles (where young people care for older people who are not their natural parents or kin by conventional definition); a great investment of time and effort by the fewer kin who *are* available; or kinship inventions (such as "step-grandchildhood" or "half-nephewhood"), which would introduce scarce young people into more kinship obligations than they would have had in the past. We may also see older people caring for foster grandchildren. These are all possible, but far from certain, changes in the future.

So the family is changing but it does seem to have a future—in fact, several possible futures. In large part, the future of the family will depend on how people come to balance family life and work life with their individual goals, and how much personal choice the economy allows people. And here we find a variety of visions in the articles excerpted in this section.

A Variety of Visions

As we have seen, a great deal depends on how much choice people will have in shaping their own lives. Certainly, people have tended—whenever given the choice—to live differently from the ways they have done in the past [on this, see Jones, Marsden and Tepperman (1990).]

Evidence to support this is provided by the excerpt by van de Kaa, which surveys findings from many European countries in the recent past. Van de Kaa reports a major shift in family formation and childbearing behaviors taking place throughout the continent. Though societies change at slightly different times and progress at somewhat different rates, they are all heading in the same direction: what van de Kaa calls "a second demographic transition."

This transition continues the downward trend in childbearing and upward trend in concern for "quality of life." It also emphasizes individualism—the rights of each individual to live in a way that is most fulfilling. As people gain ever more choice over their lives—a result of prosperity as much as new values—they are choosing against the age-old practice of surrounding themselves with family members.

They are also choosing to surround themselves with people they love. And, as we learn from a study of Chinese marriages excerpted in this section, the growth of freedom to choose seems to have a happy ending: People have happier marriages when they can choose their own mate than when their marriage is arranged by parents or relatives. Love and freedom make people happy—not an astonishing finding, perhaps, but a gratifying one.

From van de Kaa's point of view, new values are the driving force in this continued reform of family life. Along similar lines, Burch and Matthews explain why people are living in ever smaller households (more and more people living entirely on their own or in two-person households) and why this trend is likely to continue.

Sweden epitomizes a pattern some authors feel will be typical of Western family life in the future: a low marriage rate, small household size, high rates of unmarried cohabitation, high rates of divorce, and female labor-force participation. The "progressive" values van de Kaa describes are also widespread in Sweden. Yet the Swedish family is still alive and well after these many assaults on collective living (Popenoe, 1987). This fact suggests a built-in desire for family life that is unlikely to fall below a certain minimum level.

Excerpt 59 by Peres and Katz shows the importance of external threat for keeping families together. In Israel, both Jews *and* Palestinians feel this threat of war and violence at every turn. Like South Africa, India, and Northern Ireland, this is a society in a permanent state of civil unrest. Given so much uncertainty and threat, people are likely to close ranks and define their boundaries. Strengthening family life is part of that affirmation. The family will have a strong future in Israel so long as external threats to security remain strong.

Even where there is no threat to family life, countries like Italy and Hungary, with a long tradition of close familial ties, continue to display that kind of family life. And, Höllinger and Haller (Excerpt 58) show, close kin and friends remain the most important supports in the event of a personal problem—even though face-to-face contacts may be less frequent than they were in the past.

In the future we expect that families will continue to change for many reasons. For example, anything that threatens or diminishes personal choice—poverty, war or the threat of war, environmental disaster, the upsurge of powerful collective sentiments (nationalism or religious fundamentalism, for example)—will strengthen the family.

Finally, some futures of the family are entirely unknowable because we cannot make good guesses about the economic, political, or ecological context within which we will live our lives in the next fifty or so years. What we have seen in this book is that family life around the world is moving in one particular direction, of many possible ones. As humans, we seem to have chosen our next of kin.

References

CHERLIN, A. J. and F. F. FURSTENBURG. (1983) "The American family in the year 2000," *The Futurist,* June, 7–14.

GOODE, W. J. (1984) "Individual investments in family relationships over the coming decades," *Tocqueville Review,* 6(1), Spring–Summer, 51–83.

JONES C., L. MARSDEN and L. TEPPERMAN. (1990) *Lives of their Own: The Individualization of Women's Lives.* Toronto: Oxford University Press.

KELLER, S. (1971) "Does the family have a future?" *Journal of Comparative Family Studies,* Spring, 1–15.

POPENOE, D. (1987) "Beyond the nuclear family: A statistical portrait of the changing family in Sweden," *Journal of Marriage and the Family,* 29(1), February, 173–183.

Introduction

We should shape our best guesses about the future from what we know about the past and present. This is one reason we have examined such a wide variety of historical and cross-national findings in this book: they give us a better sense of what family life is about and, therefore, *can be* about.

The next excerpt surveys findings from many European countries in the recent past. The author, Dirk van de Kaa, reports a major shift in family formation and childbearing behaviors taking place throughout the continent. Though they have started at slightly different times and progress at somewhat different rates, they are all pointing in the same direction: what van de Kaa calls "a second demographic transition."

Recall that the first demographic transition began in Europe around two hundred years ago. Falling mortality rates, then falling fertility rates, were part of a large social change we call modernization. Central to this change in people's lives was a change in people's values toward smaller, healthier families. People would bear fewer children but value and care for those they bore more devotedly than before— at least, so the argument went.

The second demographic transition continues this downward trend in childbearing and upward trend in concern for "quality of life." However it also emphasizes individualism—the rights of each individual to live in a way that is most fulfilling. Viewed in this context, parenthood, and even marriage, is somewhat less attractive than it ever was before. As people gain ever more choice over their lives—surely a result of prosperity as much as new values—they are choosing against the age-old practice of surrounding themselves with family members.

55
Europe's Second Demographic Transition

Dirk J. van de Kaa

. . . According to current United Nations medium projections, Europe's population will increase a scant 6 percent between 1985 and 2025, from 492 to 524 million, while the world's population nearly doubles, from 4.5 to 8.2 billion, and nearly one in every five Europeans in 2025 will be pensioners aged 65 and over. . . .

The new stage in Europe's demographic history might be called its "second demographic transition. Europe's first demographic transition began with a gradual decline in death rates dating from the early 19th century, followed by fertility decline beginning around 1880 in most countries, though earlier in France. By the 1930s, both birth and death rates were at low levels. . . .

Source: van de Kaa, Dirk (1987) "Europe's second demographic transition," Population Bulletin, Vol. 42, No. 1, March, 1–57.

The start of the second transition can arbitrarily be set at 1965. In the interim had come World War II and the baby boom that followed it. The principal demographic feature of the second transition is the decline in fertility from somewhat above the "replacement" level of 2.1 births per woman, which ensures that births and deaths will stay in balance and population remain stationary over the long run, to a level well below replacement.

If fertility stabilizes below replacement, as seems likely in Europe, and barring immigration, population numbers will sooner or later decline, as had begun already by 1985 in four countries (Austria, Denmark, the Federal Republic of Germany, and Hungary). Changes in mortality and migration—the other two variables that shape changes in population numbers—have had relatively little impact in the second transition. . . .

Early ... theories about the demographic transition, based on Europe's experience to the 1930s, usually ended with the stage of "zero ...." population growth. The stage of long-term population decline, now imminent in Europe, has since been called "beyond the demographic transition," but its special features in Europe seem to merit the label "second demographic transition." This *Bulletin* describes the broad features of this second demographic transition as it has evolved among Europe's some 30 heterogeneous countries. . . .

SECOND DEMOGRAPHIC TRANSITION: THE BACKGROUND

Two keywords characterize the norms and attitudes behind the first and second demographic transitions and highlight the contrasts between them: *altruistic* and *individualistic*. The first transition to low fertility was dominated by concerns for family and offspring, but the second emphasizes the rights and self-fulfillment of individuals. Demographers Ron Lesthaeghe and Christopher Wilson argue convincingly that industrialization, urbanization, and secularization were the indirect determinants of the first transition.[1] The shift from family-based production to wage-paid labor that accompanied industrialization and urbanization reduced the economic utility of children. . . . Moreover, a large number of children could mean the dissipation of family assets like land after the parents' death, so birth control became a sound strategy. Secularization reduced the influence of the churches and increased couples' willingness to practice family planning.

Demographically, the first transition reflected the disappearance of the Malthusian pattern of family formation. Couples no longer had to delay marriage until they acquired a separate means of existence by succeeding their parents. The age at marriage declined and so did the number of people who remained permanently single. Within marriage, the number of children was controlled; quality replaced quantity.

The indirect determinants of the second transition cannot be summed up so neatly. . . .

In these societies, one's standard of living is largely determined by one's level and quality of education, degree of commitment to societal goals, and motivation to develop and use one's talents. This holds for women as well as men; both sexes tend to strive to earn a personal income. Getting married and/or having children may involve considerable opportunity costs. . . .

For a couple, children involve not only ... direct expenditures, but also their utility has declined even further. They are no longer either expected or legally required to support their parents in old age or help with family finances. The emotional satisfactions of parenthood can be achieved most economically by having one or perhaps two children.

Beyond the simple calculation of economic utilities, social and cultural changes play a role in people's move away from marriage and parenthood in postindustrial societies. The forces behind these changes have been described in various ways. . . .

I have argued that most European societies have shifted remarkably toward greater progressiveness in the postwar period and this helps explain many demographic changes. Philosophically, "progressiveness" characterizes a tendency to embrace the new, look critically at the present, and largely disregard the past. . . .

A SEQUENCE OF EVENTS IN FAMILY FORMATION

A Standard Sequence with Variations?

An interesting perspective on recent population change in Europe is to see the changes that have occurred in factors bearing on family formation as a sequence through which all countries pass. The timing and speed of the sequence have differed substantially between Eastern and

Western Europe and within these regions, but there is strong evidence of a logical ordering. Each step taken seems to have led to the next; each option chosen made a further choice possible. Looking back, the sequence of events that led to today's low fertility seems both logical and understandable. One wonders why it was not predicted! Reflecting the shift to progressiveness and individualism, the sequence involves shifts from marriage toward cohabitation, from children to the adult couple as the focus of a family, from contraception to prevent unwanted births to deliberate, self-fulfilling choices whether and when to conceive a child, and from uniform to widely diversified families and households. Let us sketch the sequence as it has progressed to completion in a "standard" European country.

To trace the story, one must begin with the great impact of World War II. Virtually all European countries were involved in the fighting, suffered from occupation and shortages, and experienced the uncertainties and sorrows that war brings. Many young men saw military service and became familiar with techniques to prevent conception and venereal disease. Retrospective surveys document a steady increase from cohort to cohort in the proportions of adults who have experienced premarital intercourse and a sharp postwar decline in the age at which such sexual relations begin. Geeraert, citing a long list of research in Western European countries since 1900, concludes that among young women in particular, both students and working women, premarital intercourse is increasingly common.[2] . . .

Social attitudes regarding premarital or extramarital sexual relations did not change so rapidly. Most couples therefore sought official sanction through marriage. This was also the solution in the case of an out-of-wedlock pregnancy.

Besides official sanction to live together, most couples who married in the early 1950s also wanted and were economically ready to start a family. The average age at first marriage declined, the interval between marriage and the first birth remained short, and birth rates for lower-order births began to rise. The increase in

fertility in the early childbearing ages more than made up for the decline in higher-order births, so that the total fertility rate increased—at least to the mid-1960s.

The decline in higher-order births reflected general acceptance or birth control as a means to limit family size. This was the tail end of the first demographic transition in which birth control was used not for spacing but to bring completed family size down from seven or eight children in the 1880s to two or three some 50–60 years later. But the contraceptives available before the mid-1960s were not very effective or suitable for inexperienced couples and many "unwanted" children were no doubt born.

The decline in age at first marriage loosened the link between marriage and the start of childbearing. Marriage was still desired to earn official approval of sexual relations (certainly by a couple's parents), but for many young couples it no longer marked a readiness to have children. Parents anxious to help their just-married children avoid the burdens of an immediate birth may well have introduced them to family planning. Family planning organization enrollments soared. Membership in the Dutch organization (Netherlands Association for Sexual Reform, NVSH) more than doubled from 97,000 in 1955 to a peak of 206,000 in 1965 (and now has almost evaporated). As contraception became more popular for avoiding births early in married life, the age at marriage could decline further. Young married couples could accumulate assets together before deciding to take on the care of children.

Just about that time, in the mid-1960s, the effective, as well as safe, pills and IUDs came on the market. They were readily adopted. First and second birth intervals lengthened, and there were somewhat fewer lower-order births. Doubtless due also to further reductions in family-size norms, fertility above age 30 plummeted and the birth of fourth, fifth, and later children became an exception. The proportion of unwanted births—conceived out of marriage or too late in marriage—declined.

By the early 1970s, . . . changes in abortion

law made it possible to terminate unintended premarital pregnancies safely, so the frequency of unwanted first births declined further. The gradual disappearance of "forced marriages" slowed the decline in age at first marriage and this age began to climb.

Abortion could, of course, also be used to avert unwanted births among married women—high-order births, risky and socially unacceptable births to older women, and, if so desired, births conceived extramaritally. Increased adoption of sterilization to control fertility after couples had all the children they wanted further cut the number of higher-order births in the early 1970s. Fertility fell below replacement level.

Once it was generally accepted that sexual relations in marriage were not solely or primarily aimed at procreation and contraceptives of high quality had become available, a further step was taken. Law changes had already increased the frequency of divorce and legal separation. Divorce and separation were also occurring at earlier ages and sooner after marriage. Since young people now married with the intention of delaying childbearing for several years, it is understandable that the need to seek a seal of approval for such an arrangement was questioned. Why not start living together and marry only when children were wanted or on the way? Stable unions were formed, differing from early marriage mainly in that they were "paperless." The first marriage rate began to decline and the age at first marriage went up. . . .

The proportions ever-marrying declined markedly; age at first marriage rose further. Remarriages became much less common. A rise in out-of-wedlock fertility became noticeable, particularly among somewhat older women. Some of these women deliberately chose to bear a child without having a stable relationship with a male partner. The proportions of out-of-wedlock births legitimated by marriage or the male partner declined. In addition, voluntary childlessness was no longer solely an option for men and women who elected not to marry. Being married or living in a stable union no longer differentiated people strongly with regard either to having

children or desired family size. Fertility seemed to stabilize well below replacement level.

This "standard" sequence of changes in family formation is obviously impossible to trace in detail for all 30 of Europe's heterogeneous countries and the sequence itself is likely to be different as it evolves among them. However, the countries can be grouped roughly according to their place in the sequence as it has evolved so far and fairly simple period data available for a reasonable number of the countries demonstrate the basic features of the second transition to low fertility. These features involve four related shifts . . .

1. Shift from the *golden age of marriage* to the *dawn of cohabitation*;
2. Shift from the era of the *king-child with parents* to that of the *king-pair with a child*;
3. Shift from *preventive contraception* to *self-fulfilling conception*;
4. Shift from *uniform* to *pluralistic families and households*.

WHERE COUNTRIES ARE IN THE SEQUENCE

Only two European countries appear to have experienced the full sequence of changes in family formation that have led to very low fertility—Denmark and Sweden. Even here there have been deviations from the "standard" sequence described above. However, in these two countries the proportion of out-of-wedlock births has risen from about 10 percent in 1956–60 to well over 40 percent currently. And the tremendously changed social significance of the "married" status probably best demonstrates the transition toward greater individualism.

The following four groups indicate where European countries now are in . . . the standard sequence.

First Group. In addition to Denmark and Sweden, this group includes the Northern and Western European countries which appear to be following close in their tracks. The birth rates of these countries as of the mid-1980s generally fall between 10 and 12 per 1,000 population and the rate of natural increase (births minus deaths) is no more than 0.4 percentage points above zero or actually negative. . . . Finland, Norway, the United Kingdom, Austria, Belgium, France, the Federal Republic of Germany, the Netherlands, Switzerland, and Italy (in Southern Europe) all qualify for this group. Here the second demographic transition is well advanced.

Second Group. This group includes Greece, Malta, Portugal, Spain, and Yugoslavia in Southern Europe. The fertility decline has been less marked in these countries; they follow the first group at a distance. Current birth rates range from 12 to 16 per 1,000 population and the rate of natural increase usually exceeds 0.4 percent. The second transition is late, but there is little doubt that it has begun and will be completed.

Third Group. The six Eastern European countries make up this group: Bulgaria, Czechoslovakia, the German Democratic Republic, Hungary, Poland, and Romania. . . . Here the . . . postwar trend toward greater sexual freedom appears to be less pronounced. In reaction to forcible attempts to change the structure and norms of society after the political change, many people have clung tenaciously to traditional mores in their personal lives. On the other hand, legal abortion became available in these countries earlier than in most other European countries, while government intervention to raise birth rates has had some impact on fertility trends. Current birth rates are close to 14 per 1,000 population, except for Hungary (12.2 in 1985) and Poland (18.2).

Fourth Group. This group covers the remaining countries which, for a variety of cultural and historical reasons, are all late in completing the *first* demographic transition. It includes Iceland and Ireland in Northern Europe and Albania and Turkey in Southern Europe. Even parts of the USSR belong to this

group. Whether or when they will begin the second demographic transition is not easy to predict. Their current birth rates tend to be high by European standards and rates of natural increase range from about 0.9 percent in Iceland and Ireland to 2.1 percent in Turkey. . . .

MAKING THE GIFT OF A BABY TO THE PENSION FUNDS?

In 1986 the influential Germany weekly *Der Spiegel* ran a series of articles under the heading *Den Alterskassen ein Baby schenken?*, which translates roughly as above. It sums up Europe's demographic dilemma well. Collective and individual interests do not seem to coincide. The transition to individualism appears to have led to an extended period of below-replacement-level fertility, population decline, and an age structure that will in the long run make full funding of old-age pensions virtually impossible. Yet it is difficult to imagine people having babies to please the pension funds and economic incentives, even at the level offered in France and some Eastern European countries, appear incapable of overcoming individualistic desires and raising fertility to replacement level. Relying on immigration to adjust age structures is practically out of the question. All countries of immigration have taken effective measures to end the influx and increasingly aim at rapid integration of the current minorities. . . .

What then is the answer to the predicament? Most countries will probably follow the old maxim: If in doubt, do nothing; wait and see. . . .

Another approach is to try out new, more imaginative measures to raise fertility and have them ready when needed. Thinking in this direction is developing rapidly. So far no serious proposal seems to be compatible with the shift to individualistic values. But a recent proposition by . . . demographer Paul Demeny is certainly imaginative.[3] He proposes to relink fertility behavior and economic security in old age. The pronatalist institution he sees would "earmark a socially agreed-upon fraction of the compulsory contribution from earnings that flow into the common pool from which pay-as-you-go national social security schemes are now financed and transfer that fraction to individual contributors' live parents as an additional entitlement."

It is easy to make a long list of reasons why this proposal has no chance in the world of being implemented. But then, in demographic matters the unexpected sometimes happens.

NOTES

[1]Lesthaeghe, R., and C. Wilson, *Modes of Production, Secularisation, and the Pace of the Fertility Decline in Western Europe, 1870–1930*, working paper, Brussels, 1978.

[2]Geeraert, A., *Sexualiteit bij jongeren* (Sexuality among Young People) (Brussels: De Sikkel, 1977) p. 27.

[3]Demeny, P., *Population Note No. 57* (New York: The Population Council, December 1, 1986).

Introduction

Will the freedom to choose their own mates make people happier or unhappier? This is an important question for the future, as more and more people around the world are getting the chance to choose their own marriage partners.

We can think of theories that would support both answers. On the one hand, freedom to choose *should* make people happier. It gives them more control over their own lives, and people seem to like autonomy. Free choice allows people to marry partners who are emotionally compatible, attractive, or desirable in the eyes of the spouses-to-be. And who is better equipped to judge these things than the people who will end up marrying?

On the other hand, supporters of arranged marriages have argued that people— especially, young people—are often blinded by passion. That is why they make foolish choices. But older people are better equipped, by life experience and disinterest, to choose the best mate for someone else—especially for their own children.

And, as these same supporters of arranged marriages might argue, mating on the basis of love and free choice creates uncertainty and anxiety. It may also raise unrealistic hopes about marriage and in the end cause dissatisfaction with the chosen partner. In this way, free choice may even increase the chances of divorce.

So which answer is right? The best way to find out is to compare the experiences of people who married for love and people whose marriages were arranged by family elders. Read the following excerpt, on Chinese families, to find out which kind of marriage seems to produce the greater happiness.

56

Love Matches and Arranged Marriages

Xu Xiaohe and Martin King Whyte

Throughout the world a revolution has been taking place in the way mates are selected. In societies where parents used to select marital partners for their children, the power of parents is crumbling. Through some combination of structural modernization, cultural Westernization, and governmental pressure, arranged marriages are increasingly giving way to freedom of choice, or "love matches," in which young people play the dominant role in selecting whom they will marry. (For the classic account of this transition worldwide, see Goode, 1963.)

Even though the nature of the trend is indisputable, its implications are not. Individuals reared in the West, where "youth-driven" mate choice has been the rule in most social strata for centuries, assume that this shift from arranged marriages to love matches is progressive and "healthy." As young people are increasingly freed from arbitrary family dictates and controls, they are able to select partners according to criteria of love and personal compatibility, and the result should be happier marriages and individuals. In the "bad old days" of arranged marriages, according to this view, many people found themselves stuck in marriages with persons decidedly not of their own choosing, mates selected on the basis of family status, wealth, or other criteria, whom they might find personally repulsive.[1] The shift away from arranged marriage, then, should reduce the level of marital misery in a society.

Traditionalists in many part of the world raise questions about this set of assumptions, however. They point to the high divorce rates in modern societies characterized by freedom of

mate choice as evidence of the problems inherent in love matches. They claim that arranged marriages have virtues that are not appreciated by people in Western societies. The contrast they draw is illustrated by the phrase, "love matches start out hot and grow cold, while arranged marriages start out cold and grow hot." In other words, love matches typically involve a very intense romantic involvement, accompanied by idealization of the partner and fantasies about wedded bliss, in the period prior to the wedding (the "hot" phase). Then after the wedding, reality sets in, and some combination of domestic chores, child care burdens, financial anxieties, and mundane life with a less-than-ideal real life partner leads to a more or less inevitable decline in romantic feelings and satisfaction with the relationship over the years. Here traditionalists can point to a considerable accumulation of evidence, from both cross-sectional and longitudinal studies in Western societies, showing that marital happiness and satisfaction ratings do tend to decline over the course of a marriage (see for example, Pineo, 1961; Renne, 1970; Hicks and Platt, 1970).[2]

The trajectory for arranged marriages, according to traditionalists, is different. Since they don't know each other well, or perhaps not at all, and since they don't have any romantic feelings for one another prior to the marriage, the partners in an arranged marriage "have nowhere to go but up." After the marriage the couple will have the opportunity to get to know one another and forge common bonds. As this process occurs, compatibility and mutual concern are likely to lead to a mature form of love, perhaps never as "hot" as the premarital emotions experienced in a love match, but a relationship that provides a more realistic and durable bond that can survive the test of time and family diffi-

Source: Xiaohe, Xu, and M. K. Whyte, "Love matches and arranged marriages," *Journal of Marriage and the Family*, 52 (August 1990), 709–722.

culties. In the long run, at least, the traditionalists claim, arranged marriages give more satisfaction than free-choice marriages.

But can we assume that spouses selected by parents will have any realistic basis for developing a compatible relationship? Critics of arranged marriages can point to cases that make this seem quite unlikely—of a young and vital woman married off to an old and feeble man, or to a deformed son of a wealthy family, and so forth. However, traditionalists argue that such cases are atypical and that arranged marriages are generally more likely to produce compatibility than are love matches. They argue that parents are concerned about the happiness of their offspring and will usually be in a better position to judge compatibility in the long run than their children are. They can rationally evaluate the nature of their own child and investigate the character of a prospective spouse for that child and then use their wisdom and experience to arrive at the most "suitable" match. Their offspring, in contrast, may be young and immature, and even if not they may be too swayed by emotions and hormones to make a "wise" choice of a marital partner.[3] The result of allowing young people to choose their own spouses, then, may be that they will be blinded by love and overlook areas of personal incompatibility, and the latter will become apparent and cause problems later on in the marriage. Parents are less likely to be so blinded, or so the argument goes.

A STUDY IN THE PEOPLE'S REPUBLIC OF CHINA

In the pages that follow we report the results of a love-match/arranged-marriage comparison conducted in Chengdu, the capital of Sichuan Province, in the People's Republic of China. A probability sample of 586 ever-married women between the ages of 22 and 70 residing in the two main urban districts of Chengdu (which together contained about 1.2 million people in 1982, or 97% of the urban population of that city) was interviewed in 1987, with a response rate of 87.7%. Sichuan is China's most populous province, with over 100 million people, and it is located in the Southwest. Even though Chengdu is the capital of the province, it may be less cosmopolitan than cities near the coast, such as Peking, Canton, or Shanghai. No claim is made here that Chengdu is representative of urban China in general. However, existing research on other urban areas (see Whyte and Parish, 1984) suggests that the general features of the mate-choice transition process in Chengdu are similar to what is occurring elsewhere.

Women in the Chengdu sample were first married over a 55-year period, from 1933 to 1987, and during this time period a major transformation from arranged to free-choice marriages has been under way. The results of the Chengdu survey will be used to compare Chinese love matches and arranged marriages. Unfortunately, husbands were not interviewed, so we can only examine how marriages were viewed by wives.

Arranged marriages were the dominant tradition in China for all classes for centuries, unlike the situation in Japan. Furthermore, Chinese arranged marriages often took a more extreme form than that found in China's Asian neighbor. While in the Japanese *miai* custom the young couple had a ritualized meeting and at least some opportunity to express an opinion about the partner selected for them, in China many people experienced what could be called a "blind marriage," in which the parents monopolized the decision (with the aid of hired go-betweens), and the couple did not even meet until the day of the wedding.

This arranged marriage system came under attack in the early decades of this century, with reformers and revolutionaries denouncing the personal misery and suicides that resulted (see Pa, 1933/1972). Over time a combination of increasing wage labor in China's town and cities and growing Western influence on China's culture and educational system did begin to foster a growing voice for young people in mate-choice decisions during the republican era (1912–1949—see Lang, 1946; Levy, 1949).

After the Chinese Communists came to national power in 1949, they vigorously promoted freedom of mate choice. The Marriage Law of the People's Republic of China, adopted in 1950, denounced the "arbitrary and compulsory feudal marriage system . . . which ignores the childrens' interest" and proclaimed that "marriage shall be based upon the complete willingness of the two parties. Neither party shall use compulsion and no third party shall be allowed to interfere" (quoted in Yang, 1959:221). Marriage registration offices were established nationwide, where couples were to be interviewed at the point of marriage to see whether they were doing so voluntarily. A nationwide propaganda campaign was launched during the period 1950–1953 to try to mobilize support for, and compliance with, the Marriage Law. In subsequent years socialist transformation of the economy eliminated the family as a production unit (until the post-Mao reforms, at least), and the resulting proletarianization of the population, combined with industrialization and the spread of education, helped to accelerate the process of transition from arranged to free-choice marriages (see the fuller discussion in Parish and Whyte, 1978; Whyte and Parish, 1984).

Cross-sectional data from the Chengdu survey can be used to get some picture of the timing and extent of this transition. Responses to several pertinent, closed-ended questions are displayed by time periods in Table 1. Women in the sample are arrayed in this table in terms of the years they first married, rather than by birth cohorts, and the time divisions that form marriage cohorts in the table are selected to match the major political turning points in recent Chinese history—the coming to power of the Chinese Communist Party in 1949, the launching of the Great Leap Forward in 1958, the onset of the Cultural Revolution in 1966, and the beginning of the post-Mao reform era in 1977. First, it is apparent that a major shift away from arranged marriage has occurred, with instances in which parents dominate the proceedings declining from 60% to 70% in the pre-1949 period to under 10% today. Relatedly, those who met their husbands directly rather than through an introduction, those whose introducers were peers rather than parents, those who had some romantic relationships and dates prior to marriage, and those who describe themselves as having been in love have all increased in comparison with the pre-1949 era.

The results in Table 1 also show that in spite of the increasing role that young people have played recently in selecting their own spouses, very little in the way of a "dating culture" exists yet in Chengdu. (Elements defining a dating culture might include the ability of young people to link up romantically without adult supervision in a setting that is not defined as leading directly to marriage. In such a dating culture it is acceptable for young people to "try out" a variety of romantic partners before progressing to the stage of preparing to select a spouse. See the discussion in Modell, 1983.) Most women (over 90%) never had another person they considered marrying besides their eventual husbands, and less than 30% even had had other boyfriends. Furthermore, even in recent years generally 30–50% of the women interviewed say they rarely or never dated their future husbands, and even for those who did, the dates almost always came after the decision to marry, rather than prior to it (a fact that is not obvious from the table but is made clear by ethnographic observations in China). In this setting, in which young people have to make a vital decision about their lives without being able to gain experience first via casual dating, it is understandable that in some cases parents are able to exert considerable influence. Depending upon which measure one chooses, parents play some or even a dominant role in 11–43% of recent marriages, and almost one-fifth of those who rely on introductions end up receiving these from their parents or other senior kin. So a second conclusion that can be drawn from the table is that the transition to freedom of mate choice has not produced as

TABLE 1. Changes in Aspects of Freedom of Mate Choice in Chengdu

Item	Year First Married				
	1933–48	1949–57	1958–65	1966–76	1977–87
1. Traditional arranged marriage (%)	69	22	1	0	0
2. Type of marriage (%)					
Arranged	68	27	0	1	2
Intermediate	15	33	45	40	41
Individual choice	17	40	55	59	57
3. Dominant role in mate choice (%)					
Parents	56	30	7	8	5
Mixed	15	11	6	3	6
Respondent	28	59	87	89	89
4. Introduced to husband (%)	91	76	54	59	60
5. Who provided the introduction? (%)					
Own generation	38	43	75	75	74
Other	8	17	7	6	9
Parents' generation	53	40	18	19	17
6. Dated husband prior to marriage (%)					
Often	12	17	24	40	48
Sometimes	6	18	27	13	21
Rarely	23	22	30	31	24
Never	59	44	18	16	7
7. Number of romances (%)					
None	73	29	9	5	5
One	24	63	74	66	67
More than one	3	8	18	29	28
8. Had other marital prospects (%)	4	5	2	6	9
9. How much in love when married (%)					
Completely	17	38	63	61	67
	26	29	22	26	19
	35	20	9	11	10
	9	4	4	1	3
Not at all	13	9	2	1	0
N (number of cases) =	71	107	82	116	210

much ability for young people to exercise free choice as currently exists in the West.[4]

A final pattern that becomes clear from the figures in the table is that the transition to free mate choice seems to have largely "stalled" since the late 1950s. Although there have been small increases since then in indicators such as the percentage of women with other marriage prospects and in those who often dated prior to marriage, the major shifts occurred among the early cohorts.

From this we can conclude that freedom of mate choice was already increasing during the 1930s, that this increase halted during World War II, and that a major further increase occurred during the post-war period and the 1950s.

However, there have been only incremental shifts toward even greater freedom for young people since that time. The reasons for this "stalling" of the transition (which contrasts with a more linear trend toward freedom of choice in Taiwan—see Thornton, Chang, and Lin, 1989) are too complex to go into here, but explanations are attempted in a companion paper (see Whyte, 1990). Suffice it to say here that while China's communist leaders have consistently advocated freedom for young people to choose their own mates, they have erected considerable barriers designed to inhibit young people from developing a dating culture, not to mention experimenting with premarital sex. In any case, the figures in Table 1 attest to the substantial change in the direction of freedom of mate choice that has occurred in the lives of Chengdu women, while also leaving enough variability in mate-choice experiences even recently to allow us to compare free-choice and arranged marriages.

FREEDOM OF MATE CHOICE AND MARRIAGE QUALITY

Has the shift toward greater freedom of mate choice in China produced more satisfactory marriage relations or less satisfactory ones? We examine this question first with a graphic display of the impact of the mode of mate choice on marriage quality for Chengdu and then by subjecting a marriage quality measure to multivariate analysis to see whether any impact detected is spurious or not. This exercise can only be conducted for wives, since we did not have the opportunity to interview husbands.

The main feature visible in Figure 1 is that the curve for "love matches" is consistently higher than that for arranged marriages, regardless of the length of the marriage. In other words, the Chengdu data indicate that women in free-choice marriages are consistently more satisfied with their marital relationship than are women in arranged marriages. However, the pattern in which women who have been married longer are generally less satisfied with their marriages than those recently wed, does not appear in our Chengdu results. Indeed, for both love matches and arranged marriages, wives who had been married 20–24 years reported having the highest-quality marriages of all.

We do not have a satisfactory explanation for the unexpected shape of the curves in Figure 1. Perhaps some degree of success in preserving filial piety and socializing children to respect family obligations makes having teenagers at home less stressful than it is in other societies for Chinese mothers, or even beneficial (e.g., as such children are able to take over more of the ardu-

FIGURE 1. Marriage quality by mode of mate choice in Chengdu

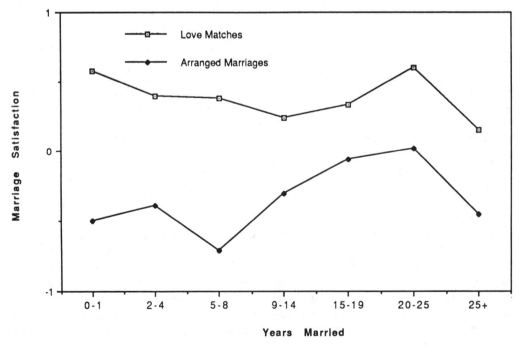

ous burden of domestic chores). Further, most older Chinese women will never see an "empty nest," since they will end their days of living in a three-generation family and tending small children once again for one or more of their grown children.

The main point we stress here is that marriage quality in a society such as China is likely to be affected not only by relations with the husband and children but also by relations with others in the family, including parents-in-law and grandchildren. To be sure, before we go too far with such speculations it would be nice to have access to longitudinal data from China to make sure that the shape of the curves in Figure 1 is not simply the product of unusual cohort effects.

The best summary of Figure 1 is that marriage quality fluctuates irregularly along the length of the marriage, that perhaps there is some modest tendency for Chinese arranged marriages to get "warmer" over time, but that, even so, love matches are rated more highly at every stage.

The final step in the present analysis involves subjecting the freedom-of-choice/marriage-quality relationship to multivariate analysis. To examine whether the association between these two realms, as shown in Figure 1, might be spurious, Marriage Quality Scale scores were used as the dependent variable in ordinary-least-squares regression, with the Freedom of Mate Choice Scale (in its full, rather than categorical, version) and a large number of other measures included as predictors in a variety of models. In all, more than 50 measures covering a broad range of topics were examined in our search for a "best model," and many predictors that had moderately strong bivariate correlations with the Marriage Quality Scale had only weak multivariate associations and were rejected from our final regression analyses.

It can be seen that the way wives perceive the quality of their marriages is affected by status characteristics of the women and her husband (her political status, his educational attainment and class origin label), the closeness of other social bonds (good relations between her parents,

close ties to her father and his approval of the man she married, and closeness to her husband's relatives). But far and away the strongest predictor is the degree of freedom of mate choice experienced in forming the marriage. Together these variables account for about one-third of the variation in Marriage Quality Scale scores, and by itself the Freedom of Mate Choice Scale explains about 11% of the variance in the dependent variable.

Thus in a major provincial city in socialist China a transition toward increasing freedom of mate choice has transformed the way spouses are selected, even though that transformation process has been "stalled" in recent years. Young people have much more say in whom they will marry then earlier generations did. Furthermore, women who had "love matches" feel better about their marriages today than do women who experienced arranged marriages, regardless of when they first married. This is not a spurious result. Even when we control for other predictors, the way in which the spouse was selected continues to have a strong and significant impact on satisfaction with the marriage currently. Indeed, this impact is stronger than for any other measure included in our study.

Partisans of family change and freedom of mate choice can rest easier now. Evidence presented here indicates that the shift toward freedom of mate choice is not only "progressive" in some ideological sense, but it also has some real benefits.

NOTES

[1] For purposes of argument we are oversimplifying the alternatives here. In reality the variations in mate selection involve not two categories but a continuum, from total parental control to total freedom of choice for the young. Few cultures can be found at the extremes of this continuum, and in many locales with arranged marriage, the young people may be consulted to some degree and may even have an ability to

veto prospects selected by their parents. In such intermediate cases the likelihood of being stuck with a repulsive partner would presumably be lower.

[2]A number of cross-sectional studies argue that the long-term trend is more complex and in fact curvilinear, with marital satisfaction improving again in the postparental or "empty nest" phase of the life cycle (see, for example, Hudson and Murphy, 1980; Lupri and Frideres, 1981; Rollins and Feldman, 1970). This possibility is not of particular concern in the present study, since such a trend would not invalidate the argument that the main trend during most of the life of a free-choice marriage is toward decreased marital satisfaction.

[3]Obviously, this argument carries greater force if the customary age at marriage in a particular society is quite early than if it is relatively late.

[4]Our conclusion here reconfirms the results of earlier research on contemporary urban marriages. See Whyte and Parish, 1984. This sort of partial shift in the mode of mate choice is visible in many other developing societies. See, for example, Vogel, 1961 (for Japan); Thornton, Chang, and Lin, 1990 (for Taiwan). Of course, by drawing this comparison with the West, we do not mean to imply that China will eventually and inevitably develop customs and norms about dating that are identical to those found in, say, the United States. We are simply stressing that even greater premarital freedom and autonomy for the young are possible and have not yet developed (and perhaps may never develop) in China.

REFERENCES

Goode, William J. 1963. World Revolution and Family Patterns, New York: Free Press.

Hicks, Mary and Marilyn Platt. 1970. "Marital happiness and stability: A review of the research in the sixties." Journal of Marriage and the Family 32: 553–574.

Hudson, Walter and Gerald Murphy. 1980. "The nonlinear relationship between marital satisfaction and stages of the family life cycle: An artifact of Type I errors?" Journal of Marriage and the Family 42:263–268.

Lang, Olga. 1946. Chinese Family and Society. New Haven, CT: Yale University Press.

Levy, Marion J., Jr. 1949. The Family Revolution in Modern China. Cambridge, MA: Harvard University Press.

Lupri, Eugen, and James Frideres. 1981. "The quality of marriage and the passage of time: Marital satisfaction over the family life cycle." Canadian Journal of Sociology 6:283–305.

Modell, John. 1983. "Dating becomes the way of American youth." pp. 91–126 in Leslie P. Moch and Gary D. Stark (eds.), Essays on the Family and Historical Change. College Station, TX: Texas A&M University Press.

Pa Chin. 1972. Family. New York: Doubleday. (Originally published 1933)

Parish, William L., and Martin K. Whyte. 1978. Village and Family in Contemporary China. Chicago: University of Chicago Press.

Pineo, Peter C. 1961. "Disenchantment in the later years of marriage." Marriage and Family Living 23: 3–11.

Renne, K. S. 1970. "Correlates of dissatisfaction in marriage." Journal of Marriage and the Family 32: 54–66.

Rollins, Boyd D., and Harold Feldman. 1970. "Marital satisfaction over the family life cycle." Journal of Marriage and the Family 32:20–28.

Thornton, Arland, Jui-shan Chang, and Hui-sheng Lin. 1989. "From arranged marriage toward love match: The transformation of marriage arrangements in Taiwan." Unpublished paper.

Vogel, Ezra F. 1961. "The go-between in a developing society: The case of the Japanese marriage arranger." Human Organization 20:112–120.

Whyte, Martin K. 1990. Dating, Mating, and Marriage. New York: Aldine de Gruyter.

Whyte, Martin K. 1990. "Changes in mate choice in Chengdu." In D. Davis and E. Vogel (eds.), China on the Eve of Tiananmen. Cambridge, MA: Harvard University Press.

Whyte, Martin K., and William L. Parish. 1984. Urban Life in Contemporary China. Chicago: University of Chicago Press.

Yang, C. K. 1959. The Chinese Family in the Communist Revolution. Cambridge, MA: MIT Press.

Introduction

In the next excerpt, Burch and Matthews explain why household formation has changed in developed societies. In particular, they explain why people have been living in ever smaller households (more people, entirely on their own or in two-person households) and why this trend is likely to continue.

Their analysis uses a "microeconomic model, stated in informal terms." Household status is a "good" that people trade off other things to maximize. At the same time, people's greater tendency to live alone is not simply a result of greater opportunities to do so, and less benefit from living with others. It also reflects a growing taste for privacy, recreation, and autonomy—none of which fits very well with traditional family life.

Burch and Matthews stop short of predicting that the trend to smaller households will continue in the future, but there is no reason for thinking otherwise. New technology and services will make family life ever more redundant. We will not need families to "take care of us" in any practical sense. We will have places to live that permit the enjoyment of solitude. We will spend our lives drifting in and out of small and medium-size households as our needs and tastes for company change.

Of course, this scenario does assume a reasonably high level of prosperity and security within which we can make our individual choices.

57
Household Formation in Developed Societies

Thomas K. Burch
Beverly J. Matthews

Within the last quarter century, the developed countries of the Western world . . . have experienced. . . :

1. The decline of fertility to below-replacement levels.

2. The postponement or avoidance of legal marriage and an increase in the prevalence of nonmarital cohabitation.

3. A sharp rise in the incidence of divorce,

along with high rates of instability in nonmarital unions that do not lead to marriage.

4. A rise in the proportion of persons living in small households—one- or two-person households, single-parent families—with a concomitant decline in average household size. Associated trends are a decline in the frequency of non-nuclear relatives or of nonrelatives in family households. . . .

The general tendency underlying the trends . . . is away from large, complex households toward smaller, simpler forms. . . . In terms of . . . size or number of adults, the trend can be characterized as a drop . . . from an optimum

Source: Burch, T.K. and B.J. Matthews (1987) "Household formation in developed societies," *Population and Development Review,* 13, 3, September, 495–511.

household of five or six, with two or more adults, to an optimum household of two or three, with two or fewer adults; and, from a minimum viable household size of three or four to a minimum viable household size of one adult.

Households are tending to become simpler in the sense of more homogeneous in age and sex composition, relationship structures, and sex or gender roles. . . .

Since all the above trends involve the same underlying tendency—toward separate living in smaller and simpler households—they should lend themselves to common explanations. This note sketches a general model of household formation and uses it to . . . develop some standard explanatory hypotheses and to suggest some new ones. No attempt is made to test any hypotheses. The model is an expanded version of a microeconomic model. . . .

ꙮ

HOUSEHOLD STATUS AS A COMPOSITE GOOD

Household status is defined . . . by the number and characteristics of other persons, if any, with whom an individual shares a housing unit. Household status is conceived of . . . as a means to other ends. . . .

In sociological . . . terms, these other ends are treated as household functions; in microeconomics they are . . . a bundle of goods or a composite good.

. . . Component goods associated with household status would include:

1. Physical shelter. . . .
2. Storage of property, both common . . . and personal.
3. Domestic service: meals, laundry and repair of clothing, etc.
4. Personal care, notably of dependent members: minor children, the ill or disabled, the dependent elderly.
5. Companionship: sexual and nonsexual.
6. Recreation, entertainment.
7. Privacy.
8. Independence/autonomy.
9. Power/authority.
10. Economies of scale in consumption of those of the above goods that are to some extent "public" goods.

PAYING FOR HOUSEHOLD GOODS

It is assumed that all household goods must be paid for . . . by individual members of the household. Money and household labor are the most obvious forms of payment, . . . but the "coin of the household realm" also includes . . . :(1) affection and companionship (love, support, and so on); (2) subordination (deference, obedience, respect, dependence); and (3) credits based on past services (e.g., for elderly parents). . . .

In the . . . traditional marriage, what Davis (1984) has termed the "breadwinner system," the husband exchanged money . . . and affection for the wife's affection (including sexual relations), household labor, and subordination. Children provided companionship, recreation, household labor, and subordination in the form of obedience.

Today, women are more apt to have income derived from labor outside the household, and are less willing to provide domestic service or subordination. A family enterprise to which they can contribute labor is the exception rather than the rule. For children, as well, work in a household firm is largely irrelevant; subordination is problematic, recreation is individually oriented and often outside the household. In general, income has risen, but even more important, perhaps, more people have or are entitled to income in their own right, through employment or transfer payments (social security, welfare). . . .

The matter is further complicated by . . . the residual obligations of kinship—social norms that call for sharing one's household even when one would rather not, or when the recipient of such sharing is unable or unwilling to reciprocate through one of the above forms of exchange. Despite the attenuation of kinship in modern society, traditional sentiments persist. . . . Such norms are not to be identified with tastes or preferences as defined by economists, unless one defines norms simply as an average of individual preferences (Ryder, 1973). But . . . inclination, conscience, and social norms often do not point in the same direction. An adequate behavioral model must allow for conflict between rational decision, individual inclination, and social norms and pressures. . . .

SOME EXPLANATORY HYPOTHESES

The above framework suggests a number of hypotheses that might explain the . . . trend toward separate living and smaller households. The hypotheses are not . . . mutually exclusive; an adequate model will involve additive and interactive elements. . . .

RISING REAL INCOME

. . . One reason so many people now live alone or in very small households is that they can afford to. They are able to forgo the economies of scale represented by larger households, and they are not particularly inclined to increase consumption of public household goods affected by such scale economies: a household does not need more than one stove or furnace. On the other hand, certain previously public household goods have tended to become private; for example, personal television sets instead of the . . . single television set in the family room. . . .

This hypothesis would follow from the assumption that separate living and its associated goods (privacy, independence) are . . . superior goods, and that, with the exception of couple cohabitation, coresidence and its associated goods are inferior. Such an assumption probably is valid for the societies in question during the period at issue. . . .

Other goods (domestic services, personal care, companionship, recreation) can now be purchased outside the household. . . .

Not only has real income risen on average, but also new institutional arrangements have increased the proportion of the population that can claim income in their own right (Duncan and Morgan, 1976b, p. 19). Married women and mothers can and do work; the elderly are entitled to pensions or social security; young adults can collect welfare or unemployment benefits. Only the minor child is totally dependent for income on other household members. . . .

This qualification to the income hypothesis is a reminder that . . . there is no such thing as a purely economic explanation. Rising real income among older persons . . . is one of the main reasons that the proportions living alone have reached such high levels. . . . But their having an independent income is the result of an institutional change—social values and norms apparently favored independence for the elderly, and society provided the income to ensure it through social security and private pension plans. . . .

AVAILABILITY OF KIN

The close identification in Western societies of the household with the family has meant that coresidence has tended to be viewed as something involving kin or relatives—a family matter. For many, sharing a house or apartment is seen as a form of intimacy, not to be indulged in with strangers or even friends. Sweet's (1972) study of older, formerly married women showed that coresidence with nonrelatives was a last resort—living alone and institutionalization were more common . . . where it was not possible to live with relatives. . . .

This availability of kin in turn is affected by . . . low fertility, since the number of kin a person has . . . is directly . . . related to fertility, both on average and in a particular extended family network.[1] Kobrin (1976) hypothesized from aggregate data and others have demonstrated with household-level data (Wister and Burch, 1983; Wolf, 1983) that the probability that an older, nonmarried woman lives alone is closely related to her completed family size and to numbers of living children. . . .

Another relevant demographic factor is the . . . rate of migration . . . from one community to another. Such migration results in a physical dispersal of kin, so that a decision to coreside often must involve a decision to migrate, and thus becomes more costly and difficult. Put differently, the supply of kin in one's . . . home community is effectively reduced.

A related sub-hypothesis . . . would note that migration of a household may provide opportunities for the loss of members who are . . ."at risk" of separate living. Thus migration may provide the occasion for home-leaving by an adult child, or institutionalization of an elderly relative. . . .

CHANGING PREFERENCES FOR PRIVACY

A third line of explanation in the literature on household formation . . . since World War II is that there has been an increase in the . . . preference for privacy relative to some other goods. There is little direct evidence such an increase has occurred and no satisfactory explanation as to why it might have. . . . The explanation is clung to partly because of residual variance after income and other "hard" variables have been accounted for (Pampel, 1983). . . .

Satisfactory empirical work on this hypothesis will require more attention to specific reasons for taste changes. Four such specifications come to mind.

1. First, a general increase in preference for . . . individual privacy could be the result of a gradual working out of the full implications of basic elements of Western culture, notably the individualism of Christianity, especially Protestant Christianity, and of the Enlightenment.

The fullest demographic treatment of this hypothesis is by Lesthaeghe. In his earlier work, the focus is on a cultural explanation for fertility decline. More recently, he has applied this cultural explanation to other aspects of household and family formation (Lesthaeghe, 1983, 1985; Lesthaeghe and Meekers, 1986).

2. Lesthaeghe also has pioneered in integrating demographic theory with social-psychological research on human needs and values (Maslow, 1954) and on the consequences of affluence and the development of a "post-materialist" society (Ingelhart, 1981). With higher real income and a sense of security provided by an extensive welfare net, the individual turns inward and becomes more concerned with self-development and personal growth and experience. Recipes for such growth often emphasize the need for solitude and privacy.

. . . This explanation is at base an economic one, since the shift to self-centeredness is correlated with high levels of material welfare. . . . This again emphasizes the simultaneity . . . of the relationships; just as income is partly a function of values, values . . . are partly a function of income.

3. . . . The increasing tolerance by society of sexual activity among persons other than young and middle-aged married couples . . . would tend to increase the preference of such persons for privacy as opposed to economies of scale or companionship of persons other than the sexual partner. It would also decrease the willingness of household heads to provide coresidence. Parents of single adults have increasingly tolerated cohabitation or even more casual sex, but often draw the line at such activity occurring in their own household.

4. A fourth hypothesis asserts that the preference for specifically household privacy has increased as opportunities for privacy outside the household have declined. . . . As more of the population live in large cities and work for large organizations, they have less control over

these environments and less opportunity to avoid contact with . . . other persons. . . . In this situation, the household may more than ever become a refuge. . . . In microeconomic terms, this hypothesis assumes an increase in the preference for household privacy, but not necessarily for privacy in general.

ROLE CHANGES AND HOUSEHOLD CROWDING

In an earlier paper, the first author hypothesized that . . . trends toward more homogeneous age-sex roles, have tended to make households more crowded given the same number of individuals (Burch, 1985). The argument was based on an ecological analogy, in which the household is viewed as a habitat. As men and women—old and young, married and unmarried—try to occupy more similar niches, increased competition results. . . . In Durkheimian terms, household solidarity declines with a decline in the division of household labor (Durkheim, 1985). . . .

Changing norms have allowed more household members to enter the market for certain household goods—notably privacy—formerly reserved to persons of specific age, sex, or marital status. . . . At the same time, the supply of household privacy per capita tends to decline as the number of members rises. . . .

DECLINE OF HOUSEHOLD SERVICES

. . . Traditionally, humans have turned to the household for meals, for storage and care of clothing, and for care in childhood, illness, and disability. And as a physical plant, the housing unit requires maintenance—housecleaning, decorating, and so on.

The traditional Western household was an ideal institution for . . . adult males and young children. But its effectiveness . . . was dependent on massive inputs of household labor by adult women and older female children. . . .

But the entry of the vast majority of women, including married women and mothers, into the labor force . . . leaves fewer and fewer households with a full-time resident housekeeper. This has two likely consequences: (1) a decline in the quantity and quality of domestic services; (2) pressure on other household members, notably men, older children, and "extended" family members, to provide more household labor. Both consequences have occurred.

A decline in household services makes coresidence less desirable. . . .

TECHNOLOGY, RECREATION, AND COMPANIONSHIP

A final hypothesis suggests modern technological developments, as well as increasing urbanization, have made the individual less dependent on other household members for companionship and recreation. Urban residence means relatives or friends are close at hand, as are opportunities for recreation. . . . The telephone and automobile have partly eliminated distance as a barrier to contact and interaction. And television has provided an alternative to human companionship; it is not a perfect substitute but it distracts and can ward off extremes of loneliness and isolation. . . .

NOTE

[1]Goodman, Keyfitz, and Pullum, 1974. The secular decline in mortality has tended to increase the number of living kin of any type, but in general has been more than offset by declining fertility.

REFERENCES

Burch, T. K. 1985. "Changing age-sex roles and household crowding: A theoretical note," in *Proceedings, International Population Conference, Flor-*

ence, *1985*, Vol. 3. Liège: International Union for the Scientific Study of Population, pp. 253–261.

CHERLIN, A. 1978. "Remarriage as an incomplete institution," *American Journal of Sociology* 84:634–650.

DAVIS, K. 1984. "Wives and work: The sex role revolution and its consequences," *Population and Development Review* 10:397–417.

DUNCAN, G. J., and J. N. MORGAN. 1976b. "Introduction, overview, summary and conclusions," in Duncan and Morgan, 1976a, pp. 1–22.

DURKHEIM, E. 1985 [1893]. *The Division of Labor in Society*, trans. by W. D. Hall. New York: The Free Press.

GOODMAN, L. A., N. KEYFITZ, and T. W. PULLUM. 1974. "Family formation and the frequency of various kinship relationships," *Theoretical Population Biology* 5: 1–27. See also 8 (1975):376–381.

INGLEHART, R. 1981. "Post-materialism in an environment of insecurity," *American Political Science Review* 75:880–900.

KOBRIN, F. 1976. "Fall of household size and the rise of the primary individual in the U.S.," *Demography* 13:127–138.

LESTHAEGHE, R. 1983. "A century of demographic and cultural change in Western Europe: An explo-ration of underlying dimensions," *Population and Development Review* 9:411–435.

—— 1985. "Value orientations, economic growth, and demographic trends—Toward a confrontation," Interuniversity Programme in Demography Working Paper No. 1985-7. Brussels: Free University.

—— and D. MEEKERS. 1986. "Value changes and the dimensions of familism in the European Community," *European Journal of Population* 2:225–268.

MASLOW, A. 1954. *Motivation and Personality*. New York: Harper and Row.

PAMPEL, F. C. 1983. "Changes in the propensity to live alone: Evidence from consecutive cross-sectional surveys, 1960–76," *Demography* 20:433–448.

RYDER, N. B. 1973. "Comment," *Journal of Political Economy* 81, no. 2, Part II: 65–69.

SWEET, J. A. 1972. "Living arrangements of separated, widowed, and divorced mothers," *Demography* 9: 143–157.

WISTER, A. V., and T. K. BURCH. 1983. "Fertility and household status of older women, Canada, 1971," *Canadian Studies in Population* 10:1–13.

WOLF, D. A. 1983. "Kinship and the living arrangements of older Americans," *Project Report*. Washington, D.C.: The Urban Institute.

Introduction

Is adult life going to become more and more individualistic, as van de Kaa seems to suggest? Are people going to invest even less of their time and emotion in family relationships, as Goode believes? And, in the future, are people going to buy as much privacy as they can afford, the way Burch and Matthews seem to suggest?

Well, not if Höllinger and Haller are right in their assessment of kinship trends in seven modern societies. These authors find that kinship ties *are* loosening, especially among Americans and Australians (somewhat less among Britons, Germans, and Austrians), but they are not loosening nearly as much among Italians and Hungarians. Indeed, there may be a geographic split here, with northern and western Europeans having much looser networks than Southern and Eastern Europeans.

Not all of this difference is due to the greater degree of socioeconomic development in Northern and Western Europe (nor in America and Australia). Generally, traditions of close kinship in the South and East date back to preindustrial times, and they will not be eroded quickly, if at all. This fact argues against "convergence theory"—the theory that all societies will become the same once they industrialize.

Finally, the authors note that even in countries where kinship ties have become looser, primary (face-to-face) groups of kin and close friends have kept their importance. They still provide people with emotional support and practical assistance when help is needed most. We are still far from substituting paid professionals for loved ones when we need an emotional "fix."

58
Kinship and Social Networks in Modern Societies

Franz Höllinger
Max Haller

... Various methods have been developed to record changes in social networks. In this context, the most relevant model is the 'ego-centred social network' (Marbach, 1986). It ... allows for quantifiable statements on the number of relations maintained, the frequency of contact as well as on the functions of these relations. This model is used for the analysis of contacts with kin as well as non-kin. . . .

There exist only few cross-national studies on this topic and they are limited to comparisons of two countries. . . .

In the present paper, we are presenting an analysis from the 1986 survey of the International Social Survey Program (ISSP) on 'Social Relations and Social Support.' . . . In this survey, seven countries were included: Australia, Austria, Britain, West Germany, Hungary, Italy and the USA. . . .

HYPOTHESES

. . . In a post-industrial society, sociocultural differences of family-patterns have become less important. . . . Today the nuclear family is the dominant family type in all advanced industrial-

ized countries. Nevertheless, . . . we assume, . . . in accordance with historical family research, . . . that in the South- and East-European culture-area primary-group ties are closer than in Northwestern-Europe and that the Anglo-Saxon nations have gone even further in the dissolution of kin ties. . . .

EMPIRICAL RESULTS

. . . The method of measuring social networks in the ISSP-project was to present a questionnaire to representative samples of the population in each of the participating countries. . . . About 10,000 persons over 18 years of age were interviewed. The size of the sample varied between 1,000 and 2,800 in the several countries. . . . People over 75 were excluded in all countries. . . .

FREQUENCY OF CONTACT WITH KIN

. . . In Italy, the proportion of children living in their parents' house until they get married is still very high. This is the case for 92 per cent of singles. Even in Hungary (85 per cent) and . . . in Britain (75 per cent), only a small percentage of young people set out to live alone before they get married. In West Germany, USA and Australia,

Source: Hollinger, Franz and Max Haller (1990), "Kinship and social networks in modern societies: A cross-cultural comparison among seven nations," European Sociological Review, Vol. 6, No. 2, September, 103–124.

however, only one-third of unmarried youth live with their parents.[1]

Intercultural variations in the spatial closeness of relations between parents and children remain the same even after children have moved out from the parents' house. The percentage of those settling in the immediate neighbourhood of their parents (at a walking distance of 15 minutes) seems to be a good indicator of the importance which spatial propinquity to the parents may have when setting up house.[2] Italians (57 per cent) and Hungarians (43 per cent) most frequently settle close to their parents while Australians and Americans are the least 'family-bound': here, only 25 per cent live at a distance of 15 minutes from their parents.

Does the different closeness of relations with kin have an impact on the varying frequency of contact at a given distance? Differences between the respective countries are not marked: 75–80 per cent of Italians and Hungarians as well as 60–70 per cent of Austrians, West Germans and Americans who live very close to their parents, . . . report that they see their parents every day or at least several times a week. However, only 50 per cent of Australians and Britons see their parents that frequently.[3]

FIGURE 1. Frequency of contact with the mother

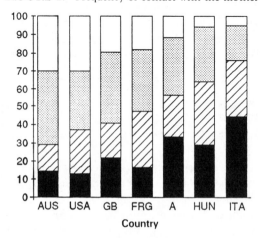

Country

☐ Less often   ▦ One a week - once mouth
▨ Daily - several times a week
■ She lives in the same household

. . . While approximately three-quarters of adult Italians with parents still alive either live in their house or go to visit them at least some days a week, only a quarter of Australians have comparably intense contacts. In Italy and Hungary, less than 10 per cent indicate that they meet their parents only a few times a year or even less frequently. The corresponding figure for America and Australia is about 30 per cent.

When talking about 'contacts', we have up to now been referring to personal encounters. The questionnaire has also included items on other contacts with the parents. . . . Two-thirds of those meeting their parents only a few times a year or less frequently indicate that they write to or call up their parents at least once a month. These results apply to all countries except Hungary which can be attributed to the much less dense telephone network in this country. Thus, when taking into account these phone calls, the percentage of Australians and Americans who have hardly any contacts with their parents is reduced to about 10 per cent. This confirms Litwak and Szelenyi's (1969) findings that the loss in permanent face-to-face contact with relatives does not mean a breakdown of social contact. . . .

The frequency of contact with the parents compared with that with brothers and sisters or the one other relative most often seen is more or less the same in all countries. . . . The respondents stated they see their brothers or sisters only half as often as their parents; the frequency of contact with one other relative (usually an in-law) is more or less the same as with the parents. . . . Most respondents have at least one relative they maintain close contact with. . . .

URBANIZATION AND CONTACTS WITH KIN

. . . The supposed association between a higher degree of urbanization and a declining frequency of contact with relatives cannot be upheld. . . . The USA and the FRG, for example, show a comparable degree of urbanization although the frequency of contact with relatives is much higher in West Germany than in the USA. . . . Although Italy is more urbanized than Austria, Italians see their relatives more frequently than Austrians. . . .

In the USA and Australia, there is practically no association between the population size of the place of residence of interviewed persons and the distance to their mother's house. In Germany, Austria, Hungary and Italy there is a significant association, i.e. the larger the place of residence of the respondents the larger the distance to their mother's house. The association between size of the hometown and the frequency of contact with the mother corresponds to the expectation, i.e. persons living in urban areas see their mothers more rarely. This association, however, is weak in all countries. . . .

Americans and Australians both in urban and rural areas have a relatively low frequency of contact with kin.

A . . . factor which . . . seems important is . . . that approximately 80 per cent of Americans, Australians and British have their own houses (one-family dwellings or semi-detached houses). In Austria this proportion is 57 per cent, in West Germany 46 per cent and in Italy only 36 per cent.[4] . . . The Britons', Americans' and Australians' . . . housing individualism . . . is an expression of their individualistic lifestyle in general (see also Willi, 1966; Münch, 1986). One aspect of this individualism is the importance ascribed to the privacy of the nuclear family. The fact that people distance themselves from their parents and other relatives is relevant also in the geographical sense. The vast settlements arising from the . . . one-family houses have the consequence that members of a family live far apart even within one town. . . .

RELATIONS WITH FRIENDS

. . . The ISSP . . . questionnaire asked for the number of friends as well as for the frequency of contacts with the best friend. . . . This question probably also measures sociocultural differences on the understanding of the term 'friend.' . . .

Table 1 shows significant differences among the various countries. About 20 per cent of West Germans and Austrians, and 34 per cent of Hungarians state they have no friend at all; in Australia and America the corresponding figure is only 5 per cent. . . .

Americans, and evidently Australians as well, define . . . 'friend' in a wider and more casual way than other nations (see also Fischer, 1982b). West Germans, Austrians and Hungarians have fewer but probably more lasting friendships. The high number of people in West Germany, Austria and Hungary stating they had no friends at all suggests, however, that a sense of social isolation is more common in these countries. . . .

Britons and Italians lie between Americans and Australians, on the one hand, and West Germans, Austrians and Hungarians on the other hand. Similar results on this question, however, do not imply the same type of friendship in these countries. . . . Italians meet their best friend more frequently than the British (56 per cent of Italians as compared to 37 per cent of Britons meet their best friend several times a week. The same difference arises when we compare Australians and Americans. Although the average number of friends is the same . . . Australians are more reserved . . . than Americans. Twenty-five per cent of Australians as opposed to 42 per cent of Americans replied that they called on their best friends several times a week. The reserved . . . personal relations, which can be shown also for the contact with close kin (controlling for the spatial distance, Australians and Britons see their parents less frequently than the other nationalities) can be attributed to sociocultural similarities between Australians and Britons. . . . This sociocultural aspect also distinguishes Australians from Americans. . . .

When comparing the average number of friends according to age cohort . . . , there are only minor differences between the countries in the youngest age group (18 to 24 years). Differences become more marked in older age groups.

TABLE 1.   Number of Friends

	AUS %	USA %	GB %	FRG %	A %	HUN %	ITA %
No friend	6	5	13	20	23	34	15
1–4 friends	38	44	45	50	48	44	53
5–9 friends	29	28	42[a]	19	18	12	18
10 or more friends	27	23		11	11	10	15
Total	100	100	100	100	100	100	100

Note: (a) GB: 5 or more friends.

Data for Hungary, West Germany and Austria confirm the assumption that the number of friends declines gradually in the course of one's life. . . . The average number of friends reported by Italians and Australians hardly varies from age group to age group. In America, surprisingly . . . the average number of friends even increases in the older age cohorts.

. . . In all countries, respondents with a higher educational level report a larger number of friends. The data do not confirm, however, . . . that the average number of friends is higher in urban areas. . . .

SOCIAL SUPPORT PROVIDED BY KIN, NON-KIN AND PROFESSIONAL ASSOCIATIONS

The ISSP questionnaire included six hypothetical situations . . .

'Who Would You Turn to If . . .

1. you needed help for work in your house or garden
2. you had the flu and had to stay in bed for some days
3. you had to borrow a large sum of money
4. you had problems with your partner and could not talk with him/her about it
5. you were depressed
6. you had to make an important decision and needed advice.'

. . . The respondents had to choose from a list of persons . . . the one they would turn to first and second for help. . . . To make the . . . data more accessible, we will limit ourselves to the two first and the two last questions, which go together.[5] 'Help in the house' and 'help during illness' might be called instrumental assistance and requires one's physical presence. 'Help during depressions' and 'advice with an important decision' involve emotional assistance, which depends less on physical proximity between the persons involved. As the proportion of certain persons (categories) being named is similar in all countries, we will present the . . . accumulated data record for all countries.

. . . Respondents named their partner by far the most frequently both for instrumental and emotional assistance. . . . Table 2.

The ratios, for example that the mother is asked for help twice as often as the father, that friends are of higher importance for emotional than for instrumental support etc. do not vary from country to country. We take this as a proof for the gross structure of social support networks being relatively similar in our sample of countries. . . .

. . . When one is in need of instrumental assistance (illness, help in the house), fifty-three per cent of respondents in all countries who live within 15 minutes of their mother's house name her as the person they would turn to in at least one of these two situations. If they live at a distance of more than one hour, the proportion is only 11 per cent in the cumulated dataset. Cross-national differences in this regard are not

TABLE 2. Who Do You Expect Help from in Emergency Situations? (Percentages of the Persons Named First and Second in the Accumulated Data Record of All Countries)

		Instrumental Assistance (Household + Sickness)	Emotional Assistance (Depression + Important Decision)
Partner	%	29.7	27.9
Mother	%	8.8	8.7
Father	%	3.9	3.7
Daughter	%	9.5	7.2
Son	%	9.8	6.0
Sister	%	3.7	4.9
Brother	%	3.6	2.7
Other Kin	%	5.7	3.5
Friend	%	10.5	18.1
Neighbour	%	7.8	1.0
Parish Priest	%		1.1
Physician	%		1.7
Psychologist	%		0.7
Others, Nobody	%	7.1	12.8
Total	%	100.0	100.0

significant. Consequently, in countries where the spatial distance between parents and children is smaller, instrumental assistance is more often granted by the closest relatives.

As far as emotional assistance is concerned, spatial distance is not that relevant. . . . When controlling for differences in spatial distance, the mother is named equally often in all countries. At a distance of less than 15 minutes, about 45 per cent name their mother, at a distance of more than one hour, the proportion is still 25 per cent. The father is named more rarely in all countries, but particularly in Italy and Hungary. This could . . . indicate that father–child relations in these countries are still rather patriarchal while in the other countries fathers are somewhat more actively involved in close family relationships. . . .

Italians and Hungarians also differ from the others . . . in how often they name their partner as 'Number One Helper'. Eighty to eighty-five per cent of Australians, West Germans, Britons and Austrians who are married and/or live with a partner named their partner at least in three out of four situations. In Hungary the figure is

down to 72 per cent and in Italy to 63 per cent. . . .

. . . Americans and Australians go for professional assistance most frequently, Italians and Hungarians most rarely. These results can, however, only partly be explained by the . . . course of modernization. What comes as a surprise is the varying frequency of the 'parish priest' being named as an important contact person. Americans name him four times, and Australians twice as frequently as Europeans. . . .

SUMMARY

. . . The frequency of face-to-face contacts with kin is much higher in Italy and Hungary than in the USA and Australia. Austria, West Germany and Britain are at an intermediate position. . . . That Hungary and . . . Italy are lagging behind the other nations economically and . . . are representatives of the South/East-European as contrasted to the Northwest-European culture area, makes our results compatible both with the hypothesis of a 'modernization' effect and with that of sociocultural differences. There is some evidence, however, that sociocultural factors are outweighing the influence of modernization. Even in the highly industrialized northern parts of Italy kin relations are much more similar to the overall Italian pattern of close kin contacts than to the loosened kin contacts ... in North-west-Europe.... And contacts with kin are considerably less frequent in America and Australia than in the comparably developed nations of West Germany and Britain. Higher geographical mobility in the countries of the New World is a main factor.... Concerning the effect of urbanization on social networks, ... the degree of urbanization is of little importance ... but differences in the prevailing type of housing are important. The dominance of single-family houses in Britain, USA and Australia leads to widespread settlements ... and to larger distances between different parts of a family even within one town. The preference for one's own house can be seen as expressing a more individualistic lifestyle in these countries....

... We have ... shown that close kin do play an important role in emergency situations even in advanced industrial societies. Although in the English- and German-speaking countries spatial distance from parents is larger than in Italy and Hungary, the data suggest that relations between parents and children do not lose their emotional strength. Emotional assistance within the nuclear family, between husband and wife, father and children is even more frequent in the English- and German-speaking countries than in Italy and Hungary. Family structures in these countries seem still to be closer to the patriarchical type. Consistently with this, extended kin relations are more important in the two latter than in the former countries....

Our results on ... friendship-networks have to be interpreted ... by sociocultural differences in the meaning of the term 'friendship'. Americans and Australians consider many persons as friends, who Europeans would ... call close acquaintances. Geographical mobility has to be considered again as a main factor for a higher

'friendship-turnover' in the countries of the New World. On the other hand, that the frequency of contact with the best friend is lower in Britain and Australia than in America and Italy might be taken as an indicator of social relations being more formal and reserved in the former ... countries. Austrians and Hungarians stand out because a high percentage of respondents say they had no friends ... and they rarely expect friends to provide social support. Differences in the concept of friendship ... might explain this result.... The Austrians' limited friend-network can also be attributed to their social characteristics ... —introverted, taboo-loving and conflict-avoiding (Magris, 1966; Johnston, 1972). This tendency not to communicate about one's personal problems has repeatedly been associated with the high suicide rate in Austria (Gaspari and Millendorfer, 1973; Ringel, 1984). ... Hungarians, who in international suicide statistics rank even higher than Austrians, also rarely name friends as persons of confidence. ...

NOTES

[1] The percentage of 18 to 24-year-olds being married is more or less the same in Britain, Australia and the USA. Approximately 20 per cent of under 25-year-olds are married. In Italy, Germany and Austria, this percentage is significantly lower (10 per cent), in Hungary it is highest (35 per cent). The varying frequency of young people living in their parents' houses until they get married in the individual countries cannot be associated with the percentages quoted above.

[2] Spatial distance and frequency of contact do not differ between father and mother in any country. Therefore, the following discussion ... is restricted to data for contact with the mother.

[3] ... The frequency of contact with kin is strongly associated with spatial distance. Re-

spondents living . . . several hours from their mother meet her only a few times a year or less. . . . When excluding those respondents who live . . . more than five hours from their mother from the calculations, . . . cross-national differences . . . become insignificant. . . .

[4]Sources: ALLBUS 1986 for the FRG, GSS 1987 for the USA, BSA Survey 1987 for Britain, ISSP-87 for Austria, Meyers Enzyklopädisches Lexikon for Australia. . . .

[5]Results on the question of 'borrowing a large sum of money' showed national characteristics very different from the rest of the questions. This suggests the need for separate analysis. The question 'whom would you turn to if you had a problem with your partner?' was not put in the same way in all countries, thus the results cannot directly be compared.

REFERENCES

GASPERI, C, MILLENDORFER H. (1973): 'Prognosen für Österreich', München: Oldenburg.

FISCHER C S. (1982b): 'What do We Mean by "friend": An Inductive Study', Social Network 3:287–306.

HALLER M. (1977): 'Austria', in Chester R, (ed), Divorce in Europe, Leiden: M. Njihoff, pp. 211–51.

JOHNSTON W M. (1972): 'The Austrian Mind: An Intellectual and Social History 1848–1938', University of California Press.

LITWAK E, SZELENYI I. (1969): 'Primary Group Structures and their Functions: Kin, Neighbours, and Friends', American Sociological Review, 34:465–81.

MARBACH J. (1986): 'Familie und soziales Netzwerk', München: Deutsches Jugendinstitut (mimeo).

MÜNCH R. (1986): 'Die Kultur der Moderne, Band I: Ihre Grundlagen und Entwicklung in England und Amerika', Frankfurt: Suhrkamp.

PFEIL E. (1970): 'Die Großstadtfamilie', Kölner Zeitschrift für Soziologie und Sozialpsychologie, SH 14: 411–32.

RINGEL E. (1984): 'Die österreichische Seele', Wien/Köln/Graz: Böhlau.

WILLI V J. (1966): 'Grundlagen einer empirischen Soziologie der Werte und Wertsysteme', Zürich: Orell Füssli.

Introduction

In the previous excerpt, we saw that the family is far from dead in many parts of Europe. Though people can choose to do otherwise, they still seem to want kin and family life. What's more, through its social policies, the State makes it easier than ever for many Europeans to bear and raise children despite problems like unemployment and divorce.

In Israel too, the State plays an important role in supporting family life. In addition, conservative forces such as orthodox religion, Asian and African attitudes about life, and small-community living also emphasize the importance of family living. For these reasons, Peres and Katz find that the nuclear family continues to be stable and central to modern Israeli living.

There is one other reason why the family is important in Israeli life—a reason that does not apply to most of Europe. This is the sense, and fact, of continuing external threat. Both Israeli Jews *and* Palestinians feel this threat of war and violence at every turn. Like South Africa, India, Northern Ireland, and Yugoslavia, Israel is a society in a permanent state of civil unrest. Unlike those others, it is also endangered by attack from neighboring countries.

In this context of uncertainty and threat, people are likely to close ranks and define their boundaries. Strengthening family life is part of that affirmation. This process is likely to occur whenever people are faced with forms of external danger (for example, recurrent famine in Eastern Africa or persistent poverty and exploitation in most of rural South America).

Because such external threats are not going to disappear overnight, the family will not disappear either.

59
The Importance of Nuclear Families in Israel

Yochanan Peres
Ruth Katz

. . . Israel is an urban society: 90 percent of its Jewish population dwells in cities or townships, 24 percent of its labor force is employed in industry, and 70 percent in services. (All data relate to the Jewish sector of the . . . population.) The average standard of living does not fall below that of European countries such as France or Italy. Due to her special relationship with the United States, Israel, to a greater extent than comparable countries, tends to adopt American attitudes and social patterns. . . .

Taking these factors into account, one would expect the Israeli family to change in the same direction as its counterparts in the Western world. . . . However, the dominant pattern in the Israeli family is one of centrality and stability.

. . . Israel's marriage and divorce rates . . . resemble those of traditional and predominantly agrarian societies . . . , whereas the Israeli birth rate falls about mid-way between European and Middle-Eastern rates. . . .

There has been virtually no change in the divorce rate over the last 18 years, while the marriage and birth rates have tended to stabilize, and even rise, during the late 1960s and 1970s

(after showing some decrease from 1950 to 1965). . . .

These indications of continuity in familial behavior should be viewed against the background of . . . rapid and intense . . . modernization . . . during the 1960s and 1970s in the technological, economic, and educational spheres. . . .

Assuming that rapid modernization usually coincides with a decline in the centrality and stability of the family, which attributes of Israeli society have forestalled or reversed this tendency?

THE EXTERNAL CONFLICT

Not only has Israel experienced four wars, but the continuous threat to her security is a salient reality. Border clashes, reserve duty, and hostile broadcasts from neighboring states are reminders . . . easily grasped by every person.

. . . External threat may reinforce familistic behavior in several ways.

1. Anxiety is likely to raise the individual's need for intimate affiliation (Freedman et al.; Mills and Mintz; Sarnoff and Zimbardo; Shachter). An Israeli study has shown that during warfare, intimate communication within the family increases (Cohen and Dotan).

One should thus anticipate a rise in mar-

Source: Peres, Yochanan and Ruth Katz (1981) "Stability and centrality: The nuclear family in modern Israel," *Social Forces,* vol. 59 (3), March, 687–704.

riage rates after an outbreak of hostilities. . . . There is, however, no reason to expect an increase in the birth rate or a decrease in the divorce rate. . . . If, due to external threats, couples who otherwise would have postponed or suspended their marriage do wed, some of these marriages may be more divorce-prone than the average. So, an increase in the divorce rate should occur shortly after the rise in the marriage rate. . . .

2. Israeli parents are aware of the danger of losing their sons in war, and this . . . might affect family planning. Women interviewed on this topic stated that one reason for raising many children is to avoid . . . remaining alone in old age (Bar-Yosef and Becher). In the same context, . . . it has become common for Israeli parents to give birth to another child when the eldest son is drafted into the army—after not having had any children for many years. . . . Generally speaking, the awareness of personal danger is more likely to affect the birth rate than marriage or divorce rates. . . .

3. . . . The main responsibilities and risks of combat are still carried by men. . . . After being exposed to hardships and sometimes danger, the married soldier feels . . . entitled to have his home kept for him as a stable emotional base.

This tacit division of responsibilities during emergencies seems to reinforce and stabilize the different primordial images of women and men.[1] Such a differentiation creates stronger interdependence between spouses and makes a separation less probable.

The postulated relationship between the external conflict and the increase of familism in Israel suggests . . . we can expect the marriage and birth rates to rise and the divorce rate to decline when . . . hostilities break out. . . .

Israel has experienced four wars . . . [including] the 1956 Sinai campaign, the June 1967 war, and the October 1973 war. . . . The relevant effects of the Sinai campaign were not outstanding: the decrease in marriage and divorce rates stopped for a year or two, while the gradual decrease in birth rates continued. The effects of the

Six Day War, however, were appreciable: marriage and birth rates rose while divorce rates remained stable. These developments cannot be explained away as balancing a forced postponement of pre-war plans to marry or have children, since the evaluation in marriage and birth rates lasted 4–5 years (from 1968 to 1971–2). The effects of the October 1973 War were similar, though less striking, and not as prolonged. . . . Apparently birth and marriage rates are more responsive to states of external tension than are divorce rates. This statement is consistent both with our first explanation (the state of anxiety created by war makes for the initiation and preservation of intimate interpersonal relationships), and with our second (the concern for the personal security of combatant sons increases the tendency to expand families). The data do not support the third explanation (during war the increased interdependence between spouses tends to stabilize the family).

THE ETHNIC FACTOR

The most important demographic change which has occurred in Israel . . . is the transition from a Jewish population of predominantly European origin (78 percent in 1949) to a mixed population with a small majority of Asian-African origin (53 percent in 1975). This development can be traced to . . . the mass immigration from Asia and Africa during the early 1950s, . . . and the greater natural increase among Jews of Asian-African (A-A) origin. . . .

Although Europeans and A-A households differ . . . in size, there is a much smaller difference between households headed by Israeli-born males of European parentage and those headed by Israeli-born males of A-A parentage. . . . The ethnic gap in family size is shrinking . . . as a result of corresponding changes on the part of *both* ethnicities. A standard medium-size Israeli family of 3–4 members seems to emerge. If these findings indicate a . . . trend of diminishing ethnic differentiation in family structure, then a growing uniformity in other properties, e.g., age at marriage, should be expected.

. . . In the early 1960s Europeans tended to marry later than A-A's, but by 1975 this difference had vanished. . . . The process of closing the ethnic gap was again symmetrical. The average age of A-A brides and grooms rose and the age of European brides and grooms fell.

The involvement of the family in the process of ethnic integration is most directly observable in the dynamics of intermarriage. . . . Between 1952 and 1975 the ratio of mixed marriages (one spouse of A-A the other of European origin) to all Jewish marriages rose consistently from 9 to 19 percent.

These facts are both an indication of ongoing ethnic integration . . . and of a powerful force toward further amalgamation. At least 20 percent of the next generation will not belong to either of the two leading ethnicities. An even larger segment of the population will have familial affiliation across ethnic lines and thus a vested interest in further integration.

. . . Mixed families are (in most years) somewhat *more* stable than homogeneous non-European families and far more stable than European ones. . . . Mixed couples are probably *less* divergent in other relevant attributes (income, education, and personality traits) than endogamous couples. Since intermarriage is still less likely to occur than intramarriage, a person will marry across ethnic lines only if *other* attributes of his mate suit him especially well.

THE RELIGIOUS FACTOR

A third source of the Israeli family's centrality and stability lies in the status and power of organized religion. . . .

One outcome of the increasing religious influence in Israel has been an inclination to conserve the family's stability and centrality. This tendency is expressed at school . . . and in mass-media programs. . . .

The most powerful religious influence on fam-

ily life is activated through law and the court. The rabbinical courts . . . are authorized to deal with all marital issues. . . . Although the rabbinical tradition does not ban divorce, such an extreme step will be taken only after all the means of restoring marital relations have been employed. . . .

In sum, Jewish religious institutions . . . promote the . . . family.

If the reasoning . . . above is correct, then those parts of the Israeli population . . . under direct religious . . . influence should have a higher birth rate and a lower divorce rate than secular sectors. . . .

Election results are published for each town or township separately, so it is possible to estimate the . . . religiosity of towns from the proportion of the electorate who voted for religious parties in the 1977 General Elections. For each township, data on ethnic composition and marriage, divorce and birth ratios were collected. . . .

About 15 percent of the population voted for religious parties in 1977. . . . It therefore seems safe to define, operationally, a town where 15 percent or more voted "religious" as . . . religious . . . and a town where religious parties polled 10 percent or less as . . . secular. We calculated the ratios of all cases of divorce to all marriages (during 1972) for "religious" and "secular" townships. As expected these ratios were significantly lower in religious (Divorce/Marriage $\times$ 100 = 9.21%) than in nonreligious (Divorce/Marriage $\times$ 100 = 10.74%) townships. . . .

SOCIAL CONTROL

Anonymity has been considered by many sociologists as a major determinant of anomie in general, and of the crisis in the nuclear family in particular.

If the individual remains unidentified most of the time, social control becomes ineffective.

Anonymity is a consequence of the dissolution of compact and stable communities. . . . In a small community, . . . a closed network of acquaintances (and therefore control) emerges (Bott). Sanctions are transferred from one sphere to another: an individual who deviates in his occupational role might experience inconvenience in his kinship relations, and vice versa. The breakdown of a marriage will be more complicated, more costly, and therefore, less likely in . . . a closed social network.

In Israel the individual feels less anonymous than his counterpart in the modern West . . . because the tradition of respect for privacy carries much less force, and values of mutual help and responsibility are somewhat more emphasized.

. . . We should expect the family to retain more stability in *small* communities than in large ones. To test this hypothesis, the ratio of divorce to marriage was calculated for small towns (35,000 inhabitants or less) and large towns (70,000 inhabitants or more). The ratio results were 8 and 10.77 percent respectively, and this is, statistically, highly significant.

We may now draw together three findings: the stability of the family is positively affected by (a) ethnic background (the percentage of Jews of Asian-African origin . . . in the township), (b) religiosity (percentage voting for religious parties), and (c) efficacy of social control (size of town).

. . . Each of these factors seems to cause a significant difference in divorce to marriage ratios. . . .Although the ratio of divorce to marriage rates in European towns do not differ significantly according to religiosity and size, . . . significant differences among non-Europeans support our hypothesis.

THE GOVERNMENT'S CONTRIBUTION

. . . Israeli leaders have emphasized . . . that a high birth rate in the Jewish population is vital to maintaining the balance of power between Israel and her neighbors. In the fifties a prize was given to mothers on the birth of their tenth child. In 1967 the Center for Demography was established by the Prime Minister's Office. The . . . purpose of the Center has been construed: "To support the government's population policy . . . to encourage a high birth rate which is essential for the future of the Jewish people." In addition . . . , the government's development policy brought about what Rosenfeld and Carmi have called: ". . . the state-made middle class and the realization of family values.". . .

Public housing projects have supported the purchase of apartments by several hundred thousand families. Until recently, however, almost no public funds were allocated for the construction of rental housing. This has contributed indirectly to the stability of many young families. The first steps . . . of a new couple usually entail an immediate heavy expenditure, and considerable long-term obligations. The cost of a standard two-bedroom apartment is equivalent to 6–7 average yearly earnings. The necessary capital is . . . obtained from . . . parents . . . , public and bank loans and the couple's own savings. All these contributors have a vested interest in the stability of the young family. . . . Also . . . most of the above-mentioned loans and contributions can be obtained only by a legally married couple. . . .

CONCLUSIONS

. . . We have analyzed some central trends of the Jewish-Israeli family in light of various characteristics of Israeli society. We conclude:

External conflicts and tensions tend to increase marriage and birth rates, while divorce rates are not systematically affected.

Jews of Asian or African background have higher marriage and birth rates and lower divorce rates than Jews of European background.

The family patterns of the two major ethnicities have become more similar. . . .

The family is involved in . . . ethnic integration through the growing rate of intermarriage.

This is also a . . . vehicle for further merging of ethnicities in the future.

The . . . Jewish religious . . . establishment has a firm impact on the centrality and stability of the family . . . throughout the Jewish population.

In small townships where the networks of social control are assumed to be dense, the family is more stable than in large cities.

Government policies contribute directly and indirectly to the establishment of a family-centered style of life.

These findings can be viewed as manifestations of . . .: (a) interdependence of the spouses, caused by gender-role differentiation, (b) social control to which the family is exposed, and (c) personal values and attitudes based on nationalism and on commitment to ethnic and religious traditions. Obviously these factors conflict . . . with some of the major ideological commitments of contemporary Western societies—personal freedom, privacy, secularism, gender equality, and internationalism. . . . Thus the preservation of the family's stability and centrality . . . takes its toll in humanistic and individualistic values. The individual must often make a painful choice between personal freedom . . . and . . . families ties and responsibilities. . . .

NOTE

[1]Bar-Yosef and Padan-Eisenshtark argue that the massive mobilization of men during 1973–74 reinforced the differentiation of gender roles. However, . . . their data shows the prolonged absence of husbands induced wives to *expand* their roles to include tasks . . . usually considered "man's work. . . ." Thus, roles might blur while primordial images are further differentiated.

REFERENCES

BAR YOSEF, R., and A. BECHER. 1972. *The Psychological and Social Causes of Fertility.* Research Report. Jerusalem.

BOTT, E. 1957. *Family and Social Networks.* London: Tavistock.

COHEN, A., and J. DOTAN. 1976. "Communication in the Family as a Function of Stress During War and Peace." *Journal of Marriage and the Family* (February): 141–48.

DESHEN, S. 1978. "Israeli Judaism Introduction to the Major Patterns." *International Journal of Middle-East Studies* (Summer): 141–69.

FREEDMAN, J. L., J. M. CARLSMITH, and D. O. SEARS. 1974. "Affiliation." In *Social Psychology.* Englewood Cliffs: Prentice-Hall.

MILLS, J., and P. MINTZ. 1972. "Effect of Unexplained Arousal on Affiliation." *Journal of Personality and Social Psychology* 24(11–13).

ROSENFELD, H., and S. CARMI. 1976. "The Privatization of Public Means: The State-Made Middle Class and the Realization of Family Values in Israel." In J. G. Peristiany (ed.), *Kinship and Modernization in Mediterranean Society.* Rome: Vatican.

SARNOFF, I. S., and P. ZIMBARDO. 1961. "Anxiety, Fear and Social Affiliation." *Journal of Abnormal and Social Psychology* 62:356–63.

SHACHTER, S. 1959. *The Psychology of Affiliation.* Stanford: Stanford University Press.

Introduction

In Buru Buru and Umoja, housing subdivisions on the edge of Nairobi (Kenya), young couples are re-enacting America's suburban drama of the 1950s. There, "father [still] knows best," according to data provided by Sharon Stichter in the next excerpt. Middle-class families have moved into shiny, if modest, new houses. How does urban middle-class life affect the relations between husbands and wives?

Well, the data suggest that these relations have not changed very much at all. Husbands still dominate in making decisions about how large amounts of money will be spent. Women still have responsibility for the household, and dominate in making decisions about how to run the household. The author concludes that "in Kenya . . . traditional subordination in marriage persists, despite contemporary economic change."

Yet Stichter also finds that wives have more decision-making power if (1) they hold paid employment, (2) they, or their husbands, have more than average education, and (3) if they are older, or are close to their husband in age. All of these factors are becoming more common in the Kenyan population; therefore, we have reason to expect that Kenyan women will gradually and inevitably gain more domestic power. (This runs counter to the author's conclusion.)

Unfortunately, this paper provides no data from one or two generations ago that would allow us to assess whether there has been a change in domestic relations. In fact, we cannot tell whether the people Stichter studied are really standing still culturally, or whether they are Kenyan versions of *Ozzie and Harriet*—deep in a 1950s-type sleep of new affluence.

Maybe what is going to happen to Kenyan families in the 2000s is what happened to American families in the 1960s and 1970s.

60

Changing Gender Relations in Middle-Class Kenyan Families

Sharon Stichter

This paper addresses the changes in women's position in the family resulting from creation of an urban middle class in Kenya. It focuses on male-female relations in terms of (1) material appropriation and exchange within the conjugal unit, (2) conjugal power and decision making, and (3) domestic labor. The underlying . . . question is whether more egalitarian, "joint" relations are coming into being in the domestic domain, such as are said to exist in contemporary European and U.S. middle class families. . . .

Source: Stichter, Sharon (1985) "The middle class family in Kenya: Changes in gender relations," *African Urban Studies,* 21 (Spring), 39–52.

MIDDLE CLASS FAMILIES IN NAIROBI

A survey of 317 families living in two . . . housing estates on the edge of Nairobi, Buru Buru and Umoja, was carried out in July and August 1979. Systematic random samples of 10 percent and 5 percent of households were chosen in Buru Buru and Umoja, respectively, and both the wife (or wives) and the husband were interviewed. . . . The two phases of Buru Buru together had about 1,897 units, and Umoja had 2,903 units at the time of interviewing. . . . The cost of the housing varies . . . , Umoja being much less expensive. . . .

The sample is representative of Nairobi's small but growing African middle class. . . .

White-collar workers predominate in the sample. . . . Nearly 70 percent of the women interviewed were active in the labor force. . . .

ASPECTS OF HOUSEHOLD STRUCTURE

. . . The fact that any African marriage is at least potentially polygynous dilutes the wife's claims on her husband's income in comparison to those she might make under monogamy. The rate of reported polygyny in this sample was only 4 percent, much below the levels found by Parkin (1978, p. 45) in 1968 in the low income estate of Kaloleni. . . . In the three estates examined here, being the only wife was significantly and positively correlated with the educational level of the wife and with being Kikuyu. It was negatively correlated with large age and education differences between husband and wife, with the age of the husband, and with being a Luo. Having only one wife was noticeably not correlated with either the education of the husband or with household income; in fact, the polygyny rate was highest in Buru Buru 2. This suggests that increasing male incomes and education levels may not lead to a decline in polygyny, but that, as Parkin argued for the Luo, increasing female education levels may. . . .

. . . Formalized polygyny is only the tip of the iceberg, however. It is impossible to assess the rate of "disguised polygyny," the practice whereby a man keeps a mistress or "outside wife" in separate accommodation. . . . Rumor had it that some of the single women in Umoja . . . were in fact "outside wives."

. . . The majority of marriages, even among the urban middle class, are contracted according to custom, even if there is also a church ceremony. The latter effectively assures the first wife of at least a superior status in relation to any succeeding co-wives and is also a sign of economic status, since the celebrations are expensive. Whatever the marriage type, a wife has little protection against her main risks: lack of support for herself and her children and physical abuse. A marriage reform bill, which would have unified marriage types, made polygyny contingent on the agreement of the first wife, and outlawed the custom of wife-beating, has twice been voted down in parliament. A . . . bill which would have enforced child support, also failed to pass.

In customary marriages (nearly all), the bridewealth payments continue to define the position of the wife as subordinate; 90 percent of the marriages in this sample involved bridewealth. The persistence of polygyny, bridewealth, large household size, frequent and extended visits from relatives, and control of older generations over land inheritance all suggest the "nuclear family" and the "conjugal estate" are at best only weakly emergent among the Kenyan middle class. Yet, the forces of change are great. . . . Wealth increasingly depends on salaries, and families are increasingly able to guarantee status and property (such as educational advantages) to only a small, rather than a large, family. Strong cultural forces for change operate through the mass media and the education system. The education of women may be particularly important. Educated Kenyan women express a desire for a more emotionally close and egalitarian relationship with their husbands, for monogamy, and for the husband's involvement in childrearing (Whiting 1977; Parkin 1978, p. 261; Kayongo-Male and Onyango 1984, pp. 65–67).

ACCESS TO CONJUGAL RESOURCES

. . . How are income resources dispersed and controlled in the domestic unit? . . .

Informal conversation suggested . . . that wives are likely to put a greater proportion of their resources into a household pool than do husbands. One indication of the husband's willingness to pool his resources with his wife is the presence of a joint bank account. Only 22 percent of the men in the sample reported they maintained such accounts, 29 percent in Buru Buru 2 and 13 percent in Buru Buru 1 and Umoja. Some of these men could also have had individual accounts. Wives were asked whether they kept their earnings separate or put them into a common household fund; 44 percent said they put most of their earnings into the common fund. Even if resources are pooled, there is not necessarily equality of control. Women were asked: "Who decides what is done with the money you contribute?" Twenty-two percent reported that they did, 66 percent said the spouses decided together, and 12 percent said the husband decided.

. . . The wives were asked: "Between you and your husband, who usually pays for the following items?" (See Table 1.) These items are assumed to be a reasonable list of the major budgetary outlays of urban African households. Any sharing of costs can be interpreted as a decline of male financial dominance and an increase in the wife's financial responsibilities. On average, husbands continue to be responsible for the major household costs. Strong wifely financial autonomy and equality in financial contributions are rare.

. . . Wives tend to be responsible for the housegirl's wages and their own clothing, while husbands tend to be responsible for the rent or mortgage, the children's school fees, large furniture items, their own clothing, and the car if there is one. Food and clothing for the children tend to be shared.

To explore the correlates of wifely financial responsibility, a scale was created from the accumulated, equally weighted scores on budgetary items. It ranges . . . from one to five; the higher the score, the greater the wifely responsibility. . . . The responsibility scale is most highly correlated with whether the wife is employed. Lower but significant relationships (positive or negative) were found with the wife's education level and age, difference in the spouses' ages, husband's education, household income, ethnicity (for Luo), whether the husband helps with the housework, and the presence of a housegirl. . . . Multiple regression analysis indicated the wife's employment explains 41 percent of the total variance, the other factors each contributing only very small increases in explanatory power. . . .

Jointness, or the "husband and wife equally" response, is more frequent as the wife's employment, education, and income rise. Responses vary markedly according to estate. Umoja, with the lowest level of female employment, also has the lowest level of "jointness" and the highest evidence of male dominance (Stichter 1987). This finding is consistent with studies in Lusaka

TABLE 1. Division of Financial Responsibility (in Percent)

	Husband			Wife		
	Only	*Mostly*	Equal	*Mostly*	*Only*	Total
Rent/mortgage	52	29	14	2	3	100
Furniture	41	27	25	3	4	100
School fees	42	23	25	4	6	100
Food	26	15	35	4	20	100
Clothing						
Husband	43	35	19	1	2	100
Children	25	13	46	4	12	100
Wife	27	16	28	8	21	100
Wages, housegirl	19	16	23	10	32	100
Average	34	22	27	4	13	100

and Lagos, where it also was found that pooling is more common among middle-class than among lower class couples and increases as income and education increase (Munachonga n.d.; Karanja-Diejomaoh 1978; Mack 1978). . . .

Domestic budgeting is acknowledged by observers and popular commentators to be a problem in Kenya . . . and . . . women are demanding more influence on decisions. For example, women protest the widespread assumption that the wife's salary is meant to be spent on the household while the husband's may be spent on entertaining friends or on rural business enterprises (Kayongo-Male and Onyango 1984, pp. 29–30). They also complain about the lack of financial trust and openness in marriage as well as and their lack of control over their own earnings. . . .

CONJUGAL DECISION MAKING

Oppong (1974) argued that the greater a woman's financial contribution to a marriage, the greater will be her decision-making power within it. This study only provides qualified support for this view. The questions were framed in hypothetical terms, asking whether the husband or wife, or both together, would decide on buying a car, buying land or investing in business, where to send the children to school, and hiring a housegirl. These are . . . major decisions for Kenyan middle class families. Equal weight was allotted to each decision, but the decision scale understates women's contribution because everyday decisions such as what to have for supper are not included. Scores ranged from 1 to 3; the higher the score, the greater is the wife's decision making power. Many of the same factors correlate with decision-making as with financial responsibility. . . . Husbands have more power over decisions in Umoja and least in Buru Buru 2. Their separate role in major decisions probably declines as income and wife's employment increase; her greater power over decisions, however, is almost solely in the area of hiring housegirls. Similarly, the "decide together" response increases as one moves from the lower to the higher income estate only if the housegirl question is omitted from the analysis (Stichter 1987).

Hiring the housegirl is usually the wife's prerogative, and paying her is frequently also her province (see Table 1). This reflects the fact that domestic work is considered the woman's responsibility, although she is allowed to hire a substitute. As her income increases, she is likely to do just that. The presence of a housegirl is significantly correlated with women's employment and with household income. None of the factors examined, including wife's financial contribution to the household, appear to account in a major way for the variance in the wife's decision making power. . . . The most likely hypothesis is that it is mainly in domestic areas such as household help and children's schooling that the wife's decision making increases as her financial contributions do. In large-scale but relatively rare decisions, such as a car, or land, or businesses, her contribution is less often seen as relevant. . . . There is no strong trend toward separate, autonomic decision making. The most frequent response shown in Table 2 is "decide together.". . . Kenyan middle class wives appear to have difficulty translating earnings into truly joint decision making.

DOMESTIC WORK

It is still the wife who performs most household tasks, with . . . help from a maid or housegirl. The wife usually purchases food, prepares and serves meals, does the washing, and takes care of the children in the evenings. The housegirl helps with all of these tasks, except shopping, at which the husband helps. The housegirl's range of tasks and total work contribution are surprisingly limited. The husband's contribution is . . . in purchasing children's clothing and furniture, making small repairs, and in some cases taking children to and from school.

. . . The wife and housegirl perform the most

TABLE 2. Spheres of Family Decision Making (in Percent)

Decision	Husband	Together	Wife	Total
Car purchase	30	69	1	100
Land/business	23	75	2	100
Schooling	13	79	8	100
Housegirl	4	40	56	100
Average	18	65	17	100

time-consuming and house-bound tasks. The husband's domestic contribution does not vary much across the estates and is not highly correlated with any of the major social background variables, such as age, education, income, or ethnicity. Segregation of tasks between husband and wife is notable. . . .

The incidence of housegirls was virtually identical in Buru Buru 2 and Buru Buru 1—79 percent and 78 percent, respectively; only 43 percent of the Umoja sample had them. Typically, they are poor, uneducated, village girls. Surprisingly, only about one-quarter of them were close relatives of their employers, which was even less likely in higher income families. . . .

The housegirl system poses a number of labor management problems for the wife. The first is finding and retaining a housegirl in a situation of fairly high turnover. This is normally the wife's responsibility, and it may involve a trip to the rural area. If a housegirl leaves, the wife may lose a week or two of work finding another one, with the result that her employer will be annoyed and inconvenienced. The second problem is in the quality of work. This is not only a question of theft or carelessness with household valuables; many women worry about the quality of childcare. . . .

Many wives worry about their inability to influence their children or to provide adequately for them. . . .

CONCLUSION

Middle income urban married couples in Nairobi usually pool at least part of their income yet adhere to much separation in decision making and household tasks. The husband's dominance in major financial decision making persists. Wives often do not have much autonomy within marriage. Housework is still largely the responsibility of wives, although most working wives are able to hire housegirls to help.

Lewis (1977) has observed that for Ivorian women of all classes, marriage remains as desirable an asset as it was traditionally. Their control over their own financial resources makes it possible for them to maintain leverage and autonomy within marriage. Smock (1977) describes Ghanaian middle class women as having moved from traditional autonomy to modern subordination. The Kenyan situation differs from . . . these West African cases in that traditional spousal decision-making arrangements do not seem to have accorded the wife as much independence as was the case in some West African societies. This research suggests that the problem in Kenya is that traditional subordination in marriage persists, despite contemporary economic change.

REFERENCES

KARANJA-DIEJOMAOH, W. 1978. "Disposition of Incomes by Husbands and Wives: An Exploratory Study of Families in Lagos." In C. Oppong, ed., *Marriage, Fertility and Parenthood in West Africa*. Canberra: Department of Demography, Australian National University.

KAYONGO-MALE, D., and P. ONYANGO. 1984. *The Sociology of the African Family*. London: Longman Group Limited.

LEWIS, B. C. 1977. "Economic Activity and Marriage among Ivorian Urban Women." In A. Schlegel, ed., *Sexual Stratification: A Cross-Cultural View.* New York: Columbia University Press: Pp. 161–91.

MACK, D. E. 1978. "Husbands and Wives in Lagos: The Effects of Socioeconomic Status on the Pattern of Family Living." *Journal of Marriage and the Family* 40:807–16.

MUNACHONGA, M. n.d. "The Conjugal Power Relationship: An Urban Case Study in Zambia." Falmer, U.K.: Sussex University. Xerox.

OPPONG, C. 1974. *Marriage among a Matrilineal Elite: A Family Study of Ghanaian Senior Civil Servants.* London: Cambridge University Press.

PARKIN, D. 1978. *The Cultural Definition of Political*

Response: Lineal Destiny among the Luo. New York: Academic Press.

SCHUSTER, I. M. G. 1979. *New Women of Lusaka.* Palo Alto, Calif.: Mayfield Publishing.

SMOCK, A. 1977. "Ghana: From Autonomy to Subordination." In J. Giele and A. Smock, eds., *Women: Roles and Status in Eight Countries.* New York: John Wiley.

STICHTER, S. 1987. "Women and the Family: The Impact of Capitalist Development in Kenya." In M. Schatzberg, ed., *The Political Economy of Kenya.* New York: Praeger. Pp. 137–60.

WHITING, B. 1977. "Changing Life Styles in Kenya." *Daedalus* (Spring): 211–25.

Discussion Questions

1. The study of Chinese marriages in this section shows that people who choose their partners freely are happier with marriage than people who are in "arranged marriages." Does this suggest that free choice is a major source of happiness in all family life; and if so, is family life around the world going to be happier in the future than it was in the past?

2. In Israel and Sweden, two very modern societies, the family is alive and well. Does this convince you that the family will still be a viable institution in America in, say, the year 2020?

3. Suppose that medical and technological means made it possible for people to live an average of two hundred years. How would this change affect family life?

4. Judging from what van de Kaa, Höllinger, and Haller have to say about family changes in modern societies, what do you predict the Kenyan family will be like fifty years from now?

5. Would prosperity or scarcity be most likely to strengthen the American family in the future? Why?

6. "Some people look at modern family life and say 'How progressive!' others say 'How rational!' and others still say 'How selfish!'" Does this quotation describe the outlooks of van de Kaa, and Burch and Matthews? Do they view the modern family as progressive, rational, selfish, or none of the above? What predictions of future family life flow from each analysis?

Data Collection Exercises

1. Peres and Katz report that the average household headed by an Israeli Jew born in Europe or America contains 2.7 persons, while one that is headed by an Israeli Jew born in Africa or Asia contains 4.5 persons. How would Burch and Mat-

thews explain this? Collect some data on Israel to test whether their (presumed) explanation is likely to be valid. Then, project what Israeli household sizes are likely to be in the year 2020.

2. One researcher predicts that people are likely to continue reducing their investments in family life in the future. Let's find out if they have actually done so in the recent past. Collect statistical data from a northern or western European country (for example, Germany or Sweden) to determine what proportion of their incomes married people currently spend on long-lasting domestic items like homes, household appliances, and expensive furniture. Compare this with the spending of married people (1) in another "more traditional" society—for example, Spain or India, and in (2) the same northern or western European country twenty-five, fifty, or one hundred years ago.

3. Into which group of countries would Israel fall in van de Kaa's sequence of family transformations? Where is it likely to be fifty years from now? Collect some data that will help you make this prediction.

4. Collect some data to determine whether Kenya today is, in *some* important respects, very much like America in the 1950s.

Writing Exercises

1. "In the future, most people will spend most of their lives living alone, with brief periods spent in family-like arrangements (some with children present.)" Write a brief (500-word) essay commenting on this statement in view of the excerpts by Burch and Matthews, and Höllinger and Haller.

2. Imagine you are a young Chinese woman who has been pushed into an "arranged marriage" with a much older man you do not love. Write brief entries in your diary just before your wedding and five, ten, fifteen, and twenty years later, to reflect your thoughts about married life.

3. "In fifty years, a Kenyan wife will have more in common with an Israeli or Dutch wife than she will with her own husband." Write a brief (500-word) essay interpreting and commenting on this statement.

4. Sociologist Ogun Grok writes in the year 2053, "Van de Kaa's analysis was good as far as it went; but it didn't tell us anything about the stages that would come *after* stage 4 (the shift from uniform to pluralistic families and households)." Imagine you are Grok. Using the material in this section, write a brief (500-word) scenario that brings van de Kaa's analysis up to date by discussing stages 5 and 6.

Glossary

Investment (in relationship)—The commitment of time, money, and emotion (or psychic energy) to creating and maintaining a bond with another person, or persons. Goode's use of this idea suggests that intimacy does not come naturally; it needs to be constantly nourished and repaired.

Second demographic transition—A second round of changes in family life and childbearing in developed nations, beginning in the 1960s. Unlike the first transition, this one is motivated by individualistic values and attitudes.

Self-interest—A pursuit of personal well-being or advantage. The French writer Toqueville believed that self-interest "rightly understood" was not the same as selfishness, since self-improvement could work to everyone's advantage in the long run.

Suggested Readings

BERNARD, JESSE. (1973) *The Future of Marriage.* New York: Bantam Books. A classic work that introduced the notion of "his marriage" and "her marriage," to emphasize the gap in husbands' and wives' experiences. Does marriage have a future? Yes. But what kind of a future, and how can we influence that future? These are the important questions Bernard answers.

EHRENREICH, BARBARA. (1983) *The Hearts of Men: American Dreams and the Flight from Commitment.* Garden City, New York: Anchor Books. Puts flesh and bones on van de Kaa's "second demographic transition" theory by focusing on the last forty years of mating and marriage in America. Unlike van de Kaa, however, Ehrenreich sees the issue at hand as (1) a problem, (2) caused by males, and (3) having economic, not cultural, origins.

KIRKENDALL, LESTER A., and ARTHUR E. GRAVATT, eds. (1984) *Marriage and the Family in the Year 2020.* Buffalo, New York: Prometheus Book. "Beam me up, Scotty, we're going to rocket into some strange galaxies!" The articles in this collection of social science speculations range from timid and ho-hum to weird and provocative, but most are standard, state-of-the-art future forecasting. They all provide some food for thought. Consider the prediction that by 2020, seventy-five percent of all American spouses will have had extramarital sex partners. One-quarter of these will have had more than 10 such partners.

MCLAUGHLIN, STEVEN D., BARBARA D. MELBER, JOHN O. G. BILLY, DENISE M. ZIMMERLE, LINDA D. WINGES, and TERRY R. JOHNSON. (1988) *The Changing Lives of American Women.* Chapel Hill, NC: University of North Carolina Press. A fine, statistically informed analysis of how American women's "life cycle" has been changing over the past three generations, with particular references to education, premarital sex, marriage and childbearing, and paid work. Also relates these behavioral changes to demographic and attitude changes and tries to figure out which comes first.

OVERALL, CHRISTINE, ed. (1989) *The Future of Human Reproduction.* Toronto: The Women's Press. Will the new reproductive technology change family life, and if so, how? What are the moral and political issues that surround likely and possible changes in this area of personal life? A variety of essays by feminist historians, philosophers, social scientists, and activists explore the changes that lie ahead.

YOUNG, MICHAEL, and PETER WILLMOTT. (1975) *The Symmetrical Family.* Harmondsworth, England: Penguin Books. Like Bernard's book, this book helps us see the future by helping us understand the present and recent past. These authors have written a number of other classic books on family life, all of them rich with believable detail and insight; this one is no exception. It covers the domestic politics of husbands and wives, and the way the growth of cities and paid work for women has changed work and leisure within the home.